GREAT ISSUES IN WESTERN CIVILIZA TION

VOLUME TWO

EDITED BY BRIAN TIERNEY,
DONALD KAGAN,
AND L. PEARCE WILLIAMS

CONSULTING EDITOR:

EUGENE RICE
Columbia University

GREAT ISSUES IN WESTERN CIVILIZATION

VOLUME TWO

Second Edition

Random House · New York

Copyright © 1967, 1972 by Random House, Inc.
All rights reserved under International and
Pan-American Copyright Conventions.
Published in the United States by Random House, Inc.,
New York, and simultaneously in Canada
by Random House of Canada Limited, Toronto.
ISBN: 0-394-31656-8
Library of Congress Catalog Card Number: 77-152715
Manufactured in the United States of America
Composed by H. Wolff Book Mfg. Co., New York, N.Y.
Printed and Bound by Colonial Press, Clinton, Mass.
Second Edition
987654321

To Frederick G. Marcham

TEACHER—SCHOLAR—COLLEAGUE—FRIEND

NOTE ON THE SECOND EDITION

Many changes have been made in this new edition of *Great Issues* in response to the helpful suggestions we received from college teachers who have been using the volumes in their courses. In particular, the amount of introductory and explanatory material has been substantially increased. In the new, extended Preface we have tried to explain to the student the kinds of real historical problems that lie behind the questions posed in the title of each "great issue." In addition, the individual sections have been given more substantial introductions that explain the historical context of each issue considered and the significance of the particular documents cited.

Experience has shown that most instructors like to begin their courses with the topic "What Is History?" Accordingly, we have moved this section to the beginning of the book. Four sections that seem to have been little used have been omitted from this edition. The treatment of three topics has been radically revised; these are the sections on ancient science, Christianity, and the cold war. The whole work has been reedited in order to make the various sections more uniform in length.

For teachers who prefer to use *Great Issues* in alternative formats, the volume *Great Issues Since 1500* and the series of individual pamphlets are still available in their original editions.

BRIAN TIERNEY
DONALD KAGAN
L. PEARCE WILLIAMS

PREFACE

A major purpose of this two-volume work is to convince students in Western civilization courses that the essential task of a historian is not to collect dead facts but to confront live issues. The issues are alive because they arise out of the tensions that men have to face in every generation—tensions between freedom and authority, between reason and faith, between human free will and all the impersonal circumstances that help to shape our lives. Such issues concern scholars other than historians, of course—philosophers, sociologists, and theologians, for instance. But the historian thinks about them in a distinctive way. We have tried, therefore, to provide for the student not only a body of information about past events and ideas but also an introduction to the ways in which modern historians seek to interpret the record of the past.

In order to achieve any sophisticated understanding of such matters, a student needs to read the views of great modern historians as they are set out in their own words. He needs to develop a measure of critical historical insight by comparing these often conflicting views with the source material on which they are based. He needs, above all, to concern himself with the great issues that have shaped the course of Western civilization and not with historical "problems" that are mere artificially contrived conundrums.

The present volume is divided into ten parts. Each of them presents both original source material and a variety of modern interpretations, and each deals with a truly great issue in Western history. The questions that we have posed in the title of each section are real questions in the sense that they are issues that great historians have really argued about. But they are not questions of a simple "true-false" type. When two capable historians fall into a dispute it is possible, of course, that one is simply wrong and the other right. A historian may be ignorant of some of the source material relevant to the topic he is considering. He may misunderstand his sources. More reprehensibly, he may distort the meaning of the sources in order to make them fit in with his own political or religious prejudices. In all such cases he is likely to be challenged by another scholar.

But differences among historians often have more complex origins than simple error on the part of a particular writer. Sometimes they arise because different authors use the same words in different senses. Thus in considering the question "Periclean Athens—Democracy, Aristocracy, or Monarchy?" it is just as important to ask what the word "democracy" means to the different authors who use it as to ask how the Athenian state was organized in the time of Pericles.

Most typically, historical controversies arise when some historian brings a novel insight to bear on an old problem. The historian's enthusiasm for his new idea can lead to a deeper understanding of the problem he considers, but it can also encourage a one-sided approach to a complex issue. Other historians will point this out and emphasize different approaches—and so a controversy ensues. A good example is provided by the historians' classical problem concerning "the decline and fall of the Roman Empire." By the early twentieth century it was evident that social and economic factors were very important in historical causation. Accordingly, various historians produced social and economic explanations of the fall of Rome. But the fact that social and economic factors were important in the process of decline does not exclude the possibility that religious, moral, and military factors were important too. Hence when we consider a problem as broad as "The Roman Empire—Why Did It Fall?" our real task is not to identify one particular cause of disintegration but to explain how all the different causes of decay interacted to produce the final downfall.

When two historians disagree it is usually because each of them is stating a truth, but each is so preoccupied with his own truth that he regards the view of the other as simply an error. Historical understanding progresses when we come to see that two truths are in fact compatible with one another and that both are necessary for the understanding of a given historical situation. Fifty years ago historians disagreed violently about the issues implied in the question "Renaissance Man—Medieval or Modern?" Nowadays virtually every sophisticated student of the problem would agree that some medieval ideas and institutions persisted as formative influences on the early modern world while others disappeared or survived only as unimportant anachronisms. In a sense, then, the historical argument that we have presented was a pseudoargument. But it led to a deeper understanding of a complex problem; for we can hardly hope to understand the course of Western history at all until we can determine what the ancient world and the Middle Ages contributed to the formation of modern civilization and what was distinctively new in the age of the Renaissance and the Scientific Revolution. This is a real problem and it is still far from settled.

In considering all the great issues in this book the reader has to ask himself not only what happened in the past but why historians disagree about what happened. Are they using the same words in different senses? Are they emphasizing one truth at the expense of another? Are they allowing their own prejudices to distort their interpretations of historical documents? Are the apparently conflicting opinions really incompatible with one another? If so, which view seems more persuasive? If not, how can the different opinions be reconciled with one another?

We believe that there are three major themes whose development and interplay have shaped the distinctive characteristics that set Western civilization apart from the other great historic cultures. They are the growth of a tradition of rational scientific inquiry, the persistence of a tension between Judaeo-Christian religious ideals and social realities, and the emergence of constitutional forms of government. These three themes are introduced in the first sections of Volume I. The reader will find them recurring in new forms and changing contexts throughout the rest of the work. We hope that in studying them he will come to a richer understanding of the heritage of Western civilization—and of the historian's approach to it.

Ithaca, 1971   BRIAN TIERNEY

                          DONALD KAGAN

                          L. PEARCE WILLIAMS

CONTENTS

THE ENGLISH CIVIL WAR

A FIGHT FOR LAWFUL GOVERNMENT?

CONTENTS

QUESTIONS FOR STUDY

1. *How do the views on fundamental law expressed by James I, Coke, Pym, Rainborow, and Ireton differ from one another?*

2. *Why did the leaders of Parliament oppose the royal government in 1604–1641?*

3. *In what ways do Macaulay and Wingfield-Stratford agree and in what ways do they differ in their accounts of the "Case of the Five Members"?*

4. *Why did civil war break out in 1642? Which side would you have fought on?*

5. *On the scaffold Charles I said he was "the martyr of the people." Was he?*

6. *How did Oliver Cromwell defend his actions? Do you find the defense convincing?*

7. *All the legislation signed by Charles before the outbreak of war remained in force after the Restoration. How would this affect future relationships between king and Parliament?*

At a time when nearly all the states of Europe were adopting absolutist forms of government, England embarked on a new experiment in parliamentary constitutionalism.

When Queen Elizabeth died in 1603 she was succeeded by her nephew James (1603–1625), who was already King of Scotland. Elizabeth had had a long and glorious reign, but she left many problems for her successor. James succeeded only in exacerbating them all. In the first place, there was a constitutional problem. Everyone agreed that the king had the right to direct affairs of state. But during the sixteenth century Parliament had grown into a powerful representative assembly whose members expected to be consulted on major issues of policy. There was no written constitution to define where the authority of the king ended and the rights of Parliament began. In King James's native Scotland no such parliamentary institution had grown up, and he never learned to understand the English Parliament or its traditions. Hence all through his reign the members of the House of Commons felt obliged to adopt an attitude of prickly self-assertiveness in upholding their rights and privileges (pp. 12–15).

Second, James inherited a serious religious problem. During Elizabeth's reign most Englishmen had come to accept the Church of England as the true church for them and the queen as its legitimate head. There were some dissident Puritans and some Roman Catholics who refused to join the established church, but they formed only small and unpopular minorities. The real problem for James was the fact that within the Church of England itself a substantial faction of reformers wanted to modify the rites and doctrines of the church in a generally Puritan, Calvinistic way. James had learned to hate Presbyterianism in Scotland, and he obdurately resisted any such changes. (An English observer remarked of the king in 1604 that "howsoever he lived among Puritans, and was kept for the most part as a ward under them, yet since he was . . . ten years old he ever disliked their opinions.") The Puritans became increasingly influential in the House of Commons during James's reign and this contributed greatly to the continuing ill-feeling between king and Parliament.

Finally, Elizabeth bequeathed a major financial problem to her successor. The basic trouble here was inflation. Most of the king's rents and traditional revenues had remained fixed while the costs of government had been constantly rising. Here again James made things worse by maintaining an ostentatiously extravagant court. By this time it was plainly established that the king could not levy direct taxation without consent of Parliament. But the situation was not so clear as regards indirect taxes, especially customs duties. Major disputes arose in 1610 and 1628 concerning the duties known as "impositions" and "tonnage and poundage" (pp. 14–15, 17–20).

Under James's son Charles I (1625–1649), events moved to a crisis. Charles was a devout Anglican by conviction, but his enemies denounced his "Arminianism" (that is, ritualistic High Church Episcopalianism) as a mere mask for popery (pp. 18–20). From the beginning of Charles's reign the king's opponents, who were now able to command a majority in the House of Commons, deliberately tried to destroy the king's power to pursue his own chosen policies in religion and foreign affairs by withholding taxation. Their opposition culminated in 1629 in a scene of unprecedented turmoil in the House of Commons (pp. 18–20). After this Charles ruled for eleven years without summoning a Parliament. His financial expedients during this period led his adversaries to formulate explicitly the doctrine that taxes could be levied only through Parliament, even in times of national emergency (pp. 21–22).

In 1640 a rebellion in Scotland (once again a consequence of the king's "Arminian" religious policies) made it impossible for Charles to carry on his government without new parliamentary grants of taxation. The Parliament that he summoned quickly took advantage of the king's weakness by enacting a series of measures designed to curtail the powers of the crown for the future (pp. 23–27). Early in 1641 the House of Commons supported these measures by overwhelming majorities. But then a split developed between the moderates, who were content with the reforms they had enacted, and the radicals, who wanted to make the king a mere figurehead and seize real power for themselves. The subsequent deterioration of the situation, which ultimately led to open civil war, can be attributed either to Charles's clumsiness in handling his opponents (pp. 34–41) or to the implacability of the king's enemies (pp. 54–64). In the course of the war the parliamentary leaders quarreled with the army that they had created to fight the king, and the army established a military dictatorship under Oliver Cromwell (pp. 42–52). The eventual outcome of the whole conflict was the restoration of monarchy—but of a monarchy limited by the important constitutional legislation that had been enacted in 1641.

A peculiar feature of the twenty-year-long "crisis of the constitution" was that, even when the situation had degenerated into a naked struggle for power, all parties in the conflict claimed to be defending lawful government and the ancient rights of Englishmen. Partly for this reason, perhaps, the English people succeeded in carrying through a constitutional revolution in the seventeenth century without abandoning any of their medieval institutions of government. King, Parliament, and courts of common law entered into new relationships with one another, and all survived into the modern world.

1
KING AND PARLIAMENT, 1604–1640

The following passage describes some views on government that were widely held in England at the beginning of the seventeenth century.

FROM The Crisis of the Constitution
BY MARGARET A. JUDSON

[*The king, as head of state—B. T.*] made the important appointments to the council, the law courts, other departments of government, and to the church. As head of the state he summoned and dismissed parliament at his pleasure. Prerogatives of this sort were seldom mentioned in the law courts and, when they were, never denied. They came to be discussed and eventually questioned and challenged in parliament, but they were not directly attacked there until 1641 and 1642. When at that time some members of parliament worked to take away these particular prerogatives from the king and transfer them to parliament, the civil war soon broke out.

In the years leading up to that war, men agreed also that the king as head of the state was peculiarly competent and solely responsible in certain realms they called government. Here he was most particularly the head of the state, practicing the art of governing, a craft possessed only by kings. Within these realms his authority was accepted as absolute. It must be, they believed, or else he would be unable to carry on his craft as a true artist. These realms of government within which his authority was accepted as absolute included foreign policy, questions of war and peace, the coinage, and the control of industries and supplies necessary for the defense of the realm.

* * *

Margaret A. Judson, *The Crisis of the Constitution* (1964), pp. 24–25, 34–35, 44–46. Reprinted by permission of Margaret A. Judson and Octagon Books, Inc.

As kings possessed prerogatives, so subjects possessed rights; and those rights, like the king's prerogative, were part of the law and basic in the constitution. Only when the nature and extent of the subjects' rights are understood is it possible to present some aspects of the prerogative and some controversies concerning it which have not been discussed up to this point.

The most important of these rights were property rights. To protect them was the principal concern of the common law. It was also the main concern of great English subjects in the sixteenth and early seventeenth centuries. According to the evidence revealed by the law reports and family papers of this time, men in the upper social classes were adding to their landed holdings. In their acquisition of property, parliament helped them by measures, like the Statute of Uses, which made the transfer of property easier than it had been before. The crown helped them also by its sale of the confiscated monastic lands. The great mistake of the Tudors if they wished to be despots (as Harrington clearly pointed out in his *Oceana* in 1656) was their encouragement of such measures. It was a mistake from the point of view of the king's position, because, at the same time as the king's authority was increasing in the sixteenth century and the concept of the divine right of kings was rising to new exalted heights, the amount of property possessed by influential subjects was also increasing and thereby strengthening the old medieval concept that property was a right belonging to subjects. Among the many reasons why the growing absolutism of the Tudors did not become complete absolutism under the Stuarts is the fact that the medieval concept of the inviolability of a man's property did not disappear or become weaker in the sixteenth or early seventeenth centuries. Tudor and Stuart noblemen, gentry, and merchants who were acquiring property did not forget that although "government belonged to kings, property belonged to subjects."

* * *

Englishmen entered into the constitutional controversies of the seventeenth century with a profound belief in the importance of law. To them law was not primarily a decree enacted by a sovereign legislature to deal with a particular problem of the moment. Law was normally regarded as more than human, as the reflection of eternal principles of justice. When men considered it in relation to their own England, they looked upon it as a binding, cohesive force in their polity without which there would be no commonwealth, no government, no rights, and no justice.

They believed that the law was impartial—serving well both the king and the subject, enabling the king to fulfill his divine mission of governing with justice and protecting the subject in his God-given rights. To the seventeenth-century mind, rule by the king and rule by law were harmonious and not competing concepts. As the king's authority gave sanction to the law, so the law gave strength to the king's rule. To Yelverton, a faithful servant of Queen Elizabeth, "to live without government is hellish and to governe without lawes is brutish." James himself remarked that both king and parliament have a "union of interest" "in the lawes of the Kingdome, without which as the Prerogative cannot subsist, soe without that the Lawe cannot be maynteyned." . . .

It is well known that the parliamentarians based much of their case against the king on the law, but it is sometimes forgotten that the royalists also looked to the law to sanction the great authority they claimed for the monarch. In the long period of controversy between 1603 and 1642, both royalists and parliamentarians turned to the law to justify their actions, and both believed that the law was on their side. Even after the civil war broke out with its appeal to force, both groups strove to prove the legality of their actions, and only a few men admitted that the law had failed them.

James I, as King of Scotland, had propounded a theory of absolute monarchy before he inherited the crown of England. The following extract is from his *True Law of Free Monarchies,* published in 1598.

FROM True Law of Free Monarchies BY JAMES I

The Kings therefore in Scotland were before any estates or ranks of men within the same, before any Parliaments were holden or laws made; and by them was the land distributed (which at the first was wholly theirs), states erected and decerned [*decreed—B. T.*], and forms of government devised and established. And it follows of necessity that the Kings were the authors and makers of the laws and not the laws of the Kings. . . . And according to these fundamental laws already alleged, we daily see that in the Parliament (which is nothing else but the head court of the King and his vassals) the laws are but craved by his subjects, and only made by him at their rogation and with their advice. For albeit the King make daily statutes and ordinances, enjoining such pains thereto as he thinks meet, without any advice of Parliament or Estates, yet it lies in the power of no Parliament to make any kind of law or statute without his sceptre be to it for giving it the force of a law. . . . And as ye see it manifest that the King is overlord of the whole land, so is he master over every person that inhabiteth the same, having power over the life and death of every one of them. For although a just prince will not take the life of any of his subjects without a clear law, yet the same laws whereby he taketh them are made by himself or his predecessors,

J. R. Tanner, *Constitutional Documents of the Reign of James I, 1603–1625* (1930), pp. 9–10. Reprinted by permission of Cambridge University Press.

and so the power flows always from himself; as by daily experience we see good and just princes will from time to time make new laws and statutes, adjoining the penalties to the breakers thereof, which before the law was made had been no crime to the subject to have committed. Not that I deny the old definition of a King and of a law which makes the King to be a speaking law and the law a dumb King; for certainly a King that governs not by his law can neither be countable to God for his administration nor have a happy and established reign. For albeit it be true, that I have at length proved, that the King is above the law as both the author and giver of strength thereto, yet a good King will not only delight to rule his subjects by the law, but even will conform himself in his own actions thereunto; always keeping that ground, that the health of the commonwealth be his chief law.

Edward Coke, Chief Justice of the Court of Common Pleas, opposed these views of James I with a doctrine of the supremacy of law. In 1607 he informed James that a king of England could administer justice only through the anciently established courts.

Edward Coke on the Supremacy of Law

Then the King said that he thought the law was founded upon reason, and that he and others had reason as well as the Judges. To which it was answered by me, that true it was that God had endowed his Majesty with excellent science and great endowments of nature, but his Majesty was not learned in the laws of his realm of England; and causes which concern the life or inheritance or goods or fortunes of his subjects are not to be decided by natural reason but by the artificial reason and judgment of law, which law is an act which requires long study and experience before that a man can attain to the cognizance of it; and that the law was the golden metwand and measure to try the causes of the subjects, and which protected his Majesty in safety and peace. With which the King was greatly offended, and said that then he should be under the law, which was treason to affirm, as he said; to which I said that Bracton saith, *quod Rex non debet esse sub homine sed sub Deo et lege* [*that the King ought not to be under man but under God and under the law—B. T.*].

J. R. Tanner, *Constitutional Documents of the Reign of James I, 1603–1625* (1930), p. 187. Reprinted by permission of Cambridge University Press.

At the very beginning of James's reign in England (1604), the members of the House of Commons thought it necessary to explain to the new king that he had been "misinformed" about their rights.

The Rights of the House of Commons, 1604

Now concerning the ancient rights of the subjects of this realm, chiefly consisting in the privileges of this House of Parliament, the misinformation openly delivered to your Majesty hath been in three things:

First, That we held not privileges of right, but of grace only, renewed every Parliament by way of donature upon petition, and so to be limited.

Secondly, That we are no Court of Record, nor yet a Court that can command view of records, but that our proceedings here are only to acts and memorials, and that the attendance with the records is courtesy, not duty.

Thirdly and lastly, That the examination of the return of writs for knights and burgesses is without our compass, and due to the Chancery.

* * *

And contrariwise, with all humble and due respect to your Majesty our Sovereign Lord and Head, against those misinformations we most truly avouch,

First, That our privileges and liberties are our right and due inheritance, no less than our very lands and goods.

Secondly, That they cannot be withheld from us, denied, or impaired, but with apparent wrong to the whole state of the realm.

Thirdly, And that our making of request in the entrance of Parliament to enjoy our privilege is an act only of manners. . . .

Fourthly, We avouch also, That our House is a Court of Record, and so ever esteemed.

Fifthly, That there is not the highest standing Court in this land that ought to enter into competency [*competition—B. T.*], either for dignity or authority, with this High Court of Parliament, which with your Majesty's royal assent gives laws to other Courts but from other Courts receives neither laws nor orders.

Sixthly and lastly, We avouch that the House of Commons is the sole

J. R. Tanner, *Constitutional Documents of the Reign of James I, 1603–1625* (1930), pp. 220–226, 230. Reprinted by permission of Cambridge University Pres.

proper judge of return of all such writs and of the election of all such members as belong to it. . . .

The rights of the liberties of the Commons of England consisteth chiefly in these three things:

First, That the shires, cities, and boroughs of England, by representation to be present, have free choice of such persons as they shall put in trust to represent them.

Secondly, That the persons chosen, during the time of the Parliament as also of their access and recess, be free from restraint, arrest, and imprisonment.

Thirdly, That in Parliament they may speak freely their consciences without check and controlment, doing the same with due reverence to the Sovereign Court of Parliament, that is, to your Majesty and both the Houses, who all in this case make but one politic body whereof your Highness is the Head. . . .

For matter of religion, it will appear by examination of truth and right that your Majesty should be misinformed if any man should deliver that the Kings of England have any absolute power in themselves either to alter Religion (which God defend should be in the power of any mortal man whatsoever), or to make any laws concerning the same otherwise than, as in temporal causes, by consent of Parliament. We have and shall at all times by our oaths acknowledge that your Majesty is Sovereign Lord and Supreme Governor in both. . . .

There remaineth, dread Sovereign, yet one part of our duty at this present which faithfulness of heart, not presumption, doth press. We stand not in place to speak or do things pleasing; our care is and must be to confirm the love and tie the hearts of your subjects the commons most firmly to your Majesty. Herein lieth the means of our well deserving of both. There was never prince entered with greater love, with greater joy and applause of all his people. This love, this joy, let it flourish in their hearts for ever. Let no suspicion have access to their fearful thoughts that their privileges, which they think by your Majesty should be protected, should now by sinister informations or counsel be violated or impaired, or that those which with dutiful respects to your Majesty speak freely for the right and good of their country shall be oppressed or disgraced. Let your Majesty be pleased to receive public information from our Commons in Parliament as to the civil estate and government, for private informations pass often by practice: the voice of the people, in the things of their knowledge, is said to be as the voice of God. And if your Majesty shall vouchsafe, at your best pleasure and leisure, to enter into your gracious consideration of our petition for the ease of these burdens under which your whole people have of long time mourned, hoping for relief by your Majesty, then may you be assured to be possessed of their hearts, and if of their hearts, of all they can do or have.

And so we your Majesty's most humble and loyal subjects, whose ancestors have with great loyalty, readiness, and joyfulness served your famous progenitors, Kings and Queens of this Realm, shall with like loyalty and joy, both we and our posterity, serve your Majesty and your most royal issue for ever, with our lives, lands, and goods, and all other our abilities, and by all means endeavour to procure your Majesty honour, with all plenty, tranquillity, content, joy and felicity.

In 1610 the Commons complained about new customs duties (impositions) levied by the king.

Parliament and Taxation, 1610

The policy and constitution of this your kingdom appropriates unto the Kings of this realm, with the assent of the Parliament, as well the sovereign power of making laws as that of taxing or imposing upon the subjects' goods or merchandises, wherein they have justly such a propriety as may not without their consent be altered or changed. This is the cause that the people of this kingdom, as they ever shewed themselves faithful and loving to their Kings and ready to aid them in all their just occasions with voluntary contributions, so have they been ever careful to preserve their own liberties and rights when anything hath been done to prejudice or impeach the same. And therefore when their Princes, occasioned either by their wars or their overgreat bounty or by any other necessity, have without consent of Parliament set impositions either within the land or upon commodities either exported or imported by the merchants, they have in open Parliament complained of it in that it was done without their consents, and thereupon never failed to obtain a speedy and full redress, without any claim made by the Kings of any power or prerogative in that point. And though the law of propriety be originally and carefully preserved by the common laws of this realm, which are as ancient as the kingdom itself, yet these famous Kings, for the better contentment and assurance of their loving subjects, agreed that this old fundamental right should be farther declared and established by Act of Parliament, wherein it is provided that no such charges should ever be laid upon the people without their common consent, as may appear by sundry records of former times.

J. R. Tanner, *Constitutional Documents of the Reign of James I, 1603–1625* (1930), p. 150. Reprinted by permission of Cambridge University Press.

We therefore, your Majesty's most humble Commons assembled in Parliament, following the example of this worthy care of our ancestors and out of a duty to those for whom we serve, finding that your Majesty, without advice or consent of Parliament, hath lately in time of peace set both greater impositions and far more in number than any your noble ancestors did ever in time of war, have with all humility presumed to present this most just and necessary petition unto your Majesty, That all impositions set without the assent of Parliament may be quite abolished and taken away.

A "protestation" of 1621 declared that any important matter of state was a fit subject for débate in Parliament.

Commons Protestation, 1621

The Commons now assembled in Parliament, being justly occasioned thereunto concerning sundry liberties, franchises, and privileges of Parliament, amongst others here mentioned, do make this Protestation following, That the liberties, franchises, privileges, and jurisdictions of Parliament are the ancient and undoubted birthright and inheritance of the subjects of England; and that the arduous and urgent affairs concerning the King, State, and defence of the realm and of the Church of England, and the maintenance and making of laws, and redress of mischiefs and grievances which daily happen within this realm, are proper subjects and matter of counsel and debate in Parliament; and that in the handling and proceeding of those businesses every member of the House of Parliament hath, and of right ought to have, freedom of speech to propound, treat, reason, and bring to conclusion the same.

The accession of Charles I did not improve matters. Charles was, by conviction, a High Church Anglican. Moreover, he had married a papist wife (Henrietta Maria of France) and was inclined to tolerate Catholicism. The leaders of the House of Commons were deeply suspicious of his religious

J. R. Tanner, *Constitutional Documents of the Reign of James I, 1603–1625* (1930), pp. 288–289. Reprinted by permission of Cambridge University Press.

policy, and they hated his chief minister, Buckingham. Accordingly, they withheld grants of taxation. Charles resorted to forced loans, which led to another constitutional protest, the Petition of Right of 1628.

Petition of Right, 1628

Humbly show unto our Sovereign Lord the King, the Lords Spiritual and Temporal, and Commons in Parliament assembled, that whereas it is declared and enacted by a statute made in the time of the reign of King Edward the First, commonly called *Statutum de Tallagio non concedendo,* that no tallage or aid shall be laid or levied by the King or his heirs in this realm, without the goodwill and assent of the Archbishops, Bishops, Earls, Barons, Knights, Burgesses, and other the freemen of the commonalty of this realm: and by authority of Parliament holden in the five and twentieth year of the reign of King Edward the Third, it is declared and enacted, that from thenceforth no person shall be compelled to make any loans to the King against his will, because such loans were against reason and the franchise of the land; and by other laws of this realm it is provided, that none should be charged by any charge or imposition, called a Benevolence, or by such like charge, by which the statutes before-mentioned, and other the good laws and statutes of this realm, your subjects have inherited this freedom, that they should not be compelled to contribute to any tax, tallage, aid, or other like charge, not set by common consent in Parliament.

Yet nevertheless, of late divers commissions directed to sundry Commissioners in several counties with instructions have issued, by means whereof your people have been in divers places assembled, and required to lend certain sums of money unto your Majesty, and many of them upon their refusal so to do, have had an oath administered unto them, not warrantable by the laws or statutes of this realm, and have been constrained to become bound to make appearance and give attendance before your Privy Council, and in other places, and others of them have been therefore imprisoned, confined, and sundry other ways molested and disquieted. . . .

And where also by the statute called, "The Great Charter of the Liberties of England," it is declared and enacted, that no freeman may be taken or imprisoned or be disseised of his freeholds or liberties, or his free customs, or be outlawed or exiled; or in any manner destroyed, but by the lawful judgment of his peers, or by the law of the land.

They do therefore humbly pray your Most Excellent Majesty, that no man hereafter be compelled to make or yield any gift, loan, benevolence, tax, or

S. R. Gardiner, *The Constitutional Documents of the Puritan Revolution,* 2nd ed. (1899), pp. 66–69. Reprinted by permission of The Clarendon Press, Oxford.

such like charge, without common consent by Act of Parliament; and that none be called to make answer, or take such oath, or to give attendance, or be confined, or otherwise molested or disquieted concerning the same, or for refusal thereof; and that no freeman, in any such manner as is before-mentioned, be imprisoned or detained. . . .

Charles accepted the Petition of Right. But a new dispute broke out at once over a tax called "tonnage and poundage," not specifically mentioned in the petition. Charles protested that he had never intended to deprive himself of this source of revenue.

FROM Charles I's Speech at the Prorogation of Parliament, 1628

Now since I am truly informed, that a second Remonstrance is preparing for me to take away the profit of my Tonnage and Poundage, one of the chiefest maintenances of my Crown, by alleging I have given away my right thereto by my answer to your Petition.

This is so prejudicial unto me, that I am forced to end this Session some few hours before I meant, being not willing to receive any more Remonstrances, to which I must give a harsh answer. And since I see that even the House of Commons begins already to make false constructions of what I granted in your Petition, lest it be worse interpreted in the country, I will now make a declaration concerning the true intent thereof.

The profession of both Houses in the time of hammering this Petition, was no ways to trench upon my Prerogative, saying they had neither intention or power to hurt it. Therefore it must needs be conceived that I have granted no new, but only confirmed the ancient liberties of my subjects; yet to show the clearness of my intentions, that I neither repent, nor mean to recede from anything I have promised you, I do here declare myself, that those things which have been done, whereby many have had some cause to expect the liberties of the subjects to be trenched upon—which indeed was the first and true ground of the Petition—shall not hereafter be drawn into example for your prejudice, and from time to time; in the word of a king, ye shall not have the like cause to complain; but as for Tonnage and Poundage, it is a

S. R. Gardiner, *The Constitutional Documents of the Puritan Revolution*, 2nd ed. (1899), pp. 73–74. Reprinted by permission of The Clarendon Press, Oxford.

thing I cannot want, and was never intended by you to ask, nor meant by me—I am sure—to grant.

To conclude, I command you all that are here to take notice of what I have spoken at this time, to be the true intent and meaning of what I granted you in your Petition; but especially, you my Lords the Judges, for to you only under me belongs the interpretation of laws, for none of the Houses of Parliament, either joint or separate (what new doctrine soever may be raised), have any power either to make or declare a law without my consent.

The Parliament of 1629 continued to attack the fiscal and religious policies of Charles's government. It ended in the unprecedented scene described next.

FROM A True Relation of . . . Proceedings in Parliament

This day, being the last day of the Assembly, as soon as prayers were ended the Speaker went into the Chair, and delivered the Kings command for the adjournment of the House until Tuesday sevennight following.

The House returned him answer, that it was not the office of the Speaker to deliver any such command unto them, but for the adjournment of the House it did properly belong unto themselves; and after they had settled some things they thought fit and convenient to be spoken of they would satisfy the King.

The Speaker told them that he had an express command from the King as soon as he had delivered his message to rise; and upon that he left the Chair, but was by force drawn to it again by Mr. Denzil Holles, son of the Earl of Clare, Mr. Valentine, and others. And Mr. Holles, notwithstanding the endeavour of Sir Thomas Edmondes, Sir Humphrey May, and other Privy Councellors to free the Speaker from the Chair, swore, Gods wounds, he should sit still until they pleased to rise. . . .

Sir John Eliot. God knows I now speak with all duty to the King. It is true the misfortunes we suffer are many, we know what discoveries have been made; how Arminianism creeps in and undermines us, and how Popery comes in upon us; they mask not in strange disguises, but expose themselves to the view of the world. In search whereof we have fixed our eyes not simply on the actors (the Jesuits and priests), but on their masters, they that are in authority, hence it comes we suffer. The fear of them makes these interruptions. You have seen prelates that are their abettors. That great Bishop of

Wallace Notestein and Frances H. Relf, eds., *Commons Debates for 1629* (1921), pp. 101–106.

Winchester, we know what he hath done to favour them; this fear extends to some others that contract a fear of being discovered, and they draw from hence this jealousy. This is the Lord Treasurer, in whose person all evil is contracted. I find him acting and building on those grounds laid by his Master, the late great Duke of Buckingham, and his spirit is moving for these interruptions. And from this fear they break Parliaments lest Parliaments should break them. I find him the head of all that great party the Papists, and all Jesuits and priests derive from him their shelter and protection.

In this great question of Tonnage and Poundage, the instruments moved at his command and pleasure; he dismays our merchants, and invites strangers to come in to drive our trade, and to serve their own ends.

The Remonstrance was put to the question, but the Speaker refused to do it; and said he was otherwise commanded from the King.

Whereupon Mr. Selden spake as followeth:

"You, Mr. Speaker, say you dare not put the question which we command you; if you will not put it we must sit still, and thus we shall never be able to do any thing; they that come after you may say they have the Kings command not to do it. We sit here by commandment of the King, under the great Seal of England; and for you, you are by his Majesty (sitting in his royal chair before both Houses) appointed our Speaker, and yet now you refuse to do us the office and service of a Speaker."

Then they required Mr. Holles to read certain Articles as the Protestations of the House, which were jointly, as they were read, allowed with a loud *Yea* by the House. The effect of which Articles are as followeth:

First, Whosoever shall bring in innovation in Religion, or by favour or countenance, seek to extend or introduce Popery or Arminianism or other opinions disagreeing from the true and orthodox Church, shall be reputed a capital enemy to this Kingdom and Commonwealth.

Secondly, Whosoever shall counsel or advise the taking and levying of the Subsidies of Tonnage and Poundage, not being granted by Parliament, or shall be an actor or instrument therein, shall be likewise reputed an innovator in the government, and a capital enemy to this Kingdom and Commonwealth.

Thirdly, If any merchant or person whatsoever shall voluntarily yield or pay the said subsidies of Tonnage and Poundage, not being granted by Parliament, he shall likewise be reputed a betrayer of the liberties of England and an enemy to the same.

These being read and allowed of, the House rose up after they had sitten down two hours.

The King hearing that the House continued to sit (notwithstanding his command for the adjourning thereof) sent a messenger for the serjeant with the mace, which being taken from the table there can be no further proceeding; but the serjeant was by the House stayed, and the key of the door taken from him, and given to a gentleman of the House to keep.

After this the King sent Maxwell [*the usher—B. T.*] with the black rod for the dissolution of Parliament, but being informed that neither he nor his message would be received by the House, the King grew into much rage and passion, and sent for the Captain of the Pensioners and Guard to force the door, but the rising of the House prevented the bloodshed that might have been spilt.

Notwithstanding the Parliament was but as yet adjourned until that day sevennight, being the tenth of March, yet were the principal gentlemen attached by pursuivants, some the next morning; and on Wednesday by order from the Council-board sent to sundry prisons.

After this incident Charles ruled for eleven years without Parliament. He obtained revenue by reviving ancient rights of the crown that had fallen into disuse. When such procedures were challenged in the courts, the judges upheld their legality. The following extracts deal with the "Case of Ship Money" (1637).

Case of Ship Money, 1637

AN ENQUIRY OF CHARLES TO THE JUDGES

When the good and safety of the kingdom in general is concerned; and the whole kingdom in danger, whether may not the King, by writ under the Great Seal of England, command all the subjects of our kingdom at their charge to provide and furnish such a number of ships, with men, victuals, and munition, and for such time as we shall think fit for the defence and safeguard of the kingdom from such danger and peril, and by law compel the doing thereof, in case of refusal or refractoriness; and whether in such a case is not the King the sole judge both of the danger, and when and how the same is to be prevented and avoided?

REPLY OF THE JUDGES

May it please your Most Excellent Majesty:
We have, according to your Majesty's command, every man by himself, and all of us together, taken into serious consideration the case and question signed by your Majesty, and inclosed in your royal letter; and we are of

S. R. Gardiner, *The Constitutional Documents of the Puritan Revolution,* 2nd ed. (1899), pp. 108–114. Reprinted by permission of The Clarendon Press, Oxford.

opinion, that when the good and safety of the kingdom in general is concerned, and the kingdom in danger, your Majesty may, by writ under the Great Seal of England, command all your subjects of this your kingdom, at their charge to provide and furnish such a number of ships, with men, victuals, and munition, and for such time as your Majesty shall think fit for the defence and safeguard of this kingdom from such danger and peril: and that by law your Majesty may compel the doing thereof in case of refusal, or refractoriness: and we are also of opinion, that in such case your Majesty is the sole judge both of the danger, and when and how the same is to be prevented and avoided.

SPEECH OF OLIVER ST. JOHN AGAINST SHIP MONEY

My Lords, not to burn daylight longer, it must needs be granted that in this business of defence the *suprema potestas* [*supreme power—B. T.*] is inherent in His Majesty, as part of his crown and kingly dignity.

So that as the care and provision of the law of England extends in the first place to foreign defence, and secondly lays the burden upon all, and for ought I have to say against it, it maketh the quantity of each man's estate the rule whereby this burden is to be equally apportioned upon each person; so likewise hath it in the third place made His Majesty the sole judge of dangers from foreigners, and when and how the same are to be prevented, and to come nearer, hath given him power by writ under the Great Seal of England, to command the inhabitants of each county to provide shipping for the defence of the kingdom, and may by law compel the doing thereof.

So that, my Lords, as I still conceive the question will not be *de persona,* in whom the *suprema potestas* of giving the authorities or powers to the sheriff, which are mentioned in this writ, doth lie, for that it is in the King; but the question is only *de modo,* by what medium or method this supreme power, which is in His Majesty, doth infuse and let out itself into this particular. . . .

And as without the assistance of his Judges, who are his settled counsel at law, His Majesty applies not the law and justice in many cases unto his subjects . . . neither can he out of Parliament alter the old laws, nor make new, or make any naturalizations or legitimations, nor do some other things; and yet is the Parliament His Majesty's Court too, as well as other his Courts of Justice.

That amongst the *ardua Regni negotia,* for which Parliaments are called, this of the defence is not only one of them, but even the chief, is cleared by this, that of all the rest none is named particularly in the summons, but only this; for all the summons to Parliament show the cause of the calling of them to be *pro quibusdam arduis negotiis nos et defensionem Regni nostri Angliae et Ecclesiae Anglicanae concernentibus* [*for certain arduous affairs concerning us and the defense of our realm of England and of the English church— B. T.*].

My Lords, the Parliament, as it is best qualified and fitted to make this supply for some of each rank, and that through all the parts of the kingdom being there met, His Majesty having declared the danger, they best knowing the estates of all men within the realm, are fittest, by comparing the danger and men's estates together, to proportion the aid accordingly.

And secondly, as they are fittest for the preservation of that fundamental propriety which the subject hath in his lands and goods, because each subject's vote is included in whatsoever is there done; so that it cannot be done otherwise, I shall endeavour to prove to your Lordships both by reason and authority.

My first reason is this, that the Parliament by the law is appointed as the ordinary means for supply upon extraordinary occasions, when the ordinary supplies will not do it. . . .

My second reason is taken from the actions of former Kings in this of the defence.

The aids demanded by them, and granted in Parliament, even for this purpose of the defence, and that in times of imminent danger, are so frequent, that I will spare the citing of any of them; it is rare in a subject, and more in a prince, to ask and take that of gift, which he may and ought to have of right, and that without so much as a *salvo,* or declaration of his right.

2
THE LIMITATION OF ROYAL POWER, 1640-1641

In 1640 Charles was compelled by a rebellion in Scotland to summon Parliament again. It promptly passed a series of acts curtailing royal power for the future. The first act decreed that Parliament was to meet at least every three years.

Triennial Act

AN ACT FOR THE PREVENTING OF INCONVENIENCES HAPPENING BY THE LONG INTERMISSION OF PARLIAMENTS

I. Whereas by the laws and statutes of this realm the Parliament ought to be holden at least once every year for the redress of grievances, but the appointment of the time and place for the holding thereof hath always belonged, as it ought, to His Majesty and his royal progenitors; and whereas it is by experience found that the not holding of Parliaments accordingly hath produced sundry and great mischiefs and inconveniences to the King's Majesty, the Church and Commonwealth; for the prevention of the like mischiefs and inconveniences in time to come.

II. Be it enacted by the King's Most Excellent Majesty, with the consent of the Lords spiritual and temporal, and the Commons in this present Parliament assembled, that the said laws and statutes be from henceforth duly kept and observed; and your Majesty's loyal and obedient subjects, in this present Parliament now assembled, do humbly pray that it be enacted; and be it

S. R. Gardiner, *The Constitutional Documents of the Puritan Revolution*, 2nd ed. (1899), pp. 144–145. Reprinted by permission of The Clarendon Press, Oxford.

enacted accordingly, by the authority of this present Parliament, that in case there be not a Parliament summoned by writ under the Great Seal of England, and assembled and held before the 10th of September, which shall be in the third year next after the last day of the last meeting and sitting in this present Parliament, the beginning of the first year to be accounted from the said last day of the last meeting and sitting in Parliament; and so from time to time, and in all times hereafter, if there shall not be a Parliament assembled and held before the 10th day of September, which shall be in the third year next after the last day of the last meeting and sitting in Parliament before the time assembled and held; the beginning of the first year to be accounted from the said last day of the last meeting and sitting in Parliament; that then in every such case as aforesaid, the Parliament shall assemble and be held in the usual place at Westminster. [*The act required the Lord Chancellor to issue writs for a new Parliament whether the king commanded it or not—B. T.*]

The Earl of Strafford was declared guilty of high treason by act of attainder and executed. Since his real offense was that he had been an exceptionally loyal and effective servant of the king, the chief prosecutor, John Pym, found it necessary to propound a new theory of treason as an offense against fundamental law.

Attainder of Strafford

My Lords, many days have been spent, in maintenance of the impeachment of the earl of Strafford, by the House of Commons, whereby he stands charged with high treason; and your lordships have heard his defence with patience and with as much favour as justice would allow. We have passed through our evidence, and the result of all this is, that it remains clearly proved, that the earl of Strafford hath endeavoured by his words, actions, and counsels, to subvert the fundamental laws of England and Ireland, and to introduce an arbitrary and tyrannical government. . . .

The law is that which puts a difference betwixt good and evil, betwixt just and unjust; if you take away the law, all things will fall into a confusion, every man will become a law to himself, which in the depraved condition of human nature, must needs produce many great enormities. Lust will become a law, and envy will become a law, covetousness and ambition will become

S. Reed Brett, *John Pym* (1940), pp. 171–172. Reprinted by permission of John Murray, London.

laws; and what dictates, what decisions such laws will produce, may easily be discovered in the late government of Ireland. . . .

The law is the boundary, the measure, betwixt the King's prerogative and the people's liberty; whilst these move in their own orbs, they are a support and a security to one another; the prerogative a cover and defence to the liberty of the people, and the people by their liberty are enabled to be a foundation to the prerogative; but if these bounds be so removed, that they enter into contestation and conflict, one of these mischiefs must ensue: if the prerogative of the King overwhelm the liberty of the people, it will be turned to tyranny; if liberty undermine the prerogative, it will grow into anarchy.

Parliament also decreed that it could not be dissolved without its own consent.

Act Against Dissolving the Long Parliament Without Its Own Consent

AN ACT TO PREVENT INCONVENIENCES WHICH MAY HAPPEN BY THE UNTIMELY ADJOURNING, PROROGUING, OR DISSOLVING THIS PRESENT PARLIAMENT

Whereas great sums of money must of necessity be speedily advanced and provided for the relief of His Majesty's army and people in the northern parts of this realm, and for preventing the imminent danger it is in, and for supply of other His Majesty's present and urgent occasions, which cannot be so timely effected as is requisite without credit for raising the said monies; which credit cannot be obtained until such obstacles be first removed as are occasioned by fears, jealousies and apprehensions of divers His Majesty's loyal subjects, that this present Parliament may be adjourned, prorogued, or dissolved, before justice shall be duly executed upon delinquents, public grievances redressed, a firm peace between the two nations of England and Scotland concluded, and before sufficient provision be made for the repayment of the said monies so to be raised; all which the Commons in this present Parliament assembled, having duly considered, do therefore most humbly beseech your Majesty that it may be declared and enacted.

And be it declared and enacted by the King, our Sovereign Lord, with the assent of the Lords and Commons in this present Parliament assembled, and by the authority of the same, that this present Parliament now assembled

S. R. Gardiner, *The Constitutional Documents of the Puritan Revolution,* 2nd ed. (1899), pp. 158–159. Reprinted by permission of The Clarendon Press, Oxford.

shall not be dissolved unless it be by Act of Parliament to be passed for that purpose.

Act Abolishing Star Chamber

AN ACT FOR THE REGULATING OF THE PRIVY COUNCIL AND FOR TAKING AWAY THE COURT COMMONLY CALLED THE STAR CHAMBER

I. Whereas by the Great Charter many times confirmed in Parliament, it is enacted that no freeman shall be taken or imprisoned, or disseized of his freehold or liberties or free customs, or be outlawed or exiled or otherwise destroyed, and that the King will not pass upon him or condemn him but by lawful judgment of his Peers or by the law of the land; and by another statute made in the fifth year of the reign of King Edward the Third, it is enacted that no man shall be attached by any accusation nor forejudged of life or limb, nor his lands, tenements, goods nor chattels seized into the King's hands against the form of the Great Charter and the law of the land . . . ; and forasmuch as all matters examinable or determinable before the Court commonly called the Star Chamber, may have their proper remedy and redress, and their due punishment and correction by the common law of the land, and in the ordinary course of justice elsewhere, and forasmuch as the reasons and motives inducing the erection and continuance of that Court do now cease, and the proceedings, censures and decrees of that Court have by experience been found to be an intolerable burden to the subjects, and the means to introduce an arbitrary power and government: and forasmuch as the Council Table hath of late times assumed unto itself a power to intermeddle in civil causes and matters only of private interest between party and party, and have adventured to determine of the estates and liberties of the subject contrary to the law of the land and the rights and privileges of the subject, by which great and manifold mischiefs and inconveniences have arisen and happened, and much uncertainty by means of such proceedings hath been conceived concerning men's rights and estates: for settling whereof and preventing the like in time to come, be it ordained and enacted by the authority of this present Parliament, that the said Court commonly called the Star Chamber, and all jurisdiction, power and authority belonging unto or exercised in the same Court, or by any of the Judges, Officers or Ministers thereof be, from the first day of August in the year of our Lord God one thousand six hundred forty and one, clearly and absolutely dissolved, taken away, and determined.

S. R. Gardiner, *The Constitutional Documents of the Puritan Revolution*, 2nd ed. (1899), pp. 179–182. Reprinted by permission of The Clarendon Press, Oxford.

The collection of ship money was declared illegal. Other acts of Parliament abolished all the other nonparliamentary procedures that Charles had used to raise taxes during the preceding ten years. It is important to note that all these acts of 1641 were signed by the king and so became valid statutes.

Act Abolishing Ship Money

Whereas divers writs of late time issued under the great seal of England, commonly called ship writs, for the charging of the ports, towns, cities, boroughs, and counties of this realm respectively to provide and furnish certain ships for his majesty's service; and whereas, upon the execution of the same writs . . . , process hath been thence made against sundry persons pretended to be charged by way of contribution for the making up of certain sums assessed for the providing of the said ships, and in especial . . . against John Hampden, esquire . . . ; and whereas some other actions and process depend . . . against other persons for the like kind of charge grounded upon the said writs commonly called ship writs, all which writs and proceedings as aforesaid were utterly against the law of the land: be it therefore declared and enacted by the king's most excellent majesty and the lords and the commons in this present parliament assembled, and by the authority of the same, that the said charge imposed upon the subject for the providing and furnishing of ships commonly called ship money . . . , and the said writs . . . and the said judgment given against the said John Hampden, were and are contrary to and against the laws and statutes of this realm, the right of property, the liberty of the subjects, former resolutions in parliament, and the Petition of Right made in the third year of the reign of his majesty that now is.

And it is further declared and enacted . . . that all . . . particulars prayed or desired in the said Petition of Right shall from henceforth be put in execution accordingly, and shall be firmly and strictly holden and observed as in the same petition they are prayed and expressed; and that all . . . the records . . . of all . . . the judgment, enrolments . . . , and proceedings as aforesaid, and all . . . the proceedings whatsoever, upon or by pretext . . . of any of the said writs commonly called ship writs . . . , shall be deemed . . . to be utterly void.

Sources of English Constitutional History, p. 482, edited and translated by Carl Stephenson and Frederick G. Marcham. Copyright 1937 by Harper & Brothers. Reprinted by permission of Harper & Row, Publishers.

3
THE
OUTBREAK
OF WAR

Toward the end of 1641 a division between the more moderate and the more radical members of the House of Commons became apparent in debates over the Grand Remonstrance. This document was a diffuse statement of all the grievances of the preceding twenty years. The petition accompanying the Grand Remonstrance, given below, sets out its main points..

Petition Accompanying the Grand Remonstrance

MOST GRACIOUS SOVEREIGN,

Your Majesty's most humble and faithful subjects the Commons in this present Parliament assembled, do with much thankfulness and joy acknowledge the great mercy and favour of God, in giving your Majesty a safe and peaceable return out of Scotland into your kingdom of England, where the pressing dangers and distempers of the State have caused us with much earnestness to desire the comfort of your gracious presence, and likewise the unity and justice of your royal authority, to give more life and power to the dutiful and loyal counsels and endeavours of your Parliament, for the prevention of that eminent ruin and destruction wherein your kingdoms of England and Scotland are threatened. The duty which we owe to your Majesty and our country, cannot but make us very sensible and apprehensive, that the multiplicity, sharpness and malignity of those evils under which we have now many years suffered, are fomented and cherished by a corrupt and ill-affected party, who amongst other their mischievous devices for the alteration

S. R. Gardiner, *The Constitutional Documents of the Puritan Revolution*, 2nd ed. (1899), pp. 202–205. Reprinted by permission of The Clarendon Press, Oxford.

of religion and government, have sought by many false scandals and imputations, cunningly insinuated and dispersed amongst the people, to blemish and disgrace our proceedings in this Parliament. . . .

* * *

And because we have reason to believe that those malignant parties, whose proceedings evidently appear to be mainly for the advantage and increase of Popery, is composed, set up, and acted by the subtile practice of the Jesuits and other engineers and factors for Rome, and to the great danger of this kingdom, and most grievous affliction of your loyal subjects, have so far prevailed as to corrupt divers of your Bishops and others in prime places of the Church, and also to bring divers of these instruments to be of your Privy Council, and other employments of trust and nearness about your Majesty, the Prince, and the rest of your royal children.

And by this means have had such an operation in your counsel and the most important affairs and proceedings of your government, that a most dangerous division and chargeable preparation for war betwixt your kingdoms of England and Scotland, the increase of jealousies betwixt your Majesty and your most obedient subjects, the violent distraction and interruption of this Parliament, the insurrection of the Papists in your kingdom of Ireland, and bloody massacre of your people, have been not only endeavoured and attempted, but in a great measure compassed and effected.

* * *

We, your most humble and obedient subjects, do with all faithfulness and humility beseech your Majesty:

1. That you will be graciously pleased to concur with the humble desires of your people in a parliamentary way, for the preserving the peace and safety of the kingdom from the malicious designs of the Popish party:

For depriving the Bishops of their votes in Parliament, and abridging their immoderate power usurped over the Clergy, and other your good subjects, which they have perniciously abused to the hazard of religion, and great prejudice and oppression to the laws of the kingdom, and just liberty of your people:

For the taking away such oppressions in religion, Church government and discipline, as have been brought in and fomented by them:

For uniting all such your loyal subjects together as join in the same fundamental truths against the Papists, by removing some oppressions and unnecessary ceremonies by which divers weak consciences have been scrupled, and seem to be divided from the rest, and for the due execution of those good laws which have been made for securing the liberty of your subjects.

2. That your Majesty will likewise be pleased to remove from your council all such as persist to favour and promote any of those pressures and corruptions wherewith your people have been grieved, and that for the future your Majesty will vouchsafe to employ such persons in your great and public

affairs, and to take such to be near you in places of trust, as your Parliament may have cause to confide in; that in your princely goodness to your people you will reject and refuse all mediation and solicitation to the contrary, how powerful and near soever.

The last part of the preceding petition was, in effect, a demand by Parliament to take control of the king's government. Charles refused to assent to it and, in January 1642, tried to arrest its leading sponsors.

. Case of the Five Members

And as his Majesty came through Westminster Hall, the Commanders, etc., that attended him made a lane on both sides the Hall (through which his Majesty passed and came up the stairs to the House of Commons) and stood before the guard of Pensioners and Halbedeers (who also attended the king's person) and, the door of the House of Commons being thrown open, his Majesty entered the House, and as he passed up towards the Chair he cast his eye on the right hand near the Bar of the House, where Mr. Pym used to sit; but his Majesty not seeing him there (knowing him well) went up to the Chair, and said, "By your leave, Mr. Speaker, I must borrow your chair a little." Whereupon the Speaker came out of the Chair and his Majesty stepped up into it; after he had stood in the Chair a while, casting his eye upon the members as they stood up uncovered, but could not discern any of the five members to be there, nor indeed were they easy to be discerned (had they been there) among so many bare faces all standing up together. Then his Majesty made this speech.

"Gentlemen, I am sorry for this occasion of coming unto you. Yesterday I sent a Serjeant at Arms upon a very important occasion, to apprehend some that by my command were accused of high treason; whereunto I did expect obedience and not a message. And I must declare unto you here that, albeit no king that ever was in England shall be more careful of your privileges, to maintain them to the uttermost of his power, than I shall be; yet you must know that in cases of treason no person hath a privilege. And therefore I am come to know if any of these persons that were accused are here. For I must tell you, Gentlemen, that so long as these persons that I have accused (for no light crime, but for treason) are here, I cannot expect that this House will be in the right way that I do heartily wish it. Therefore I am come to tell you that I must have them wheresoever I find them. Well, since I see all the birds

John Rushworth, *Historical Collections,* IV (1721), 477–478.

are flown, I do expect from you that you shall send them unto me as soon as they return hither. But I assure you, on the word of a king, I never did intend any force, but shall proceed against them in a legal and fair way, for I never did intend any other.

"And now, since I cannot do what I came for, I think this no unfit occasion to repeat what I have said formerly, that whatsoever I have done in favor and to the good of my subjects, I do mean to maintain it.

"I will trouble you no more, but tell you I do expect as soon as they come to the House you will send them to me; otherwise I must take my own course to find them."

When the king was looking about the House, the Speaker standing below by the Chair, his Majesty asked him whether any of these persons were in the House. Whether he saw any of them? And where they were? To which the Speaker, falling on his knee, thus answered, "May it please your Majesty, I have neither eyes to see, nor tongue to speak in this place but as the House is pleased to direct me, whose servant I am here; and humbly beg your Majesty's pardon, that I cannot give any other answer than this to what your Majesty is pleased to demand of me."

The king, having concluded his speech, went out of the House again, which was in great disorder, and many members cried out aloud, so as he might hear them, "Privilege! Privilege!" and forthwith adjourned till the next day at one of the clock.

After this abortive attempt Charles withdrew from London. The decisive breach came when the houses of Parliament, without royal consent, raised an army on their own authority. (An army was urgently needed to suppress a rebellion in Ireland.)

Militia Ordinance

AN ORDINANCE OF THE LORDS AND COMMONS IN
PARLIAMENT, FOR THE SAFETY AND DEFENCE OF THE
KINGDOM OF ENGLAND AND DOMINION OF WALES

Whereas there hath been of late a most dangerous and desperate design upon the House of Commons, which we have just cause to believe to be an effect of the bloody counsels of Papists and other ill-affected persons, who have al-

S. R. Gardiner, *The Constitutional Documents of the Puritan Revolution,* 2nd ed. (1899), pp. 245–246. Reprinted by permission of The Clarendon Press, Oxford.

ready raised a rebellion in the kingdom of Ireland; and by reason of many discoveries we cannot but fear they will proceed not only to stir up the like rebellion and insurrections in this kingdom of England, but also to back them with forces from abroad.

For the safety therefore of His Majesty's person, the Parliament and kingdom in this time of imminent danger.

It is ordained by the Lords and Commons now in Parliament assembled, that Henry Earl of Holland shall be Lieutenant of the County of Berks, Oliver Earl of Bolingbroke shall be Lieutenant of the County of Bedford, &c.

* * *

And shall severally and respectively have power to assemble and call together all and singular His Majesty's subjects, within the said several and respective counties and places, as well within liberties as without, that are meet and fit for the wars, and them to train and exercise and put in readiness, and them after their abilities and faculties well and sufficiently from time to time to cause to be arrayed and weaponed, and to take the muster of them in places most fit for that purpose.

The king, in reply, insisted on his ancient right to command the armed forces of the realm.

Charles I's Proclamation Condemning the Militia Ordinance

Whereas, by the statute made in the seventh year of King Edward the First, the Prelates, Earls, Barons and Commonalty of the realm affirmed in Parliament, that to the King it belongeth, and his part it is by his royal seigniory straightly to defend wearing of armour and all other force against the peace, at all times when it shall please him, and to punish them which do the contrary according to the laws and usages of the realm; and hereunto all subjects are bound to aid the King as their sovereign lord, at all seasons when need shall be; and whereas we understand that, expressly contrary to the said statute and other good laws of this our kingdom, under colour and pretence of an Ordinance of Parliament, without our consent, or any commission or war-

S. R. Gardiner, *The Constitutional Documents of the Puritan Revolution,* 2nd ed. (1899), pp. 248–249. Reprinted by permission of The Clarendon Press, Oxford.

rant from us, the trained bands and militia of this kingdom have been lately, and are intended to be put in arms, and drawn into companies in a warlike manner, whereby the peace and quiet of our subjects is, or may be, disturbed; we being desirous, by all gracious and fair admonitions, to prevent that some malignant persons in this our kingdom do not by degrees seduce our good subjects from their due obedience to us and the laws of this our kingdom . . . do therefore, by this our Proclamation, expressly charge and command all our sheriffs, and all colonels, lieutenant-colonels, sergeant-majors, captains, officers and soldiers, belonging to the trained bands of this our kingdom, and likewise all high and petty constables, and other our officers and subjects whatsoever, upon their allegiance, and as they tender the peace of this our kingdom, not to muster, levy, raise or march, or to summon or warn, upon any warrant, order or ordinance from one or both of our Houses of Parliament.

4
A WHIG INTERPRETATION OF THE CIVIL WAR

FROM The History of England BY T. B. MACAULAY

And now [*1624—B. T.*] began that hazardous game on which were staked the destinies of the English people. It was played on the side of the House of Commons with keenness, but with admirable dexterity, coolness, and perseverance. Great statesmen who looked far behind them and far before them were at the head of that assembly. They were resolved to place the King in such a situation that he must either conduct the administration in conformity with the wishes of his Parliament, or make outrageous attacks on the most sacred principles of the constitution. They accordingly doled out supplies to him very sparingly. He found that he must govern either in harmony with the House of Commons, or in defiance of all law. His choice was soon made. He dissolved his first Parliament, and levied taxes by his own authority. He convoked a second Parliament, and found it more intractable than the first. He again resorted to the expedient of dissolution, raised fresh taxes without any show of legal right, and threw the chiefs of the opposition into prison. At the same time a new grievance, which the peculiar feelings and habits of the English nation made insupportably painful, and which seemed to all discerning men to be of fearful augury, excited general discontent and alarm. Companies of soldiers were billeted on the people; and martial law was, in some places, substituted for the ancient jurisprudence of the realm.

The King called a third Parliament, and soon perceived that the opposition was stronger and fiercer than ever. He now determined on a change of tactics. Instead of opposing an inflexible resistance to the demands of the Com-

Thomas Babington Macaulay, *The History of England*, 9th ed., I (1853), 83–88, 96–111.

mons, he, after much altercation and many evasions, agreed to a compromise which, if he had faithfully adhered to it, would have averted a long series of calamities. The Parliament granted an ample supply. The King ratified, in the most solemn manner, that celebrated law, which is known by the name of the Petition of Right, and which is the second Great Charter of the liberties of England. By ratifying that law he bound himself never again to raise money without the consent of the Houses, never again to imprison any person, except in due course of law, and never again to subject his people to the jurisdiction of courts martial.

The day on which the royal sanction was, after many delays, solemnly given to this great act, was a day of joy and hope. The Commons, who crowded the bar of the House of Lords, broke forth into loud acclamations as soon as the clerk had pronounced the ancient form of words by which our princes have, during many ages, signified their assent to the wishes of the Estates of the realm. Those acclamations were reechoed by the voice of the capital and of the nation; but within three weeks it became manifest that Charles had no intention of observing the compact into which he had entered. The supply given by the representatives of the nation was collected. The promise by which that supply had been obtained was broken. A violent contest followed. The Parliament was dissolved with every mark of royal displeasure. Some of the most distinguished members were imprisoned; and one of them, Sir John Eliot, after years of suffering, died in confinement.

Charles, however, could not venture to raise, by his own authority, taxes sufficient for carrying on war. He accordingly hastened to make peace with his neighbours, and thenceforth gave his whole mind to British politics.

Now commenced a new era. Many English Kings had occasionally committed unconstitutional acts: but none had ever systematically attempted to make himself a despot, and to reduce the Parliament to a nullity. Such was the end which Charles distinctly proposed to himself. From March 1629 to April 1640, the Houses were not convoked. Never in our history had there been an interval of eleven years between Parliament and Parliament. Only once had there been an interval of even half that length. This fact alone is sufficient to refute those who represent Charles as having merely trodden in the footsteps of the Plantagenets and Tudors.

It is proved, by the testimony of the King's most strenuous supporters, that, during this part of his reign, the provisions of the Petition of Right were violated by him, not occasionally, but constantly, and on system; that a large part of the revenue was raised without any legal authority; and that persons obnoxious to the government languished for years in prison, without being ever called upon to plead before any tribunal.

For these things history must hold the King himself chiefly responsible. From the time of his third Parliament he was his own prime minister. Several persons, however, whose temper and talents were suited to his purposes, were at the head of different departments of the administration.

Thomas Wentworth, successively created Lord Wentworth and Earl of

Strafford, a man of great abilities, eloquence, and courage, but of a cruel and imperious nature, was the counsellor most trusted in political and military affairs. . . . His object was to do in England all, and more than all, that Richelieu was doing in France; to make Charles a monarch as absolute as any on the Continent; to put the estates and the personal liberty of the whole people at the disposal of the crown; to deprive the courts of law of all independent authority, even in ordinary questions of civil rights between man and man; and to punish with merciless rigour all who murmured at the acts of the government, or who applied, even in the most decent and regular manner, to any tribunal for relief against those acts.

This was his end; and he distinctly saw in what manner alone this end could be attained. There was, in truth, about all his notions a clearness, coherence, and precision which, if he had not been pursuing an object pernicious to his country and to his kind, would have justly entitled him to high admiration. He saw that there was one instrument, and only one, by which his vast and daring projects could be carried into execution. That instrument was a standing army. To the forming of such an army, therefore, he directed all the energy of his strong mind. In Ireland, where he was viceroy, he actually succeeded in establishing a military despotism, not only over the aboriginal population, but also over the English colonists, and was able to boast that, in that island, the King was as absolute as any prince in the whole world could be.

The ecclesiastical administration was, in the meantime, principally directed by William Laud, Archbishop of Canterbury. Of all the prelates of the Anglican Church, Laud had departed farthest from the principles of the Reformation, and had drawn nearest to Rome. . . . Under his direction every corner of the realm was subjected to a constant and minute inspection. Every little congregation of separatists was tracked out and broken up. Even the devotion of private families could not escape the vigilance of his spies. Such fear did his rigour inspire that the deadly hatred of the Church, which festered in innumerable bosoms, was generally disguised under an outward show of conformity. On the very eve of troubles, fatal to himself and to his order, the Bishops of several extensive dioceses were able to report to him that not a single dissenter was to be found within their jurisdiction.

* * *

In November 1640 met that renowned Parliament which, in spite of many errors and disasters, is justly entitled to the reverence and gratitude of all who, in any part of the world, enjoy the blessings of constitutional government.

During the year which followed, no very important division of opinion appeared in the Houses. The civil and ecclesiastical administration had, through a period of near twelve years, been so oppressive and so unconstitutional that even those classes of which the inclinations are generally on the side of order and authority were eager to promote popular reforms, and to bring the instruments of tyranny to justice. It was enacted that no interval of more than three years should ever elapse between Parliament and Parliament, and that, if writs under the Great Seal were not issued at the proper time, the returning officers should, without such writs, call the constituent bodies together for the choice of representatives. The Star Chamber, the High Commission, the Council of York, were swept away. Men who, after suffering cruel mutilations, had been confined in remote dungeons, regained their liberty. On the chief ministers of the crown the vengeance of the nation was unsparingly wreaked. The Lord Keeper, the Primate, the Lord Lieutenant were impeached. Finch saved himself by flight. Laud was flung into the Tower. Strafford was impeached, and at length put to death by act of attainder. On the same day on which this act passed, the King gave his assent to a law by which he bound himself not to adjourn, prorogue, or dissolve the existing Parliament without its own consent.

* * *

At a later period the Royalists found it convenient to antedate the separation between themselves and their opponents, and to attribute the Act which restrained the King from dissolving or proroguing the Parliament, the Triennial Act, the impeachment of the ministers, and the attainder of Strafford, to the faction which afterwards made war on the King. But no artifice could be more disingenuous. Every one of those strong measures was actively promoted by the men who were afterwards foremost among the Cavaliers. No republican spoke of the long misgovernment of Charles more severely than Colepepper. The most remarkable speech in favour of the Triennial Bill was made by Digby. The impeachment of the Lord Keeper was moved by Falkland. The demand that the Lord Lieutenant should be kept close prisoner was made at the bar of the Lords by Hyde. Not till the law attaining Strafford was proposed did the signs of serious disunion become visible. Even against that law, a law which nothing but extreme necessity could justify, only about sixty members of the House of Commons voted. It is certain that Hyde was not in the minority, and that Falkland not only voted with the majority, but spoke strongly for the bill. Even the few who entertained a scruple about inflicting death by a retrospective enactment thought it necessary to express the utmost abhorrence of Strafford's character and administration.

But under this apparent concord a great schism was latent; and when, in October 1641, the Parliament reassembled after a short recess, two hostile parties, essentially the same with those which, under different names, have ever since contended, and are still contending, for the direction of public affairs, appeared confronting each other. During some years they were designated as Cavaliers and Roundheads. They were subsequently called Tories and Whigs; nor does it seem that these appellations are likely soon to become obsolete.

* * *

Neither party wanted strong arguments for the measures which it was disposed to take. The reasonings of the most enlightened Royalists may be summed up thus:—"It is true that great abuses have existed; but they have been redressed. It is true that precious rights have been invaded; but they have been vindicated and surrounded with new securities. The sittings of the Estates of the realm have been, in defiance of all precedent and of the spirit of the constitution, intermitted during eleven years; but it has now been provided that henceforth three years shall never elapse without a Parliament. The Star Chamber, the High Commission, the Council of York, oppressed and plundered us; but those hateful courts have now ceased to exist. . . . Henceforth it will be our wisdom to look with jealousy on schemes of innovation, and to guard from encroachment all the prerogatives with which the law has, for the public good, armed the sovereign."

Such were the views of those men of whom the excellent Falkland may be regarded as the leader. It was contended on the other side with not less force, by men of not less ability and virtue, that the safety which the liberties of the English people enjoyed was rather apparent than real, and that the arbitrary projects of the court would be resumed as soon as the vigilance of the Commons was relaxed. True it was,—such was the reasoning of Pym, of Hollis, and of Hampden,—that many good laws had been passed: but, if good laws had been sufficient to restrain the King, his subjects would have had little reason ever to complain of his administration. The recent statutes were surely not of more authority than the Great Charter or the Petition of Right. Yet neither the Great Charter, hallowed by the veneration of four centuries, nor the Petition of Right, sanctioned, after mature reflection, and for valuable consideration, by Charles himself, had been found effectual for the protection of the people. If once the check of fear were withdrawn, if once the spirit of opposition were suffered to slumber, all the securities for English freedom resolved themselves into a single one, the royal word; and it had been proved by a long and severe experience that the royal word could not be trusted.

The two parties were still regarding each other with cautious hostility, and had not yet measured their strength, when news arrived which inflamed the passions and confirmed the opinions of both. The great chieftains of Ulster, who, at the time of the accession of James, had, after a long struggle, submitted to the royal authority, had not long brooked the humiliation of dependence. They had conspired against the English government, and had been attainted of treason. Their immense domains had been forfeited to the crown, and had soon been peopled by thousands of English and Scotch emigrants. The new settlers were, in civilisation and intelligence, far superior to the native population, and sometimes abused their superiority. The animosity produced by difference of race was increased by difference of religion. Under the iron rule of Wentworth, scarcely a murmur was heard: but, when that strong pressure was withdrawn, when Scotland had set the example of successful resistance, when England was distracted by internal quarrels, the smothered rage of the Irish broke forth into acts of fearful violence. . . . To raise a great army had always been the King's first object. A great army must now be raised. It was to be feared that, unless some new securities were devised, the forces levied for the reduction of Ireland would be employed against the liberties of England. Nor was this all. A horrible suspicion, unjust indeed, but not altogether unnatural, had arisen in many minds. The Queen was an avowed Roman Catholic: the King was not regarded by the Puritans, whom he had mercilessly persecuted, as a sincere Protestant; and so notorious was his duplicity, that there was no treachery of which his subjects might not, with some show of reason, believe him capable. It was soon whispered that the rebellion of the Roman Catholics of Ulster was part of a vast work of darkness which had been planned at Whitehall.

After some weeks of prelude, the first great parliamentary conflict between the parties which have ever since contended, and are still contending, for the government of the nation, took place on the twenty-second of November 1641. It was moved by the opposition, that the House of Commons should present to the King a remonstrance, enumerating the faults of his administration from the time of his accession, and expressing the distrust with which his policy was still regarded by his people. That assembly, which a few months before had been unanimous in calling for the reform of abuses, was now divided into two fierce and eager factions of nearly equal strength. After a hot debate of many hours, the remonstrance was carried by only eleven votes.

The result of this struggle was highly favourable to the conservative party. It could not be doubted that only some great indiscretion could prevent them from shortly obtaining the predominance in the Lower House. The Upper House was already their own. Nothing was wanting to insure their success, but that the King should, in all his conduct, show respect for the laws and scrupulous good faith towards his subjects.

His first measures promised well. He had, it seemed, at last discovered that an entire change of system was necessary, and had wisely made up his mind to what could no longer be avoided. He declared his determination to govern in harmony with the Commons, and, for that end, to call to his councils men in whose talents and character the Commons might place confidence. Nor was the selection ill made. Falkland, Hyde, and Colepepper, all three distinguished by the part which they had taken in reforming abuses and in punishing evil ministers, were invited to become the confidential advisers of the crown, and were solemnly assured by Charles that he would take no step in any way affecting the Lower House of Parliament without their privity.

Had he kept this promise, it cannot be doubted that the reaction which was already in progress would very soon have become quite as strong as the most respectable Royalists would have desired. Already the violent members of the opposition had begun to despair of the fortunes of their party, to tremble for their own safety, and to talk of selling their estates and emigrating to America. That the fair prospects which had begun to open before the King were suddenly overcast, that his life was darkened by adversity, and at length shortened by violence, is to be attributed to his own faithlessness and contempt of law.

The truth seems to be that he detested both the parties into which the House of Commons was divided: nor is this strange; for in both those parties the love of liberty and the love of order were mingled, though in different proportions. The advisers whom necessity had compelled him to call round him were by no means men after his own heart. They had joined in condemning his tyranny, in abridging his power, and in punishing his instruments. They were now indeed prepared to defend by strictly legal means his strictly legal prerogatives; but they would have recoiled with horror from the thought of reviving Wentworth's projects of Thorough. They were, therefore, in the King's opinion, traitors, who differed only in the degree of their seditious malignity from Pym and Hampden.

He accordingly, a few days after he had promised the chiefs of the constitutional Royalists that no step of importance should be taken without their knowledge, formed a resolution the most momentous of his whole life, carefully concealed that resolution from them, and executed it in a manner which overwhelmed them with shame and dismay. He sent the Attorney General to impeach Pym, Hollis, Hampden, and other members of the House of Commons of high treason at the bar of the House of Lords. Not content with this flagrant violation of the Great Charter and of the uninterrupted practice of centuries, he went in person, accompanied by armed men, to seize the leaders of the opposition within the walls of Parliament.

The attempt failed. The accused members had left the House a short time before Charles entered it. A sudden and violent revulsion of feeling, both in the Parliament and in the country, followed. The most favourable view that has ever been taken of the King's conduct on this occasion by his most partial advocates is that he had weakly suffered himself to be hurried into a gross indiscretion by the evil counsels of his wife and of his courtiers. But the general voice loudly charged him with far deeper guilt. At the very moment at which his subjects, after a long estrangement produced by his maladministration, were returning to him with feelings of confidence and affection, he had aimed a deadly blow at all their dearest rights, at the privileges of Parliament, at the very principle of trial by jury. . . . Had Charles remained much longer in his stormy capital, it is probable that the Commons would have found a plea for making him, under outward forms of respect, a state prisoner.

He quitted London, never to return till the day of a terrible and memorable reckoning had arrived. A negotiation began which occupied many months. Accusations and recriminations passed backward and forward between the contending parties. All accommodation had become impossible. The sure punishment which waits on habitual perfidy had at length overtaken the King.

* * *

The change which the Houses proposed to make in our institutions, though it seems exorbitant, when distinctly set forth and digested into articles of capitulation, really amounts to little more than the change which, in the next generation, was effected by the Revolution [*of 1688—B. T.*]. It is true that, at the Revolution, the sovereign was not deprived by law of the power of naming his ministers: but it is equally true that, since the Revolution, no ministry has been able to remain in office six months in opposition to the sense of the House of Commons. It is true that the sovereign still possesses the power of creating peers, and the more important power of the sword: but it is equally true that in the exercise of these powers the sovereign has, ever since the Revolution, been guided by advisers who possess the confidence of the representatives of the nation. In fact, the leaders of the Roundhead party in 1642, and the statesmen who, about half a century later, effected the Revolution, had exactly the same object in view. That object was to terminate the contest between the crown and the Parliament, by giving to the Parliament a supreme control over the executive administration. The statesmen of the Revolution effected this indirectly by changing the dynasty. The Roundheads of 1642, being unable to change the dynasty, were compelled to take a direct course towards their end.

5
MONARCHY, OLIGARCHY, DEMOCRACY, OR DICTATORSHIP?

The parliamentary regime can reasonably be called an oligarchy in that it represented men of property (the masses of the common people had no vote). The idea of instituting a democratic system was put forward in the course of a debate held among the army leaders in 1647 concerning the future form of government. The views expressed by Colonel Rainborow in the following exchange, however, proved totally unacceptable to the monarchists, the parliamentary leaders, and the generals. There was never any serious possibility of their being put into practice.

FROM The Army Debates

COL. RAINBOROW. . . . Really I thinke that the poorest hee that is in England hath a life to live as the greatest hee; and therefore truly, Sir, I thinke itt's cleare, that every man that is to live under a Governement ought first by his owne consent to putt himself under that Governement; and I doe thinke that the poorest man in England is not att all bound in a stricte sence to that Governement that hee hath not had a voice to putt himself under; and I am confident that when I have heard the reasons against itt, something will bee

---

C. H. Firth, ed., *The Clarke Papers* (1891), pp. 301–309. Reprinted by permission of The Royal Historical Society.

said to answer those reasons, insoemuch that I should doubt whether he was an Englishman or noe that should doubt of these thinges.

COMMISSARY IRETON. Give mee leave to tell you, that if you make this the rule I thinke you must flie for refuge to an absolute naturall Right, and you must deny all Civill Right; and I am sure itt will come to that in the consequence. . . . For my parte I thinke itt is noe right att all. I thinke that noe person hath a right to an interest or share in the disposing or determining of the affaires of the Kingedome, and in chusing those that shall determine what lawes wee shall bee rul'd by heere, noe person hath a right to this, that hath nott a permanent fixed interest in this Kingedome; and those persons together are properly the Represented of this Kingedome, and consequentlie are to make uppe the Representors of this Kingedome, who taken together doe comprehend whatsoever is of reall or permanent interest in the Kingedome. And I am sure I cannott tell what otherwise any man can say why a forraigner coming in amongst us—or as many as will coming in amongst us, or by force or otherwise setling themselves heere, or att least by our permission having a being heere—why they should nott as well lay claime to itt as any other. We talk of birthright. Truly [by] birthright there is thus much claime. Men may justly have by birthright, by their very being borne in England, that wee should nott seclude them out of England, that wee should nott refuse to give them aire, and place, and ground, and the freedome of the high wayes and other things, to live amongst us; nott [to] any man that is borne heere, though by his birth there come nothing att all to him that is parte of the permanent interest of this Kingedome. That I thinke is due to a man by birth. Butt that by a man's being borne heere hee shall have a share in that power that shall dispose of the lands heere, and of all thinges heere, I doe nott thinke itt a sufficient ground. I am sure if wee looke uppon that which is the utmost within man's view of what was originally the constitution of this Kingedome, [if wee] looke uppon that which is most radicall and fundamentall, and which if you take away there is noe man hath any land, any goods, [or] any civill interest, that is this: that those that chuse the Representors for the making of Lawes by which this State and Kingedome are to bee govern'd, are the persons who taken together doe comprehend the locall interest of this Kingedome; that is, the persons in whome all land lies, and those in Corporations in whome all trading lies. This is the most fundamentall Constitution of this Kingedome, which if you doe nott allow you allow none att all. . . .

COL. RAINBOROW. Truly, Sir, I am of the same opinion I was; and am resolved to keepe itt till I know reason why I should nott. . . . I doe heare nothing att all that can convince mee, why any man that is borne in England ought nott to have his voice in Election of Burgesses. Itt is said, that if a man have nott a permanent interest, hee can have noe claime, and wee must bee noe freer then the lawes will lett us to bee, and that there is no Chronicle will lett us bee freer then what wee enjoy. Something was said to this yesterday. I doe thinke that the maine cause why Almighty God gave men reason, itt was, that they should make use of that reason, and that they should improve itt for that end and purpose that God gave itt them. And truly, I thinke that halfe a loafe is better then none if a man bee an hungry, yett I thinke there is nothing that God hath given a man that any else can take from him. Therefore I say, that either itt must bee the law of God or the law of man that must prohibite the meanest man in the Kingedome to have this benefitt as well as the greatest. I doe nott finde any thinge in the law of God, that a Lord shall chuse 20 Burgesses, and a Gentleman butt two, or a poore man shall chuse none. I finde noe such thinge in the law of nature, nor in the law of nations. . . . And truly I have thought somethinge [else], in what a miserable distressed condition would many a man that hath fought for the Parliament in this quarrell bee? I will bee bound to say, that many a man whose zeale and affection to God and this Kingedome hath carried him forth in this cause hath soe spent his estate that in the way the State, the Army are going hee shall nott hold uppe his head; and when his estate is lost, and nott worth 40s. a yeare, a man shall nott have any interest; and there are many other wayes by which estates men have doe fall to decay, if that bee the rule which God in his providence does use. A man when hee hath an estate hath an interest in making lawes, when hee hath none, hee hath noe power in itt. Soe that a man cannott loose that which hee hath for the maintenance of his family, butt hee must loose that which God and nature hath given him. Therefore I doe [think] and am still of the same opinion; that every man born in England cannot, ought nott, neither by the law of God nor the law of nature, to bee exempted from the choice of those who are to make lawes, for him to live under, and for him, for ought I know, to loose his life under.

* * *

COMMISSARY GEN. IRETON. . . . All the maine thinge that I speake for is because I would have an eye to propertie. I hope wee doe nott come to contend for victorie, butt lett every man consider with himself that hee doe nott goe that way to take away all propertie. For heere is the case of the most fundamentall parte of the Constitution of the Kingedome, which if you take away, you take away all by that. Heere are men of this and this qualitie who are determined to bee the Electors of men to the Parliament, and they are all those who have any permanent interest in the Kingedome, and who taken together doe comprehend the whole interest of the Kingedome. . . . Now I wish wee may all consider of what right you will challenge, that all the people should have right to Elections. Is itt by the right of nature? If you will hold forth that as your ground, then I thinke you must deny all property too, and this is my reason. For thus: by that same right of nature, whatever itt bee that you pretend, by which you can say, "one man hath an equall right with another to the chusing of him that shall governe him"—by the same right of nature, hee hath an equal right in any goods hee sees: meate, drinke, cloathes, to take and use them for his sustenance. Hee hath a freedome to the land, [to take] the ground, to exercise itt, till itt; he hath the [same] freedome to any thinge that any one doth account himself to have any propriety in. Why now I say then, if you, against this most fundamentall parte of [the] civill Constitution (which I have now declar'd), will pleade the law of nature, that a man should, paramount [to] this, and contrary to this, have a power of chusing those men that shall determine what shall bee law in this state, though he himself have noe permanent interest in the State, [but] whatever interest hee hath hee may carry about with him. If this be allowed, [because by the right of nature] wee are free, wee are equall, one man must have as much voice as another, then shew mee what steppe or difference [there is], why by the same right of necessity to sustaine nature [I may not claim property as well]?

COL. RAINBOROW. . . . For my parte, as I thinke, you forgott somethinge that was in my speech, and you doe nott only your selves believe that [we] are inclining to anarchy, butt you would make all men believe that. And Sir, to say because a man pleades, that every man hath a voice [by the right of nature], that therefore itt destroyes [by] the same [argument all property]— that there's a propertie the law of God sayes itt; else why [hath] God made that law, "Thou shalt nott steale"? If I have noe interest in the Kingedome I must suffer by all their lawes bee they right or wronge. I am a poore man, therefore I must bee prest. . . . Therefore I thinke that to that itt is fully answered. God hath sett downe that thinge as to propriety with this law of his, "Thou shalt not steale." For my parte I am against any such thought, and as for yourselves I wish you would nott make the world believe that wee are for anarchy.

By the autumn of 1648 the parliamentary armies had defeated both the Cavaliers and the Scots—with whom Charles had formed an alliance in 1647. But at this point a quarrel broke out between the leaders of Parliament and the generals. Parliament wanted to continue negotiating with the king; the army was determined to kill him. Parliament wanted to impose a rigid Presbyterian discipline on the English church; the army sought toleration for the various extremist Protestant sects included in its rank. Oliver Cromwell justified a takeover of power by the army in the following letter (November 25, 1648).

Oliver Cromwell's Letter to Colonel Hammond

Dear Robin, thou and I were never worthy to be door-keepers in this service. If thou wilt seek, seek to know the mind of God in all that chain of Providence, whereby God brought thee thither, and that person to thee; how, before and since, God has ordered him, and affairs concerning him: and then tell me, whether there be not some glorious and high meaning in all this, above what thou hast yet attained? And, laying aside thy fleshly reason, seek of the Lord to teach thee what that is; and He will do it. . . .

You say: "God hath appointed authorities among the nations, to which active or passive obedience is to be yielded. This resides in England in the Parliament. Therefore active or passive [*obedience should be yielded to Parliament"—B. T.*].

Authorities and powers are the ordinance of God. This or that species is of human institution, and limited, some with larger, others with stricter bands, each one according to its constitution. "But" I do not therefore think the authorities may do anything, and yet such obedience "be" due, but all agree there are cases in which it is lawful to resist. If so, your ground fails, and so likewise the inference. Indeed, dear Robin, not to multiply words, the query is, Whether ours be such a case? This ingenuously is the true question.

To this I shall say nothing, though I could say very much; but only desire thee to see what thou findest in thy own heart as to two or three plain considerations. First, whether *Salus Populi* be a sound position? [*Cromwell referred to the maxim "The safety of the people is the supreme law"—B. T.*] Secondly, whether in the way in hand, really and before the Lord, before whom conscience must stand, this be provided for, or the whole fruit of the war like to be frustrated, and all most like to turn to what it was, and worse? And this, contrary to engagements, declarations, implicit covenants with those who ventured their lives upon those covenants and engagements, without whom perhaps, in equity, relaxation ought not to be? Thirdly, Whether this Army be not a lawful power, called by God to oppose and fight against the King upon some stated grounds; and being in power to such ends, may not oppose one name of authority, for those ends, as well as another, the outward authority that called them, not by their power making the quarrel lawful, but it being so in itself? If so it may be acting will be justified *in foro*

Thomas Carlyle, *The Letters and Speeches of Oliver Cromwell,* I (1904), 394–397, edited by S. C. Lomas. Reprinted by permission of Methuen & Co., Ltd., London.

humano.—But truly these kinds of reasonings may be but fleshly, either with or against: only it is good to try what truth may be in them. And the Lord teach us.

My dear friend, let us look into providences; surely they mean somewhat. They hang so together; have been so constant, so clear and unclouded. Malice, swoln malice against God's people, now called Saints, to root out their name; and yet they, "these poor Saints," by providence, having arms, and therein blessed with defence and more. . . .

What think you of Providence disposing the hearts of so many of God's people this way, especially in this poor Army, wherein the great God has vouchsafed to appear. I know not one officer among us but is on the increasing hand. And let me say it is here in the North, after much patience, we trust the same Lord who hath framed our minds in our actings, is with us in this also. And this contrary to a natural tendency, and to those comforts our hearts could wish to enjoy with others. And the difficulties probably to be encountered with, and the enemies, not few, even all that is glorious in this world, with appearance of united names, titles and authorities, and yet not terrified, only desiring to fear our great God, that we do nothing against His will. Truly this is our condition.

And to conclude. We in this Northern Army were in a waiting posture, desiring to see what the Lord would lead us to.

On December 6, 1648, a Colonel Pride "purged" Parliament of all the members opposed to the army's policies. The surviving remnant then enacted the following decree.

Declaration of the Supremacy of Parliament

(Resolved) That the commons of England, in parliament assembled, do declare that the people are, under God, the original of all just power. And do also declare, that the commons of England, in parliament assembled, being chosen by and representing the people have the supreme power in this nation. And do also declare, that whatsoever is enacted, or declared for law, by the commons in parliament assembled, hath the force of a law; and all the people of this nation are concluded thereby, although the consent of king, or house of peers, be not had thereunto.

W. Cobbett, *Parliamentary History of England,* III (1808), column 1257.

This decree was followed by an act creating a high court of justice to try the king. The act was passed by the Commons but not by the Lords.

Act Erecting a High Court of Justice for the King's Trial

Whereas it is notorious that Charles Stuart, the now King of England, not content with the many encroachments which his predecessors had made upon the people in their rights and freedom, hath had a wicked design totally to subvert the ancient and fundamental laws and liberties of this nation, and in their place to introduce an arbitrary and tyrannical government, and that besides all other evil ways and means to bring his design to pass, he hath prosecuted it with fire and sword, levied and maintained a civil war in the land, against the Parliament and kingdom; whereby this country hath been miserably wasted, the public treasure exhausted, trade decayed, thousands of people murdered, and infinite other mischiefs committed; for all which high and treasonable offences the said Charles Stuart might long since have justly been brought to exemplary and condign punishment: whereas also the Parliament, well hoping that the restraint and imprisonment of his person, after it had pleased God to deliver him into their hands, would have quieted the distempers of the kingdom, did forbear to proceed judicially against him, but found, by sad experience, that such their remissness served only to encourage him and his accomplices in the continuance of their evil practices, and in raising new commotions, rebellions and invasions: for prevention therefore of the like or greater inconveniences, and to the end no Chief Officer or Magistrate whatsoever may hereafter presume, traitorously and maliciously, to imagine or contrive the enslaving or destroying of the English nation, and to expect impunity for so doing; be it enacted and ordained by the [Lords] and Commons in Parliament assembled, and it is hereby enacted and ordained by the authority thereof, that the Earls of Kent, Nottingham, Pembroke, Denbigh and Mulgrave, the Lord Grey of Wark, Lord Chief Justice Rolle of the King's Bench, Lord Chief Justice St. John of the Common Pleas, and Lord Chief Baron Wylde, the Lord Fairfax, Lieutenant-General Cromwell, &c. [in all about 150], shall be and are hereby appointed and required to be Commissioners and Judges for the hearing, trying and judging of the said Charles Stuart.

S. R. Gardiner, *The Constitutional Documents of the Puritan Revolution,* 2nd ed. (1899), pp. 357–358. Reprinted by permission of The Clarendon Press, Oxford.

Charles was not permitted to speak at his trial. He said at that time: "I am not suffered to speak. Expect what justice other people will have." On the scaffold he gave a last defense of his reign.

Charles I's Defense of His Reign

I think it is my duty, to God first, and to my country, for to clear myself both as an honest man, a good king, and a good Christian.

I shall begin first with my innocence. In truth I think it not very needful for me to insist long upon this, for all the world knows that I never did begin a war with the two Houses of Parliament; and I call God to witness, to whom I must shortly make an account, that I never did intend to incroach upon their privileges. They began upon me. It was the Militia they began upon. They confessed that the Militia was mine but they thought it fit to have it from me. . . . So that the guilt of these enormous crimes that are laid against me, I hope in God that God will clear me of it. I will not (I am in charity) God forbid that I should lay it upon the two Houses of Parliament. There is no necessity of either. I hope that they are free of this guilt, for I do believe that ill instruments between them and me have been the chief cause of all this bloodshed. . . . I will only say this, that an unjust sentence that I suffered to take effect [*i.e., the execution of Strafford—B. T.*] is punished now by an unjust sentence upon me. That is, so far as I have said, to show you that I am an innocent man.

Now for to show you that I am a good Christian. I hope there is a good man that will bear me witness that I have forgiven all the world, and even those in particular that have been the chief causes of my death. Who they are God knows. I do not desire to know. I pray God forgive them. But this is not all. My charity must go further. I wish that they may repent, for indeed they have committed a great sin in that particular. I pray God, with St. Stephen, that this be not laid to their charge; nay, not only so, but that they may take the right way to the peace of the kingdom, for my charity commands me, not only to forgive particular men, but my charity commands me to endeavor to the last gasp the peace of the kingdom. . . .

[As] for the people—truly I desire their liberty and freedom as much as anybody whosoever. But I must tell you that their liberty and freedom consists in having of government those laws by which their lives and goods may be most their own. It is not for having share in government. That is nothing

England's Black Tribunal, 5th ed. (1720), pp. 43–46.

pertaining to them. A subject and a sovereign are clean different things, and therefore, until they do that—I mean that you do put the people in that liberty as I say—certainly they will never enjoy themselves.

Sirs, it was for this that now I am come here. If I would have given way to an arbitrary way, for to have all laws changed according to the power of the sword, I needed not to have come here. And therefore I tell you (and I pray God it be not laid to your charge) that I am the matyr of the people.

Act Declaring England To Be a Commonwealth, 1649

Be it declared and enacted by this present Parliament, and by the authority of the same, that the people of England, and of all the dominions and territories thereunto belonging, are and shall be, and are hereby constituted, made, established, and confirmed, to be a Commonwealth and Free State, and shall from henceforth be governed as a Commonwealth and Free State by the supreme authority of this nation, the representatives of the people in Parliament, and by such as they shall appoint and constitute as officers and ministers under them for the good of the people, and that without any King or House of Lords.

Cromwell finally dismissed the surviving "rump" of Parliament in 1653 in the following fashion.

Oliver Cromwell's Dismissal of the Rump Parliament

Calling to Major-General Harrison, who was on the other side of the House, to come to him, he told him, that he judged the Parliament ripe for a dissolution, and this to be the time of doing it. The Major-General answered, as he since told me, "Sir, the work is very great and dangerous, therefore I desire you seriously to consider of it before you engage in it." "You say well," replied the General, and thereupon sat still for about a quarter of an hour; and

S. R. Gardiner, *The Constitutional Documents of the Puritan Revolution*, 2nd ed. (1899), p. 388. Reprinted by permission of The Clarendon Press, Oxford.
C. H. Firth, ed., *The Memoirs of Edmund Ludlow*, I (1894), 352–354. Reprinted by permission of The Clarendon Press, Oxford.

then the question for passing the Bill being to be put, he said again to Major-General Harrison, "this is the time I must do it"; and suddenly standing up, made a speech, wherein he loaded the Parliament with the vilest reproaches, charging them not to have a heart to do any thing for the publick good, to have espoused the corrupt interest of Presbytery and the lawyers, who were the supporters of tyranny and oppression, accusing them of an intention to perpetuate themselves in power, had they not been forced to the passing of this Act, which he affirmed they designed never to observe, and thereupon told them, that the Lord had done with them, and had chosen other instruments for the carrying on his work that were more worthy. This he spoke with so much passion and discomposure of mind, as if he had been distracted. Sir Peter Wentworth stood up to answer him, and said, that this was the first time that ever he had heard such unbecoming language given to the Parliament, and that it was the more horrid in that it came from their servant, and their servant whom they had so highly trusted and obliged: but as he was going on, the General stept into the midst of the House, where continuing his distracted language, he said, "Come, come, I will put an end to your prating"; then walking up and down the House like a mad-man, and kicking the ground with his feet, he cried out, "You are no Parliament, I say you are no Parliament; I will put an end to your sitting; call them in, call them in": whereupon the serjeant attending the Parliament opened the doors, and Lieutenant-Colonel Worsley with two files of musqueteers entered the House; which Sir Henry Vane observing from his place, said aloud, "This is not honest, yea it is against morality and common honesty." Then Cromwell fell a railing at him, crying out with a loud voice, "O Sir Henry Vane, Sir Henry Vane, the lord deliver me from Sir Henry Vane." Then looking upon one of the members, he said, "There sits a drunkard"; and giving much reviling language to others, he commanded the mace to be taken away, saying, "What shall we do with this bauble? here, take it away." Having brought all into this disorder, Major-General Harrison went to the Speaker as he sat in the chair, and told him, that seeing things were reduced to this pass, it would not be convenient for him to remain there. The Speaker answered, that he would not come down unless he were forced. "Sir," said Harrison, "I will lend you my hand"; and thereupon putting his hand within his, the Speaker came down. Then Cromwell applied himself to the members of the House, who were in number between 80 and 100, and said to them, "It's you that have forced me to this, for I have sought the Lord night and day, that he would rather slay me than put me upon the doing of this work."

Six years of army rule made most Englishmen long for a restoration of monarchy. Charles II smoothed the way for his return to the throne by issuing the following declaration.

Declaration of Breda

We do make it our daily suit to the Divine Providence, that He will, in compassion to us and our subjects, after so long misery and sufferings, remit and put us into a quiet and peaceful possession of that our right, with as little blood and damage to our people as is possible; nor do we desire more to enjoy what is ours, than that all our subjects may enjoy what by law is theirs, by a full and entire administration of justice throughout the land, and by extending our mercy where it is wanted and deserved.

And to the end that the fear of punishment may not engage any, conscious to themselves of what is past, to a perseverance in guilt for the future, by opposing the quiet and happiness of their country, in the restoration of King, Peers and people to their just, ancient and fundamental rights, we do, by these presents, declare, that we do grant a free and general pardon, which we are ready, upon demand, to pass under our Great Seal of England, to all our subjects, of what degree or quality soever, who, within forty days after the publishing hereof, shall lay hold upon this our grace and favour, and shall, by any public act, declare their doing so, and that they return to the loyalty and obedience of good subjects; excepting only such persons as shall hereafter be excepted by Parliament, those only to be excepted. . . .

And because the passion and uncharitableness of the times have produced several opinions in religion, by which men are engaged in parties and animosities against each other (which, when they shall hereafter unite in a freedom of conversation, will be composed or better understood), we do declare a liberty to tender consciences, and that no man shall be disquieted or called in question for differences of opinion in matter of religion, which do not disturb the peace of the kingdom; and that we shall be ready to consent to such an Act of Parliament, as, upon mature deliberation, shall be offered to us, for the full granting that indulgence.

And because, in the continued distractions of so many years, and so many and great revolutions, many grants and purchases of estates have been made to and by many officers, soldiers and others, who are now possessed of the same, and who may be liable to actions at law upon several titles, we are

S. R. Gardiner, *The Constitutional Documents of the Puritan Revolution*, 2nd ed. (1899), pp. 465–466. Reprinted by permission of The Clarendon Press, Oxford.

likewise willing that all such differences, and all things relating to such grants, sales and purchases, shall be determined in Parliament, which can best provide for the just satisfaction of all men who are concerned.

And we do further declare, that we will be ready to consent to any Act or Acts of Parliament to the purposes aforesaid, and for the full satisfaction of all arrears due to the officers and soldiers of the army under the command of General Monk; and that they shall be received into our service upon as good pay and conditions as they now enjoy.

6
THE CASE
FOR THE
KING

FROM Charles King of England 1600–1637
BY ESMÉ WINGFIELD-STRATFORD

It was now [*1629—B. T.*] just upon four years since King Charles had come to the throne, years of continued difficulty and frustration, that had brought him to a pass unprecedented in the history of English monarchy. For now one tremendous fact stared him in the face: Parliamentary government had broken down; had become, for the time being, impossible, from the standpoint of a monarch who aspired to govern as well as to reign.

That riot in the House had been enough to prove that under such leadership as Eliot's, there were no lengths to which the Commons could not be driven along the path to revolution. Not content with openly defying the King's authority, they were capable of inciting his subjects in general to set it at naught—nay more, of actually intimidating them into doing so. They were determined to take all before giving him anything; to destroy everyone on whom he leaned, or on whose loyalty he could count, in Church or State; to strip him of the barest minimum of necessary revenue; and to leave him as abject a puppet as Richard II had been in the days of the Merciless Parliament, or Henry III when he was the crowned captive of Simon de Montfort.

It is therefore misleading to talk as if, after that memorable scene which closed the career of his third Parliament, Charles had formed some novel and sinister design of governing without Parliament. Humanly speaking, he had no choice in the matter. He had to do so if he was to govern at all and the only question was—how to do it?

Esmé Wingfield-Stratford, *Charles King of England 1600–1637* (1949), pp. 241, 245–246, 318–322. Reprinted by permission of The Bodley Head Ltd., London, and Christy & Moore Ltd., London.

* * *

It is odd that even so prejudiced an historian as John Richard Green should have chosen to describe this period in a section of his famous *Short History* entitled *The Tyranny*. The idea of setting up a despotism on the Continental model had never entered Charles's mind. It was Parliament and not he that had been trying to upset the balance of the Constitution. There was nothing in the law or practice of that Constitution to compel him to summon Parliament before he needed its help. If he could carry on without it—so much the better for the Taxpayer!

Meanwhile the law, stiffened up as it had recently been against the Crown, remained supreme, and the King had not the power, even if he had the will, to set it at defiance. For unlike the real tyrants overseas, he had practically no armed force to back him. The handful of royal guards would not have been equal to defending his royal person against a really determined mob. Thus the King was compelled to govern with at least the passive acquiescence of a people, who certainly would not have endured any flagrant assertion of arbitrary power.

* * *

All that it is essential to know about the affair of ship-money, and Hampden's part in it, can be briefly set down.

Let us remember that the object of King Charles's government was to tide over a situation in which it was only too plain that to summon a Parliament would be to open the flood gates of revolution. The policy of which Wentworth and Laud were to become the two leading exponents, was to observe the strictest bounds of constitutional propriety, narrowed as these were by the Petition of Right; to scrape along on the peace-time income of the Crown without resort to taxation; to withdraw from any attempt to interfere in the politics of the Continent; and to devote all the energy and resources available to building up such a Utopia of ordered prosperity as would in time cause the revolutionary fires to die from lack of fuel, and enable the normal course of Parliamentary government to be resumed in an atmosphere of loyal co-operation between King, Church, Parliament, and people.

Now Hampden, who was an enormously wealthy multiple estate owner, was among those who were determined at all costs to upset this programme.

Sooner or later the Thorough plan, if it were allowed to go through smoothly, would revolutionize the situation the wrong way. You could not go on indefinitely playing propaganda against prosperity. Sooner or later the people would discover that they were well off, and that life under King Charles, without war, without taxes, and without want, was the sort of life that the common Englishman would like to prolong indefinitely. And even the 160,000 or so who constituted the entire electorate, might come round sufficiently to this point of view to return a majority willing to carry on with the existing Constitution.

But that time had not come yet, and the King's position was one of the utmost precariousness. For one thing, the necessity of realizing the last farthing of an income that largely consisted of petty and antiquated calls on the resources of the wealthy, made the government extremely unpopular with just that class which alone could have been said, in any intelligible sense of the word, to be represented in Parliament. And again, the King's isolationist and pacifist foreign policy, though in the long run it might come to be reckoned as the most priceless boon ever conferred by any English Sovereign on his people and their posterity, was not of the sort to appeal to a public opinion inflamed with ideologist propaganda, and demanding a firm line and decisive intervention on behalf of God's, and the Prince Palatine's cause, without counting the cost. And there was a third factor of weakness, in the personnel of the government itself. The King and his ministers were weakest just where Pym and his friends were strongest, in the now indispensable art of propaganda. They could confer benefits much more easily than advertise them. Neither King Charles, with his tongue-tied dignity, nor Wentworth, with his thunder-charged brow and explosive temper, nor the little, bustling, rather old-maidish Archbishop Laud, could be described as competent advertisers of their own goods. No doubt, in course of time, the goods might be trusted to advertise themselves; but he who waits for that time, as any slick salesman will tell you, will be in danger of missing his market.

To bring down the King, then, it was necessary to act with the least possible delay, in order to catch him at a disadvantage that would grow steadily less the longer time he had for his policy to develop. The best thing of all would be for him to get involved in war—but to count on this would be wishful thinking. But what if he could be compelled, with his resources already strained to breaking point, to foot some extra item of expenditure that his income would not cover? That—in his extremely delicate position of the moment—would be just enough to do the trick.

It was only to be expected that Charles's difficulties with the navy should have presented themselves, to the conspirators, as a golden opportunity for upsetting that precarious equilibrium between income and expenditure, that alone enabled him, from year to year, to stave off the revolution that they were engineering. That they were in the least affected by urgency of the need for ships, or sympathetic with His Majesty's efforts to meet it, there is no reason to believe. If he wanted to police the seas, let him come to Parliament with his crown in his hand, and hear what conditions Parliament was going to exact for his privilege of performing the most elementary duty to his subjects. Verily he should not come out thence till he had parted with its uttermost jewel! That he should find means, legal or otherwise, of escaping from this dilemma, was sheer tyranny; it was not to be borne!

All that was needed was for some champion to come forward and bring this new grievance into the light of fullest publicity, by challenging the legality of ship-money in the courts.

* * *

Hampden was selected, possibly because he was known to be excellently versed in the law; and he chose to resist an assessment of twenty shillings on one of his many estates. As money was no object to him, he was able to brief the most eloquent counsel at the Bar, including one of his own group, Oliver St John, who, though of a saturnine and jaundiced disposition, rose magnificently to the occasion. And Hampden displayed his strategic insight in fighting the case, not on the obvious legal ground of the difference between maritime and inland districts, but on the King's right to make the levy at all, except with Parliamentary sanction. In view of the fact that the judges had already certified, by an overwhelming majority, the legality of ship-money, he could hardly have hoped to win. But he could obtain such nation-wide publicity for the opposition propaganda as had not been possible since the doors at Westminster had been locked.

He succeeded probably beyond his expectations. The case came on early in November, 1637, and was argued by counsel till within a week of Christmas. So well had St John, and his colleague, Holborn, done their work, that even the Barons of the Exchequer were sufficiently impressed with the importance of the issue at stake to insist on referring its decision to the entire body of judges. It was not until the following June that all their opinions were collected, and this time the majority for the Crown was no longer 10 to 2, but a bare 7 to 5. Hampden had had a rare piece of luck, in the fact that two of their Lordships had decided the matter for him on technical grounds that had nothing to do with the main contention. The fact that legal technicalities could be strained in this way against the Crown, at least shows how fair, according to their lights, the judges endeavoured to be. To put it mildly, this is not the sort of thing one expects during a tyranny. . . .

Charles had thus got the decision he wanted, and got it fairly enough. But it was one of those victories whose fruits are reaped by the vanquished. The King's zeal for the navy was likely to prove his undoing. Ship-money might be legal, but it had now been advertised throughout the length and breadth of the country as another grievance of grievances.

It was the most fatal time such a thing could have happened. For now clouds of war and rebellion had begun to darken the Northern sky, and the King would have need of all his prestige, and all the loyalty of his subjects, if he were not to be swept off his feet by the plainly impending storm.

FROM King Charles and King Pym 1637–1643
BY ESMÉ WINGFIELD-STRATFORD

When the bells of the London steeples were heard ringing in the year 1642, the same thought must surely have come to the mind of every hearer. Long before the end of the year England would again, as in that unforgotten time of troubles when White Rose had contended with Red, be a house divided against itself—a self-created shambles. It was the horror of all others that had been most deeply seared into the English soul. Even Pym, in his lodging at Westminster, must have regarded the prospect with apprehension. Nature had not made him a man of war, nor even a man of blood; he would no doubt have far preferred to arrive at his goal in what he himself would have described as a Parliamentary way. But having once set his face towards it, neither remorse nor scruple would turn him aside. Though the steeples themselves should be silenced, he at least would see this year out with his head on.

Meanwhile in Whitehall, with its improvised guard house and its informal garrison, King Charles must have been listening to the same sounds with an even keener anxiety, in proportion as he lacked his rival's unimaginative toughness of fibre. To him, with his almost feminine horror of violence, the prospect of civil war must have been more bitter than that of death itself, of which he was never to show the least fear. But in these last months he had come to realize that for him too the die was cast. Nothing of all that he had conceded, nothing that he ever could concede short of the trust that he held for his people, could satisfy these few who were banded together to make their will law for the rest of the community.

And yet it would seem that in the dawn of their New Year, he could not abandon all hope of finding some honourable means of averting this unthinkable catastrophe—a solution by reason and conciliation and not by the sword. That such thoughts must have been passing through his mind is clear from the fact that he chose that very day for making one last desperate effort to give his enemies all that they demanded of him short of the actual overthrow of the Constitution. For the last time he offered to govern the realm through a ministry of their own choice and composition—a Pym ministry.

Of the form in which this offer was made, we are even more in the dark than we are about the two previous occasions, but that it *was* made seems beyond all reasonable doubt, and it is equally certain that Pym turned it down out of hand. We can well believe that his suspicious mind scented a trap in the invitation to take up an office from which his Sovereign retained

Esmé Wingfield-Stratford, *King Charles and King Pym 1637–1643* (1949), pp. 260–270. Reprinted by permission of The Bodley Head Ltd., London, and Christy & Moore Ltd., London.

the right to dismiss him at will. And in any case, it seems certain that he and his friends were now determined to go through to the last item with their programme of revolution, which envisaged a perpetual government in control of a perpetual Parliament. And Pym, conscious of the trump card that he had been keeping all this time up his sleeve and was now ready to produce, can have been in no mood for compromise. Why—we can imagine him putting it to himself—walk into the King's trap, when the jaws of his own trap were ready to close on the King?

Did the King realize what Pym was about to spring on him? And did Pym divine that he realized it? In the light of subsequent events the overwhelming probability would seem to be that they did, both of them. [*The following day Charles appointed three leaders of the moderate party in Parliament to his government—B. T.*]

* * *

This prompt action of the King was none the less calculated to infuriate the revolutionaries, from its having been the result of their own refusal to take office. Instead of the surrender to which they had meant to drive him, he had gone quietly ahead and challenged them, by implication, to do their worst. And he must have known them well enough, by now, to realize that the challenge would be accepted.

Some days must needs elapse before the two new ministers, who were quite without administrative experience, would be ready to take over their departments, and by that time the whole face of the situation was destined to be transformed. For on Monday, the third day of the year, the Attorney General, Sir Edward Herbert, appeared before the Lords, to present, in the King's name, articles of impeachment for treason against Pym, Hampden, and three others of the extremist stalwarts in the Commons, Haslerigg, Denzil Holles, and Strode, as well as one of the Peers, Lord Kimbolton. . . .

It was an amazing and, to those not in the secret, must have seemed an unaccountable move. It is certain that the King's new advisers had had no part in it, and they can hardly have failed to regard it with consternation, since they must have realized to what an extent it was calculated to frustrate all their efforts, and to give the game, in which their Constitutional party had built up for itself a position of winning advantage, into the hands of Pym and his extremists. But the fact that none of the trio, not even Falkland, did what might have seemed the obvious thing, and retired from the service of a master who had to all appearance let them down so hopelessly, suggests that they may have had a more discerning insight into his motives than that of the conventional version in which he figures as a crowned villain plotting to establish his absolute power by eliminating the noblest champions of his peoples' liberties. The truth was not so crudely melodramatic.

Not improbably the person who was least surprised at the news, was Pym himself, who must have felt all the satisfaction of a chess player who has forced his opponent to make a fatal move. Paradoxical as it may seem to characterize him as the prime mover in getting himself arraigned by the highest legal authority in the land on the most heinous charge known to the law, we have only to regard the matter from what must have been his standpoint, to realize that this offered him his only way of escape from otherwise practically certain ruin. He had committed himself to destroying the King, and the King had entrenched himself in a constitutional position from which, so long as he sat quiet, there appeared to be no means of dislodging him, before the not distant date when the forces gathering to his support had rendered him strong enough to turn the tables on his assailants.

It had come to this. The only person who could defeat the King now was the King himself. Once let him quit his secure defensive to launch out with some premature counter-stroke, and the revolutionary forces in the field, with public opinion rallied to their support, would have him at a fatal disadvantage. It is true that the King had hitherto not shown the faintest disposition to oblige his enemies in this way, and that with Hyde at his elbow, he would be even less likely to do so now. But what if his hand could be forced? What if means could be found of compelling him at the last moment to throw patience to the winds, and to rush, with suicidal precipitation, into the trap prepared for him?

Anyone who had followed Pym's strategy up to this point would have seen that such a design was its necessary culmination. For it had been his invariable principle to repeat every once successful manoeuvre as nearly as possible to pattern when the next opportunity occurred. The former great royal surrender he had forced by bringing all his pressure to bear on the King's most vulnerable point, which was constituted by his love for the Queen. In the even more difficult and delicate operation he had now to perform, Pym could not fail to exploit the same weakness. He would force the King to move, by a threat to the Queen. He would confront his opponent with the choice between attacking him, and sacrificing her. Or what was equally to the purpose, bluff him into thinking so.

* * *

For months he had waged a war of nerves against her, and through her, against her husband. He had played cat and mouse with her. Every time she had tried to escape, even for a respite, out of his invisible clutches, she had been drawn back with just sufficient firmness. Her feelings had been played upon with that gentle skill which modern progress has prescribed for its technique of the Third Degree. Her love for her children, her sympathy for her persecuted co-religionists, her sensitiveness to calumny—never for one moment had she been allowed the least respite from a menace that was all the more nerve-racking from the fact of its always lurking just out of sight behind the forms of fulsomeness and loyalty. Meanwhile opinion in the country was being exacerbated against her in every conceivable way—the ordinary man was being conditioned to associate her with Army plots, Popish plots, and now with the monstrous libel of having been accessory, before the fact, to all the horrors of the Irish rebellion.

* * *

On the last day of the year, a Friday, it had been proposed that a committee of the Commons should sit over the week-end behind closed doors in the city Guild Hall, to deliberate over the safety of the Kingdom. What lay behind this may be gathered from the coded report of the Venetian Ambassador:

"These persons, supplied with arms, proceeded publicly to the destined place, giving every one the impression that there was a plot against the liberty of Parliament. By this device they redeemed their credit generally and won back the affection of ignorant people. Shut up there in long secret discussions, they persuaded themselves that the King's action [in appointing a guard for the palace] and his resentment were due to the advice of the Queen. Accordingly they decided to accuse her in Parliament of conspiring against the public liberty, and of secret intelligence of the rebellion in Ireland. When their Majesties learned this they decided to put aside all dissimulation, and denounce to the Lower House as guilty of high treason five members of the Lower Chamber and one of the Upper, of the most powerful and factious individuals."

Even if we did not know, specifically, that the committee was open to any member who liked to attend, it is incredible that intelligence of its dire intent can have failed to get through to the King almost at once. Nor can we doubt that this was just what Mr Pym wanted, since such a master in the arts of concealment would never have chosen this theatrical way of wrapping up his bombshell unless he had meant to advertise it. And that such warning was conveyed to the King, probably on Friday night, may be inferred from his desperate last minute attempt to come to terms with Pym on the Saturday, and the energy with which he acted on the two following days.

For the thing that of all others he must have feared was now upon him, and to his troubled conscience it may well have seemed the Nemesis of Strafford. For it had been his love for the Queen, and assuredly no fear for either his life or his Crown, that had induced him to make that fatal compromise with his honour. And his mind may have travelled back to that other failure of his from which it had all started; when at his urgent request, Strafford had come up to London to confront the then all-powerful Parliamentary leaders with the proofs of their own treason; and how he, Charles, had by his failure to appreciate the urgency of the situation, succeeded in delaying his minister's stroke for just the few hours required to enable Pym to get in with his framed up impeachment, and thus keep out of court and publicity the evidence of the real treason that would have branded its perpetrators with a stigma as ineffaceable as that of Guy Fawkes.

And now the same hand that had struck down his friend was lifted to strike down his wife. Behind those doors at the Guild Hall another charge of treason was being framed up. Parliament was resuming its sittings on Monday, and Pym was not the man to let the grass grow under his feet. At any moment he might be expected to rise in his place to read out the list of charges, drawn up with all his proved skill in denigration; and then the Sergeant at Arms, followed by the trained bands, would arrive at the palace, to conduct her through the insults of the mob away from him and her children, to eat her heart out in some gloomy chamber of the Tower until she left it to mingle her dust with that of two other Queens of England beneath the floor of St Peter's Chapel.

On the previous occasion it had been through no disloyalty that he had failed Strafford. He had not realized—and who has to this day!—what sort of an opponent, in Pym, he had had to deal with. But if he were to fail again in the same circumstances and through a similar hesitation to grasp the nettle— what excuse could he plead? This time there should be not a second's delay in getting the true charge brought home to the real traitors. So he must have thought; and so Mr Pym must have known, and counted on his thinking.

But *were* the circumstances the same? Are they ever, in life? There was one difference that the King may have failed to notice. Last time, Pym had taken very good care that his victim should not have the least warning of what was in store for him till the moment of his arrest. This time he positively went out of his way to warn him in advance—all the more by that ostentatious make-believe of secrecy. Pym was not likely to act in this way without some sufficient motive.

If Charles had been playing political chess with the same cold calculation as his opponent, it might have occurred to him that just because the threat to the Queen was being made with such ostentation, it was his game to ignore it. But this was more a matter of the heart than of the head with him. And that, I think, accounts for the fact that he went ahead without pausing to take the advice of his new counsellors, who, just because of their loyalty, would have taken a more detached view than his own. Perhaps he may have divined, in his innermost soul, the sort of advice he would have received from Hyde:

"Have no fear, Sir. Pym is desperate, and you can safely dare him to do his worst. It is to the last degree unlikely that he will go to the length of moving an impeachment against Her Majesty. That he could get a majority for it in the Commons is at least doubtful; that he could ever get the Lords to condemn her is unthinkable. Pym is no fool. Even if he could get her as far as the Tower, he knows that she would be safer in the care of Sir John Byron than she would at Whitehall. And the spectacle of its Queen in distress would rally nine tenths of the nation, in its present mood, to your support. Be advised, Sir! Hold your hand for a very little longer and all will be well. But give Pym the opportunity he is seeking, to transfer the issue to one of Parliamentary privilege, and you give him the one chance he has left of turning the tide against you."

That would, I believe, have been not only a just appreciation, but one that Charles, if he had felt himself free to do so, would have been the first to endorse. A masterly restraint had been the keynote of his policy during all these months, and now that he was just about to harvest its fruits, why should he wish to jettison it unless it was that policy had to give way to honour? Rather than run the slightest risk of harm to the Queen, he was ready to forgo any advantage to himself. And the bitter repentance, that haunted him to the scaffold, for his surrender of Strafford, had planted in him a resolve, from which he never wavered, that his loyalty even to the humblest of his followers—and how much more to the wife he adored—should be unconditional, and unswayed by prudential considerations.

And if this had not been enough to spur him to action, there was the indignation that he must have felt against these men who were striking down right and left his ministers, judges, and bishops, and were now preparing to strike down his Consort, on charges of treason so impudently unsubstantiated that an impeachment had come to signify, in effect, a proscription for loyalty. Whereas they themselves . . .

But let us examine the charges one by one on which he had directed Sir Edward Herbert to proceed against them.

1. *That they have traitorously endeavoured to subvert the fundamental laws and government of this Kingdom; and deprive the King of his regal power; and place his subjects under an arbitrary and tyrannical power.*

A more modestly worded, or historically correct, description of the aims unswervingly held by Pym and his associates, from the days of the Providence Island Company and their Broughton Castle caballing to those of the plot against the Queen, it would be hard, even now, to frame.

2. *That they have endeavoured, by many foul aspersions upon His Majesty, and his government, to alienate the affections of his people and to make His Majesty odious to them.*

Not only endeavoured, but largely succeeded, owing to Pym's consummate mastery of the arts of propaganda.

3. *That they have endeavoured to draw His Majesty's late army to disobedience to His Majesty's command and to side with them in their traitorous design.*

To what other purpose had been their endeavours to place it under the command of their own stooges, to prevent it taking the least step to oppose the invasion or interfere with the occupation of English soil, their relentless proscription of all officers suspected of disloyalty to their faction, and now their open conspiracy to wrest the control of it out of the King's hands altogether and lodge it in their own?

4. *That they have traitorously invaded, and encouraged a foreign power to invade His Majesty's Kingdom of England.*

Their most ardent supporters have not denied the substantial truth of this.

5. *That they have traitorously endeavoured to subvert the very rights and being of Parliament.*

What milder description could be applied to their Perpetual Parliament Act and the means whereby it had been jockeyed through Parliament and forced on the Crown?

6. *That . . . they have endeavoured . . . by force and terror to compel the Parliament to join with them in their traitorous designs, and to that end have actually raised and countenanced tumults against King and Parliament.*

Notoriously and consistently, and Pym had recently gone out of his way openly to applaud and justify such tumults.

7. *That they have traitorously conspired to levy and actually have levied, war against the King.*

By foreign invasion, by terror of the mob, and now—though it had not yet got beyond the stage of conspiracy—by civil war.

I have set down the terms of this brief indictment in order to show that every item of it is as indisputable a statement of historical fact as that England was conquered in 1066, or that Queen Anne died in 1714. Nor are they, in point of fact, any more disputed, the invariable line of justification being that even if these things were done, provided they were done by men like John Hampden against a King like Charles Stuart, they *must* be justified, and that to count them as treason is one of those things that are not done. But even so, it seems a little hard on the King to blame him for being too biased to have anticipated this convenient standpoint.

THE ABSOLUTISM OF LOUIS XIV

THE END OF ANARCHY OR THE BEGINNING OF TYRANNY?

CONTENTS

QUESTIONS FOR STUDY

1. *In what ways does Bossuet's king differ from the medieval king?*

2. *How does Bossuet define absolutism?*

3. *How successful did Louis XIV think his absolute rule had been?*

4. *How well did absolutism work?*

5. *What did absolutism in France accomplish?*

6. *In your opinion, was absolutism as practiced by Louis XIV a good thing for France?*

The reign of Louis XIV, which extended from 1643 until 1715, was both the longest and most "glorious" in French history. During this period France established its supremacy over every rival for power on the Continent and at the same time made French culture dominant in the Western world. French replaced Latin as the universal language of the cultivated class and the royal palace at Versailles served as the model for petty princelings all over Europe. All this, seemingly, was the result of the new system of government created by Louis XIV and his ministers. The Sun King's government was based upon the principle that the king was absolute. No other power existed or should exist in the state but his. This power was given to him by God and he was responsible to God alone for its proper use. The king was literally the father of his people and, like the old Roman *paterfamilias,* had the power of life and death over his "children."

Surprisingly enough, absolutism seems to have been perfectly acceptable to the French people, at least in the early stages of Louis' reign. Our surprise at this vanishes when we examine the alternatives. For almost two generations France had been wracked by civil and religious wars of a particularly bitter and brutal kind. The French protestants—the Huguenots—had been able to force the royal power to grant them certain privileges, which in some parts of the country were used to create semi-independent Protestant enclaves. Cardinal Richelieu, Louis XIII's great minister, had managed to curtail the independence of the Huguenots, but they still existed apart from the main body of the French state when Louis XIV at age 22 picked up the effective reins of power in 1660. The wars that had established the political privileges of the Huguenots had not been fought solely over religious matters. The great noble families whose ancestors had shared the royal power in the Middle Ages were increasingly jealous of the increased power of the king brought about by military innovations such as gunpowder and by the financial support of the middle class, or bourgeoisie. In Louis XIV's childhood this jealousy erupted into another civil war, this time nakedly exposed as noble ambitions directed against the king. The Fronde, or War of the Chamber Pots, as it was called, was a comic-opera war in which the total inability of the nobles to govern was starkly revealed. Also evident was the ability of the nobles to disrupt the orderly processes of government, and it was undoubtedly this aspect that struck the great mass of the French people. A strong king could guarantee internal peace, order, and tranquillity. If it took absolute power to do this, then so be it.

The threat of the nobility was perfectly clear to Louis. He remembered all his life the intrusion of hostile men into his bedroom in his childhood during the Fronde and took a vow never to permit such *lèse majesté* again. He set out to restore royal authority, and this meant that all competing authority throughout France had to be either eliminated or brought under royal control. To do this, he had first to tame the nobility. To this end the great palace at Versailles was built, where Louis could house all the important nobles and literally keep an eye on them. It is a mark of Louis' political genius that he was able, in fact, to lure the great nobles to Versailles and keep them obedient throughout his reign. To govern the provinces Louis and his great minister Colbert created a bureaucracy responsible to the crown alone. From this bureaucratic network information flowed to Colbert and Louis, and on the basis of this information Louis exercised his absolute control of the French state.

There are two problems that immediately come to mind after contemplating the French state in the seventeenth century. The first is: Just how absolute was Louis in reality? It is one thing to give orders at Versailles, where one can immediately see to their execution. It is another thing to give orders that must pass down a chain of command and that are to be carried out far from the royal presence. Was Louis as absolute as he thought he was? If not, who were the men who diluted his authority? how did they do it? and did they get away with it? These questions should be asked of the documents that make up the problem.

The second and perhaps more important problem is that of the uses to which absolute power was put. No doubt, the French people as a whole felt that absolutism was a good thing in 1660. Did they still feel so in 1715? Had Louis really been a "father" to his people, or was the proper word "tyrant"? The reign of Louis XIV was to raise some fundamental questions in political theory, not the least of which was whether anyone—even a competent, hardworking king like Louis XIV—could be trusted to exercise absolute power wisely.

1
THE FRANCE OF LOUIS XIV— A BRIEF PERSPECTIVE

FROM A History of the Modern World
BY R. R. PALMER AND JOEL COLTON

THE DEVELOPMENT OF ABSOLUTISM IN FRANCE

This ascendancy of French culture went along with a regime in which political liberties were at a discount. It was an embellishment to the absolute monarchy of Louis XIV. France had a tradition of political freedom in the feudal sense. It had the same kind of background of feudal liberties as did the other countries of Europe. It had an Estates-General, which had not met since 1615 but was not legally abolished. In some regions Provincial Estates, still meeting frequently, retained a measure of self-government and of power over taxation. There were about a dozen bodies known as parliaments, which, unlike the English Parliament, had developed as courts of law, each being the supreme court for a certain area of the country. The parliaments upheld certain "fundamental laws" which they said the king could not overstep, and they often refused to enforce royal edicts which they declared to be unconstitutional. We have already observed how France, beneath the surface, was almost as composite as Germany. French towns had won charters of acknowledged rights, and many of the great provinces enjoyed liberties written into old agreements with the Crown. These local liberties were the main reason for a good deal of institutional complication. There were some three hundred "customs" or regional systems of law; it was observed that a traveller some-

Reprinted by permission of the publisher from *A History of the Modern World*, pp. 156–163, by Robert R. Palmer with Joel Colton. Copyright, 1950, 1956, 1964, by Alfred A. Knopf, Inc.

times changed laws more often than he changed horses. Internal tariffs ran along the old provincial borders. Tolls were levied by manorial lords. The king's taxes fell less heavily on some regions than on others. Neither coinage nor weights and measures were uniform throughout the country. France was a bundle of territories held together by allegiance to the king.

This older kind of freedom discredited itself in France at the very time when by triumphing in Germany it pulled the Holy Roman Empire to pieces, and when in England it successfully made the transition to a more modern form of political liberty, embodied in the Parliamentary though aristocratic state. In France the old medieval, feudal or local type of liberty became associated with disorder. It has already been related how after the disorders of the sixteenth-century religious wars people had turned with relief to the monarchy and how Henry IV and then Richelieu had begun to make the monarchy strong. The troubles of the Fronde provided additional incentive for absolutism in France.

The Fronde broke out immediately after the Peace of Westphalia, while Louis XIV was still a child, and was directed against Cardinal Mazarin, who was governing in his name. It was an abortive revolution, led by the same elements, the parliaments and the nobility, which were to precipitate the great French Revolution in 1789. The parliaments, especially the Parliament of Paris, insisted in 1648 on their right to pronounce certain edicts unconstitutional. Barricades were thrown up and street fighting broke out in Paris. The nobility rebelled, as often in the past. Leadership was assumed by certain prominent noblemen who, roughly like the great Whigs of England, had enough wealth and influence to believe that, if the king's power were kept down, they might govern the country themselves. The nobility demanded a calling of the Estates-General, expecting to dominate over the bourgeoisie and the clergy in that body. Armed bands of soldiers, unemployed since the Peace of Westphalia and led by nobles, roamed about the country terrorizing the peasants. If the nobles had their way, it was probable that the manorial system would fall on the peasants more heavily, as in Eastern Europe, where triumphant lords were at this very time exacting increased labor services from the peasants. Finally the rebellious nobles called in Spanish troops, though France was at war with Spain. By this time the bourgeoisie, represented in the parliaments, had withdrawn support from the rebellious nobles. The agitation subsided in total failure, because bourgeoisie and aristocracy could not work together, because the nobles outraged the loyalty of many Frenchmen by joining with a power with which France was at war, and because the *frondeurs,* especially after the parliaments deserted them, had no systematic or constructive program, aiming only at the overthrow of the unpopular Cardinal Mazarin, and at obtaining offices and favors for themselves.

After the Fronde, as after the religious wars, the bourgeoisie and peasantry of France, to protect themselves against the claims of the aristocracy, were in a mood to welcome the exercise of strong power by the kings. And in the young Louis XIV they had a man more than willing to grasp all the power he could get. Louis, on Mazarin's death in 1661, announced that he would govern the country himself. He was the third king of the Bourbon line. It was the Bourbon tradition, established by Henry IV and by Richelieu, to draw the teeth from the feudal aristocrats, and this tradition Louis XIV followed. He was not a man of any transcendent abilities, though he had the capacity, often found among successful executives, of learning a good deal from conversation with experts. His education was not very good, having been made purposely easy; but he had the ability to see and stick to definite lines of policy, and he was extremely methodical and industrious in his daily habits, scrupulously loading himself with administrative business throughout his reign. He was extremely fond of himself and his position of kingship, with an insatiable appetite for admiration and flattery; he loved magnificent display and elaborate etiquette, though to some extent he simply adopted them as instruments of policy rather than as a personal whim.

With the reign of Louis XIV the "state" in its modern form took a long step forward. The state in the abstract has always seemed theoretical to the English-speaking world. Let us say, for simplicity, that the state represents a fusion of justice and power. A sovereign state possesses, within its territory, a monopoly over the administration of justice and the use of force. Private persons neither pass legal judgments on others, nor control private armies of their own. For private and unauthorized persons to do so, in an orderly state, constitutes rebellion. This was in contrast to the older feudal practice, by which feudal lords maintained manorial courts and led their own followers into battle. Against these feudal practices Louis XIV energetically worked, though not with complete success, claiming to possess in his own person, as sovereign ruler, a monopoly over the law-making processes and the armed forces of the kingdom. This is the deeper meaning of his reputed boast, *L'état, c'est moi*—"the state is myself." In the France of the seventeenth century, divided by classes and by regions, there was in fact no means of consolidating the powers of state except in a single man.

The state, however, while representing law and order within its borders, has generally stood in a lawless and disorderly relation to other states, since no higher monopoly of law and force has existed. Louis XIV, personifying the French state, had no particular regard for the claims of other states or rulers. He was constantly either at war or preparing for war with his neighbors. The modern state, indeed, was created by the needs of peace at home and war abroad. Machinery of government, as devised by Louis XIV and others, was a means of giving order and security within the territory of the state, and of raising, supporting and controlling armies for use against other states.

The idea that law and force within a country should be monopolized by the lawful king was the essence of the seventeenth-century doctrine of absolutism. Its principal theorist in the time of Louis XIV was Bishop Bossuet. Bossuet advanced the old Christian teaching that all power comes from God, and that all who hold power are responsible to God for the way they use it. He held that kings were God's representatives in the political affairs of earth. Royal power, according to Bossuet, was absolute but not arbitrary: not arbitrary because it must be reasonable and just, like the will of God which it reflected; absolute in that it was free from dictation by parliaments, estates or other subordinate elements within the country. Law, therefore, was the will of the sovereign king, so long as it conformed to the higher law which was the will of God. This doctrine, affirming the divine right of kings, was popularly held in France at the time, and was taught in the churches. It was fortified by the principles of Roman law, which also held that laws could be made and unmade, modified and amended, by act of the sovereign power. In addition, the authority of Louis XIV rested on purely practical considerations. Experience showed absolutism to be the corrective to anarchy, and the king was widely believed to represent the interests of the country better than anyone else. . . .

Possibly the most fundamental step taken by Louis XIV was to assure himself of control of the army. Armed forces had formerly been almost a private enterprise. Specialists in fighting, leading their own troops, worked for governments more or less as they chose, either in return for money or to pursue political aims of their own. This was especially common in Central Europe, but even in France great noblemen had strong private influence over the troops, and in times of disorder nobles led armed retainers about the country. Colonels were virtually on their own. Provided with a general commission and with funds by some government, they recruited, trained and equipped their own regiments, and likewise fed and supplied them, often by preying upon bourgeois and peasants in the vicinity. In these circumstances it was often difficult to say on whose side soldiers were fighting. It was hard for governments to set armies into motion, and usually hard to make them stop fighting, for commanders fought for their own interests and on their own momentum. War was not a "continuation of policy"; it was not an act of the state; it easily degenerated, as in the Thirty Years' War, into a kind of aimless and perpetual violence.

Louis XIV made war an activity of state. He saw to it that all armed persons in France fought only for him. This produced peace and order in France, while strengthening the fighting power of France against other states. Under the older conditions there was also little integration among different units and arms of the army. Infantry regiments and troops of horse went largely their own way, and the artillery was supplied by civilian technicians under contract. Louis XIV created a stronger unity of control, put the artillery organically into the army, systematized the military ranks and grades, and clarified the chain of command, placing himself at the top. The government supervised recruiting, required colonels to prove that they were maintaining the proper number of soldiers, and assumed most of the responsibility for equipping, provisioning, clothing and housing the troops. Higher officers, thus becoming dependent on the government, could be subjected to discipline. The soldiers were put into uniforms, taught to march in step, and housed in barracks; thus they too became more susceptible to discipline and control. Armed forces became less of a terror to their own people, and a more effective weapon in the hands of the government. They were employed usually against other governments, but if necessary to suppress rebellion at home. Louis XIV also increased the French army in size, raising it from about 100,000 to about 400,000. These changes, both in size and in degree of government control, were made possible by the growth of a large civilian administration. The heads of this administration under Louis XIV were civilians. They were in effect the first ministers of war, and their assistants, officials, inspectors, and clerks constituted the first organized war ministry.

Louis XIV was not only a vain man, but made it a political principle to overawe the country with his own grandeur. He built himself a whole new city at the old village of Versailles about ten miles from Paris. Where the Escorial had the atmosphere of a monastery, Versailles was a monument to worldly splendor. Tremendous in size alone, fitted out with polished mirrors, gleaming chandeliers, and magnificent tapestries, opening on to a formal park with fountains and shaded walks, the palace of Versailles was the marvel of Europe and the envy of lesser kings. It was virtually a public building, much of it used for government offices, and with nobles, churchmen, notable bourgeois and servants milling about on the king's affairs. The more exclusive honors of the château were reserved for the higher aristocrats. The king surrounded his daily routine of rising, eating, and going to bed (known as the *lever, dîner,* and *coucher*) with an infinite series of ceremonial acts, so minute and so formalized that there were, for example, six different entries of persons at the *lever,* and a certain gentleman at a specified moment held the right sleeve of the king's nightshirt as he took it off. The most exalted persons thought themselves the greater for thus waiting on so august a being. In this way, and by more material favors, many great lords were induced to live habitually at court. Here, under the royal eye, they might engage in palace intrigue, but were kept away from real political mischief. Versailles completed the political and moral ruin of the French aristocracy as a class. The king himself was one of the few who could proceed through such rounds of elaborate living and still be able to attend regularly to public affairs. Neither the nobles whom he kept about him, nor his own successors Louis XV and Louis XVI, were able to carry the burden.

For positions in the government, as distinguished from his personal entourage, Louis XIV preferred to use men of the bourgeois class, who were dependent on him for salaries and careers, and who unlike noblemen could aspire to no independent political influence of their own. He never called the Estates-General, which in any case no one except some of the nobility wanted. Some of the Provincial Estates, because of local and aristocratic pressures, he allowed to remain functioning. He temporarily destroyed the independence of the parliaments, commanding them to accept his orders, as Henry IV had commanded them to accept the Edict of Nantes. He stifled the old liberties of the towns, turning their civic offices into empty and purchasable honors, and likewise regulating the operation of the gilds. He developed a strong system of administrative coordination, centering in a number of councils of state, which he attended in person, and in "intendants" who represented these councils throughout the country. Councillors of state and intendants were generally of bourgeois origin. Each intendant, within his district, embodied all aspects of the royal government, supervising the flow of taxes and recruiting of soldiers, keeping an eye on the local nobility, dealing with towns and gilds, controlling the more or less hereditary officeholders, stamping out bandits, smugglers and wolves, policing the market places, relieving famine, watching the local law courts and often deciding cases himself. In this way a firm and uniform administration was superimposed upon the heterogeneous mass of the old France. In contrast to England, all local questions were handled by agents of the central government, usually honest and often efficient, but essentially bureaucrats constantly instructed by, and referring back to, their superiors at Versailles.

To support the reorganized and enlarged army, the panoply of Versailles, and the growing civil administration the king needed a good deal of money. Finance was always the weak spot in the French monarchy. Methods of collecting taxes were costly and inefficient. Direct taxes passed through the hands of many intermediate officials; indirect taxes were collected by private concessionnaires called tax-farmers, who made a substantial profit. The state always received far less than what the taxpayers actually paid. But the main weakness arose from an old bargain between the French crown and nobility; the king might raise taxes without consent if only he refrained from taxing the nobles. Only the "unprivileged" classes paid direct taxes, and these came almost to mean the peasants only, since many bourgeois in one way or another obtained exemptions. The system was outrageously unjust in throwing the tax burden on the poor and helpless. It was ruinous to the government, since the government could never raise enough money, however hard it taxed the poor, being unable to tap the real source of ready wealth, namely the wealthier people. It was ruinous also to the French nobility, who in paying no direct taxes lost their hold over the government, lacked incentive to interest themselves in public affairs, and were unable to assume leadership of the bulk of the population. Louis XIV was willing enough to tax the nobles, but was unwilling to fall under their control, and only toward the close of his reign, under extreme stress of war, was he able, for the first time in French history, to impose direct taxes on the aristocratic elements of the population. This was a great step toward equality before the law and toward sound public finance, but so many concessions and exemptions were won by nobles and bourgeois that the reform lost much of its value.

Like his predecessors, Louis resorted to all manner of expedients to increase his revenues. He raised the tax-rates, always with disappointing results. He devaluated the currency. He sold patents of nobility to ambitious bourgeois.

He sold government offices, judgeships, and commissions in the army and navy. For both financial and political reasons the king used his sovereign authority to annul the town charters, then sell back reduced rights at a price; this produced a little income but demoralized local government and civic spirit. The need for money, arising from the fundamental inability to tax the wealthy, which in turn reflected the weakness of absolutism, of a government which would not or could not share its rule with the propertied classes, corrupted much of the public life and political aptitude of the French people.

Louis XIV wished, if only for his own purposes, to make France economically powerful. His great minister Colbert worked for twenty years to do so. Colbert went beyond Richelieu in the application of mercantilism, aiming to make France a self-sufficing economic unit and to increase the wealth from which taxes were drawn. He managed to abolish local tariffs in a large part of Central France, where he set up a tariff-union oddly entitled the Five Great Farms (since the remaining tolls were collected by tax-farmers); and although vested interests and provincial liberties remained too strong for him to do away with all internal tariffs, the area of the Five Great Farms was in itself one of the largest free-trade areas in Europe, being about the size of England. For the convenience of business men Colbert promulgated a Commercial Code, replacing much of the local customary law, and long a model of business practice and business regulation. He improved communications by building roads and canals, of which the most famous was one joining the Bay of Biscay with the Mediterranean. Working through the gilds, he required the handicraft manufacturers to produce goods of specified kind and quality, believing that foreigners, if assured of quality by the government, would purchase French products more freely. He gave subsidies, tax exemptions, and other privileges to expand the manufacture of silks, tapestries, glassware, and woollens. He helped to found colonies, built up the navy, and established the French East India Company. Export of some goods, notably foodstuffs, was forbidden, for the government wished to keep the populace quiet by holding down the price of bread. Export of other goods, mainly manufactures, was encouraged, partly as a means of bringing money into the country, where it could be funneled into the royal treasury. The growth of the army, and the fact that under Louis XIV the government clothed and equipped the soldiers, and hence placed unprecedentedly large orders for uniforms, overcoats, weapons, and ammunition, greatly stimulated the employment of weavers, tailors and gunsmiths, and advanced the commercial capitalism by which such labors were organized. In general, trade and manufacture developed in France under more direct government guidance than in England. They long gave the English an extremely brisk competition. Not until the age of iron and coal did France begin economically to lag.

2
THE THEORY OF
ABSOLUTISM

Jacques Bénigne Bossuet (1627–1704) was a bishop, popular preacher, and tutor to the Dauphin under Louis XIV. His political writings provided the most eloquent justification of the divine right of kings.

FROM Politics Drawn from the Very Words of Holy Scripture BY J. B. BOSSUET

To His Lordship the Dauphin,
God is the king of kings: it is his place to instruct them and to regulate them as his ministers. Hence listen well, Your Lordship, to the lessons that he gives to them in his Scripture, and learn from him the rules and the examples on which they should base their conduct.

BOOK I

In order to form nations and unite peoples, it was necessary to establish a government.

PROPOSITION I
It is not enough that men live in the same country or speak the same language, because becoming unsociable by the violence of their passions, and incompatible by their different humors, they cannot act as one unless they submit themselves altogether to a single government which rules over all.

J. B. Bossuet, *Politique tirée des propres paroles de l'Écriture Sainte,* I (1870), 299, 305, 306, 308, 313, 322, 325, 326, 333, 335, translated by L. Pearce Williams (citations from the Bible are taken directly from the King James Version).

Without that, even Abraham and Lot could not get along together and were forced to separate. . . .

If Abraham and Lot, two just men who were moreover closely related, could not get along with one another because of their servants, what kind of disorder must be expected among those who are bad! . . .

Justice has no other support than authority and the subordination of powers.

It is this order which restrains license. When everyone does what he wishes and has only his own desires to regulate him, everything ends up in confusion.

* * *

PROPOSITION 3

It is only by the authority of the government that union is established amongst men.

The effect of this legitimate commandment is marked by these words often repeated in Scripture: to the command of Saul and of legitimate power, "all Israel obeyed as one man. They were forty thousand men, and all this multitude was as one." This is what is meant by the unity of a people, when each man renouncing his own will takes it and joins it to that of the prince and the magistrate. Otherwise there is no union; the people wander as vagabonds like a dispersed flock. . . .

* * *

PROPOSITION 5

By means of government each individual becomes stronger.

The reason is that each is helped. All the forces of the nation concur in one and the sovereign magistrate has the right to reunite them. . . .

Thus the sovereign magistrate has in his hand all the forces of the nation which submits itself to obedience to him. . . .

Thus, an individual is not troubled by oppression and violence because he has an invincible defender in the person of the prince and is stronger by far than all those who attempt to oppress him.

The sovereign magistrate's own interest is to preserve by force all the individuals of a nation because if any other force than his own prevails among the people his authority and his life is in peril. . . .

PROPOSITION 6

The law is sacred and inviolable.

In order to understand perfectly the nature of the law it is necessary to note that all those who have spoken well on it have regarded it in its origin as a pact and a solemn treaty by which men agree together under the authority of princes to that which is necessary to form their society.

This is not to say that the authority of the laws depends on the consent and acquiescence of the people; but only that the prince who, moreover by his

very station has no other interest than that of the public good, is helped by
the sagest heads in the nation and leans upon the experience of centuries gone
by.

BOOK II

PROPOSITION 7
A monarchy is the most common, the oldest, and the most natural form of
government.

The people of Israel themselves formed a monarchy as being the universally received government. "Make us a king to judge us like all the nations."

If God was annoyed it was because up to then he had governed this people
by himself and that he had been their true king. This is why he said to
Samuel: "They have not rejected thee but they have rejected me, that I
should not reign over them."

For the rest, this government was so clearly the most natural, that it is to be
found at the beginning in all peoples.

We have seen it in sacred history: but here a short look at profane histories
will show us that even those who lived in republics had begun first of all
under kings.

Rome started that way and finally came back to it as to its natural state.

It was only later and little by little that the Greek cities formed their republics. The old opinion of Greece was that expressed by Homer in this
famous sentence in the *Iliad*: "Many princes is not a good thing: let there be
only one prince and one king."

At the present time there is no republic which was not at one time subject to a monarch. The Swiss were the subjects of the princes of the house of
Austria. The United Provinces have only just escaped the domination of
Spain and that of the house of Burgundy. The free cities of Germany have
their individual lords other than the emperor who was the common head of
the entire Germanic body. The cities of Italy which turned themselves into
republics at the time of the emperor Rudolf bought their liberty from him.
Venice even, which so boasts of having been a republic since its founding,
was yet subject to the emperors, under the reign of Charlemagne and even
long after: since then she has become a popular state from which she has now
only recently become the state which we see.

Everybody thus begins with a monarchy and almost everybody has retained it as being the most natural state.

We have also seen that it has its foundation and its model in the rule of the
father, that is to say in nature itself.

All men are born subjects: and paternal authority which accustoms them
to obey, accustoms them at the same time to have only one chief.

PROPOSITION 8
Monarchical government is the best.

If it is the most natural, it is consequently the most durable and from that it follows also the strongest.

It is also the most opposed to divisiveness, which is the worst evil of states, and the most certain cause of their ruin. . . . "Every kingdom divided against itself is brought to desolation; and every city or house divided against itself shall not stand."

We have seen that Our Lord in this sentence has followed the natural progress of government and seems to have wished to show to realms and to cities the same means of uniting themselves that nature has established in families.

Thus, it is natural that when families wish to unite to form a body of State, they will almost automatically coalesce into the government that is proper to them.

When states are formed there is the impulse to union and there is never more union than under a single leader. Also there is never greater strength because everything works in harmony. . . .

BOOK III

Where we begin to explain the nature and properties of royal authority.

Article I

There are four characters or qualities essential to royal authority:
First, royal authority is sacred; second, it is paternal; third, it is absolute; fourth, it is ruled by reason. . . .

Article II

Royal authority is sacred.

PROPOSITION I
God established kings as his ministers and rules peoples by them.

We have already seen that all power comes from God. "The prince," St. Paul adds, "is the minister of God to thee for good. But if thou do that which is evil, be afraid; for he beareth not the sword in vain; for he is the minister of God, a revenger to execute wrath upon him that doeth evil."

Thus princes act as ministers of God, and as his lieutenants on earth. It is by them that he exercises his rule. . . .

Thus we have seen that the royal throne is not the throne of a man, but the throne of God himself. . . .

He thus governs all peoples and gives to them all their kings; even though he governs Israel in a more particular and more explicit way. . . .

PROPOSITION 2

The person of kings is sacred.

It thus appears that the person of kings is sacred and that to make an attempt on their lives is a sacrilege.

God has had them anointed by his prophets with a sacred unction as he has his pontiffs and his altars anointed.

But without the external application of this unction, they are sacred by their office, as being the representatives of the divine majesty, deputized by his providence to the execution of his designs. . . .

The title of Christ is given to kings; and they are everywhere called christs, or the anointed of the lord.

Article III

Royal authority is paternal and its proper character is goodness.

After what has been said, this truth has no need of proof.

We have seen that kings take the place of God, who is the true father of the human species. We have also seen that the first idea of power which exists among men is that of the paternal power; and that kings are modeled on fathers.

Everybody is also in accord, that the obedience which is owed to the public power can be found in the ten commandments only in the precept which obliges him to honor his parents.

Thus it follows from this that the name of king is a name for father and that goodness is the most natural character of kings. . . .

PROPOSITION 3

The prince must provide for the needs of the people.

It is a royal right to provide for the needs of the people. He who undertakes it at the expense of the prince undertakes royalty: this is why it has been established. The obligation to care for the people is the foundation of all the rights that sovereigns have over their subjects.

This is why, in time of great need, the people have the right to have recourse to its prince. . . .

BOOK IV

Article I

The royal authority is absolute.

In order to make this term odious and insupportable, many wish to confuse absolute government and arbitrary government. But there is nothing more distinct than these two as we shall see when we speak of justice.

PROPOSITION 1
The prince owes no account to anyone on what he orders.

"I counsel thee to keep the king's commandments, and that in regard to the oath of God. Be not hasty to go out of his sight, stand not in an evil thing; for he doeth whatsoever pleaseth him. Where the word of a king is, there is power: and who may say unto him what doest thou? Who so keepeth the commandment shall feel no evil thing."

Without this absolute authority, he cannot do good nor can he repress evil: it is necessary that his power be such that no one can hope to escape him; and finally the only defense of individuals against the public power ought to be their innocence. . . .

The prince is by his office the father of his people; he is placed by his grandeur above all petty interests; even more: all his grandeur and his natural interests are that the people shall be conserved, for once the people fail him he is no longer prince. There is thus nothing better than to give all the power of the state to him who has the greatest interest in the conservation and greatness of the state itself.

* * *

PROPOSITION 4
Kings are not by this above the laws.

"Thou shalt in any wise set him king over thee . . . but he shall not multiply horses to himself. . . . Neither shall he multiply wives to himself that his heart turn not away: neither shall he greatly multiply to himself silver and gold. And it shall be, when he sitteth upon the throne of his kingdom, that he shall write him a copy of this law in a book out of that which is before the priest the Levite: and it shall be with him and he shall read therein all the days of his life: that he may learn to fear the Lord his god, to keep all the words of this law and these statutes to do them: that his heart be not lifted up above his brethren and that he turn not aside from the commandment to the right hand, or to the left: to the end that he may prolong his days in his kingdom, he, and his children."

It should be noticed that this law does not include only religion, but the law of the realm as well to which the prince was subject as much as any other, or even more than others by the justness of his will.

It is this that princes find difficult to understand. . . .

Kings therefore are subject like any others to the equity of the laws both because they must be just and because they owe to the people the example of protecting justice; but they are not subject to the penalties of the laws: or, as theology puts it, they are subject to the laws, not in terms of its coactive power but in terms of its directive power.

Louis XIV was in the habit of keeping a journal in which he noted the course of his reign. He was also concerned to pass on to his heirs the lessons he had learned over the years. The selection that follows reveals his thoughts from the age of twenty-one—when he first assumed full control of the state —to the end of his reign, when he took stock of what he had accomplished.

FROM Louis XIV's Letters to His Heirs

Many reasons, all very important, my son, have decided me, at some labour to myself, but one which I regard as forming one of my greatest concerns, to leave you these Memoirs of my reign and of my principal actions. I have never considered that kings, feeling in themselves, as they do, all paternal affection, are dispensed from the obligation common to fathers of instructing their children by example and by precept. On the contrary, it has seemed to me that in the high rank in which we are placed, you and I, a public duty is added to private, and that in the midst of all the respect which is given us, all the abundance and brilliancy with which we are surrounded—which are nothing more than the reward accorded by Heaven itself in return for the care of the peoples and States confided to our charge—this solicitude would not be very lofty if it did not extend beyond ourselves by making us communicate all our enlightenment to the one who is to reign after us.

I have even hoped that in this purpose I might be able to be more helpful to you, and consequently to my subjects, than any one else in the world; for there cannot be men who have reigned of more talents and greater experience than I, nor who have reigned in France; and I do not fear to tell you that the higher the position the greater are the number of things which cannot be viewed or understood save by one who is occupying that position.

I have considered, too, what I have so often experienced myself—the throng who will press round you, each for his own ends, the trouble you will have in finding disinterested advice, and the entire confidence you will be able to feel in that of a father who has no other interest but your own, no ardent wish but for your greatness.

* * *

I have given, therefore, some consideration to the condition of Kings—hard and rigorous in this respect—who owe, as it were, a public account of their

Louis XIV, *Letters to His Heirs,* in Jean Longnon, *A King's Lessons in Statecraft: Louis XIV* (1925), pp. 39–45, 47–53, 58, 66–70, 129–131, 149–151, 177–178, translated by Herbert Wilson. Reprinted by permission of Albert & Charles Boni, Inc., and Routledge & Kegan Paul Ltd., London.

actions to the whole world and to all succeeding centuries, and who, nevertheless, are unable to do so to all and sundry at the time without injury to their greatest interests, and without divulging the secret reasons of their conduct. And, not doubting that the somewhat important and considerable affairs in which I have taken part, both within and without my kingdom, will one day exercise diversely the genius and passions of writers, I should not be sorry for you to possess in these Memoirs the means of setting history aright if it should err or not rightly interpret, through not having faithfully reported or well divined my plans and their motives. I will explain them to you without disguise, even where my good intentions have not been happily conceived, being persuaded that only a small mind and one usually at fault could expect never to make a mistake, and that those who have sufficient merit to succeed the more often, discover some magnanimity in recognising their faults.

* * *

I made a beginning by casting my eyes over all the different parties in the State, not indifferently, but with the glance of experience, sensibly touched at seeing nothing which did not invite and urge me to take it in hand, but carefully watching what the occasion and the state of affairs would permit. Everywhere was disorder. My Court as a whole was still very far removed from the sentiments in which I trust you will find it. Men of quality and officials, accustomed to continual intrigue with a minister who showed no aversion to it, and to whom it had been necessary, arrogated to themselves an imaginary right to everything that suited them. There was no governor of a city who was not difficult to govern; no request was preferred without some complaint of the past, or some hint of discontent for the future, which I was allowed to expect and to fear. The favours demanded, and extorted, rather than awaited, by this one and that, and always considerable, no longer were binding on any one, and were only regarded as useful in order to maltreat thenceforth those to whom they wished me to refuse them.

The finances, which give movement and action to the great organisation of the monarchy, were entirely exhausted, so much so that we could hardly find the ways and means. Much of the most necessary and most privileged expenses of my house and of my own privy purse were in arrears beyond all that was fitting, or maintained only on credit, to be a further subsequent burden. At the same time a prodigality showed itself among public men, masking on the one hand their malversations by every kind of artifice, and revealing them on the other in insolent and daring luxury, as though they feared I might take no notice of them.

The Church, apart from its usual troubles, after lengthy disputes on matters of the schools, a knowledge of which they allowed was unnecessary to salvation for any one, with points of disagreement augmenting day by day through the heat and obstinacy of their minds, and ceaselessly involving fresh human interests, was finally threatened with open schism by men who were all the more dangerous because they were capable of being very serviceable and greatly deserving, had they themselves been less opinionated. It was not a question only of a few private and obscure professors, but of Bishops established in their Sees and able to draw away the multitude after them, men of high repute, and of piety worthy of being held in reverence had it been accompanied by submission to the sentiments of the Church, by gentleness, moderation, and charity. Cardinal de Retz, Archbishop of Paris, whom for well-known reasons of State I could not permit to remain in the kingdom, encouraged all this rising sect from inclination or interest, and was held in favour by them.

The least of the ills affecting the order of Nobility was the fact of its being shared by an infinite number of usurpers possessing no right to it, or one acquired by money without any claim from service rendered. The tyranny exercised by the nobles over their vassals and neighbours in some of my provinces could no longer be suffered or suppressed save by making severe and rigorous examples. The rage for duelling—somewhat modified by the exact observance of the latest regulations, over which I was always inflexible—was only noticeable in a now well advanced recovery from so inveterate an ill, so that there was no reason to despair of the remedy.

The administration of Justice itself, whose duty it is to reform others, appeared to me the most difficult to reform. An infinity of things contributed to this state of affairs: the appointments filled haphazard or by money rather than by selection and merit; scant experience and less knowledge on the part of some of the judges; the regulations referring to age and service almost everywhere eluded; chicanery firmly established through many centuries, and fertile in inventing means of evading the most salutary laws. And what especially conduced to this was the fact that these insatiable gentry loved litigation and fostered it as their own peculiar property, applying themselves only to prolong and to add to it. Even my Council, instead of supervising the other jurisdictions, too often only introduced disorder by issuing a strange number of contrary regulations, all in my name and as though by my command, which rendered the confusion far more disgraceful.

All this collection of evils, their consequences and effects, fell principally upon the people, who, in addition, were loaded with impositions, some crushed down by poverty, others suffering want from their own laziness since the peace, and needing above all to be alleviated and occupied.

Amid so many difficulties, some of which appeared to be insurmountable, three considerations gave me courage. The first was that in these matters it is not in the power of Kings—inasmuch as they are men and have to deal with men—to reach all the perfection they set before themselves, which is too far removed from our feebleness; but that this impossibility of attainment is a poor reason for not doing all we can, and this difficulty for not always making progress. This, moreover, is not without its uses, nor without glory. The second was that in all just and legitimate enterprises, time, the fact of doing them even, and the aid of Heaven, open out as a rule a thousand channels, and discover a thousand facilities which we had not looked for. And the last was one which of itself seemed to me to hold out visibly that help, by disposing everything to the same end with which it inspired me.

In fact, all was calm everywhere. There was no movement, nor fear or seeming of any movement in my kingdom which might interrupt or oppose my designs. Peace was established with my neighbours, and to all seeming for as long as I myself wished it, owing to the conditions of affairs then prevailing.

It would assuredly have been to make a bad use of conditions of such perfect tranquillity, such as might only be met with very rarely in several centuries, not to turn them to the only account capable of making me appreciate them, at a time when my youth and the pleasure of being at the head of my armies would have caused me to wish to have more matters to deal with abroad. But inasmuch as my chief hope in these reforms was based on my will, their foundation at the outstart rested on making absolute my will by conduct which should impose submission and respect: by rendering scrupulous justice to all to whom I owed it; but in the bestowing of favours, giving them freely and without constraint to whomsoever I would, and when it should please me, provided that my subsequent action should let others know that while giving reasons to no one for my conduct I ruled myself none the less by reason, and that in my view the remembrance of services rendered, the favouring and promoting of merit—in a word, doing the right thing—should not only be the greatest concern but the greatest pleasure of a prince.

Two things without doubt were absolutely necessary: very hard work on my part, and a wise choice of persons capable of seconding it.

As for work, it may be, my son, that you will begin to read these Memoirs at an age when one is far more in the habit of dreading than loving it, only too happy to have escaped subjection to tutors and to have your hours regulated no longer, nor lengthy and prescribed study laid down for you.

On this heading I will not warn you solely that it is none the less toil *by which* one reigns, and *for which* one reigns, and that the conditions of royalty, which may seem to you sometimes hard and vexatious in so lofty a position, would appear pleasant and easy if there was any doubt of your reaching it.

There is something more, my son, and I hope that your own experience will never teach it to you: nothing could be more laborious to you than a great amount of idleness if you were to have the misfortune to fall into it through beginning by being disgusted with public affairs, then with pleasure, then with idleness itself, seeking everywhere fruitlessly for what can never be found, that is to say, the sweetness of repose and leisure without having the preceding fatigue and occupation.

I laid a rule on myself to work regularly twice every day, and for two or three hours each time with different persons, without counting the hours which I passed privately and alone, nor the time which I was able to give on particular occasions to any special affairs that might arise. There was no moment when I did not permit people to talk to me about them, provided that they were urgent; with the exception of foreign ministers who sometimes find too favourable moments in the familiarity allowed to them, either to obtain or to discover something, and whom one should not hear without being previously prepared.

I cannot tell you what fruit I gathered immediately I had taken this resolution. I felt myself, as it were, uplifted in thought and courage; I found myself quite another man, and with joy reproached myself for having been too long unaware of it. This first timidity, which a little self-judgment always produces and which at the beginning gave me pain, especially on occasions when I had to speak in public, disappeared in less than no time. The only thing I felt then was that I was King, and born to be one. I experienced next a delicious feeling, hard to express, and which you will not know yourself except by tasting it as I have done. For you must not imagine, my son, that the affairs of State are like some obscure and thorny path of learning which may possibly have already wearied you, wherein the mind strives to raise itself with effort above its purview, more often to arrive at no conclusion, and whose utility or apparent utility is repugnant to us as much as its difficulty. The function of Kings consists principally in allowing good sense to act, which always acts naturally and without effort. What we apply ourselves to is sometimes less difficult than what we do only for our amusement. Its usefulness always follows. A King, however skilful and enlightened be his ministers, cannot put his own hand to the work without its effect being seen. Success, which is agreeable in everything, even in the smallest matters, gratifies us in these as well as in the greatest, and there is no satisfaction to equal that of noting every day some progress in glorious and lofty enterprises, and in the happiness of the people which has been planned and thought out by oneself. All that is most necessary to this work is at the same time agreeable; for, in a word, my son, it is to have one's eyes open to the whole earth; to learn each hour the news concerning every province and every nation, the secrets of every court, the mood and the weaknesses of each Prince and of every foreign minister; to be well-informed on an infinite number of matters about which we are supposed to know nothing; to elicit from our subjects what they hide from us with the greatest care; to discover the most remote opinions of our own courtiers and the most hidden interests of those who come to us with quite contrary professions. I do not know of any other pleasure we would not renounce for that, even if curiosity alone gave us the opportunity.

I have dwelt on this important subject longer than I had intended, and far more for your sake than for my own; for while I am disclosing to you these methods and these alleviations attending the greatest cares of royalty I am not unaware that I am likewise depreciating almost the sole merit which I can hope for in the eyes of the world. But in this matter, my son, your honour is dearer to me than my own; and if it should happen that God call you to govern before you have yet taken to this spirit of application and to public affairs of which I am speaking, the least deference you can pay to the advice of a father, to whom I make bold to say you owe much in every kind of way, is to begin to do and to continue to do for some time, even under constraint and dislike, for love of me who beg it of you, what you will do all your life from love of yourself, if once you have made a beginning.

I gave orders to the four Secretaries of State no longer to sign anything whatsoever without speaking to me; likewise to the Controller, and that he should authorise nothing as regards finance without its being registered in a book which must remain with me, and being noted down in a very abridged abstract form in which at any moment, and at a glance, I could see the state of the funds, and past and future expenditure.

The Chancellor received a like order, that is to say, to sign nothing with the seal except by my command, with the exception only of letters of justice, so called because it would be an injustice to refuse them, a procedure required more as a matter of form than of principle; and I allowed to remain the administering and remissions of cases manifestly pardonable, although I have since changed my opinion on this subject, as I will tell you in its proper place. I let it be understood that whatever the nature of the matter might be, direct application must be made to me when it was not a question that depended only on my favour; and to all my subjects without distinction I gave liberty to present their case to me at all hours, either verbally or by petitions.

At first petitions came in very great numbers, which nevertheless did not discourage me. The disorder in which my affairs had been placed was productive of many; the novelty and expectation, whether vain or unjust, attracted not less. A large number were presented connected with law-suits, which I could not and ought not to take out of the ordinary tribunals in order to have them adjudicated before me. But even in these things, apparently so unprofitable, I found great usefulness. By this means I informed myself in detail as to the state of my people; they saw that I was mindful of them, and nothing won their heart so much. Oppression on the part of the ordinary tribunals might be represented to me in such a way as to make me feel it desirable to gain further information in order to take special measures when they were required. One or two examples of this kind prevented a thousand similar ills; the complaints, even when they were false and unjust, hindered my officers from giving a hearing to those which were more genuine and reasonable.

Regarding the persons whose duty it was to second my labours, I resolved at all costs to have no prime minister; and if you will believe me, my son, and all your successors after you, the name shall be banished for ever from France, for there is nothing more undignified than to see all the administration on one side, and on the other, the mere title of King.

To effect this, it was necessary to divide my confidence and the execution of my orders without giving it entirely to one single person, applying these different people to different spheres according to their diverse talents, which is perhaps the first and greatest gift that Princes can possess.

I also made a resolution on a further matter. With a view the better to unite in myself alone all the authority of a master, although there must be in all affairs a certain amount of detail to which our occupations and also our dignity do not permit us to descend as a rule, I conceived the plan, after I should have made choice of my ministers, of entering sometimes into matters with each one of them, and when they least expected it, in order that they might understand that I could do the same upon other subjects and at any moment. Besides, a knowledge of some small detail acquired only occasionally, and for amusement rather than as a regular rule, is instructive little by little and without fatigue, on a thousand things which are not without their use in general resolutions, and which we ought to know and do ourselves were it possible that a single man could know and do everything.

* * *

Time has shown what to believe, and I have now been pursuing for ten years fairly consistently, as it seems to me, the same course, without relaxing my application; kept well-informed of everything; listening to the least of my subjects; at any hour knowing the number and quality of my troops, and the state of my fortified towns; unremitting in issuing my orders for all their requirements; dealing at once with foreign ministers; receiving and reading dispatches; doing myself a portion of the replies and giving to my secretaries the substance of the others; regulating the State receipts and expenditure; requiring those whom I placed in important posts to account directly to me; keeping my affairs to myself as much as any one before me had ever done; distributing my favours as I myself chose; and retaining, if I mistake not, those who served me in a modest position which was far removed from the elevation and power of prime ministers, although loading them with benefits for themselves and their belongings.

The observation by others of all these things doubtless gave rise to some opinion of me in the world; and this opinion has in no small measure contributed to the success of what I have since undertaken, inasmuch as nothing could have produced such great results in so short a time as the reputation of the Prince.

* * *

After having thus fully informed myself in private discussions with them I entered more boldly into practical action. There was nothing that appeared more pressing to me than to alleviate the condition of my people, to which the poverty of the provinces and the compassion I felt for them strongly urged me. The state of my finances, as I have shown you, seemed to oppose this, and in any case counselled delay; but we must always be in haste to do well. The reforms I took in hand, though beneficial to the public, were bound to be irksome to a large number of private people. It was appropriate to make a beginning with something that could only be agreeable, and besides, there was no other way of maintaining any longer even the name of peace without its being followed by some sort of sop of this kind as a promise of greater hopes for the future. I therefore put aside any other considerations and, as a pledge of further alleviation, I first remitted three millions of the taxes for the following year which had already been prescribed and were awaiting collection.

At the same time, but with the intention of having them better observed than heretofore, I renewed the regulations against wearing gold and silver on clothes, and a thousand other foreign superfluities which were a kind of charge and contribution, outwardly voluntary but really obligatory, which my subjects, especially those most qualified and the persons at my Court, paid daily to neighbouring nations, or, to be more correct, to luxury and vanity.

For a thousand reasons, and also to pave the way for the reform of the administration of justice so greatly needed, it was necessary to diminish the authority of the chief jurisdictions which, under the pretext that their judgments were without appeal, and, as we say, sovereign and of final resort, regarded themselves as separate and independent sovereignties. I let it be known that I would no longer tolerate their assumptions. The *Cour des Aides* in Paris having been the first to exceed its duties and in some degree its jurisdiction, I exiled a few of its most offending officers, believing that if this remedy were thoroughly employed at the outset, it would relieve me of the necessity of its frequent application afterwards; and my action has been successful.

Immediately afterwards I gave them to understand my intentions still better in a solemn decree by my Supreme Council. For it is quite true that these jurisdictions have no cause to regulate each other in their different capacities, which are defined by laws and edicts. In former times these sufficed to make them live in peace with each other, or in the event of certain differences arising between them, especially in matters regarding private individuals, these were so rare and so little difficult of adjustment, that the Kings themselves decided them with a word, more often than not during a walk, on the report of the Magistrates, who then consisted of a very small number, until, owing to the growth in the kingdom of these matters and still more of chicanery, this duty was entrusted principally to the Chancellor of France and to the Administrative Council of which I have spoken already to you. Now these officials of necessity should be fully authorised to regulate the competence of the other jurisdictions (and also all other matters of which from time to time we deem it suitable for reasons of public utility, or of our own proper service, to give them cognisance exceptionally) by taking it over from them inasmuch as they derive their power only from us. Notwithstanding, owing to this spirit of self-sufficiency and the disorder of the times, they only yielded in so far as seemed good to them, and outstepped their powers daily and in all manner of cases in spite of their proper limitations, often enough going so far as to say that they recognised the King's will in no other form than that contained in the Ordinances and the authorised Edicts.

By this decree I forbade them all in general to give any judgments contrary

to those of my Council under any pretext whatsoever, whether in their own
jurisdiction or in their private capacity, and I commanded them, when one or
the other felt they had suffered hurt to make their complaint to me and have
recourse to my authority, inasmuch as I had only entrusted to them to exercise justice towards my subjects and not to create their own justice of themselves, which thing constitutes a part of sovereignty so closely united to the
Crown and so much the prerogative of the King alone that it cannot be
communicated to any other.

In the same year, but a little later, for I shall not observe too closely the
order of dates, in a certain matter connected with the finances of all the
record offices in general, and one which they had never dared carry through
in connection with those of the Parliament in Paris, because the property
belonged to the officers of that body and sometimes to the chambers as a
whole, I made it be seen that these officers must submit to the common law,
and that there was nothing to prevent my absolving them from it when it
pleased me to give this reward for their services.

About the same time, I did a thing which seemed even too bold, so greatly
had the gentlemen of the law profited by it up till then, and so full were their
minds of the importance they had acquired in the recent troubles through the
abuse of their power. From three quarters I reduced to two all the fresh
mortgages which were charged upon my revenue, which had been effected at
a very extortionate rate during the war, and which were eating up the best of
my farms of which the officials of the corporations had acquired the greater
part. And this made them regard it as a fine thing to treat them as harshly as
possible in their most vital interests. But at bottom this action of mine was
perfectly just, for two quarters was still a great deal in return for what they
had advanced. The reform was necessary. My affairs were not in such a state
that I had nothing to fear from their resentment. It was more to the purpose
to show them that I feared nothing they could do and that the times were
changed. And those who from different interests had wished that these corporations might win the day learnt on the contrary from their submission
what was due to me.

*   *   *

I also made a change in my household at that time, in which all the nobility of the realm had an interest. This had to do with my chief stables in
which I increased the number of pages by more than half, and took pains
both that the selection was made with more care and that they were better
instructed than they had been up till then.

I was aware that what had prevented people of quality from aspiring to
these kinds of positions was either the ease with which all conditions of folk
had been recommended and admitted to them, or the scant opportunity
afforded to them as a rule of approaching my person, or the neglect to perfect
them in their duties which had insensibly arisen. To remedy all this I determined to take care to appoint all the pages myself, to make them share with

those of my private stables all the domestic services which the latter rendered me, and to choose the best instructors in my realm to train them.

As regards the public, the results I hoped to obtain were to provide an excellent education for a large number of gentlemen, and for my own private benefit to have always a supply of people coming from this school more capable, and better disposed than the general run of my subjects, to enter my service.

I had yet another object for my personal attention which concerned principally people of substance, but the effect of which was afterwards spread over my kingdom generally. I knew what immense sums were spent by private individuals and were perpetually being withdrawn from the State by the trade in lace of foreign manufacture. I saw that the French were wanting neither in industry nor in the material for undertaking this work themselves, and I had no doubt that if they did this on the spot they could provide it far more cheaply than what they imported from such a distance. From these considerations I determined to establish works here, the effect of which would be that the great would moderate their expenditure, the people would derive the entire benefit of what the rich spent, and the large sums leaving the State would insensibly produce additional abundance and wealth by being retained in it, and beyond this would provide occupation for many of my subjects who up till then had been forced either to become slack through want of work or to go in search of it among our neighbours.

However, inasmuch as the most laudable plans are never carried out without opposition, I foresaw well that the lace merchants would oppose this with all their power, because I had no doubt that they found it paid them better to sell their wares which came from a distance, whereof the proper value could not be known, than those which were manufactured here within sight of everybody.

But I was determined to cut short by my authority all the trickery they might use, and so I gave them sufficient time to sell the foreign lace which they had before my edict was published, and when this time had expired I caused all that they still had to be seized as having come in since my prohibition, while, on the other hand, I caused shops filled with new manufactures to be opened, at which I obliged private individuals to make their purchases.

The example of this in a short while set up the manufacture of many other things in my State, such as sheets, glass, mirrors, silk stockings, and similar wares.

I took special plans to find out how to augment and assure to my subjects their maritime trade by making the ports I possessed safer, and seeking places to construct new ones. But while doing this I took in hand another enterprise of no lesser utility, which was to link by a canal the Ocean with the Mediterranean, in such wise that it would be no longer necessary to go round Spain to pass from one sea to the other. It was a great and difficult undertaking. But it was infinitely advantageous to my realm, which thus became the centre, and as it were the arbiter of the trade of the whole of Europe. And it was no less glorious for me who in the accomplishing of this object raised myself above the greatest men of past centuries who had undertaken it without result.

* * *

I have never failed, when an occasion has presented itself, to impress upon you the great respect we should have for religion, and the deference we should show to its ministers in matters specially connected with their mission, that is to say, with the celebration of the Sacred Mysteries and the preaching of the doctrine of the Gospels. But because people connected with the Church are liable to presume a little too much on the advantages attaching to their profession, and are willing sometimes to make use of them in order to whittle down their most rightful duties, I feel obliged to explain to you certain points on this question which may be of importance.

The first is that Kings are absolute *seigneurs,* and from their nature have full and free disposal of all property both secular and ecclesiastical, to use it as wise dispensers, that is to say, in accordance with the requirements of their State.

The second is that those mysterious names, the Franchises and Liberties of the Church, with which perhaps people will endeavour to dazzle you, have equal reference to all the faithful whether they be laymen or tonsured, who are all equally sons of this common Mother; but that they exempt neither the one nor the other from subjection to Sovereigns, to whom the Gospel itself precisely enjoins that they should submit themselves.

The third is that all that people say in regard to any particular destination of the property of the Church, and to the intention of founders, is a mere scruple without foundation, because it is certain that, inasmuch as the founders of benefices when transmitting their succession were not able to free them either from the quit-rental or the other dues which they paid to particular *seigneurs,* so for a far stronger reason they could not release them from the first due of all which is payable to the Prince as *Seigneur* over all, for the general welfare of the whole realm.

The fourth is that if up till now permission has been given to ecclesiastics to deliberate in their assemblies on the amount which it is their duty to provide, they should not attribute this custom to any special privilege, because the same liberty is still left to the people of several provinces as a former mark of the probity existing in the first centuries, when justice was sufficient to animate each individual to do what he should according to his ability and, notwithstanding, this never prevented either laymen or ecclesiastics when they refused to fulfil their obligations of their own free will, from being compelled to do so.

And the fifth and last is that if there are dwellers in our Empire more bound than others to be of service to us as regards their property as a whole, these should be the beneficiaries who only hold all they have at our option. The claims attaching to them have been established as long as those of their benefices, and we have titles to them which have been preserved from the first period of the monarchy. Even Popes who have striven to despoil us of this right have made it more clear and more incontestable by the precise retraction of their ambitious pretensions which they have been obliged to make.

But we might say that in this matter there is no need of either titles or examples, because natural equity alone is sufficient to illustrate this point. Would it be just that the Nobility should give its services and its blood in the defence of the realm and so often consume its resources in the maintenance of the offices with which it is charged, and that the people (with so little substance and so many mouths to fill) should bear in addition the sole weight of all the expenses of the State, while ecclesiastics, exempt by their profession from the dangers of war, from the profusion of luxury and the burden of families, should enjoy in abundance all the advantages of the general public without ever contributing anything to its necessities?

* * *

I have sustained this war with the high hand and pride which becomes this realm; through the valour of my Nobility and the zeal of my subjects I have been successful in the undertakings I have accomplished for the good of the State; I have given my whole concern and application to reach a successful issue; I have also put in motion the measures I thought necessary in fulfilling my duties, and in making known the love and tenderness I have for my people, by procuring by my labours a peace which will bring them rest for the remainder of my reign so that I need have no other care than for their welfare. After having extended the boundaries of this Empire, and protected my frontiers with the important strongholds I have taken, I have given ear to the proposals of peace which have been made to me, and I have exceeded perhaps on this occasion the limits of prudence in order to accomplish so great a work. I may say that I stepped out of my own character and did extreme violence to myself in order promptly to secure repose for my subjects at the expense of my reputation, or at least of my own particular satisfaction, and perhaps of my renown, which I willingly risked for the advantage of those who have enabled me to acquire it. I felt that I owed them this mark of gratitude. But seeing at this hour that my most vehement enemies have only wished to play with me and that they have employed all the artifices they could to deceive me as well as their allies by forcing them to contribute to the immense expenditure which their disordered ambition demanded, I do not see any other course to take than that of considering how to protect ourselves securely, making them understand that a France thoroughly united is stronger than all the powers they have got together at so great pains, by force and artifice, to overwhelm her. Up to now I have made use of the extraordinary measures which on similar occasions I have put into practice in order to provide sums proportionate to the expenditure indispensable to uphold the glory and safety of the State. Now that all sources are *quasi*-exhausted I come to you at this juncture to ask your counsel and your assistance, whence a safe issue will arise. Our enemies will learn from the efforts we shall put forth together that we are not in the condition they would have people believe, and by means of the help which I am asking of you and which I believe to be indispensable, we shall be able to force them to make a peace which shall be honourable to ourselves, lasting for our tranquillity, and agreeable to all the Princes of Europe. This is what I shall look to up to the moment of its conclusion, even in the greatest stress of the war, as well as to the welfare and happiness of my people which have always been, and will continue to be to the last moment of my life, my greatest and most serious concern.

3
ABSOLUTISM
IN PRACTICE

The Duke of Saint-Simon (1675–1755) came from one of the oldest noble families in France. He was, in many ways, typical of the feudal nobility that Louis XIV was concerned to tame and bring under the authority of the monarchy. His *memoirs* describe court life and give considerable insight into the ways in which Louis XIV tried to control the aristocracy. His reports on politics in the provinces were clearly influenced by his own position at court.

FROM The Memoirs of the Duke of Saint-Simon

Louis XIV was made for a brilliant Court. In the midst of other men, his figure, his courage, his grace, his beauty, his grand mien, even the tone of his voice and the majestic and natural charm of all his person, distinguished him till his death as the King Bee, and showed that if he had only been born a simple private gentleman, he would equally have excelled in fêtes, pleasures, and gallantry, and would have had the greatest success in love. The intrigues and adventures which early in life he had been engaged in—when the Comtesse de Soissons lodged at the Tuileries as superintendent of the Queen's household, and was the centre figure of the Court group—had exercised an unfortunate influence upon him: he received those impressions with which he could never after successfully struggle. From this time, intellect, education, nobility of sentiment, and high principle in others, became objects of suspicion to him, and soon of hatred. The more he advanced in years the more this sentiment was confirmed in him. He wished to reign by himself. His jealousy on this point unceasingly, became weakness. He reigned, indeed, in little

The Memoirs of the Duke of Saint-Simon on the Reign of Louis XIV and the Regency, I (1857), 315–319; II (1857), 3–6, 64–66, 95–98, 214–219, 354–357; III (1857), 225–228, 232–233, translated by Bayle St. John.

things; the great he could never reach: even in the former, too, he was often governed. The superior ability of his early ministers and his early generals soon wearied him. He liked nobody to be in any way superior to him. Thus he chose his ministers, not for their knowledge, but for their ignorance; not for their capacity, but for their want of it. He liked to form them, as he said; liked to teach them even the most trifling things. It was the same with his generals. He took credit to himself for instructing them; wished it to be thought that from his cabinet he commanded and directed all his armies. Naturally fond of trifles, he unceasingly occupied himself with the most petty details of his troops, his household, his mansions; would even instruct his cooks, who received, like novices, lessons they had known by heart for years. This vanity, this unmeasured and unreasonable love of admiration, was his ruin. His ministers, his generals, his mistresses, his courtiers, soon perceived his weakness. They praised him with emulation and spoiled him. Praises, or to say truth, flattery, pleased him to such an extent, that the coarsest was well received, the vilest even better relished. It was the sole means by which you could approach him. Those whom he liked owed his affection for them to their untiring flatteries. This is what gave his ministers so much authority, and the opportunities they had for adulating him, of attributing everything to him, and of pretending to learn everything from him. Suppleness, meanness, an admiring, dependent, cringing manner—above all, an air of nothingness—were the sole means of pleasing him.

This poison spread. It spread, too, to an incredible extent, in a prince who, although of intellect beneath mediocrity, was not utterly without sense, and who had had some experience. Without voice or musical knowledge, he used to sing, in private, the passages of the opera prologues that were fullest of his praises! He was drowned in vanity; and so deeply, that at his public suppers —all the Court present, musicians also—he would hum these selfsame praises between his teeth, when the music they were set to was played!

And yet, it must be admitted, he might have done better. Though his intellect, as I have said, was beneath mediocrity, it was capable of being formed. He loved glory, was fond of order and regularity; was by disposition prudent, moderate, discreet, master of his movements and his tongue. Will it be believed? He was also by disposition good and just! God had sufficiently gifted him to enable him to be a good King; perhaps even *a tolerably great King!* All the evil came to him from elsewhere. His early education was so neglected that nobody dared approach his apartment. He has often been heard to speak of those times with bitterness, and even to relate that, one evening he was found in the basin of the Palais Royale garden fountain, into which he had fallen! He was scarcely taught how to read or write, and remained so ignorant, that the most familiar historical and other facts were utterly unknown to him! He fell, accordingly, and sometimes even in public, into the grossest absurdities.

It was his vanity, his desire for glory, that led him, soon after the death of the King of Spain, to make that event the pretext for war; in spite of the renunciations so recently made, so carefully stipulated, in the marriage contract. He marched into Flanders; his conquests there were rapid; the passage of the Rhine was admirable; the triple alliance of England, Sweden, and Holland only animated him. In the midst of winter he took Franche Comté, by restoring which at the peace of Aix-la-Chapelle, he preserved his conquests in Flanders. All was flourishing then in the state. Riches everywhere. Colbert had placed the finances, the navy, commerce, manufactures, letters even, upon the highest point; and this age, like that of Augustus, produced in abundance illustrious men of all kinds,—even those illustrious only in pleasures.

* * *

Thus, we see this monarch grand, rich, conquering, the arbiter of Europe; feared and admired as long as the ministers and captains existed who really deserved the name. When they were no more, the machine kept moving some time by impulsion, and from their influence. But soon afterwards we saw beneath the surface; faults and errors were multiplied, and decay came on with giant strides; without, however, opening the eyes of that despotic master, so anxious to do everything and direct everything himself, and who seemed to indemnify himself for disdain abroad by increasing fear and trembling at home.

* * *

A short time after the death of Mademoiselle de l'Enclos, a terrible adventure happened to Courtenvaux, eldest son of M. de Louvois. Courtenvaux was commander of the Cent-Suisses, fond of obscure debauches; with a ridiculous voice, miserly, quarrelsome, though modest and respectful; and in fine a very stupid fellow. The King, more eager to know all that was passing than most people believed, although they gave him credit for not a little curiosity in this respect, had authorised Bontemps to engage a number of Swiss in addition to those posted at the doors, and in the parks and gardens. These attendants had orders to stroll morning, noon, and night, along the corridors, the passages, the staircases, even into the private places, and, when it was fine, in the court-yards and gardens; and in secret to watch people, to follow them, to notice where they went, to notice who was there, to listen to all the conversation they could hear, and to make reports of their discoveries. This was assiduously done at Versailles, at Marly, at Trianon, at Fontainebleau, and in all the places where the King was. These new attendants vexed Courtenvaux considerably, for over such new-comers he had no sort of authority. This season, at Fontainebleau, a room, which had formerly been occupied by a party of the Cent-Suisses and of the body-guard, was given up entirely to the new corps. The room was in a public passage of communication indispensable to all in the château, and in consequence, excellently well adapted for watching those who passed through it. Courtenvaux more than ever vexed by this new arrangement, regarded it as a fresh encroachment upon his authority, and flew into a violent rage with the new-comers, and railed at them in good set terms. They allowed him to fume as he would; they had their orders; and were too wise to be disturbed by his rage. The King, who heard of all this, sent at once for Courtenvaux. As soon as he appeared in the cabinet, the King called to him from the other end of the room, without giving him time to approach, and in a rage so terrible, and for him so novel, that not only Courtenvaux, but Princes, Princesses, and everybody in the chamber, trembled. Menaces that his post should be taken away from him, terms the most severe and the most unusual, rained upon Courtenvaux, who, fainting with fright, and ready to sink under the ground, had neither the time nor the means to prefer a word. The reprimand finished by the King saying, "Get out." He had scarcely the strength to obey.

The cause of this strange scene was that Courtenvaux, by the fuss he had made, had drawn the attention of the whole Court to the change effected by the King, and that, when once seen, its object was clear to all eyes. The King, who hid his spy system with the greatest care, had counted upon this change passing unperceived, and was beside himself with anger when he found it made apparent to everybody by Courtenvaux's noise. He never regained the King's favour during the rest of his life; and but for his family he would certainly have been driven away, and his office taken from him.

* * *

The death of the Abbé de Vatteville occurred at the commencement of this year, and made some noise, on account of the prodigies of the Abbé's life. This Vatteville was the younger son of a Franche Comté family; early in life he joined the Order of the Chartreux monks, and was ordained priest. He had much intellect, but was of an impetuous spirit, and soon began to chafe under the yoke of a religious life. He determined, therefore, to set himself free from it, and procured some secular habits, pistols, and a horse. Just as he was about to escape over the walls of the monastery by means of a ladder, the prior entered his cell. Vatteville made no to-do, but at once drew a pistol, shot the prior dead, and effected his escape.

Two or three days afterwards, travelling over the country and avoiding as much as possible the frequented places, he arrived at a wretched road-side inn, and asked what there was in the house. The landlord replied—"A leg of mutton and a capon." "Good!" replied our unfrocked monk; "put them down to roast."

The landlord replied that they were too much for a single person, and that he had nothing else for the whole house. The monk upon this flew in a passion, and declared that the least the landlord could do was to give him what he would pay for; and that he had sufficient appetite to eat both leg of mutton and capon. They were accordingly put down to the fire, the landlord not daring to say another word. While they were cooking, a traveller on horseback arrived at the inn, and learning that they were for one person, was much astonished. He offered to pay his share to be allowed to dine off them with the stranger who had ordered this dinner; but the landlord told him he was afraid the gentleman would not consent to the arrangement. Thereupon the traveller went up stairs and civilly asked Vatteville if he might dine with him on paying half of the expense. Vatteville would not consent, and a dispute soon arose between the two; to be brief, the monk served this traveller as he had served the prior, killed him with a pistol shot. After this he went down stairs tranquilly, and in the midst of the fright of the landlord and of the whole house, had the leg of mutton and capon served up to him, picked both to the very bone, paid his score, remounted his horse, and went his way.

Not knowing what course to take, he went to Turkey, and in order to succeed there, had himself circumcised, put on the turban, and entered into the militia. His blasphemy advanced him, his talents and his colour distinguished him; he became *Bacha,* and the confidential man in the Morea, where the Turks were making war against the Venetians. He determined to make use of this position in order to advance his own interests, and entering into communication with the generalissimo of the Republic, promised to betray into his hands several secret places belonging to the Turks, but on certain conditions. These were, absolution from the Pope for all crimes of his life, his murders and his apostasy included; security against the Chartreux and against being placed in any other Order; full restitution of his civil rights, and liberty to exercise his profession of priest with the right of possessing all benefices of every kind. The Venetians thought the bargain too good to be refused, and the Pope, in the interest of the Church, accorded all the demands of the Bacha. When Vatteville was quite assured that his conditions would be complied with, he took his measures so well that he executed perfectly all he had undertaken. Immediately after he threw himself into the Venetian army, and passed into Italy. He was well received at Rome by the Pope, and returned to his family in Franche Comté, and amused himself by braving the Chartreux.

At the first conquest of the Franche Comté, he intrigued so well with the Queen-mother and the ministry, that he was promised the Archbishopric of Besançon; but the Pope cried out against this on account of his murders, circumcision, and apostasy. The King sided with the Pope, and Vatteville was obliged to be contented with the abbey of Baume, another good abbey in Picardy, and divers other advantages.

Except when he came to the Court, where he was always received with great distinction, he remained at his abbey of Baume, living there like a grand seigneur, keeping a fine pack of hounds, a good table, entertaining jovial company, keeping mistresses very freely; tyrannising over his tenants and his neighbours in the most absolute manner. The intendants gave way to him, and by express orders of the Court allowed him to act much as he pleased, even with the taxes, which he regulated at his will, and in his conduct was oftentimes very violent. With these manners and this bearing, which caused him to be both feared and respected, he would often amuse himself by going to see the Chartreux, in order to plume himself on having quitted their frock. He played much at *hombre,* and frequently gained *codille* (a term of the game), so that the name of the Abbé Codille was given to him. He lived in this manner, always with the same licence and in the same consideration, until nearly ninety years of age.

* * *

Such was our military history of the year 1706—a history of losses and dishonour. It may be imagined in what condition was the exchequer with so many demands upon its treasures. For the last two or three years the King had been obliged, on account of the expenses of the war, and the losses we had sustained, to cut down the presents that he made at the commencement of the year. Thirty-five thousand louis in gold was the sum he ordinarily spent in this manner. This year, 1707, he diminished it by ten thousand louis. It was upon Madame de Montespan that the blow fell. Since she had quitted the Court the King gave her twelve thousand louis of gold each year. This year he sent word to her that he could only give her eight. Madame de Montespan testified not the least surprise. She replied, that she was only sorry for the poor, to whom indeed she gave with profusion. A short time after the King had made this reduction,—that is, on the 8th of January,—Madame La Duchesse de Bourgogne gave birth to a son. The joy was great, but the King prohibited all those expenses which had been made at the birth of the first-born of Madame de Bourgogne, and which had amounted to a large sum. The want of money indeed made itself felt so much at this time, that the King was obliged to seek for resources as a private person might have done. A mining speculator, named Rodes, having pretended that he had discovered many veins of gold in the Pyrenees, assistance was given him in order that he might bring these treasures to light. He declared that with eighteen hundred workmen he would furnish a million (francs' worth of gold) each week. Fifty-two millions a-year would have been a fine increase of revenue. However, after waiting some little time, no gold was forthcoming, and the money that had been spent to assist this enterprise was found to be pure loss.

The difficulty of finding money to carry on the affairs of the nation continued to grow so irksome that Chamillart, who had both the finance and the war departments under his control, was unable to stand against the increased trouble and vexation which this state of things brought him. More than once he had represented that this double work was too much for him. But the King had in former times expressed so much annoyance from the troubles that arose between the finance and war departments, that he would not separate them, after having once joined them together. At last, Chamillart could bear up against his heavy load no longer. The vapours seized him: he had attacks of giddiness in the head; his digestion was obstructed; he grew thin as a lath. He wrote again to the King, begging to be released from his duties, and frankly stated that, in the state he was, if some relief was not afforded him, everything would go wrong and perish. He always left a large margin to his letters, and upon this the King generally wrote his reply. Chamillart showed me this letter when it came back to him, and I saw upon it with great surprise, in the handwriting of the King, this short note: "Well! let us perish together."

The necessity for money had now become so great, that all sorts of means were adopted to obtain it. Amongst other things, a tax was established upon baptisms and marriages. This tax was extremely onerous and odious. The result of it was a strange confusion. Poor people, and many of humble means, baptised their children themselves, without carrying them to the church, and were married at home by reciprocal consent and before witnesses, when they could find no priest who would marry them without formality. In consequence of this there were no longer any baptismal extracts; no longer any certainty as to baptisms or births; and the children of the marriages solemnised in the way I have stated above were illegitimate in the eyes of the law. Researches and rigours in respect to abuses so prejudicial were redoubled therefore; that is to say, they were redoubled for the purpose of collecting the tax.

From public cries and murmurs the people in some places passed to sedition. Matters went so far at Cahors, that two battalions which were there had great difficulty in holding the town against the armed peasants; and troops intended for Spain were obliged to be sent there. It was found necessary to suspend the operation of the tax, but it was with great trouble that the movement of Quercy was put down, and the peasants, who had armed and collected together, induced to retire into their villages. In Perigord they rose, pillaged the bureaux, and rendered themselves masters of a little town and some castles, and forced some gentlemen to put themselves at their head. They declared publicly that they would pay the old taxes to King, curate, and lord, but that they would pay no more, or hear a word of any other taxes or vexation. In the end it was found necessary to drop this tax upon baptism and marriages, to the great regret of the tax-gatherers, who, by all manner of vexations and rogueries, had enriched themselves cruelly.

It was one thing to claim that the royal will was absolute; it was another thing to enforce it throughout France. To do this, Louis XIV and his great minister Jean Baptiste Colbert (1619–1683) set out to create a bureaucracy that would extend into the farthest reaches of the realm. Through this bureaucracy, information would flow to Versailles and orders could be carried out in the localities. The effectiveness of absolutism was determined by the efficiency of both operations.

FROM Memoirs of Nicolas-Joseph Foucault

Colbert to the Commissioners in the Field, April 28, 1679

You know that I have written you by order of the king every year before this in order to stimulate you to make your visit to all the elections [an administrative unit] of the generality of . . . with great care and also in order to let you know what you should occupy yourself with principally in this visit. Since this is a way of procuring the easing of the people's lot, almost equal to that which the king has given them by the great decrease that he has made in the taxes, His Majesty has ordered me to tell you that he wishes that this year you will make a more complete visit of all the elections and parishes of the above generality that you have not yet made, and that you should start this immediately and without any hesitation; and to this effect I will give you, in a few words, the principal points that you should examine.

The first and the most important is the imposition of the *tailles* [*a property tax from which the nobility and clergy were exempt—L. P. W.*], on which, although I am persuaded that the application that you already have shown prevents many abuses, nevertheless, since it is certain that, either in the drawing up of the tax rolls, or in the levying and collection of the *tailles,* or in the actual reception that the receivers make of the collectors, or in the pressures that one exercises and the expenses that the taxable people are forced to pay, there is still a good deal of disorder of which you are not aware since those who are guilty and who profit from it take care to hide it from you—this being the case the king wants you to enter into detail on all these points, in order that there is nothing on which you are not exactly informed and to which you will not be able to apply whatever remedies may be necessary.

His Majesty also wishes that you should examine the state of commerce and manufactures in the same generality, together with the food supply and the number of domestic animals, and that you should consider these three points as the fertile sources from which the people draw their money, not only for their own subsistence, but also for paying all their taxes; so that His Majesty desires that you should look into with care the means not only of maintaining them but even of augmenting them and of re-establishing commerce and manufactures which have disappeared because of not having received any help. . . .

Mémoires de Nicolas-Joseph Foucault (1850), pp. 417 ff., translated by L. Pearce Williams.

You know well enough the intentions of the king regarding the garrisoning of troops. . . . This is why I shall rest content merely to add that His Majesty has been informed that in the greatest number of cities and places where the inhabitants have furnished the housing of troops for the last ten or twelve years, the mayors and aldermen have kept and distributed amongst themselves the money which was given to them by the general receivers of finances for the reimbursement of the said inhabitants; and since there is no theft more obvious than this, and none which merits more to be punished, since the people are in the hands of their magistrates and since this theft can consequently begin again every day, His Majesty wishes that in the visit that you are going to make, you will examine carefully if the inhabitants of the cities and places of your generality which have furnished housing for troops make the same complaints against the mayors and aldermen, and in case you find someone who has been in charge for five or six years and who has applied for his own profit a large enough sum, let me know about it so that I can render an account to His Majesty and he will be able to send you orders so that you can give an exemplary punishment of this crime. . . .

FROM Administrative Correspondence Under the Reign of Louis XIV

The Bishop of Marseilles to Colbert, Lambesc, November 20, 1668

No matter with what care I tried, I was unable to get the deputies to this assembly to go beyond the sum of 400,000 [*French pounds—L. P. W.*] without certain conditions. The main ones are compensation for the expense that the troops have caused this year, the revocation of the edict on soap, and the revocation of the edict on genealogical experts.

They defend themselves in terms of the sum of money by pointing to the exhaustion of money in the province which is, in truth, very great, and which proceeds from the taxes on the businessmen, from the inquest on false nobility, which has drawn out enormous amounts of money by rather extraordinary avenues, the considerable expenses which have fallen on the communities with the arrangement of the [*royal—L. P. W.*] domain, from which apparently the money does not come back into the treasury, and the circulation of counterfeit five-sous pieces which has used up a great deal of good money and which will destroy commerce if there is not a true remedy forthcoming. In truth, if the province was only assessed for what the King wishes to draw from it and which he demands as his free gift there would be no trouble in arranging that and in persuading the deputies.

G. B. Depping, ed., *Correspondance administrative sous le règne de Louis XIV*, I (1850), 381–382, 384–385, 389, 390, 398, 399, translated by L. Pearce Williams.

The province by law has a right to compensation [*for garrisoning—L. P. W.*], and this year it has cost almost one hundred thousand livres, and since the King, no doubt, will not wish to subtract this amount from his gift this will mean it will cost the province five hundred thousand pounds and there is some justice to the position that the province should be assured of this compensation for the future in order to dismiss the apprehension under which these people labor that in giving to H. M. a considerable gift they will at the same time be asked, in the province, to pay for the lodging of troops or any other expense that may be demanded.

As for the affair of the soap, it is certain that not everything is being done to carry out the ordinance of H. M. as the price of soap has gone up. Since the old manufactories no longer work and since new ones are being established in neighboring provinces, there is the fear that this manufacture, which is one of the largest in the realm and which gives so much profit in this province, will be destroyed in the end if something is not done about it. You will do, Monsieur, what you will consider just.

As for the edict on the genealogical experts, if this is carried out it will mean the establishment of more than 800 officers at the same time that the King is working so well to abolish those who are useless and a burden on the people; moreover, paying them will force the disbursement of immense sums.

I also feel it necessary, Monsieur, to inform you that the nobility of this province, having the desire to sell their wheat at an excessive price, would like to restrain the public liberty (the right to import wheat by sea) on a foodstuff so necessary to life. They have worked, by all kinds of means, to force this assembly to join with them; but the deputies know the famine that would affect all the poor people of the province, and on this affair I have no doubt that they will oppose themselves to this unjust proposition, which is so harmful to the public. . . . Since the assembly has been meeting for almost three months without accomplishing much, and as it cannot disband until the return of the courier that has been sent to you, you would be doing a great favor to send him back soon, and you will find complete acquiescence to all that H. M. may order.

Colbert to President d'Oppède, Saint-Germain, March 6, 1671

I have given an account to the King of the request that you have made to the assembly of the communities of Provence, in conformity to the order of H. M. He orders me to tell you that it is necessary to terminate this affair promptly considering how long it has been going on. . . .

I have already received several complaints that the aldermen of the city of Marseilles are not carrying out the execution of the edicts for the liberation (of the port) and particularly for the payment of the 20 per cent, and the confiscation of merchandise which would enter without paying. . . .

March 13 . . . I will not even answer the offer that the province has made of giving 200,000 pounds as the free gift, since you know that the King wishes the amount that is mentioned in your instructions and is waiting for you to get it done.

Colbert to the Count de Grignan, Saint-Germain, March 20, 1671

I have reported to the King what you have been pleased to write me on the offer that the assembly of the communities of Provence have made for his free gift and the difficulty that you are encountering in raising it to the sum that H. M. desires; but he has told me at the same time to let you know that he will not rest content with less than what he has asked for and thus has no doubt that you will employ all the means that you consider necessary to oblige the said assembly to give him this satisfaction.

Colbert to the Count de Grignan, Saint-Germain, October 16, 1671

I can assure you that H. M. wanted 500,000 pounds from the province last year, as this, and it was only the pleading of your letters and those of Monsieur d'Oppède, that led H. M. to reduce it to 450,000 pounds for particular reasons that I cannot remember at present; but this year H. M. wants 500,000 pounds. . . .

Colbert to President d'Oppède, Saint-Germain, October 23, 1671

The King was somewhat surprised to hear that the deputies of the communities have returned to their homes under the pretext of holidays and that after a negotiation of three weeks you have only obtained from them the sum of 300,000 pounds. I ought to tell you that I really fear that the King may take the resolution to dismiss this assembly without taking anything from it since H. M. is not accustomed, by the conduct of other estates, to all these long negotiations for such a modest sum as that which he demands from Provence. . . .

Colbert to the Count de Grignan, Paris, December 25, 1671

I have reported to the King on the bad conduct of the assembly of the communities of Provence and, since H. M. is not disposed to suffer it any longer, he has given the necessary orders to dismiss it and at the same time has sent *lettres de cachet* intended to exile the ten deputies who caused the most trouble to Grandville, Cherbourg, Saint-Malo, Morlaix, and Concarneau. The said letters and orders will be sent to you by the first ordinary post, and I do not think it necessary to recommend that you be punctual and exact in executing them, knowing with how much warmth and zeal you act in everything that concerns the service of the King.

Colbert to the Bishop of Marseilles, Versailles, December 31st, 1671

The King accepts the four hundred and fifty thousand pounds that the assembly of the communities of Provence offered for the free gift, but H. M. is so indignant at the conduct of the deputies in making their deliberation that he has sent orders to exile 10 of the worst troublemakers to the provinces of Normandy and Brittany, which orders have been addressed to Monsieur the Count de Grignan. Provence should easily know how disadvantageous it has been to it to have chosen deputies so little attached to its true interest, but I do not know if these complaints may not be useless since it looks as though H. M. will not permit another such assembly of the communities in Provence.

4
THE EVALUATION OF THE REIGN

Absolutism depended upon the efficiency of the bureaucracy created to make it effective. This machinery of government is the subject studied by James E. King, who sees its development as the result of the new science of the seventeenth century. Just as the new science emphasized facts over theories, so the government of Louis XIV was an attempt to apply reason to actual situations. To do so, channels of information and chains of command had to be created.

FROM Science and Rationalism in the Government of Louis XIV BY JAMES E. KING

Such was the central government of France in the period 1661 to 1683. It is necessary to remind oneself that most of its actual work was performed in committees, subcommittees of the councils, and in the bureaus functioning under the various ministers and secretaries of state. In the provinces the will of this organization was exercised, in the main, through four distinct structures: that of justice, finances, the military, and the church. The last of these we can omit from our considerations as it has no direct bearing on our story.

The justice of the King was carried to the kingdom by the "sovereign" parlements. These were, for all but extraordinary cases, the supreme courts of the realm. To them came appeals from all the lower courts, as the *présidiaux, bailliages,* or *sénéchaussées,* in their particular jurisdictions. The chief of these parlements in prestige and real authority was that at Paris. This might be called the King's parlement. Other parlements were situated at Toulouse, Rouen, Grenoble, Bordeaux, Dijon, Aix, Rennes, Pau, Metz, and Besançon,

James E. King, *Science and Rationalism in the Government of Louis XIV, 1661–1683* (1950), pp. 124–130, 136–137. Reprinted by permission of The Johns Hopkins Press.

and several sovereign courts functioned elsewhere. The natural head, excluding the king, of all these courts was the chancellor of France, and it was through his department that appointments to them were made. The *conseil du Roi,* as represented in any of its four divisions, might override the decisions or opinions of the parlements.

The financial administration of the kingdom, and this must be extended to include economic as well as tax administration, was carried on, primarily, by the intendants with their subordinates. In our period, France was divided into twenty-six large tax districts, for administrative purposes, called generalities. These were headed by twenty-five intendants. The generalities, in turn, were subdivided into smaller districts called elections and the elections into parishes. A regular hierarchy of officials, within these areas, supervised the levying and collection of taxes, judged cases involving taxation, performed accounting, kept tax rolls, and allocated sums for local costs of government. Under the intendants operated a separate group of officials, with undefined powers, who supervised or interfered in these functions.

The so-called military government of the king was exercised by royal governors in thirty-seven governments. These men were ordinarily the peers of the realm or princes of the blood. Many of the ancient prerogatives of these gentlemen, as governors, had been drained off by the agents of the secretary of state for war and the intendants, but their prestige was still very considerable and if the governor was a man of capacity, cooperated with the intendants, was friendly to and trusted by the King and ministers, he could still wield considerable influence. Below the governor were usually four or five lieutenant-generals and, beneath them, governors of local places, cities or royal chateaux. Lieutenant-generals and these local governors were often almost independent of the provincial governor and were also usually chosen from the higher nobility. The primary duties of the governors were to maintain order and obedience to the crown in the provinces and to give armed support, if necessary, to the executions and functions of the other administrations.

The administrative prerogatives of the intendant as supervisor of the royal services of justice, police, and finances in the provinces had been rather clearly defined by the time that Colbert assumed his full role in the government. During the personal reign of Louis XIV, these powers were even more definitely organized and solidified and the monarchy assumed the form which it was to retain almost to the end of the *ancien régime.* At the center of this monarchy was the officer called the *contrôleur général,* and, intimately allied to his functions and carrying his authority throughout the realm, were the intendants of the provinces. This close relationship, or interdependence, was largely the creation of Colbert. The expression of it was the development of the practice of regular correspondence between the intendants and the *contrôleur général.* From the very beginning of his administration, Colbert maintained a prodigious correspondence with his subordinates and, particularly, with the intendants. The reciprocal necessity of submitting reports, surveys and memoirs to the *contrôleur général* became a regular duty of these officials. This was the most striking innovation of the minister in the government. As Usher writes in his *History of the grain trade in France,* "The development of the informing function of the intendants was thus one of the most direct results of the personal influence of Colbert. Nor was any function of the new administration more important or more literally unique."

Under the regime of Colbert and Louis XIV, the intendant assumed the part of delegate administrator in the most obscure sections that the royal power penetrated. . . . A literal reading of the instructions and circular letters sent to the intendants or *commissaires départis* into the generalities and *pays d'élections* from 1663 through 1683 would probably leave the researcher at a loss to imagine any possible field of government which was not committed to their inspection. But every inspection required the return of a report or written survey to the King, the secretaries of state, or the *contrôleur général,* and it was on such reports that *ordonnances* were formed, policies decreed, and projects drawn up by the ministry for presentation to the councils and the King.

It was the desire of the King, according to his Minister, that the intendants should come to know "perfectly all abuses" in the area of their responsibility, and to know them appears to have been considered as equal to remedying them. The insistence on thorough penetration into the most obscure corners of provincial affairs was the theme dominating instructions. The King recognized the physical limitations of his own personal desire to learn of the details of his realm "piece by piece," details which he would acquire himself if it were possible; therefore, trusted emissaries must perform the vicarious functions of a protean crown.

* * *

The intendants were, then, the legal eyes of the Monarchy. Colbert wrote his intendants and ordered them carefully, and personally, to investigate the levying of all taxes in all the elections of their generality "in a way that nothing escapes you." He spurred them on to greater thoroughness by representing these requests as being relayed from "His Majesty" who urged them to make "a serious reflection on all that which happens in the area of the Generality in which you serve . . . that you enter into the detail of the conduct of all those who are employed thereto." He acknowledged the difficulty of knowing all the various matters to "the depth," but this difficulty only emphasized the need of more continuous application to the task, in order that he might give to "His Majesty all your advice on all that which can apply in the future to the end which he sets for himself."

* * *

The multifarious functions of the intendants and the essentially informative character of these functions are progressively evident in early correspondence of Colbert with them. Usher asserts that technical and statistical information was less frequently required of the intendant than a statement of the general impression of conditions in his generality; however, as time passed the Minister became ever more exacting in his demands and increasingly discriminating in the segregation of fact from rumor. His persistency in insisting on adequate and valid information had the end result of developing an administrative standard of expectation and compliance which accounts for the fullness of the reports of the intendants after Colbert's death. The requirement of continuous reporting, the necessity for presenting, to the ministry, digested summary statements of the most diverse facts in his generality, placed the intendant, perforce, as another writer has observed, in the midst of numbers. By the very nature of his functions, he became a statistical agent of the central government.

The general pattern of government by inquiry was precisely laid down in the *Instruction pour les maîtres des requêtes, commissaires départis dans les provinces* of September 1663. This circular letter significantly and, in a sense, officially underlined the henceforth consistent policy of Colbert and Louis XIV in regard to the duties of the intendants. It initiated a vast inquest into the state of the realm with the intendants as the royal investigators; an inquest which was never completed in the life of its originator. The correspondence of Colbert reveals that most of the information requested at this time was still being sought by him twenty years later. Twenty years after that the Duke of Beauvillier made almost the same inquiries when forming his famous memoirs for the instruction of Louis XIV's grandson, the Duke of Burgundy. However imperfectly the designs of the inquest might be carried out, the instruction of 1663 was an unqualified endorsement by Louis XIV and his Minister of the ideal of administration based on the accumulation of political and social statistics.

* * *

Among the memoirs resulting from the inquest of 1663 those of Charles Colbert de Croissy, a brother of the Minister, are singled out by Clement as of superior quality, displaying, besides a diversity of information, an unusual frankness. His reports on Poitou, Touraine, Anjou, Alsace and the three bishoprics of Metz, Toul and Verdun were notably detailed and revealed the sad plight of their peoples. Other such memoirs have been discovered on Brittany, Rouen, Champagne, Burgundy, Bourges, Berry, and Moulins dating from the early years of Colbert's administration.

The utility of a summary account of the personal qualities of the members of the parlements, and other superior courts, probably seemed particularly pointed to Louis XIV and Colbert, both of whom always kept the lessons of the Fronde carefully nurtured in their memories. We have seen the attention given to this detail in the third section of the memoir. All the intendants of the provinces were requested to submit careful notes on the morals, capacities, influence, property, connections, and functions of the personnel of these courts. The resulting reports were in many cases partial and in most cases must have appeared inadequate. But this might be expected at a time when the intendants were but beginning to assume the new role assigned to them by an exacting Minister. At any rate, the *"Notes sécrètes"* sent to Colbert in response to this request form an extensive and entertaining part of the administrative correspondence edited by Depping.

M. Lamoignon of the Parlement of Paris was a pompous person with an "affectation of great probity and of a great integrity hiding a great ambition." M. Bailleul had a "gentle and easy disposition, acquiring through his civility many friends in the Palais [of the Parlement] and at the court." One de Nesmond "married to the sister of Mr the first president, is governed by her." M. Menardeau-Sampré was "very capable, firm, obstinate . . . governed by a damlle of the rue Saint-Martin." As for M. Fayet, he was "less than nothing." In the *Chambre des Enquestes,* M. Faure was "stupid, ignorant, brutal, fearing extraordinarily M. Hervé; he is a man of letters, but loves extraordinarily his own interests." But this was a report on all the major courts of the kingdom; in the Parlement of Brittany, the sieur De Brequingy had good intention "but he is weak and of a very mediocre mind." Jacquelot, sieur de la Motte, was "without capacity, and addicted to debauches with women and wine," but M. Montigny had "many of all kinds of good qualities and no bad ones." The reporter on the councillors of the *cours des Aydes* at Rouen contented himself almost entirely with variations on the two words: *"probité"* and *"capacité."* If his subject was very commendable he had both *"probité"* and *"capacité."*

However deficient some of the first reports of the intendants might be, it would appear that, with practice, the technique could be too well mastered. In July 1676, Colbert wrote in perplexity to M. Le Blanc at Rouen, "I have received the account of the provender which has been consumed in your generality during the winter quarter; but you fail to explain for what reason you send it to me, and I cannot supply it."

François-Marie Arouet (1694–1778), who took the name of Voltaire, was one of the most prominent and prolific writers of the Enlightenment in France. The age of Louis XIV was, to him, the golden age of French culture, and he attributed much of this excellence to the regime of absolutism instituted by the Sun King.

FROM The Age of Louis XIV BY VOLTAIRE

We owe it to public men who have benefited their age to look at the point from which they started in order better to appreciate the changes they have brought about in their country. Posterity owes them an eternal debt of gratitude for the examples they have given, even when their achievements have been surpassed, and this well-deserved glory is their only reward. It was certainly the love of this sort of glory that inspired Louis XIV when, as soon as he began to govern for himself, he set out to reform his kingdom, embellish his court and perfect the arts.

Not only did he impose upon himself the duty of working regularly with each one of his ministers, but any man of repute could obtain a private audience with him, and every citizen was free to present him with petitions and projects. The petitions were received, first of all, by a master of requests, who noted his comments in the margin and sent them on to the offices of the ministers. The projects were examined in Council when they deserved it and their authors were more than once admitted to discuss their proposals with the ministers in the King's presence. In this way, despite Louis's absolute power, the nation could still communicate with the monarch.

Louis XIV trained and accustomed himself to work, and this work was all the more difficult because it was new to him and because he could easily be distracted by the lures of pleasure. The first dispatches he sent to his ambassadors he wrote himself, and he later often minuted the most important letters in his own hand. None were written in his name without his having them read to him.

After the fall of Fouquet, Colbert had scarcely re-established order in the finances when the King canceled all the arrears due on taxes from 1647 to 1656 and, above all, three millions of the taille. Five hundred thousand crowns' worth of onerous duties were abolished. So the Abbé de Choisi seems to be either very misinformed or very unjust when he says that the receipts were not decreased. It is clear that they were decreased by these remissions, though they were later increased again as a result of better administration.

The efforts of the First President of Bellièvre, helped by the generosity of the Duchess of Aiguillon and several other citizens, had already established the general hospital in Paris. The King enlarged it and had others built in all the principal towns of the kingdom.

The highways, which up till then had been impassable, were no longer neglected and gradually became what they are today under Louis XV— the admiration of all foreigners. Whatever direction one goes from Paris, one can now travel for nearly two hundred miles, except for a few places, on well-surfaced roads lined with trees. The roads built by the ancient Romans were more lasting, but not as spacious or as beautiful.

Colbert directed his genius principally toward commerce, which was still largely undeveloped and whose basic principles were still unknown. The English, and still more the Dutch, carried almost all French trade in their ships. The Dutch in particular loaded their ships with our goods in our ports and distributed them throughout Europe. In 1662 the King began to exempt his subjects from a duty called the freight tax, which all foreign vessels had to pay, and he gave French merchants every facility for transporting their goods themselves more cheaply. It was then that our maritime trade began to develop. The council of commerce, which still exists today, was established, and the King presided over it every fortnight.

The ports of Dunkirk and Marseilles were declared free, and very soon this advantage attracted the trade of the Levant to Marseilles and that of the North to Dunkirk.

* * *

The West India company was encouraged no less than the others; the King supplied a tenth of all its funds. He gave thirty francs a ton on exports and forty on imports. All those who had ships built in French ports received five francs for each ton their vessel could carry.

* * *

Paris in those days was very far from being what it is now. There was neither lighting, police protection nor cleanliness. Provision had to be made for the continual cleaning of the streets and for lighting them every night with five thousand lamps; the whole town had to be paved; two new gates had to be built and the old ones restored; a permanent guard, both mounted and on foot, was needed for the security of citizens. All this the King took upon himself, allotting the funds for these necessary expenses. In 1667 he appointed a magistrate whose sole duty was to supervise the police. Most of the large cities of Europe only initiated these examples many years later; none has equaled them. There is no city paved like Paris, and even Rome has no street lighting.

Everything was beginning to improve so noticeably that the second holder of the office of lieutenant of police in Paris acquired a reputation which placed him among the distinguished men of his age; and indeed he was a man of great ability. He was afterward in the Ministry and he would have made a fine general. The post of lieutenant of police was below his birth and merit, and yet it gained him a much greater reputation than did the uneasy and transient ministerial office which he obtained toward the end of his life.

It is worth noting here that M. d'Argenson was not the only member of the old nobility to hold the office of magistrate. Far from it; France is almost the only country in which the old nobility has often worn magisterial robes. Almost all other states, from motives which are a remnant of Gothic barbarity, fail to realize that there is greatness in this profession.

From 1661 onward, the King was continually occupied in building the Louvre, Saint-Germain and Versailles. Private individuals, following his example, built hundreds of superb, spacious buildings in Paris. Their number increased to such an extent that there sprang up around the Palais-Royal and Saint-Sulpice two new towns vastly superior to the old one. This same time saw the invention of that splendid convenience, the coach, ornamented with mirrors and suspended on springs; thus a citizen of Paris could travel about this great city in far greater luxury than that in which the ancient Romans rode in triumph to the Capitol. This custom, which began in Paris, soon spread to the rest of Europe and has become so common that it is no longer a luxury.

Louis XIV had a taste for architecture, gardens and sculpture, and his taste was characterized by a liking for grandeur and impressiveness. In 1664, Controller General Colbert assumed the office of director of buildings (which is really the Ministry of the Arts), and no sooner had he done so than he set about furthering his master's schemes. The first task was to complete the Louvre. François Mansart, one of the greatest architects France has ever had, was chosen to construct the vast buildings that were planned. He was unwilling to undertake this commission unless he had freedom to reconstruct any parts of the edifice which seemed to him defective when he had completed them, and this mistrust of himself, which might have involved too great an expenditure, led to his exclusion. The chevalier Bernini was then sent for from Rome, a man whose name was famous by virtue of the colonnade surrounding St. Peter's Square, the equestrian statue of Constantine and the Navonna fountain. Carriages were provided for his journey. He was brought to Paris like a man who came to honor France. Apart from five louis a day during the eight months he stayed, he also received a present of fifty thousand crowns, together with a pension of two thousand, and one of five hundred for his son. Louis XIV's generosity to Bernini was even greater than that of Francis I to Raphael. By way of acknowledgment, Bernini later made, in Rome, the equestrian statue of the King which is now to be seen at Versailles. But when he arrived in Paris with so much circumstance, he was amazed to see the plan of the façade of the Louvre which faces Saint-Germain l'Auxerrois, and which soon after, when executed, became one of the most august monuments of architecture in the world. Claude Perrault had made this plan, and it was put into execution by Louis Levau and Dorbay. Perrault invented the machines by which were transported the stones, fifty-two feet long, that formed the pediment of this majestic edifice. Sometimes people go a long way to find what they already have at home. No palace in Rome has an entrance comparable to that of the Louvre, for which we are indebted to the Perrault whom Boileau dared to ridicule. Travelers admit that the famous Italian villas are inferior to the château of Maisons, which was built at such a small cost by François Mansart. Bernini was magnificently rewarded and did not deserve his rewards; he merely furnished plans which were never put into execution.

While building the Louvre, the completion of which is so greatly to be desired, while creating a town at Versailles near the Château which has cost so many millions, while building the Trianon and Marly and embellishing many other edifices, the King also built the Observatory, which was begun in 1666, at the same time as he founded the Academy of Sciences. But his most glorious monument, by its usefulness and its greatness as much as by the difficulties of its construction, was the canal which joins the two seas and which finds an outlet at the port of Sète, built especially for the purpose. All this work was begun in 1664 and continued without interruption until 1681. The foundation of the Invalides, with its chapel, the finest in Paris, and the establishment of Saint-Cyr, the last of many works built by the King—these by themselves would suffice to make his memory revered. Four thousand soldiers and a large number of officers find consolation in their old age and relief for their wounds and wants in the first of these great institutions; two hundred and fifty daughters of noblemen receive an education worthy of them in the other; together they are like so many voices praising Louis XIV. The establishment of Saint-Cyr will be surpassed by the one which Louis XV has just created for the education of five hundred noblemen; but so far from causing Saint-Cyr to be forgotten, it serves to remind one of it; the art of doing good has been brought to perfection.

At the same time, Louis XIV wanted to achieve something even greater and more generally useful, though more difficult; he wanted to reform the laws. For this task he employed the Chancellor Seguier, Lamoignon, Talon, Bignon, and above all, the councilor of state, Pussort. Sometimes he attended their meetings himself. The year 1667 was marked both by his first laws and by his first conquests. The civil ordinance appeared first and was followed by the code for the rivers and forests, and then by statutes concerning all the industries, by a criminal code, one for commerce and one for the marine. These followed one another in an almost annual succession. New laws were even established in favor of the Negroes of our colonies, a race of men who had hitherto not enjoyed the common rights of humanity.

One cannot expect a sovereign to possess a profound knowledge of jurisprudence, but the King was well informed about the principal laws; he was imbued with their spirit and knew how to enforce or mitigate them as the occasion demanded. He often judged his subjects' cases, not only in the Council of the Secretaries of State, but also in the so-called Council of Parties.

There are two celebrated judgments of his in which he decided against his own interest.

In the first, in 1680, the issue was one between himself and some private citizens of Paris who had built on his land. He decided that they should keep the houses, together with the land which belonged to him and which he ceded to them.

The other case concerned a Persian called Roupli, whose goods had been seized by his revenue commissioners in 1687. His decision was that all should be returned to him, and the King added a present of three thousand crowns. Roupli returned to his country full of admiration and gratitude. When we later met Mehemet Rizabeg, the Persian ambassador to Paris, we found that he had known about this incident for a long time, for it had become famous.

* * *

He was the legislator of his armies as well as of his people as a whole. It is surprising that, before his time, there was no uniform dress among the troops. It was he who, in the first year of his administration, ordered that each regiment should be distinguished by the color of its dress or by different badges; this regulation was soon adopted by all other nations. It was he who instituted brigadiers and who put the household troops on their present footing. He turned Cardinal Mazarin's guards into a company of musketeers and fixed the number of men in the companies at five hundred; moreover, he gave them the uniform which they still wear today.

Under him there were no longer constables, and after the death of the Duke of Epernon, no more colonel generals of infantry; they had become too powerful, and he quite rightly wanted to be sole master. Marshal Grammont, who was only colonel of horse of the French Guards under the Duke of Epernon and who took his orders from this colonel general, now took them only from the King, and was the first to be given the title of Colonel of the Guards. The King himself installed his colonels at the head of their regiments, giving them with his own hand a gilt gorget with a pike, and afterward, when the use of pikes was abolished, a spontoon, or kind of half-pike. In the King's Regiment, which he created himself, he instituted grenadiers, on the scale of four to a company in the first place; then he formed a company of grenadiers in each regiment of infantry. He gave two to the French Guards. Nowadays there is one for each battalion throughout the whole infantry. He greatly enlarged the Corps of Dragoons, and gave them a colonel general. The establishment of studs for breeding horses, in 1667, must not be forgotten, for they had been completely abandoned beforehand and they were of great value in providing mounts for the cavalry, an important resource which has since been too much neglected.

It was he who instituted the use of the bayonet affixed to the end of the musket. Before his time, it was used occasionally, but only a few companies fought with this weapon. There was no uniform practice and no drill; everything was left to the general's discretion. Pikes were then thought of as the most redoubtable weapon. The first regiment to have bayonets and to be trained to use them was that of the Fusiliers, established in 1671.

The manner in which artillery is used today is due entirely to him. He founded artillery schools, first at Douai, then at Metz and Strasbourg; and the Regiment of Artillery was finally staffed with officers who were almost all capable of successfully conducting a siege. All the magazines in the kingdom were well stocked, and they were supplied annually with eight hundred thousand pounds of powder. He created a regiment of bombardiers and one of hussars; before this only his enemies had had hussars.

In 1688 he established thirty regiments of militia, which were provided and equipped by the communes. These militia trained for war but without abandoning the cultivation of their fields.

Companies of cadets were maintained in the majority of frontier towns; there they learned mathematics, drawing and all the drills, and carried out the duties of soldiers. This institution lasted for ten years, but the government finally tired of trying to discipline these difficult young people. The Corps of Engineers, on the other hand, which the King created and to which he gave its present regulations, is an institution which will last forever. During his reign the art of fortifying strongholds was brought to perfection by Marshal Vauban and his pupils, who surpassed Count Pagan. He built or repaired a hundred and fifty fortresses.

To maintain military discipline, the King created inspectors general and later directors, who reported on the state of the troops; from their reports it could be seen whether the war commissioners had carried out their duties.

He instituted the Order of Saint-Louis, an honorable distinction which was often more sought after than wealth. The Hôtel des Invalides put the seal on his efforts to merit loyal service.

It was owing to measures such as these that he had, by 1672, a hundred and eighty thousand regular troops, and that, increasing his forces as the number and strength of his enemies increased, he finished with four hundred and fifty thousand men under arms, including the troops of the navy.

Before his time such powerful armies were unknown. His enemies could scarcely muster comparable forces, and to do so they had to be united. He showed what France, on her own, was capable of, and he always had either great successes or great resources to fall back on.

* * *

This short account is enough to illustrate the changes which Louis XIV brought about in the state; and that they were useful changes is shown by the fact that they still exist. His ministers vied with each other in furthering his plans. They were responsible for all the details and for the actual execution, but the over-all plan was his. Of one thing one can be certain: the magistrates would not have reformed the laws; order would not have been restored in the finances; discipline would not have been introduced into the armies and into the general policing of the kingdom; there would have been no fleets; the arts would not have been encouraged; and all this would not have been achieved in such an organized and determined fashion at one single time (though under different ministers) if there had not been at the head of affairs a master who conceived in general terms all these great aims, and had the will power to accomplish them.

He never separated his own glory from the well-being of France, and he never looked on his kingdom in the same light as a lord looks on the lands from which he extracts all he can in order to live a life of luxury. Every king who loves glory loves the public welfare; Colbert and Louvois were no longer there when, in 1698, he ordered each intendant to produce a detailed description of his province for the instruction of the Duke of Burgundy. In this way it was possible to have an exact account of his kingdom and an accurate census of his peoples. This was a most useful achievement, although not every intendant had the capacity or the attention to detail of M. de Lamoignon de Bâville. If the King's intentions had been carried out as thoroughly in every other province as they were by this magistrate in his census of Languedoc, this collection of reports would have been one of the finest monuments of the age. Several others were well done; but a general plan was lacking, insofar as the intendants did not all receive the same instructions. What would have been most desirable was for each intendant to give, in columns, an account of the number of inhabitants of each district—nobles, citizens, farm workers, artisans and workmen—together with livestock of all kinds, lands of various degrees of fertility, the whole of the regular and secular clergy, their revenues, those of the towns and those of the communes.

In most of the reports returned, these aims are confused; some subjects are dealt with superficially and inaccurately, and it is often quite difficult to find the information one is looking for and which should be immediately available to a minister wanting to discover, at a glance, the forces, needs and resources of the community. The plan was an excellent one, and it would be most useful if someday it is executed in a uniform manner.

This, then, in general terms, is what Louis XIV did or tried to do to make his country more flourishing. It seems to me hardly possible to consider all this work and all these efforts without a feeling of gratitude and without being filled with the concern for the welfare of the people which inspired them. Consider what the country was like at the time of the *Fronde* and what it is like today. Louis XIV did more for his people than twenty of his predecessors put together; and even then he did not do everything he might have done. The war which ended with the Peace of Rijswijk began the ruin of the flourishing commerce established by his minister Colbert, and the War of Spanish Succession completed it.

He spent immense sums on the aqueducts and works of Maintenon and on conveying water to Versailles, and both these projects were abandoned and thereby rendered useless. If he had spent this money, or a fifth part of what it cost to force nature at Versailles, on embellishing his capital, Paris today would be, throughout its whole extent, as beautiful as is the area around the

Tuileries and the Pont-Royal, and would have become the most magnificent city in the universe.

It is a great achievement to have reformed the laws, but legal chicanery could not be abolished by legislation. The government tried to make justice uniform, and it has become so in criminal matters and in those of commerce and procedure; it could become so in the laws regulating the fortunes of individual citizens. It is most inconvenient that the same tribunal often has to give judgment on the basis of a hundred different customs. Certain land rights, which are either equivocal, onerous or harmful to society, still exist like remnants of a feudal government which no longer survives; they are the rubbish from a ruined Gothic building.

We are not claiming that the different orders in the state should all be subjected to the same laws. It will be realized that the customs of the nobility, the clergy, the magistracy and the peasantry must be different. But there is no doubt that it is desirable that each order should have its own law, which should be uniform throughout the kingdom, and that what is just or true in Champagne should not be considered false or unjust in Normandy. In every branch of administration, uniformity is a virtue; but the difficulties of achieving it have deterred people from the attempt.

Louis XIV could much more easily have done without the dangerous assistance of tax-farmers, to whom he was forced to have recourse because he almost always anticipated on his revenues, as will be seen in the chapter on finances.

If he had not believed that his will was sufficient to make a million men change their religion, France would not have lost so many citizens. Yet despite these upsets and losses, the country is still one of the most prosperous in the world, because all the good which Louis did remains and the evil which it was difficult to avoid doing in those stormy times has been repaired. In the final analysis it is posterity which judges kings and of whose judgment they must always be mindful; and when it comes to weigh up the virtues and weaknesses of Louis XIV, posterity will admit that, although he received too much praise during his lifetime, he deserves the praise of all future ages and was worthy of the statue which was erected to him at Montpellier, with a Latin inscription the sense of which is "To Louis the Great after his death." Don Ustariz, a statesman who has written on the finances and commerce of Spain, calls Louis XIV "an astounding man."

All these changes in government and in all the orders of society, which we have just examined, necessarily produced a vast change in our manners. The spirit of faction, intemperance and rebellion which had possessed the citizens of France ever since the time of Francis II gave place to a desire to excel in serving the King. The lords of large estates no longer remained quartered at home; the governors of provinces no longer had important posts to bestow; and as a result, the sovereign's favors were the only ones people strove to deserve; in this way, the state acquired a sort of geometrical unity, with each line leading to the center.

Charles Guignebert was for many years professor of history at the University
of Paris. Educated under the Third Republic, he saw the age of Louis XIV
with somewhat different eyes from Voltaire's.

FROM A Short History of the French People
BY CHARLES GUIGNEBERT

THE DESPOTISM OF LOUIS XIV

It was a great misfortune for France and the monarchy that every means of
resisting royal absolutism and every desire to do so should have disappeared
towards 1661. The evolution of royalty, which might have proceeded in closer
and closer adaptation to the needs of the country, was cut short and crystal-
lised into a practical *deification of the king*. And since, in fact, *the uncontrolled authority* of the prince cannot possibly do all that is needed, it gives
less than it takes away, and any government which it provides has inevitably
many shortcomings; further, by supplanting every other principle on which
public action can be based, *it rapidly vitiates its own administration and
transforms it into a mere exploitation of the subjects for the benefit of the
monarch.*

The character and the political theories of Louis XIV largely contributed to
this disastrous result; but this character assumed its visible shape under the
influence of a definite environment. These theories did not spring spontaneously to birth in the spirit of the young king; they are the result of impressions made on him by his surroundings. When Bossuet, preaching before him
in the Lent of 1662, said, *"Il se remue pour votre Majesté quelque chose
d'illustre et de grand et qui passe la destinée des rois vos prédécesseurs"*
(*There broods over your Majesty something illustrious and great, foreshad-
owing a destiny above that of the kings your predecessors*), he expressed a
prevalent opinion. It was with the complicity of his own subjects that Louis
XIV developed his despotic egotism. Neither they nor he understood from
the start the danger they were running.

At the death of Mazarin the king was twenty-two, and was commonly considered the handsomest man in his kingdom. It was said at court that only
the poet Racine could compare with him. In other words, he fulfilled the
ideal of royal beauty, formed by his contemporaries. Though he was but of

Charles Guignebert, *A Short History of the French People* (1930), pp. 86–105, translated by
F. G. Richmond.

moderate stature, he had a perfect nobility and majesty of deportment, so natural as never to seem in the least affected. Easy and gracious, with the most courteous manners in the world, he exercised an extraordinary attraction when he cared to trouble himself so far. Saint-Simon, who had no affection for him, nevertheless praises his fine manners and his perfect politeness. His subjects had a genuine admiration for him. *"The respect aroused by his presence, no matter where or when,"* writes Saint-Simon, *"imposed silence and almost terror on all."* Even in old age and depression he never lost his grand air.

His mind without being *"below mediocrity,"* as the redoubtable memorialist alleges, was ordinary and above all *passive,* but *"capable of forming itself,"* being well able both to attend and to reflect. It was, in other respects, ill-served by a most inadequate education, conducted without order or method during the Fronde, which Mazarin made no effort to remedy effectively, in so far as essentially political knowledge was concerned, until the last of his life. Louis XIV in compensation for these insufficiencies had indeed the precious gift of *knowing how to be silent, and how to listen,* and another, even rarer among absolute monarchs: he could tolerate ability in those about him and turn it to his own use and profit.

His character was headstrong and his temper in all probability violent, but he could keep it under control; a perfect self-mastery seemed to him essential to his dignity, and Saint-Simon assures us that he did not lose his self-control *"more than ten times in the whole of his life";* that is to say, he did not allow himself to be visibly angered more than ten times. He was endowed with a certain instinct for right, justice and equity which he did not always follow, but never completely lost. His politeness, too, tempered and controlled his keen susceptibilities, but it unfortunately fostered a tendency to dissimulation, a fault to which he was by nature only too prone, and this dissimulation was accompanied by a tendency to be vindictive which led him at times to ill-feeling and ill-dealing. His *pride* was unbounded, such that *"but for the fear of the devil which God never took from him, however disturbed he might be, he would have caused himself to be worshipped."* His pride never pardoned an offense, and to offend him was easy.

It is possible that his good will, his diligence, certain qualities of prudence and moderation, his basic benevolence, if not real generosity—an assortment, in fact, of inconspicuous but by no means negligible virtues—might, after some years of experience of life, if each reinforced the other, have made him a type of much that a king should be, had not all been ruined by flattery. Unfortunately Louis XIV was the prey *"of flattery so egregious as to deify him in the very heart of Christianity."* During his whole life he drank deep of this deadly poison. It gave him extreme pleasure and cost him his sense of reality. Thus he came to believe himself of a different kind and of a different clay from other men, to find it both natural and necessary that all men and everything should be sacrificed to him. His egotism developed into a kind of unconscious ferocity and his *Ego,* his *"Moi,"* became a monstrosity. The in-

terested and ingenious servility of courtiers, the crowd of adulators constantly
pressing about him, were more responsible than himself for this disastrous
distortion of his judgment.

He was extremely devout, or at least he became so when his early youthful
fires had waned. He believed himself in all respects a good Christian. In
reality he neither professed nor comprehended any but a religion of outward
show, compounded of habit, ceremony, superstition and *"fear of the devil."* It
was impotent either to make him moral or repress his inordinate sensuality.
His private life was a scandal up to the threshold of middle age and he
paraded his irregularities before the world with a sedate absence of all shame,
apparently in the belief that he was privileged by Heaven and need not concern himself with the code that must rule the rest of the world. Not only did
he live openly in adultery, but he had the assurance to give his bastards the
rank of princes of the blood. It is probable that the eminent preachers whose
office it was, every Lent, to remind him of the Christian virtues and of repentance for sin, sometimes found themselves in an embarrassing position.
The warnings and the stern rebukes, to which he had to listen from some
among them, fell on deaf ears till he had grown old, or at least was aging
after 1681.

He owed the dignity of the latter part of his life, in all probability, to
Madame de Maintenon. It was she who brought him and the queen again
together in 1681, and after the death of the latter, in 1683, she was secretly
married to the king, probably in January, 1684. Thenceforward he was a
faithful husband and grew steadily more absorbed in religious devotion. On
his death-bed he asked pardon from the bystanders for the scandals occasioned by his transgressions.

His political theories, which he took the trouble to embody by his own
hand in writing for the instruction of his son, were in keeping with the
education which had persuaded him that for him there was no law but his
own will, and no control but that of God. One of his childish copybook
headings, which has been preserved, is in these words, *"Homage is due to
kings, they do everything that pleases them."* His youth was spent in hearing
this reiterated by all about him, and the Fronde itself helped to convince him
that all hung attendant on the king's will.

That kings were *"instituted by God,"* held their sceptre from Him alone,
need render no account of their acts but to Him alone, was the complete
conviction of his contemporaries as of himself and the few bold spirits who
still recalled the political doctrines of the jurists of the Renaissance and their
chimeras concerning *Organised Monarchy*—that is to say, monarchy controlled and limited—were careful after the end of the troubles to raise no
voice in France. The work of Bossuet *Politique tirée des propres paroles de
l'Ecriture sainte* has been commonly considered as the classical presentation
of the doctrine of the divine right of kings. Its chief merit was the exposition
of this doctrine in precise propositions and in a style of great magnificence.
Fundamentally it added nothing essential to what had been said again and

again for forty or fifty years by every political theorist of royalty. Is it not curious to hear on the lips of Parliamentarians formulas which no servility could surpass, taken as a matter of course as the expression of received opinion?—the king is *"a visible divinity"* or *"a divine image of the divinity . . . , an august law-giver, who with one hand has access to the laws in the breast of God himself, and with the other communicates the gathered treasure through us to his people."*

Louis XIV was thus naturally led to believe himself of a *"station above that of other men."* He saw himself as *"standing in the place of God"* and as *"sharing in his knowledge as well as in his authority."* He persuaded himself that for a man of his rank to be under *"the necessity of receiving the law from his people"* was the *"greatest calamity"* into which he could fall, that every man who was his *"born subject"* must *"blindly obey,"* and that *"however bad"* a prince might be, revolt against him was *"always infinitely criminal,"* because a prince could be judged only by God. These convictions were held by him to be clearly established both by direct evidence and by the sovereign strength of revelation.

However, he did not, for a moment, imagine that divine favour had raised him to the throne merely to indulge himself with a life of ease and material satisfaction. He believed thoroughly that the *interest of the State must come first* and that his own duty was clear: he must never *"reproach himself in any important matter with having done less than his best."* It was borne in upon him that the *"trade"* he practised was one which exacted abnegation and forgetfulness of self. *"The trade of king,"* he wrote, *"is great, noble and delightful when the workman can feel that he has acquitted himself worthily in all his undertakings, but it does not exempt him from pain, fatigue and anxiety."* Above all, it exacts continual labour: *"it is by this he reigns, for this he reigns, and it were ingratitude and insolence towards God, injustice and tyranny towards men to desire the one without the other."*

Louis XIV was indeed a life-long labourer; that is to say, he devoted several hours a day to audiences with his ministers and councils, he made decisions, he really believed that he himself transacted all the chief business of the State, though in this he was not free from illusions; neither in quantity nor in quality was his work all that he believed it to be. Nevertheless he did his best according to the measure of his ability and was persuaded that he was the inspirer of his ministers.

There is certainly some grandeur in this conception which shows the sovereign, rising superior to human frailty, to all individual interests and to his own inclinations, bending his mind and will to the sole service of his State. Unfortunately Louis XIV thought that *"when one has the State in view one works for oneself"* and he held that *the nation* had no embodiment in France, save as it might express itself solely *"in the person of the king."* Thus *it was easy for him to confuse the State with his person, and the public service with worship of himself.*

A strange phenomenon indeed is the feeling displayed at this time towards the monarch, professed as it is by men in whom a genuine revival of faith has engendered an energetic Catholicism and amounting as it does to a kind of *idolatry*. Louis XIV had merely to make a gesture to inaugurate a cult. Did not, in 1686, the Marshal of La Feuillade go so far as to have lighted lanterns placed at night about the prince's statue on the Place des Victoires at Paris? Other acts of like servility are met with; we feel that more than one of those courtiers to whom the king's countenance was *"felicity complete,"* as La Bruyère puts it, tended to accept as truth the ejaculation of Bossuet, *"O kings, ye are gods!"* And this devotional sentiment and this religious respect undoubtedly are a better explanation than the universal lassitude which followed the Fronde, of the abasement of character and the abdication of all will in face of the king.

* * *

Louis XIV always claimed to govern by himself; the examples of his father dominated by Richelieu, and of his mother led by Mazarin, the memories of his youth, which were certainly not unmixed so far as his associations and personal relations with the late cardinal were concerned, had taught him a salutary lesson. He was determined that another should never be *"king in function"* while he was but King in name. Thus he decided to do without a prime minister and entrusted the preparation and the execution of business only to *commis* (clerks). Nor did he ever make of any man a favourite, or at any rate he allowed no one with whom he formed a friendship to exercise any influence whatever in State affairs any more than he allowed his mistresses to do so.

Saint-Simon alleges that in reality he was led by his ministers, even the least able among them, and that he was master only in his own imagination. There is undoubtedly some truth in this view, but it should not be unreservedly accepted. The Fronde had taught him suspicion of men; he knew that they might deceive him and he was always on his guard. Those of his *commis* who really influenced him successfully were those who, as students of human nature, had the address to persuade him that the ideas and the resolutions which he owed to their suggestion were originated by himself. Le Tellier, father of Louvois, relates that of twenty agenda submitted by himself to a Council meeting there was always one which the king returned for examination after refusing the proposed solution, but it was impossible to know beforehand which one it would be. Louis XIV said *No* to show that he was master and in a position to do so, not because he had come to any opinion of his own upon the case in question. As he could not possibly know or examine everything for himself, it may be considered as certain that his ministers sometimes duped him, that they wielded more power than he wished, but this was only achieved surreptitiously and by running a risk from the authority which hung over them, always ready to strike. The perfidious and tenacious rancour which the king displayed towards Fouquet, his superintendent of finance, after his disgrace and arrest, helps us to realise to what lengths he could go when he felt certain that he had been deceived.

He was not a man to think of great innovations in matters of government or even to realise that they might be necessary. On the other hand, he showed himself capable of approving improvements, more or less considerable, on the tradition which he received from the hands of Mazarin, provided that they seemed likely to advance his power or add lustre to his name.

During his reign the organisation of central government on the lines laid down by Francis I was completed. His ministers were six: *the Chancellor,* for justice; *the Controller-General of Finance*—the title of *superintendent* was thus altered, as being unacceptable to the king—*the four Secretaries of State:* of the *King's Household,* of *Foreign Affairs,* of *War* and of the *Navy.* But it must not be assumed that the apparent precision of their titles implied a clear and invariable ascription of duties among these four last functionaries. The limits of their respective jurisdictions are always giving rise to doubt, dispute and transpositions between them. The confusion is still further increased by the fact that each retains the general administration of one of the four sections into which the kingdom is still divided; each minister has a numerous staff, assigned to different *bureaux.* In these, current business is considered and carried on by the officials who form their staff, and are soon to become an important factor in the State. *The reign of the bureaucracy is beginning.*

The traditional practice of the French monarchy was to surround itself with competent advisers. These came to form what were practically government Councils. Under Louis XIV the tendency to specialisation, already frequently mentioned, has reached a definite result; we see four regular and largely specialised *Councils* now at work. The *Council* "par excellence," called also the *High Council,* examines all great questions of policy and government, as does our Council of Ministers today. Its numbers do not exceed four or five persons, including the king. They are entitled *Ministers of State.* The *Council of Despatches* has cognisance of all business affecting the interior administrative life of the kingdom. It conducts, with the four Secretaries of State as intermediaries, correspondence with the intendants. It consists of not more than a dozen or so members and is presided over by the king: it includes the dauphin, the Ministers of State, the Chancellor, the Controller-General of Finance and the Secretaries of State. The *Council of Finance* dealt with the assessment and distribution of direct taxes, conducted negotiations with the financiers and examined all that the financial administration thought fit to submit to it. The king sat as its president twice a week.

The *Privy Council* or *Council of Parties* was essentially, like our present Council of State, a *superior* court; that is to say, all the administrative difficulties, conflicts as to jurisdiction, besides a number of purely judicial affairs that the king consigned to it, came within its province which was both extremely vague and extensive. It consisted of thirty members assisted by eighty-eight *Masters of Requests,* who examined and reported upon cases. These masters paid high prices for their posts, since their work prepared them for that of higher administration and the king chose his provincial *Intendants* from among them. The Privy Council was presided over by the Chancellor, the king rarely attending, though its business was conducted in his name as though he himself were present.

This organisation of the central government of Louis XIV is undoubtedly still far from perfection. It still fails in the distinct differentiation between functions which we know to be necessary to the smooth working of a political machine. It is nevertheless a great advance on its predecessor though it runs on similar lines. The *Duke of Beauvilliers,* who was head of the Council of Finance and afterwards Minister of State, was almost the only exception to the rule that no authentic noble had part or portion in this central government; no prince of the blood except the dauphin had even the right to membership on any of the four Councils. This despotism meant, as Saint-Simon said, *"the reign of the long robe"* in all things. The titles of nobility borne by many among these confidential men or ministers of the king should not mislead us as to their origin; they are bourgeois or they come from the ranks of the *officers* of the robe. Ennoblement was the reward for their services.

The provincial government likewise becomes better defined; the provinces are now fixed areas, each has its governor, a noble and a swordsman, well paid and much looked up to, but in reality now no more than a figurehead, indeed so much so that except on special ceremonial occasions the majority of these great personages dispense with residence in their "government." The real authority is in the hands of the *Intendant.* As the experiment attempted by Richelieu proved successful, it was continued by Mazarin and completed by Louis XIV. In his reign the kingdom was divided into financial districts, known as *Généralités* or *Intendances,* of which there were thirty-one in 1700. Their limits did not coincide with those of the provinces in which they were established.

The *Intendant,* his appointment being decided by the Council of the Parties, was chosen by the king, under whose control he remained. He started his career in an intendantship of small importance and his advancement depended on his zeal and success in the *"execution of the orders of his Majesty."* His powers may be described as extending over the whole provincial administration and his work as comprising all duties such as now fall to the heads of the various services in a modern department. Taxes, police, public works, commerce, industry, religious matters, recruiting, supervision and control of the courts of justice and of the administrators of all ranks, the judgment of many contentious or even criminal cases and the selection of those chosen for submission to the king; his work and his authority both covered an immense field.

Louis XIV would naturally wish to abolish such *Provincial States* as still survived, many of which did, in fact, disappear during his reign, for instance, those of Auvergne, Normandy, Quercy and others. If he left some as they were (Brittany, Flanders, Artois, Burgundy, Provence, Languedoc) this would be because they gave him no trouble and because he had probably no intention of abolishing wholesale all the institutions of the past still extant in the provinces. He allowed various anomalies in local administrative usage to continue, and left uncorrected defects of organisation, highly detrimental to those who came under them. They could be justified by established custom and the king seems to have been little concerned with them, being, as he always was, supremely preoccupied with securing two things from his people: *passive obedience and money*.

The government is one which settles all questions in secret. It is absolutely uncontrolled. The *nobility* are no longer a separate body, and politically they count for nothing; to the prince they are *"mere people,"* says Saint-Simon. The *Assembly of the Clergy*, held at regular intervals, deals only with its own affairs, except that it is attempting to secure the abolition of the Edict of Nantes. All ecclesiastical appointments are in the hands of the king. The *States-General* are now altogether out of the field. Their name alone was sufficient to set Louis XIV beside himself. There was now not even an Assembly of Notables. The *Parliament*, deprived of all right of remonstrance, could now do no more than register the edicts of the king without comment. As to the *subjects*, they had merely to take their orders. Discussion is considered as revolt and as a kind of sacrilege. It will be only towards the end of the reign that *opposition*, born from the misery of the country and from the failures of the king, will venture to find a home in men's minds and occasionally an outward expression. Not even a genius could have succeeded in realising the immeasurable pretensions of this appalling despotism; and Louis XIV was no genius.

The administration of the kingdom is entirely directed for the service and benefit of the king, against which no consideration whatever can prevail. The care, which it outwardly devotes to the public interest, is no more than a way of promoting the king's. If the subjects are well off and contented they will be able to pay better and more. Although men of all ranks are merely "people" before the king, equally subjected to his will, in practice the administration takes account of the *social inequalities* that the founders of the French monarchy had never attempted to abolish, which were so unfortunately confirmed by the States-General of 1614 and which were now maintained by Louis XIV. It seems probable that no idea that they were unjust or detrimental to the State ever entered his head; all prescription was in their favour. His absolutism, in fact, heavy as it was upon all men, was particularly severe upon the *small folk*, on whose shoulders it laid the greater portion of public expenditure.

In principle, they are the sole bearers of the direct impost (*la taille*, a tax on real property), besides most of those which are indirect, the chief of which are *aids*, diverse taxes upon merchandise of prime necessity and common consumption, and *gabelle*, a tax upon salt. These imposts are raised in a way which makes them particularly difficult to bear. The State farms them out to private companies which can appeal to public force for support; they greatly abuse the power thus given them to bring pressure upon the defenceless tax-payers. In those times it was no honour to a man to say that he was in the *Farms* or *Parties;* this last word designating the tenders made to the State by financiers in relation to the adjudication of taxes. From this deplorable system the peasants were the sufferers in chief.

After the death of Colbert (1683), who had done his best to restrain the insane extravagance of the king, the impoverishment of the country proceeded apace, assisted by the exigencies of an expensive foreign policy. The returns from the ordinary taxes then diminished as the need of the royal treasury for money grew greater. The government had recourse to various expedients, not altogether honourable, which furthermore were far from fulfilling expectation. The verses of Boileau are well known (*Satire* III).

> *D'où vous vient aujourd'hui cet air sombre et sévère,*
> *Et ce visage enfin plus pâle qu'un rentier*
> *A l'aspect d'un édit qui supprime un quàrtier?*

> Why do you look so sombre and severe today,
> With a face indeed paler than a rentier's
> At the appearance of an edict which abrogates a quarter?

A *quartier* of the *rentes* covers a *trimestre,* period of three months; to abrogate it was a method of raising a special tax on the creditors of the State. The creation of useless and sometimes ridiculous posts is an indirect method of establishing new taxes, as the newly created officials will not fail to reimburse themselves from the pockets of the public; thus we find controllers appointed for faggots, fresh butter, oysters and the like, without mentioning *conseillers semestres* (semestrial councillors) who, sitting in their courts for six months only, enable the State to double the number of those functionaries.

The fiscal necessities became so great that even a restriction in the number of the *privileged* had to be accepted. The poll-tax, established in 1695, was to be paid by all Frenchmen without distinction in proportion to their income; only the poorest were exempted. As a matter of fact the privileged, by diverse expedients, for instance, by paying a composition by which they escaped on good terms—as was done by the Assembly of the Clergy—or by obtaining the appointment of special receivers, materially decreased their obligations. This was similarly the case with another tax upon income, the *tenth,* superimposed in 1710, upon all contributions and upon all subjects.

The government was not unaware of the defects in its fiscal system and could easily realise the disastrous results to which they must lead, but it seems to have been only concerned to fill the treasury by no matter what means, and to have considered inevitable, if not natural, evils for which it had neither leisure nor will to devise adequate remedies. Those which were suggested to it from without, for instance by *Vauban* beginning in 1695 and by *Boisguil-lebert* starting from 1699, left it indifferent or brought more or less disagreeable consequences upon the heads of their authors.

Justice remained in the hands of the old local jurisdictions, over which were the *Présidiaux,* which went back to Henry II (over them again were the *Parliaments,* then about twelve in number), but its orderly working is disturbed by the privileges of the clergy, who have their own tribunals, and of the nobles, who still often enjoy the abusive right to be judged only by the Parliament of Paris; above all, it is impaired by the *right of evocation* retained by the king. He, being theoretically supreme judge and the fountainhead of all justice, is able, when he thinks fit, to transfer any case from its regular judges and bring it before the *Council of Parties.* These exceptions and privileges are detrimental to the proper working of one of the essential functions of the State.

The diversity of laws and customs had similar effects. It is impossible to find a way through their inextricable confusion. A methodical synopsis would have been indispensable. Colbert thought of having one made and of drafting a kind of civil code, but his plans came to nothing.

The criminal procedure remains barbarous and the penalties are harsh in the extreme. When the king wants oarsmen for his galleys, conviction for any petty crime is enough to send a man to the benches. Generally speaking, the law takes no thought for the moral improvement of delinquents; its one aim is to induce terror by extreme severity. Here as elsewhere the government follows its most immediate interest, regardless of equity, of the needs of its subjects, or of the progress of manners, which are much milder than those of the Middle Ages though its spirit still survives in the practice of torture.

The administration of Louis XIV is in close correspondence with the principles and intentions of the government for which it acts. Rigorous, exacting, and generally exact, it confounds the service of the king with the good of the State, and for the good of the State it deliberately sacrifices individual interests, even those which most call for respect. It is, in fact, an instrument of despotism and not in the least an organism established and set to work for the good of the nation.

In a general work on the sixteenth and seventeenth centuries, the modern
French historian Roland Mousnier, a professor at the University of Strasbourg, defined the dimensions of Louis XIV's absolutism and its effect.

FROM The XVIth and XVIIth Centuries
BY ROLAND MOUSNIER

THE ABSOLUTE MONARCHY

Absolutism was the wish of the crowds who saw their salvation in the concentration of powers in the hands of one man—the incarnation of the realm,
the living symbol of order and of the desired unity. Everyone wished to see in
the king the image of God: "You are God on earth. . . ." To this conception
was added, with many, the old humanist dream: the king ought to be a hero,
lover of glory as in antiquity, protector of Letters like Augustus, protector of
the Church like Constantine, a legislator like Justinian, but with a "predilection for arms," because "the role of conqueror is esteemed to be the most
noble and the highest of titles," by all contemporaries.

As lieutenant of God, the king is sovereign. "The sovereign Prince makes
the law, consequently he is absolved of the law." He acts according to his
own good pleasure. Thus it results that kings "naturally have the full and
free disposition of all properties, secular as well as ecclesiastic, to make wise
use of like good stewards, that is to say according to the needs of their states."
Public good is above the right of property. Thus it follows that the Church is
subject to the sovereign and owes him rental on its possessions which have
been given to it "for the general welfare of the entire realm. . . ." (The comparison with the sun arose by itself, and Louis XIV, Nec Pluribus Impar
[None His Equal], did no more than insist on an old monarchical symbol.)

But, as an image of God, the king ought to be a providence on earth. He
should make justice reign, "precious trust that God has put in the hand of
kings as a participation in his wisdom and his power." He ought to bring to
perfection each of the professions of which society is constituted, because
"each of them has its functions, which the others may do without only with
great difficulty. . . . This is why, far from disdaining any of these conditions,
or of raising one at the expense of others, we should take care to bring them
all, if it can be done, to the perfection of which they are capable," [realizing]

Roland Mousnier, *Les XVIè et XVIIè Siècles. Les progrès de la civilisation européenne et le
déclin de l'Orient (1492–1715)*, Tome IV, *Histoire Générale des Civilisations* (1954), pp. 229–
236. Translated by L. Pearce Williams by permission of Presses Universitaires de France, Paris.

the ideal of a society where social work is directed and the professions form a hierarchy according to the needs of man. Finally, the king should be the protector of the weak; he ought "to give to the people who are subject to us the same marks of paternal goodness that we receive from God every day," to have "nothing more at heart than to guarantee the most feeble from the oppression of the most powerful and to find some ease for the neediest in their misery."

The king mistrusted his ministers and his secretaries of state. He reverted to a division of labor, and tried to divide up the affairs which were interconnected in such a way that no specialist would be able to block his will. He opposed his officials to one another, provoked them, divided them, stimulated their mutual jealousies, saw in the opposition of Colbert and of Le Tellier a guarantee of his power.

. . . The problem for the king is not only to make his subjects obey, but also to subject to his will his own officers who had become independent thanks to the venality of office, and to exercise the fullness of the legislative judiciary police or administrative powers.

For this purpose the king used *lettres de cachet* by which he made known his will directly to individuals or to bodies. By *lettres de cachet,* the king arrested, imprisoned, exiled; at the request of families, he punished the bad conduct of a son or of a spouse; he weakened resistance, arbitrarily punished seditions and plots with the enemy. When the king himself had spoken, there was nothing else to do but to bow before his authority, the legal source of justice.

More and more, the king utilized commissioners named by him and removeable at his will. The Counselors of State of the administrative councils were only commissioners. . . .

The king used the intendants of the army and the intendants of justice, police, and finance. They were above all inspectors, charged with the surveillance of the officers and subjects of the king, and were required to give an account to the council. The council could then either deal with the question itself by a decree or give the necessary powers to the intendant to decide, judge, or regulate the problem by means of an ordinance. The intendant could thus meet with the council of the governor and give his advice; he could preside over courts of justice, reform justice by means of ordinances, make sure that the officers carried out their functions and suspend them if they did not, listen to the complaints of the king's subjects and make sure justice was given them by the judges. The intendant presided over the assemblies of the cities, . . . elections, checked the debts of communities, and oversaw the carrying out of orders and regulations. . . . The intendant supervised the raising of taxes, presided over the bureau of finances, and guaranteed the observance of ordinances and regulations. Only in two cases did he have a general and discretionary power and a sovereign judgment: malpractices and falsification of accounts by financial officers, and illicit assemblies, seditions, riots, and raising of armed men.

The intendant was a very supple instrument. In time of war or of internal crisis, the council could extend his powers indefinitely, to the point that the intendant could perform all the functions of the officers and leave them only their hollow title. At these times, with their assistants the intendants formed an administration of commissioners in competition with the administration of the regular officers. But the royal government, Richelieu, and Colbert considered such times as exceptional and as an unhappy necessity. In time of peace, the king strove to keep the intendant, who always wanted to extend his powers, in his role of inspector. He forbade him to substitute himself for the royal officers—he was instructed only to supervise them, and, if they were not working well, to let the council know and to wait for the necessary powers to remedy the situation.

The king used a political police. It was run by the intendants, by spies and agents to be found everywhere—at Paris by the governor of the Bastille, the chief criminal officer, and, since 1667, the lieutenant general of police, La Reynie. One misinterpretation and, duke or lackey, one was in the Bastille. On such feeble suspicions, the intendants or the council constructed accusations of *lèse majesté;* judgment was given on mere suspicion because Richelieu, Louis XIII, and Louis XIV all believed that when conspiracy was concerned it was almost impossible to have mathematical proofs, and one should not wait for the event itself by which everything would be lost. More often than for mere trials, the king had recourse to preventive imprisonment of indefinite length by means of the *lettres de cachet.* . . .

In all important offices, like that of ministers, secretaries of state, controller general, and so on, Louis XIV desired only "devoted servants" who joined to their public functions domestic services and, like Colbert, carried the notes from the monarch to his favorites or received the adulterine children of the king at the childbirth of the royal mistresses. He used the sentiments of vassalage but he wished to be the sole object of them. He wished to achieve absolutism by tying all Frenchmen directly to the king by means of a personal connection, just as vassals were tied to their suzerain. He wished to be the unique and universal suzerain or at least the universal patron. . . . All ties of sentiment and of interest converged on the king, who thus incarnated the wishes and the hopes of all his subjects, and in this way, not less than by the personal exercise of power, concentrated the State in himself; achieved in himself the unity of the State and thus prepared his subjects, by means of very old sentiments, to pass to the concept of the abstract State. Through the intermediary of medieval survivals, Louis XIV prepared the foundations of the modern State.

The king prepared them by opposing class to class and by making the bourgeois rise in a social scale. His ministers, his counselors, and his intendants were drawn more and more in the course of the century from among the bourgeois officers. These were his men, "rising from pure and perfect commonness," but "exalted above all grandeur." The king ennobled the Le Tellier and the Colbert families, made marquises of them, lords were known by the name of their estates, Louvois, Barbeziux, Croissy, Torcy. He created dynasties of ministers, bourgeois family groups and dynasties whose strength he used in face of the dynasties and noble family groups. . . .

The gentlemen grumbled. They despised these "bourgeois." "It was the reign of the vile bourgeoisie," complained Saint-Simon. They suffered by the leveling accomplished by a state which broke all resistance. The prisons were filled with eminent prisoners: the Count of Cramaing, the Marshal of Bassompierre, Barabas—one of the favorites of Louis XIII. The kings also sought, however, to procure honors and a means of existence for the nobility. The place of governor was reserved for them, and they filled most of the grades in the army. To their younger sons went the greater part of the ecclesiastical functions; they [the Kings] used them in their service, inculcating in them the spirit of subordination and little by little turning them into functionaries. Louis XIV succeeded in organizing the court. Around him he grouped, at Saint Germain, at Fontainebleau, at Versailles, all who counted among the nobility. He ruined them by alternating between the onerous life of military camps and the ostentatious life of the Court. He had no hesitation in waging war to find them employment and the opportunity for glory and reputation. He rendered them servile by pensions, dowries, and properties of the church. . . . He even provided a psychological alibi to this nobility. In a series of marvelous fairy-like festivals, the king appeared costumed as a god from Olympus, the courtiers appearing as secondary divinities or as heroes. Thus they could transpose their false dreams of power and grandeur to this copy of the life of the immortals, raised above common humanity and, if it had to obey, at least obeyed the "Lord Jupiter," the king-god. Etiquette habituated them to see in the king a superhuman being. Men uncovered themselves before the king's bed, women curtsied to it as in church before the high altar. The princes of the blood disputed the honor of handing him the sleeve of his shirt at his rising. A whole ceremonial filled with reverences was present at his rising in the morning, at his retiring, at his meals, and for his whole life. . . .

Thus the king, by dividing governmental functions between two classes but reserving the most important to the lower one—the bourgeoisie—and by systematically raising this one and opposing the other—the strongest— brought the class struggle to an equilibrium which assured his personal power and—both in the government and in the state—unity, order, and hierarchy. But also, perhaps forced by crises and war, and without wishing to change the social structure of the realm, the king leveled and equalized more and more in the service due to the state. When Louis XIV had achieved total submission and limitless obedience his power became autocratic and revolutionary.

THE SCIENTIFIC REVOLUTION

FACTUAL OR METAPHYSICAL?

CONTENTS

QUESTIONS FOR STUDY

1. *How do the methods proposed by Bacon and Descartes for the study of nature differ?*

2. *What practical problems could the new science actually solve?*

3. *Compare Galileo's view of ultimate reality* (The Assayer) *with Newton's view* (Third Rule of Reasoning).

4. *In what ways do Merton and Bernal agree? disagree?*

5. *What would Koyré insist is the weakness in Bernal's interpretation? How would Bernal defend himself?*

In 1543 a book was published in Poland entitled *De Revolutionibus Orbium Coelestium* (*On the Revolutions of the Heavenly Spheres*). Its author was a canon in the Catholic Church, Nicholas Copernicus. One hundred and forty-four years later another work appeared in London with the forbidding title *Philosophiae Naturalis Principia Mathematica* (*The Mathematical Principles of Natural Philosophy*). Its author, Isaac Newton, Lucasion Professor of Mathematics at Cambridge University, there set out the principles that were the foundations of modern physics. The period encompassed by these two dates is known to historians as the Scientific Revolution. What was overthrown was the world view of the Middle Ages, which had relied heavily upon the science and philosophy of Aristotle. Aristotle's physics, it may be remembered (see "Ancient Science—Observed Facts, Mathematical Systems, or Philosophical Fancies?" Volume I, pp. 29–37), was "biological" in form, asking questions of the physical world that today we ask only of living organisms. Aristotle had wanted to know primarily what end an object or a process served in the overall divine plan of the cosmos. Thus the "final cause" had been of primary importance. Once known, the final cause permitted the philosopher to deduce and understand the other causes (material, efficient, and formal) that, taken together, completely defined an object or a process. This philosophical pattern had been particularly attractive in the Middle Ages, when Aristotle's treatises were recovered and translated into Latin. The primary concern of the devout was salvation, and salvation was the Final cause of man's existence, the purpose for which he had been created.

In the fifteenth and sixteenth centuries the Aristotelian system of the world encountered severe criticism. Out of this criticism was to come the creative outburst known as the Scientific Revolution.

The most obvious weakness in Aristotelian physics was that it simply did not fit the facts. This failure had been recognized as early as the fourteenth century in the treatment of uniformly accelerated motion, as in the trajectory of a falling stone. Early critics had been able to cut and patch the theory so that it could be stretched to cover this case with reasonable accuracy so long as one did not look too closely. In another field, however, the failure of theory to match appearances could not be hidden. This was in the area of astronomy, which was the basis of the calendar. By the end of the sixteenth century the calendar was seriously out of whack, and this was a matter of some ecclesiastical concern. For example, Easter, the most important religious day in the Christian year, is determined astronomically as the first Sunday after the first full moon after the vernal equinox. The astronomical models provided by Aristotelian physics or by the later mathematical reasonings of Claudius Ptolemy (c. A.D. 150) were either too inaccurate or too clumsy to provide the basis for really accurate calendrical computations. It might be added that this was also true for computations used in navigation. Copernicus was urged by the Pope himself to undertake his investigations with the purpose of calendrical reform. The Gregorian calendar of the modern world was the direct result.

Copernicus did more than merely increase the accuracy of astronomical calculations, which could have been done simply by leaving theory alone and introducing corrections to make the calculations fit the observations. Copernicus, however, was no mere mathematical tinkerer but a philosopher who grasped the astronomical nettle firmly. Despite all evidence to the contrary and despite *no* observational support, Copernicus proposed to put the sun at the center of the universe and make the earth merely one of the planets. If this substitution were made, the whole of astronomy looked neater. There was a symmetry and a beauty in the Copernican system notably lacking in its Aristotelian rival. But there was also a price to pay. To move the earth from the center of the universe was to move man from his central position in the cosmos, to which both the Old and New Testaments had seemingly assigned him. It also meant, as the followers of Copernicus emphasized, the expansion of the universe to infinity and, for some, the consequent diminution of man both in relative size and in absolute importance. Finally, it required the denial of common-sense observations. Aristotle had been the master of common sense. The earth, he had argued, was obviously inert and incapable of motion; therefore it must rest at the center of the universe, unmoving and dead. The sun obviously rose in the east, passed across the hemisphere of the sky and set in the west, and somewhat less obviously, turned about the earth once every year, giving rise to the seasons. "Mere appearance," argued the Copernicans. Things are not what they may (obviously) appear, and it was the task of the new science to reveal the reality behind the appearances. We are, in short, right back to the old methodological problem that had tormented the Greeks. The only difference is that there were new answers to be found in the sixteenth and seventeenth centuries.

The problem that follows concentrates on this question of scientific method, since it would be impossible to compress the achievements of the Scientific Revolution into so few pages. At issue is a matter of some contemporary importance. Does science flourish best if it is stimulated by and directed toward specific technological problems of obvious social importance, or is science more fruitful in the long run if it concerns itself with general philosophical issues from which scientific theories may be deduced and checked against observations? The issue is still joined today in the battle between "pure" and "applied" science, and it is likely that it will continue. The arguments of the seventeenth century are still relevant.

1
THE DIMENSIONS
OF THE SCIENTIFIC
REVOLUTION

J. D. Bernal, one of England's leading scientists, has for many years concerned himself with the mutual interactions of science and society. To Bernal, science is essentially an intellectual response to changing social and economic needs. In the following selection he maps out the ways in which this response led to the Scientific Revolution in the seventeenth century.

FROM Science in History BY J. D. BERNAL

The period roughly from 1540 to 1650 has no convenient name in history. It has been called the Counter-Renaissance, but this would indicate a far greater degree of reaction to the earlier phase than actually took place. It includes the Counter-Reformation, with the Baroque style that was its visible expression, the Wars of Religion that raged in turn in France (1560–98), in the Low Countries (1572–1609), and in Germany (1618–48), and the establishment of the States General of Holland in 1576 and the Commonwealth of England in 1649. Of these events it was the last two that were to have the greatest ultimate significance. They point to the political triumph of the new bourgeoisie in the two countries in which was concentrated the bulk of the world's trade and manufacture.

In science the period includes the first great triumphs of the new observational, experimental approach. It opens fresh from the first exposition of the solar system by Copernicus and closes with its firm establishment—despite

J. D. Bernal, *Science in History,* 2nd ed. (1957), pp. 281–282, 287–288, 291–293, 295–298, 304–305, 307, 334–342. Reprinted by permission of C. A. Watts & Co. Ltd., London.

the condemnation of the Church—through the work of Galileo. It includes in its scope Gilbert's description in 1600 of the earth as a magnet and Harvey's discovery in 1628 of the circulation of the blood. It witnesses the first use of the two great extenders of visible Nature, the telescope and the microscope.

Economically the century was dominated by the cumulative effects of the navigations, which by then involved a trade comparable with the old internal trade of Europe. It was specially marked by the great increase in prices brought about by the influx of American silver. The breakdown of feudal land-holding in western Europe, especially in Holland and England, had thrown on the market landless people, and, at the same time, the real wages of hired workers were seriously depressed. This had the effect of lowering the cost of products in a period of rising prices and increasing markets, and at the same time of providing an abundant labour force for manufacturers. The result was an unprecedented increase in the wealth of those traders and manufacturers who were on the new oceanic trade routes and could draw on new resources and supply new markets.

* * *

Galileo Galilei

The telescope was to prove the greatest scientific instrument of the age. The bare news of it reaching the ears of the professor of physics and military engineering at Padua, Galileo Galilei (1564–1642), determined him to make one himself and turn it on the heavens. Galileo was already a convinced Copernican, as well as being deeply interested in the movements of pendulums and the related problems of the fall of bodies. In the first few nights of observation of the heavens he saw enough to shatter the whole of the Aristotelian picture of that serene element. For the moon, instead of being a perfect sphere, was found to be covered with seas and mountains; the planet Venus showed phases like the moon; while the planet Saturn seemed to be divided into three. Most important of all, he observed that around Jupiter there circled three stars or moons, a small-scale model of the Copernican system, which anyone who looked through a telescope could see for himself.

With his keen sense of publicity and of the material value of his discoveries, which he found in no way incompatible with the pure joy of discovery, Galileo immediately tried to sell the titles of these stars in succession to the Duke of Florence (a Medici), to the King of France, and to the Pope, but the celestial honours seemed too expensive to all of them. Later, when the more practical end of using their motion to determine longitude at sea occurred to him, he tried to sell the secret to the King of Spain and the States General of Holland, who had both offered prizes for the discovery of the longitude, but still found no takers.

These attempts, however, were to Galileo mere side-shows. He sensed at

once the really revolutionary character of the new observations. Here he had
for everyone to see the very model of Copernicus' system in the sky. This was
knowledge not to keep but to broadcast. Within a month, in 1610, he had
published what was clearly a scientific best seller, *Siderius Nuntius,* i.e. "Messenger from the Stars," in which his observations were set out briefly and
plainly. . . .

The Fall of Bodies: Dynamics

But Galileo felt it was not sufficient to have verified by observation the aes-
thetic preference of Copernicus. It was also necessary to justify it by explaining how such a system could exist, and by removing the objections which
both philosophy and good sense had raised to it in the past. It was necessary
to explain how the rotation of the earth could occur without a mighty wind
blowing in the opposite direction and how bodies projected through the air
would not be left behind. This meant a serious study of bodies in free motion,
a problem which had already become of great practical importance in relation to the aiming of projectiles.

* * *

The first intellectual object of the scientific revolution had been achieved:
the classical world-picture had been destroyed, though only the bare outlines
of a new one had been put in its place. In doing so new means for understanding and conquering Nature had been found, but little had as yet emerged that
could be claimed to be of general practical use. The telescope itself was a
technical rather than a scientific invention. Before the effects of the revolution
in thought could make themselves felt in practice, it was necessary that the
possibilities the new science offered should be brought home not only to the
learned but to the new class of enterprising people that were making their
own political revolution—merchants, navigators, manufacturers, statesmen,
and the early and progressive capitalists. Galileo had started to do this, but he
was living in a country that had already lost its *élan* and that was rapidly
being frozen into reaction by the Counter-Reformation.

The Prophets: Bacon and Descartes

Two men from the less cultured but far more active northern countries were
to take on the task—Bacon and Descartes. These two major figures stood at
the turning point between medieval and modern science. Both were essentially prophets and publicists, men who had seen a vision of the possibility of
knowledge and were making it their business to show it to the world. Both
were universal in scope, though their approaches to knowledge were very
different. Temperamentally, too, it would be difficult to find two more different people than the shrewd, self-seeking, and afterwards rather pompous
lawyer, always at the centre of public affairs, and the intensely introspective,

solitary ex-soldier of fortune. Each too is characteristic of the nature of the scientific revolution in his own country.

* * *

The Novum Organum *and the* Discours de la Méthode

Both thinkers were preoccupied with methods, though their ideas of scientific method were very different. Bacon's was that of collecting materials, carrying out experiments on a large scale, and finding the results from a sheer mass of evidence—an essentially *inductive* method. Descartes, on the other hand, believed in the rapier thrust of pure intuition. He held that with clarity of thought it should be possible to discover everything rationally knowable, experiment coming in essentially as an auxiliary to *deductive* thought. The major difference, however, was that while Descartes used his science to construct a *system* of the world, a system which, though now almost forgotten, was able in its time completely to supersede that of the medieval schoolmen, Bacon put forward no system of his own but was content to propose an *organization* to act as a collective builder of new systems. His function as he saw it was only to provide the builders with the new tool—the logic of the *Novum Organum*—with which to do it.

In this sense they were strictly complementary. Bacon's concept of organization led directly to the formation of the first effective scientific society, the Royal Society. Descartes' system, by breaking definitely with the past, put up a set of concepts which could be the basis of argument about the material world in a strictly quantitative and geometric manner.

Bacon was taken to be, and rightly, the first great man who had given a new direction to science and who had linked it definitely once more to the progress of material industry.

With his empirical bent Bacon was inevitably an opponent of all predetermined systems in Nature; he believed that, given a well-organized and well-equipped body of research workers, the weight of facts would ultimately lead to truth. Descartes' method, on the other hand, was a more direct successor of that of the schools, with this absolute difference: that it was not *their* system that he wanted to establish but *his own*. In this he exhibited that individual arrogance which was one of the great liberating features of the Renaissance, the same arrogance that expressed itself in the great navigators, in the *conquistadores,* in all the defiances of authority that characterized the end of the feudal period and the beginning of one of individual enterprise.

Unconsciously, Descartes' system incorporated very much of the system which he wished to destroy. There was the same insistence on deductive logic and self-evident propositions, but starting with these he used the *mathematics,* of which he was a master, to arrive at conclusions far beyond the reach of his medieval or even of his classical predecessors. His major mathematical contribution was the use of co-ordinate geometry, by which a curve could be completely represented by an equation relating the values of the co-ordinates of its points referred to fixed axes. This was more than the mapping of geometry. It broke down the old distinction between the Greek science of the continuum—*geometry*—and the Babylonian-Indian-Arabic calculus of numbers—*algebra*. Henceforth their two powers would be joined to attack problems never before attempted.

CELESTIAL MECHANICS: THE NEWTONIAN SYNTHESIS

While all these achievements bear witness to the great flowering of scientific activity in many fields, the central interest and the greatest scientific triumph of the seventeenth century was undoubtedly the completion of a general system of *mechanics* capable of accounting for the motion of the stars in terms of the observable behaviour of matter on earth. Here the moderns were in effect settling their accounts once and for all with the ancient Greeks. Ancients and moderns were both agreed on the importance of the study of the heavens. But because the interests of the latter were now more practical than philosophic, they required a very different kind of answer. . . .

The intrinsic interest of the problem of the movements of the solar system was still very great, though, in fact, its philosophical and theological significance had already vanished with the destruction of the cosmology of the Ancients. The trial of Galileo was indeed in the nature of a futile parting shot by clerical Aristotelianism. But the new edifice that was to take its place would not be complete unless an acceptable physical explanation of the system of Copernicus and Kepler could be found. That was one reason why almost every natural philosopher speculated, experimented, and calculated with the aim of finding this explanation. Some got very close to it, particularly Hooke, until Newton's success ended the chase.

Finding the Longitude

The astronomers had another and even more compelling reason for discovering the laws of motion of the solar system. This was the need for astronomical tables far more accurate than had sufficed in the days when astronomy was required mainly for astrological prediction. The needs of navigation were far more stringent. The determination of a ship's position at sea, and particularly the more difficult part of the position, the longitude, was a recurring problem. It became more and more urgent as a larger and larger share of the economic and military effort of countries was spent in overseas ventures, especially of those countries that were themselves the centres of scientific advance: England, France, and Holland. The finding of the longitude was a question that was to occupy both the learned astronomers and the practical sailors for many decades, even centuries. It was for the purpose of assisting in the solution of this practical problem that the first nationally financed scientific institutions were set up—the Observatoire Royal at Paris in 1672 and the Royal Observatory at Greenwich in 1675.

The question of the determination of longitude is essentially one of determining absolute time—or, as we now would call it, Greenwich time—at any place. This, compared with the local times, gives the time interval which is directly convertible to longitude. At any place there are, or were before the invention of radio, only two methods of determining the Greenwich time: one by observing the movements of the moon among the stars—a clock already fixed in the sky; and the other by carrying around an accurate clock originally set at that time. The first required extremely accurate tables for the prediction of the place of heavenly bodies, the second absolutely reliable clock mechanisms. All through the seventeenth and a large part of the eighteenth centuries both lines of attack were pursued without definite advantage falling to either. There was an immediate stimulus to thought, observation, and experiment in both directions, a stimulus in part simply mercenary but also one of national and individual prestige.

* * *

Newton Replaces Aristotle: An Established Universe Against a Maintained One

Newton's theory of gravitation and his contribution to astronomy mark the final stage of the transformation of the Aristotelian world-picture begun by Copernicus. For a vision of spheres, operated by a first mover or by angels on God's order, Newton had effectively substituted that of a mechanism operating according to a simple natural law, requiring no continuous application of force, and only needing divine intervention to create it and set it in motion.

Newton himself was not quite sure about this, and left a loophole for divine intervention to maintain the stability of the system. But this loophole was closed by Laplace and God's intervention dispensed with. Newton's solution, which contains all the quantities necessary for the practical prediction of the positions of the moon and the planets, stops short of any fundamental questioning of the existence of a divine plan. Indeed Newton felt he had revealed this plan and wished to ask no further questions.

He got over the awkward assumption he had made on the existence of absolute motion by saying, following his Platonist friends, that space was the sensorium—awareness or brain—of God, and must therefore be absolute. In this way he avoided confusing himself in relativistic theories. His own theory gave no reasons why the planets should all be more or less in a plane and all go round the same way—for which Descartes' whirlpool had given a facile explanation. Newton honestly disguised his ignorance of origins by postulating that this was the will of God at the beginning of creation.

By this time the destructive phase of the Renaissance and Reformation was over; a new compromise between religion and science was needed just as much as those between monarchy and republic and between the upper bourgeoisie and the nobility. Newton's system of the universe did represent a considerable concession on the part of religious orthodoxy, for by it the hand of God could no longer be clearly seen in every celestial or terrestrial event but only in the general creation and organization of the whole. God had, in fact, like his anointed ones on earth, become a constitutional monarch. On their side the scientists undertook not to trespass into the proper field of religion—the world of man's life with its aspirations and responsibilities. This compromise, wisely advocated by Bishop Sprat, and preached by the redoubtable Dr Bentley in his Boyle sermons of 1692, was to last until Darwin upset it in the nineteenth century.

Although the system of universal gravitation appeared to be at the time, and still remains, Newton's greatest work, his influence on science and outside it was even more effective through the methods he employed in achieving his results. His calculus provided a universal way of passing from the changes of quantities to the quantities themselves, and vice versa. He provided the mathematical key adequate for the solution of physical problems for another 200 years. By setting out his laws of motion, which linked force not with motion itself but with change of motion, he broke definitely with the old commonsense view that force was needed to maintain motion, and relegated the friction, which makes this necessary in all practical mechanisms, to a secondary role which it was the object of the good engineer to abolish. In one word Newton established, once and for all, the *dynamic* view of the universe instead of the *static* one that had satisfied the Ancients. This transformation, combined with his atomism, showed that Newton was in unconscious harmony with the economic and social world of his time, in which individual enterprise, where each man paid his way, was replacing the fixed hierarchical order of the late classical and feudal period where each man knew his place.

2
WHAT IS THE PROPER SCIENTIFIC METHOD?

René Descartes (1596–1650) was one of the foremost "revolutionaries" in the Scientific Revolution. He not only contributed such fundamental instruments to the advance of science as analytical geometry but also laid down what he considered to be the only proper method for the pursuit of scientific truth. His *Discourse on Method* was intended to lay out the future course of the Scientific Revolution.

FROM A Discourse on Method BY RENÉ DESCARTES

Among the branches of Philosophy, I had, at an earlier period, given some attention to Logic, and among those of the Mathematics of Geometrical Analysis and Algebra,—three Arts or Sciences which ought, as I conceived, to contribute something to my design. But, on examination, I found that, as for Logic, its syllogisms and the majority of its other precepts are of avail rather in the communication of what we already know, or even as the Art of Lully, in speaking without judgment of things of which we are ignorant, than in the investigation of the unknown; and although this Science contains indeed a number of correct and very excellent precepts, there are, nevertheless, so many others, and these either injurious or superfluous, mingled with the former, that it is almost quite as difficult to effect a severance of the true from

René Descartes, *A Discourse on the Method of Rightly Conducting the Reason*, in *The Philosophy of Descartes* (1901), pp. 60–64, 74–76, 102–106, translated by John Veitch. Reprinted by permission of Tudor Publishing Company.

the false as it is to extract a Diana or a Minerva from a rough block of marble. Then as to the Analysis of the ancients and the Algebra of the moderns, besides that they embrace only matters highly abstract, and, to appearance, of no use, the former is so exclusively restricted to the consideration of figures, that it can exercise the Understanding only on condition of greatly fatiguing the Imagination; and, in the latter, there is so complete a subjection to certain rules and formulas, that there results an art full of confusion and obscurity calculated to embarrass, instead of a science fitted to cultivate the mind. By these considerations I was induced to seek some other Method which would comprise the advantages of the three and be exempt from their defects. And as a multitude of laws often only hampers justice, so that a state is best governed when, with few laws, these are rigidly administered; in like manner, instead of the great number of precepts of which Logic is composed, I believed that the four following would prove perfectly sufficient for me, provided I took the firm and unwavering resolution never in a single instance to fail in observing them.

The *first* was never to accept anything for true which I did not clearly know to be such; that is to say, carefully to avoid precipitancy and prejudice, and to comprise nothing more in my judgment than what was presented to my mind so clearly and distinctly as to exclude all ground of doubt.

The *second,* to divide each of the difficulties under examination into as many parts as possible, and as might be necessary for its adequate solution.

The *third,* to conduct my thoughts in such order that, by commencing with objects the simplest and easiest to know, I might ascend by little and little, and, as it were, step by step, to the knowledge of the more complex; assigning in thought a certain order even to those objects which in their own nature do not stand in a relation of antecedence and sequence.

And the *last,* in every case to make enumerations so complete, and reviews so general, that I might be assured that nothing was omitted.

The long chains of simple and easy reasonings by means of which geometers are accustomed to reach the conclusions of their most difficult demonstrations, had led me to imagine that all things, to the knowledge of which man is competent, are mutually connected in the same way, and that there is nothing so far removed from us as to be beyond our reach, or so hidden that we cannot discover it, provided only we abstain from accepting the false for the true, and always preserve in our thoughts the order necessary for the deduction of one truth from another. And I had little difficulty in determining the objects with which it was necessary to commence, for I was already persuaded that it must be with the simplest and easiest to know, and, considering that of all those who have hitherto sought truth in the Sciences, the mathematicians alone have been able to find any demonstrations, that is, any certain and evident reasons, I did not doubt but that such must have been the rule of their investigations. I resolved to commence, therefore, with the examination of the simplest objects, not anticipating, however, from this any other advantage than that to be found in accustoming my mind to the love and nourishment of truth, and to a distaste for all such reasonings as were unsound. But I had no intention on that account of attempting to master all the particular Sciences commonly denominated Mathematics: but observing that, however different their objects they all agree in considering only the various relations or proportions subsisting among those objects, I thought it best for my purpose to consider these proportions in the most general form possible, without referring them to any objects in particular, except such as would most facilitate the knowledge of them, and without by any means restricting them to these, that afterwards I might thus be the better able to apply them to every other class of objects to which they are legitimately applicable. Perceiving further, that in order to understand these relations I should sometimes have to consider them one by one, and sometimes only to bear them in mind, or embrace them in the aggregate, I thought that, in order the better to consider them individually, I should view them as subsisting between straight lines, than which I could find no objects more simple, or capable of being more distinctly represented to my imagination and senses; and on the other hand, that in order to retain them in the memory, or embrace an aggregate of many, I should express them by certain characters the briefest possible. In this way I believed that I could borrow all that was best both in Geometrical Analysis and in Algebra, and correct all the defects of the one by help of the other.

And, in point of fact, the accurate observance of these few precepts gave me, I take the liberty of saying, such ease in unravelling all the questions embraced in these two sciences, that in the two or three months I devoted to their examination, not only did I reach solutions of questions I had formerly deemed exceedingly difficult, but even as regards questions of the solution of which I continued ignorant, I was enabled, as it appeared to me, to determine the means whereby, and the extent to which, a solution was possible; results attributable to the circumstance that I commenced with the simplest and most general truths, and that thus each truth discovered was a rule available in the discovery of subsequent ones. Nor in this perhaps shall I appear too vain, if it be considered that, as the truth on any particular point is one, whoever apprehends the truth, knows all that on that point can be known. The child, for example, who has been instructed in the elements of Arithmetic, and has made a particular addition, according to rule, may be assured that he has found, with respect to the sum of the numbers before him, all that in this instance is within the reach of human genius. Now, in conclusion, the Method which teaches adherence to the true order, and an exact enumeration of all the conditions of the thing sought includes all that gives certitude to the rules of Arithmetic.

* * *

I am in doubt as to the propriety of making my first meditations in the place above mentioned matter of discourse; for these are so metaphysical, and so uncommon, as not, perhaps, to be acceptable to every one. And yet, that it may be determined whether the foundations that I have laid are sufficiently secure, I find myself in a measure constrained to advert to them. I had long before remarked that, in relation to practice, it is sometimes necessary to adopt, as if above doubt, opinions which we discern to be highly uncertain, as has been already said; but as I then desired to give my attention solely to the search after truth, I thought that a procedure exactly the opposite was called for, and that I ought to reject as absolutely false all opinions in regard to which I could suppose the least ground for doubt, in order to ascertain whether after that there remained aught in my belief that was wholly indubitable. Accordingly, seeing that our senses sometimes deceive us, I was willing to suppose that there existed nothing really such as they presented to us; and because some men err in reasoning, and fall into paralogisms, even on the simplest matters of Geometry, I, convinced that I was as open to error as any other, rejected as false all the reasonings I had hitherto taken for demonstrations; and finally, when I considered that the very same thoughts (presentations) which we experience when awake may also be experienced when we are asleep, while there is at that time not one of them true, I supposed that all the objects (presentations) that had ever entered into my mind when awake, had in them no more truth than the illusions of my dreams. But immediately upon this I observed that, whilst I thus wished to think that all was false, it was absolutely necessary that I, who thus thought, should be somewhat; and as I observed that this truth, *I think, hence I am,* was so certain and of such evidence, that no ground of doubt, however extravagant, could be alleged by the Sceptics capable of shaking it, I concluded that I might, without scruple, accept it as the first principle of the Philosophy of which I was in search.

In the next place, I attentively examined what I was, and as I observed that I could suppose that I had no body, and that there was no world nor any place in which I might be; but that I could not therefore suppose that I was not; and that, on the contrary, from the very circumstance that I thought to doubt of the truth of other things, it most clearly and certainly followed that I was; while, on the other hand, if I had only ceased to think, although all the other objects which I had ever imagined had been in reality existent, I would have had no reason to believe that I existed; I thence concluded that I was a substance whose whole essence or nature consists only in thinking, and which, that it may exist, has need of no place, nor is dependent on any material thing; so that "I," that is to say, the mind by which I am what I am, is wholly distinct from the body, and is even more easily known than the latter, and is such, that although the latter were not, it would still continue to be all that it is.

After this I inquired in general into what is essential to the truth and certainty of a proposition; for since I had discovered one which I knew to be true, I thought that I must likewise be able to discover the ground of this certitude. And as I observed that in the words *I think, hence I am,* there is nothing at all which gives me assurance of their truth beyond this, that I see very clearly that in order to think it is necessary to exist, I concluded that I might take, as a general rule, the principle, that all the things which we very clearly and distinctly conceive are true, only observing, however, that there is some difficulty in rightly determining the objects which we distinctly conceive.

* * *

I have never made much account of what has proceeded from my own mind; and so long as I gathered no other advantage from the Method I employ beyond satisfying myself on some diffculties belonging to the speculative sciences, or endeavouring to regulate my actions according to the principles it taught me, I never thought myself bound to publish anything respecting it. For in what regards manners, every one is so full of his own wisdom, that there might be found as many reformers as heads, if any were allowed to take upon themselves the task of mending them, except those whom God has constituted the supreme rulers of his people, or to whom he has given sufficient grace and zeal to be prophets; and although my speculations greatly pleased myself, I believed that others had theirs, which perhaps pleased them still more. But as soon as I had acquired some general notions respecting Physics, and beginning to make trial of them in various particular difficulties, had observed how far they can carry us, and how much they differ from the principles that have been employed up to the present time, I believed that I could not keep them concealed without sinning grievously against the law by which we are bound to promote, as far as in us lies, the general good of mankind. For by them I perceived it to be possible to arrive at knowledge highly useful in life; and in room of the Speculative Philosophy usually taught in the Schools, to discover a Practical, by means of which, knowing the force and action of fire, water, air, the stars, the heavens, and all the other bodies that surround us, as distinctly as we know the various crafts of our artizans, we might also apply them in the same way to all the uses to which they are adapted, and thus render ourselves the lords and possessors of nature. And this is a result to be desired, not only in order to the invention of an infinity of arts, by which we might be enabled to enjoy without any trouble the fruits of the earth, and all its comforts, but also and especially for the preservation of health, which is without doubt, of all the blessings of this life, the first and fundamental one; for the mind is so intimately dependent upon the condition and relation of the organs of the body, that if any means can ever be found to render men wiser and more ingenious than hitherto, I believe that it is in Medicine they must be sought for. It is true that the science of Medicine, as it now exists, contains few things whose utility is very remarkable: but without any wish to depreciate it, I am confident that there is no one, even among those whose profession it is, who does not admit that all at present known in it is almost nothing in comparison of what remains to be discovered; and that we could free ourselves from an infinity of maladies of body as well as of mind, and perhaps also even from the debility of age, if we had sufficiently ample knowledge of their causes, and of all the remedies provided for us by Nature. But since I designed to employ my whole life in the search after so necessary a Science, and since I had fallen in with a path which seems to me such, that if any one follow it he must inevitably reach the end desired, unless he be hindered either by the shortness of life or the want of experiments, I judged that there could be no more effectual provision against these two impediments than if I were faithfully to communicate to the public all the little I might myself have found, and incite men of superior genius to strive to proceed farther, by contributing, each according to his inclination and ability, to the experiments which it would be necessary to make, and also by informing the public of all they might discover, so that, by the last beginning where those before them had left off, and thus connecting the lives and labours of many, we might collectively proceed much farther than each by himself could do.

I remarked, moreover, with respect to experiments, that they become always more necessary the more one is advanced in knowledge; for, at the commencement, it is better to make use only of what is spontaneously presented to our senses, and of which we cannot remain ignorant, provided we bestow on it any reflection, however slight, than to concern ourselves about more uncommon and recondite phaenomena: the reason of which is, that the more uncommon often only mislead us so long as the causes of the more ordinary are still unknown; and the circumstances upon which they depend are almost always so special and minute as to be highly difficult to detect. But in this I have adopted the following order: first, I have essayed to find in general the principles, or first causes of all that is or can be in the world, without taking into consideration for this end anything but God himself who has created it, and without educing them from any other source than from certain germs of truths naturally existing in our minds. In the second place, I examined what were the first and most ordinary effects that could be deduced from these causes; and it appears to me that, in this way, I have found heavens, stars, and earth, and even on the earth, water, air, fire, minerals, and some other things of this kind, which of all others are the most common and simple, and hence the easiest to know. Afterwards, when I wished to descend to the more particular, so many diverse objects presented themselves to me, that I believe it to be impossible for the human mind to distinguish the forms or species of bodies that are upon the earth, from an infinity of others which might have been, if it had pleased God to place them there, or consequently to apply them to our use, unless we rise to causes through their effects, and avail ourselves of many particular experiments. Thereupon, turning over in my mind all the objects that had ever been presented to my senses, I freely venture to state that I have never observed any which I could not satisfactorily explain by the principles I had discovered. But it is necessary also to confess that the power of nature is so ample and vast, and these principles so simple and general, that I have hardly observed a single particular effect which I cannot at once recognise as capable of being deduced in many different modes from the principles, and that my greatest difficulty usually is to discover in which of these modes the effect is dependent upon them; for out of this difficulty I cannot otherwise extricate myself than by again seeking certain experiments, which may be such that their result is not the same, if it is in the one of these modes that we must explain it, as it would be if it were to be explained in the other. As to what remains, I am now in a position to discern, as I think, with sufficient clearness what course must be taken to make the majority of those experiments which may conduce to this end: but I perceive likewise that they are such and so numerous, that neither my hands nor my income, though it were a thousand times larger than it is, would be sufficient for them all; so that, according as henceforward I shall have the means of making more or fewer experiments, I shall in the same proportion make greater or less progress in the knowledge of nature. This was what I had hoped to make known by the Treatise I had written, and so clearly to exhibit the advantage that would thence accrue to the public, as to induce all who have the common good of man at heart, that is, all who are virtuous in truth, and not merely in appearance, or according to opinion, as well to communicate to me the experiments they had already made, as to assist me in those that remain to be made.

Sir Francis Bacon (1561–1626) was a lawyer who rose to be Lord Chancellor of England under James I. As a "practical" man, he had little patience with what he considered to be the hairsplitting of academic philosophers. To him, the only way to know nature was to look at it, not to argue about it. In his "science-fiction" essay *The New Atlantis* he pointed out what might be accomplished if men only organized their assault on nature properly.

FROM The New Atlantis BY FRANCIS BACON

This fable my Lord devised, to the end that he might exhibit therein a model or description of a college instituted for the interpreting of nature and the producing of great and marvellous works for the benefit of men, under the name of Salomon's House, or the College of the Six Days' Works. And even so far his Lordship hath proceeded, as to finish that part. Certainly the model is more vast and high than can possibly be imitated in all things; notwithstanding most things therein are within men's power to effect. His Lordship thought also in this present fable to have composed a frame of Laws, or of the

Sir Francis Bacon, *The New Atlantis* (1936), pp. 544, 574–584.

best state or mould of a commonwealth; but foreseeing it would be a long work, his desire of collecting the Natural History diverted him, which he preferred many degrees before it.

* * *

"God bless thee, my son; I will give thee the greatest jewel I have. For I will impart unto thee, for the love of God and men, a relation of the true state of Salomon's House. Son, to make you know the true state of Salomon's House, I will keep this order. First, I will set forth unto you the end of our foundation. Secondly, the preparations and instruments we have for our works. Thirdly, the several employments and functions whereto our fellows are assigned. And fourthly, the ordinances and rites which we observe.

"The End of our Foundation is the knowledge of Causes, and secret motions of things; and the enlarging of the bounds of Human Empire, to the effecting of all things possible.

"The Preparations and Instruments are these. We have large and deep caves of several depths: the deepest are sunk six hundred fathom; and some of them are digged and made under great hills and mountains: so that if you reckon together the depth of the hill and the depth of the cave, they are (some of them) above three miles deep. For we find that the depth of a hill, and the depth of a cave from the flat, is the same thing; both remote alike from the sun and heaven's beams, and from the open air. These caves we call the Lower Region. And we use them for all coagulations, indurations, refrigerations, and conservations of bodies. We use them likewise for the imitation of natural mines; and the producing also of new artificial metals, by compositions and materials which we use, and lay there for many years. We use them also sometimes, (which may seem strange,) for curing of some diseases, and for prolongation of life in some hermits that choose to live there, well accommodated of all things necessary; and indeed live very long; by whom also we learn many things.

"We have burials in several earths, where we put divers cements, as the Chineses do their porcellain. But we have them in greater variety, and some of them more fine. We have also great variety of composts, and soils, for the making of the earth fruitful.

"We have high towers; the highest about half a mile in height; and some of them likewise set upon high mountains; so that the vantage of the hill with the tower is in the highest of them three miles at least. And these places we call the Upper Region: accounting the air between the high places and the low, as a Middle Region. We use these towers, according to their several heights and situations, for insolation, refrigeration, conservation; and for the view of divers meteors; as winds, rain, snow, hail; and some of the fiery meteors also. And upon them, in some places, are dwellings of hermits, whom we visit sometimes, and instruct what to observe.

"We have great lakes both salt and fresh, whereof we have use for the fish and fowl. We use them also for burials of some natural bodies: for we find a difference in things buried in earth or in air below the earth, and things buried in water. We have also pools, of which some do strain fresh water out of salt; and others by art do turn fresh water into salt. We have also some rocks in the midst of the sea, and some bays upon the shore, for some works wherein is required the air and vapour of the sea. We have likewise violent streams and cataracts, which serve us for many motions: and likewise engines for multiplying and enforcing of winds, to set also on going divers motions.

"We have also a number of artificial wells and fountains, made in imitation of the natural sources and baths; as tincted upon vitriol, sulphur, steel, brass, lead, nitre, and other minerals. And again we have little wells for infusions of many things, where the waters take the virtue quicker and better than in vessels or basins. And amongst them we have a water which we call Water of Paradise, being, by that we do to it, made very sovereign for health, and prolongation of life.

"We have also great and spacious houses, where we imitate and demonstrate meteors; as snow, hail, rain, some artificial rains of bodies and not of water, thunders, lightnings; also generations of bodies in air; as frogs, flies, and divers others.

"We have also certain chambers, which we call Chambers of Health, where we qualify the air as we think good and proper for the cure of divers diseases, and preservation of health.

"We have also fair and large baths, of several mixtures, for the cure of diseases, and the restoring of man's body from arefaction: and others for the confirming of it in strength of sinews, vital parts, and the very juice and substance of the body.

"We have also large and various orchards and gardens, wherein we do not so much respect beauty, as variety of ground and soil, proper for divers trees and herbs: and some very spacious, where trees and berries are set whereof we make divers kinds of drinks, besides the vineyards. In these we practise likewise all conclusions of grafting and inoculating, as well of wild-trees as fruit-trees, which produceth many effects. And we make (by art) in the same orchards and gardens, trees and flowers to come earlier or later than their seasons; and to come up and bear more speedily than by their natural course they do. We make them also by art greater much than their nature; and their fruit greater and sweeter and of differing taste, smell, colour, and figure, from their nature. And many of them we so order, as they become of medicinal use.

"We have also means to make divers plants rise by mixtures of earths without seeds; and likewise to make divers new plants, differing from the vulgar; and to make one tree or plant turn into another.

"We have also parks and inclosures of all sorts of beasts and birds, which we use not only for view or rareness, but likewise for dissections and trials; that thereby we may take light what may be wrought upon the body of man.

Wherein we find many strange effects; as continuing life in them, though divers parts, which you account vital, be perished and taken forth; resuscitating of some that seem dead in appearance; and the like. We try also all poisons and other medicines upon them, as well of chirurgery as physic. By art likewise, we make them greater or taller than their kind is; and contrariwise dwarf them, and stay their growth: we make them more fruitful and bearing than their kind is; and contrariwise barren and not generative. Also we make them differ in colour, shape, activity, many ways. We find means to make commixtures and copulations of different kinds; which have produced many new kinds, and them not barren, as the general opinion is. We make a number of kinds of serpents, worms, flies, fishes, of putrefaction; whereof some are advanced (in effect) to be perfect creatures, like beasts or birds; and have sexes, and do propagate. Neither do we this by chance, but we know beforehand of what matter and commixture what kind of those creatures will arise.

"We have also particular pools, where we make trials upon fishes, as we have said before of beasts and birds.

"We have also places for breed and generation of those kinds of worms and flies which are of special use; such as are with you your silk-worms and bees.

"I will not hold you long with recounting of our brew-houses, bake-houses, and kitchens, where are made divers drinks, breads, and meats, rare and of special effects. Wines we have of grapes; and drinks of other juice of fruits, of grains, and of roots; and of mixtures with honey, sugar, manna, and fruits dried and decocted. Also of the tears or woundings of trees, and of the pulp of canes. And these drinks are of several ages, some to the age or last of forty years. We have drinks also brewed with several herbs, and roots, and spices; yea with several fleshes, and white meats; whereof some of the drinks are such, as they are in effect meat and drink both: so that divers, especially in age, do desire to live with them, with little or no meat or bread. And above all, we strive to have drinks of extreme thin parts, to insinuate into the body, and yet without all biting, sharpness, or fretting; insomuch as some of them put upon the back of your hand will, with a little stay, pass through to the palm, and yet taste mild to the mouth. We have also waters which we ripen in that fashion, as they become nourishing; so that they are indeed excellent drink; and many will use no other. Breads we have of several grains, roots, and kernels: yea and some of flesh and fish dried; with divers kinds of leavenings and seasonings: so that some do extremely move appetites; some do nourish so, as divers do live of them, without any other meat; who live very long. So for meats, we have some of them so beaten and made tender and mortified, yet without all corrupting, as a weak heat of the stomach will turn them into good chylus, as well as a strong heat would meat otherwise prepared. We have some meats also and breads and drinks, which taken by men enable them to fast long after; and some other, that used make the very flesh of men's bodies sensibly more hard and tough, and their strength far greater than otherwise it would be.

"We have dispensatories, or shops of medicines. Wherein you may easily think, if we have such variety of plants and living creatures more than you have in Europe, (for we know what you have,) the simples, drugs, and ingredients of medicines, must likewise be in so much the greater variety. We have them likewise of divers ages, and long fermentations. And for their preparations, we have not only all manner of exquisite distillations and separations, and especially by gentle heats and percolations through divers strainers, yea and substances; but also exact forms of composition, whereby they incorporate almost, as they were natural simples.

"We have also divers mechanical arts, which you have not; and stuffs made by them; as papers, linen, silks, tissues; dainty works of feathers of wonderful lustre; excellent dyes, and many others; and shops likewise, as well for such as are not brought into vulgar use amongst us as for those that are. For you must know that of the things before recited, many of them are grown into use throughout the kingdom; but yet if they did flow from our invention, we have of them also for patterns and principals.

"We have also furnaces of great diversities, and that keep great diversity of heats; fierce and quick; strong and constant; soft and mild; blown, quiet; dry, moist; and the like. But above all, we have heats in imitation of the sun's and heavenly bodies' heats, that pass divers inequalities and (as it were) orbs, progresses, and returns, whereby we produce admirable effects. Besides, we have heats of dungs, and of bellies and maws of living creatures, and of their bloods and bodies; and of hays and herbs laid up moist; of lime unquenched; and such like. Instruments also which generate heat only by motion. And farther, places for strong insolations; and again, places under the earth, which by nature or art yield heat. These divers heats we use, as the nature of the operation which we intend requireth.

"We have also perspective-houses, where we make demonstrations of all lights and radiations; and of all colours; and out of things uncoloured and transparent, we can represent unto you all several colours; not in rain-bows, as it is in gems and prisms, but of themselves single. We represent also all multiplications of light, which we carry to great distance, and make so sharp as to discern small points and lines; also all colorations of light: all delusions and deceits of the sight in figures, magnitudes, motions, colours: all demonstrations of shadows. We find also divers means, yet unknown to you, of producing of light originally from divers bodies. We procure means of seeing objects afar off; as in the heaven and remote places; and represent things near as afar off, and things afar off as near; making feigned distances. We have also helps for the sight, far above spectacles and glasses in use. We have also glasses and means to see small and minute bodies perfectly and distinctly; as the shapes and colours of small flies and worms, grains and flaws in gems, which cannot otherwise be seen; observations in urine and blood, not otherwise to be seen. We make artificial rain-bows, halos, and circles about light. We represent also all manner of reflexions, refractions and multiplications of visual beams of objects.

"We have also precious stones of all kinds, many of them of great beauty, and to you unknown; crystals likewise; and glasses of divers kinds; and amongst them some of metals vitrificated, and other materials besides those of which you make glass. Also a number of fossils, and imperfect minerals, which you have not. Likewise loadstones of prodigious virtue; and other rare stones both natural and artificial.

"We have also sound-houses, where we practice and demonstrate all sounds, and their generation. We have harmonies which you have not, of quarter-sounds, and lesser slides of sounds. Divers instruments of music likewise to you unknown, some sweeter than any you have; together with bells and rings that are dainty and sweet. We represent small sounds as great and deep; likewise great sounds extenuate and sharp; we make divers tremblings and warblings of sounds, which in their original are entire. We represent and imitate all articulate sounds and letters, and the voices and notes of beasts and birds. We have certain helps which set to the ear do further the hearing greatly. We have also divers strange and artificial echoes, reflecting the voice many times, and as it were tossing it: and some that give back the voice louder than it came; some shriller, and some deeper; yea, some rendering the voice differing in the letters or articulate sound from that they receive. We have also means to convey sounds in trunks and pipes, in strange lines and distances.

"We have also perfume-houses; wherewith we join also practices of taste. We multiply smells, which may seem strange. We imitate smells, making all smells to breathe out of other mixtures than those that give them. We make divers imitations of taste likewise, so that they will deceive any man's taste. And in this house we contain also a confiture house; where we make all sweet-meats, dry and moist, and divers pleasant wines, milks, broths, and sallets, far in greater variety than you have.

"We have also engine-houses, where are prepared engines and instruments for all sorts of motions. There we imitate and practise to make swifter motions than any you have, either out of your muskets or any engine that you have; and to make them and multiply them more easily, and with small force, by wheels and other means: and to make them stronger, and more violent than yours are; exceeding your greatest cannons and basilisks. We represent also ordnance and instruments of war, and engines of all kinds: and likewise new mixtures and compositions of gun-powder, wildfires burning in water, and unquenchable. Also fireworks of all variety both for pleasure and use. We imitate also flights of birds; we have some degrees of flying in the air; we have ships and boats for going under water, and brooking of seas; also swimming-girdles and supporters. We have divers curious clocks, and other like motions of return, and some perpetual motions. We imitate also motions of living creatures, by images of men, beasts, birds, fishes, and serpents. We have also a great number of other various motions, strange for equality, fineness, and subtilty.

"We have also a mathematical house, where are represented all instruments, as well of geometry as astronomy, exquisitely made.

"We have also houses of deceits of the senses; where we represent all manner of feats of juggling, false apparitions, impostures, and illusions; and their fallacies. And surely you will easily believe that we that have so many things truly natural which induce admiration, could in a world of particulars deceive the senses, if we would disguise those things and labour to make them seem more miraculous. But we do hate all impostures and lies: insomuch as we have severely forbidden it to all our fellows, under pain of ignominy and fines, that they do not shew any natural work or thing, adorned or swelling; but only pure as it is, and without all affectation of strangeness.

"These are (my son) the riches of Salomon's House.

"For the several employments and offices of our fellows; we have twelve that sail into foreign countries, under the names of other nations, (for our own we conceal;) who bring us the books, and abstracts, and patterns of experiments of all other parts. These we call Merchants of Light.

"We have three that collect the experiments which are in all books. These we call Depredators.

"We have three that collect the experiments of all mechanical arts; and also of liberal sciences; and also of practices which are not brought into arts. These we call Mystery-men.

"We have three that try new experiments, such as themselves think good. These we call Pioneers or Miners.

"We have three that draw the experiments of the former four into titles and tables, to give the better light for the drawing of observations and axioms out of them. These we call Compilers.

"We have three that bend themselves, looking into the experiments of their fellows, and cast about how to draw out of them things of use and practice for man's life, and knowledge as well for works as for plain demonstration of causes, means of natural divinations, and the easy and clear discovery of the virtues and parts of bodies. These we call Dowry-men or Benefactors.

"Then after divers meetings and consults of our whole number, to consider of the former labours and collections, we have three that take care, out of them, to direct new experiments, of a higher light, more penetrating into nature than the former. These we call Lamps.

"We have three others that do execute the experiments so directed, and report them. These we call Inoculators.

"Lastly, we have three that raise the former discoveries by experiments into greater observations, axioms, and aphorisms. These we call Interpreters of Nature.

"We have also, as you must think, novices and apprentices, that the succession of the former employed men do not fail; besides a great number of servants and attendants, men and women. And this we do also: we have consultations, which of the inventions and experiences which we have discovered shall be published, and which not: and take all an oath of secrecy, for the concealing of those which we think fit to keep secret: though some of those we do reveal sometimes to the state, and some not.

"For our ordinances and rites: we have two very long and fair galleries: in one of these we place patterns and samples of all manner of the more rare and excellent inventions: in the other we place the statua's of all principal inventors. There we have the statua of your Columbus, that discovered the West Indies: also the inventor of ships: your monk that was the inventor of ordnance and of gunpowder: the inventor of music: the inventor of letters: the inventor of printing: the inventor of observations of astronomy: the inventor of works in metal: the inventor of glass: the inventor of silk of the worm: the inventor of wine: the inventor of corn and bread: the inventor of sugars: and all these by more certain tradition than you have. Then have we divers inventors of our own, of excellent works; which since you have not seen, it were too long to make descriptions of them; and besides, in the right understanding of those descriptions you might easily err. For upon every invention of value, we erect a statua to the inventor, and give him a liberal and honourable reward. These statua's are some of brass; some of marble and touchstone; some of cedar and other special woods gilt and adorned; some of iron; some of silver; some of gold.

"We have certain hymns and services, which we say daily of laud and thanks to God for his marvellous works: and forms of prayers, imploring his aid and blessing for the illumination of our labours, and the turning of them into good and holy uses.

"Lastly, we have circuits or visits of divers principal cities of the kingdom; where, as it cometh to pass, we do publish such new profitable inventions as we think good. And we do also declare natural divinations of diseases, plagues, swarms of hurtful creatures, scarcity, tempests, earthquakes, great inundations, comets, temperature of the year, and divers other things; and we give counsel thereupon what the people shall do for the prevention and remedy of them."

And when he had said this, he stood up; and I, as I had been taught, kneeled down; and he laid his right hand upon my head, and said: "God bless thee, my son, and God bless this relation which I have made. I give thee leave to publish it for the good of other nations; for we here are in God's bosom, a land unknown." And so he left me; having assigned a value of about two thousand ducats, for a bounty to me and my fellows. For they give great largesses where they come upon all occasions.

3
THE SEARCH FOR TRUTH

Galileo Galilei (1564-1642) was one of the principal architects of the Scientific Revolution. His observations of the surface of the moon and of sunspots and his discovery of the moons of Jupiter did much to destroy faith in the old Aristotelian cosmology. His laws of motion were fundamental in creating a new picture of the physical universe. In *The Assayer*, Galileo defends himself from the attacks of an Aristotelian, Sarsi, who felt that Galileo's way could lead only to confusion and error.

FROM The Assayer BY GALILEO GALILEI

In Sarsi I seem to discern the firm belief that in philosophizing one must support oneself upon the opinion of some celebrated author, as if our minds ought to remain completely sterile and barren unless wedded to the reasoning of some other person. Possibly he thinks that philosophy is a book of fiction by some writer, like the *Iliad* or *Orlando Furioso,* productions in which the least important thing is whether what is written there is true. Well, Sarsi, that is not how matters stand. Philosophy is written in this grand book, the universe, which stands continually open to our eyes.

Perhaps Sarsi believes that all the host of good philosophers may be enclosed within four walls. I believe that they fly, and that they fly alone, like eagles, and not in flocks like starlings. It is true that because eagles are rare birds they are little seen and less heard, while birds that fly like starlings fill the sky with shrieks and cries, and wherever they settle befoul the earth be-

From *Discoveries and Opinions of Galileo*, pp. 237, 239-241, 270-271, 273-278, translated by Stillman Drake. Copyright © 1957 by Stillman Drake. Reprinted by permission of Doubleday & Company, Inc.

neath them. Yet if true philosophers are like eagles they are not [unique] like
the phoenix. The crowd of fools who know nothing, Sarsi, is infinite. Those
who know very little of philosophy are numerous. Few indeed are they who
really know some part of it, and only One knows all.

To put aside hints and speak plainly, and dealing with science as a method
of demonstration and reasoning capable of human pursuit, I hold that the
more this partakes of perfection the smaller the number of propositions it
will promise to teach, and fewer yet will it conclusively prove. Consequently
the more perfect it is the less attractive it will be, and the fewer its followers.
On the other hand magnificent titles and many grandiose promises attract the
natural curiosity of men and hold them forever involved in fallacies and
chimeras, without ever offering them one single sample of that sharpness of
true proof by which the taste may be awakened to know how insipid is the
ordinary fare of philosophy. Such things will keep an infinite number of men
occupied, and that man will indeed be fortunate who, led by some unusual
inner light, can turn from dark and confused labyrinths in which he might
have gone perpetually winding with the crowd and becoming ever more entangled.

Hence I consider it not very sound to judge a man's philosophical opinions
by the number of his followers. Yet though I believe the number of disciples
of the best philosophy may be quite small, I do not conclude conversely that
those opinions and doctrines are necessarily perfect which have few followers,
for I know well enough that some men hold opinions so erroneous as to be
rejected by everyone else. But from which of those sources the two authors
mentioned by Sarsi derive the scarcity of their followers I do not know, for I
have not studied their works sufficiently to judge.

Guidicci has written, "Many stars completely invisible to the naked eye are
made easily visible by the telescope; hence their magnification should be
called infinite rather than nonexistent." Here Sarsi rises up and, in a series of
long attacks, does his best to show me to be a very poor logician for calling
this enlargement "infinite." At my age these altercations simply make me
sick, though I myself used to plunge into them with delight when I too was
under a schoolmaster. So to all this I answer briefly and simply that it appears
to me Sarsi is showing himself to be just what he wants to prove me; that is,
little cognizant of logic, for he takes as absolute that which was spoken relatively.

* * *

Sarsi goes on to say that since this experience of Aristotle's has failed to
convince us, many other great men also have written things of the same sort.
To this I reply that if in order to refute Aristotle's statement we are obliged to
represent that no other men have believed it, then nobody on earth can ever
refute it, since nothing can make those who have believed it not believe it.
But it is news to me that any man would actually put the testimony of writers ahead of what experience shows him. To adduce more witnesses serves no

purpose, Sarsi, for we have never denied that such things have been written and believed. We did say they are false, but so far as authority is concerned yours alone is as effective as an army's in rendering the events true or false. You take your stand on the authority of many poets against our experiments. I reply that if those poets could be present at our experiments they would change their views, and without disgrace they could say they had been writing hyperbolically—or even admit they had been wrong.

I cannot but be astonished that Sarsi should persist in trying to prove by means of witnesses something that I may see for myself at any time by means of experiment. Witnesses are examined in doubtful matters which are past and transient, not in those which are actual and present. A judge must seek by means of witnesses to determine whether Peter injured John last night, but not whether John was injured, since the judge can see that for himself. But even in conclusions which can be known only by reasoning, I say that the testimony of many has little more value than that of few, since the number of people who reason well in complicated matters is much smaller than that of those who reason badly. If reasoning were like hauling I should agree that several reasoners would be worth more than one, just as several horses can haul more sacks of grain than one can. But reasoning is like racing and not like hauling, and a single Arabian steed can outrun a hundred plowhorses. So when Sarsi brings in this multitude of authors it appears to me that instead of strengthening his conclusion he merely ennobles our case by showing that we have outreasoned many men of great reputation.

* * *

It now remains for me to tell Your Excellency, as I promised, some thoughts of mine about the proposition "motion is the cause of heat," and to show in what sense this may be true. But first I must consider what it is that we call heat, as I suspect that people in general have a concept of this which is very remote from the truth. For they believe that heat is a real phenomenon, or property, or quality, which actually resides in the material by which we feel ourselves warmed. Now I say that whenever I conceive any material or corporeal substance, I immediately feel the need to think of it as bounded, and as having this or that shape; as being large or small in relation to other things, and in some specific place at any given time; as being in motion or at rest; as touching or not touching some other body; and as being one in number, or few, or many. From these conditions I cannot separate such a substance by any stretch of my imagination. But that it must be white or red, bitter or sweet, noisy or silent, and of sweet or foul odor, my mind does not feel compelled to bring in as necessary accompaniments. Without the senses as our guides, reason or imagination unaided would probably never arrive at qualities like these. Hence I think that tastes, odors, colors, and so on are no more than mere names so far as the object in which we place them is concerned, and that they reside only in the consciousness. Hence if the living creature were removed, all these qualities would be wiped away and annihilated. But since we have imposed upon them special names, distinct from those of the other and real qualities mentioned previously, we wish to believe that they really exist as actually different from those.

I may be able to make my notion clearer by means of some examples. I move my hand first over a marble statue and then over a living man. As to the effect flowing from my hand, this is the same with regard to both objects and my hand; it consists of the primary phenomena of motion and touch, for which we have no further names. But the live body which receives these operations feels different sensations according to the various places touched. When touched upon the soles of the feet, for example, or under the knee or armpit, it feels in addition to the common sensation of touch a sensation on which we have imposed a special name, "tickling." This sensation belongs to us and not to the hand. Anyone would make a serious error if he said that the hand, in addition to the properties of moving and touching, possessed another faculty of "tickling," as if tickling were a phenomenon that resided in the hand that tickled. A piece of paper or a feather drawn lightly over any part of our bodies performs intrinsically the same operations of moving and touching, but by touching the eye, the nose, or the upper lip it excites in us an almost intolerable titillation, even though elsewhere it is scarcely felt. This titillation belongs entirely to us and not to the feather; if the live and sensitive body were removed it would remain no more than a mere word. I believe that no more solid an existence belongs to many qualities which we have come to attribute to physical bodies—tastes, odors, colors, and many more.

A body which is solid and, so to speak, quite material, when moved in contact with any part of my person produces in me the sensation we call touch. This, though it exists over my entire body, seems to reside principally in the palms of the hands and in the finger tips, by whose means we sense the most minute differences in texture that are not easily distinguished by other parts of our bodies. Some of these sensations are more pleasant to us than others. . . . The sense of touch is more material than the other sense; and, as it arises from the solidity of matter, it seems to be related to the earthly element.

Perhaps the origin of two other senses lies in the fact that there are bodies which constantly dissolve into minute particles, some of which are heavier than air and descend, while others are lighter and rise up. The former may strike upon a certain part of our bodies that is much more sensitive than the skin, which does not feel the invasion of such subtle matter. This is the upper surface of the tongue; here the tiny particles are received, and mixing with and penetrating its moisture, they give rise to tastes, which are sweet or unsavory according to the various shapes, numbers, and speeds of the particles. And those minute particles which rise up may enter by our nostrils and strike upon some small protuberances which are the instrument of smelling; here likewise their touch and passage is received to our like or dislike according as they have this or that shape, are fast or slow, and are numerous or few. The tongue and nasal passages are providently arranged for these things, as the one extends from below to receive descending particles, and the other is adapted to those which ascend. Perhaps the excitation of tastes may be given a certain analogy to fluids, which descend through air, and odors to fires, which ascend.

Then there remains the air itself, an element available for sounds, which come to us indifferently from below, above, and all sides—for we reside in the air and its movements displace it equally in all directions. The location of the ear is most fittingly accommodated to all positions in space. Sounds are made and heard by us when the air—without any special property of "sonority" or "transonority"—is ruffled by a rapid tremor into very minute waves and moves certain cartilages of a tympanum in our ear. External means capable of thus ruffling the air are very numerous, but for the most part they may be reduced to the trembling of some body which pushes the air and disturbs it. Waves are propagated very rapidly in this way, and high tones are produced by frequent waves and low tones by sparse ones.

To excite in us tastes, odors, and sounds I believe that nothing is required in external bodies except shapes, numbers, and slow or rapid movements. I think that if ears, tongues, and noses were removed, shapes and numbers and motions would remain, but not odors or tastes or sounds. The latter, I believe, are nothing more than names when separated from living beings, just as tickling and titillation are nothing but names in the absence of such things as noses and armpits. And as these four senses are related to the four elements, so I believe that vision, the sense eminent above all others in the proportion of the finite to the infinite, the temporal to the instantaneous, the quantitative to the indivisible, the illuminated to the obscure—that vision, I say, is related to light itself. But of this sensation and the things pertaining to it I pretend to understand but little; and since even a long time would not suffice to explain that trifle, or even to hint at an explanation, I pass this over in silence.

Having shown that many sensations which are supposed to be qualities residing in external objects have no real existence save in us, and outside ourselves are mere names, I now say that I am inclined to believe heat to be of this character. Those materials which produce heat in us and make us feel warmth, which are known by the general name of "fire," would then be a multitude of minute particles having certain shapes and moving with certain velocities. Meeting with our bodies, they penetrate by means of their extreme subtlety, and their touch as felt by us when they pass through our substance is the sensation we call "heat." This is pleasant or unpleasant according to the greater or smaller speed of these particles as they go pricking and penetrating; pleasant when this assists our necessary transpiration, and obnoxious when it causes too great a separation and dissolution of our substance. The operation of fire by means of its particles is merely that in moving it penetrates all bodies, causing their speedy or slow dissolution in proportion to the number and velocity of the fire-corpuscles and the density or tenuity of the bodies. Many materials are such that in their decomposition the greater part of them passes over into additional tiny corpuscles, and this dissolution continues so long as these continue to meet with further matter capable of being so resolved. I do not believe that in addition to shape, number, motion, penetration, and touch there is any other quality in fire corresponding to "heat"; this belongs so intimately to us that when the live body is taken away, heat becomes no more than a simple name. . . .

Since the presence of fire-corpuscles alone does not suffice to excite heat, but their motion is needed also, it seems to me that one may very reasonably say that motion is the cause of heat. . . . But I hold it to be silly to accept that proposition in the ordinary way, as if a stone or piece of iron or a stick must heat up when moved. The rubbing together and friction of two hard bodies, either by resolving their parts into very subtle flying particles or by opening an exit for the tiny fire-corpuscles within, ultimately sets these in motion; and when they meet our bodies and penetrate them, our conscious mind feels those pleasant or unpleasant sensations which we have named heat, burning, and scalding. And perhaps when such attrition stops at or is confined to the smallest quanta, their motion is temporal and their action calorific only; but when their ultimate and highest resolution into truly indivisible atoms is arrived at, light is created. This may have an instantaneous motion, or rather an instantaneous expansion and diffusion, rendering it capable of occupying immense spaces by its—I know not whether to say its subtlety, its rarity, its immateriality, or some other property which differs from all these and is nameless.

The last great treatise by Galileo was his *Dialogues Concerning Two New Sciences*. It was in these dialogues that Galileo laid the foundations for the two sciences of the strength of materials and dynamics.

FROM Dialogues Concerning Two New Sciences
BY GALILEO GALILEI

SALV. The constant activity which you Venetians display in your famous arsenal suggests to the studious mind a large field for investigation, especially that part of the work which involves mechanics; for in this department all types of instruments and machines are constantly being constructed by many artisans, among whom there must be some who, partly by inherited experi-

Galileo Galilei, *Dialogues Concerning Two New Sciences* (1914), pp. 1–6, translated by Henry Crew and Alfonso de Salvio. Reprinted by permission of Northwestern University Press.

ence and partly by their own observations, have become highly expert and clever in explanation.

SAGR. You are quite right. Indeed, I myself, being curious by nature, frequently visit this place for the mere pleasure of observing the work of those who, on account of their superiority over other artisans, we call "first rank men." Conference with them has often helped me in the investigation of certain effects including not only those which are striking, but also those which are recondite and almost incredible. At times also I have been put to confusion and driven to despair of ever explaining something for which I could not account, but which my senses told me to be true. And notwithstanding the fact that what the old man told us a little while ago is proverbial and commonly accepted, yet it seemed to me altogether false, like many another saying which is current among the ignorant; for I think they introduce these expressions in order to give the appearance of knowing something about matters which they do not understand.

SALV. You refer, perhaps, to that last remark of his when we asked the reason why they employed stocks, scaffolding and bracing of larger dimensions for launching a big vessel than they do for a small one; and he answered that they did this in order to avoid the danger of the ship parting under its own heavy weight [*vasta mole*], a danger to which small boats are not subject?

SAGR. Yes, that is what I mean; and I refer especially to his last assertion which I have always regarded as a false, though current, opinion; namely, that in speaking of these and other similar machines one cannot argue from the small to the large, because many devices which succeed on a small scale do not work on a large scale. Now, since mechanics has its foundation in geometry, where mere size cuts no figure, I do not see that the properties of circles, triangles, cylinders, cones and other solid figures will change with their size. If, therefore, a large machine be constructed in such a way that its parts bear to one another the same ratio as in a smaller one, and if the smaller is sufficiently strong for the purpose for which it was designed, I do not see why the larger also should not be able to withstand any severe and destructive tests to which it may be subjected.

SALV. The common opinion is here absolutely wrong. Indeed, it is so far wrong that precisely the opposite is true, namely, that many machines can be constructed even more perfectly on a large scale than on a small; thus, for instance, a clock which indicates and strikes the hour can be made more accurate on a large scale than on a small. There are some intelligent people who maintain this same opinion, but on more reasonable grounds, when they cut loose from geometry and argue that the better performance of the large machine is owing to the imperfections and variations of the material. Here I trust you will not charge me with arrogance if I say that imperfections in the material, even those which are great enough to invalidate the clearest mathematical proof, are not sufficient to explain the deviations observed between machines in the concrete and in the abstract. Yet I shall say it and will affirm that, even if the imperfections did not exist and matter were absolutely perfect, unalterable and free from all accidental variations, still the mere fact that it is matter makes the larger machine, built of the same material and in the same proportion as the smaller, correspond with exactness to the smaller in every respect except that it will not be so strong or so resistant against violent treatment; the larger the machine, the greater its weakness. Since I assume matter to be unchangeable and always the same, it is clear that we are no less able to treat this constant and invariable property in a rigid manner than if it belonged to simple and pure mathematics. Therefore, Sagredo, you would do well to change the opinion which you, and perhaps also many other students of mechanics, have entertained concerning the ability of machines and structures to resist external disturbances, thinking that when they are built of the same material and maintain the same ratio between parts, they are able equally, or rather proportionally, to resist or yield to such external disturbances and blows. For we can demonstrate by geometry that the large machine is not proportionately stronger than the small. Finally, we may say that, for every machine and structure, whether artificial or natural, there is set a necessary limit beyond which neither art nor nature can pass; it is here understood, of course, that the material is the same and the proportion preserved.

SAGR. My brain already reels. My mind, like a cloud momentarily illuminated by a lightning-flash, is for an instant filled with an unusual light, which now beckons to me and which now suddenly mingles and obscures strange, crude ideas. From what you have said it appears to me impossible to build two similar structures of the same material, but of different sizes and have them proportionately strong; and if this were so, it would not be possible to find two single poles made of the same wood which shall be alike in strength and resistance but unlike in size.

SALV. So it is, Sagredo. And to make sure that we understand each other, I say that if we take a wooden rod of a certain length and size, fitted, say, into a wall at right angles, i.e., parallel to the horizon, it may be reduced to such a length that it will just support itself; so that if a hair's breadth be added to its length it will break under its own weight and will be the only rod of the kind in the world.[1] Thus if, for instance, its length be a hundred times its breadth, you will not be able to find another rod whose length is also a hundred times its breadth and which, like the former, is just able to sustain its own weight and no more: all the larger ones will break while all the shorter ones will be strong enough to support something more than their own weight. And this

---

[1] The author here apparently means that the solution is unique. [Trans.]

which I have said about the ability to support itself must be understood to apply also to other tests; so that if a piece of scantling [corrente] will carry the weight of ten similar to itself, a beam [trave] having the same proportions will not be able to support ten similar beams.

Please observe, gentlemen, how facts which at first seem improbable will, even on scant explanation, drop the cloak which has hidden them and stand forth in naked and simple beauty. Who does not know that a horse falling from a height of three or four cubits will break his bones, while a dog falling from the same height or a cat from a height of eight or ten cubits will suffer no injury? Equally harmless would be the fall of a grasshopper from a tower or the fall of an ant from the distance of the moon. Do not children fall with impunity from heights which would cost their elders a broken leg or perhaps a fractured skull? And just as smaller animals are proportionately stronger and more robust than the larger, so also smaller plants are able to stand up better than larger. I am certain you both know that an oak two hundred cubits [braccia] high would not be able to sustain its own branches if they were distributed as in a tree of ordinary size; and that nature cannot produce a horse as large as twenty ordinary horses or a giant ten times taller than an ordinary man unless by miracle or by greatly altering the proportions of his limbs and especially of his bones, which would have to be considerably enlarged over the ordinary. Likewise the current belief that, in the case of artificial machines, the very large and the small are equally feasible and lasting is a manifest error. Thus, for example, a small obelisk or column or other solid figure can certainly be laid down or set up without danger of breaking, while the very large ones will go to pieces under the slightest provocation, and that purely on account of their own weight. And here I must relate a circumstance which is worthy of your attention as indeed are all events which happen contrary to expectation, especially when a precautionary measure turns out to be a cause of disaster. A large marble column was laid out so that its two ends rested each upon a piece of beam; a little later it occurred to a mechanic that, in order to be doubly sure of its not breaking in the middle by its own weight, it would be wise to lay a third support midway; this seemed to all an excellent idea; but the sequel showed that it was quite the opposite, for not many months passed before the column was found cracked and broken exactly above the new middle support.

SIMP. A very remarkable and thoroughly unexpected accident, especially if caused by placing that new support in the middle.

SALV. Surely this is the explanation, and the moment the cause is known our surprise vanishes; for when the two pieces of the column were placed on level ground it was observed that one of the end beams had, after a long while, become decayed and sunken, but that the middle one remained hard and strong, thus causing one half of the column to project in the air without any support. Under these circumstances the body therefore behaved differently from what it would have done if supported only upon the first beams; because no matter how much they might have sunken the column would have gone with them. This is an accident which could not possibly have happened to a small column, even though made of the same stone and having a length corresponding to its thickness, i.e., preserving the ratio between thickness and length found in the large pillar.

SAGR. I am quite convinced of the facts of the case, but I do not understand why the strength and resistance are not multiplied in the same proportion as the material; and I am the more puzzled because, on the contrary, I have noticed in other cases that the strength and resistance against breaking increase in a larger ratio than the amount of material. Thus, for instance, if two nails be driven into a wall, the one which is twice as big as the other will support not only twice as much weight as the other, but three or four times as much.

SALV. Indeed you will not be far wrong if you say eight times as much; nor does this phenomenon contradict the other even though in appearance they seem so different.

SAGR. Will you not then, Salviati, remove these difficulties and clear away these obscurities if possible: for I imagine that this problem of resistance opens up a field of beautiful and useful ideas; and if you are pleased to make this the subject of to-day's discourse you will place Simplicio and me under many obligations.

The greatest scientist of the Scientific Revolution, and perhaps of all time, was Isaac Newton (1642–1727). In his letter to his friend Francis Aston, Newton pointed out what might be learned by Aston in his travels.

Isaac Newton's Letter to Francis Aston

Trin. Coll. Cambr. May 18. 1699.

Fr.

Since in your letter you give mee so much liberty of spending my Judgment about wt may bee to your advantage in travelling, I shall doe it more freely then perhaps would otherwise have beene decent. First therefore I will lay down some generall rules most of wch I beleve you have considered already; but if any of them bee new to you they may excuse ye rest, if none at all yet tis my punishment more in writing them then yours in reading ym.

When you come into any fresh company, 1, observe their humours; 2, suit your own carriage thereto, by wch insinuation you will make their converse more free & open; 3, let your discours bee more in Quaerys & doubtings yn peremptory assertions or disputings, it being ye designe of Travellers to learne not teach; besides it will persuade your acquaintance yt you have the greater esteem of them & soe make ym more ready to communicate wt they know to you; whereas nothing sooner occasions disrespect & quarrells yn peremptorinesse. You will find little or noe advantage in seeming wiser or much more ignorant yn your company. 4, seldome discommend any thing though never so bad, or doe it but moderatly, least you bee unexpectedly forced to an unhansom retraction. Tis safer to commend any thing more then it deserves yn to discommend a thing so much as it deserves. For commenda-ntions [*sic*] meet not soe often wth oppositions or at least are not usually so ill resented by men that think otherwise as discommendations. And you will insinuate into mens favour by nothing sooner then seeming to approve & commend wt they like; but beware of doing it by a comparison. 5, If you bee affronted, tis better in a forrain Country to passe it by in silence or wth a jest though wth some dishonour then to endeavour revenge; For in the first case your credit's ne're the wors when you return into England or come into other company yt have not heard of the quarrell, but in the second case you may beare ye marks of ye quarrell while you live, if you out live it att all. But if you find your self unavoydably engaged tis best, I think, if you can command

H. W. Turnbull, ed., *The Correspondence of Isaac Newton*, I (Cambridge University Press, 1959), 9–11. Reprinted by permission of the copyright holder.

your passion & language, to keep them pretty eavenly at some certain moderate pitch, not much heightning them to exasperate ye adversary or provoke his freinds nor letting them grow overmuch dejected to make him insult. In a word if you can keep reason above passion, yt & watchfulnesse will bee your best defendants. To wch purpose you may consider yt though such excuses as this [He provok't mee so much I could not forbeare] may passe amongst freinds yet amongst strangers they are insignificant & only argue a Travellers weaknesse.

To these I may ad some generall heads for inquirys or observations such as at present I can think on. As 1 to observe ye policys wealth & state affaires of nations so far as a solitary Traveller may conveniently doe. 2 Their impositions upon all sorts of People Trades or commoditys yt are remarkeable. 3 Their Laws & Customes how far they differ from ours. 4 Their Trades & Arts wherin they excell or come short of us in England. 5 Such fortifications as you shall meet wth, their fashion strength & advantages for defence; & other such military affaires as are considerable. 6 The power & respect belonging to their degrees of nobility or Magistracy. 7 It will not bee time mispent to make a Catalogue of the names & excellencys of those men that are most wise learned or esteemed in any nation. 8 Observe ye Mechanisme & manner of guiding ships. 9 Observe the products of nature in severall places especially in mines wth ye circumstances of mining & of extracting metalls or mineralls out of their oare and refining them and if you meet wth any transmutations out of one species into another (as out of Iron into Copper, out of any metal into quicksilver, out of one salt into another or into an insipid body &c) those above all others will bee worth your noting being ye most luciferous & many times luciferous experiments too in Philosophy. 10 The prizes of diet & other things. 11 And the staple commoditys of Places.

These Generalls (such as at present I could think of) if they will serve for nothing else yet they may assist you in drawing up a Modell to regulate your Travels by.

As for particulars these yt follow are all yt I can now think of, viz: Whither at Schemnitium in Hungary (where there are Mines of Gold, copper, Iron, vitrioll, Antimony, &c) they change Iron into Copper by dissolving it in a Vitriolate water wch they find in cavitys of rocks in the mines & then melting the slymy solution in a strong fire wch in ye cooling proves copper. The like is said to bee done in other places wch I cannot now remember. Perhaps too it may bee done in Italy; For about 20 or 30 years agone there was a certain Vitrioll came from thence (called Roman Vitrioll, but of a nobler vertue yn yt wch is now called by yt name) wch Vitrioll is not now to bee gotten becaus perhaps they make a greater gain by some such trick as turning Iron into Copper wth it then by selling it. 2 Wither in Hungary, Sclavonia, Bohemia neare the town Eila, or at ye Mountains of Bohemia neare Silesia there be rivers whose waters are impregnated wth gold; perhaps ye Gold being dissolved by som corrosive waters like *Aqua Regis* & ye solution carried along wth ye streame that runs through ye mines. And whither ye practise of laying mercury in the rivers till it be tinged wth gold & then straining ye mercury through leather yt ye gold may stay behind, bee a secret yet or openly practised. 3 There is newly contrived in Holland a mill to grind glasses plane wthall & I think polishing them too, perhaps it will bee worth ye while to see it. 4 There is in Holland one—Bory, who some yeares since was imprisoned by the Pope to have extorted from him some secrets (as I am told) of great worth both as to medicine & profit, but hee escaped into Holland where they have granted him a guard. I think he usually goes clothed in green, pray enquire wt you can of him, & whither his ingenuity bee any profit to the Dutch. 5 You may inform your selfe whither ye Dutch have any tricks to keep their ships from being all worm eaten in their voyages to ye Indys. Whither Pendulum clocks doe any service in finding out ye longitude &c. I am very weary & shall not stay to part wth a long complement only I wish you a Good Journey & God bee wth you.

Is NEWTON.

Pray let us heare from you in your Travells. I have given your 2 books to Ds Arrowsmith.

Newton's masterpiece, and the work that more than any other created the new science, was *Philosophiae Naturalis Principia Mathematica* (*The Mathematical Principles of Natural Philosophy*), published in 1687. In the *Principia,* Newton laid out his rules of reasoning, which presumably had led him to his great discoveries.

Rules of Reasoning in Philosophy BY ISAAC NEWTON

RULE I

We are to admit no more causes of natural things than such as are both true and sufficient to explain their appearances.

To this purpose the philosophers say that Nature does nothing in vain, and more is in vain when less will serve; for Nature is pleased with simplicity, and affects not the pomp of superfluous causes.

Sir Isaac Newton's Mathematical Principles of Natural Philosophy and His System of the World (1947), pp. 398–400, translated by Andrew Motte (1729); translation revised by Florian Cajori. Reprinted by permission of University of California Press.

RULE II

Therefore to the same natural effects we must, as far as possible, assign the same causes.

As to respiration in a man and in a beast; the descent of stones in *Europe* and in *America;* the light of our culinary fire and of the sun; the reflection of light in the earth, and in the planets.

RULE III

The qualities of bodies, which admit neither intensification nor remission of degrees, and which are found to belong to all bodies within the reach of our experiments, are to be esteemed the universal qualities of all bodies whatsoever.

For since the qualities of bodies are only known to us by experiments, we are to hold for universal all such as universally agree with experiments; and such as are not liable to diminution can never be quite taken away. We are certainly not to relinquish the evidence of experiments for the sake of dreams and vain fictions of our own devising; nor are we to recede from the analogy of Nature, which is wont to be simple, and always consonant to itself. We no other way know the extension of bodies than by our senses, nor do these reach it in all bodies; but because we perceive extension in all that are sensible, therefore we ascribe it universally to all others also. That abundance of bodies are hard, we learn by experience; and because the hardness of the whole arises from the hardness of the parts, we therefore justly infer the hardness of the undivided particles not only of the bodies we feel but of all others. That all bodies are impenetrable, we gather not from reason, but from sensation. The bodies which we handle we find impenetrable, and thence conclude impenetrability to be an universal property of all bodies whatsoever. That all bodies are movable, and endowed with certain powers (which we call the inertia) of persevering in their motion, or in their rest, we only infer from the like properties observed in the bodies which we have seen. The extension, hardness, impenetrability, mobility, and inertia of the whole, result from the extension, hardness, impenetrability, mobility, and inertia of the parts; and hence we conclude the least particles of all bodies to be also all extended, and hard and impenetrable, and movable, and endowed with their proper inertia. And this is the foundation of all philosophy. Moreover, that the divided but contiguous particles of bodies may be separated from one another, is matter of observation; and, in the particles that remain undivided, our minds are able to distinguish yet lesser parts, as is mathematically demonstrated. But whether the parts so distinguished, and not yet divided, may, by the powers of Nature, be actually divided and separated from one another, we cannot certainly determine. Yet, had we the proof of but one experiment that any undivided particle, in breaking a hard and solid body, suffered a division, we might by virtue of this rule conclude that the undivided as well as the divided particles may be divided and actually separated to infinity.

Lastly, if it universally appears, by experiments and astronomical observations, that all bodies about the earth gravitate towards the earth, and that in proportion to the quantity of matter which they severally contain; that the moon likewise, according to the quantity of its matter, gravitates towards the earth; that, on the other hand, our sea gravitates towards the moon; and all the planets one towards another; and the comets in like manner towards the sun; we must, in consequence of this rule, universally allow that all bodies whatsoever are endowed with a principle of mutual gravitation. For the argument from the appearances concludes with more force for the universal gravitation of all bodies than for their impenetrability; of which, among those in the celestial regions, we have no experiments, nor any manner of observation. Not that I affirm gravity to be essential to bodies: by their *vis insita* I mean nothing but their inertia. This is immutable. Their gravity is diminished as they recede from the earth.

RULE IV

In experimental philosophy we are to look upon propositions inferred by general induction from phenomena as accurately or very nearly true, notwithstanding any contrary hypotheses that may be imagined, till such time as other phenomena occur, by which they may either be made more accurate, or liable to exceptions.

This rule we must follow, that the argument of induction may not be evaded by hypotheses.

4
THE ORIGINS
OF THE SCIENTIFIC
REVOLUTION

The late Alexandre Koyré was one of the leading historians of the Scientific Revolution. He is the strongest advocate of the position that the Scientific Revolution was basically a philosophical reorientation of Western thought and had nothing to do with the needs of society or anything else.

FROM Galileo and Plato BY ALEXANDRE KOYRÉ

The name of Galileo Galilei is indissolubly linked with the scientific revolution of the sixteenth century, one of the profoundest, if not the most profound, revolution of human thought since the invention of the Cosmos by Greek thought: a revolution which implies a radical intellectual "mutation," of which modern physical science is at once the expression and the fruit.

This revolution is sometimes characterized, and at the same time explained, as a kind of spiritual upheaval, an utter transformation of the whole fundamental attitude of the human mind; the active life, the *vita activa* taking the place of the θεωρία, the *vita contemplativa,* which until then had been considered its highest form. Modern man seeks the domination of nature, whereas medieval or ancient man attempted above all its contemplation. The mechanistic trend of classical physics—of the Galilean, Cartesian, Hobbesian physics, *scientia activa, operativa,* which was to render man "master and possessor of nature"—has, therefore, to be explained by this desire to dominate, to act; it has to be considered purely and simply an outflow of this attitude, an application to nature of the categories of thinking of *homo faber.* The

Alexandre Koyré, "Galileo and Plato," *Journal of the History of Ideas,* IV (1943), 400–405, 406–408, 417–419, 421–424.

science of Descartes—and *a fortiori* that of Galileo—is nothing else than (as has been said) the science of the craftsman or of the engineer.

I must confess that I do not believe this explanation to be entirely correct. It is true, of course, that modern philosophy, as well as modern ethics and modern religion, lays much more stress on action . . . than ancient and medieval thought. And it is just as true of modern science: I am thinking of the Cartesian physics and its analogies of pulleys, strings and levers. Still the attitude we have just described is much more that of Bacon—whose rôle in the history of science is not of the same order—than that of Galileo or Descartes. Their science is made not by engineers of craftsmen, but by men who seldom built or made anything more real than a theory. The new ballistics was made not by artificers and gunners, but against them. And Galileo did not learn *his* business from people who toiled in the arsenals and shipyards of Venice. Quite the contrary: he taught them *theirs*. Moreover, this theory explains too much and too little. It explains the tremendous scientific progress of the seventeenth century by that of technology. And yet the latter was infinitely less conspicuous than the former. Besides, it forgets the technological achievements of the Middle Ages. It neglects the lust for power and wealth which, throughout its history, inspired alchemy.

Other scholars have insisted on the Galilean fight against authority, against tradition, especially against that of Aristotle: against the scientific and philosophical tradition, upheld by the Church and taught in the universities. They have stressed the rôle of observation and experience in the new science of nature. It is perfectly true, of course, that observation and experimentation form one of the most characteristic features of modern science. It is certain that in the writings of Galileo we find innumerable appeals to observation and to experience, and bitter irony toward men who didn't believe their eyes because what they saw was contrary to the teaching of the authorities, or, even worse, who (like Cremonini) did not want to look through Galileo's telescope for fear of seeing something which would contradict their traditional theories and beliefs. It is obvious that it was just by building a telescope and by looking through it, by careful observation of the moon and the planets, by his discovery of the satellites of Jupiter, that Galileo dealt a crushing blow to the astronomy and the cosmology of his times.

Still one must not forget that observation and experience, in the sense of brute, common-sense experience, did not play a major rôle—or, if it did, it was a negative one, the rôle of obstacle—in the foundation of modern science. The physics of Aristotle . . . was . . . much nearer to common-sense experience than those of Galileo and Descartes. It is not "experience," but "experiment," which played—but only later—a great positive rôle. Experimentation is the methodical interrogation of nature, an interrogation which presupposes and implies a *language* in which to formulate the questions, and a dictionary which enables us to read and to interpret the answers. For Galileo, as we know well, it was in curves and circles and triangles, in mathematical or even more precisely, in *geometrical language*—not in the language of common sense or in that of pure symbols—that we must speak to Nature and receive her answers. Yet obviously the choice of the language, the decision to employ it, could not be determined by the experience which its use was to make possible. It had to come from other sources.

I shall not try to explain here the reasons and causes that produced the spiritual revolution of the sixteenth century. It is for our purpose sufficient to describe it, to describe the mental or intellectual attitude of modern science by two (connected) characteristics. They are: 1) the destruction of the Cosmos, and therefore the disappearance in science of all considerations based on that notion; 2) the geometrization of space—that is, the substitution of the homogeneous and abstract space of Euclidian geometry for the qualitatively differentiated and concrete world-space conception of the pre-Galilean physics. These two characteristics may be summed up and expressed as follows: the mathematization (geometrization) of nature and, therefore, the mathematization (geometrization) of science.

The dissolution of the Cosmos means the destruction of the idea of a hierarchically-ordered finite world-structure, of the idea of a qualitatively and ontologically differentiated world, and its replacement by that of an open, indefinite and even infinite universe, united and governed by the same universal laws; a universe in which, in contradiction to the traditional conception with its distinction and opposition of the two worlds of Heaven and of Earth, all things are on the same level of Being. The laws of Heaven and the laws of Earth are merged together. Astronomy and physics become interdependent, and even unified and united. And this implies the disappearance from the scientific outlook of all considerations based on value, on perfection, on harmony, on meaning and on purpose. They disappear in the infinite space of the new Universe. It is in this new Universe, in this new world of a geometry made real, that the laws of classical physics are valid and find their application.

The dissolution of the Cosmos—I repeat what I have already said: this seems to me to be the most profound revolution achieved or suffered by the human mind since the invention of the Cosmos by the Greeks. It is a revolution so profound and so far-reaching that mankind—with very few exceptions, of whom Pascal was one—for centuries did not grasp its bearing and its meaning; which, even now, is often misvalued and misunderstood.

Therefore what the founders of modern science, among them Galileo, had to do, was not to criticize and to combat certain faulty theories, and to correct or to replace them by better ones. They had to do something quite different. They had to destroy one world and to replace it by another. They had to reshape the framework of our intellect itself, to restate and to reform its concepts, to evolve a new approach to Being, a new concept of knowledge, a new concept of science—and even to replace a pretty natural approach, that of common sense, by another which is not natural at all.

This explains why the discovery of things, of laws, which today appear so simple and so easy as to be taught to children—the laws of motion, the law of falling bodies—required such a long, strenuous, and often unsuccessful effort of some of the greatest geniuses of mankind, a Galileo, a Descartes. This fact in turn seems to me to disprove the modern attempt to minimize, or even to deny, the originality, or at least the revolutionary character, of Galileo's thinking; and to make clear that the apparent continuity in the development of medieval and modern physics (a continuity so emphatically stressed by Caverni and Duhem) is an illusion.

Aristotelian physics is false, of course; and utterly obsolete. Nevertheless, it is a "physics," that is, a highly though non-mathematically elaborated science. It is not a childish phantasy, nor a brute and verbal restatement of common sense, but a theory, that is, a doctrine which, starting of course with the data of common sense, subjects them to an extremely coherent and systematic treatment.

The facts or data which serve as a basis for this theoretical elaboration are very simple, and in practice we admit them just as did Aristotle. It still seems to all of us "natural" to see a heavy body fall "down." And just like Aristotle or St. Thomas, we should be deeply astonished to see a ponderous body—a stone or a bull—rise freely in the air. This would seem to us pretty "unnatural"; and we would look for an explanation in the action of some hidden mechanism.

In the same way we still find it "natural" that the flame of a match points "up," and that we place our pots and pans "on" the fire. We should be astonished and should seek for an explanation if, for instance, we saw the flame turn about and point "down." Shall we call this conception, or rather this attitude, childish and simple? Perhaps. We can even point out that according to Aristotle himself science begins precisely by looking for an explanation for things that appear natural. Still, when thermodynamics asserts as a principle that "heat" passes from a hot to a cold body, but not from the cold to a hot one, does it not simply translate an intuition of common sense that a "hot" body "naturally" becomes cold, but that a cold one does not "naturally" become hot? And even when we are stating that the center of gravity of a system tends to take the lowest position and does not rise by itself, are we not simply translating an intuition of common sense, the self-same intuition which Aristotelian physics expresses by its distinction of movement into "natural" and "violent"?

Moreover, Aristotelian physics no more rests content than thermodynamics with merely expressing in its language the "fact" of common sense just mentioned; it transposes it, and the distinction between "natural" and "violent" movements takes its place in a general conception of physical reality, a conception of which the principal features seem to be: (a) the belief in the existence of qualitatively determined "natures," and (b) the belief in the existence of a Cosmos—that is, the belief in the existence of principles of order in virtue of which the entirety of real beings form a hierarchically-ordered whole.

Whole, cosmic order, and harmony: these concepts imply that in the Universe things are (or should be) distributed and disposed in a certain determined order; that their location is not a matter of indifference (neither for them, nor for the Universe); that on the contrary each thing has, according to its nature, a determined "place" in the Universe, which is in some sense its own. A place for everything, and everything in its place: the concept of "natural place" expresses this theoretical demand of Aristotelian physics.

We are too well acquainted with, or rather too well accustomed to, the principles and concepts of modern mechanics; so well that it is almost impossible for us to see the difficulties which had to be overcome for their establishment. They seem to us so simple, so natural, that we do not notice the paradoxes they imply and contain. Yet the mere fact that the greatest and mightiest minds of mankind—Galileo, Descartes—had to struggle in order to make them theirs, is in itself sufficient to indicate that these clear and simple notions—the notion of movement or that of space—are not so clear and simple as they seem to be. Or they are clear and simple only from a certain point of view, only as part of a certain set of concepts and axioms, apart from which they are not simple at all. Or, perhaps, they are too clear and too simple: so clear and so simple that, like all prime notions, they are very difficult to grasp.

Movement, space—let us try to forget for a while all we have learnt at school; let us try to think out what they mean in mechanics. Let us try to place ourselves in the situation of a contemporary of Galileo, a man accustomed to the concepts of Aristotelian physics which *he* learnt at *his* school, and who encounters for the first time the modern concept of motion. What is it? In fact something pretty strange. It is something which in no way affects the body which is endowed with it: to be in motion or to be at rest does not make any difference for, nor any change in, the body in motion or at rest. The body, as such, is utterly and absolutely indifferent to both. Therefore, we are not able to ascribe motion to a determined body considered in itself. A body is in motion only in relation to some other body which we assume to be at rest. All motion is relative. And therefore we may ascribe it to the one or to the other of the two bodies, *ad libitum*.

Thus motion seems to be a relation. But at the same time it is a *state,* just as rest is another *state,* utterly and absolutely opposed to the former; besides which they are both *persistent states.* The famous first law of motion, the law of inertia, teaches us that a body left to itself persists eternally in its state of motion or of rest, and that we must apply a force in order to change a state of motion to a state of rest, and *vice versa.* Yet every kind of motion is thus endowed with an eternal being, but only uniform movement in a straight line. Modern physics affirms, as well we know, that a body once set in motion conserves eternally its direction and speed, provided of course it is not subject to the action of any external force. Moreover, to the objection of the Aristotelian that though as a matter of fact he is acquainted with eternal motion, the eternal circular motion of the heavenly spheres, he has never yet encountered a persistent rectilinear one, modern physics replies: of course! rectilinear, uniform motion is utterly impossible, and can take place only in a vacuum.

Let us think it over, and perhaps we will not be too harsh on the Aristotelian who felt himself unable to grasp and to accept this unheard-of notion, the notion of a persistent, substantial relation-state, the concept of something which to him seemed just as abstruse, and just as impossible, as the ill-fated substantial forms of the scholastics appear to us. No wonder that the Aristotelian felt himself astonished and bewildered by this amazing attempt to explain the real by the impossible—or, which is the same thing, to explain real being by mathematical being, because, as I have mentioned already, these bodies moving in straight lines in infinite empty space are not *real* bodies moving in *real* space, but *mathematical* bodies moving in *mathematical* space.

Once more, we are so accustomed to mathematical science, to mathematical physics, that we no longer feel the strangeness of a mathematical approach to Being, the paradoxical daring of Galileo's utterance that the book of Nature is written in geometrical characters. For us it is a foregone conclusion. But not for the contemporaries of Galileo. Therefore it is the right of mathematical science, of the mathematical explanation of Nature, in opposition to the non-mathematical one of common sense and of Aristotelian physics, much more than the opposition between two astronomical systems, that forms the real subject of the *Dialogue on the Two Greatest Systems of the World*. As a matter of fact the *Dialogue,* as I believe I have shown . . . is not so much a book on *science* in our meaning of the term as a book on philosophy—or to be quite correct and to employ a disused but time-honored expression, a book on *natural philosophy*—for the simple reason that the solution of the astronomical problem depends on the constitution of a new Physics; which in turn implies the solution of the *philosophical* question of the rôle played by mathematics in the constitution of the science of Nature.

One sees that for the scientific and philosophical consciousness of the time —Buonamici and Mazzoni are only giving expression to the *communis opinio*—the opposition, or rather the dividing line, between the Aristotelian and the Platonist is perfectly clear. If you claim for mathematics a superior status, if more than that you attribute to it a real value and a commanding position in Physics, you are a Platonist. If on the contrary you see in mathematics an abstract science, which is therefore of a lesser value than those— physics and metaphysics—which deal with real being; if in particular you pretend that physics needs no other basis than experience and must be built directly on perception, that mathematics has to content itself with the secondary and subsidiary rôle of a mere auxiliary, you are an Aristotelian.

What is in question in this discussion is not certainty—no Aristotelian has ever doubted the certainty of geometrical propositions or demonstrations— but Being; not even the use of mathematics in physical science—no Aristotelian has ever denied our right to measure what is measurable and to count what is numerable—but the structure of science, and therefore the structure of Being.

These are the discussions to which Galileo alludes continuously in the course of his *Dialogue*. Thus at the very beginning Simplicio, the Aristotelian, points out that "concerning natural things we need not always seek the necessity of mathematical demonstrations." To which Sagredo, who allows himself the pleasure of misunderstanding Simplicio, replies: "Of course, when you cannot reach it. But, if you can, why not?" Of course. If it is possible in questions pertaining to natural things to achieve a demonstration possessing a mathematical necessity, why shouldn't we try to do it? But is it possible? That is precisely the problem, and Galileo, in the margin of the book, sums up the discussion and formulates the real meaning of the Aristotelian: "In natural demonstrations," says he, "one must not seek mathematical exactitude."

One must not. Why? Because it is impossible. Because the nature of physical being is qualitative and vague. It does not conform to the rigidity and the precision of mathematical concepts. It is always "more or less." Therefore, as the Aristotelian will explain to us later, philosophy, that is the science of the real, does not need to look at details, nor need it have recourse to numerical determinations in formulating its theories of motion; all that it has to do is to develop its chief categories (natural, violent, rectilinear, circular) and to describe its general qualitative and abstract features.

The modern reader is probably far from being convinced. He finds it difficult to admit that "philosophy" had to content itself with abstract and vague generalization and not try to establish precise and concrete universal laws. The modern reader does not know the real reason of this necessity, but Galileo's contemporaries knew it quite well. They knew that quality, as well as form, being non-mathematical by nature, cannot be treated in terms of mathematics. Physics is not applied geometry. Terrestrial matter can never exhibit exact mathematical figures; the "forms" never "inform" it completely and perfectly. There always remains a gap. In the skies, of course, it is different; and therefore mathematical astronomy is possible. But astronomy is not physics. To have missed that point is precisely the error of Plato and of those who follow Plato. It is useless to attempt to build up a mathematical philosophy of nature. The enterprise is doomed even before it starts. It does not lead us to truth but to error.

"All these mathematical subtleties," explains Simplicio, "are true *in abstracto*. But applied to sensible and physical matter, they do not work." In real nature there are no circles, no triangles, no straight lines. Therefore it is useless to learn the language of mathematical figures: the book of Nature, in spite of Galileo and Plato, is not written in them. In fact, it is not only useless, it is dangerous: the more a mind is accustomed to the precision and to the rigidity of geometrical thought, the less it will be able to grasp the mobile, changing, qualitatively determined variety of Being.

This attitude of the Aristotelian is very far from being ridiculous. To me, at least, it seems perfectly sensible. You cannot establish a mathematical theory of quality, objects Aristotle to Plato; not even one of motion. There is no motion in numbers. . . . And the Aristotelian of Galileo's time could add that the greatest of the Platonists, the *divus* Archimedes himself, was never able to establish more than a statics. Not a dynamics. A theory of rest. Not one of motion.

The Aristotelian was perfectly right. It is impossible to furnish a mathematical deduction of quality. And well we know that Galileo, like Descartes somewhat later, and for just the same reason, was forced to drop the notion of quality, to declare it subjective, to ban it from the realm of nature. This at the same time implies that he was obliged to drop sense-perception as the source of knowledge and to proclaim that intellectual, and even *a priori* knowledge, is our sole and only means of apprehending the essence of the real.

As for dynamics, and the laws of motion—the *posse* is only to be proved by the *esse;* in order to show that it is possible to establish mathematical laws of nature, you have to do it. There is no other way and Galileo is perfectly conscious of it. It is therefore by giving mathematical solutions to concrete physical problems—the problem of falling bodies, the problem of projectile motion—that he leads Simplicio to the confession "that to want to study natural problems without mathematics is to attempt something that cannot be done."

It is of this science, the true "philosophic" knowledge which is knowledge of the very essence of Being, that Galileo proclaims: "And I, I say to you that if one does not know the truth by himself, it is impossible for anyone else to give him that knowledge. It is indeed possible to teach those things that are neither true nor false; but the true, by which I mean necessary things, that is, those for which it is impossible to be otherwise, every average mind either knows by itself, or it is impossible for it ever to learn them." Assuredly. A Platonist cannot be of a different opinion because for him to know is nothing else than to understand.

Robert Merton is a sociologist at Columbia University who has turned the instruments of modern sociology on the Scientific Revolution. His analysis is based upon the use of sociological method to resolve a historical problem.

FROM Science and Economy of 17th Century England
BY ROBERT K. MERTON

The interplay between socio-economic and scientific development is scarcely problematical. To speak of socio-economic influences upon science in general unanalyzed terms, however, barely poses the problem. The sociologist of science is specifically concerned with the *types* of influence involved (facilitative and obstructive); the *extent* to which these types prove effective in different social structures; and the *processes* through which they operate. But these questions cannot be answered even tentatively without a clarification of the conceptual tools employed. All too often, the sociologist who repudiates the mythopeic or heroic interpretation of the history of science lapses into a vulgar materialism which seeks to find simple parallels between social and scientific development. Such misguided efforts invariably result in a seriously biased and untenable discussion.

FORMULATION OF THE PROBLEM

At least three common but unsound postulates must be avoided. The first and most illusive is the identification of personal utilitarian motivation of scientists with the structural determinants of their research. Second is the belief that socio-economic factors serve to account exhaustively for the entire complex of scientific activity; and third is the imputation of "social needs" where these needs are, in any significant sense, absent.

* * *

Motives may range from the desire for personal aggrandisement to a wholly "disinterested desire to know" without necessarily impugning the demonstrable fact that the thematics of science in seventeenth century England were in large part determined by the social structure of the time. Newton's own motives do not alter the fact that astronomical observations, of which he made considerable use, were a product of Flamsteed's work in the

Reprinted with permission of The Macmillan Company from Robert K. Merton, *Social Theory and Social Structure*, pp. 347–357, 361–363. Copyright 1949 The Free Press.

Greenwich Observatory, which was constructed at the command of Charles II for the benefit of the Royal Navy. Nor do they vitiate the striking influence upon Newton's work of such practically-oriented scientists as Halley, Hooke, Wren, Huyghens and Boyle. . . . It is neither an idle nor unguarded generalization that *every English scientist of this time* who was of sufficient distinction to merit mention in general histories of science at one point or another explicitly related at least some of his scientific research to immediate practical problems. But in any case, analysis exclusively in terms of (imputed) motives is seriously misleading and tends to befog the question of the modes of socioeconomic influence upon science.

Thus it is important to distinguish the personal attitudes of individual men of science from the social role played by their research. Clearly, some scientists were sufficiently enamored of their subject to pursue it "for its own sake," at times with little consideration of its practical bearings. Nor need we assume that *all* individual researches are directly linked to technical tasks. The relation between science and social needs is two-fold: direct, in the sense that some research is advisedly and deliberately pursued for utilitarian purposes; and indirect, insofar as certain problems and materials for their solution come to the attention of scientists although they need not be cognizant of the practical exigencies from which they derive.

* * *

There remains the third problem—of ascertaining social needs—which can best be handled in specific empirical terms. The widely accepted notion that need precipitates appropriate inventions and canalizes scientific interests demands careful restatement. Specific emergencies have often focused attention upon certain fields, but it is equally true that a multitude of "human needs" have gone unsatisfied throughout the ages. In the technical sphere, needs far from being exceptional, are so general that they explain little. Each invention *de facto* satisfies a need or is an attempt to achieve such satisfaction. It is necessary to realize that certain needs may not exist for the society under observation, precisely because of its particular social structure. It is only when the goal is actually part and parcel of the culture in question, only when it is actually perceived as such by some members of the society, that one may properly speak of a need directing scientific and technological interest in certain channels. Moreover, economic needs may be satisfied not only technologically but also by changes in social organization. But given the routine of fulfilling certain types of needs by technologic invention, a pattern which was becoming established in the seventeenth century; given the prerequisite accumulation of technical and scientific knowledge which provides the basic fund for innovation; given (in this case) an *expanding* capitalistic economy; and it may be said that necessity is the (foster) mother of invention and the grandparent of scientific advance.

* * *

A CASE: PROBLEM OF THE LONGITUDE

This engrossing problem of finding the longitude perhaps illustrates best the way in which practical considerations focused scientific interest upon certain fields. There can be no doubt that the contemporary astronomers were thoroughly impressed with the importance of discovering a satisfactory way of finding the longitude, particularly at sea. . . .

The various methods proposed for finding longitude led to the following investigations:

1. Computation of lunar distances from the sun or from a fixed star. First widely used in the first half of the sixteenth century and again in the latter seventeenth century.
2. Observations of the eclipses of the satellites of Jupiter. First proposed by Galileo in 1610; adopted by Hooke, Halley, G. D. Cassini, Flamsteed and others.
3. Observations of the moon's transit of the meridian. Generally current in the seventeenth century.
4. The use of pendulum clocks, and other chronometers, at sea, aided by Huyghens, Hooke, Halley, Messy, Sully and others.

Newton clearly outlined these procedures, as well as the scientific problems which they involved, upon the occasion of Ditton's claim of the reward for an accurate method of determining longitude at sea. The profound interest of English scientists in this subject is marked by an article in the first volume of the *Philosophical Transactions,* describing the use of pendulum clocks at sea. As Sprat put it, the Society had taken the problem "into its peculiar care." Hooke attempted to improve the pendulum clock and, as he says, "the success of these [trials] made me further think of improving it for finding the Longitude, and . . . quickly led me to the use of Springs instead of Gravity for the making a Body vibrate in any posture. . . ." A notorious controversy then raged about Hooke and Huyghens concerning priority in the successful construction of a watch with spiral balance spring. Howsoever the question of priority be settled, the very fact that two such eminent men of science, among others, focused their attention upon this sphere of inquiry is itself significant. These simultaneous inventions are a resultant of two forces: the intrinsically scientific one which provided the theoretical materials employed in solving the problem in hand, and the non-scientific, largely economic, factor which served to direct interest toward the general problem. The limited range of practicable possibilities leads to independent duplicate inventions.

* * *

It is precisely these examples, with their acknowledged practical implications, which clearly illustrate the role of utilitarian elements in furthering scientific advance. For it may be said, upon ample documentary grounds, that

Giovanni Domenico Cassini's astronomical discoveries were largely a result of utilitarian interests. In almost all of Cassini's papers in the *Transactions* he emphasizes the value of observing the moons of Jupiter for determining longitude, by means of the method first suggested by Galileo. It is perhaps not too much to say that from this interest derived his discovery of the rotation of Jupiter, the double ring of Saturn, and the third, fourth, fifth, sixth and eighth satellites of Saturn for, as he suggests, astronomical observations of this sort were "incited" because of their practical implications. . . .

Newton was likewise deeply interested in the same general problem. Early in his career, he wrote a now famous letter of advice to his friend, Francis Aston, who was planning a trip on the Continent, in which he suggested among other particulars that Aston "inform himself whether pendulum clocks be of any service in finding out the longitude." In a correspondence which we have reason to believe ultimately led Newton to the completion of the *Principia,* both Halley and Hooke urged Newton to continue certain phases of his research because of its utility for navigation.

* * *

THE EXTENT OF ECONOMIC INFLUENCE

In a sense, the foregoing discussion provides materials illustrative only of the connections we have been tracing. We still have to determine the extent to which socio-economic influences were operative. The minutes of the Royal Society as transcribed in Birch's *History of the Royal Society* provide one basis for such a study. A feasible, though in several manifest respects inadequate, procedure consists of a classification and tabulation of the researches discussed at these meetings, together with an examination of the context in which the various problems came to light. This should afford some ground for deciding *approximately* the extent to which extrinsic factors operated.

Meetings during the four years 1661, 1662, 1686 and 1687 will be considered. There is no reason to suppose that these did not witness meetings "typical" of the general period. The classification employed is empirical rather than logically symmetrical. Items were classified as "directly related" to socio-economic demands when the individual conducting the research explicitly indicated some such connection or when the immediate discussion of the research evidenced a prior appreciation of some such relation. Items classified as "indirectly related" comprise researches which had a clear-cut connection with current practical needs, intimated in the context, but which were not definitely so related by the investigators. Researches which evidenced no relations of this sort were classified as "pure science." Many items have been classified in this category which have (for the present-day observer) a conceivable relation to practical exigencies but which were not so regarded explicitly in the seventeenth century. Thus, investigations in the field of meteorology could readily be related to the practical desirability of forecasting the weather but when these researches were not explicitly related to specific problems they were classified as pure science. Likewise, much of the work in anatomy and physiology was undoubtedly of value for medicine and surgery, but the same criteria were employed in the classification of these items. It is likely, therefore, that if any bias was involved in this classification, it was in the direction of over-estimating the scope of "pure science."

Each research discussed was "counted" as one "unit." It is obvious that this procedure provides only a gross approximation to the extent of extrinsic influences upon the selection of subjects for scientific study, but when greater precision is impossible one must perforce rest temporarily content with less. The results can merely suggest the relative extent of the influences which we have traced in a large number of concrete instances.

From this tabulation it appears that less than half (41.3%) of the investigations conducted during the four years in question are classifiable as "pure science." If we add to this the items which were but indirectly related to practical needs, then about seventy per cent of this research had no explicit practical affiliations. Since these figures are but grossly approximate, the results may be summarized by saying that from forty to seventy per cent occurred in the category of pure science; and conversely that from thirty to sixty per cent were influenced by practical requirements.

Again, considering only the research directly related to practical needs, it appears that problems of marine transport attracted the most attention. This is in accord with one's impression that the contemporary men of science were well aware of the problems raised by England's insular position—problems both military and commercial in nature—and were eager to rectify them. Of almost equal importance was the influence of military exigencies. Not only were there some fifty years of actual warfare during this century, but also the two greatest revolutions in English history. Problems of a military nature left their impress upon the culture of the period, including scientific development.

Likewise, mining, which developed so markedly during this period, as we may see from the studies of Nef and other economic historians, had an appreciable influence. In this instance, the greater part of scientific, if one may divorce it from technologic, research was in the fields of mineralogy and metallurgy with the aim of discovering new utilizable ores and new methods of extracting metals from the ore.

It is relevant to note that, in the latter years considered in this summary, there was an increasing proportion of investigation in the field of pure science. A conjectural explanation is not far to seek. It is probable that at the outset the members of the Society were anxious to justify their activities (to the Crown and the lay public generally) by deriving practical results as soon as possible. Hence, the initially marked orientation toward practical problems. Furthermore, many of the problems which were at first advisedly investigated because of their utilitarian importance may later be studied with no awareness of their practical implications. On the basis of the (perhaps biased) criteria adopted in this compilation, some of the later researches would arbitrarily be classified as pure science.

On the grounds afforded by this study it seems justifiable to assert that the range of problems investigated by seventeenth century English scientists was appreciably influenced by the socio-economic structure of the period.

Rupert Hall, professor of the history of science at Imperial College, London, has published extensively on the nature of the Scientific Revolution. The selection that follows was delivered as a lecture at a symposium at the University of Wisconsin in 1957.

FROM The Scholar and the Craftsman in the Scientific Revolution BY RUPERT HALL

Never has there been such a time as that during the later sixteenth and the seventeenth centuries for the great diversity of men in the forefront of scientific achievement. A proportion of those who contributed to the swelling literature of science were in a broad sense professionals: indeed, a sizable proportion, since many minor figures enlarge this group. Among these professionals were university teachers, professors of mathematics, anatomy, and medicine; teachers of these subjects, especially applied mathematics, outside the universities; and their various practitioners—physicians, surveyors, mariners, engineers, and so on; and lastly the instrument-makers, opticians, apothecaries, surgeons, and other tradesmen, though their great period in science is to be found rather in the eighteenth century than in the seventeenth. These men, widely divergent as they were in social origins and intellectual attainments, at least occupied positions in a recognizable scientific hierarchy. Some had won them through academic study, others through private education and research, others again by apprenticeship and pursuit of an occupation closely related to scientific inquiry. All were trained men in some way, whether in mathematics, physic and dissection, or the exercise of a manual craft. Now it is surprising enough, whether we make comparison with the scientific world of recent times, or with that of the later Middle Ages, to find such disparity in the professional group, that is, to find that the definition of

Reprinted with permission of the copyright owners, the Regents of the University of Wisconsin, from Rupert Hall, "The Scholar and the Craftsman in the Scientific Revolution," in Marshall Clagett, *Critical Problems in the History of Science*, 1959, pp. 3–23, The University of Wisconsin Press.

scientific professionalism must be so loosely drawn; yet it is still more aston-ishing that many minor figures in the history of seventeenth-century science, and not a few notable ones, constitute an even more heterogeneous collec-tion. Among these true "amateurs" of science (the distinction has really little meaning), some, it is true, had been exposed to scientific influences of a kind in college or university; yet the creation of a permanent interest thus, in an ordinary passing student, must have been as rare then as the acquisition of a taste for Latin verse is now. A few also, no doubt, were quietly encouraged by discerning fathers or by private patrons. The rest remain as "sports"; diffu-sionist and environmental principles hardly suffice to explain their appear-ance on the scene. One thinks of such men as William Petty, son of a clothier, Otto von Guericke, Mayor of Magdeburg, John Flamsteed, an independent gentleman of modest means, or, most extraordinary of all, Antony van Leeuwenhoek, an unschooled borough official.

Thus one can never predict the social circumstances or personal history of a seventeenth-century scientist. Given the taste, the ability, and freedom from the immediate necessities of the struggle for subsistence, any man who could read and write might become such. Latin was no longer essential, nor mathe-matics, nor wide knowledge of books, nor a professorial chair. Publication in journals, even membership in scientific societies, was open to all; no man's work needed the stamp of academic approval. This was the free age between the medieval M.A. and the modern Ph.D. In the virtual absence of systematic scientific training, when far more was learned from books than from lectures, the wholly self-educated man was hardly at a disadvantage as compared with his more fortunate colleague who had attended the seats of learning, except perhaps in such special fields as theoretical astronomy or human anatomy. There were no important barriers blocking entry into the newer areas of exploration, such as chemistry, microscopy, qualitative astronomy, where all types of ability, manual and intellectual, were almost equally required. Obvi-ously it was statistically more probable that a scientist would spring from the gentry class (if I may use this disputed term) than any other, and that he would be a university man rather than not. But the considerations determin-ing the probability were sociological rather than scientific; if the texture of science was almost infinitely receptive of first-rate ability of any kind, the texture of society was such that it was more likely to emerge from some quarters than from others.

It is needful to traverse this familiar ground in order to set in perspective the dichotomy to which I shall turn—that of craftsman and scholar. It is a quadruple dichotomy—social, intellectual, teleological, and educational. It marks off, broadly, men of one class in society from another—those who earn their bread from scientific trades of one kind or another from those who do not. It distinguishes likewise those achievements in science which are in the main practical or operational from those which are cerebral or conceptual. Thirdly, it draws attention to the different objects of those who seek mainly practical success through science, and those who seek mainly understanding.

And finally, if we consider only the group whom I have previously called professional, we may discern on the one hand the "scholars" who have been introduced to science by university or similar studies, and on the other the "craftsmen" who have learnt something of practical science in a trade. But we must be cautious in detecting polar opposites where there is in reality a spectrum. The scientific movement of the seventeenth century was infinitely varied, its successes demanded an infinite range of different qualities, and it is against this background of wide inclusion that we must set any attempt at analysis in particular terms.

By far the most closely-knit, homogeneous, and intellectually influential of the groups I have described was that of the university men, including both those who remained as teachers and those who departed to other walks of life. Some of the harshest critics of the contemporary "schools," like Bacon, Descartes, or Webster, were nevertheless their products. The opponents of the Aristotelian "forms and qualities" had been firmly grounded in that doctrine; many future scientists found stimulus in the universally required mathematical studies. To exemplify this point, one may consider the earliest membership of the Royal Society in 1663. Of the 115 names listed, I find that 65 had definitely attended a university, while only 16 were certainly non-academic. The remaining 34 are doubtful, but at any rate the university men had the majority. It is still more telling to single out the names which have a definite association-value on inspection; I rate 38 on this test, of whom 32 are "U" and only 6 "non-U." Whether or not we term such men "scholars" is largely a rather unimportant question of definition: at any rate they had in common a knowledge of Latin, some training in mathematics, and an introduction at least to logic and natural philosophy; quite a proportion would also have had such experience of the biological and medical sciences as was available at the time.

It appears then that the medieval association of scientific activity with the universities was weakened, but not disrupted, in the seventeenth century, though the association certainly became less strong as the century advanced. It was weakened not only by the importance in science of men who were not academically trained at all, but by the shift in the locus of scientific activity from the universities, where it had remained securely fixed throughout the Middle Ages, to new institutions like Gresham College, to the scientific societies meeting in capital cities, and to the circles basking in the patronage of a Montmor or a Medici. If a majority of creative scientists had been at the university, they were so no longer in their mature age. Moreover, while in the medieval university there had been little disparity between the instruction given to the student, and the advanced researches of the master, this was no longer the case in the seventeenth century. In the schools of the fourteenth century the master who remained to teach pushed forward his knowledge, in the main, within the framework of ideas, and through study of authorities, with which he had become familiar at a more elementary level. The seventeenth-century university, on the other hand, almost ignored observational and experimental science. The unprecedented advances in scientific technique occurring in physics, astronomy, botany and zoology, and chemistry were not made widely available to students: there was a fairly good grounding only in mathematics and human medicine. The potential investigator had to learn the techniques he required from practice, by the aid of books, and through personal contact with an experienced scientist, often only obtainable else-where. Perhaps even more serious was the absence from university courses of the leading principles of the scientific revolution and of the ideas of the new natural philosophy. In the last quarter of the seventeenth century Cartesian science was indeed expounded in some of the colleges of France, and less widely elsewhere, but dissemination of the thought of Galileo, of Bacon, and of the exponents of the mechanical philosophy owed little to university courses. . . . If the universities could produce scholars, they were ill-adapted to turning out scientists; the scientist had to train himself. Many who accom-plished this transition regarded it, indeed, as a revulsion from the ordinary conception of scholarship. The learning they genuinely prized, in their own scientific disciplines, they had hardly won for themselves. It would surely be absurd to argue that Newton was less a self-made scientist than Huyghens, or Malpighi than Leeuwenhoek, because the former had attended a univer-sity and the latter not.

It lies outside my brief to discuss the fossilization of the universities, which, from what I can learn, the Renaissance did little to diminish so far as science was concerned, nor the rise of the new science as a rejection of academic dogma. Recent investigations would, I believe, tend to make one hesitant in concluding that the innovations and criticisms in the academic sciences—astronomy, physics, anatomy—which we call the scientific revolution, were the product solely, or even chiefly, of forces and changes operating outside the universities. Rather it would seem that, in relation to these subjects, it was a case of internal strife, one party of academic innovators trying to wrest the field from a more numerous one of academic conservatives. Certainly this was the case with Vesalius and his fellow-anatomists, with Copernicus, with Galileo. It was the academic and professional world that was passionately divided on the question of the inviolability of the Galenic, Aristotelian, or Ptolemaic doctrines; these quarrels of learned men had as little to do with capitalism as with the protestant ethic. Only towards the middle of the seven-teenth century were they extended through the wider range of the educated class.

In the long run—that is to say within a century or so in each instance—the innovators won. In the short run they were defeated; academic conservatism prevented the recognition and implementation of the victories of the revolu-tion in each science until long after they were universally applauded by thoughtful men outside. Whereas in the thirteenth century the schools had swung over to the Greeks and Muslims, despite their paganism and their often unorthodox philosophy, whereas in the fourteenth century the devel-opment of mechanics, of astronomy theoretical and practical, of anatomical and other medical studies, had been centered upon them, in the later six-teenth and seventeenth centuries teaching failed to adapt itself to the pace with which philosophy and science were moving. In the mid-sixteenth cen-tury the universities could still have formed the spear-head of this astonishing intellectual advance; in Galileo's life-time the opportunity was lost, and de-spite the invaluable efforts of individual teachers, as institutions the universi-ties figured only in the army of occupation, a fantastic position not reversed until the nineteenth century. The innovators really failed, at the critical pe-riod, to capture the universities and bring them over to their side as centers of teaching and research in the new scientific manner. There were, for instance, many schemes in the seventeenth century for organizing scientific research, and for the provision of observatories, museums, laboratories and so on: yet no one, I think, thought of basing such new institutions on a university.

* * *

The passage in the *Discourse on Method* may be recalled, in which Des-cartes reviews critically the content of education and learning as ordinarily understood:

Of philosophy I will say nothing, except that when I saw it had been cultivated for many ages by the most distinguished men, and that yet there is not a single matter within its sphere which is not still in dispute, and nothing therefore which is above doubt, I did not presume to anticipate that my success would be greater in it than that of others; and further, when I considered the number of conflicting opinions touching a single matter that may be upheld by learned men, while there can be but one true, I reckoned as well-nigh false all that was only probable.

After observing that the other sciences derived their principles from philoso-phy, which was itself infirm, so that "neither the honour nor the gain held out by them was sufficient to determine one to their cultivation," Descartes abandoned the study of letters "and resolved no longer to seek any other sci-ence than the knowledge of myself, or of the great book of the world." With this one may compare Bacon's "surprise, that among so many illustrious col-leges in Europe, all the foundations are engrossed by the professions, none being left for the free cultivation of the arts and sciences." This restriction, he declares, "has not only dwarfed the growth of the sciences, but been prejudi-cial to states and governments themselves." The candid appraisal of the first chapter of the *Advancement of Learning* could have been applied to many academic institutions more than two centuries after it was penned.

* * *

The object of the preceding remarks is to justify my conception of the scientific scholar of the sixteenth and seventeenth centuries, as a man learned not merely in recent scientific activities and methods, but in the thought of the past. It seems superfluous to argue that the majority of the scientists of the time were of this type, neither technicians nor ignorant empiricists. Certainly the learning of Galileo, or Mersenne, or Huyghens, or Newton, was not quite like learning in the medieval or Renaissance conception; they may have been as deficient in the subtleties of Thomist philosophy as in the niceties of Greek syntax; but to deny that they were learned scholars in their field and in their outlook, would be to deny that any scientist is entitled to be called learned.

I have tried also to trace in outline the way in which, at this time, scientific learning diverged from other branches of scholarship, without wholly severing its affiliations with academic institutions. One might also ask the question: how far was the new scientific spirit of the seventeenth century brought into being by activities of a purely scholarly kind—for example, through the evolution of certain principles of logic during the Middle Ages, or through the activities of the persistent students of Greek science in the Renaissance?

The latter especially furnished the core of an interpretation of the scientific revolution which held favor until recent times. To put it crudely, the scientific revolution was seen, according to this view, as the terminal stage of a scientific renaissance beginning about the mid-fifteenth century, and characterized chiefly by its full exploration of classical scientific texts, which was aided particularly by the invention of printing; the scientific renaissance was itself regarded as a classical reaction against the gothic barbarity of the Middle Ages. This interpretation is in effect an extension of Bacon's, to which I referred earlier; an extension which Bacon himself was unable to make because he did not know that the revolution he sought was going on around him. Clearly, if such a view is accepted, it attaches a very great importance indeed to the activity of the scholar-scientists of the Renaissance, who besides polishing and extending the works of the most authoritative ancient authors, shed a full light on others, such as Lucretius, Celsus, and Archimedes, whose writings had not previously been widely studied.

The merits of this hypothesis of the origin of the scientific revolution are as obvious as its defects. It draws attention to the weight of the contribution of sheer scholarship, and of the amazing Hellenophile instinct of the Renaissance, to the change in science which occurred between 1550 and 1700. No one would deny the connection between the mechanical, corpuscular philosophy of the seventeenth century, and *De natura rerum;* nor the significance for anatomy of the intensive study of Galen; nor would he dispute that the virtual rediscovery of Archimedes transformed geometry, and ultimately algebra. Equally, however, it is clear that this is far from being the whole story: the instances I have quoted are not universally typical ones. The history of mechanics before Galileo, which has been so elaborately worked out in the present half-century, proves the point. Medieval science was not abruptly cut short by a classical revival called a renaissance: it had much—how much must be the subject of continuing research—to contribute to the formation of modern science. Very important threads in the scientific revolution are not really traceable to antiquity at all, at least not through the channels of scholarship; here the chemical sciences furnish examples. Above all, the Renaissance-scholarship interpretation fails to account for the *change* in science. If anything is fairly certain, it is that the intention of the Renaissance was the imitation of antiquity, and there is evidence that this ideal extended to the scholar-scientists. Yet the pursuit of this ideal seems to have endured least long in science, of all the learned subjects; it had ceased to have force long before the end of the sixteenth century. There never was a true Palladian age in science, and the limitations that had bound the Greeks themselves were relatively soon transcended in Europe. Why this was so is really the whole point at issue, and the Renaissance-scholarship interpretation does not squarely face it.

*   *   *

There is a point here . . . that deserves fuller consideration, and allows the craftsman to enter on the scene. For while we recognize science as a scholarly activity, and the reform of science as an act of learned men, it may plausibly be asked whether the impulse to reform was spontaneously generated among the learned. Was it perhaps stimulated elsewhere? Some support for this suspicion might seem to spring from the emphasis that has been laid on empiricism, not merely in the scientific revolution itself, but among its philosophical precursors. Thus, to quote Dr. Crombie: "The outstanding scientific event of the twelfth and thirteenth centuries was the confrontation of the empiricism long present in the West in the practical arts, with the conception of rational explanation contained in scientific texts recently translated from Greek and Arabic." It is unnecessary to dwell on the well-known interest of at least a few learned men, during the Middle Ages, in such fruits of empirical invention as the magnetic compass, the grinding of lenses, and above all, the important advances in the chemical and metallurgical arts. Similarly, everyone is familiar with the arguments of the Baconian school: that true command— and therefore real if unwitting knowledge—of natural processes had been won by the arts rather than by sciences, and that the scholar would often become more learned if he would consent to apprentice himself to the craftsman. All this might suggest that the increasingly spectacular achievements of empirical technology arrested the attention of scholarly scientists, enforcing some doubt of the rectitude of their own procedures, and still more, leading them to accept as an ideal of science itself that subjection of the natural environment to human purposes which had formerly seemed to belong only to the arts and crafts.

There are two issues here. One is the fact of technological progress, which some philosophical critics contrasted with the stagnation of science. The other is the reaction of learned men to the state of technology, and this is more properly our concern. Technological progress was not simply a feature of the Middle Ages and Renaissance: it occurred in the ancient empires, in the Greek world, under the Roman dominion, and even in the so-called "Dark Ages." It would be difficult to think of a long period of complete technical stagnation in European history, though individual arts suffered temporary periods of decline. Some craftsmen at some places seem always to have been making their way forward by trial and error. In short, a philosopher of antiquity had as great an opportunity of appreciating the inventiveness of craftsmen as his successors of the sixteenth and seventeenth centuries, and of drawing the same lessons as were drawn then. Indeed, ancient writers were aware of the importance of the crafts in creating the means of civilized existence, and praised works of ingenuity and dexterity; where they differed from the moderns was in their preservation of the distinction between *understanding* and *doing*. They did not conclude that the progressive success of the crafts set up any model of empiricism for philosophy to emulate. They would not have written, as Francis Bacon did, in the opening lines of the *Novum Organum:* "Man, as the minister and interpreter of nature, does and understands as much as his observations on the order of nature, either with regard to things or the mind, permit him, and neither knows nor is capable of more. The unassisted hand and the understanding left to itself possess but little power. . . . Knowledge and human power are synonymous."

It is the philosopher who has modified his attitude, not the craftsman, and the change is essentially subjective. The success of craft empiricism was nothing new in late medieval and early modern times, and if the philosopher became conscious of its significance for science it was not because such success was more dramatic now than in the past. It was always there to be seen, by those who had eyes to see it, and the change was in the eye of the beholder. It is absurd, for instance, to suppose that the introduction of gunpowder and cannon into warfare was in any serious sense the cause of a revival of interest in dynamics, and especially in the theory of the motion of projectiles, during the sixteenth and early seventeenth century. The ancient torsion artillery provided equally dramatic machines in its day, not to mention the crossbow, mangonel, and trebuchet of the Middle Ages. The simplest methods of hurling projectiles—the human arm, the sling, the bow—pose problems of motion no less emphatically than more complex or powerful devices, and as everyone knows, appeal to practical experience of this primitive kind was the basis for the development of the concept of impetus. The earliest "scientific" writers on explosive artillery . . . did no more than transfer this concept to the operation of a different device.

Such an example reminds us that it may be naive to assume that even major technological advances suggested, contemporaneously, such questions worthy of scientific enquiry as would, indeed, immediately spring to our own minds. The scientific examination of the three useful forms of iron—cast-iron, wrought iron, and steel—did not begin until the early eighteenth century; the geometrical theory of gear-wheels was initiated about fifty years earlier; the serious study of the chemistry of the ceramics industry was undertaken a little later. I choose deliberately examples of practical science each associated with notable developments in late-medieval craftsmanship: the introduction, respectively, of the effective blast-furnace; of the gear-train in the windmill, water-mill, mechanical clock, and other devices; and of fine, brightly pigmented, tin-glazed earthenware. The time-lag in each instance between the establishment of a new craft-skill, and the effective appearance of scientific interest in it, is of the order of 250 years, and in each of these examples it appears *after* the scientific revolution was well under way. If there is some truth in the view that interest in crafts promoted a change in scientific procedures, it is also true that, at a later date, the very success of the new scientific knowledge and methods opened up the possibility of examining craft procedures systematically, which had not existed before.

* * *

In any case, I hesitate to conclude that the behavior of an empirical scientist —that is, I take it, one who observes and experiments, both to discover new information and to confirm his statements and ideas—is derivable by virtually direct imitation from the trial-and-error, haphazard, and fortuitous progress of the crafts. This seems to me to be the defect of the view that sees the new scientist of the seventeenth century as a sort of hybrid between the older natural philosopher and the craftsman. It is easy enough to say that the philosopher thought much and did little, while the craftsman did much but had no ideas, and to see the scientist as one who both thinks and does. But is such a gross simplification really very helpful in describing or explaining a complex historical transition? Neither Copernicus, nor Vesalius, nor Descartes, to name only three, were more craftsmanlike than Ptolemy, Galen, or Aristotle. Surely scientific empiricism is itself a philosophical artifact, or at least the creation of learned men . . . and it stands in about the same relation to craftsmanship as the theory of evolution does to the practices of pigeon-fanciers. It is a highly sophisticated way of finding out about the world in which we live; on the other hand, the notion that direct immersion in the lore of tradesmen was the essential baptism preceding scientific discovery was one of the sterile by-paths from which the scientists of the seventeenth century fortunately emerged after a short time. Modern studies combine in revealing that the empirical element in the scientific revolution, taking the word in its crudest, least philosophical, and most craftsmanlike sense, has been greatly exaggerated; correspondingly we are learning to attach more and more significance to its conceptual and intellectual aspects.

* * *

Perhaps I may illustrate this in the following way. The contributions of craftsmanship to the development of scientific knowledge in the sixteenth and seventeenth centuries seem to be analyzable under five heads:

1. the presentation of striking problems worthy of rational and systematic enquiry;
2. the accumulation of technological information susceptible to scientific study;
3. the exemplification of techniques and apparatus adaptable from the purposes of manufacture to those of scientific research;

4. the realization of the scientific need for instruments and apparatus;

5. the development of topics not embraced in the organization of science proper.

The incidence of these contributions is highly variable among the individual sciences. None are strongly relevant in anatomy, medicine, or indeed any biological science, except that 4 would apply to microscopy. All the sciences demonstrate an increasing dependence on the instrument-maker's craft. Again, 4 is relevant to astronomy, while mechanics draws very slightly upon 1 and 2. Chemistry, on the other hand, exemplifies all these possible contributions, and most forms of applied science—other than mathematical sciences—owe much to the fifth contribution. All we can conclude, therefore, is an obvious truism: that those sciences in whose development empiricism played the greatest part are those in which elements derived from craftsmanship have the most effect. It does not follow, however, that the empirical sciences are those that best exhibit the profundity or the nature of the change in scientific thought and work, nor that the theoretical function of scholars is insignificant even in these sciences. . . . The academic and above all the mathematical sciences were not only those that advanced fastest, but they were already regarded as the models for the structure of other sciences, when these should have reached a sufficiently mature stage. In an ascending scale of sophistication, it was regarded as desirable to render all physical science of the same pattern as mechanics and astronomy, and to interpret all other phenomena in terms of the basic physical laws. The first great step towards the attainment of such an ambition was Newton's *Principia,* a work soon regarded by many as the ultimate manifestation of man's capacity for scientific knowledge. I believe it would be wrong to suppose that the scientists of the late seventeenth century, with such rich examples before them, were content to remain indefinitely at the level of empiricism or sublimated craftsmanship, though indeed in many branches of enquiry it was not yet possible to soar far above it. They were aware that the more abstruse and theoretical sciences, where the contributions of learned men had been greatest, were of a higher type than this.

Perhaps I may now summarize the position I have sought to delineate and justify in the following six propositions, in which it is assumed as an axiom that a science is distinguished by its coherent structure of theory and explanation from a mass of information about the way the world is, however carefully arranged.

1. The scientific revolution appears primarily as a revolution in theory and explanation, whether we view it in the most general fashion, considering the methods and philosophy of the new scientists, or whether we consider the critical points of evolution in any single science.

2. There is a tradition of logical (or, more broadly, philosophical) preoccupation with the problem of understanding natural phenomena of which the later stages, from the thirteenth to the seventeenth century, have at the

lowest estimate some bearing on the attitudes to this problem of seventeenth-century scientists.

3. Some of the most splendid successes of the scientific revolution sprang from its novel treatment of questions much discussed by medieval scholars.

4. These may be distinguished from the "contrary instances" of success (or an approximation to it) in handling types of natural phenomena previously ignored by philosophers, though familiar in technological experience.

5. While "scholars" showed increasing readiness to make use of the information acquired by craftsmen, and their special techniques for criticizing established ideas and exploring phenomena afresh, it is far less clear that craftsmen were apt or equipped to criticize the theories and procedures of science.

6. Though the early exploitation of observation and experiment as methods of scientific enquiry drew heavily on straightforward workshop practice, the initiative for this borrowing seems to be with scholars rather than craftsmen.

I dislike dichotomies: of two propositions, so often neither *a* nor *b* by itself can be wholly true. The roles of the scholar and the craftsman in the scientific revolution are complementary ones, and if the former holds the prime place in its story, the plot would lack many rich overtones had the latter also not played his part. The scholar's function was active, to transform science; the craftsman's was passive, to provide some of the raw material with which the transformation was to be effected. If science is not constructed from pure empiricism, neither can it be created by pure thought. I do not believe that the scientific revolution was enforced by a necessity for technological progress, but equally in a more backward technological setting it could not have occurred at all. If the genesis of the scientific revolution is in the mind, with its need and capacity for explanation, as I believe, it is also true that the nascent movement would have proved nugatory, had it not occurred in a world which offered the means and incentive for its success.

THE ORIGINS
OF THE FRENCH
REVOLUTION

POPULAR MISERY, SOCIAL AMBITIONS, OR PHILOSOPHICAL IDEAS?

CONTENTS

QUESTIONS FOR STUDY

1. *In what ways do Montesquieu and Rousseau criticize the foundations of the French state in the eighteenth century?*

2. *How desperate was the plight of the peasantry in France in 1789?*

3. *How does the Declaration of the Rights of Man reflect the influence of ideas on the makers of the Revolution? In what ways does it deal with very practical concerns?*

4. *Who were the makers of the French Revolution? In what ways could their motives be affected by misery, social ambitions, and ideas?*

5. *What do you feel to be sufficient motives for revolutionary action?*

The reign of Louis XIV in France revealed some of the problems associated with the exercise of absolute power by the king. Although Louis created a brilliant society and stimulated the development of the arts and sciences—so much so that the age of Louis XIV was later regarded as a golden age—he also bled France white with his interminable wars and search for "glory." The wars and the Revocation of the Edict of Nantes in 1685 struck heavy blows at French commercial development, and this, along with the sheer expense of continuous fighting, brought France to the brink of bankruptcy in 1715. Throughout the eighteenth century France was to remain tottering on the verge of financial collapse, and it should not be forgotten that it was this collapse that led directly to the convocation of the Estates-General in 1789. In the financial sense, the origins of the French Revolution go back to Louis XIV.

Finances, however, were not the whole story. Had the French state been sound in 1789, the financial system might simply have been reformed and the monarchy restored to strength. The crisis in France went much deeper. The whole constitution of the state was in question. Several important flaws of absolutism had become apparent under Louis XIV, primary of which was that of the misuse of power. Except for his megalomania and pursuit of *la gloire,* however, Louis was a competent and hard-working executive. His successors, Louis XV and Louis XVI, were not. Louis XV was a poorly educated, rather dull fellow who ultimately found his goal in life to be the care and feeding of a series of royal mistresses. One of them, Madame de Pompadour, had the intelligence and political ambition that Louis lacked and took advantage of her position to exercise both. For some twenty years she was the most important politician in France. Her successor, Madame du Barry, inherited Madame de Pompadour's power without the latter's intellectual attributes. Madame du Barry had received only a rudimentary education, having plied the trade of prostitute in Paris before her elevation to royal mistress, and she was incompetent to succeed Madame de Pompadour, at least politically.

Louis XVI was virtuous but uninterested in governing. His twin passions were hunting and the mechanisms of locks. The entry in his diary for July 14, 1789, when the Bastille fell, was *"rien"* (nothing), referring to the fact that his hunting had been unsuccessful.

The reigns of Louis XV and Louis XVI could not help but raise some political questions. They might be no more general than whether France could afford such royal incompetents at a critical time in its history—a position taken by the Duke of Orleans, for example, who had royal ambitions. This was not to question the monarchy, only the monarchs. Others went further in their criticism. Did not the experience of Louis XIV, XV, and XVI indicate that no monarch could be trusted with absolute power? And if this were the case, with whom should power be shared? In 1788 there were a number of candidates for political participation in the French state. The nobles, of course, could and did argue that they had traditionally shared power with the king and had in ages past prevented the abuses of absolutism from appearing. By 1788, however, another group was eager for political action. The bourgeoisie had grown in wealth and numbers in the eighteenth century. Its members were educated, competent, and ambitious. They had read the philosophes, whose abstract theories they felt competent to translate into concrete realities. As men of affairs, who were better suited to steer the French ship of state through the financial shoals than they?

Nobility and bourgeoisie made up but a small fraction of the French people. The majority were peasants and artisans. What of them? Did they read Voltaire, Montesquieu, and Rousseau? Did they dream of political power? What were their grievances and what did they expect from the government? Fortunately, we have sources that permit us to evaluate the aspirations of this great mass of the French people on the eve of the French Revolution. By royal decree, every parish and corporate group in France was to compose a *cahier des doléances* (notebook of grievances) in which the people could spell out the evils that afflicted them.

There is no doubt that the woes of France in 1789 were many and grievous. Nor can there be any doubt that reform was necessary. What is puzzling is the reasons for the transformation of cries for reform into cries for revolution. For many, if not most, Frenchmen the old regime became intolerable, and it is the historian's task to try to discover who found it so, for what reasons, and how this discontent was channeled into politically effective action. Could the Revolution have succeeded without the energies produced by the frustrated masses demanding bread? Could it have succeeded without the ambitions of the middle class, who saw the road to power open before it? Finally, could the Revolution have been successful without the theories of the philosophes, which provided the only chart for those who wished to embark upon the uncertain seas of rebellion? And in any case, were these frustrations, ambitions, and theories sufficient to cause the Revolution? We are left with the fundamental question: Why do men revolt against their legal government when they know that the price of failure is their very lives?

1
MAN AND THE STATE IN THE AGE OF REASON

Charles de Secondat, Baron de Montesquieu (1689–1755), was one of the keenest political analysts of the eighteenth century. His most influential work was *The Spirit of the Laws*.

FROM The Spirit of the Laws BY BARON DE MONTESQUIEU

OF THE LAWS WHICH ESTABLISH POLITICAL LIBERTY, WITH REGARD TO THE CONSTITUTION

A General Idea

I make a distinction between the laws that establish political liberty, as it relates to the constitution, and those by which it is established, as it relates to the citizen. . . .

Different Significations of the Word, Liberty

There is no word that admits of more various significations, and has made more different impressions on the human mind, than that of *liberty*. Some have taken it for a facility of deposing a person on whom they had conferred a tyrannical authority: others, for the power of choosing a superior whom they are obliged to obey: others, for the right of bearing arms, and of being

---

The Complete Works of M. de Montesquieu, translated from the French in Four Volumes, I (1778), 195–212.

thereby enabled to use violence: others, in fine, for the privilege of being governed by a native of their own country, or by their own laws. A certain nation, for a long time, thought liberty consisted in the privilege of wearing a long beard. Some have annexed this name to one form of government exclusive of others: those who had a republican taste applied it to this species of polity: those who liked a monarchical state gave it to monarchy. Thus they have all applied the name of *liberty* to the government most suitable to their own customs and inclinations; and as, in republics, the people have not so constant and so present a view of the causes of their misery, and as the magistrates seem to act only in conformity to the laws, hence liberty is generally said to reside in republics, and to be banished from monarchies. In fine, as in democracies the people seem to act almost as they please, this sort of government has been deemed the most free, and the power of the people has been confounded with their liberty.

In What Liberty Consists

It is true that, in democracies, the people seem to act as they please; but political liberty does not consist in an unlimited freedom. In governments, that is, in societies directed by laws, liberty can consist only in the power of doing what we ought to will, and in not being constrained to do what we ought not to will.

We must have continually present to our minds the difference between independence and liberty. Liberty is a right of doing whatever the laws permit; and, if a citizen could do what they forbid, he would be no longer possessed of liberty, because all his fellow-citizens would have the same power.

The Same Subject Continued

Democratic and aristocratic states are not in their own nature free. Political liberty is to be found only in moderate governments; and even in these it is not always found. It is there only when there is no abuse of power: but constant experience shews us that every man invested with power is apt to abuse it, and to carry his authority as far as it will go. Is it not strange, though true, to say, that virtue itself has need of limits?

To prevent this abuse, it is necessary, from the very nature of things, power should be a check to power. A government may be so constituted, as, no man shall be compelled to do things to which the law does not oblige him, nor forced to abstain from things which the law permits.

Of the End or View of Different Governments

Though all governments have the same general end, which is that of preservation, yet each has another particular object. Increase of dominion was the object of Rome; war, that of Sparta; religion, that of the Jewish laws; commerce, that of Marseilles; public tranquility, that of the laws of China; navigation, that of the laws of Rhodes; natural liberty, that of the policy of the savages; in general, the pleasure of the prince, that of despotic states; that of monarchies, the prince's and the kingdom's glory: the independence of individuals is the end aimed at by the laws of Poland; from thence results the oppression of the whole.

One nation there is also in the world, that has, for the direct end of its constitution, political liberty. We shall presently examine the principles on which this liberty is founded: if they are sound, liberty will appear in its highest perfection.

To discover political liberty in a constitution, no great labour is requisite. If we are capable of seeing it where it exists, it is soon found, and we need not go far in search of it.

Of the Constitution of England

In every government there are three sorts of power; the legislative; the executive in respect to things dependent on the law of nations; and the executive in regard to matters that depend on the civil law.

By virtue of the first, the prince or magistrate enacts temporary or perpetual laws, and amends or abrogates those that have been already enacted. By the second, he makes peace or war, sends or receives embassies, establishes the public security, and provides against invasions. By the third, he punishes criminals, or determines the disputes that arise between individuals. The latter we shall call the judiciary power, and the other, simply, the executive power of the state.

The political liberty of the subject is a tranquility of mind arising from the opinion each person has of his safety. In order to have this liberty, it is requisite the government be so constituted as one man need not be afraid of another.

When the legislative and executive powers are united in the same person, or in the same body of magistrates, there can be no liberty; because apprehensions may arise, lest the same monarch or senate should enact tyrannical laws, to execute them in a tyrannical manner.

Again, there is no liberty if the judiciary power be not separated from the legislative and executive. Were it joined with the legislative, the life and liberty of the subject would be exposed to arbitrary controul; for the judge would be then the legislator. Were it joined to the executive power, the judge might behave with violence and oppression.

There would be an end of every thing, were the same man, or the same body, whether of the nobles or of the people, to exercise those three powers, that of enacting laws, that of executing the public resolutions, and of trying the causes of individuals.

Most kingdoms in Europe enjoy a moderate government, because the prince, who is invested with the two first powers, leaves the third to his subjects.

In Turkey, where these three powers are united in the sultan's person, the subjects groan under the most dreadful oppression.

In the republics of Italy, where these three powers are united, there is less liberty than in our monarchies. Hence their government is obliged to have recourse to as violent methods, for its support, as even that of the Turks; witness the state-inquisitors, and the lion's mouth into which every informer may at all hours throw his written accusation.

In what a situation must the poor subject be, under those republics! The same body of magistrates are possessed, as executors of the laws, of the whole power they have given themselves in quality of legislators. They may plunder the state by their general determinations; and, as they have likewise the judiciary power in their hands, every private citizen may be ruined by their particular decisions.

The whole power is here united in one body; and, though there is no external pomp that indicates a despotic sway, yet the people feel the effects of it every moment.

Hence it is that many of the princes of Europe, whose aim has been levelled at arbitrary power, have constantly set out with uniting, in their **own** persons, all the branches of magistracy, and all the great offices of state.

I allow, indeed, that the mere hereditary aristocracy of the Italian republics does not exactly answer to the despotic power of the Eastern princes. The number of magistrates sometimes moderates the power of the magistracy; the whole body of the nobles do not always concur in the same design; and different tribunals are erected, that temper each other. Thus, at Venice, the legislative power is in the *council,* the executive in the *pregadi,* and the judiciary in the *quarantia.* But the mischief is, that these different tribunals are composed of magistrates all belonging to the same body; which constitutes almost one and the same power.

The judiciary power ought not to be given to a standing senate; it should be exercised by persons taken from the body of the people, at certain times of the year, and consistently with a form and manner prescribed by law, in order to erect a tribunal that should last only so long as necessity requires.

By this method, the judicial power, so terrible to mankind, not being annexed to any particular state or profession, becomes, as it were, invisible. People have not then the judges continually present to their view; they fear the office, but not the magistrate.

In accusations of a deep and criminal nature, it is proper the person accused should have the privilege of choosing, in some measure, his judges, in concurrence with the law; or, at least, he should have a right to except against so great a number, that the remaining part may be deemed his own choice.

The other two powers may be given rather to magistrates or permanent bodies, because they are not exercised on any private subject; one being no more than the general will of the state, and the other the execution of that general will.

But, though the tribunals ought not to be fixt, the judgements ought; and to such a degree, as to be ever conformable to the letter of the law. Were they to be the private opinion of the judge, people would then live in society without exactly knowing the nature of their obligations.

The judges ought likewise to be of the same rank as the accused, or, in other words, his peers; to the end, that he may not imagine he is fallen into the hands of persons inclined to treat him with rigour.

If the legislature leaves the executive power in possession of a right to imprison those subjects who can give security for their good behaviour, there is an end of liberty; unless they are taken up in order to answer, without delay, to a capital crime; in which case they are really free, being subject only to the power of the law.

But, should the legislature think itself in danger, by some secret conspiracy against the state, or by a correspondence with a foreign enemy, it might authorize the executive power, for a short and limited time, to imprison suspected persons, who, in that case, would lose their liberty only for a while, to preserve it for ever.

And this is the only reasonable method that can be substituted to the tyrannical magistracy of the *Ephori,* and to the *state inquisitors* of Venice, who are also despotical.

As, in a country of liberty, every man who is supposed a free agent ought to be his own governor, the legislative power should reside in the whole body of the people. But, since this is impossible in large states, and in small ones is subject to many inconveniences, it is fit the people should transact by their representatives what they cannot transact by themselves.

The inhabitants of a particular town are much better acquainted with its wants and interests than with those of other places; and are better judges of the capacity of their neighbours than of that of the rest of their countrymen. The members, therefore, of the legislature should not be chosen from the general body of the nation; but it is proper, that, in every considerable place, a representative should be elected by the inhabitants.

The great advantage of representatives is their capacity of discussing public affairs. For this, the people collectively are extremely unfit, which is one of the chief inconveniences of a democracy.

* * *

When the deputies, as Mr. Sidney well observes, represent a body of people, as in Holland, they ought to be accountable to their constituents; but it is a different thing in England, where they are deputed by boroughs.

All the inhabitants of the several districts ought to have a right of voting at the election of a representative, except such as are in so mean a situation as to be deemed to have no will of their own.

* * *

Neither ought the representative body to be chosen for the executive part of government, for which it is not so fit; but for the enacting of laws, or to see whether the laws in being are duly executed; a thing suited to their abilities, and which none indeed but themselves can properly perform.

In such a state, there are always persons distinguished by their birth, riches, or honours: but, were they to be confounded with the common people, and to have only the weight of a single vote, like the rest, the common liberty would be their slavery, and they would have no interest in supporting it, as most of the popular resolutions would be against them. The share they have, therefore, in the legislature ought to be proportioned to their other advantages in the state; which happens only when they form a body that has a right to check the licentiousness of the people, as the people have a right to oppose any encroachment of theirs.

The legislative power is, therefore, committed to the body of the nobles, and to that which represents the people; each having their assemblies and deliberations apart, each their separate views and interests.

Of the three powers abovementioned, the judiciary is, in some measure, next to nothing: there remain, therefore, only two: and, as these have need of a regulating power to moderate them, the part of the legislative body composed of the nobility is extremely proper for this purpose.

The body of the nobility ought to be hereditary. In the first place, it is so in its own nature; and, in the next, there must be a considerable interest to preserve its privileges; privileges that, in themselves, are obnoxious to popular envy, and of course, in a free state, are always in danger.

But, as an hereditary power might be tempted to pursue its own particular interests, and forget those of the people, it is proper, that, where a singular advantage may be gained by corrupting the nobility, as in the laws relating to the supplies, they should have no other share in the legislation than the power of rejecting, and not that of resolving.

By the *power of resolving* I mean the right of ordaining by their own authority, or of amending what has been ordained by others. By the *power of rejecting,* I would be understood to mean the right of annulling a resolution taken by another, which was the power of the tribunes at Rome. And, though the person possessed of the privilege of rejecting may likewise have the right of approving, yet this approbation passes for no more than a declaration that he intends to make no use of his privilege of rejecting, and is derived from that very privilege.

The executive power ought to be in the hands of a monarch, because this branch of government, having need of dispatch, is better administered by one than by many: on the other hand, whatever depends on the legislative power, is oftentimes better regulated by many than by a single person.

But, if there were no monarch, and the executive power should be committed to a certain number of persons, selected from the legislative body, there would be an end of liberty, by reason the two powers would be united; as the same persons would sometimes possess, and would be always able to possess, a share in both.

Were the legislative body to be a considerable time without meeting, this would likewise put an end to liberty. For, of two things, one would naturally follow: either that there would be no longer any legislative resolutions, and then the state would fall into anarchy; or that these resolutions would be taken by the executive power, which would render it absolute.

* * *

The legislative body should not meet of itself. For a body is supposed to have no will but when it is met: and besides, were it not to meet unanimously, it would be impossible to determine which was really the legislative body, the part assembled, or the other. And if it had a right to prorogue itself, it might happen never to be prorogued; which would be extremely dangerous, in case it should ever attempt to encroach on the executive power. Besides, there are seasons (some more proper than others) for assembling the legislative body: it is fit, therefore, that the executive power should regulate the time of meeting, as well as the duration, of those assemblies, according to the circumstances and exigences of a state, known to itself.

Were the executive power not to have a right of restraining the encroachments of the legislative body, the latter would become despotic: for, as it might arrogate to itself what authority it pleased, it would soon destroy all the other powers.

But it is not proper, on the other hand, that the legislative power should have a right to stay the executive. For, as the execution has its natural limits, it is useless to confine it: besides, the executive power is generally employed in momentary operations.

* * *

Here, then, is the fundamental constitution of the government we are treating of. The legislative body being composed of two parts, they check one another by the mutual privilege of rejecting. They are both restrained by the executive power, as the executive is by the legislative.

These three powers should naturally form a state of repose or inaction: but, as there is a necessity for movement in the course of human affairs, they are forced to move, but still in concert.

As the executive power has no other part in the legislative than the privilege of rejecting, it can have no share in the public debates. It is not even necessary that it should propose; because, as it may always disapprove of the resolutions that shall be taken, it may likewise reject the decisions on those proposals which were made against its will.

* * *

Were the executive power to determine the raising of public money other-wise than by giving its consent, liberty would be at an end; because it would become legislative in the most important point of legislation.

If the legislative power were to settle the subsidies, not from year to year, but for ever, it would run the risk of losing its liberty, because the executive power would be no longer dependent; and, when once it was possessed of such a perpetual right, it would be a matter of indifference whether it held it of itself or of another. The same may be said if it should come to a resolution of intrusting, not an annual, but a perpetual, command of the fleets and ar-mies to the executive power.

To prevent the executive power from being able to oppress, it is requisite that the armies with which it is intrusted should consist of the people, and have the same spirit as the people, as was the case at Rome till the time of *Marius*. To obtain this end, there are only two ways; either that the persons employed in the army should have sufficient property to answer for their conduct to their fellow-subjects, and be enlisted only for a year, as was cus-tomary at Rome; or, if there should be a standing-army composed chiefly of the most despicable part of the nation, the legislative power should have a right to disband them as soon as it pleased; the soldiers should live in com-mon with the rest of the people; and no separate camp, barracks, or fortress should be suffered.

Of the Monarchies We Are Acquainted With

The monarchies we are acquainted with have not, like that we have been speaking of, liberty for their direct view: the only aim is the glory of the subject, of the state, and of the sovereign. But from hence there results a spirit of liberty, which, in those states, is capable of achieving as great things, and of contributing as much, perhaps, to happiness, as liberty itself.

Here the three powers are not distributed and founded on the model of the constitution abovementioned: they have each a particular distribution, ac-cording to which they border more or less on political liberty; and, if they did not border upon it, monarchy would degenerate into despotic government.

As the French Revolution developed, increasing attention was given to the ideas of Jean Jacques Rousseau (1712–1778). It soon became possible to claim Rousseau as the most important philosophical instigator of the Revolution. Robespierre himself was proud to be known as a disciple. Some of Rousseau's most important ideas are to be found in his essay on the social contract.

FROM An Inquiry into the Nature of the Social Contract
BY J. J. ROUSSEAU

OF THE SOCIAL COMPACT

We will suppose that men in a state of nature are arrived at that crisis, when the strength of each individual is insufficient to defend him from the attacks he is subject to. This primitive state can therefore subsist no longer; and the human race must perish, unless they change their manner of life.

As men cannot create for themselves new forces, but merely unite and direct those which already exist, the only means they can employ for their preservation is to form by aggregation an assemblage of forces that may be able to resist all assaults, be put in motion as one body, and act in concert upon all occasions.

This assemblage of forces must be produced by the concurrence of many: and as the force and the liberty of a man are the chief instruments of his preservation, how can he engage them without danger, and without neglecting the care which is due to himself? This doubt, which leads directly to my subject, may be expressed in these words:

"Where shall we find a form of association which will defend and protect with the whole aggregate force the person and the property of each individual; and by which every person, while united with ALL, shall obey only HIMSELF, and remain as free as before the union?" Such is the fundamental problem, of which the Social Contract gives the solution.

The articles of this contract are so unalterably fixed by the nature of the act, that the least modification renders them vain and of no effect. They are the same everywhere, and are everywhere understood and admitted, even though they may never have been formally announced: so that, when once the social pact is violated in any instance, all the obligations it created cease; and each

An Inquiry into the Nature of the Social Contract; or Principles of Political Right, translated from the French of John James Rousseau (1971), pp. 33–49.

individual is restored to his original rights, and resumes his native liberty, as the consequence of losing that conventional liberty for which he exchanged them.

All the articles of the social contract will, when clearly understood, be found reducible to this single point—THE TOTAL ALIENATION OF EACH ASSOCIATE, AND ALL HIS RIGHTS, TO THE WHOLE COMMUNITY. For every individual gives himself up entirely—the condition of every person is alike; and being so, it would not be the interest of anyone to render himself offensive to others.

Nay, more than this—the alienation is made without any reserve; the union is as complete as it can be, and no associate has a claim to anything: for if any individual was to retain rights not enjoyed in general by all, as there would be no common superior to decide between him and the public, each person being in some points his own proper judge, would soon pretend to be so in everything; and thus would the state of nature be revived, and the association become tyrannical or be annihilated.

In fine, each person gives himself to ALL, but not to any INDIVIDUAL: and as there is no one associate over whom the same right is not acquired which is ceded to him by others, each gains an equivalent for what he loses, and finds his force increased for preserving that which he possesses.

If, therefore, we exclude from the social compact all that is not essentially necessary, we shall find it reduced to the following terms:

"We each of us place, in common, his person, and all his power, under the supreme direction of the general will; and we receive into the body each member as an indivisible part of the whole."

From that moment, instead of so many separate persons as there are contractors, this act of association produces a moral collective body, composed of as many members as there are voices in the assembly; which from this act receives its unity, its common self, its life, and its will. This public person, which is thus formed by the union of all the private persons, took formerly the name of *city,* and now takes that of *republic* or *body politic.* It is called by its members *state* when it is passive, and *sovereign* when in activity: and whenever it is spoken of with other bodies of a similar kind, it is denominated *power.* The associates take collectively the name of *people,* and separately that of *citizens,* as participating in the sovereign authority: they are also styled *subjects,* because they are subjected to the laws. But these terms are frequently confounded, and used one for the other; and a man must understand them well to distinguish when they are properly employed.

OF THE SOVEREIGN POWER

It appears from this form that the act of association contains a reciprocal engagement between the public and individuals; and that each individual contracting as it were with himself, is engaged under a double character; that is, as a part of the *sovereign power* engaging with individuals, and as a member of the *state* entering into a compact with the *sovereign power*. But we cannot apply here the maxim of civil right, that no person is bound by any engagement which he makes with himself; for there is a material difference between an obligation contracted towards *one's self* individually, and towards a collective body of which *one's self* constitutes a part.

It is necessary to observe here that the will of the public, expressed by a majority of votes—which can enforce obedience from the subjects to the sovereign power in consequence of the double character under which the members of that body appear—cannot bind the sovereign power to itself; and that it is against the nature of the body politic for the sovereign power to impose any one law which it cannot alter. Were they to consider themselves as acting under one character only, they would be in the situation of individuals forming each a contract with himself: but this is not the case; and therefore there can be no fundamental obligatory law established for the body of the people, not even the social contract. But this is of little moment, as that body could not very well engage itself to others in any manner which would not derogate from the contract. With respect to foreigners, it becomes a single being, an individual only.

But the body politic, or sovereign power, which derives its existence from the sacredness of the contract, can never bind itself, even towards others, in any thing that would derogate from the original act; such as alienating any portion of itself, or submitting to another sovereign: for by violating the contract its own existence would be at once annihilated; and by nothing nothing can be performed.

As soon as the multitude is thus united in one body, you cannot offend one of its members without attacking the whole; much less can you offend the whole without incurring the resentment of all the members. Thus duty and interest equally oblige the two contracting parties to lend their mutual aid to each other; and the same men must endeavour to unite under this double character all the advantages which attend it.

The sovereign power being formed only of the individuals which compose it, neither has, or can have, any interest contrary to theirs; consequently the sovereign power requires no guarantee towards its subjects, because it is impossible that the body should seek to injure all its members: and we shall see presently that it can do no injury to any individual. The sovereign power by its nature must, while it exists, be everything it ought to be: but it is not so with subjects towards the sovereign power; to which, notwithstanding the common interest subsisting between them, there is nothing to answer for the performance of their engagements, if some means is not found of ensuring their fidelity.

In fact, each individual may, as a man, have a private will, dissimilar or contrary to the general will which he has as a citizen. His own particular interest may dictate to him very differently from the common interest; his mind, naturally and absolutely independent, may regard what he owes to the common cause as a gratuitous contribution, the omission of which would be less injurious to others than the payment would be burthensome to himself; and considering the moral person which constitutes the state as a creature of the imagination, because it is. not a man, he may wish to enjoy the rights of a citizen, without being disposed to fulfil the duties of a subject: an injustice which would in its progress cause the ruin of the body politic.

In order therefore to prevent the social compact from becoming a vain form, it tacitly comprehends this engagement, which alone can give effect to the others—That whoever refuses to obey the general will, shall be compelled to it by the whole body, which is in fact only forcing him to be free; for this is the condition which guarantees his absolute personal independence to every citizen of the country: a condition which gives motion and effect to the political machine; which alone renders all civil engagements legal; and without which they would be absurd, tyrannical, and subject to the most enormous abuses.

OF THE CIVIL STATE

The passing from a state of nature to a civil state, produces in man a very remarkable change, by substituting justice for instinct, and giving to his actions a moral character which they wanted before.

It is at the moment of that transition that the voice of duty succeeds to physical impulse; and a sense of what is right, to the incitements of appetite. The man who had till then regarded none but himself, perceives that he must act on other principles, and learns to consult his reason before he listens to his propensities.

2
CONDITIONS OF LIFE ON THE EVE OF THE REVOLUTION

Arthur Young (1741–1820) was a wealthy English farmer whose passion was the study of agriculture. In 1787 he set out to see how England's neighbor, France, conducted farming operations. His descriptions of various parts of France provide a vivid picture of the peasant's standard of living in the years immediately preceding the Revolution.

FROM Travels in France During the Years 1787, 1788, 1789
BY ARTHUR YOUNG

Poverty and poor crops to Amiens; women are now ploughing with a pair of horses to sow barley. The difference of the customs of the two nations is in nothing more striking than in the labours of the sex; in England, it is very little that they will do in the fields except to glean and make hay; the first is a party of pilfering, and the second of pleasure: in France, they plough and fill the dung cart. . . .

* * *

To La Ferté Lowendahl, a dead flat of hungry sandy gravel, with much heath. The poor people, who cultivate the soil here, are *métayers,* that is, men who hire the land without ability to stock it; the proprietor is forced to pro-

Arthur Young, *Travels in France During the Years 1787, 1788, 1789* (1889), pp. 8–9, 19, 27, 61, 123, 125, 189, 198, 201.

vide cattle and seed, and he and his tenant divide the produce; a miserable system, that perpetuates poverty and excludes instruction. . . .

* * *

The same wretched country continues to La Loge; the fields are scenes of pitiable management, as the houses are of misery. Yet all this country is highly improveable, if they knew what to do with it: the property, perhaps, of some of those glittering beings, who figured in the procession the other day at Versailles. Heaven grant me patience while I see a country thus neglected—and forgive me the oaths I swear at the absence and ignorance of the possessors. . . .

Pass Payrac, and meet many beggars, which we had not done before. All the country, girls and women, are without shoes or stockings; and the ploughmen at their work have neither sabots nor feet to their stockings. This is a poverty, that strikes at the root of national prosperity; a large consumption among the poor being of more consequence than among the rich; the wealth of a nation lies in its circulation and consumption; and the case of poor people abstaining from the use of manufacturers of leather and wool ought to be considered as an evil of the first magnitude. It reminded me of the misery of Ireland. .

* * *

Take the road to Moneng, and come presently to a scene which was so new to me in France, that I could hardly believe my own eyes. A succession of many well built, tight, and COMFORTABLE farming cottages, built of stone, and covered with tiles; each having its little garden, inclosed by clipt thorn hedges, with plenty of peach and other fruit-trees, some fine oaks scattered in the hedges, and young trees nursed up with so much care, that nothing but the fostering attention of the owner could effect any thing like it. To every house belongs a farm, perfectly well inclosed, with grass borders mown and neatly kept around the corn fields, with gates to pass from one inclosure to another. The men are all dressed with red caps, like the highlanders of Scotland. There are some parts of England (where small yeomen still remain) that resemble this country of Bearne; but we have very little that is equal to what I have seen in this ride of twelve miles from Pau to Moneng. It is all in the hands of little proprietors, without the farms being so small as to occasion a vicious and miserable population. An air of neatness, warmth, and comfort breathes over the whole. It is visible in their new built houses and stables; in their little gardens; in their hedges; in the courts before their doors; even in the coops for their poultry, and the sties for their hogs. A peasant does not think of rendering his pig comfortable, if his own happiness hangs by the thread of a nine years lease. We are now in Bearne, within a few miles of the cradle of Henry IV. Do they inherit these blessings from that good prince? The benignant genius of that good monarch, seems to reign still over the country; each peasant has *the fowl in the pot.*

* * *

September 1st. To Combourg, the country has a savage aspect; husbandry not much further advanced, at least in skill, than among the Hurons, which appears incredible amidst inclosures; the people almost as wild as their country, and their town of Combourg one of the most brutal filthy places that can be seen; mud houses, no windows, and a pavement so broken, as to impede all passengers, but ease none—yet here is a château, and inhabited; who is this Mons. de Chateaubriant, the owner that has nerves strung for a residence amidst such filth and poverty? Below this hideous heap of wretchedness is a fine lake, surrounded by well wooded inclosures. . . .

* * *

1788

To Montauban. The poor people seem poor indeed; the children terribly ragged, if possible worse clad than if with no cloaths at all; as to shoes and stockings they are luxuries. A beautiful girl of six or seven years playing with a stick, and smiling under such a bundle of rags as made my heart ache to see her: they did not beg and when I gave them any thing seemed more surprized than obliged. One third of what I have seen of this province seems uncultivated, and nearly all of it in misery. What have kings, and ministers, and parliaments, and states, to answer for their prejudices, seeing millions of hands that would be industrious, idle and starving, through the execrable maxims of despotism, or the equally detestable prejudices of a feudal nobility. . . .

* * *

1789

The 12th. Walking up a long hill, to ease my mare, I was joined by a poor woman, who complained of the times, and that it was a sad country; demanding her reasons, she said her husband had but a morsel of land, one cow, and a poor little horse, yet they had a *franchar* (42 lb.) of wheat, and three chickens, to pay as a quit-rent to one Seigneur; and four *franchar* of oats, one chicken and 1 £. to pay to another, besides very heavy tailles and other taxes. She had seven children, and the cow's milk helped to make the soup. But why, instead of a horse, do not you keep another cow? Oh, her husband could not carry his produce so well without a horse; and asses are little used in the country. It was said, at present, that *something was to be done by some great folks for such poor ones, but she did not know who nor how,* but God send us better, *car les tailles & les droits nous écrasent.*—This woman, at no great distance, might have been taken for sixty or seventy, her figure was so bent, and her face so furrowed and hardened by labour,—but she said she was only twenty-eight. An Englishman who has not travelled cannot imagine the figure made by infinitely the greater part of the country women in France; it speaks, at the first sight, hard and severe labour: I am inclined to think, that they work harder than the men, and this, united with the more miserable labour of bringing a new race of slaves into the world, destroys absolutely all symmetry of person and every feminine appearance. To what are we to attribute this difference in the manners of the lower people in the two kingdoms? To GOVERNMENT. . . .

* * *

Nangis is near enough to Paris for *the people* to be politicians; the per-ruquier that dressed me this morning tells me, that every body is determined to pay no taxes, should the National Assembly so ordain. But the soldiers will have something to say. No, Sir, never:—be assured as we are, that the French soldiers will never fire on the people: but, if they should, it is better to be shot than starved. He gave me a frightful account of the misery of the people; whole families in the utmost distress; those that work have a pay insufficient to feed them—and many that find it difficult to get work at all. I enquired of Mons. de Guerchy concerning this, and found it true. By order of the magistrates no person is allowed to buy more than two bushels of wheat at a market, to prevent monopolizing. It is clear to common sense, that all such regulations have a direct tendency to increase the evil, but it is in vain to reason with people whose ideas are immovably fixed. Being here on a market-day, I attended, and saw the wheat sold out under this regulation, with a party of dragoons drawn up before the market-cross to prevent violence. The people quarrel with the bakers, asserting the prices they demand for bread are beyond the proportion of wheat, and proceeding from words to scuffling, raise a riot, and then run away with bread and wheat for nothing: this has happened at Nangis, and many other markets; the consequence was, that neither farmers nor bakers would supply them till they were in danger of starving, and, when they did come, prices under such circumstances must necessarily rise enormously, which aggravated the mischief, till troops became really necessary to give security to those who supplied the markets. . . .

* * *

Letters from Paris! all confusion! the ministry removed: Mons. Necker ordered to quit the kingdom without noise. The effect on the people of Nancy was considerable.—I was with Mons. Willemet when his letters arrived, and for some time his house was full of enquires; all agreed, that it was fatal news, and that it would occasion great commotions. *What will be the result at Nancy?* The answer was in effect the same from all I put this question to: *We are a provincial town, we must wait to see what is done at Paris;*

*but every thing is to be feared from the people, because bread is so dear, they
are half starved, and are consequently ready for commotion.*—This is the
general feeling; they are as nearly concerned as Paris; but they dare not stir;
they dare not even have an opinion of their own till they know what Paris
thinks; so that if a starving populace were not in question, no one would
dream of moving. This confirms what I have often heard remarked, that the
deficit would not have produced the revolution but in concurrence with the
price of bread. Does not this shew the infinite consequence of great cities to
the liberty of mankind? Without Paris, I question whether the present revolution, which is fast working in France, could possibly have had an origin.

The peasant was not always as miserable as he seemed.

FROM The Confessions of Jean Jacques Rousseau

One day, amongst others, having purposely turned out of my way to get a
nearer view of a spot which appeared worthy of admiration, I was so delighted with it, and went round it so often that, at last, I completely lost
myself. After several hours of useless walking, tired, and dying of hunger and
thirst, I entered a peasant's hut, not much to look at, but the only dwelling I
saw in the neighbourhood. I expected to find it the same as in Geneva, or
Switzerland, where all the well-to-do inhabitants are in a position to show
hospitality. I begged him to give me dinner, and offered to pay for it. He
offered me some skimmed milk and coarse barley bread, saying that that was
all he had. I drank the milk with delight, and ate the bread, husks and all;
but it was not very invigorating fare for a man exhausted by fatigue. The
peasant, who examined me closely, estimated the truth of my story by my
appetite, and immediately afterwards declared that he could see that I was a
good and honourable young man, who had not come there to betray him for
money. He opened a little trapdoor near the kitchen, went down, and came
up a minute afterwards with a nice brown wheaten loaf, a very tempting-
looking ham, although considerably cut down, and a bottle of wine, the sight
of which rejoiced my heart more than all the rest; to this he added a substantial omelette, and I made a dinner such as none but a pedestrian ever enjoyed.
When it came to the question of payment, his uneasiness and alarm returned;
he would take none of my money, and refused it with singular anxiety; and
the amusing thing was that I could not imagine what he was afraid of. At

---

The Confessions of Jean Jacques Rousseau (Modern Library ed., n.d.), pp. 169–170.

last, with a shudder, he uttered the terrible words, "Revenue officers and excisemen." He gave me to understand that he hid his wine on account of the excise, that he hid his bread on account of the tax, and that he was a lost man, if anyone had a suspicion that he was not starving. All that he said to me on this subject, of which I had not the least idea, made an impression upon me which will never be forgotten. It was the germ of the inextinguishable hatred which subsequently grew up in my heart against the oppression to which these unhappy people are subject, and against their oppressors. This man, although in good circumstances, did not dare to eat the bread which he had obtained by the sweat of his brow, and could only escape utter ruin by displaying the same poverty as prevailed around him. I left his house, equally indignant and touched, lamenting the lot of these beautiful countries, upon which Nature has only lavished her gifts to make them the prey of barbarous farmers of taxes.

The French Revolution is unique among revolutions in that there was an extensive sampling of public opinion immediately preceding the Revolution itself. Once the decision was made to call the Estates-General, the king was prevailed upon to order the compilation of notebooks of grievances (*cahiers des doléances*) to be drawn up by the three estates (Clergy, Nobility, Third). It was the first attempt to sample "grass-roots" opinion, for literally every French subject was forced to think of the ills that afflicted France and was given the opportunity to make his views known.

The number of *cahiers* that have survived is immense. The one that follows is typical of those submitted by the Third Estate.

FROM The Notebook of Grievances of the Third Estate of the Parish of Saint-Vaast

Today, Sunday, the twenty-ninth day of March 1789, following vespers, at the sound of the church bell, in the customary way, the inhabitants of the parish of Saint-Vaast, Bailiwick of Auge, citizens of the Third-Estate, assembled according to the terms of the letters of convocation given by His Majesty at Versailles, the 24th of January 1789, for the convocation and holding of the Estates-general of the realm, and according to the ordinance of the Lieuten-

M. J. Mavidal and M. E. Laurent, *Archives parlementaires de 1787 à 1860*, Première Série, V (1879), 609–612, translated by L. Pearce Williams.

ant General of the Bailiwick of Auge at Pont-l'Evêque, dated the 16th of this month and announced in the pulpit of this parish on Sunday the 22nd of this month, and affixed to the main door of the Church on the same day, to the effect that they should confer among themselves and proceed to the writing of their notebook of grievances, complaints and remonstrances, means and advice that they wish to propose to the general assembly of the nation:

Begin, by assuring the King that they are ready to sacrifice their fortunes and their very persons for him and for the State;

And vote unanimously that the representatives of this province, in the Assembly of the Estates-general, before consenting to any new taxes to pay the debts of the government, shall employ their efforts and their zeal to the end that there shall be drawn up a *Declaration of the Rights of the French Nation* as a charter between the King, head of the nation and sole executor of the laws, and the nation, which will include the following:

NATIONAL CONSTITUTION

1. That the King consents to a law of *habeas corpus* which will guarantee every citizen, no matter how low his condition, from ever being subjected to the abuse of *lettres de cachet* or letters of exile, as well as from the actions and the arbitrary power of ministers, of governors and of intendants of provinces exercised through sealed letters.

2. That only the nation has the right to tax itself, that is to say, to accede to or refuse taxes, to regulate their size, their use, their assessment and their scope; the nation can also ask for an account and must be consulted before loans are made. Any other means of taxation or of borrowing are declared unconstitutional, illegal and of no force.

3. That the periodical and regular reconvening of the Estates-general be set for every four years, at a specific time of the year, so that the nation can there consider the state of the realm, the use of taxes granted in the previous session in order to decide whether to continue or suppress them, and to propose, besides, reforms and other helps for all branches of the political economy.

4. That in the case (unhappily too frequent) where, by the intrigues of an ambitious minister intent upon administering everything according to his caprice, the lines of communication between the nation and its king are broken so that the convocation of the Estates-general does not take place as provided for in the *national charter,* the particular Estates of this province (of which more later) shall be authorized to oppose the levy of all taxes, and the parlements shall be authorized to publish their opposition by an ordinance which shall be sent to all lesser tribunals in their circuit and which will permit the public authorities to prosecute those who continue to collect them for malfeasance of office.

5. That all taxes on real and personal property shall be levied equally on all the goods of ecclesiastics, nobles and commoners, on perpetual rents and those

of recent creation, and that all privileges which are really subsidies shall be wiped out.

6. That the Third-Estate, greatly superior in number to the two other orders, in order that it may be judged at least in part by its peers, as it was in the old exchequer court, will have, in the parlement of this undivided and indivisible province, forty magistrates drawn from this Estate; reason and experience have shown that the laws which guarantee the property, the liberty and the rights of the Third-Estate from the attacks and pretensions of the clergy and the nobility are illusory, useless and poorly obeyed so long as the maintenance and execution of justice rest in the hands of the two first orders to the exclusion of the third.

These representatives of the Third-Estate, presented to the King by the province and armed by the King with their powers, will be chosen among those of his subjects who have shown proof of their capacity by their study of the law and in the exercise of their talents at the bar, during ten years, either before the parlement or before other, lesser, courts. But, they shall cease to be the representatives of the Third-Estate, and their mandate shall become null and void if and when they are ennobled, no matter by what means.

*   *   *

The small income of a commoner should be no reason for exclusion from the parlement. The magistrature should not be based on the brilliance coming from opulence but on the brilliance of knowledge; this is especially true of a sense of justice which nothing can tarnish. How worthy of respect is the man who is always just!

The undersigned also vote that the representatives of this province to the Estates-general will insist that His Majesty grant, before they consent to any new taxes:

PROVINCIAL ESTATES

1. The re-establishment of the particular Estates of this province, which shall meet at Caen, center of Normandy, or elsewhere, each year, composed of a number of members of the Third-Estate equal to those of the two orders of the clergy and of the nobility together. . . .

2. *The unlimited liberty of the press,* with the requirement that the printer or the author place his name at the bottom of the printed matter so that he may be held responsible for whatever is contrary to dominant religious sentiments, or to the respect of the sovereign, public decency and the honor of citizens.

3. The destruction of all particular commissions of attribution or evocation, for whatever cause, so that no citizen can ever be transferred from out his own jurisdiction. . . .

4. Great modifications in the ordinance of 1669, called the *Hunting Code,* most of which turns free commoners into true serfs. It is contrary to human rights that a cultivator who owns his land cannot lift a finger to destroy the wild animals which devastate his harvest, which is even more destroyed by those who chase these animals with great noise and numbers. The too abundant nature of the wild game (hitherto given greater privileges than the cultivator) leads to the real destruction of property; it also is contrary to reason as well as to the principle of liberty that a peaceful inhabitant of the country, merely because he is a commoner, can be seized from the center of his family and sent to prison by order of the governor of the province, simply because he has a gun to assure his own safety and is, therefore, suspect of having killed a Lord's rabbit.

In order to reconcile the interests of the possessors of fiefs with those of the commoner vassal (who is, after all, a man), it is necessary that the representatives of the Third-Estate solicit and obtain from the sovereign a hunting law such that:

No game warden can be believed on his own word unless he produce two witnesses who will swear to the day and the hour of the crime and to the person of the criminal. . . .

* * *

That game wardens who have killed commoners who were armed or caught hunting, or without authorization in the woods, shall no longer be immune from punishment, as has been the case recently in this province, among others in four recent cases of killing by the wardens of Madame A. . . . , of Madame N. . . . , of a prelate and of a Marshal of France, and others, all residents of this province.

That the cultivator be authorized to shoot, but not to carry away, the pigeons which devastate his harvest, from July 15 to August 20, as well as during the sowing season. This is the only way to force the Lords to close their dovecotes during this short time, since the laws passed on this point are not enforced since their enforcement is in the hands of those who have an interest in perpetuating the abuse.

Madame Roland was the wife of a moderate revolutionary who served for a time as Minister of the Interior before his execution in the Terror. Madame Roland followed him to the scaffold. Her memoirs were written as she awaited execution; in them she recalls her own feelings as a young girl confronted with the pretensions of the nobility.

FROM The Private Memoirs of Madame Roland

My grandmother one day took it into her head to pay a visit to Madame de Boismorel, either for the pleasure of seeing her, or of displaying her little daughter. Great preparations in consequence; long toilet in the morning: at length behold us setting off with Aunt Angélique for the *rue Saint-Louis, au Marais,* where we arrived about noon. On entering the house every one, beginning with the *portier,* salutes Madame Phlipon with an air of respect and affection, emulous who shall treat her with the greatest civility. She repays their attention with courtesy, tinged at the same time with dignity. So far very well; but her granddaughter is perceived; and, not satisfied with pointing her out to one another, they proceed to pay her a number of compliments. . . . We go on; a tall lackey announces us, and we enter the *salon,* and find the lady seated, with her lap-dog beside her, upon what we called then, not an *ottomane,* but a *canapé,* gravely embroidering tapestry. Madame de Boismorel was about the age, the height, and the figure of my grandmother; but her dress betokened the pride of wealth, rather than taste; and her countenance, far from expressing any plebeian desire to please, plainly demanded that all attention should be bestowed upon herself, and manifested her consciousness of deserving it. . . . The rouge, spread one layer over another, lent to eyes naturally dull a much greater air of fierceness than was sufficient to make me fix mine upon the ground.

"Ah, Mademoiselle Rotisset, good morning to you," cried, in a loud and cold tone, Madame de Boismorel, as she rose to meet us. (*"Mademoiselle!"* So my grandmother is mademoiselle in this house.) "Upon my honor I am very glad to see you. And this pretty child is your granddaughter? She will make a fine woman. Come here, my dear, sit down by my side. . . . Did you never venture in the lottery?"

"Never, madame; I am not fond of gaming."

"So, so! very likely indeed! At your age children are apt to think their game is sure. . . . She is so grave too: I suppose you have a devotional turn?"

The Private Memoirs of Madame Roland (1900), pp. 121–125, 136–137, 200–205, edited, with an Introduction, by Edward Gilpin Johnson.

"I know my duty to God, and I endeavor to fulfil it."

"That is a good girl! You wish to take the veil: is it not so?"

"I do not know my future destination, and I do not seek to pry into it." . . .

The conversation next turned upon the family and friends of the mistress of the house, . . . for example of Madáme Roudé, who, notwithstanding her great age, was still absurd enough to pretend to a fine bosom, and accordingly greatly exposed this part of her person, except when she got in and out of her carriage, for which occasion she had always an immense handkerchief ready in her pocket, because, as she observed, it is not decent to make such an exhibition to the footmen. . . . I did not at this age ask myself, why my grandmother did not sit upon the *canapé,* or for what reason in particular Madame de Boismorel always called her *"Mademoiselle"* Rotisset; but I had the feeling that led to this reflection, and I saw the end of the visit with joy, as if I were just liberated from some hard confinement.

* * *

Mademoiselle d'Hannache, at that time at law for the inheritance of her uncle, "the captain," was accommodated in the house of my mother, and resided with us nearly a year and a half. During this interval I was her secretary; I wrote her letters, copied her precious genealogy, drew up the petitions she presented to the president and the attorney-general of the Parliament of Paris, the administrators of some annuities bequeathed by a M. de Saint-Vallier to females of rank in reduced circumstances, and accompanied her sometimes in her solicitations to various persons, which her affairs made necessary. I observed upon these occasions that, notwithstanding her ignorance, her illiterate language, her starched manners, her old-fashioned dress, and her other absurdities, she was treated with respect on account of her pedigree. They listened with attention to the names of her ancestors, which she never failed to enumerate, and were ready to side with her in her claims to the disputed inheritance. I could not but contrast this honorable treatment with the reception I had met with at Madame de Boismorel's, which had left a deep impression on my mind. It was impossible to conceal from myself my superiority to Mademoiselle d'Hannache, who, with all her genealogy and her forty years to boot, could not write a letter that was either legible, or dignified with a word of common sense; and I thought mankind extremely unjust, and the institutions of society extravagantly absurd.

* * *

The old Haudry, creator of the vast fortune of the family, was deceased, and had left a large estate to his son, who, born and educated in opulence, was fashioned to dissipate it. This son, who had already lost a charming wife, lived extravagantly, and, according to the custom of the rich, spent a part of the year at his château of Soucy, whither he transplanted the manners and mode of life of the town, instead of adopting those of the country. He had several neighboring estates, of which that nearest to Soucy (Fontenay), had an old mansion belonging to it that he loved to have occupied; and he had prevailed on M. and Madame Besnard to accept apartments there, in which they passed a part of the summer. This at once contributed to keep up the place, and to give that air of magnificence to his establishments, of which he was ambitious. M. and Madame Besnard were well accommodated, and enjoyed the use of the park, the wildness of which made an agreeable contrast with that of Soucy, and delighted me more than the artificial luxury, which distinguished the abode of the *fermier-général*. Soon after our arrival, Madame Besnard requested us to make a visit with her to Soucy, where the sister-in-law and stepmother of Haudry resided with him and did the honors of his house. This visit was modestly paid before dinner; and I entered, without the least feeling of pleasure, into the *salon,* where Madame Pénault and her daughter received us, with great politeness, it is true, but a politeness that savored a little of superiority. The propriety of my mother's behavior, and something too that appeared in me, in spite of that air of timidity which is produced by a feeling of our value and a doubt whether it will be appreciated by others, scarcely allowed them to exercise it. . . .

The ladies did not fail, a few days after, to return our visit. Three or four persons accompanied them, who happened to be at the château, their paying their respects to us serving merely for the termination of their walk. Upon this occasion I was more agreeable, and succeeded in infusing into my part of the reception the proportion of modest and decent politeness which reestablished the equilibrium. Madame Pénault invited us to dinner; but I was never more astonished than on learning that it was not to her own table, but to that of the servants. I was sensible, however, that, as M. Besnard had formerly been in that station, I ought not, out of respect to him, to appear averse to accompanying them; but I felt that Madame Pénault ought to have arranged things otherwise, or spared us this contemptuous civility. My aunt saw it in the same light; but, to avoid any little scene, we accepted the invitation. These inferior household deities were a new spectacle to me, for I had formed no conception of ladies'-maids personating grandeur. They were prepared to receive us; and, indeed, aped their superiors admirably well. Toilet, gesture, affectation, graces, nothing was forgotten. The cast-off dresses of their mistresses gave to the female part of the household a richness of appearance that honest tradespeople would think out of character to themselves. The caricature of *bon ton* added to their garb a sort of elegance, not less foreign to *bourgeois* simplicity than odious in the eye of an artist. In spite of all this, however, the fluency of their prate and the multiplicity of their grimaces would no doubt have inspired awe into rustics. It was still worse with the men. The sword of "M. *le maître,*" the attentions of "M. *le chef,*" the graces and fine clothes of the valets, could not cloak their *gaucheries* or the jargon they affected when they wished to seem distinguished, or their native vulgarity of speech when for a moment they forgot their assumed gentility. The conversation glittered with marquises, counts, financiers, whose titles, fortunes, and alliances shed a second-hand splendor on those who so glibly discoursed of them. The superfluities of the first table were transferred to the second with an order and despatch that made them appear as if then served for the first time, and with a profusion that sufficed to deck a third table, that of the servants—for it seems the domestics of the first grade called themselves *"officiers."* After dinner, cards were introduced: the stake was high; it was that for which these *"demoiselles"* were accustomed to play, and they played every day. I was introduced to a new world, in which were reflected the prejudices, the vices, and the follies of the great world, the value of which is not really superior, though the show be somewhat more dazzling. I had heard a thousand times of the beginnings of old Haudry, of his coming to Paris from his village, and rising by degrees to the accumulation of thousands at the expense of the public; of his marrying his daughter to Montule, his granddaughters to the Marquis du Chillau and Count Turpin, and leaving his son heir to immense treasures. I agreed with Montesquieu that financiers support the state, just as the cord supports the criminal. I judged that publicans who found means to enrich themselves to this degree, and to use their wealth as an engine by which to unite themselves with families of rank, which the policy of courts regards as essential to the glory and safety of a kingdom—I judged that characters like these could belong only to a detestable government and a depraved nation.

3
THE
IDEALS OF THE
REVOLUTION

On August 27, 1789, the National Assembly decreed the Declaration of the Rights of Man as the preamble to the constitution of France yet to be written. It was, like the American Bill of Rights, to serve as the basic definition of the goals of the Revolution.

Declaration of the Rights of Man and of the Citizen

The representatives of the French people, organized as a national assembly, believing that the ignorance, neglect or contempt of the rights of man are the sole causes of public calamities and of the corruption of governments, have determined to set forth in a solemn declaration, the natural, inalienable and sacred rights of man, in order that this declaration, being constantly before all the members of the social body, shall remind them continually of their rights and duties; in order that the acts of the legislative power, as well as those of the executive power, may be compared at any moment with the ends of all political institutions and may thus be more respected; in order that the grievances of the citizens, based hereafter upon simple and incontestable principles, shall tend to the maintenance of the constitution and redound to the happiness of all. Hence the national assembly recognizes and proclaims in the presence and under the auspices of the Supreme Being the following rights of man and of the citizen:

ARTICLE I. Men are born and remain free and equal in rights. Social distinctions can only be founded upon the general good.

J. H. Robinson, ed., "The French Revolution, 1789–91," in *Translations and Reprints from the Original Sources of European History,* I, No. 5 (1897), 6–8.

2. The aim of all political association is the preservation of the natural and imprescriptible rights of man. These rights are liberty, property, security, and resistance to oppression.

3. The principle (*principe*) of all sovereignty resides essentially in the nation. No body nor individual may exercise any authority which does not proceed directly from the nation.

4. Liberty consists in being able to do everything which injures no one else; hence the exercise of the natural rights of each man has no limits except those which assure to the other members of the society the enjoyment of the same rights. These limits can only be determined by law.

5. Law can only prohibit such actions as are hurtful to society. Nothing may be prevented which is not forbidden by law, and no one may be forced to do anything not provided for by law.

6. Law is the expression of the general will. Every citizen has a right to participate personally or through his representative in its formation. It must be the same for all, whether it protects or punishes. All citizens being equal in the eyes of the law are equally eligible to all dignities and to all public positions and occupations according to their abilities and without distinction except that of their virtues and talents.

7. No person shall be accused, arrested or imprisoned except in the cases and according to the forms prescribed by law. Any one soliciting, transmitting, executing or causing to be executed any arbitrary order shall be punished. But any citizen summoned or arrested in virtue of the law shall submit without delay as resistance constitutes an offence.

8. The law shall provide for such punishments only as are strictly and obviously necessary, and no one shall suffer punishment except it be legally inflicted in virtue of a law passed and promulgated before the commission of the offence.

9. As all persons are held innocent until they shall have been declared guilty, if arrest shall be deemed indispensable all severity not essential to the securing of the prisoner's person shall be severely repressed by law.

10. No one shall be disquieted on account of his opinions, including his religious views, provided their manifestation does not disturb the public order established by law.

11. The free communication of ideas and opinions is one of the most precious of the rights of man. Every citizen may, accordingly, speak, write and print with freedom, being responsible, however, for such abuses of this freedom as shall be defined by law.

12. The security of the rights of man and of the citizen requires public military force. These forces are, therefore, established for the good of all and not for the personal advantage of those to whom they shall be entrusted.

13. A common contribution is essential for the maintenance of the public forces and for the cost of administration. This should be equitably distributed among all the citizens in proportion to their means.

14. All the citizens have a right to decide either personally or by their representa-

tives as to the necessity of the public contribution, to grant this freely, to know to what uses it is put, and to fix the proportion, the mode of assessment, and of collection, and the duration of the taxes.

15. Society has the right to require of every public agent an account of his administration.

16. A society in which the observance of the law is not assured nor the separation of powers defined has no constitution at all.

17. Property being an inviolable and sacred right, no one shall be deprived thereof except where public necessity, legally determined, shall clearly demand it, and then only on condition that the owner shall have been previously and equitably indemnified.

4
THE ORIGINS OF THE REVOLUTION

The most eloquent opponent of the French Revolution in Europe was Edmund Burke (1729–1797). He is the classic spokesman for conservatism, and he used the events of the French Revolution to illustrate his thesis that abstract reasoning is no substitute for a slow, careful, organic growth of the state.

FROM Reflections on the Revolution in France
BY EDMUND BURKE

Dear Sir,
You are pleased to call again, and with some earnestness, for my thoughts on the late proceedings in France.

I flatter myself that I love a manly, moral, regulated liberty as well as any gentleman of that society, be he who he will; and perhaps I have given as good proofs of my attachment to that cause, in the whole course of my public conduct. I think I envy liberty as little as they do, to any other nation. But I cannot stand forward, and give praise or blame to any thing which relates to human actions, and human concerns, on a simple view of the object, as it stands stripped of every relation, in all the nakedness and solitude of metaphysical abstraction. Circumstances (which with some gentlemen pass for nothing) give in reality to every political principle its distinguishing colour, and discriminating effect. The circumstances are what render every civil and

Edmund Burke, *Reflections on the Revolution in France, and on the Proceedings in Certain Societies in London Relative to that Event,* 6th ed. (1790), pp. 1, 7–9, 11, 35–36, 50–51, 74–75, 86–89, 90–92, 115.

political scheme beneficial or noxious to mankind. Abstractedly speaking, government, as well as liberty, is good; yet could I, in common sense, ten years ago, have felicitated France on her enjoyment of a government (for she then had a government) without enquiry what the nature of that government was, or how it was administered? Can I now congratulate the same nation upon its freedom? Is it because liberty in the abstract may be classed amongst the blessings of mankind, that I am seriously to felicitate a madman, who has escaped from the protecting restraint and wholesome darkness of his cell, on his restoration to the enjoyment of light and liberty? Am I to congratulate an highwayman and murderer, who has broke prison, upon the recovery of his natural rights? This would be to act over again the scene of the criminals condemned to the gallies, and their heroic deliverer, the metaphysic Knight of the Sorrowful Countenance.

The effect of liberty to individuals is, that they may do what they please: We ought to see what it will please them to do, before we risque congratulations, which may be soon turned into complaints. Prudence would dictate this in the case of separate insulated private men; but liberty, when men act in bodies, is *power*. Considerate people before they declare themselves will observe the use which is made of *power;* and particularly of so trying a thing as *new* power in *new* persons, of whose principles, tempers, and dispositions, they have little or no experience, and in situations where those who appear the most stirring in the scene may possibly not be the real movers.

It looks to me as if I were in a great crisis, not of the affairs of France alone, but of all Europe, perhaps of more than Europe. All circumstances taken together, the French revolution is the most astonishing that has hitherto happened in the world. The most wonderful things are brought about in many instances by means the most absurd and ridiculous; in the most ridiculous modes; and apparently, by the most contemptible instruments. Every thing seems out of nature in this strange chaos of levity and ferocity, and of all sorts of crimes jumbled together with all sorts of follies. In viewing this monstrous tragi-comic scene, the most opposite passions necessarily succeed, and sometimes mix with each other in the mind; alternate contempt and indignation; alternate laughter and tears; alternate scorn and horror.

A few years ago I should be ashamed to overload a matter, so capable of supporting itself, by the then unnecessary support of any argument; but this seditious, unconstitutional doctrine is now publicly taught, avowed, and printed. The dislike I feel to revolutions, the signals for which have so often been given from pulpits; the spirit of change that is gone abroad; the total contempt which prevails with you, and may come to prevail with us, of all ancient institutions, when set in opposition to a present sense of convenience, or to the bent of a present inclination: all these considerations make it not unadviseable, in my opinion, to call back our attention to the true principles of our own domestic laws; that you, my French friend, should begin to know, and that we should continue to cherish them. We ought not, on either side of the water, to suffer ourselves to be imposed upon by the counterfeit wares which some persons, by a double fraud, export to you in illicit bottoms, as raw commodities of British growth though wholly alien to our soil, in order afterwards to smuggle them back again into this country, manufactured after the newest Paris fashion of an improved liberty.

You might, if you pleased, have profited of our example, and have given to your recovered freedom a correspondent dignity. Your privileges, though discontinued, were not lost to memory. Your constitution, it is true, whilst you were out of possession, suffered waste and dilapidation; but you possessed in some parts the walls, and in all the foundations of a noble and venerable castle. You might have repaired those walls; you might have built on those old foundations. Your constitution was suspended before it was perfected; but you had the elements of a constitution very nearly as good as could be wished. In your old states you possessed that variety of parts corresponding with the various descriptions of which your community was happily composed; you had all that combination, and all that opposition of interests, you had that action and counteraction which, in the natural and in the political world, from the reciprocal struggle of discordant powers, draws out the harmony of the universe. These opposed and conflicting interests, which you considered as so great a blemish in your old and in our present constitution, interpose a salutary check to all precipitate resolutions. They render deliberation a matter not of choice, but of necessity; they make all change a subject of *compromise,* which naturally begets moderation; they produce *temperaments,* preventing the sore evil of harsh, crude, unqualified reformations; and rendering all the headlong exertions of arbitrary power, in the few or in the many, for ever impracticable. Through that diversity of members and interests, general liberty had as many securities as there were separate views in the several orders; whilst by pressing down the whole by the weight of a real monarchy, the separate parts would have been prevented from warping and starting from their allotted places.

You had all these advantages in your antient states; but you chose to act as if you had never been moulded into civil society, and had everything to begin anew. You began ill, because you began by despising every thing that belonged to you. You set up your trade without a capital. If the last generations of your country appeared without much lustre in your eyes, you might have passed them by, and derived your claims from a more early race of ancestors. Under a pious predilection of those ancestors, your imaginations would have realized in them a standard of virtue and wisdom, beyond the vulgar practice of the hour; and you would have risen with the example to whose imitation you aspired. Respecting your forefathers, you would have been taught to respect yourselves. You would not have chosen to consider the French as a people of yesterday, as a nation of low-born servile wretches until the emancipating year of 1789.

* * *

Nothing is a due and adequate representation of a state, that does not represent its ability, as well as its property. But as ability is a vigorous and active principle, and as property is sluggish, inert, and timid, it never can be safe from the invasions of ability, unless it be, out of all proportion, predominant in the representation. It must be represented too in great masses of accumulation, or it is not rightly protected. The characteristic essence of property, formed out of the combined principles of its acquisition and conservation, is to be *unequal*. The great masses therefore which excite envy, and tempt rapacity, must be put out of the possibility of danger. Then they form a natural rampart about the lesser properties in all their gradations. The same quantity of property, which is by the natural course of things divided among many, has not the same operation. Its defensive power is weakened as it is diffused. In this diffusion each man's portion is less than what, in the eagerness of his desires, he may flatter himself to obtain by dissipating the accumulations of others. The plunder of the few would indeed give but a share inconceivably small in the distribution to the many. But the many are not capable of making this calculation; and those who lead them to rapine, never intend this distribution.

* * *

Far am I from denying in theory; full as far is my heart from withholding in practice (if I were of power to give or to withhold) the *real* rights of men. In denying their false claims of right, I do not mean to injure those which are real, and are such as their pretended rights would totally destroy. If civil society be made for the advantage of man, all the advantages for which it is made become his right. It is an institution of beneficence; and law itself is only beneficence acting by a rule. Men have a right to live by that rule; they have a right to justice; as between their fellows, whether their fellows are in politic function or in ordinary occupation. They have a right to the fruits of their industry; and to the means of making their industry fruitful. They have a right to the acquisitions of their parents; to the nourishment and improvement of their offspring; to instruction in life, and to consolation in death. Whatever each man can separately do, without trespassing upon others, he has a right to do for himself; and he has a right to a fair portion of all which society, with all its combinations of skill and force, can do in his favour. In this partnership all men have equal rights; but not to equal things. He that has but five shillings in the partnership, has as good a right to it, as he that has five hundred pound has to his larger proportion. But he has not a right to an equal dividend in the product of the joint stock; and as to the share of power, authority, and direction which each individual ought to have in the management of the state, that I must deny to be amongst the direct original rights of man in civil society; for I have in my contemplation the civil social man, and no other. It is a thing to be settled by convention.

If civil society be the offspring of convention, that convention must be its law. That convention must limit and modify all the descriptions of constitution which are formed under it. Every sort of legislative, judicial, or executory power are its creatures. They can have no being in any other state of things; and how can any man claim, under the conventions of civil society, rights which do not so much as suppose its existence? Rights which are absolutely repugnant to it? One of the first motives to civil society, and which becomes one of its fundamental rules, is, *that no man should be judge in his own cause*. By this each person has at once divested himself of the first fundamental right of uncovenanted man, that is, to judge for himself, and to assert his own cause. He abdicates all right to be his own governor. He inclusively, in a great measure, abandons the right of self-defence, the first law of nature. Men cannot enjoy the rights of an uncivil and of a civil state together. That he may obtain justice he gives up his right of determining what it is in points the most essential to him. That he may secure some liberty, he makes a surrender in trust of the whole of it.

Government is not made in virtue of natural rights, which may and do exist in total independence of it; and exist in much greater clearness, and in a much greater degree of abstract perfection: but their abstract perfection is their practical defect. By having a right to every thing they want every thing. Government is a contrivance of human wisdom to provide for human *wants*. Men have a right that these wants should be provided for by this wisdom. Among these wants is to be reckoned the want, out of civil society, of a sufficient restraint upon their passions. Society requires not only that the passions of individuals should be subjected, but that even in the mass and body as well as in the individuals, the inclinations of men should frequently be thwarted, their will controlled, and their passions brought into subjection. This can only be done *by a power out of themselves;* and not, in the exercise of its function, subject to that will and to those passions which it is its office to bridle and subdue. In this sense the restraints on men, as well as their liberties, are to be reckoned among their rights. But as the liberties and the restrictions vary with times and circumstances, and admit of infinite modifications, they cannot be settled upon any abstract rule; and nothing is so foolish as to discuss them upon that principle.

* * *

The science of constructing a commonwealth, or renovating it, or reforming it, is like every other experimental science, not to be taught *a priori*. Nor is it a short experience that can instruct us in that practical science; because the real effects of moral causes are not always immediate; but that which in the first instance is prejudicial may be excellent in its remoter operation; and its excellence may arise even from the ill effects it produces in the beginning. The reverse also happens; and very plausible schemes, with very pleasing commencements, have often shameful and lamentable conclusions. In states there are often some obscure and almost latent causes, things which appear at first view of little moment, on which a very great part of its prosperity or adversity may most essentially depend. The science of government being therefore so practical in itself, and intended for such practical purposes, a matter which requires experience, and even more experience than any person can gain in his whole life, however sagacious and observing he may be, it is with infinite caution that any man ought to venture upon pulling down an edifice which has answered in any tolerable degree for ages the common purposes of society, or on building it up again, without having models and patterns of approved utility before his eyes.

These metaphysic rights entering into common life, like rays of light which pierce into a dense medium, are, by the laws of nature, refracted from their straight line. Indeed in the gross and complicated mass of human passions and concerns, the primitive rights of men undergo such a variety of refractions and reflections, that it becomes absurd to talk of them as if they continued in the simplicity of their original direction. The nature of man is intricate; the objects of society are of the greatest possible complexity; and therefore no simple disposition or direction of power can be suitable either to man's nature, or to the quality of his affairs. When I hear the simplicity of contrivance aimed at and boasted of in any new political constitutions, I am at no loss to decide that the artificers are grossly ignorant of their trade, or totally negligent of their duty. The simple governments are fundamentally defective, to say no worse of them. If you were to contemplate society in but one point of view, all these simple modes of polity are infinitely captivating. In effect each would answer its single end much more perfectly than the more complex is able to attain all its complex purposes. But it is better that the whole should be imperfectly and anomalously answered, than that, while some parts are provided for with great exactness, others might be totally neglected, or perhaps materially injured, by the over-care of a favourite member.

The pretended rights of these theorists are all extremes; and in proportion as they are metaphysically true, they are morally and politically false. The rights of men are in a sort of *middle,* incapable of definition, but not impossible to be discerned. The rights of men in governments are their advantages; and these are often in balances between differences of good; in compromise sometimes between good and evil, and sometimes, between evil and evil. Political reason is a computing principle; adding, subtracting, multiplying, and dividing, morally and not metaphysically or mathematically, true moral denominations.

* * *

On the scheme of this barbarous philosophy, which is the offspring of cold hearts and muddy understandings, and which is as void of solid wisdom, as it is destitute of all taste and elegance, laws are to be supported only by their own terrors, and by the concern, which each individual may find in them, from his own private speculations, or can spare to them from his own private interests. In the groves of *their* academy, at the end of every vista, you see nothing but the gallows. Nothing is left which engages the affections on the part of the commonwealth. On the principles of this mechanic philosophy, our institutions can never be embodied, if I may use the expression, in persons; so as to create in us love, veneration, admiration, or attachment. But that sort of reason which banishes the affections is incapable of filling their place. These public affections, combined with manners, are required sometimes as supplements, sometimes as correctives, always as aids to law. . . . There ought to be a system of manners in every nation which a well-formed mind would be disposed to relish. To make us love our country, our country ought to be lovely.

But power, of some kind or other, will survive the shock in which manners and opinions perish, and it will find other and worse means for its support. The usurpation which, in order to subvert antient institutions, has destroyed antient principles, will hold power by arts similar to those by which it has acquired it. When the old feudal and chivalrous spirit of *Fealty,* which, by freeing kings from fear, freed both kings and subjects from the precautions of tyranny, shall be extinct in the minds of men, plots and assassinations will be anticipated by preventive murder and preventive confiscation, and that long roll of grim and bloody maxims, which form the political code of all power, not standing on its own honour, and the honour of those who are to obey it. Kings will be tyrants from policy when subjects are rebels from principle.

When antient opinions and rules of life are taken away, the loss cannot possibly be estimated. From that moment we have no compass to govern us; nor can we know distinctly to what port we steer. Europe undoubtedly, taken in a mass, was in a flourishing condition the day on which your Revolution was compleated. How much of that prosperous state was owing to the spirit of our old manners and opinions is not easy to say; but as such causes cannot be indifferent in their operation, we must presume, that, on the whole, their operation was beneficial.

Hippolyte Taine (1828–1893) was a literary critic by training. After having lived through the upheaval of the Paris Commune of 1871, he turned to the study of the French Revolution in order to find the origins of the class struggle that racked the France of his day. He found it in the misery of the lower orders of society on the eve of the Revolution.

FROM The Ancient Regime BY HIPPOLYTE TAINE

I

Examine administrative correspondence for the last thirty years preceding the Revolution. Countless statements reveal excessive suffering, even when not terminating in fury. Life to a man of the lower class, to an artisan, or workman, subsisting on the labor of his own hands, is evidently precarious; he obtains simply enough to keep him from starvation and he does not always get that. Here, in four districts, "the inhabitants live only on buckwheat," and for five years, the apple crop having failed, they drink only water. There, in a country of vineyards, "the vine-dressers each year are reduced, for the most part, to begging their bread during the dull season." Elsewhere, several of the day-laborers and mechanics, obliged to sell their effects and household goods, die of the cold; insufficient and unhealthy food generates sickness, while in two districts, thirty-five thousand persons are stated to be living on alms. In a remote canton the peasants cut the grain still green and dry it in the oven, because they are too hungry to wait. The intendant of Poitiers writes that "as soon as the workhouses open, a prodigious number of the poor rush to them, in spite of the reduction of wages and of the restrictions imposed on them in behalf of the most needy." The intendant of Bourges notices that a great many *métayers* have sold off their furniture and that "entire families pass two days without eating," and that in many parishes the famished stay in bed most of the day because they suffer less. The intendant of Orléans reports that "in Sologne, poor widows have burned up their wooden bedsteads and others have consumed their fruit trees" to preserve themselves from the cold, and he adds, "nothing is exaggerated in this statement; the cries of want cannot be expressed; the misery of the rural districts must be seen with one's own eyes to obtain an idea of it." From Rioni, from La Rochelle, from Limoges, from Lyons, from Montauban, from Caen, from Alençon, from Flanders, from Moulins come similar statements by other intendants. One

Hippolyte Taine, *The Ancient Regime* (1876), pp. 335–348, translated by John Durand.

might call it the interruptions and repetitions of a funeral knell; even in years
not disastrous it is heard on all sides. In Burgundy, near Chatillon-sur-Seine,
"taxes, seignioral dues, the tithes, and the expenses of cultivation, divide up
the productions of the soil into thirds, leaving nothing for the unfortunate
cultivators, who would have abandoned their fields, had not two Swiss manufacturers of calicoes settled there and distributed about the country forty
thousand francs a year in cash." In Auvergne, the country is depopulated
daily; many of the villages have lost, since the beginning of the century, more
than one-third of their inhabitants. "Had not steps been promptly taken to
lighten the burden of a downtrodden people," says the provincial assembly in
1787, "Auvergne would have forever lost its population and its cultivation."
In Comminges, at the outbreak of the Revolution, certain communities
threaten to abandon their possessions, should they obtain no relief. "It is a
well-known fact," says the assembly of Haute-Guyenne, in 1784, "that the lot
of the most severely taxed communities is so rigorous as to have led their proprietors frequently to abandon their property. Who is not aware of the inhabitants of Saint-Servin having abandoned their possessions ten times and of
their threats to resort again to this painful proceeding in their recourse to the
administration? Only a few years ago an abandonment of the community of
Boisse took place through the combined action of the inhabitants, the seignior and the *décimateur* of the community"; and the desertion would be still
greater if the law did not forbid persons liable to the *taille* abandoning over-
taxed property, except by renouncing whatever they possessed in the community. In the Soissonais, according to the report of the provincial assembly,
"misery is excessive." In Gascony the spectacle is "heart-rending." In the envi-
rons of Toule, the cultivator, after paying his taxes, tithes and other dues,
remains empty-handed. "Agriculture is an occupation of steady anxiety and
privation, in which thousands of men are obliged to painfully vegetate." In a
village in Normandy, "nearly all the inhabitants, not excepting the farmers
and proprietors, eat barley bread and drink water, living like the most
wretched of men, so as to provide for the payment of taxes with which they
are overburdened." In the same province, at Forges, "many poor creatures eat
oat bread, and others bread of soaked bran, this nourishment causing many
deaths among infants." People evidently live from day to day; whenever the
crop proves poor they lack bread. Let a frost come, a hailstorm, an inunda-
tion, and an entire province is incapable of supporting itself until the coming
year; in many places even an ordinary winter suffices to bring on distress. On
all sides hands are seen outstretched to the king, who is the universal al-
moner. The people may be said to resemble a man attempting to wade
through a pool with the water up to his chin, and who, losing his footing at
the slightest depression, sinks down and drowns. Existent charity and the
fresh spirit of humanity vainly strive to rescue them; the water has risen too
high. It must subside to a lower level and the pool be drawn off through
some adequate outlet. Thus far the poor man catches breath only at intervals,
running the risk of drowning at every moment.

II

Between 1750 and 1760, the idlers who eat suppers begin to regard with compassion and alarm the laborers who go without dinners. Why are the latter so impoverished, and by what mischance, on a soil as rich as that of France, do those lack bread who grow the grain? In the first place many farms remain uncultivated, and, what is worse, many are deserted. According to the best observers "one-quarter of the soil is absolutely lying waste . . . Hundreds and hundreds of *arpents* of heath and moor form extensive deserts." "Let a person traverse Anjou, Maine, Brittany, Poitou, Limousin, la Marche, Berry, Nivernais, Bourbonnais and Auvergne, and he finds one-half of these provinces in heaths, forming immense plains all of which might be cultivated." In Touraine, in Poitou and in Berry they form solitary expanses of thirty thousand *arpents*. In one canton alone, near Preuilly, forty thousand *arpents* of good soil consist of heath. The agricultural society of Rennes declares that two-thirds of Brittany is lying waste. This is not sterility but decadence. The régime invented by Louis XIV has produced its effect; the soil for a century past is reverting back to a wild state. "We see only abandoned and ruinous châteaux; the principal towns of the fiefs, in which the nobility formerly lived at their ease, are all now occupied by poor *métayer* herdsmen whose scanty labor hardly suffices for their subsistence and a remnant of tax ready to disappear through the ruin of the proprietors and the desertion of the settlers." In the election-district of Confolens a piece of property rented for 2,956 *livres* in 1665, brings in only 900 *livres* in 1747. On the confines of la Marche and of Berry a domain which, in 1660, honorably supported two seignioral families is now simply a small unproductive *métayer*-farm; "the traces of the furrows once made by the ploughshare being still visible on the surrounding heaths." Sologne, once flourishing, becomes a marsh and a forest; a hundred years earlier it produced three times the quantity of grain; two-thirds of its mills are gone; not a vestige of its vineyards remains; "grapes have given way to the heath." Thus abandoned by the spade and the plough, a vast portion of the soil ceases to feed man, while the rest, poorly cultivated, scarcely provides the simplest necessities.

In the first place, on the failure of a crop, this portion remains untilled; its occupant is too poor to purchase seed; the intendant is often obliged to distribute seed, without which the disaster of the current year would be followed by sterility the following year. Every calamity, accordingly, in these days affects the future as well as the present; during the two years of 1784 and 1785, around Toulouse, the drought having caused the loss of all draft animals, many of the cultivators are obliged to let their fields lie fallow. In the second place, cultivation, when it does take place, is carried on according to mediaeval modes. Arthur Young, in 1789, considers that French agriculture has not progressed beyond that of the tenth century. Except in Flanders and on the plains of Alsace, the fields lie fallow one year out of three and oftentimes one year out of two. The implements are poor; there are no ploughs made of iron; in many places the plough of Virgil's time is still in use. Cart-axles and wheel-tires are made of wood, while a harrow often consists of the trestle of a cart. There are few animals and but little manure; the capital bestowed on cultivation is three times less than that of the present day. The yield is slight; "our ordinary farms," says a good observer, "taking one with another return about six times the seed sown." In 1778, on the rich soil around Toulouse, wheat returns about five for one, while at the present day it yields eight to one and more. Arthur Young estimates that, in his day, the English acre produces twenty-eight bushels of grain, and the French acre eighteen bushels, and that the value of the total product of the same area for a given length of time is thirty-six pounds sterling in England and only twenty-five in France. As the parish roads are frightful, and transportation often impracticable, it is clear that, in remote cantons, where poor soil yields scarcely three times the seed sown, food is not always obtainable. How do they manage to live until the next crop? This is the question always under consideration previous to, and during, the Revolution. I find, in manuscript correspondence, the syndics and mayors of villages estimating the quantities for local subsistence at so many bushels in the granaries, so many sheaves in the barns, so many mouths to be filled, so many days to wait until the August wheat comes in, and concluding on short supplies for two, three and four months. Such a state of inter-communication, and of agriculture condemns a country to periodical famines, and I venture to state that, alongside of the small-pox which, out of eight deaths, causes one, another endemic disease exists, as prevalent and as destructive, and this disease is starvation.

We can easily imagine the people as sufferers by it, and, especially, the peasant. An advance in the price of bread prevents him from getting any, and even without that advance, he obtains it with difficulty. Wheat bread costs, as at the present day, three *sous* per pound, but as the average day's work brought only nineteen *sous* instead of forty, the day-laborer, working the same time, could buy only the half of a loaf instead of a full loaf. Taking everything into account, and wages being estimated according to the price of grain, we find that the husbandman's manual labor then procured him 959 *litres* of wheat, while nowadays it gives him 1,851 *litres;* his well-being, accordingly, has advanced ninety-three per cent; which suffices to show to what extent his predecessors suffered privations. And these privations are peculiar to France. Through analogous observations and estimates Arthur Young shows that in France those who lived on field labor, and they constituted the great majority, are seventy-six per cent less comfortable than the same laborers in England, while they are seventy-six per cent less well in health. The result is that, in seven-eighths of the kingdom, there are no farmers but simply *métayers*. The peasant is too poor to undertake cultivation on his own account, possessing no agricultural capital. "The proprietor, desirous of improving his land, finds no one to cultivate it but miserable creatures possessing only a pair of hands; he is obliged to advance everything for its cultivation at his own expense, animals, implements and seed, and even to advance the wherewithal to this *métayer* to feed him until the first crop comes in." "At Vatan, for example, in Berry, the *métayers,* almost every year, borrow bread of the proprietor in order to await the harvesting." "Very rarely is one found who is not indebted to his master at least one hundred *livres* a year." Frequently the latter proposes to abandon the entire crop to them on condition that they demand nothing of him during the year; "these miserable creatures" have refused; left to themselves, they would not be sure of keeping themselves alive. In Limousin and in Angoumois their poverty is so great "that, deducting the taxes to which they are subject, they have no more than from twenty-five to thirty *livres* each person per annum to spend; and not in money, it must be stated, but counting whatever they consume in kind out of the crops they produce. Frequently they have less, and when they cannot possibly make a living the master is obliged to support them. . . . The *métayer* is always reduced to just what is absolutely necessary to keep him from starving." As to the small proprietor, the villager who ploughs his land himself, his condition is but little better. "Agriculture, as our peasants practise it, is a veritable drudgery; they die by thousands in childhood, and in maturity they seek places everywhere but where they should be." In 1783, throughout the plain of the Toulousain they eat only maize, a mixture of flour, common seeds and very little wheat; those on the mountains feed, a part of the year, on chestnuts; the potato is hardly known, and, according to Arthur Young, ninety-nine out of a hundred peasants would refuse to eat it. According to the reports of intendants, the basis of food, in Normandy, is oats; in the election-district of Troyes, buckwheat; in the Marche and in Limousin, buckwheat with chestnuts and radishes; in Auvergne, buckwheat, chestnuts, milk-curds and a little salted goat's meat; in Beauce, a mixture of barley and rye; in Berry, a mixture of barley and oats. There is no wheat bread; the peasant consumes inferior flour only because he is unable to pay two *sous* a pound for his bread. There is no butcher's meat; at best he kills one pig a year. His dwelling is built of clay (*pise*), roofed with thatch, without windows, and the floor is the beaten ground. Even when the soil furnishes good building materials, stone, slate and tile, the windows have no sashes. In a parish in Normandy, in 1789, "most of the dwellings consist of four posts." They are often mere stables or barns "to which a chimney has been added made of four poles and some mud." Their clothes are rags, and often, in winter these are muslin rags. In Quercy and elsewhere, they have no stockings, or shoes or *sabots* (wooden shoes). "It is not in the power of an English imagination," says Arthur Young, "to figure the animals that waited on us here at the *Chapeau Rouge.* Some things that called themselves by courtesy Souillac women, but in reality walking dung-hills. But a neatly dressed, clean waiting-girl at an inn, will be looked for in vain in France." On reading descriptions made on the spot we see in France a similar aspect of country and of peasantry as in Ireland, at least in its broad outlines.

III

In the most fertile regions, for instance, in Limagne, both cottages and faces denote "misery and privation." "The peasants are generally feeble, emaciated and of slight stature." Nearly all derive wheat and wine from their home-steads, but they are forced to sell this to pay their rents and imposts; they eat black bread, made of rye and barley, and their sole beverage is water poured on the lees and the husks. "An Englishman who has not travelled can not imagine the figure made by infinitely the greater part of the countrywomen in France." Arthur Young, who stops to talk with one of these in Cham-pagne, says that "this woman, at no great distance, might have been taken for sixty or seventy, her figure was so bent and her face so hardened and fur-rowed by labor, but she said she was only twenty-eight." This woman, her husband and her household, afford a sufficiently accurate example of the con-dition of the small proprietary husbandmen. Their property consists simply of a patch of ground, with a cow and a poor little horse; their seven children consume the whole of the cow's milk. They owe to one seignior a *franchard* (forty-two pounds) of flour, and three chickens; to another three *franchards* of oats, one chicken and one *sou,* to which must be added the *taille* and other imposts. "God keep us!" she said, "for the *tailles* and the dues crush us." What must it be in districts where the soil is poor! "From Ormes (near Chatellerault), as far as Poitiers," writes a lady, "there is a good deal of ground which brings in nothing, and from Poitiers to my residence (in Li-mousin) twenty-five thousand *arpents* of ground consist wholly of heath and sea-grass. The peasantry live on rye, of which they do not remove the bran, and which is as black and heavy as lead. In Poitou, and here, they plough up only the skin of the ground with a miserable little plough without wheels. . . . From Poitiers to Montmorillon it is nine leagues, equal to sixteen of Paris, and I assure you that I have seen but four men on the road and, be-tween Montmorillon and my own house, which is four leagues, but three; and then only at a distance, not having met one on the road. You need not be surprised at this in such a country. . . . Marriage takes place as early as with the grand seigniors," doubtless for fear of the militia. "But the population of the country is no greater because almost every infant dies. Mothers having scarcely any milk, their infants eat the bread of which I spoke, the stomach of a girl of four years being as big as that of a pregnant woman. . . . Their rye crop this year was ruined by the frost on Easter day; flour is scarce; of the twelve *métairies* owned by my mother, four of them may, perhaps, have some on hand. There has been no rain since Easter; no hay, no pasture, no vegeta-bles, no fruit. You see the lot of the poor peasant. There is no manure, and there are no cattle. . . . My mother, whose granaries used to be always full, has not a grain of wheat in them, because, for two years past, she has fed all her *métayers* and the poor."

"The peasant is assisted," says a seignior of the same province, "protected, and rarely maltreated, but he is looked upon with disdain. If kindly and pliable he is made subservient, but if ill-disposed he becomes soured and irritable. . . . He is kept in misery, in an abject state, by men who are not at all inhuman but whose prejudices, especially among the nobles, lead them to regard him as of a different species of being. . . . The proprietor gets all he can out of him; in any event, looking upon him and his oxen as domestic animals, he puts them into harness and employs them in all weathers for every kind of journey, and for every species of carting and transport. On the other hand, this *métayer* thinks of living with as little labor as possible, converting as much ground as he can into pasturage, for the reason that the product arising from the increase of stock costs him no labor. The little ploughing he does is for the purpose of raising low-priced provisions suitable for his own nourishment, such as buckwheat, radishes, etc. His enjoyment consists only of his own idleness and sluggishness, hoping for a good chestnut year and doing nothing voluntarily but procreate"; unable to hire farming hands he begets children. The rest, ordinary laborers, have small supplies, "living on the spontaneous, and on a few goats which devour everything." Often again, these, by order of Parlement, are killed by the keepers. A woman, with two children in swaddling clothes, having no milk, "and without an inch of ground," whose two goats, her sole resource, had thus been slain, and another, with one goat slain in the same way, and who begs along with her boy, present themselves at the gate of the château; one receives twelve *livres,* while the other is admitted as a domestic, and henceforth, "this village is all bows and smiling faces." In short, they are not accustomed to benefactions; the lot of all these poor people is to endure. "As with rain and hail, they regard as inevitable the necessity of being oppressed by the strongest, the richest, the most skillful, the most in repute," and this stamps on them, "if one may be allowed to say so, an air of painful suffering."

In Auvergne, a feudal country, covered with extensive ecclesiastic and seignioral domains, the misery is the same. At Clermont-Ferrand, "there are many streets that can for blackness, dirt and scents only be represented by narrow channels cut in a night dunghill." In the inns of the largest bourgs, "closeness, misery, dirtiness and darkness." That of Pradelles is "one of the worst in France." That of Aubenas, says Young, "would be a purgatory for one of my pigs." The senses, in short, are paralyzed. The primitive man is content so long as he can sleep and get something to eat. He gets something to eat, but what kind of food? To put up with the indigestible mess a peasant here requires a still tougher stomach than in Limousin; in certain villages where, ten years later, every year twenty or twenty-five hogs are to be slaughtered, they now slaughter but three. On contemplating this temperament, rude and intact since Vercingetorix, and, moreover, rendered more savage by suffering, one cannot avoid being somewhat alarmed. The Marquis de Mirabeau describes "the votive festival of Mont-Doré, savages descending from the mountain in torrents, the curate with stole and surplice, the justice in his wig, the police corps with sabres drawn, all guarding the open square before letting the bagpipers play; the dance interrupted in a quarter of an hour by a fight; the hootings and cries of children, of the feeble and other spectators, urging them on as the rabble urge on so many fighting dogs; frightful-looking men, or rather wild beasts covered with coats of coarse wool, wearing wide leather belts pierced with copper nails, gigantic in stature, which is increased by high *sabots,* and making themselves still taller by standing on tiptoe to see the battle, stamping with their feet as it progresses and rubbing each other's flanks with their elbows, their faces haggard, and covered with long matted hair, the upper portion pallid, and the lower distended, indicative of cruel delight and a sort of ferocious impatience. And these folks pay the *taille!* And now they want to take away their salt! And they know nothing of those they despoil, of those whom they think they govern, believing that, by a few strokes of a cowardly and careless pen, they may starve them with impunity up to the final catastrophe! Poor Jean-Jacques, I said to myself, had any one despatched you, with your system, to copy music amongst these folks he would have had some sharp replies to make to your discourses!" Prophetic warning and admirable foresight in one whom an excess of evil does not blind to the evil of the remedy! Enlightened by his feudal and rural instincts, the old man at once judges both the government and the philosophers, the Ancient Régime and the Revolution.

IV

Misery begets bitterness in a man; but ownership coupled with misery renders him still more bitter. He may have submitted to indigence but not to spoilation—which is the situation of the peasant in 1789, for, during the eighteenth century, he had become the possessor of land. But how could he maintain himself in such destitution? The fact is almost incredible, but it is nevertheless true. We can only explain it by the character of the French peasant, by his sobriety, his tenacity, his rigor with himself, his dissimulation, his hereditary passion for property and especially for that of the soil. He had lived on privations, and economized *sou* after *sou*. Every year a few pieces of silver are added to his little store of crowns buried in the most secret recess of his cellar; Rousseau's peasant, concealing his wine and bread in a pit, assuredly had a yet more secret hiding-place; a little money in a woolen stocking or in a jug escapes, more readily than elsewhere, the search of the clerks. Dressed in rags, going barefoot, eating nothing but coarse black bread, but cherishing the little treasure in his breast on which he builds so many hopes, he watches for the opportunity which never fails to come. "In spite of privileges," writes a gentleman in 1775, "the nobles are daily being ruined and reduced, the Third-Estate making all the fortunes." A number of domains, through forced or voluntary sales, thus pass into the hands of financiers, of men of the quill, of merchants, and of the well-to-do bourgeois. Before undergoing this total dispossession, however, the seignior, involved in debt, is evidently resigned to partial alienations of his property. The peasant who has bribed the steward is on hand with his hoard. "It is poor property, my lord, and it costs you more than you get from it." This may refer to an isolated patch, one end of a field or meadow, sometimes a farm whose farmer pays nothing, and generally worked by a *métayer* whose wants and indolence make him an annual expense to his master. The latter may say to himself that the alienated parcel is not lost since, some day or other, through his right of repurchase, he may take it back, while in the meantime, he enjoys a *cens,* drawbacks, and the lord's dues. Moreover, there is on his domain and around him, extensive open spaces which the decline of cultivation and depopulation have left a desert. To restore the value of this he must surrender its proprietorship. There is no other way by which to attach man permanently to the soil. And the government helps him along in this matter. Obtaining no revenue from the abandoned soil, it assents to a provisional withdrawal of its too weighty hand. By the edict of 1766, a piece of cleared waste land remains free of the *taille* for fifteen years, and, thereupon, in twenty-eight provinces four hundred thousand *arpents* are cleared in three years.

This is the mode by which the seignioral domain gradually crumbles away and decreases. Towards the last, in many places, with the exception of the château and the small adjoining farm, which brings in two or three thousand francs a year, nothing is left to the seignior but his feudal dues; the rest of the soil belongs to the peasantry. Forbonnais already remarks, towards 1750, that many of the nobles and of the ennobled "reduced to extreme poverty but with titles to immense possessions," have sold off portions to small cultivators at low prices, and often for the amount of the *taille.* Towards 1760, one-quarter of the soil is said to have already passed into the hands of agriculturists. In 1772, in relation to the *vingtième,* which is levied on the net revenue of real property, the intendant of Caen, having completed the statement of his quota, estimates that out of one hundred and fifty thousand "there are perhaps fifty thousand whose liabilities did not exceed five *sous* and perhaps still as many more not exceeding *twenty sous.*" Contemporary observers authenticate this passion of the peasant for real property. "The savings of the lower classes, which elsewhere are invested with individuals and in the public funds, are wholly destined in France to the purchase of land." "Accordingly the number of small rural holdings is always on the increase. Necker says that there is an *immensity* of them." Arthur Young, in 1789, is astonished at their great number and "inclines to think that they form one-third of the kingdom." That would already be about the proportion, and the proportion would still be the same, were we to compare the number of proprietors with the number of inhabitants.

The small cultivator, however, in becoming a possessor of the soil assumes its charges. Simply as day-laborer, and with his arms alone, he was only partially affected by the taxes; "where there is nothing the king loses his dues." But now, vainly is he poor and declaring himself still poorer; the fisc has a hold on him and on every portion of his new possessions. The collectors,

peasants like himself, and jealous, by virtue of being his neighbors, know
how much his property, exposed to view, brings in; hence they take all they
can lay their hands on. Vainly has he labored with renewed energy; his hands
remain as empty, and, at the end of the year, he discovers that his field has
produced him nothing. The more he acquires and produces the more burdensome do the taxes become. In 1715, the *taille* and the poll-tax, which he alone
pays, or nearly alone, amounts to sixty-six millions of *livres;* the amount is
ninety-three millions in 1759 and one hundred and ten millions in 1789. In
1757, the imposts amount to 283,156,000 *livres;* in 1789 to 476,294,000 *livres.*

Theoretically, through humanity and through good sense, there is, doubtless, a desire to relieve the peasant and pity is felt for him. But, in practice,
through necessity and routine, he is treated according to Cardinal Richelieu's
precept, as a beast of burden to which oats are measured out for fear that he
may become too strong and kick, "a mule which, accustomed to his load, is
spoiled by more long repose than by work."

Alphonse Aulard was the leading historian of the French Revolution in the
generation after Taine. He was also the foremost proponent of the primary
role of the ideas of the eighteenth century in bringing about the French
Revolution.

FROM The French Revolution BY A. AULARD

On August 10, 1792, the Legislative Assembly, in establishing universal
suffrage, constituted France a democratic State, and the Convention, in establishing the Republic on the following September 22nd, gave to this democracy
the form of government which in the eyes of the Convention was logically
expedient.

Can we say that by these two acts a preconceived system was brought into
being? Many have thought so; many of our teachers and writers, with much
eloquence, have advanced the theory that democracy and the Republic
sprang, fully fledged, from the eighteenth-century philosophy, from the
works of the Encyclopaedists, from the doctrine of the precursors of the Revolution. Let us see if the facts, and the written word, justify these assertions.

One prime and important fact is this: that in 1789, at the time of the convocation of the Estates-General, there was no Republican party in France.

Reprinted with the permission of Charles Scribner's Sons from *The French Revolution,* pp.
79–81, 89–99, 125–126, 127–132, by A. Aulard, translated by Bernard Miall (1910).

Now the best testimony to be found as to contemporary French opinion is contained in the *cahiers* in which the people embodied their grievances and their desires. Of these we have many, different in origin and in kind, and in none is a republic demanded, nor even a change of dynasty; and I think my study of these justifies the assertion that in none is there found any criticism, even indirect, of the King's conduct. It would seem that none of the petitioners dream of attributing their stated grievances to the Monarchy, nor even to the King. In all these documents the French are seen imbued with an ardent royalism, a warm devotion to the person of Louis XVI. Above all, in documents of the more humble kind, petitions from parishes, and the like, there is a note of confidence, love, and gratitude. "Our good King! The King our father!"—so the peasants and the workers address him. The nobles and the clergy, less ingenuously enthusiastic, appear equally loyal.

* * *

If all Frenchmen were at one in wishing to maintain the Monarchy, they were not agreed as to the manner of regulating the royal authority, and we may go so far as to say that they did not all see the throne with the same eyes.

The masses of the people, in their unreasoned loyalty, did not, it would appear, discern the excesses of the royal prerogative. No doubt the commissaries were unpopular. But complaints of "ministerial despotism," as they preferred to call it, came from the nobles, the *bourgeoisie,* the rich and enlightened classes, rather than from the peasantry. The latter more especially lamented a "feudal despotism," because, in fact, they were the greatest sufferers from it.

Far from regarding the King as responsible for the conduct of his agents, the people would say that his agents deceived the King, that they annulled or hampered his power of doing good. The popular idea was to deliver the King from these unjust stewards in order that he might be enlightened, the better to direct his omnipotent power, to the profit of the nation, against the remnants of feudalism. The masses were beginning to have a certain idea of their rights, yet, so far were they from thinking to restrain his royal omnipotence, that it was precisely on that omnipotence that all their hopes were based. One petition said that, in order that all should go well, it was only necessary for the King to cry: *"To me, my people!"*

Enlightened Frenchmen, on the other hand, knowing well what manner of men Louis XIV and XV had been, feared the abuse of the royal power, and were not all reassured by the paternal character of Louis XVI's despotism. They wished to restrain, by means of political institutions, this fantastic and capricious power, so that it should no longer be dangerous to liberty, while leaving it sufficient force to destroy the aristocracy and what remained of the feudal system, thus making France a nation. To ensure that the King should govern according to the laws—this was what they called "organising the Monarchy."

The way to this organisation of the Monarchy was prepared by the writers of the eighteenth century.

They, with the logical spirit natural to the French, did not attempt merely to prevent abuses and to regulate the exercise of sovereign power; they discussed the very essence of this power, of the pretended right Divine; they sapped the Catholic faith by which the throne was propped, sought publicly for the origins of sovereignty and authority, in history, in the assent of subjects, and in the national will.

Thus, without desiring to establish a republic, and solely with a view to "organising" the Monarchy, they attacked the monarchical principle, and put in circulation republican ideals of such a nature that, although in 1789 no one wished for a republic, yet whoever thought at all was impregnated with these republican ideas; and this is why, in 1792, when circumstances made the Republic necessary, there was a sufficient number of thinking men prepared to accept, and to force on others, a form of government of which they had already adopted the principles.

A few examples will show the diffusion and elaboration of republican ideas before the Revolution.

* * *

Montesquieu, in 1748, in his *l'Esprit des Lois,* defined a republic: "The republican form of government," he says, "is that in which the people as a whole, or one party only of the people, exercises the sovereign power." This definition became classic. In 1765 it was reproduced in the article on "republics" in the *Encyclopédie* (vol. xiv.), which consists entirely of quotations from Montesquieu.

Could not such a republic exist under a king? Montesquieu does not think so; but Mably does—when, for instance, he dreams of a "republican monarchy"; and the same idea is held by those whom we shall find, in 1789, speaking of a "monarchical democracy."

Montesquieu undoubtedly pronounces against a republic, and is of opinion that in a republic "the laws are evaded with greater danger than they can be violated by a prince, who, being always the chief citizen of the State, has the greatest interest in its conservation. None the less, we see how he elsewhere commends the republican form of government, as when he says that virtue is its very mainspring, while a monarchy is founded upon respect and honour; or when, in approval of the popular elections, he writes: "It is an admirable thing that the people should select those to whom they are bound to confide some part of their authority."

It was after reading Montesquieu that Frenchmen became accustomed to regard the republican form of government—which they did not desire to see in France—as a theoretically noble and interesting form.

This theorist of the Monarchy thus found that he had deprived monarchical government of some of its prestige; and, by his views upon the separation of the three forms of authority, he touched royalty itself to the quick—that royalty which pretended, by Divine right, to concentrate all authority in itself.

In this manner did Montesquieu, so admired, so widely read, contribute towards the development of republican ideas and the formation of the republican spirit.

* * *

Jean-Jacques Rousseau, in his *Contrat social,* had written "that, in general, government by democracy was suited to small States, government by aristocracy to those of medium size, and government by Monarchy to large States." He further stated "that there is no form of government so liable to civil wars and internecine tumult as the democratic or popular," and that "if there existed a nation of gods, they would govern themselves by a democracy: so perfect a government is unsuited to mankind." But he was preparing for the ruin of the monarchical system when he said that "the two principal objects of every system of legislation should be liberty and equality." Prudent and reserved though he was in theory, he preached revolt by his conduct, in his speeches, and in his romantic writings—revolt, in the name of Nature, against the vicious and artificial social system of his time; and, although fundamentally a Christian, he replaced the mystical ideals of charity and humility by the republican ideal of fraternity.

* * *

From the writings of these philosophers one idea stands out, an idea that quickly became almost general: that the nation is above the King; and is not this a republican idea? Although these writers wish to maintain the Monarchy, they habitually speak of the republican system in honourable terms. A posthumous work of d'Argenson's, *Considérations sur le Gouvernement,* published in 1765, recommends the fortification of the Monarchy by an "infusion" of republican institutions; and d'Argenson praises the government which he does not desire for his own country in terms so sympathetic as to invite misconception, so greatly does this work of royalist tendencies, which was much read at the time, do honour to the republican idea.

* * *

The idea that the King should be only a citizen subject to the law, causing the law to be executed, had gradually become popularised; of its popularity there is endless proof. When Voltaire wrote, in his tragedy of *Don Pèdre* (1775):

> A king is but a man with name august,
> First subject of the laws: and, by law, just,

he knew well that he would win applause. And if it be objected that this tragedy was not presented, that these lines were not actually heard by the

theatre-going public, I will cite the line borrowed by Favart from a poem by
Louis Racine, published in 1744, which drew applause in the *Trois Sultanes,*
at the *Théâtre des Italiens,* on April 9, 1761:

> Each citizen a king, under a citizen king.

That such maxims were applauded in the theatre, nearly thirty years before
the Revolution, that the Government was obliged to tolerate them: does not
this prove that public opinion had already, so to say, despoiled the King and
his kingship of the mystical principle of sovereignty? And is not this idea of
the "citizen king," so unanimously applauded, one of the most startling signs
of the republicanisation of the general mind?

* * *

To sum up: no one on the eve of the Revolution had ever dreamed of the
establishment of a republic in France: it was a form of government that
seemed impossible in a great State in course of unification. It was through the
King that men sought to establish a free government. Men wished to organise the Monarchy, not to destroy it. No one dreamed of calling the ignorant
mass of the people to political life; the necessary revolution was to be brought
about by the better class of the nation, the educated, property-owning class. It
was believed that the people, blind and inconstant as they were thought,
could only prove an instrument of reaction in the hands of the privileged.
However, the future date of democracy was announced in the proclamation
of the principle of the sovereignty of the people: and the republic, the logical
form of democracy, was prepared by the diffusion of republican ideas—for
example, from America; by the sight of an impotent monarchy, and by the
continual proclamation of the necessity of a violent revolution, which, undertaken in order to reform the monarchy, was to expose its very existence to the
dangers of a general upheaval. The ruling classes of society were steeped in
republicanism. Such a state of mind was so prevalent that if the King, in
whom men saw the historically indispensable guide to a new France, were to
fail in his mission, or discard, for example, his authority as hereditary defender of French independence, a republic would be accepted without dislike
and without enthusiasm, first by the better class, and then by the mass of the
nation.

* * *

We have seen that in 1789 there appeared to be two Frances; the enlightened France and the ignorant France, a rich France and a poor France. As
for the political rights which the publicists of the day were demanding, it was
only for the well-to-do and the educated that these rights were claimed. Owners of property were to be "active citizens"; they alone having the right to
vote. Those without property were to be "passive citizens." In short, "the
nation is the *bourgeoisie.*"

Between the *bourgeoisie* and the people there is a gulf. The richer classes exaggerate the stupidity and obliviousness of the people—above all, of the rural masses. There is ill-feeling and misunderstanding between the two classes. To clear up this misunderstanding will require a conference, a general meeting and mingling of the middle classes with the people as a whole.

Such a result will follow the convocation of the Estates-General.

At the Parish Assemblies the Third Estate is admitted almost without exception, under a slight property restriction, to fulfil the condition of being "included in the roll of taxpayers." This is very nearly universal suffrage.

Had royalty established this suffrage, so contrary to the ideas of the century, for the very reasons that induced the philosophers and the writers in favour of reform to reject it? Did the King hope, in the poor and ignorant masses, to find an element of resistance against the new and revolutionary ideas of the middle class? I have not found any documentary evidence which will allow me to answer this question precisely, but to me it does not seem impossible that the King did have some confused idea of appealing to universal suffrage against the opposition of the middle class, to darkness against light.

If such a calculation did really exist, it was disproved by the event.

To be sure, the *cahiers* are more timid than the books and pamphlets of the time; but as a general thing they demand a Constitution, and a Constitution is the end of absolutism—it is, to some extent, the Revolution.

Moreover, there are *cahiers* which are bold in the extreme.

However, neither the hopes of royalty nor the fears of the *bourgeoisie* were realised—supposing that such hopes and fears existed.

In any case, we must note how the misunderstanding between the *bourgeoisie* and the people was dissipated or diminished on the occasion of convocation and the drawing up of the *cahiers*.

Collaboration took place between the *bourgeoisie* and the people in the drafting of the *cahiers* of the first degree, or the parish *cahiers;* and in general we must not, in the case of rural communities, regard these *cahiers* as the personal work of peasants. It was usually a man of the middle classes who held the pen, and in most localities, even in the most rustic, there were a few educated men. The majority of the parish *cahiers* that we possess testify to a considerable amount of culture—a culture higher than that of the provincial middle classes of today.

If the *cahier* is not dictated by peasants, it is at least read to and approved by them. There is an assembly at which peasants and middle classes mingle together, chat with one another, and publicly discuss and debate. It is the first time such a colloquy has taken place; the occasion is a fraternal one, and the classes are quickly in agreement. The middle-class man sees that the peasant is more intelligent or less imbecile than he had supposed; that—by what obscure channels who knows?—the spirit of the times has touched him. The peasants, once they have met together, soon rise to the idea of a common interest; they have the sense that they are many and powerful, and they obtain, from the middle classes, a perception of their rights. For them this Parish Assembly is a civic apprenticeship.

We must not picture the whole peasantry rising at once to the revolutionary idea of the mother-country. But they take the Convocation seriously; they feel that it will bring about an event which will be beneficial to themselves, and they conceive an image of the King, an image which is a reflection of the idea of country. To them, it appears in deadly earnest that the King is going to concern himself with the cure of the ills which afflict them; it is in earnest that they recount these ills, or, rather, accept the account of them that the gentlemen of the village write for them; and when they sign with a cross at the bottom of the document, they have no fear that this cross will subject them to surcharges of taxation and the nuisance of collectors. By no means; their signature is an act of confidence and hope.

We have here no longer the vile populace, slighted and feared by Mably, Rousseau, and Condorcet. But it is not as yet the sovereign people. They are men who at last are counting on being treated as men; almost candidates for the dignity of citizen; and who, tomorrow, by an electric impulse issuing, at the fall of the Bastille, from Paris, will feel themselves animated by an impetus of union and agglomeration from which will issue the new nation, the new France.

Let us repeat that the middle classes also have found somewhat to learn at these assemblies—namely, to be less scornful of the poor and the ignorant. It is true that men will still declaim against the populace, and the middle class will even establish itself as a caste politically privileged. But enlightened Frenchmen will no longer, after this royal experiment in universal suffrage, be unanimous in declaring the unlettered to be incapable of exercising political rights. A democratic party is about to declare itself, and will soon be fully formed. The method of convening the Third Estate at the Estates-General allows us almost to foretell the advent of universal suffrage, and, as a consequence, the establishment of the Republic, the national form of Democracy.

Georges Lefebvre devoted his whole scholarly life to the study of the French Revolution. In 1939 his unmatched knowledge of the origins of the Revolution was distilled into the little book from which the following selection is drawn.

FROM The Coming of the French Revolution
BY GEORGES LEFEBVRE

THE PEASANTRY

There was scarcely any question of the peasants before July 14. Yet they formed at least three quarters of the population of the kingdom, and we realize today that without their adherence the Revolution could with difficulty have succeeded. Their grievances had been disregarded in the drafting of the bailiwick petitions, or had at best received little emphasis. Their complaints were by no means uppermost among the interests of the National Assembly, in which there were no peasant members. Then suddenly they too revolted, taking their cause into their own hands and delivering a death blow to what was left of the feudal and manorial system. The peasant uprising is one of the most distinctive features of the Revolution in France.

The Peasant and the Land

In 1789 the great majority of the French peasants had been free for many generations, i.e., they could move about and work as they wished, possess property and bring suit in the law courts. Some "serfs" could still be found, principally in Franche-Comté and the Nivernais, but they were no longer really attached to the soil, and in 1779 the king had even abolished the right of pursuit, which had allowed the lord to make good his claims over the serf wherever the latter might go. The main characteristic of serfdom in France was lack of freedom in disposing of goods. The serf was a *mainmortable* or man under a mortmain; if, at his death, he did not have at least one living child residing with him, all his possessions reverted to the lord. In France the serf was far better off than in central and eastern Europe, where the peasantry was left under the nobleman's arbitrary jurisdiction. In France the king's justice protected the rights and person of both serf and free man.

Georges Lefebvre, *The Coming of the French Revolution*, pp. 131–137, 140–147, 209–212, 214–220, translated by R. R. Palmer. Reprinted by permission of Princeton University Press. Copyright 1947 by Princeton University Press.

Not only were most French peasants not serfs. Many were landowners, differing in this respect from the peasants of England, who in general had been reduced by the landed aristocracy to the status of wage laborers. The size and number of peasant properties varied greatly from one region to another. They were most extensive in Alsace, Flanders, Limousin, parts of Normandy, the Loire valley, the plains of the Saône and the Garonne and generally throughout southern France more than in the North. In these regions peasants owned from half to three-quarters of the soil. Elsewhere the proportion fell much lower, notably in barren, marshy or forested regions and in the neighborhood of cities. Of the land around Versailles peasant ownership accounted for no more than one or two per cent. Thirty per cent is a probable average for the kingdom as a whole. The remaining land was owned by the clergy (probably a tenth of the kingdom), the nobles (over twice as much) and the bourgeoisie (perhaps a fifth). The clergy was especially wealthy in the North, less so as one went west and south. The nobles seem to have been wealthiest in the North, East and West. Bourgeois ownership of rural land was characteristic of the South.

Yet everywhere there were propertyless peasants. Rarely was the number of these rural proletarians negligible: it has been estimated at about a fifth of family heads in Limousin, 30 to 40 per cent in the Norman woodlands, 70 per cent around Versailles and as high as 75 per cent in maritime Flanders. Some of these unpropertied peasants found land to rent. Ecclesiastics, noblemen and bourgeois seldom exploited their own lands, except in the wine country and in some parts of the South. Instead, they put them in the hands of farmers, or more often of sharecroppers with whom they divided the produce. Moreover, their estates consisted in many small unconnected parcels, which they were glad to lease out separately bit by bit. Hence the laborer could manage to procure a patch for himself, and the peasant owner, for his part, could supplement his own holdings with additional parcels taken on lease. In this way the rural proletariat in the strict sense, or peasants who had no land either by ownership or by leasehold, was substantially reduced while never disappearing entirely. Hence also rural society had as many gradations as society in the cities. The most well to do were the large farmers, who often owned no land themselves. Next came the substantial class, called *laboureurs,* who worked considerable tracts which they owned wholly or in part. They were followed, in downward order, by the small farmer, the sharecropper, the peasant having the use of some land but not enough to live on, the laborer possessing a house and garden plus some small parcel on lease and finally the laborer who had nothing but his hands.

Unfortunately the holdings of the overwhelming majority of the peasants were not large enough to support them and their families. Backward methods of cultivation were in part the cause. In the North and East the village lands were subdivided into countless long and narrow strips, which were grouped in three "fields." One field was sown with winter wheat, one with a spring crop, while the third lay fallow, i.e., uncultivated, each field changing its role from year to year. South of a line running from eastern Normandy to Burgundy and passing by Beauce there were only two fields, of which one always lay fallow. In the West, in Limousin and in the mountains, the cultivated areas, enclosed by hedges, comprised an even smaller fraction of the soil, the remaining land being worked only from time to time, sometimes only one year in ten, sometimes even less often. In any case, triennial or biennial rotation left a third or half the arable soil unproductive. Hence the peasant needed more land than today. In the region later comprised in the department of Nord nine families out of ten had too little to live on. The situation had grown worse since the middle of the eighteenth century, for the population had increased perceptibly, probably by three million. The number of proletarians had risen, while through division of inheritances the shares of property owners had become smaller. There was, therefore, at the end of the Old Regime, an agrarian crisis.

Hence many peasants invaded the commons when the king, in 1764 and 1766, granted exemption from tithes and taxes to persons who cleared new land. Borders of the forests, and open places within them, swarmed with barefoot pioneers who built themselves cabins, cleared what they could and felled timber either for sale or for conversion into charcoal. The marshes likewise hid a wretched population which lived by fishing or cutting peat. Peasant landowners, in the grievance-lists, roundly criticized the nobles and clergy who exploited their own estates directly, and demanded also that the big properties be leased out, not to a few large farmers, but to many small ones. In Picardy and Hainaut, when the owners tried to change farmers, the latter fought back against eviction, even to the point of arson and murder. It is therefore not surprising to find some parishes asking for alienation of the crown lands and even of part of the property of the clergy. But it is characteristic of the time that the property of individuals was never questioned. At the height of the Terror, when the property of *émigrés* and of persons condemned for political offenses was sold, and when it was decided also to confiscate the property of mere suspects, the principle was always that of penalizing enemies of the country. Nobles who stayed in France, and remained peaceable, never at any time during the Revolution saw their property threatened. This was because the land, when it was not the property of the peasants, was already in their hands on leasehold terms. Farm rentals, it is true, had almost doubled during the eighteenth century, while prices had gone up on the average not more than sixty-five per cent. Sharecropping too had become less favorable to the peasant; in general, the owner still took only half the crop or half the increment of livestock, but he increasingly imposed obligations of many kinds and even a supplemental payment in cash, especially in cases where sharing arrangements were managed through a "farmer-general," who found it to his advantage to bring pressure on the croppers. There was much bitter complaint on this score in Bourbonnais, Nivernais and Beaujolais. Nevertheless, despite all these grievances, the farmer or share-cropper would have nothing to gain by exchanging his leased holdings for the tiny parcel which a general redistribution of property would procure for him. And it is obvious that those peasants who already owned property would not have favored any such redistribution.

Taxes, Tithes, Fees, Dues

Keeping in mind that the agrarian crisis was real and pressing, we must recognize that there was only one matter on which the whole rural population could unanimously agree—namely, the obligations imposed by the king and the aristocracy.

The peasant was almost alone in paying the *taille* and drawing lots for militia service. He alone was held for road work and for aid in military transportation. From him came most of the proceeds of the poll-tax and the twentieth-taxes. Yet it was the indirect taxes that he detested the most, especially the government salt monopoly, which held the price of salt as high as thirteen sous a pound in a large part of the kingdom. The royal demands had steadily risen during the eighteenth century, and the parish grievance-lists of 1789 invariably complained of them, but we cannot say, in view of the general rise in the price level, whether they actually took a greater part of the national income in 1789 than a half century before. Probably they did. In Walloon Flanders, a region having Provincial Estates and hence getting off fairly lightly, the increase in direct taxes in the reign of Louis XVI alone has been estimated at twenty-eight per cent. The peasants, while critical of the bourgeois, observing that commercial wealth paid less than its proper share, were most especially aroused to a state of fury by the privileges of the aristocracy.

The royal taxation, a relatively new burden superimposed on the payments made from time immemorial to the aristocracy, undoubtedly had the indirect consequence of making these payments far more hateful. To the clergy was due the tithe, variable in amount but almost always less than a tenth, levied on the "great" grains, wheat, rye, oats and barley (the "great tithe"), and on other grains and vegetables and fruits (the "small tithe"), and on a few animal products. From the peasant grievance-lists it is evident that the tithe would have been more willingly paid if the proceeds, instead of going in most cases to bishops, abbeys or chapters, or even to lay lords to whom the tithe might be "subinfeudated" (the parish priest receiving the small tithe at most), had been used, as they should have been, to support public worship, the parish church and parsonage and above all the poor. But the peasant, after paying the tithe, saw most of the expense for such purposes still falling upon himself. In addition the tithe had all the disadvantages of a levy collected in kind. The tithe owner had to come and take it away himself; if he delayed, the whole crop might suffer from bad weather; the peasant was deprived of straw, a material necessary to manure, and the only one known to him. The tithe also blocked the progress of land clearance and of new methods of cultivation. Since it was collected in kind, a rise in prices made it more profitable to the collector; in 1789 the gross product was thought to be worth

120,000,000 livres. The profit was greatest in times of scarcity, at the cost of the peasant's very subsistence; and in any case, at all times, the tithe collector seemed a food hoarder by his very nature.

What there was left of feudalism was even more disliked. The strictly feudal should be distinguished from the manorial. From the feudal point of view land consisted of fiefs, depending one upon another and all finally upon the king. Fiefs were subject to a law of their own, of which the law of primogeniture is the best known; and with each change of owner the suzerain required the vassal to make due acknowledgment, submit a survey of the estate and pay a fee. Unless the peasant had bought a fief, which was rare at least in the North, this system did not concern him. If he had bought a fief he paid the king, as did the bourgeois in the same circumstances, a special fee called the *franc-fief*.

During the eighteenth century the demands of manorial lords, like those of the king, had become more burdensome for the peasants. Since the system had been criticized by the philosophers and economists, manorial lords thought it necessary to reaffirm their rights by frequently renewing the manor rolls in which they were written down and by requiring exact payment. Increasingly they farmed out their rights to professional collectors, who were inexorable in their work, reviving and enforcing almost obsolete obligations, if indeed not broadening them in a way that was positively an abuse. Where claims were contested, the manorial courts and the Parliaments always decided against the peasants. But what exasperated the rural people, since they had in any case too little land for a livelihood, was the encroachment on their collective rights, on which their existence depended.

* * *

Numerous are the peasant grievance-lists which complain, and complain bitterly, of these constant encroachments, as of the generally growing exactions of the feudal class. They insist on the damage done to agriculture by the hunting rights, the dovecotes and the rabbit warrens in the absence of proper regulation and of any recourse. Payments in kind were subject to the same criticism as was the tithe. The petitions call attention to the crushing weight of all these dues taken together, finding it heavier than the parallel burden of the royal taxes. More rare are the petitions which propose remedies, such as suppression of certain rights considered particularly repugnant, or authorization to buy up the manorial dues. The principle of the system is never questioned, but we must note that the peasants did not express all that was on their minds, and that on the matter of manorial rights the bourgeois who assumed leadership over them were often reticent in their opinions, since manorial rights were a form of property, which some bourgeois had themselves purchased, and in which others had an interest as judges or agents for the manorial lords. Still, the deeper workings of the peasant mind can be seen in one way, when their petitions demand that the original document specifying payments in return for holdings be produced, and that in its absence such payments be brought to an end. The peasant proprietor, it is clear, thought himself the only legitimate owner of his land, and considered the payments due the lord, unless there was proof to the contrary, to have originated in nothing but violence. In some cases peasant rancor against lordly "bloodsuckers" did in fact express itself plainly. . . .

Against the aristocracy the peasants had far more substantial grievances than did the people of the cities, and it is natural therefore that they took it upon themselves to deal the blow by which the aristocracy was laid low.

THE AGRARIAN REVOLTS AND THE GREAT FEAR

The hatred of the peasants for the lords was not a thing of yesterday. The history of France abounds in *jacqueries*. In the eighteenth century the collection of manorial dues more than once led to troubles, and in particular engendered innumerable lawsuits which the peasants sustained with incredible tenacity. Yet if they were brought to a state of general rebellion in 1789 one reason is to be found in the convocation of the Estates-General. . . . The bailiwick lieutenant of Saumur observed, as the most unsettling feature of convocation of the Estates, that the electoral assemblies of the parishes thought themselves invested with sovereign authority, and that the rustics believed themselves already rid of the manorial dues. Cries of alarm rose everywhere in the kingdom in the course of the spring: the peasants were declaring their intention to make no payments at the coming harvest. Class solidarity asserted itself strongly. During the disturbances at Chatou the peasants took aside one of their number who seemed suspect, demanded of him, "Are you for the Third Estate?" and when he gave a negative answer told him, "Then we'll give you the idea!" The agrarian insurrections, more even than those of the cities, were genuine mass movements.

At the same time the idea of an "aristocratic conspiracy" grew up and rooted itself even more strongly than in the bourgeois, for the peasants knew by centuries of experience that in the eyes of the lord the manorial dues were untouchable—his social superiority depending on them as well as his income. That the lord would make every effort to deceive the "good king"; that if he failed in this he would take up arms to crush the Third Estate—all this seemed obvious and inevitable to the peasants. The inaction of the Estates-General and their silence on matters of concern to the peasants were attributed to an aristocratic conspiracy. When news came of the resort to force, what doubt could there be? And when it was learned that the king, visiting his insurgent capital, had given his approval to the resistance which had blocked the aristocrats, what reservations could any longer be felt? During the ensuing revolts the peasants insisted that they were executing the king's will. Smuggled orders circulated among them, ostensibly emanating from the king.

* * *

Yet the same observation must be made of the country as of the towns. The peasant rising would be inconceivable without the excitement produced by the calling of the Estates-General. But it is undeniable also that the economic crisis contributed powerfully to it, and reinforced also the idea of an aristocratic plot. The rural masses suffered cruelly from food shortages, contrary to what might be supposed, for most peasants raised too little to subsist on, and when the harvest was bad the number of those in want increased perceptibly as the year went on. They would go to make purchases at the neighboring market, become involved in the disturbances there and on returning spread trouble and a sense of insecurity through their home parishes. In the open country they would stop shipments of food without hesitation, so that during the summer of 1789 disorder became universal. As for the causes and possible remedies for the problem, they held the same views as the small people of the towns. Regulation was their panacea, the hoarder their enemy.

* * *

Hence the economic crisis had revolutionary consequences in two ways. On the one hand it enflamed the peasants by turning them against the tithe owners and lords who took away part of their livelihood through the manorial dues. On the other hand, by multiplying the number of those in want, it generalized a sense of insecurity which in the end was blamed on a conspiracy of the aristocrats.

The Agrarian Revolts

Just as fear in no sense dated from July 14, so it would be wrong to imagine that the peasant waited for the example of the capital to revolt. The example of the nearest town was sufficient, and even this was by no means indispensable. At the end of March the high price of bread led to popular uprisings at Toulon and Marseilles, from which agitation spread immediately to all upper Provence. The villages of the Avance Valley, in the region of Gap, rose in insurrection against their lord on April 20. On May 6 a riot broke out at Cambrai; the whole Cambrésis was instantly aflame; the contagion spread to Picardy. Near Paris and Versailles the peasants organized a systematic extermination of game, pillaged the forests and fired on the wardens.

* * *

These disturbances were all aimed against the aristocracy.

CONCLUSION

The Revolution of 1789 consisted first of all in the fall of absolute monarchy and advent of a liberty henceforth guaranteed by constitutional government; nor on this score can it be doubted that it was a national revolution, since the privileged orders as well as the Third Estate demanded a constitution and a regime in which individual rights would be respected.

But it was also the advent of equality before the law, without which liberty would be but another privilege of the powerful. For the French of 1789 liberty and equality were inseparable, almost two words for the same thing; but had they been obliged to choose, it is equality that they would have chosen; and when the peasants, who formed the overwhelming majority, cheered the conquest of liberty they were in fact thinking of the disappearance of the authority of the manorial lord, and his reduction to the status of a mere citizen. They were thinking, that is, of equality.

Thus made free and equal in rights, the French founded the nation anew, one and indivisible, by voluntary consent, in the movements called federations and especially in the Federation of July 14, 1790. This third characteristic of the Revolution of 1789 was one of its most original features, and the assertion that a people has the right to dispose of itself, and cannot be annexed to another without its own adherence freely expressed, has exerted an influence by no means yet exhausted in the world.

Moreover, the men of 1789 never entertained the idea that the rights of man and citizen were reserved for Frenchmen only. Christianity drew no distinction among men; it called on them all to meet as brothers in the divine city. In the same way the revolutionaries thought of liberty and equality as the common birthright of mankind. Imagining that all peoples would emulate their example, they even dreamed for an instant that the nations, in becoming free, would be reconciled forever in universal peace.

In the view of the lawyers, who represented and guided the bourgeoisie, the Revolution was to be a peaceful readjustment, imposed by opinion and translated rather simply into new juridical formulations. And in fact the essential work of the Revolution of 1789 may be found registered in the resolutions of August 4 and in the Declaration of Rights of Man and the Citizen. But it would be childish to emphasize only these legislative enactments, throwing into the background the events which gave them birth; childish likewise, and indeed more so, to select from among these events certain ones to compose a legend. The Estates-General skillfully and boldly defended the cause of the Third Estate which was the cause of the nation, but as even Buchez admitted, a peace-loving and Catholic democrat of 1848, "The Assembly would have achieved nothing without the insurrections." The Old Regime did not bend before the juridical revolution. Having taken to force, it was destroyed by force, which the people, descending into the street, put at the service of what they regarded as right, though even their own representatives had not dared to ask such assistance from them.

Whether the resort to violence was *in principle* necessary or unnecessary the historian cannot know. He observes simply that in the spring of 1789 the French people still had no thought of it, and that two years earlier they did not even suspect the regime to be nearing its end. It was the aristocracy that precipitated the Revolution by forcing the king to call the Estates-General.

Once the Third Estate obtained the right to express itself, the possibility of concessions which would have satisfied it for a time depended on the nobles and on the king. The issue was not so much political in character as social; for the transformation of the monarchy into a constitutional government was a reform on which nobles and bourgeois agreed, and by which Louis XVI would have lost little authority; but the great majority of the nobles, while prepared to make concessions in the direction of fiscal equality, were determined, more from pride than from material interest, to preserve their other privileges and remain a nation within the nation. One wonders whether the year 1789 might not have become the first phase of an evolutionary movement, during which the nobles would have gradually come to accept the status of mere citizens. It is possible, and, if one likes, even probable; but, since we cannot run history over like an experiment in a laboratory, opinions on this question will always be divided. In any case, what actually happened is that the necessary decisions were not made in time, that the Court turned to force to protect the aristocracy and that the problem was therefore presented in all its fullness. The Third Estate, driven to the wall, had to choose between resistance and surrender, so that in fact insurrection became inevitable, considering that fundamentally the Third was resolved to stand its ground.

* * *

Still it need hardly be said that many motives combined to bring the French people to their supreme dilemma. We have attempted to single them out. Class interests and personal interests, humbled pride, mass suffering, philosophical propaganda all made their contribution, in proportions different for each individual, but with the net effect of producing in the Third Estate a collective mentality that was strangely complex, but which in summary expressed itself as a belief in an aristocratic conspiracy, a belief which in turn aroused passionate feelings, the fear, the frenzy for fighting, the thirst for revenge that characterized the days of July.

Dismayed by popular excesses, the bourgeoisie tried to blame them on provocative agents, foreigners, "brigands" and criminals such as inevitably mingled with the insurgents. It is true that men who are the dregs of society are not the last to take part in mobs. But the allegations of the Assembly and the bourgeois authorities have a note of apology. The ordinary people neither condemned nor repudiated the murders of July, nor did Barnave or Mme. Roland. The elements in the revolutionary complex cannot be taken apart. In this sense Clemenceau was right: the Revolution is a *bloc,* a single thing. The moralist must praise heroism and condemn cruelty; but the moralist does not explain events.

* * *

Much labor has been spent in contesting the originality of the Declaration, in deducing its substance, for example, from the bills of rights adopted by the

American colonists in the struggle that won their independence. The men of
the Constituent Assembly were undoubtedly familiar with these documents,
especially the one issued by Virginia on May 10, 1776. The inspiration and
content of the American and French declarations were the same. It was in
fact with Jefferson, as early as January 1789, that La Fayette discussed his
project; the text that he presented to the Assembly on July 11, with the accompanying letter, has been found in the papers of the ambassador of the
United States, annotated by his own hand. The influence of America is beyond question. But this is not to say that without America the French declaration would not have seen the light. The whole philosophic movement in
France in the eighteenth century pointed to such an act; Montesquieu, Voltaire and Rousseau had collaborated in its making. In reality, America and
France, like England before them, were alike tributaries to a great stream of
ideas, which, while expressing the ascendancy of the bourgeoisie, constituted
a common ideal that summarized the evolution of western civilization.

* * *

Many objections have been made to the Declaration. Some have already
been mentioned because they apply to the circumstances in which it was
debated in the Assembly. Others of more general bearing merit a moment's
further attention.

The Declaration, it has been said, is a mere abstraction from real life. Some
men may be worthy of the rights it proclaims; some are less so; some, indeed,
are hardly human. For cannibals, for example, the rights of man can have no
real application; and if it be argued that even cannibals are human beings,
still they are scarcely human in our sense. Nor, it is alleged, does the Declaration allow for circumstances. If war or economic crisis endanger a nation's
existence, are the rights of its citizens to have the same free scope as in times
of prosperity? And if individual rights are not inherently limited, will not the
government be granted the power to limit them?

There is no force in this criticism except when the Declaration is confused
with a legal code, whereas its nature is that of moral principle, not of positive
legislation. We are bound by moral principle, for example—as well as by the
Declaration—not to do to another what we should not wish him to do to us.
Moral principle does not specify what our conduct should be in each particular case; it leaves this task to the moralist or the casuist. Similarly the Declaration proclaims the rights of man, but leaves to the law, which may vary
with circumstances, the task of determining the extent, which may also vary
with circumstances, to which these rights may be exercised, always providing
that the law is the true expression of the general will, i.e., of the majority of
the community. That the members of the National Assembly considered this
to be the character of the Declaration is clear from the debates in which,
a month before its adoption, they discussed the operations of counter-
revolutionaries and considered setting up a special court: governing in wartime is not like governing in peacetime, observed Gouy d'Arsy, anticipating

Robespierre. Again, when the question of slavery arose, the relativism in the Declaration became apparent; it was judged impossible to transfer the Negroes abruptly, without apprenticeship in freedom, from slavery to the full status of citizenship. And the Assembly reached by implication the same conclusion for France, when it made the right to vote depend on degree of economic well-being, and the right to be elected depend on the owning of real estate, because, rightly or wrongly, it regarded such economic well-being, and especially the ownership of land, as the only means of assuring the enlightenment and self-restraint thought necessary to the exercise of the rights of man and of citizenship. These rights then are relative to circumstances. The Declaration is an ideal to be realized. It is a *direction of intention*.

Another criticism, vehemently raised in our day, is that it favored one class at the expense of others, namely the bourgeoisie that drew it up, and that it thus provoked a disorder that threatens the community with disruption. The Declaration did indeed list property among the rights of man, and its authors meant property as it then existed and still does; moreover, economic liberty, though not mentioned, is very much in its spirit. This amounts to saying that the man who holds the land and the other instrumentalities of labor, i.e., capital, is in fact master of those who possess nothing but their muscles and their intelligence, because they depend on him for the opportunity to earn their living. The evil is made worse, it is added, by the inheritance of property, which endows certain children, irrespective of merit or capacity, with the *means* over and above the *rights* which are all that others receive. The Declaration, in short, is blamed for having allowed capitalism to develop without control and for having thus caused the proletariat to rise against it—to have had as a consequence a new class struggle of an always accelerating violence, all for want of some power of arbitration that can be granted only to the state. Contrariwise, those who deny such a power to the state have not failed to invoke the Declaration, elaborating upon it with ideas drawn from its own authors, who undoubtedly held to *laissez-faire* and unlimited competition as universal panaceas, and conceived of property as an absolute right to use or to abuse.

Here again, for a reply, we must appeal to the Constituents themselves. They had before their eyes a society in which modern capitalism was barely beginning, and in which the increase of productive capacity seemed the essential corrective to poverty and want. Even to those who gave thought to the poor it seemed not impossible that every man might own a few acres or a shop that would make him self-sufficient; and this ideal, which was that of the *sans-culottes,* remained alive well into the nineteenth century. Experience has not justified these hopes. Rousseau had already observed, long before 1789, that democracy is not compatible with an excessive inequality of wealth. It is for the community to examine whether the changes since 1789 in the economic and social structure of society do not justify intervention by the law, so that the excess of *means* in the hands of some may not reduce the *rights* of others to an empty show. By what procedure? That too is for the community to decide, in the spirit of the Declaration, which in proclaiming liberty did not mean an aristocratic liberty reserved for a few, such as Montalambert demanded in 1850, but which rather, confiding to the law the task of delimiting the rights of citizens, left it to take the measures that may be suitable to prevent social disruption.

Finally, according to other critics, the Declaration regards law as simply the will of the citizens; but what would become of the nation if the majority oppressed the minority, or if it refused to make the necessary sacrifices which in time of war may reach to life itself? The community, this school concludes, cannot be identified with the citizens who make it up at a given moment; extending beyond them in time, it is hierarchically above them, for without it they would not exist; it is really embodied in the state, which in consequence cannot depend on the will of ephemeral citizens, and for that reason has the right to coerce them. With this idea, it need hardly be said, we return to the personal absolutism of the Old Regime, for the state, whatever may be said, has itself no effective existence except in individual persons, who by and large would confer their mandates upon themselves. Still less need it be remarked that this system is in radical contradiction with the Declaration in reducing the individual to be a mere instrument in the hands of the state, depriving him of all liberty and all self-determination.

But these answers do not remove the difficulty, as too often we delude ourselves into believing. It is perfectly true that the Declaration carries with it a risk, as do absolutism and dictatorship, though the risk is of another kind. The citizens must be made to face their responsibilities. Invested with the rights of governing themselves, if they abuse their powers with respect to one another, above all if they refuse from personal selfishness to assure the welfare of the community, the community will perish, and with it their liberty, if not indeed their existence.

We come here to the deeper meaning of the Declaration. It is a direction of intention; it therefore requires of the citizens an integrity of purpose, which is to say a critical spirit, patriotism in the proper sense of the word, respect for the rights of others, reasoned devotion to the national community, "virtue" in the language of Montesquieu, Rousseau and Robespierre. "The soul of the Republic," wrote Robespierre in 1792, "is virtue, love of country, the generous devotion that fuses all interests into the general interest." The Declaration in proclaiming the rights of man appeals at the same time to discipline freely consented to, to sacrifice if need be, to cultivation of character *and to the mind*. Liberty is by no means an invitation to indifference or to irresponsible power; nor is it the promise of unlimited well-being without a counterpart of toil and effort. It supposes application, perpetual effort, strict government of self, sacrifice in contingencies, civic and private virtues. It is therefore more difficult to live as a free man than to live as a slave, and that is why men so often renounce their freedom; for freedom is in its way an invitation to a life of courage, and sometimes of heroism, as the freedom of the Christian is an invitation to a life of sainthood.

THE INDUSTRIAL REVOLUTION IN ENGLAND

BLESSING OR CURSE TO THE WORKING MAN?

CONTENTS

QUESTIONS FOR STUDY

1. *What was the condition of the rural workers in the eighteenth century?*

2. *What were the essential changes required of a person when a shift was made from the country to a manufacturing city?*

3. *What working conditions were detrimental to the children employed in factories? What conditions might be beneficial?*

4. *What are the main points at issue between the Hammonds and Ashton?*

5. *By what criteria can a judgment be made on whether the Industrial Revolution was a blessing or a curse to the working man?*

During the eighteenth century a series of economic changes in agricultural and industrial production in Great Britain gave rise to what historians later labeled the Industrial Revolution. There can be no doubt that this revolution has drastically altered all the old relationships—economic, political, and social—and has led to new conditions and problems with which we are still wrestling. Industrialization was and is a painful process, requiring considerable upheaval, individual and mass dislocations, and needless suffering. We may still ask the question: Was it worth it? Does industrialization profit only the few, or is industrialization necessary for everyone's well-being? Today half the world is rushing into industrialization, while the industrialized half is once more pausing to take stock. The passage of almost two centuries may permit us to assess the Industrial Revolution with dispassion and some claim to objectivity. To do so, however, we must have some idea of what conditions were before and after industrialization took place.

At the beginning of the eighteenth century the great mass of the English people lived on the land and from it. Some were wealthy independent farmers, others were tenant farmers whose wealth was determined in large part by their industry, and some were cottagers living in rural poverty, barely able to glean a living from the common land and their small patches of rented land. This last group was particularly subject to the vagaries of weather and agricultural production. If there was a food shortage they were the first to suffer, and in famine they were the first to die. Their cottages were hovels and they had little incentive for improvement, since they could never hope to rise above the subsistence level. It took a good deal of capital to set oneself up as an independent farmer, and the cottager could never hope to amass the necessary amount. The diet of the cottager was poor and monotonous, rarely including meat. Infant mortality was high, illiteracy was the rule, and life was brutish, boring, and short. It seemed impossible that it could get worse, but it did. The Enclosure Acts of the eighteenth century enclosed common land to the profit of the landowner and at the expense of the cottager. Sometimes the cottager found himself immediately expelled, since his cottage was on the common land, or—what ultimately amounted to the same thing—he found his cow or pigs excluded from the common. With this margin of survival removed, he and his family had to leave or go on the poor rolls. From this ever-widening pool of misery came the people who migrated to the cities, particularly London, and there created that urban poverty-stricken mass familiar in Hogarth's etchings and in such works as *The Beggar's Opera*. It is important to realize that these effects were present *before* the Industrial Revolution properly got under way.

The Industrial Revolution began simply enough. The British conquest of India in the Seven Years' War introduced Britons and Europeans to the wonders and cheapness of cotton goods. Their gay colors and low price created a mass market that could not be satisfied by importation from India. Mills were built in England and raw cotton was imported, particularly from Egypt and India. American cotton, it may be noted, did not assume importance until the invention of the cotton gin in the 1790s, which permitted the cheap production of the short staple variety that thrived in the American South. The inventions that spurred production were extremely simple in the beginning. Kay's flying shuttle and Crompton's and Arkwright's improvements of spinning machinery were the products of inspired whittling, not of engineering or applied science. One innovation had far-reaching effects—namely, the use of water power to provide the energy for spinning and weaving on a mass scale. The old method, used in the woolens industry and hallowed by centuries of tradition, had relied on spinners and weavers working in their cottages with individual spinning wheels and handlooms to produce woolen cloth. Such a system could not satisfy the mass demand for cotton goods and the new machines permitted the concentration of production in one place, the factory. In order to be profitable factory production required full-time labor and strict discipline. Fortunately for the British capitalist, a large pool of labor was available in the displaced agricultural population victimized by the Enclosure Acts. This population had to submit to the new discipline or face starvation. The substitution of the factory for the cottage worked a social revolution, for what was created was a new industrial working class that depended upon the factory for its livelihood. With the invention of the Watt steam engine, factories were freed geographically from dependence upon water power and tended to cluster in new cities. Manchester is the classic example, growing from a sleepy village to a bustling city in one generation.

It is Manchester's and Birmingham's "red, Satanic mills" that have served ever since the eighteenth century to characterize the effects of industrialization. The concomitant evils of slums, epidemic diseases, exploitation, and the sweating of labor were now both obvious and obtrusive even to the casual observer. Rural misery had been discreetly hidden behind hedges; urban squalor was there for everyone to see. The reaction in England was immediate, and critics of industrialization were both numerous and vociferous. The question is: Were they also right? Did industrialization dehumanize men and plunge them into economic slavery, or did it rescue them from starvation and from what Karl Marx later called "the idiocy of rural life"?

1
THE
INDUSTRIAL
REVOLUTION
DEFINED

The term "Industrial Revolution" was first given common currency in the lectures of Arnold Toynbee (1852–1883). It is in one of these lectures that he gave the classic definition of the fundamental economic changes that England had undergone in the years following 1750.

FROM Lectures on the Industrial Revolution of the 18th Century in England BY ARNOLD TOYNBEE

The essence of the Industrial Revolution is the substitution of competition for the mediaeval regulations which had previously controlled the production and distribution of wealth. . . .

Coming to the facts of the Industrial Revolution, the first thing that strikes us is the far greater rapidity which marks the growth of population. Before 1751 the largest decennial increase, so far as we can calculate from our imperfect materials, was 3 per cent. For each of the next three decennial periods the increase was 6 per cent.; then between 1781 and 1791 it was 9 per cent.; between 1791 and 1801, 11 per cent.; between 1801 and 1811, 14 per cent.; between 1811 and 1821, 18 per cent. This is the highest figure ever reached in England, for since 1815 a vast emigration has been always tending to moderate it; between 1815 and 1880 over eight millions (including Irish) have left

Arnold Toynbee, *Lectures on the Industrial Revolution of the 18th Century in England* (1887), pp. 85, 87–93.

our shores. But for this our normal rate of increase would be 16 or 18 instead of 12 per cent. in every decade.

Next we notice the relative and positive decline in the agricultural population. In 1811 it constituted 35 per cent. of the whole population of Great Britain; in 1821, 33 per cent.; in 1831, 28 per cent. And at the same time its actual numbers have decreased. In 1831 there were 1,243,057 adult males employed in agriculture in Great Britain; in 1841 there were 1,207,989. In 1851 the whole number of persons engaged in agriculture in England was 2,084,-153; in 1861 it was 2,010,454, and in 1871 it was 1,657,138. Contemporaneously with this change, the centre of density of population has shifted from the Midlands to the North; there are at the present day 458 persons to the square mile in the countries north of the Trent, as against 312 south of the Trent. And we have lastly to remark the change in the relative population of England and Ireland. Of the total population of the three kingdoms, Ireland had in 1821 32 per cent., in 1881 only 14.6 per cent.

An agrarian revolution plays as large part in the great industrial change of the end of the eighteenth century as does the revolution in manufacturing industries, to which attention is more usually directed. Our next inquiry must therefore be: What were the agricultural changes which led to this noticeable decrease in the rural population? The three most effective causes were: the destruction of the common-field system of cultivation; the enclosure, on a large scale, of common and waste lands; and the consolidation of small farms into large. We have already seen that while between 1710 and 1760 some 300,000 acres were enclosed, between 1760 and 1843 nearly 7,000,000 underwent the same process. Closely connected with the enclosure system was the substitution of large for small farms. In the first half of the century Laurence, though approving of consolidation from an economic point of view, had thought that the odium attaching to an evicting landlord would operate as a strong check upon it. But these scruples had now disappeared. Eden in 1795 notices how constantly the change was effected, often accompanied by the conversion of arable to pasture; and relates how in a certain Dorsetshire village he found two farms where twenty years ago there had been thirty. The process went on uninterruptedly into the present century. Cobbett, writing in 1826, says: "In the parish of Burghclere one single farmer holds, under Lord Carnarvon, as one farm, the lands that those now living remember to have formed fourteen farms, bringing up in a respectable way fourteen families." The consolidation of farms reduced the number of farmers, while the enclosures drove the labourers off the land, as it became impossible for them to exist without their rights of pasturage for sheep and geese on common lands.

Severely, however, as these changes bore upon the rural population, they wrought, without doubt, distinct improvement from an agricultural point of view. They meant the substitution of scientific for unscientific culture. "It has been found," says Laurence, "by long experience, that common or open fields

are great hindrances to the public good, and to the honest improvement
which every one might make of his own." Enclosures brought an extension
of arable cultivation and the tillage of inferior soils; and in small farms of 40
to 100 acres, where the land was exhausted by repeated corn crops, the farm
buildings of clay and mud walls and three-fourths of the estate often saturated with water, consolidation into farms of 100 to 500 acres meant rotation
of crops, leases of nineteen years, and good farm buildings. The period was
one of great agricultural advance; the breed of cattle was improved, rotation
of crops was generally introduced, the steam-plough was invented, agricultural societies were instituted. In one respect alone the change was injurious.
In consequence of the high prices of corn which prevailed during the French
war, some of the finest permanent pastures were broken up. Still, in spite of
this, it was said in 1813 that during the previous ten years agricultural
produce had increased by one-fourth, and this was an increase upon a great
increase in the preceding generation.

Passing to manufactures, we find here the all-prominent fact to be the substitution of the factory for the domestic system, the consequence of the mechanical discoveries of the time. Four great inventions altered the character of
the cotton manufacture: the spinning-jenny, patented by Hargreaves in 1770;
the water-frame, invented by Arkwright the year before; Crompton's mule
introduced in 1779, and the self-acting mule, first invented by Kelly in 1792,
but not brought into use till Roberts improved it in 1825. None of these by
themselves would have revolutionised the industry. But in 1769—the year in
which Napoleon and Wellington were born—James Watt took out his patent
for the steam-engine. Sixteen years later it was applied to the cotton manufacture. In 1785 Boulton and Watt made an engine for a cotton-mill at Papplewick in Notts, and in the same year Arkwright's patent expired. These two
facts taken together mark the introduction of the factory system. But the
most famous invention of all, and the most fatal to domestic industry, the
power-loom, though also patented by Cartwright in 1785, did not come into
use for several years, and till the power-loom was introduced the workman
was hardly injured. At first, in fact, machinery raised the wages of spinners
and weavers owing to the great prosperity it brought to the trade. In fifteen
years the cotton trade trebled itself; from 1788 to 1803 has been called "its
golden age"; for, before the power-loom but after the introduction of the
mule and other mechanical improvements by which for the first time yarn
sufficiently fine for muslin and a variety of other fabrics was spun, the demands became such that "old barns, cart-houses, out-buildings of all descriptions were repaired, windows broke through the old blank walls, and all
fitted up for loom-shops; new weavers' cottages with loom-shops arose in
every direction, every family bringing home weekly from 40 to 120 shillings
per week." At a later date, the condition of the workman was very different.
Meanwhile, the iron industry had been equally revolutionised by the invention of smelting by pit-coal brought into use between 1740 and 1750, and by
the application in 1788 of the steam-engine to blast furnaces. In the eight

years which followed this latter date, the amount of iron manufactured nearly doubled itself.

A further growth of the factory system took place independent of machinery, and owed its origin to the expansion of trade, an expansion which was itself due to the great advance made at this time in the means of communication. The canal system was being rapidly developed throughout the country. In 1777 the Grand Trunk canal, 96 miles in length, connecting the Trent and Mersey, was finished; Hull and Liverpool were connected by one canal while another connected them both with Bristol; and in 1792, the Grand Junction canal, 90 miles in length, made a waterway from London through Oxford to the chief midland towns. Some years afterwards, the roads were greatly improved under Telford and Macadam; between 1818 and 1829 more than a thousand additional miles of turnpike road were constructed; and the next year, 1830, saw the opening of the first railroad. These improved means of communication caused an extraordinary increase in commerce, and to secure a sufficient supply of goods it became the interest of the merchants to collect weavers around them in great numbers, to get looms together in a workshop, and to give out the warp themselves to the workpeople. To these latter this system meant a change from independence to dependence; at the beginning of the century the report of a committee asserts that the essential difference between the domestic and the factory system is, that in the latter the work is done "by persons who have no property in the goods they manufacture." Another direct consequence of this expansion of trade was the regular recurrence of periods of over-production and of depression, a phenomenon quite unknown under the old system, and due to this new form of production on a large scale for a distant market.

These altered conditions in the production of wealth necessarily involved an equal revolution in its distribution. In agriculture the prominent fact is an enormous rise in rents. Up to 1795, though they had risen in some places, in others they had been stationary since the Revolution. But between 1790 and 1833, according to Porter, they at least doubled. In Scotland, the rental of land, which in 1795 had amounted to £2,000,000, had risen in 1815 to £5,278,-685. A farm in Essex, which before 1793 had been rented at 10s. an acre, was let in 1812 at 50s., though, six years after, this had fallen again to 35s. In Berks and Wilts, farms which in 1790 were let at 14s., were let in 1810 at 70s., and in 1820 at 50s. Much of this rise, doubtless, was due to money invested in improvements—the first Lord Leicester is said to have expended £400,000 on his property—but it was far more largely the effect of the enclosure system, of the consolidation of farms, and of the high price of corn during the French war. Whatever may have been its causes, however, it represented a great social revolution, a change in the balance of political power and in the relative position of classes. The farmers shared in the prosperity of the landlords; for many of them held their farms under beneficial leases, and made large profits by them. In consequence, their character completely changed; they ceased to work and live with their labourers, and became a distinct class. The high prices of the war time thoroughly demoralised them, for their wealth then increased so fast, that they were at a loss what to do with it. Cobbett has described the change in their habits, the new food and furniture, the luxury and drinking, which were the consequences of more money coming into their hands than they knew how to spend. Meanwhile, the effect of all these agrarian changes upon the condition of the labourer was an exactly opposite and most disastrous one. He felt all the burden of high prices, while his wages were steadily falling, and he had lost his common-rights. It is from this period, viz., the beginning of the present century, that the alienation between farmer and labourer may be dated.

Exactly analogous phenomena appeared in the manufacturing world. The new class of great capitalist employers made enormous fortunes, they took little or no part personally in the work of their factories, their hundreds of workmen were individually unknown to them; and as a consequence, the old relations between masters and men disappeared, and a "cash nexus" was substituted for the human tie. The workmen on their side resorted to combination, and Trades-Unions began a fight which looked as if it were between mortal enemies rather than joint producers. The misery which came upon large sections of the working people at this epoch was often, though not always, due to a fall in wages, for, as I said above, in some industries they rose. But they suffered likewise from the conditions of labour under the factory system, from the rise of prices, especially from the high price of bread before the repeal of the corn-laws, and from those sudden fluctuations of trade, which, ever since production has been on a large scale, have exposed them to recurrent periods of bitter distress. The effects of the Industrial Revolution prove that free competition may produce wealth without producing wellbeing. We all know the horrors that ensued in England before it was restrained by legislation and combination.

2
THE WORLD
THAT WAS
LOST

Arthur Young (1741–1820) was a prosperous farmer who devoted his life to the improvement of agriculture. He traveled widely, keeping a journal in which he noted the condition of the countryside and reporting what he saw in the journal *Annals of Agriculture* or in separate publications. These reports give an excellent insight into the conditions of Great Britain just as it plunged into the Industrial Revolution.

In the first document Young provides figures for the amount of capital required to set up as a farmer, leasing enough land to bring in an annual income of one hundred pounds a year. Then he gives indications of the standard of living of cottagers (the poorest farmers).

FROM Tours in England and Wales BY ARTHUR YOUNG

To Hire a Farm of 100l. a Year.

5 Horses at 15l.	£.75	0	0
12 Cows at 7l.	84	0	0
8 Young cattle 3l.	24	0	0
60 Sheep at 10s.	30	0	0
2 Sows at 50s.	5	0	0
1 Waggon,	25	0	0
2 Tunbrils 10l.	20	0	0
1 Harvest cart,	7	0	0

Arthur Young, *Tours in England and Wales Selected from the Annals of Agriculture* (1932), pp. 1, 2–3, 5, 9, 45, 47–49, 87–90, 145, 157–158, 205, 217, 223–224, 274–275. Reprinted by permission of The London School of Economics and Political Science, London.

2 Ploughs,	3	0	0
2 Harrows,	3	0	0
1 Roller,	1	0	0
Harness,	5	0	0
Sundries,	15	0	0
Furniture,	50	0	0
Tythe,	12	0	0
Rates, &c.	5	0	0
Housekeeping,	25	0	0
2 Men and 1 boy,	19	0	0
2 Maids,	6	0	0
1 Labourer,	18	0	0
60 Acres seed 12s.	36	0	0
	468	0	0

Land sells at 30 years purchase, in 10 years risen much, now at a stand. Land-tax at 4s. not more than 1s. the county through. Tythes not much gathered; computed 2s. to 3s. in the pound. Poor rates, 1s. to 1s. 6d. doubled in 10 years. Tea general, leases 7s. to 14s. or 21s. many, but going out.

Labour

In harvest 1s. 4d. 1s. 6d. and board
—Hay 1s. 2d. 1s. 4d. and beer.
—Winter 1s.
Man's wages 8l.
Lad 3l.
Maid 3l. to 3l. 10s.
Woman at hay 6d. and beer.
   Rise of labour, none for 6 years, but in 15 years ⅓d.

Provision

Cheese 3d.

Butter 6d. 9d.

Beef 4d.

Bacon 6d. 7d.

Potatoes 1s. 6d. 2s. strike,

Labourer's house rent 40s.

Mutton 4d.

Veal 4d.

Pork 4d.

Firing, seldom buy more
   than 12s. for 1 stack coal.

Tools 5s.

Building

Bricks 15s. formerly 9s.
Tiles 20s.
Oak 40s. a ton, very little advanced.
Ash do.
Poplar 30s.
Carpenter 1s. 6d. 1s. 8d.

Mason do.
Building a cottage 25l.

A Farm

300 Acres	8 Horses
124 Grass	16 Cows
176 Arable	4 Fatting
33 Wheat	30 Young
50 Barley	100 Sheep
8 Oats	3 Men
17 Pease	2 Maids
60 Clover	2 Labourers
8 Fallow	

* * *

The state of the poor, in general, in this country is advantageous, owing very much to lace making. The following account will shew this, in the receipt and expenditure of a poor family, viz. a man, his wife, and five children, the eldest sixteen years of age.

Earnings

	£.	s.	d.
Twenty-six weeks winter, at 7s. raised to that rate by taking work by the great	9	2	0
Five harvest, at 9s.	2	5	0
Four week's hay, going upwards (towards London)	3	3	0
Seventeen weeks summer, at 8s.	6	16	0
The son 3s. a week, and 16s. extra in hay and harvest	8	12	0
The rest of the family, 2s. a week	5	4	0
	35	2	0

Expenses

	£.	s.	d.
Bread, half the year (winter), barley, and half wheaten, at 6s. 6d. a week, on an average including baking, 4d. barm, 2d. and salt, 1d.	0	6	6
Salt for other uses,	0	0	0½
Bacon, 2 lb. a week	0	1	4
Tea, sugar, and butter	0	1	0
Cheese, half a pound	0	0	2½
Beer (four bushel of malt, at 5s. 6d. and 3 lb. hops, 3s.) per week	0	0	6

Soap (half a pound in three weeks), and starch, and blue			0	0	2
Candles			0	0	3
Thread, half an ounce a week, 1½d. worsted, 2d.			0	0	3½
			0	10	3¼
Per annum			26	15	2
Rent			1	15	0
Wood			0	12	0
Lying in and sickness			1	0	0
Cloaths. The man's shoes	0	15	0		
shirts	0	8	0		
stockings	0	4	0		
hat, &c.	0	1	6		
jacket	0	6	0		
	1	14	6		
Family	2	0	0		
			3	14	6
			33	16	8
Earnings			35	2	0
Expenses			33	16	8
To lay up, or expend in additional cloaths			1	5	4

In the selections that follow, Young describes the conditions of rural life in a number of places throughout England and Wales.

October 23, 1776, landed at Milford haven from Ireland. The whole country is inclosed, without such a thing as a common field. The food of the poor, bread and cheese, with broth made of salt meat, paid in at the cheapest season; much fish also eaten by them. Many keep cows; no goats on the mountains. The cottages many of them not a whit better than Irish cabbins, without an equal show of pigs, poultry and cows. Labour 8d. in the winter, and 10d. in summer, the year round. The whole country is in gentle inequalities; and, if wooded would be beautiful.

To Narbarth. Several cottages building in the Irish way, of mud with straw. The poor people seem well cloathed and fed. They use through all this country small heavy carts with two oxen and two or three horses, the driver sits on the front of the cart, and drives with reins.

October 24th to St. Clear. From Narbarth to Hubberston the course is, Rents 7s. 6d. to 10s. the whole farm through; to 14s. on some farms. Farms rise to very large ones, but in general small. The Irish cottar system is found here—3 or 4 cottages to a farm of 40 or 50l. a year. They are always at the call of the farmers, they are allowed two or three grass fields at a moderate rent, a cow or two, but no pigs, unless one in a year, to kill at Christmas. Strangers get in winter 4d. a day, and food; without food 8d. in harvest 1s. 1s. 6d. and food. They live on bread and cheese, and milk, or water; no beer, nor meat, except on a Sunday. The culture of potatoes increases much, more planted last year than ever known before. The poor eat them; and every cabbin has a garden with some in it. Many iron furnaces, the ore dug in the country. The poor spin a good deal of wool, and weave it into flannel for their own wear, no linen is worn by them, flannel supplying the place. Query, to the physicians of the country—Is the rheumatism known here as much as in other countries where linen is worn? They make cloth also for their own wear. Weavers earn 1s. a day, and sometimes more. The poor live on barley-bread, cheese, and butter; not one in ten have either cows or pigs, fare very poorly and rarely touch meat. Their little gardens they plant with cabbages, carrots, leeks, and potatoes. Rent of a cottage and garden, 10s. to 20s. Building a mud cabbin costs 10l.

* * *

Crossed the Severn at the ferry at Lincoln Hill, in the midst of a most noble scenery of exceeding bold mountainous tracts, with that river rolling at the bottom. The opposite shore is one immense steep of hanging wood, which has the finest effect imaginable. Mounted through that wood, thickly scattered with cottages, the inhabitants busily employed in the vast works of various kinds carried on in the neighbourhood. One circumstance I remarked which gave me much pleasure. There was not a single cottage in which a fine hog did not seem to make a part of every family; not a door without a stone trough with the pig eating his supper, in company with the children at the same business playful about the threshold. It was a sight which shewed that chearfulness and plenty crowned the board of the humble but happy inhabitants of this romantic spot.

About St. Neot's a vast improvement by an inclosure, which took place 16 years ago, which makes the country much more beautiful, and has been a great benefit to the community. A gentleman of the town however complained, as I rode thither with him, that, notwithstanding the productiveness of the soil was certainly greater, yet that the poor were ill-treated by having about half a rood given them in lieu of a *cow keep,* the inclosure of which land costing more than they could afford, they sold the lots at 5l. the money was drank out at the ale-house, and the men, spoiled by the habit, came, with their families, to the parish; by which means poor rates had risen from 2s. 6d.

to 3s. and 3s. 6d. But pray, sir, have not rates arisen equally in other parishes, where no inclosure has taken place? Admitted. And what can be the good of commons, which would not prevent poor rates coming to such a height? Better modes of giving the poor a share might easily, and have been, as in other cases, adopted.

* * *

In the open fields the farms are generally small, usually about 70l. a-year: these little occupations with which the Duke of Grafton, and other good landlords have patience in order to nurse up industrious families, are yet a heavy loss in repairs: and sometimes in other circumstances: inclosed farms rise to 300l. which is the greatest; there are but few of 200l. to 250l. In farms of a tolerable size, the tenantry are substantial, and it gave me great pleasure to find them with such confidence in their landlord, as to raise considerable erections on the Duke's farms at their own expence, in articles beyond the common demands of the country; as a hay barn, &c. &c. and this while tenants at will; a sure proof that they regard their landlord as their father and their friend.

The 7th. To Measham, where Mr. Wilkes shewed us his many and great improvements; the manor and estate he purchased some years ago of Mr. Wollaston, of Finborough, in Suffolk, for 50,000l. The buildings erected and erecting will speedily change the face of it. Here are two cotton and a corn mill, two steam engines; many weaving-shops, and a number of cottages built; a large and handsome inn; . . . a few of the old thatched hovels remain to shew what this place was; what it will be may easily be conceived. But what is done here in ten or a dozen years by one man, who has been at the same time engaged in many other great undertakings, who, in union with Mr. Peele, is giving a new face to Faseley and Tamworth, cannot but make any one from the Continent admire at the wonderful exertions active in this kingdom—and in this kingdom only, for there is nothing out of it in the manufacturing world that is not, comparatively speaking, fast asleep.

A manufacturing town—Birmingham in the 1790s.

These immense works, which wear so animated a face of business, correspond well with the prodigious increase of the town, which I viewed to good advantage from the top of the new church of St. Paul: it is now a very great city indeed; and it was abundantly curious to have it pointed out to me the parts added since I was here. They form the greatest part of the town, and carry in their countenance undoubted marks of their modern date. In 1768 the population was under 30,000; now the common calculation is 70,000, but more accurate calculation extends it to 80,000, which I am told is the number assigned by Dr. Priestley. In the last 10 years above 4000 new houses have been built: and the increase is at present going on much more rapidly, for I was told that the number this year is not less than 700.

The earnings of the workmen in the manufacture are various, but in general very high: a boy of 10 or 12 years, 2s. 6d. to 3s. a week; a woman from 4s. to 20s. a week, average about 6s.; men from 10s. to 25s. a week, and some much higher; colliers earn yet more. These are immense wages, when it is considered that the whole family is sure of constant steady employment; indeed they are so great, that I am inclined to think labour higher at Birmingham than in any place in Europe: a most curious circumstance for the politician to reflect on, and which shews of how little effect to manufactures is cheap labour, for here is the most flourishing fabric that was perhaps ever known, paying the highest rates of labour. Such an instance ought to correct those common notions that have been retailed from hand to hand a thousand times, that cheap provisions are necessary for the good of manufactures, because cheap provisions suppose cheap labour, which is a combination founded in ignorance and error. Provisions at Birmingham are at the same rate as every where else in England, for it is remarkable that the level of price at present is very general, except the division of the east and west of the kingdom for corn; but while Birmingham and Norwich eat their provisions at nearly the same price (with allowance that the former is much the more quick, ready, and active market), the price of labour is at least 150 per cent. higher in one of those places than the other. Why then I enquire, what has provisions to do with the rate of labour? If one was to form our ideas from a very enlarged view of all the great fabrics in Europe, we should be apt to think that a great and flourishing fabric could not subsist, either with cheap provisions, or with cheap labour.

I tried hard to pick up some data, on which to calculate the amount of the fabric, but difficulties of various kinds prevented any accuracy in the estimation. In conversation with a very ingenious gentleman, who has written an able work on the town, and who was rewarded for it by having his house burnt down in the late riots, I mean Mr. Hutton, he informed me that ten years ago there were many estimates made with a good deal of care; and that on multiplied experiments it was found, that the returns per week, was equal to the rent per annum; including all the houses of the town on an average; all shops; all trades: the houses were then about 9000, and the rent 9l. each, on a medium; now the houses are about 13,000, and as I find, on enquiry, that the little houses, which have been built in such numbers for manufacturers, are let at 6l. 10s. the lowest; 7l. and 8l. each; 9l. on a general average of rents must now be much too low; however let us call it no more than 10l; this would make the rental of the town 130,000l. a year, and the returns of all its trade 6,760,000l. per annum: out of which a very great deduction is to be made for all the trades and professions of common life, supported by the manufacture, but not composing it. If I should form any idea corrective of this, it would be that the estimate is carried too high: let us suppose the population 80,000, then there are about 40,000 males, of these deduct 5000 not employed in the manufacture, remain 35,000; three-fourths of that number are of an age to be employed, or 26,250. Suppose these to earn, including manufacturers and merchants profit, 15s. a week, it amounts to 1,023,724l. a year. Of the 40,000 women 20,000 may be supposed to be employed, and to earn 6s. including, as above; the year's earnings will be 312,000l. in all 1,335,000l. double this, to include all raw materials, and you have 2,670,000l. for the amount of the manufacture. Now I am ready to grant, that here is a great deal of supposition in this estimate, but at the same time it is not altogether without data; and though the total may exceed this, possibly half a million, yet I think as much might be said to shew the calculation high, as to prove it low. It is true the ratio of the earnings is taken rather low, including, as it ought to do, the profit both of the manufacturer and of the merchant, which cannot well be less than 20 per cent.; but then the number of the workmen can scarcely exceed the supposition, probably not equal to it, 20,000 females, in particular are a high allowance.

Robert Southey (1774–1843) was poet laureate of England and intimately connected with the Romantic school of William Wordsworth and Samuel Taylor Coleridge. The Romantics tended to idealize the rural life and see in it a purity and simplicity that were often invisible to their contemporaries.

The following selection takes the form of a dialogue between Sir Thomas More's ghost and a man who speaks for Southey's time.

FROM Sir Thomas More BY ROBERT SOUTHEY

SIR THOMAS MORE. . . . The spirit which built and endowed monasteries is gone. Are you one of those persons who think it has been superseded for the better by that which erects steam-engines and cotton mills?

MONTESINOS. They are indeed miserable politicians who mistake wealth for welfare in their estimate of national prosperity; and none have committed this great error more egregiously than some of those who have been called statesmen by the courtesy of England. Yet the manufacturing system is a

---

Robert Southey, *Sir Thomas More; or, Colloquies on the Progress and Prospects of Society,* I (1829), 158–159, 166–167, 170–171, 173–174.

necessary stage in the progress of society. Without it this nation could not have supported the long and tremendous conflict which has delivered Europe from the yoke of military despotism, . . . the worst of all evils. If England had not been enabled by the use of steam-engines to send out every year myriads of brave men, and millions of specie, . . . what had Europe, and what had England itself been now? This inestimable benefit we have seen and felt. And from the consequences of that skill in machinery which the manufacturing system alone could have produced, we may expect ultimately to obtain the greatest advantages of science and civilization at the least expense of human labour.

* * *

SIR THOMAS MORE. There is an example before our eyes. Yonder children are on the way to a manufactory, where they pass six days out of the seven, from morning till night. Is it likely that the little they learn at school on the seventh (which ought to be their day of recreation as well as rest), should counteract the effects of such an education, when the moral atmosphere wherein they live and move and have their being, is as noxious to the soul, as the foul and tainted air which they inhale is to their bodily constitution?

MONTESINOS. Yet the most celebrated minister of the age, the only minister who for many generations has deserved to be called a Premier, the minister whom our best and wisest statesmen at this day profess entirely to admire and implicitly to follow, . . . he made his boast of this very evil, and congratulated Parliament that the nation had a new source of wealth and revenue in the labour of children: so completely had the political system in which he was trained up seared his heart and obscured his understanding.

SIR THOMAS MORE. Confess that this is an evil which had no existence in former times! There are new things under the sun, . . . new miseries, . . . new enormities, . . . this portentous age produces them.

* * *

SIR THOMAS MORE. What then shall we say of a system which in its direct consequences debases all who are engaged in it? a system that employs men unremittingly in pursuits unwholesome for the body, and unprofitable for the mind, . . . a system in which the means are so bad, that any result would be dearly purchased at such an expense of human misery and degradation, and the end so fearful, that the worst calamities which society has hitherto endured may be deemed light in comparison with it?

MONTESINOS. Like the whole fabric of our society it has been the growth of circumstances, not a system foreplanned, foreseen and deliberately chosen. Such as it is we have inherited it, . . . or rather have fallen into it, and must get out of it as well as we can. We must do our best to remove its evils, and to mitigate them while they last, and to modify and reduce it till only so much remains as is indispensable for the general good.

SIR THOMAS MORE. The facts will not warrant you in saying that it has come upon the country unsought and unforeseen. You have prided yourselves upon this system; you have used every means for extending it; you have made it the measure of your national prosperity. It is a wen, a fungous excrescence from the body politic: the growth might have been checked if the consequences had been apprehended in time; but now it has acquired so great a bulk, its nerves have branched so widely, and the vessels of the tumour are so inosculated into some of the principal veins and arteries of the natural system, that to remove it by absorption is impossible, and excision would be fatal.

MONTESINOS. Happily, this is but a metaphor; and the body politic, like its crowned head, never dies.

By this time we had reached the bank above Applethwaite. The last question of my companion was one to which I could make no reply, and as he neither talked for triumph, nor I endeavoured to elude the force of his argument, we remained awhile in silence, looking upon the assemblage of dwellings below. Here, and in the adjoining hamlet of Millbeck, the effects of manufactures and of agriculture may be seen and compared. The old cottages are such as the poet and the painter equally delight in beholding. Substantially built of the native stone without mortar, dirtied with no white-lime, and their long low roofs covered with slate, if they had been raised by the magic of some indigenous Amphion's music, the materials could not have adjusted themselves more beautifully in accord with the surrounding scene; and time has still farther harmonized them with weather stains, lichens and moss, short grasses and short fern, and stone plants of various kinds. The ornamented chimnies, round or square, less adorned than those which, like little turrets, crest the houses of the Portugueze peasantry, and yet not less happily suited to their place; the hedge of clipt box beneath the windows, the rose bushes beside the door, the little patch of flower ground with its tall holyocks in front, the garden beside, the bee-hives, and the orchard with its bank of daffodils and snowdrops, (the earliest and the profusest in these parts,) indicate in the owners some portion of ease and leisure, some regard to neatness and comfort, some sense of natural and innocent and healthful enjoyment. The new cottages of the manufacturers, are . . . upon the manufacturing pattern . . . naked, and in a row.

How is it, said I, that every thing which is connected with manufactures, presents such features of unqualified deformity? From the largest of Mammon's temples down to the poorest hovel in which his helotry are stalled, the edifices have all one character. Time cannot mellow them; Nature will neither clothe nor conceal them; and they remain always as offensive to the eye as to the mind!

3
WORKING CONDITIONS IN THE INDUSTRIAL REVOLUTION

The rapid industrialization of Great Britain, added to the hardships of the wars of the French Revolution and Napoleon, created serious conditions among the poor. Many members of the upper classes were troubled by the burgeoning of manufactures and by the use of young children in producing them. The children were a necessary part of the new cotton textile industry, for their small size enabled them to move freely under the machinery to repair broken threads and keep the looms and spindles working. The moral question raised by such employment could not long be ignored, and in 1816 a parliamentary committee was appointed to find out if the employment of children was detrimental to their health and morals.

FROM Report . . . on the State of the Children Employed . . .

The first witness is Matthew Baillie, M.D. The chairman of the committee is Sir Robert Peel, himself an industrialist and the father of the future Prime Minister.

Report of the Minutes of Evidence taken before the Select Committee on the State of the Children employed in the Manufactories of the United Kingdom, 25 April–18 June, 1816, pp. 30–31, 46–48, 50–52, 178–181, 222–223.

In speaking of the injury to young persons arising from labour, do you mean to speak of labour which requires great bodily exertion?—I did not suppose that children at so early an age were employed in great bodily exertion, but I meant any bodily exertion in which they were confined in a given space, and their minds not allowed to wander into the various channels of thought, and their limbs allowed the sort of irregular exercise which takes place in children who are living in the usual manner.

Is not the state of maturity of children very different in those brought up in the country, to those brought up in town?—With regard to children who are brought up in the country, they are more vigorous; and I have no doubt, in many instances, their progress towards maturity may be more rapid than in children who are reared in a large town.

And your experience has principally been in town?—Entirely, I may say.

Have you been called to give any opinion, or to know the state of health in different manufactories?—I have not.

What is the state of heat, as ascertained by a thermometer, in which children might work without injury?—I should say, that the temperature which is upon the whole most favourable, is about sixty degrees of heat.

In giving your opinion upon this subject, do you take into your consideration the situation in which children would be placed, if, at an early period, they were not employed in such factories?—I do not know that the whole of this pressed on my mind, but certainly it was not absent from it; I drew the comparison between those children as employed in manufactories, and the ordinary employment of children in the country.

Would children of the age of ten be employed in the ordinary business of the country?—No; but they would be doing a good deal of work of various kinds, as going of errands, or weeding, and a thousand employments, which I cannot at present call up to my mind.

That answer seems to refer more particularly to children in the country, as the manufactories are generally in towns, it does not apply to them; therefore the Committee wish to know whether you conceive, if children at an early period of life were prevented by Act of Parliament from working in factories, their situation would be better than it is?—I conceive it would be more favourable to health to be at large, although they might sometimes be not well nourished; and although sometimes they would be in hot rooms, they would have a great deal more time in which they could be playing about, and using their faculties of observation.

Then if those children were left on the parish for support, and many sent to the workhouse, their situation would be better than at present?—I think that children would be better situated in a workhouse, were they not so employed, than in manufactories.

Do you give this as an opinion that you derive from an accurate observation of facts, with respect to the condition of children in factories, or do you give it upon general reasoning?—Upon general reasoning.

Then you are not really acquainted with the condition of children employed in such manufactories?—I am not really acquainted with the condition of children employed in such manufactories; but I mention what I suppose must be more or less the influence of confinement which children are subject to in those manufactories upon their health, from the general principles that guide us in ascertaining the causes that maintain health or lead to sickness, with respect to the human body generally.

In a factory consisting of 875 persons, the annual deaths in which were not more than from two to five, should you conceive that the employment was inconsistent with the health of the people employed?—I should say it does not appear from that statement to have been inconsistent; I conceive, a great many of those children might not be in vigorous health, not in the same health in which they would otherwise be, and yet not be attacked with diseases which would occasion death.

Your answer refers to the number of deaths in a particular year; but if the average for seven years should be about the same, would not you consider that fact as tolerable evidence of the health of the employment?—Indeed I should think so.

Then if in another factory consisting of 289 persons, two only died in the year 1815; and on the 13th of April, one only was sick; would not that afford a tolerable inference of the healthiness of the persons employed in that factory?—It certainly would; but as I stated before, I can easily believe that those children may not be attacked by diseases which should lead to death; but at the same time, be many of them less vigorous than they otherwise would be if employed in the usual manner.

Then in factories, where on the average persons are employed seven years, and where a great portion remain from fourteen to twenty; if the general state of health has been good, would not that be tolerably good evidence of the healthiness of the employment?—I think so.

Have you ever had reason to conceive that there exists in the lower classes of people, a want of affection and tenderness for their children?—I believe you will find very often less affection, both of fathers and mothers for their children in the lower classes, than in the middle ranks: But at the same time there are many strong instances of the purest maternal and paternal affection in the lowest classes of society, where there may be very great difficulty to rear children: they will often submit to every kind of privation respecting themselves, in order to rear the children with some degree of comfort.

Then the lowest class are not the persons where the greatest degree of affection is found for their children?—I think not.

Does not a family press much harder on a poor man, than on any other class?—No doubt.

And is it not of greater importance to him to superintend the care of those children, than to any other class of persons in life?—It must be of more importance to him to superintend, if he can, the education and the bringing up of his children, because in other ranks of life, there are persons who can be procured to do that office for them.

Does not any sickness or want of health in the children of the poor, press upon the parents more than upon any other class of persons?—Certainly.

In the communications you have received from other practitioners, have you ever heard of any great detriment that has occurred to children from too intense employment in manufactories?—I do not recollect that I have ever received a communication upon the subject.

Have you had opportunities of observation upon the condition of the children of the poor not employed in manufactories in large towns?—I have been engaged almost from the beginning of my medical life, in the middle and higher ranks of society.

Sir Gilbert Blane, M.D., was also examined.

May it not happen, by those children being kept employed not in hard labour but in that kind of gentle occupation that gives exercise without super-inducing too great fatigue, for twelve hours in a day, in factories, where the air was pure and salutary?—That is a question that, from my want of knowing in detail what is the nature of the employment, I cannot answer; if it was not sedentary but loco-motive, ten hours would not be too much.

Must not a great deal of the power of performance on the part of children, depend on the nourishment and cloathing which they receive?—Not the least doubt much must depend upon the quantity and quality of food.

May not, both in men and animals, an increased degree of maturity be attained in consequence of the food that they receive?—No doubt of it; but there is a greater latitude in the human species than in any other; a man, so speaking, is more an animal of mixed food than any other.

May not children of ten years of age, by being better fed and better care taken of them, be capable of doing more work, without injury to his health, than a child of the same age could have done twenty years ago?—I am clearly of that opinion, from the habits of life, which I have watched with great accuracy.

In referring to the powers of children, are we not to refer, not to what they were, but to what they actually are, from the improvements that have been made?—No doubt of it.

Has it ever occurred to you, to contemplate what has been the increased consumption of animal food within the last fifty years?—I have frequently attended to it, and I think with advantage to mankind, particularly to the young.

Is not the increase of animal food, to young and old, ten times what it was fifty years ago?—It has certainly increased, but I should think that was too high a ratio; it has been increased, to the benefit of all ages, and particularly to the young.

In your observations, has not the consumption of animal food greatly increased within the last fifty years?—It has greatly increased.

Has it not greatly increased within the last twenty years?—Certainly it has, according to my observation.

And that has had a material influence on the strength and health of the people?—I suppose that that has had some share in the decreased mortality which appears.

Is the Committee to understand, that you consider the employment of children, under the age of ten years, to be wholly improper and inconvenient?—By no means wholly improper; I should think if it was limited to five or six hours, that would not only not be pernicious, but salutary.

And you think the employment of children from ten to sixteen, ought not to exceed ten hours a day?—Yes, that might be without prejudice.

You were understood to say, you conceived the state of the atmosphere in which the children worked, was of more importance than the labour itself?—Certainly; they would suffer more from foul air than from the actual labour: the manual labour is the least evil I think.

You say, that the employment of children under ten, might, under certain restrictions, not only be not detrimental, but even beneficial?—I should have no objection to five or six hours.

Are there any restrictions, in point of time or kind of work, that would make it proper to employ children under six years old?—I am so little acquainted with the nature of the occupations in manufactories, I cannot answer that.

Suppose a great number are kept together in the same room, and not exposed to the open air, and in a sedentary posture, or at any rate not taking exercise, do you conceive that at the age of five or six, such occupation, however limited in point of time, is wholesome?—I should apprehend it is wholesome if very limited.

At the age of five or six?—Even as low as that, very limited in time, and in apartments well ventilated and not crowded.

Do you mean, if during the other parts of the day the children should be allowed to play or amuse themselves in the open air?—Most assuredly I understood it so.

Is the proportion between the cubic feet of air in a room, and the number of persons employed in it, of great importance to their health?—Very great; that is a subject I have particularly studied.

In rooms properly ventilated, and where the quantity of respirable air allowed to each person is 1,440 cubic feet, do you think that employment is likely to be prejudicial to such persons?—There is ample space for pure air there; in a hospital there is 700 feet to a patient, and we consider that a safe and proper space, still more so where they are in health and walk about. In a hospital well ventilated, we find 700 cubic feet is a safe and proper space for each patient.

Are you of opinion, that the air in such rooms as have been alluded to, and the employment in them, are likely to be more or less healthy than such rooms as children are employed in by inferior tradesmen, such as tailors and shoemakers?—I apprehend that is a superior degree of ventilation to what they have in the apartments of the labouring poor.

Is it important to the health of children and others, that the temperature of the rooms in which they are employed in winter should be comfortable, and as nearly uniform as is consistent with proper ventilation?—There is no doubt of it; I think comfortable and salutary to be one and the same thing; nature points out what is salutary.

Your attention seems to have been particularly called to the proportion of deaths in different places in this country; do you conceive, that in a factory where in 1811 the number being 873, the deaths in that year being only three; in 1812 the number being 891, the deaths only two; and in 1813 the number being 879, and the deaths only two, such facts to be an indication of the healthiness of the employment in such factory?—It is an indication of the greatest possible health; but it so far exceeds the common course of nature, that if I had it not from such respectable authority I should greatly doubt it.

Would you be surprized at the statement, if you were informed that when children are ill, and likely to die, they are removed from the manufactories? —That alters the case totally.

Are you of opinion, that in another factory, wherein the numbers were 289 employed in 1815, the deaths being two, and where, on the 13th of April only one person out of all that number was sick, such facts are evidence that such factory is healthy?—The same answer; it is evidence of extreme healthiness.

Are you aware, in the most healthy communities, what the proportion of deaths to the persons in life, usually is?—The average in England is one in forty-nine, including Wales one in fifty; and according to the Parliamentary Returns of the beginning of this century, it was one in forty-four; by the Parliamentary Return of 1801.

Healthiness has been somewhat increasing?—Yes.

Did the surprize expressed in a former question, refer to this turning out to be six times less than the average mortality in healthy situations in this country?—To be sure, that made me say it was against the common course of nature; there are no tables that I ever saw, that quoted so high a proportion in the most healthy period of life.

Are you of opinion, that in no situation peculiarly favourable to health in this country, the proportion of deaths is less than that which you have just now stated?—I should have said, had I not been assured of this fact, that that was a rate of mortality that was not to be found any where in the world.

You stated one in forty-four as the average health in healthy districts; the question is, whether, in any particular districts, you have heard of the proportion being smaller than one in forty-four?—Yes; according to the last enumeration the mortality in Cardiganshire is only one in seventy-three, in Monmouthshire one in sixty-four, in Cornwall one in sixty-two, in Gloucestershire one in sixty-one; all the others are under one in sixty. The highest mortality is in the Metropolis and the aguish districts.

Would your surprize of the small mortality cease, if you were informed that no persons are employed under nine years of age, only fifty-nine of the number under ten at the larger factory, and perhaps not forty out of the number above forty years of age, and the factory situated in the healthful county of Ayr, with which you are acquainted?—That renders it somewhat less marvellous.

Have you the means of informing the Committee, what the general mortality is in healthy districts in this country, upon healthy persons between the age of ten and eighteen?—I had lately occasion to make enquiry about that. From some calculations I have made, I found that the mortality in England, between twenty and forty, was about one in eighty.

A deposition was later offered on the part of Charles Pennington, M.D., as a report on the health of the people employed in the mill at Papplewick.

Nottingham, 6th May 1816.

Gentlemen,

Having been desired to communicate to you, as delegates in London from the proprietors of cotton mills and factories in Nottingham and its neighbourhood, my opinion respecting the general state of health of the persons employed in the cotton mills in and near Papplewick, belonging to Mr. James Robinson and Son, I hereby certify to you and to the Honourable the Committee of the House of Commons, that for more than thirty years I have been very frequently called upon in my professional character to attend the family of Mr. Robinson, and the persons employed in his extensive manufactory; and that I have uniformly remarked the most humane attention and careful regard to the health, the morals and the comforts of all engaged in this concern; and that when under medical care, every thing, without any regard to its cost, has been always freely and largely afforded. Further, I may add, that during the greater part of this period, I have had a considerable practice in the town of Nottingham, in a very populous district, for many miles around it, and also in the Infirmary and Lunatic Asylum, amongst all classes and descriptions of people; and after a careful review of the more important circumstances connected with the health of the parties, my conviction is, that the persons employed in the cotton-spinning manufactories are as healthy and strong as any engaged in sedentary pursuits in general; more healthy and strong than the frame-work-knitter; and much more so than the shoemaker and the tailor.

> I am, very respectfully, Gentlemen,
> Your obedient Servant,
> *Charles Pennington,* M.D.
> Honorary Physician to the General Hospital,
> and Physician to the Lunatic Asylum

Messrs. Stanton and Heygate.

Mr. Archibald Buchanan, a mill owner, also took the stand.

Do you know of any person whose health was beginning to fail, leaving the manufactory?—I have known many instances of that kind; and I have known many instances of persons of delicate health coming into the manufactory, as being an easy employment.

Did you ever know of a sickly or delicate child coming into the manufactory?—A great many.

And did they, from a more regular life and a more constant supply of food and regular habits, get better?—Their parents had difficulty in getting employment for them otherwise, and they were glad to get them into the works as being easy; there are some parts of it where they may either sit or stand; and there are many parts of the work where lame people can be employed; and gentlemen in the neighbourhood, and frequently parishes, make application to me to have these people taken in to obtain a subsistence.

And from these circumstances, particularly the material one of having a regular supply of good food, did you observe that those children improved in their health?—I have observed very great improvement from their getting good food.

* * *

Do you know what proportion the persons employed in the manufactory bear to the whole population of the village?—The village contains something above 2,000.

Including those employed in the manufactory?—Yes.

Do you know any thing of the total number of deaths in the village?—I do not.

Do you mean to give to the Committee the impression, that the average number of deaths of the persons employed in the manufactory, at all resembles the total average number of deaths in the village?—I should think that the deaths belonging to the manufactory were less; I have been frequently told by the medical gentleman who attends our people, that in the course of his practice, he finds less disease existing with the people employed in the works, than in the general population of the surrounding country.

Do you mean to lead the Committee to apprehend, that the deaths, upon the remaining eleven hundred who live in the village, are in any thing resembling an equal proportion to that of the deaths in the manufactory?—I am of opinion that they are considerably more; I beg leave to state, that parents with a large family often come to the village and get their children employed; the parents frequently do little or nothing at home, and of course there are a smaller proportion of grown up people in our works than are to be found among the inhabitants of the village.

Those in your works are at the more healthy periods of life?—Yes.

* * *

In the population of the village, are the greater proportion of those not now in your works out of employment?—I have stated in my former evidence, that a great number of those who have formerly been employed in the mills have grown up and gone to other trades; a great number of them are masons, joiners, shoemakers, tailors, and in fact, engaged in every kind of trade almost.

And you have not observed, that those people who have been formerly employed in the works, have been affected in their health?—They are very similar to those who have been brought up in the country; and I mentioned also, that tradesmen generally prefer those brought up in the works to people from the country, on account of their having been brought up in industry, and having acquired a great degree of ingenuity.

* * *

MR. JOHN MOSS, CALLED IN, AND EXAMINED

Where do you live?—At Preston workhouse.

In Lancashire?—Yes.

What is your occupation?—My present occupation is that of governor of the workhouse.

Were you ever employed as the master of the apprentices at a cotton mill?—I was engaged to attend the apprentice-house at Backbarrow. I was over the children.

* * *

Up to what period were they apprenticed?—One-and-twenty.

What were the hours of work?—From five o'clock in the morning till eight at night.

Were fifteen hours in the day the regular hours of work?—Those were their regular hours of work.

Was that the regular time all the year through?—Yes.

What time was allowed for meals?—Half an hour for breakfast and half an hour for dinner.

* * *

Had they any refreshment in the afternoon?—Yes, they had their drinking taken to the mill; their bagging, they call it.

You mean luncheon?—Yes.

Did they work while they ate their afternoon refreshment?—Yes.

They had no cessation after dinner till eight o'clock at night?—No.

At what hour was the breakfast?—At seven in the morning; they came to their breakfast at seven o'clock, and then the bell rang for them at half past seven.

Did they leave the mill at breakfast time?—Yes, they always left the mill and came to the house.

What was the dinner hour?—Twelve o'clock.

And at what time did they return to the mill?—Half past twelve.

Did they, beyond working those fifteen hours, make up for any loss of time?—Yes, always.

Did the children actually work fourteen hours in the day?—Yes.

And one hour was allowed for the two meals, making fifteen hours in the whole?—Yes.

When the works were stopped for the repair of the mill, or for any want of cotton, did the children afterwards make up for the loss of that time?—Yes.

When making up lost time, how long did they continue working at night? —Till nine o'clock, and sometimes later; sometimes ten.

Was this before the Apprentice Bill or after?—It was last year, and it is in practice now.

How long were they making up lost time?—I have known them to be three weeks or more making up lost time.

Have you known them for three weeks together working from five in the morning till nine or ten at night, with the exception of the hour for meals?— Yes, I have.

What time did they rise from bed?—I always got up at half past four to get them ready to be at the mill by five.

How far was their sleeping room from the mill?—It might be not above a hundred yards; hardly so much.

Did they rise at half past four in the winter season?—They were always to be at the mill by five o'clock winter and summer, and never later.

Were there two mills?—Yes.

When you had only water for one mill, did the children work night and day?—When there was only water for one mill, one worked in the day and the other at night.

Have you ever known the children work all night on Saturday, until six o'clock on Sunday morning?—Yes, I have once; they have gone to work at eight o'clock on Saturday night, and stayed till six on Sunday morning.

At what hour on Sunday night did those children begin to work again?— They have begun at twelve o'clock on Sunday night again, and worked till five in the morning; then the other children for the day began at the other mill, and worked till eight at night.

Did they work as late on Saturday night as on other nights?—Always the same; I never knew any abatement.

Did any children work on the Sundays as cleaners of the machinery?—Yes.

Did they do this regularly?—Regularly every Sunday; I do not know that ever they missed one Sunday while I was there.

Through the year?—Yes.

How many hours did they work on a Sunday?—Their orders were from six till twelve.

Did you remonstrate against this?—Yes, I did.

Frequently?—Yes.

What was the consequence of your remonstrance?—It was never much better; there were not so many went to the mill; I believe that they went from their own accord sometimes, and I wished the book-keeper to give in a paper of the names of those who were to attend.

Did the children take it in rotation?—It was just according to what wanted cleaning.

Who gave orders what children were to work on a Sunday?—The book-keeper sent me a written note of the names of those who were to attend.

Did he give you a written order in consequence of your remonstrance?— Yes.

Do you remember any Sunday when they did not work while you were at the mills?—I do not remember one Sunday when they did not go to work.

If they had left off work a little earlier on Saturday, could not they have avoided the necessity of going to the mills on a Sunday?—Yes.

Were the children paid for the Sunday-work?—Yes.

Did the children ever attend church?—Yes.

Would the children rather get money by working on a Sunday than attend church?—I thought there was a motive, which made me put a stop to it, by having a written order who was to attend.

Did they absent themselves sometimes from church, under the pretence of going to the mill to clean the machinery?—Yes.

Did the overlookers ever give you any orders for the children to work till twelve o'clock on Saturday night?—Yes.

Did you remonstrate against this also?—Yes.

For what reason?—Because we had the children to wash and clean after they had done work on Saturday night, therefore it was late before we got to bed; but they have sometimes worked till ten, the whole of the children; and when they have been short of water, that set that went on to work at eight at night was worked till twelve.

Did the masters ever express any concern for such excessive labour?—No.

Was it at the desire of the proprietors of the mill, or of the overlookers, that the children worked till twelve o'clock on Saturday night?—It was the master of the mill that wished them to work till twelve o'clock at night, when they were short of water; but it was the overlookers that wished the whole of them to work till twelve o'clock at night, in order to make up lost time, that they might get done the sooner; the whole of them never did work together later than ten.

Were they very strict in keeping them to their time?—Yes.

Did the children sit or stand to work?—Stand.

The whole of their time?—Yes.

Were there any seats in the mill?—None.

Were they usually much fatigued at night?—Yes, some of them were very much fatigued.

Where did they sleep?—They slept in the apprentice-house.

Did you inspect their beds?—Yes, every night.

For what purpose?—Because there were always some of them missing, some sometimes might be run away, others sometimes I have found have been asleep in the mill.

Upon the mill-floor?—Yes.

Did the children frequently lie down upon the mill-floor at night when their work was over, and fall asleep before their supper?—I have found them frequently upon the mill-floors, after the time they should have been in bed.

At what time did they go to bed?—Nine o'clock was their hour, when they worked their usual time.

In summer time did you allow them to sit up a little later?—Yes, sometimes till half past nine.

Were any children injured by the machinery?—Very frequently.

Were their fingers often crushed?—Very often their fingers were caught; and one had his arm broken.

Were any of the children deformed?—Yes, several of them were deformed; there were two or three that were very crooked.

Do you know whether those children were straight when they first came to the mill?—They told me they were.

Who told you they were?—The children themselves.

Were any of the children in-kneed, or what is called knock-kneed?—Yes, there were ten or a dozen of them, I dare say, that were in-kneed.

Did you understand from them whether they were so when they came to the mill?—I do not know that they were.

Do you think they were not?—I am pretty sure some of them were not, but some of them were lame when they came.

Did the parish officers of the parishes to which they belonged, ever come to the mills to visit and inspect the children?—No; there was one from Liverpool; the overseer of Liverpool.

Do you remember his name?—Hardman, I believe.

Was there any other inspection by magistrates, or any other persons?—No, there was no magistrates ever came into the childrens house.

Is the mill in a healthy situation?—Very.

Remarkably so?—Yes.

As the children grew up, did they in general appear to be healthy, or otherwise?—There were some who were very healthy children, and there were others that were sickly looking.

What was their general appearance?—Their general appearance was as well as most of the farmers children, some of them; some of them looked sickly, but then they were not sick.

They appeared to be sick, but were not so?—Yes; we scarcely ever had any sickness in the house.

How many died during the year you were at the mill?—There was only one.

How were the children lodged?—They had very good lodgings when we left them.

Had they good lodgings when you first went there?—No.

Did you make any complaints of their bedding when you first went?—Yes.

Will you state to the Committee what was the condition of their bedding when you first went?—When I first went there, their bedding was very bad, they had only a blanket to lie on, and a thin blanket to lie at top, and a horse cover, and some of them were very bad.

Could they be preserved cleanly with sleeping only on blankets?—They were not altogether clean.

Did you make complaint of that?—Yes.

Did the parish officer from Liverpool complain of it?—Yes.

Was it in consequence of his complaints and yours, that the bedding was improved?—Yes, it was; we got after that sheets and covers for every bed, and there never were sheets for any bed in the house I believe, before.

Did they spin fine or coarse yarn at those mills?—Very coarse.

Were the rooms as warm as where they spin fine?—No, I believe not.

Do you understand that they require greater heat for fine threads?—I have heard them say so; they have no heat in their rooms in the summer, in the winter they have heat from steam.

Were the children fed well?—Very well.

Before your time at Backbarrow mill, were the children turned out on the high road to beg their way to their former parishes, when the former proprietor stopped payment?—I was informed they were.

Did you converse with any of the children that were so turned out?—Yes.

Were they taken from the mill in a cart, and then turned adrift near the sands on the Lancaster road?—Yes, I was informed they were.

Do you know what became of them afterwards?—There was one of them I heard was taken in at Caton factory, and employed there for some time; and I heard there were some of them taken into Lancaster workhouse.

Did you hear that the gentlemen of Lancaster complained of this inhumanity?—Yes.

Were any fetched back in consequence of these complaints?—Yes, I believe there were.

Were they then turned over to Messrs. Ainsworth the present proprietors? —Yes.

After they had served out their apprenticeship to Messrs. Ainsworth, were they not compelled to serve extra time, under the pretence that so much time was lost by being turned out on the road and obliged to go to Lancaster?— Yes, there was one boy out of his time while I was there, and when the day came his master said that he had to serve six weeks, I think, longer, in consequence of his having run away; he said he never had ran away, he was turned out, and he had worked at Caton factory, and they made him serve that time out; his name is Henry Carter.

Do you know of Messrs. Watson's apprentices being turned out in the same manner?—I have heard it said so, but I never knew anything of it.

Were the children bad in their morals?—Yes, they were.

How did they behave one to another?—They did not behave well one to another.

Who looked over them in the mill?—Generally the older apprentices were overlookers over the younger ones.

Did the bigger boys beat the others?—Yes.

Frequently?—Yes.

What was the general character of the children?—Very bad characters.

What was the reason you left the mill?—It was in consequence of their bad behaviour.

4
EVALUATION OF THE INDUSTRIAL REVOLUTION

Thomas Babington Macaulay (1800–1859) is most generally remembered for his history of England in the seventeenth century. He was also an essayist of devastating wit and power. Nothing was more calculated to arouse his ire than an attack on the idea of progress; and Southey's romanticism seemed to him such an attack. This review reveals Macaulay at his polemical best.

FROM Southey's Colloquies BY T. B. MACAULAY

It would be scarcely possible for a man of Mr. Southey's talents and acquirements to write two volumes so large as those before us, which should be wholly destitute of information and amusement. Yet we do not remember to have read with so little satisfaction any equal quantity of matter, written by any man of real abilities. We have, for some time past, observed with great regret the strange infatuation which leads the Poet Laureate to abandon those departments of literature in which he might excel, and to lecture the public on sciences of which he has still the very alphabet to learn. He has now, we think, done his worst. The subject which he has at last undertaken to treat is one which demands all the highest intellectual and moral qualities of a philosophical statesman, an understanding at once comprehensive and acute, a heart at once upright and charitable. Mr. Southey brings to the task two

Critical and Historical Essays contributed to the Edinburgh Review by Lord Macaulay, I (1903), 205, 207, 215–218.

faculties which were never, we believe, vouchsafed in measure so copious to any human being, the faculty of believing without a reason, and the faculty of hating without a provocation.

It is, indeed, most extraordinary, that a mind like Mr. Southey's, a mind richly endowed in many respects by nature, and highly cultivated by study, a mind which has exercised considerable influence on the most enlightened generation of the most enlightened people that ever existed, should be utterly destitute of the power of discerning truth from falsehood. Yet such is the fact. Government is to Mr. Southey one of the fine arts. He judges of a theory, of a public measure, of a religion or a political party, of a peace or a war, as men judge of a picture or a statue, by the effect produced on his imagination. A chain of associations is to him what a chain of reasoning is to other men; and what he calls his opinions are in fact merely his tastes.

* * *

Now in the mind of Mr. Southey reason has no place at all, as either leader or follower, as either sovereign or slave. He does not seem to know what an argument is. He never uses arguments himself. He never troubles himself to answer the arguments of his opponents. It has never occurred to him, that a man ought to be able to give some better account of the way in which he has arrived at his opinions than merely that it is his will and pleasure to hold them. It has never occurred to him that there is a difference between assertion and demonstration, that a rumour does not always prove a fact, that a single fact, when proved, is hardly foundation enough for a theory, that two contradictory propositions cannot be undeniable truths, that to beg the question is not the way to settle it, or that when an objection is raised, it ought to be met with something more convincing than "scoundrel" and "blockhead."

* * *

We now come to the conversations which pass between Mr. Southey and Sir Thomas More, or rather between two Southeys, equally eloquent, equally angry, equally unreasonable, and equally given to talking about what they do not understand. Perhaps we could not select a better instance of the spirit which pervades the whole book than the passages in which Mr. Southey gives his opinion of the manufacturing system. There is nothing which he hates so bitterly. It is, according to him, a system more tyrannical than that of the feudal ages, a system of actual servitude, a system which destroys the bodies and degrades the minds of those who are engaged in it. He expresses a hope that the competition of other nations may drive us out of the field; that our foreign trade may decline; and that we may thus enjoy a restoration of national sanity and strength. But he seems to think that the extermination of the whole manufacturing population would be a blessing, if the evil could be removed in no other way.

Mr. Southey does not bring forward a single fact in support of these views; and, as it seems to us, there are facts which lead to a very different conclusion.

In the first place, the poor-rate is very decidedly lower in the manufacturing than in the agricultural districts. If Mr. Southey will look over the Parliamentary returns on this subject, he will find that the amount of parochial relief required by the labourers in the different counties of England is almost exactly in inverse proportion to the degree in which the manufacturing system has been introduced into those counties. The returns for the years ending in March 1825, and in March 1828, are now before us. In the former year we find the poor-rate highest in Sussex, about twenty shillings to every inhabitant. Then come Buckinghamshire, Essex, Suffolk, Bedfordshire, Huntingdonshire, Kent, and Norfolk. In all these the rate is above fifteen shillings a head. We will not go through the whole. Even in Westmoreland and the North Riding of Yorkshire, the rate is at more than eight shillings. In Cumberland and Monmouthshire, the most fortunate of all the agricultural districts, it is at six shillings. But in the West Riding of Yorkshire, it is as low as five shillings; and when we come to Lancashire, we find it at four shillings, one fifth of what it is in Sussex. The returns of the year ending in March 1828 are a little, and but a little, more unfavourable to the manufacturing districts. Lancashire, even in that season of distress, required a smaller poor-rate than any other district, and little more than one fourth of the poor-rate raised in Sussex. Cumberland alone, of the agricultural districts, was as well off as the West Riding of Yorkshire. These facts seem to indicate that the manufacturer is both in a more comfortable and in a less dependent situation than the agricultural labourer.

As to the effect of the manufacturing system on the bodily health, we must beg leave to estimate it by a standard far too low and vulgar for a mind so imaginative as that of Mr. Southey, the proportion of births and deaths. We know that, during the growth of this atrocious system, this new misery, to use the phrases of Mr. Southey, this new enormity, this birth of a portentous age, this pest which no man can approve whose heart is not seared or whose understanding has not been darkened, there has been a great diminution of mortality, and that this diminution has been greater in the manufacturing towns than any where else. The mortality still is, as it always was, greater in towns than in the country. But the difference has diminished in an extraordinary degree. There is the best reason to believe that the annual mortality of Manchester, about the middle of the last century, was one in twenty-eight. It is now reckoned at one in forty-five. In Glasgow and Leeds a similar improvement has taken place. Nay, the rate of mortality in those three great capitals of the manufacturing districts is now considerably less than it was, fifty years ago, over England and Wales, taken together, open country and all. We might with some plausibility maintain that the people live longer because they are better fed, better lodged, better clothed, and better attended in sickness, and that these improvements are owing to that increase of national wealth which the manufacturing system has produced.

Much more might be said on this subject. But to what end? It is not from bills of mortality and statistical tables that Mr. Southey has learned his political creed. He cannot stoop to study the history of the system which he abuses, to strike the balance between the good and evil which it has produced, to compare district with district, or generation with generation. We will give his own reason for his opinion, the only reason which he gives for it, in his own words:—

"We remained awhile in silence looking upon the assemblage of dwellings below. Here, and in the adjoining hamlet of Millbeck, the effects of manufactures and of agriculture may be seen and compared. The old cottages are such as the poet and the painter equally delight in beholding. Substantially built of the native stone without mortar, dirtied with no white lime, and their low roofs covered with slate, if they had been raised by the magic of some indigenous Amphion's music, the materials could not have adjusted themselves more beautifully in accord with the surrounding scene; and time has still further harmonized them with weather stains, lichens, and moss, short grasses, and short fern, and stone-plants of various kinds. The ornamented chimneys, round or square, less adorned than those which, like little turrets, crest the houses of the Portuguese peasantry; and yet not less happily suited to their place, the hedge of clipt box beneath the windows, the rose-bushes beside the door, the little patch of flower ground, with its tall hollyhocks in front; the garden beside, the beehives, and the orchard with its bank of daffodils and snow-drops, the earliest and the profusest in these parts, indicate in the owners some portion of ease and leisure, some regard to neatness and comfort, some sense of natural, and innocent, and healthful enjoyment. The new cottages of the manufacturers are upon the manufacturing pattern—naked, and in a row.

"How is it," said I, "that every thing which is connected with manufactures presents such features of unqualified deformity? From the largest of Mammon's temples down to the poorest hovel in which his helotry are stalled, these edifices have all one character. Time will not mellow them; nature will neither clothe nor conceal them; and they will remain always as offensive to the eye as to the mind."

Here is wisdom. Here are the pinciples on which nations are to be governed. Rose-bushes and poor-rates, rather than steam-engines and independence. Mortality and cottages with weather-stains, rather than health and long life with edifices which time cannot mellow. We are told, that our age has invented atrocities beyond the imagination of our fathers; that society has been brought into a state compared with which extermination would be a blessing; and all because the dwellings of cotton-spinners are naked and rectangular. Mr. Southey has found out a way, he tells us, in which the effects of manufactures and agriculture may be compared. And what is this way? To stand on a hill, to look at a cottage and a factory, and to see which is the prettier. Does Mr. Southey think that the body of the English peasantry live, or ever lived, in substantial or ornamented cottages, with box-hedges, flower-gardens, beehives, and orchards? If not, what is his parallel worth? We despise those mock philosophers, who think that they serve the cause of science by depreciating literature and the fine arts. But if any thing could excuse their narrowness of mind, it would be such a book as this. It is not strange that, when one enthusiast makes the picturesque the test of political good, another should feel inclined to proscribe altogether the pleasures of taste and imagination.

The Hammonds, both educated at Oxford, could find little good in the Industrial Revolution. To them, it was comparable to slavery, and they make their case with skill and verve.

FROM The Rise of Modern Industry
BY JOHN L. AND BARBARA HAMMOND

Rome imported slaves to work in Italy: Englishmen counted it one of the advantages of the slave trade that it discouraged the competition of British colonists with British manufacturers. For the slaves were chiefly needed for industries like sugar planting, in which Englishmen at home were not engaged. Thus it might be argued that England had escaped the fate of Rome and that she so used the slave trade as to make it a stimulus rather than a discouragement to native energy and skill.

Yet England did not escape the penalty. For it was under this shadow that the new industrial system took form and grew, and the immense power with which invention had armed mankind was exercised at first under conditions that reproduced the degradation of the slave trade. The factory system was not like war or revolution a deliberate attack on society: it was the effort of men to use will, energy, organization and intelligence for the service of man's needs. But in adapting this new power to the satisfaction of its wants England could not escape from the moral atmosphere of the slave trade: the atmosphere in which it was the fashion to think of men as things.

In the days of the guilds the workman was regarded as a person with some kind of property or status; the stages by which this character is restricted to a smaller and smaller part of the working classes, and more and more of the journeymen and apprentices fall into a permanently inferior class, have been described by historians. In the early nineteenth century the workers, as a class, were looked upon as so much labour power to be used at the discretion of,

John L. and Barbara Hammond, *The Rise of Modern Industry* (1925), pp. 194–195, 196–199, 200–201, 210, 211–213, 217–220, 222–224, 226–232. Reprinted by permission of Methuen & Co. Ltd., London.

and under conditions imposed by, their masters; not as men and women who are entitled to some voice in the arrangements of their life and work. The use of child labour on a vast scale had an important bearing on the growth of this temper.

The children of the poor were regarded as workers long before the Industrial Revolution. Locke suggested that they should begin work at three; Defoe rejoiced to see that in the busy homes of the Yorkshire clothiers "scarce anything above four years old, but its hands were sufficient for its own support." The new industrial system provided a great field for the employment of children, and Pitt himself, speaking in 1796, dwelt on this prospect with a satisfaction strange to modern minds, and disturbing even to some who heard him. One of the most elaborate of all Bentham's fantasies was his scheme for a great series of Industry Houses, 250 in number, each to hold 2,000 persons, for whose work, recreation, education, and marriage most minute regulations were laid down. An advantage he claimed for his system was that it would enable the apprentices to marry at "the earliest period compatible with health," and this was made possible by the employment of children. "And to what would they be indebted for this gentlest of all revolutions? To what, but to economy? Which dreads no longer the multiplication of man, now that she has shown by what secure and unperishable means infant man, a drug at present so much worse than worthless, may be endowed with an indubitable and universal value." Infant man soon became in the new industrial system what he never was in the old, the basis of a complicated economy.

Most children under the old domestic system worked at home under their parents' eyes, but in addition to such children there were workhouse children, who were hired out by overseers to every kind of master or mistress. Little care was taken to see that they were taught a trade or treated with humanity by their employers, and though London magistrates like Fielding did what they could to protect this unhappy class, their state was often a kind of slavery. The number of children on the hands of the London parishes was largely increased in the latter part of the eighteenth century, because an Act of Parliament, passed in 1767 in consequence of the exertions of Jonas Hanway, compelled the London parishes to board out their young children, and to give a bonus to every nurse whose charge survived. Until this time very few parish pauper children grew up to trouble their betters.

The needs of the London workhouses on the one hand, and those of the factory on the other, created a situation painfully like the situation in the West Indies. The Spanish employers in America wanted outside labour, because the supply of native labour was deficient in quantity and quality. The new cotton mills placed on streams in solitary districts were in the same case. The inventions had found immense scope for child labour, and in these districts there were only scattered populations. In the workhouses of large towns there was a quantity of child labour available for employment, that was even more powerless and passive in the hands of a master than the stolen negro, brought from his burning home to the hold of a British slave ship. Of these children it could be said, as it was said of the negroes, that their life at best was a hard one, and that their choice was often the choice between one kind of slavery and another. So the new industry which was to give the English people such immense power in the world borrowed at its origin from the methods of the American settlements.

How closely the apologies for this child serf system followed the apologies for the slave trade can be seen from Romilly's description of a speech made in the House of Commons in 1811. "Mr. Wortley, who spoke on the same side, insisted that, although in the higher ranks of society it was true that to culti- vate the affections of children for their family was the source of every virtue, yet that it was not so among the lower orders, and that it was a benefit to take them away from their miserable and depraved parents. He said too that it would be highly injurious to the public to put a stop to the binding of so many apprentices to the cotton manufacturers, as it must necessarily raise the price of labour and enhance the price of cotton manufactured goods."

It was not until 1816 that Parliament would consent to reform this system of transportation. In that year a Bill that had been repeatedly introduced by Mr. Wilbraham Bootle passed both Houses, and it was made illegal for Lon- don children to be apprenticed more than forty miles away from their parish. But by this time the problem had changed, for steam-power had super- seded water-power and mills could be built in towns; in these towns there were parents who were driven by poverty to send their children to the mills. In the early days of the factory system there had been a prejudice against sending children to the mill, but the hand-loom weaver had been sinking steadily from the beginning of the century into deeper and deeper poverty, and he was no longer able to maintain himself and his family. Sometimes too an adult worker was only given work on condition that he send his child to the mill. Thus the apprentice system was no longer needed. It had carried the factories over the first stage and at the second they could draw on the popula- tion of the neighbourhood.

These children, who were commonly called "free-labour children," were employed from a very early age. Most of them were piecers: that is they had to join together or piece the threads broken in the several roving or spinning machines. But there were tasks less skilled than these, and Robert Owen said that many children who were four or five years old were set to pick up waste cotton on the floor. Their hours were those of the apprentice children. They entered the mill gates at five or six in the morning and left them again at seven or eight at night. They had half an hour for breakfast and an hour for dinner, but even during meal hours they were often at work cleaning a stand- ing machine; Fielden calculated that a child following the spinning machine could walk twenty miles in the twelve hours. Oastler was once in the com- pany of a West Indian slave-master and three Bradford Spinners. When the slave-master heard what were the children's hours he declared: "I have always thought myself disgraced by being the owner of slaves, but we never in the West Indies thought it possible for any human being to be so cruel as to require a child of nine years old to work twelve and a half hours a day."

This terrible evil fastened itself on English life as the other fastened itself on the life of the Colonies. Reformers had an uphill struggle to get rid of its worst abuses. Throughout this long struggle the apologies for child labour were precisely the same as the apologies for the slave trade. Cobbett put it in 1833 that the opponents of the Ten Hours Bill had discovered that England's manufacturing supremacy depended on 30,000 little girls. This was no travesty of their argument. The champions of the slave trade pointed to the £70,-000,000 invested in the sugar plantations, to the dependence of our navy on our commerce, and to the dependence of our commerce on the slave trade. This was the argument of Chatham in one generation and Rodney in another. When Fox destroyed the trade in 1806 even Sir Robert Peel complained that we were philosophizing when our looms were idle, and George Rose, that the Americans would take up the trade, and that Manchester, Stockport and Paisley would starve. . . .

The argument for child labour followed the same line. In the one case the interests of Liverpool, in the other those of Lancashire, demanded of the nation that it should accept one evil in order to escape from another. Cardwell, afterwards the famous army reformer, talked of the great capital sunk in the cotton industry and the danger of the blind impulse of humanity. Sir James Graham thought that the Ten Hours Bill would ruin the cotton industry and with it the trade of the country. The cotton industry had taken the place in this argument that had been held by the navy in the earlier controversy. Our population, which had grown so rapidly in the Industrial Revolution, was no longer able to feed itself: the food it bought was paid for by its manufactures: those manufactures depended on capital: capital depended on profits: profits depended on the labour of the boys and girls who enabled the manufacturer to work his mills long enough at a time to repay the cost of the plant and to compete with his foreign rivals. This was the circle in which the nation found its conscience entangled.

The life of man had been regulated before by the needs of a particular order or the pattern of a particular society: the government of king or church or lord had defined narrow limits within which a man was to run his course. The new master was a world force, for this economy could make its profits, so it was believed, where it chose, and when Englishmen rebelled against its rule it would seek its gains and bestow its blessings elsewhere. This way of looking at the new industrial system put man at the mercy of his machines, for if the new power was not made man's servant, it was bound to become his master. If at every point the governing claim was not man's good but the needs of the machine, it was inevitable that man's life and the quality of his civilization should be subordinated to this great system of production.

Nobody could argue that the ordinary worker before the Industrial Revolution was a free man, whether he was a peasant in the country or a journeyman in the town, but the age which watched the change from domestic to factory industry in Lancashire and Yorkshire could see that a great many men and women lost what they had possessed of initiative and choice.

* * *

What happened at the Industrial Revolution was that all the restraints that the law imposed on workmen in particular industries, were standardized into a general law for the whole of the expanding world of industry, and all the regulations and laws that recognized him as a person with rights were withdrawn or became inoperative. The workman, as we have seen, lost one by one the several Acts of Parliament that gave him protection from his master in this or that industry. His personal liberty was circumscribed by a series of Acts beginning with the Act of 1719, which made it a crime for him to take his wits and his skills into another country: a law that applied to the artisan but not to the inventor. At the end of the century the masters were given complete control of their workmen, by a Combination Act which went far beyond the Acts against combinations already on the Statute book. By the Combination Act of 1799 any workman who combined with any other workman to seek an improvement in his working conditions was liable to be brought before a single magistrate—it might be his own employer—and sent to prison for three months. This Act, the chief authors of which were Pitt and Wilberforce, was modified next year, when Parliament decided that two magistrates were necessary to form a court, and that a magistrate who was a master in the trade affected should not try offences, but these modifications did not affect in practice the power that the law gave to employers. Under cover of this Act it often happened that a master would threaten his workman with imprisonment or service in the fleet in order to compel him to accept the wages he chose to offer. In 1824 Place and Hume, taking advantage of the reaction from the worst of the panics produced by the French Revolution, managed to carry the repeal of the Combination Laws. Next year, after their repeal had been celebrated by an outburst of strikes, a less stringent law was put in their place. But the view of the new system as a beneficent mechanism which the mass of men must serve with a blind and unquestioning obedience was firmly rooted in the temper of the time, and thus anyone who tried to think of Englishmen in the spirit of Burke's description of a man, found himself strangely out of tune in a world where the workman was refused education, political rights and any voice in the conditions of his employment.

"At Tyldesley," it was said in a pamphlet published during a strike, "they work fourteen hours per day, including the nominal hour for dinner; the door is locked in working hours, except half an hour at tea time; the workpeople are not allowed to send for water to drink, in the hot factory: and even the rain water is locked up, by the master's order, otherwise they would be happy to drink even that." In this mill a shilling fine was inflicted on a spinner found dirty, or found washing, heard whistling or found with his window open in a temperature of 84 degrees. The men who were thrust into this discipline, however hard and bare their lives, had been accustomed to work in their own homes at their own time. The sense of servitude that was impressed on the age by this discipline, by the methods of government, the look of the towns and the absence of choice or initiative in the lives of the mass of the work-people, was strengthened by the spectacle of the new power. "While the engine runs," wrote an observer, "the people must work—men, women and children yoked together with iron and steam. The animal machine—breakable in the best case, subject to a thousand sources of suffering— is chained fast to the iron machine which knows no suffering and no weariness."

"Two centuries ago not one person in a thousand wore stockings; one century ago not one person in five hundred wore them; now not one person in a thousand is without them." This sentence from *The Results of Machinery* (1831), one of the publications of the Society for the Diffusion of Useful Knowledge, illustrates a feature of the Industrial Revolution that made a profound impression on the imagination of the time. When capital was applied to production on a large scale, it gained its profits by producing in bulk; producing, that is, for mass consumption. Energy and brains were now devoted to satisfying, not the luxurious taste of the classes that were served by the commerce of medieval Europe, but the needs of the poor consumer.

It was natural for the age that witnessed the first triumphs of the new system to worship production for profit. This great addition to the wealth of the world seemed to follow automatically when men were left to acquire at their pleasure. Swift success is a dazzling spectacle, and the new industrial system provided a new miracle every day. . . .

The English people, from the whole tone and cast of its thought and politics, was specially liable to be swept off its balance by this revolution. The positive enthusiasms of the time were for science and progress: for material development and individual liberty. The restraints of custom, tradition and religion had never been so frail over the classes that held power. In the Middle Ages the Church had laid a controlling or checking hand on manners: the Guilds had hampered individual enterprise by a corporate discipline. But the Church of the eighteenth century was merely part of the civil order, without standards, authority or conscience of its own; the Guilds were dead, and their successors stood not for corporate spirit, but for property and nothing else. Thus neither Church nor Guild survived to offer any obstacle to the view that headlong wealth was the sovereign good for society and for the individual, for cities and for men.

This view was powerfully encouraged by the philosophy of confidence which the eighteenth century had substituted for a religion of awe. Medieval religion had watched man's instincts with anxious eyes, as instincts needing to be disciplined, coerced, held fast by Pope and priest; the Puritans, though they gave him different masters, were not less suspicious of the natural man. The new philosophy, on the other hand, regarded man's instincts as the best guide to conduct, and taught that left to himself man so acted as to serve rather than injure the society to which he belonged. Capital was a magical power; man was a benevolent creature. Thus so far as an age lives by a system of belief, this age drew its wisdom from a philosophy that found nothing but good in the new force to which it had submitted.

The state of politics was also congenial to this impulse. Neither Conservative nor Radical offered any distracting or competing motive, for while they disagreed about political and administrative reform, they did not disagree about the advantages of a system under which acquisition and profit-making were unimpeded. If it was the manufacturers who promoted the new system in industry, the landowners were equally active in promoting it on their estates. The most important force in making the English an industrial people was the destruction of the village. Nations that kept the peasant could never be completely absorbed in the new industrial system, and it was the landowner, often of course the new landowner, who had come from the world of finance and industry, who pushed the English peasant out.

England was on the eve of a great expansion of resources, numbers, wealth and power. What were the new towns to be like? What their schools, their pleasures, their houses, their standards of a good life, their plans for cooperation and fellowship? What the fate of the mass of people who did not feel or force their way through the doors thrown open to enterprise? To all these questions the Industrial Revolution gave the same answer: "Ask Capital." And neither Conservative nor Radical, the man defending or the man attacking bad laws and bad customs, thought that answer wrong. But that answer meant that the age had turned aside from making a society in order to make a system of production.

The effect of this concentration is seen in the towns of the age. They were left, like everything else, to the mercy and direction of the spirit of profit. . . .

Yet the Industrial Revolution which had given these men their fortunes had made it much easier to supply the needs of the towns that sprang up beside their great establishments. One of the products of that revolution was gas lighting; the Soho Works were lighted with gas in 1802 to celebrate the Peace of Amiens. Great factories at Manchester and Leeds soon followed the example of Boulton and Watt. Another product was the cheap water-pipe. At the end of the American War English ironmasters were exporting water-pipes to Paris and New York. The Romans had no cheap water-pipes made by the help of mechanical power, but they could supply their towns with clean water, whereas the people of Merthyr Tydfil, their streets echoing by day and night with the clamour of forge and furnace, had to drink whatever the river brought them.

The rage for production had swept England, as the rage for piety had swept the age of the monarchists. And production had taken a form that was intensely isolating; the successful man kept his secrets, tried to find his neighbours' secrets, strove for personal gain, took personal risks, made his way by personal initiative and personal enterprise.

This concentration led to the complete neglect of the most urgent tasks of the age. In the first twenty years of the nineteenth century the population of Manchester increased from 94,000 to 160,000; of Bolton from 29,000 to 50,000; Leeds more than doubled its population between 1801 and 1831; Bradford, which had 23,000 inhabitants in 1831, grew grass in its streets at the end of the eighteenth century. Oldham, which had 38,000 inhabitants in 1821, had three or four hundred in 1760. In the twenty years from 1801 to 1821 the population of Lancashire grew from 672,000 to 1,052,000; in the next twenty years it grew to 1,701,000. The population of Merthyr increased from 7,700 to 35,000 between 1801 and 1841, and that of the two counties of Glamorgan and Monmouth from 126,000 to 305,000. Industry was accumulating dense masses of people into particular districts, where the workman was shut up in melancholy streets, without gardens or orchards. England was passing from a country to a town life, as she passed from a peasant to an industrial civilization. What this meant is clear if we compare the state of the towns as revealed in the health statistics, with that of the country districts. In 1757 Dr. Percival put the death-rate for Manchester at 1 in 25, for Liverpool at 1 in 27. In Monton, a few miles from Manchester, the ratio was at that time 1 in 68, at Horwich, between Bolton and Chorley, 1 in 66, at Darwen, three miles from Blackburn, 1 in 56. The Industrial Revolution was to spread the conditions of town life over places like Monton, Horwich and Darwen.

The problem of arranging and controlling the expansion of the towns was thus the most urgent of the problems created by the Industrial Revolution. Its importance was illustrated by a picture of some cottages near Preston published by the Health of Towns Commission in 1844. These cottages stood in two rows, separated by little back yards, with an open sewer running the whole length. The picture was given as an example of dangerous and disgusting drainage. But this is not its chief significance. One would suppose that these huddled cottages, without gardens of any kind, were built in a crowded town, where not an inch of space was available for amenities. They were in fact in the open country. Clearly then there was more here than a problem of drainage, for if it was left to private enterprise to develop this district, under the guidance of an uncontrolled sense for profit, these rows would spring up all round, and Preston would have another slum on her hands. This is what happened in the new industrial districts. When the Health of Towns Commission investigated towns like Manchester, they were told that the worst evils were not the evils of the past, for new Manchester was reproducing the slums and alleys of the old, and spreading them, of course, over a far wider surface. Of no other problem was it so true that neglect by one generation tied the hands and the mind of the next. . . .

The importance of preserving amenities, footpaths, and something of the look of the country was impressed on Parliament. The most significant comment of the neglect of these proposals is to be found in the recurring complaint that runs through all the Reports on Health and Housing that were issued in the nineteenth century. Town planning never found its way into an

Act of Parliament until the twentieth century, and back-to-back houses (made illegal in 1909) were built in great numbers two generations after Normanby's Bill had proposed to forbid them. The Commission which sat in 1867 found in existence the main evils that were revealed by the Committee of 1840; the Commission of 1884 found in existence the main evils that had been revealed by the Commission of 1867. In many towns the death-rate was higher in 1867 than in 1842, and Cross, speaking as Home Secretary in 1871, could match the terrible revelations by which Chadwick had tried to rouse the indignation and fear of the Parliaments of Melbourne and Peel.

Before each Commission the large towns disclosed the same difficulties. The law did not enable them to control expansion, or to prevent the creation on their circumference of the evils they were trying to suppress at the centre. The Committee of 1840 had pointed out that back-to-back houses were being introduced into towns that had been free from them. Town Clerks told the Commission of 1867 that whole streets were still being built on "a foundation composed of old sweepings, refuse from factories, old buildings and other objectionable matter." Parliament passed Public Health Acts and set up authorities with sharply limited powers, but the fatal blindness to the character of the problem, as a problem in the organization and planning of town life, which marked the early phases of the Industrial Revolution, persisted. England learnt sooner than other countries how to cleanse her towns, but towns still continued to grow at the pleasure of the profit seeker. Each generation looked wistfully back to its predecessor as living in a time when the evil was still manageable, and over the reforms of the century could be inscribed the motto "the Clock that always loses." For the creed of the first age of the Industrial Revolution, that the needs of production must regulate the conditions of life, and that the incidence of profits must decide in what kind of town, in what kind of streets, and in what kind of houses a nation shall find its home, had cast its melancholy fatalism over the mind of the generations that followed. The trouble was not merely that the evil was greater when a town had a quarter of a million of inhabitants instead of a hundred thousand. It was that men still saw with the eyes of their grandfathers, and that they were busy polishing the life of the slum, when a race that was free and vigorous in its mind could have put an end to it. With the consequences and the traditions of this neglect industrial civilization is still fighting an up-hill battle.

The other task that became immensely more important with the Industrial Revolution was the task of education. Adam Smith had pointed out that the division of labour, though good for production, was bad for the mind of the labourer. Men, women and children lost range, diversity and incentive in their work, when that work was simplified to a single process, or a monotonous routine. Life was more versatile and interesting when craftsmanship was combined with agriculture. Under the new system a boy or youth learnt one process and one process only; a great part of his mind was never exercised; many of his faculties remained idle and undeveloped. Moreover, apprenticeship was declining, and thus an important method of education was passing out of fashion.

Nor were these the only reasons why popular education was needed more urgently in this than in previous ages. Men learn from their leisure as well as from their work. Now the common life of the time was singularly wanting in inspiration, comparing in this respect unfavourably with the life of the ancient or that of the medieval world. The Greeks and the Romans put a great deal of beauty into their public buildings; they made provision, in some cases barbarous provision, for public amusement; they did not isolate art and pleasure for the delight of a small class. Life in Manchester or Merthyr was very different. Mr. and Mrs. Webb, who have described the work of the several bodies of Improvement Commissioners at this time, remark that even the most energetic among them made no provision for parks, open spaces, libraries, picture galleries, museums, baths, or any kind of education. The workmen put it that their sports had been converted into crimes, and their holidays into fast days. Rich men in the Roman Empire spent their money on things that were for common enjoyment as rich men in the Middle Ages spent their money on things that were for common salvation. Pliny gave to his native Como, a library, a school endowment, a foundation for the nurture of poor children and a Temple of Ceres with spacious colonnades to shelter the traders who visited the great fair. The wealthy Herodes Atticus, tutor of Marcus Aurelius, gave a theatre to Athens with a roof of cedar to hold 6,000 persons, another theatre to Corinth, and a race-course to Delphi. Such gifts were common in the days of the Antonines. But in the England of the early Industrial Revolution all diversions were regarded as wrong, because it was believed that successful production demanded long hours, a bare life, a mind without temptation to think or to remember, to look before or behind. Some Lancashire magistrates used to refuse on this ground to license public-houses where concerts were held. Long hours did not begin with the Industrial Revolution, but in the Middle Ages the monotony of industrial work was broken for the journeyman by frequent holidays, saints' days and festivals; for medieval Europe, like Rome, gave some place in common life to the satisfaction of the imagination and the senses.

Perhaps nothing served so directly to embitter the relations of class in the Industrial Revolution as this fashionable view, that the less amusement the worker had, the better. The love of amusement has a place of special significance in the English character. If the English workman stints himself for his holiday week at Blackpool, as the Scottish peasant stints himself to send his son into the Ministry, or the Irish or French peasant stints himself to own a little property, it is not merely because he sets his holiday high among the enjoyments of life. The satisfaction of this desire is connected with his self-respect. The football field and the holiday resort represent a world in which the poor man feels himself the equal of the rich: a corner of life in which he has not bargained away any rights or liberties. It might be said of the early Radicals, that they sought to extend to his view of politics, and of the early

Socialists, that they sought to extend to his view of property, the spirit that ruled the workman's outlook on his pleasures: that they sought to make him resent in those spheres the inequalities he was so quick to resent, when employer or magistrate tried to keep from him amusements that other classes enjoyed.

The need for popular education became in these circumstances specially urgent. The reading of print is one way of using and exercising the mind, and its value at any moment depends on circumstances. In the days of pageants and spectacles, when story-tellers went from village to village, when pedlars and pilgrims brought tales of adventure or war or the habits of foreign countries, a man might be unable to read or write, and yet take a share in the culture of the time. Buildings, plays, music, these may be greater influences on the mind than book or pamphlet or newspaper. But the youth of the early nineteenth century who found no scope for initiative or experiment or design in his work, found no stimulus or education for his fancy from the spectacles and amusements provided for his recreation. Science was improving the mechanical contrivances of life, but the arts of life were in decline. To take advantage of these improvements, the power to read and write was essential. In a world depending on newspapers, the man who cannot read lives in the darkest exile; when the factory was taking the place of the craft, the newspaper the place of the pageant, illiteracy was the worst disfranchisement a man could suffer.

Horner, reporting in 1839 that a population of over a hundred thousand persons in a district of Lancashire comprising Oldham and Ashton was without a single public day-school for poor scholars, the Commissioner who said of South Wales in 1842 that not one grown male in fifty could read, both spoke of an age in which the story-teller had left the village, and the apprenticeship system was leaving the town. Adam Smith had argued that as the division of labour deprived the worker of opportunities of training his mind, the State ought to provide opportunities by public education. The ruling class argued, on the contrary, that with the new methods of specialization, industry could not spare a single hour for the needs of the men who served it. In such a system education had no place. The great majority of the ruling class believed, as one of them put it, that the question to ask was not whether education would develop a child's faculties for happiness and citizenship, but whether it "would make him a good servant in agriculture and other laborious employments to which his rank in society had destined him."

Thus England asked for profits and received profits. Everything turned to profit. The towns had their profitable dirt, their profitable smoke, their profitable slums, their profitable disorder, their profitable ignorance, their profitable despair. The curse of Midas was on this society: on its corporate life, on its common mind, on the decisive and impatient step it had taken from the peasant to the industrial age. For the new town was not a home where man could find beauty, happiness, leisure, learning, religion—the influences that civilize outlook and habit; but a bare and desolate place, without colour, air or laughter, where man, woman and child worked, ate and slept. This was to be the lot of the mass of mankind: this the sullen rhythm of their lives. The new factories and the new furnaces were like the Pyramids, telling of man's enslavement, rather than of his power, casting their long shadow over the society that took such pride in them.

The foremost proponent of the necessity for revising the traditional accounts of the Industrial Revolution is T. S. Ashton, professor emeritus of economic history at the University of London.

FROM The Treatment of Capitalism by Historians
BY T. S. ASHTON

The student of English economic history is fortunate in having at his disposal the reports of a long series of Royal Commissions and Committees of Inquiry beginning in the eighteenth century but reaching full stream in the 1830's, 1840's, and 1850's. These reports are one of the glories of the early Victorian age. They signalized a quickening of social conscience, a sensitiveness to distress, that had not been evident in any other period or in any other country. Scores of massive folios provided statistical and verbal evidence that all was not well with large numbers of the people of England and called the attention of legislators and the reading public to the need for reform. The economic historians of the succeeding generations could do no other than draw on their findings; and scholarship, no less than society, benefited. There was, however, loss as well as gain. A picture of the economic system constructed from Blue Books dealing with social grievances, and not with the normal processes of economic development, was bound to be one-sided. It is such a picture of early Victorian society that has become fixed in the minds of popular writers. . . . A careful reading of the reports would, indeed, lead to the conclusion that much that was wrong was the result of laws, customs, habits, and forms of organization that belonged to earlier periods and were rapidly becoming obsolete. It would have brought home to the mind that it was not among the factory employees but among the domestic workers, whose traditions and methods were those of the eighteenth century, that earnings were at their lowest. It would have provided evidence that it was not in the large establishments making use of steam power but in the garret or cellar workshops that conditions of employment were at their worst. It would have led to the conclusion that it was not in the growing manufacturing towns or the developing coal fields but in remote villages and the countryside that restrictions on personal freedom and the evils of truck were most marked. But few had the patience to go carefully through these massive volumes. It was so much easier to pick out the more sensational evidences of distress and work them into a dramatic story of exploitation. The result has been that a generation that had the enterprise and industry to assemble the facts, the honesty to reveal them, and the energy to set about the task of reform has been held up to obloquy as the author, not of the Blue Books, but of the evils themselves. Conditions in the mills and the factory town were so bad, it seemed, that there must have been deterioration; . . . and, since the supposed deterioration had taken place at a time when machinery had increased, the machines, and those who owned them, must have been responsible.

At the same time the romantic revival in literature led to an idyllic view of the life of the peasant. The idea that agriculture is the only natural and healthy activity for human beings has persisted, and indeed spread, as more of us have escaped from the curse of Adam—or, as the tedious phrase goes, "become divorced from the soil." A year ago an examinee remarked profoundly that "in earlier centuries agriculture was widespread in England" but added sorrowfully, "Today it is confined to the rural areas." There was a similar idealization of the condition of the domestic worker, who had taken only the first step in the proceedings for divorce. Bear with me while I read some passages with which Friedrich Engels (who is usually acclaimed a realist) opens his account of *The Condition of the Working Classes in England in 1844.* It is, of course, based on the writings of the Reverend Philip Gaskell, whose earnestness and honesty are not in doubt, but whose mind had not been confused by any study of history. Engels' book opens with the declaration that "the history of the proletariat in England begins with the invention of the steam-engine and of machinery for working cotton." Before their time, he continues,

the workers vegetated throughout a passably comfortable existence, leading a righteous and peaceful life in all piety and probity; and their material condition was far better than that of their successors. They did not need to overwork; they did no more than they chose to do, and yet earned what they needed. They had leisure for healthful work in garden or field, work which, in itself, was recreation for them, and they could take part beside in the recreation and games of their neighbours, and all these games—bowling, cricket, football, etc. contributed to their physical health and vigour. They were, for the most part, strong, well-built people, in whose physique little or no difference from that of their peasant neighbours was discoverable. Their children grew up in fresh country air, and, if they could help their parents at work, it was only occasionally; while of eight or twelve hours work for them there was no question.

It is difficult to say whether this or the lurid picture of the lives of the grandchildren of these people presented in later pages of the book is more completely at variance with the facts. Engels had no doubt whatsoever as to the cause of the deterioration in the condition of labor. "The proletariat," he repeats, "was called into existence by the introduction of machinery." "The consequences of improvement in machinery under our present social conditions," he asserts, "are, for the working-man, solely injurious, and often in the highest degree oppressive. Every new advance brings with it loss of employment, want and suffering."

Engels has had many disciples, even among those who do not accept the historical materialism of Marx, with which such views are generally connected. Hostility to the machine is associated with hostility to its products and, indeed, to all innovation in consumption. One of the outstanding accomplishments of the new industrial age is to be seen in the greatly increased supply and variety of fabrics offered on the market. Yet the changes in dress are taken as evidence of growing poverty: "The clothing of the working-people in a majority of cases," Engels declares, "is in a very bad condition. The material used for it is not of the best adapted. Wool and linen have almost vanished from the wardrobes of both sexes, and cotton has taken their place. Skirts are made of bleached or coloured cotton goods, and woollen petticoats are rarely to be seen on the wash-line." The truth is that they never had been greatly displayed on the wash line, for woolen goods are liable to shrink. The workers of earlier periods had to make their garments last (second or third hand as many of these were), and soap and water were inimical to the life of clothing. The new, cheap textiles may not have been as hard-wearing as broadcloth, but they were more abundant; and the fact that they could be washed without suffering harm had a bearing, if not on their own life, at least on the lives of those who wore them.

The same hostility is shown to innovation in food and drink. Generations of writers have followed William Cobbett in his hatred of tea. One would have thought that the enormous increase in consumption between the beginning of the eighteenth and the middle of the nineteenth century was one element in a rising standard of comfort; but only a few years ago Professor Parkinson asserted that it was "growing poverty" that made tea increasingly essential to the lower classes as ale was put beyond their means. (This, I may add, unfortunately meant that they were forced to consume sugar, and one must suppose that this practice also led to a fall in the standard of living.) Similarly, Dr. Salaman has recently assured us that the introduction of the potato into the diet of the workers at this time was a factor detrimental to health and that it enabled the employers to force down the level of wages—which, it is well known, is always determined by the minimum of food required for subsistence.

Very gradually those who held to these pessimistic views of the effects of industrial change have been forced to yield ground. The painstaking researches of Bowley and Wood have shown that over most of this period, and later, the course of real wages was upward. The proof is not at all easy, for it is clear that there were sections of the working classes of whom it was emphatically not true. In the first half of the nineteenth century the population of England was growing, partly because of natural increase, partly as the result of the influx of Irish. For those endowed with little or no skill, marginal productivity, and hence earnings, remained low. A large part of their incomes was spent on commodities (mainly food, drink, and housing), the cost of which had hardly been affected by technical development. That is why so many of the economists, like McCulloch and Mill, were themselves dubious about the beneficial nature of the industrial system. There were, however, large and growing sections of skilled and better-paid workers whose money incomes were rising and who had a substantial margin to spend on the products of the machine, the costs of which were falling progressively. The controversy really rests on which of the groups was increasing most. Generally it is now agreed that for the majority the gain in real wages was substantial.

But this does not dispose of the controversy. Real earnings might have risen, it was said, but it was the quality of life and not the quantity of goods consumed that mattered. In particular, it was the evil conditions of housing and the insanitary conditions of the towns that were called as evidence that the circumstances of labor had worsened. "Everything which here arouses horror and indignation," wrote Engels of Manchester in 1844, "is of recent origin, belongs to the industrial epoch"—and the reader is left to infer that the equally repulsive features of cities like Dublin and Edinburgh, which were scarcely touched by the new industry, were, somehow or other, also the product of the machine.

This is the legend that has spread round the world and has determined the attitude of millions of men and women to labor-saving devices and to those who own them. Indians and Chinese, Egyptians and Negroes, to whose fellow-countrymen today the dwellings of the English of the mid-nineteenth century would be wealth indeed, solemnly declare, in the scripts I have to read, that the English workers were living in conditions unworthy of beasts. They write with indignation about the inefficiency of the sanitation and the absence of civic amenities—the very nature of which is still unknown to the urban workers of a large part of the earth.

Now, no one who has read the reports of the Committee on the Sanitary Condition of the Working Classes of 1842 or that of the Commission on the Health of Towns of 1844 can doubt that the state of affairs was, from the point of view of modern Western civilization, deplorable. But, equally, no one who has read Dorothy George's account of living conditions in London in the eighteenth century can be sure that they had deteriorated. Dr. George herself believes that they had improved, and Clapham declared that the English towns of the mid-century were "less crowded than the great towns of other countries and not, universally, more insanitary." The question I wish to raise, however, is that of responsibility. Engels, as we have seen, attributed the evils to the machine; others are no less emphatic in attributing them to the Industrial Revolution, which comes to much the same thing. No historian, as far as I know, has looked at the problem through the eyes of those who had the task of building and maintaining the towns.

There were two main aspects: the supply of houses in relation to the demand and the technical matters of drainage, sanitation, and ventilation. In the early nineteenth century, according to one of these scripts, "the workers were pressed into back-to-back houses, like sardines in a rabbit warren." Many of the houses were certainly unsubstantial and insanitary, and for this it is usual to blame the industrialist who put them up, a man commonly spoken of as the jerry-builder. I had often wondered who this man was. When I was young, the parson of the church I attended once preached a sermon on Jerry, who, he asserted with complete conviction, was at that very moment burning in hell for his crimes. I have searched for records of him, but in vain. It appears from Weekley's *Etymological Dictionary of Modern English* that "jerry" is a corruption of "jury"—a word of nautical origin applied to any part of a ship contrived for temporary use, as in "jury mast" and "jury rig," and extended to other things, such as "jury leg" for "wooden leg." "Jerry," then, means temporary, or inferior, or makeshift; and no doubt other uses of the word as a makeshift in an emergency will come to the mind. According to Partridge's *Dictionary of Slang and Unconventional English,* it was first used in Liverpool about 1830. The place and time are significant. Liverpool was the port for the rapidly developing industrial area of southeastern Lancashire; it was the chief gate of entry for the swarms of Irish immigrants. It was probably here that the pressure of population on the supplies of accommodation was most acute. Houses were run up rapidly, and many of them were flimsy structures, the outer walls of which were only 4½ inches in thickness. On December 5, 1822, some of them, along with many buildings elsewhere, were blown down in a great storm that swept over the British Isles; and in February, 1823, the grand jury at Liverpool called the attention of the magistrates "to the dreadful effects of the late storm . . . in consequence of the modern insecure mode of building." A year later the same body referred again to "the slight and dangerous mode of erecting dwelling houses now practised in this town and neighbourhood" and asked for steps to be taken "to procure a Legislative enactment, which might empower a proper Officer carefully to survey every building hereafter to be erected, and in case of insecurity to cause the danger to be removed."

The sudden collapse of buildings was no new experience. In 1738 Samuel Johnson had written of London as a place where "falling houses thunder on your head"; and, to give a specific instance, in 1796 two houses fell, burying sixteen people, in Houghton Street, where the concrete buildings of the School of Economics now stand. The chief trouble seems to have been the use of inferior material, such as ashes and street sweepings, in the making of bricks and the unsubstantial walls erected whenever the building lease was for only a short run of years. It would appear from the Liverpool evidence, however, that matters had taken a turn for the worse in the early 1820's; and complaints of inferior building in other quarters reinforce the belief. The explanation is not far to seek. It lies in the fact that the early twenties saw a revival of housebuilding after a long period of suspension (or, at best, feeble activity) during nearly a quarter of a century of war and that this revival took place in circumstances when building costs had been raised to an inordinate height.

It is necessary to take account of the organization of the industry. The typical builder was a man of small means, a bricklayer or a carpenter who bought a small plot of land, carried out himself only a single operation, such as that of laying the bricks, and employed craftsmen on contract for the other processes of construction. By the middle of the nineteenth century, it is true, large-scale firms were growing up, controlled by men like Thomas Cubitt, but these were concerned with the erection of public buildings or mansions and not with the dwellings of the poor. The jerry-builders were not, in the usual sense of the word, capitalists, but workingmen. Says Chadwick's *Report* of 1842:

In the rural districts, the worst of the new cottages are those erected on the borders of commons by the labourers themselves. In manufacturing districts, the tenements erected by building clubs and by speculating builders of the class of workmen, are frequently the subject of complaint, as being the least substantial and the most destitute of proper accommodation. The only conspicuous instances of improved residences found in the rural districts are those which have been erected by opulent and benevolent landlords for the accommodation of the labourers on their own estates: and in the manufacturing districts, those erected by wealthy manufacturers for the accommodation of their own workpeople.

In Liverpool the builders of so-called "slop houses," or scamped houses, were usually Welshmen, drawn largely from the quarrymen of Caernarvonshire. They were backed by attorneys who had land to dispose of on lease but were not themselves willing to become builders. They bought their materials, which were of a cheap and shoddy type, on three months' credit. They tended to employ a high proportion of apprentices, and so, it was said, workmanship was of low quality. They needed credit at every stage: to obtain the building lease, to purchase the materials, and to meet the claims of the joiners, plasterers, slaters, plumbers, painters, etc., who performed their special tasks as contractors or subcontractors. The price of money was an important element in building costs. Under the operation of the usury laws it was illegal to offer, or demand, more than 5 per cent, and this meant that, at times when the state itself was offering 4½ or more per cent, it was impossible for the builders to obtain loans at all. By allowing the rate of interest to rise to 4½ or 5 per cent on the public debt, and prohibiting the industrialist from offering more, the state had been successful in damping down the activities of the builders for more than twenty years and so had deflected to itself the resources of men and materials required for the prosecution of the war against Napoleon. After 1815 the rate of interest fell tardily; it was not until the early twenties that the builders could resume operations. They were faced with a demand that had swollen enormously as the result of a vast increase of population, which now included an abnormally large number of young adults seeking homes of their own.

They were faced also by an enormous increase in costs. In 1821, according to Silberling's index number, wholesale prices in general stood about 20 per cent above the level of the year 1788. In the same period the price of building materials had risen far more: bricks and wainscot had doubled; deals had risen by 60 per cent and lead by 58 per cent. The wages of craftsmen and laborers had gone up by anything from 80 to 100 per cent. The costs of a large number of specific operations are given annually in the *Builders' Price Books* published in London. They show an increase in the cost of plain brickwork of 120 per cent. Oak for building purposes had gone up by 150 per cent, and fir by no less than 237 per cent. The cost of common painting had doubled, and that of glazing with crown glass had increased by 140 per cent.

It was not, in the main, the producer of materials who was responsible. During the war the duties levied by the state on bricks and tiles, stone, slate, and wallpaper had increased enormously. At this time the cost of timber was the chief element in the total cost of building materials, amounting, according to one estimate, to fully a half of the whole. Almost prohibitive duties had been laid on the supplies of timber and deals from the Baltic, and the builders of working-class houses had to make use of what were generally said to be inferior woods, brought at great cost across the Atlantic from Canada. Joseph Hume declared, in 1850, that, if the duties on bricks and timber were removed, a cottage which cost £60 to build, as things were, could be put up for £40.

* * *

In the years that followed the long war, then, the builders had the task of making up arrears of housing and of meeting the needs of a rapidly growing population. They were handicapped by costs, a large part of which arose from fiscal exactions. The expenses of occupying a house were loaded with heavy local burdens, and so the net rent that most workingmen could afford to pay was reduced. In these circumstances, if the relatively poor were to be housed at all, the buildings were bound to be smaller, less substantial, and less well provided with amenities than could be desired. It was emphatically not the machine, not the Industrial Revolution, not even the speculative bricklayer or carpenter that was at fault. Few builders seem to have made fortunes, and the incidence of bankruptcy was high. The fundamental problem was the shortage of houses. Those who blame the jerry-builder remind one of the parson, referred to by Edwin Cannan, who used to upbraid the assembled worshipers for the poor attendance at church.

Stress has rightly been laid by many writers on the inadequacy of the provisions for safeguarding the public against overcrowding of houses on limited sites. But London, Manchester, and other large towns had had their Building Acts for generations, and no one who has looked at the *Builders' Price Books* can possibly believe that Londoners suffered from a deficiency of regulations. Mr. John Summerson, indeed, has suggested that the depressing monotony of the newer streets of the capital were the direct result, not, as is often assumed, of free enterprise, but of the provisions of what the builders called the Black Act of 1774—a measure that runs to about thirty-five thousand words. It is true that what was uppermost in the minds of those who framed this act was the avoidance of fire. But some writers like the Webbs (as Redford has shown) have done less than justice to the work of the early organs of local government in such matters as the paving, lighting, and cleaning of streets. If more was not done, the fault did not rest on the builders. Thomas Cubitt told the House of Commons that he would not allow a house to be built any-where unless it could be shown that there was a good drainage and a good way to get rid of water. "I think there should be a public officer paid at the public expense, who should be responsible for that." If the towns were ridden with disease, some at least of the responsibility lay with legislators who, by taxing windows, put a price on light and air and, by taxing bricks and tiles, discouraged the construction of drains and sewers. Those who dwell on the horrors that arose from the fact that the products of the sewers often got mixed up with the drinking water, and attribute this, as all other horrors, to the Industrial Revolution, should be reminded of the obvious fact that with-out the iron pipe, which was one of the products of that revolution, the prob-lem of enabling people to live a healthy life together in towns could never have been solved.

If my first complaint against commonly accepted views of the economic developments of the nineteenth century is concerned with their pessimism, my second is that they are not informed by any glimmering of economic sense. In the generation of Adam Smith and his immediate successors many treatises appeared dealing with the history of commerce, industry, coinage, public revenue, population, and pauperism. Those who wrote them—men like Anderson, Macpherson, Chalmers, Colquhoun, Lord Liverpool, Sinclair, Eden, Malthus, and Tooke—were either themselves economists or at least were interested in the things that were the concern of Adam Smith, Ricardo, and Mill. There were, it is true, many rebels, on both the right and the left, against the doctrines propounded by the economists; but few of these, it so happened, were historically minded. There was, therefore, no sharply defined cleavage between history and theory. In the second half of the nineteenth century, however, a wide breach appeared. How far it was due to the direct influence of the writings of Marx and Engels, how far to the rise of the Historical School of economists in Germany, and how far to the fact that the English economic historians, following Toynbee, were primarily social re-formers, I must not stay to discuss. There can be no doubt, however, that the tendency was to write the story in other than economic terms. A whole series of labels were introduced to indicate what were believed to be the dominant characteristics of successive periods of time, and most of these were political rather than economic in connotation. The arresting phrase, the "Industrial Revolution," was coined (as Miss Bezanson has shown) not by English industrialists or economists but by French writers of the late eighteenth century, under the spell of their own great political ferment. It was seized upon by Engels and Marx and was used by Arnold Toynbee as the title of his pioneer work. It may be questioned whether it has not now outlived its usefulness, for it has tended to support the view that the introduction of large-scale production was catastrophic, rather than beneficial, in its effects. Even more unfortunate, I would urge, has been the intrusion into economic history of another phrase of political intent, struck at the same mint but at an even earlier period. Professor Macgregor has traced back the term "laissez faire" to 1755, when it was first used by the Marquis d'Argenson as both a political and an economic principle. He has charted its curious evolution from the time when it meant noninterference with industry to its use, in 1907, by Alfred Marshall to mean "let the State be up and doing." In view of the dubiety of its intention, it is perhaps not to be wondered at that it should have been fastened by some onto a period of English history that is known to others as the Age of Reform—again a phrase drawn from the vocabulary of politics and not of economics. One could not feel too harshly, therefore, about the candidate who declared that "about the year 1900 men turned their backs on laissez-faire and began to do things for themselves." The title of a work written by Mr. Fisher Unwin in 1904 has fastened on the decade that saw the railway boom and the repeal of the Corn Laws the stigma of "the hungry forties," and only the other day a magazine called *Womanfare* referred to the decade before the recent war as "the hungry thirties." A legend is growing up that the years 1930–39 were marked throughout by misery. In the next generation "the hungry thirties" may be common form.

For two generations economic historians have shirked economic questions or have dealt with them superficially. They have never made up their minds on such elementary matters as to whether it is abundance or scarcity that is to be sought, but generally it is restrictionism they favor. The efforts of Lancashire to provide cheap cottons for people who had previously gone seminaked is acknowledged only in a sentence to the effect that "the bones of the cotton weavers whitened the plains of India." In the same elementary textbook I am told that the tax on imports of wheat led to poverty and distress in the first half of the nineteenth century and that the absence of such a tax to act as a dam against the flood of cheap wheat that poured across the Atlantic was the prime cause of the poverty and distress of the later decades of the century—the period so unhappily known as the Great Depression. Some economic historians have written chapters designed to answer such questions as to whether trade arises from industry or industry from trade, whether transport develops markets or markets give occasion for transport. They have concerned themselves with inquiries as to where the demand comes from that makes production possible. Whenever a real problem is encountered, it is passed over with some such comment as that "a crisis arose" or that "speculation became rife," though why or what nature is rarely disclosed. And, when details are given, logic is often thrown to the winds. In explaining the French depression of 1846, Professor Clough declares that "reduced agricultural production lowered the purchasing power of the farmers, and the high cost of living prevented the industrial population from buying much else than food." This surely is a case of making the worst of both worlds. It has often been said that, at least before Keynes, the economic theorist moved in a world of abstractions and had nothing worth while to offer the historian. But, if only historians had pondered a little on marginal analysis, they would have been saved from such foolish assertions as that trade can arise only when there is a surplus or that investment abroad takes place only when the capital market at home is sated. Ignorance of the elements of economic theory led historians to give political interpretations to every favorable trend. In scores of books the improvement in conditions of labor in the nineteenth century has been attributed to factory legislation; in hardly any is it pointed out that rising productivity of male labor had something to do with the decline of the number of children exploited in the factories or the number of women degraded in the mines. Until Professor Rostow wrote his work on the *British Economy of the Nineteenth Century* in 1948, there had been scarcely any discussion by historians of the relation between investment and earnings.

No one has laid more stress on the need for theory in the writing of history than Sombart. "Facts are like beads," he declares; "they require a string to hold them together. . . . No theory—no history." It is to be deplored that he found his own theory, not in the writings of the economists of his day, but in those of Karl Marx; for, although later he reacted strongly against the interpretations of Marx, his writings have led large numbers of historians in Germany, Britain, and the United States to thread their facts on a Marxist string. In particular, everything that has happened, since the early Middle Ages, is explained in terms of capitalism—a term if not coined at least given wide currency by Marx. Marx, of course, associated it with exploitation. Sombart used it to mean a system of production differing from the handicraft system by reason of the fact that the means of production are owned by a class distinct from the workers—a class whose motive is profit and whose methods are rational, as opposed to the traditional methods, of the handicraftsmen. Above all, he stressed the capitalist spirit. Other elements, such as that innovations in the system are carried out by borrowed money, or credit, have been added by later writers like Schumpeter. But nearly all agree that capitalism implies the existence of a rational technique, a proletariat that sells its labor (and not the product of its labor), and a class of capitalists whose aim is unlimited profit. The assumption is that at some stage of human history— perhaps in the eleventh century A.D.—men became, for the first time, rational and acquisitive. The main business of the economic historians who followed Sombart was to trace the origins of rationality and acquisitiveness. It was what they called the "genetic approach" to the problem of capitalism.

A thousand years is an unmanageably long period, and so capitalism had to be presented as a series of stages—the epochs, respectively, of early, full, and late capitalism, or of mercantile capitalism, industrial capitalism, finance capitalism, and state capitalism. It is admitted, of course, by those who make use of these categories that there is overlapping: that the late stage of one epoch is the early (or, as they say, the emergent) stage of the next. But to teach economic history in this way—to suggest that commerce, industry, finance, and state control are *successive* dominant forces—is to hide from the student, I suggest, the interaction and interdependence of all these at every period of time. It is bad economics.

Those who write so tend to torture the facts. It is part of the legend that the dominant form of organization under industrial capitalism, the factory, arose out of the demands, not of ordinary people, but of the rich and the rulers. Let me quote Professor Nussbaum here. "In personal terms," he says, "it was the interests of the princes [the state] and of the industrialists; in impersonal terms, war and luxury favoured—one might almost say, caused—the development of the factory system." To support this monstrous thesis, he gives a list of the capitalized industries about the year 1800. It includes "sugar, chocolate, lace, embroidery, novelties, tapestries, mirrors, porcelains, jewellery, watches and book printing." All I can say is that, apart from that of sugar, I cannot find a single instance of the production of any one of these things in a factory in England at this time. Nussbaum admits that cotton clothes "offered a field for almost exclusively capitalistic organisation" but says that this was because they were "at first and for a long time luxury goods." Apparently he thinks Arkwright and his fellows were making fine muslins and cambrics for royal courts and not calicoes for English workers and the peasants of India. But this legend about war and luxury is too absurd to need refutation by anyone who has taken the trouble to glance at the records of the first generation of factory masters in England.

FROM The Industrial Revolution BY T. S. ASHTON

Much has been written about the effects of the industrial revolution on the workers. Some, impressed by the lot of those who went down in the struggle against the machine, have declared that technological change brought little but misery and poverty, and a statistician of repute has set on record his opinion that by the early years of the nineteenth century the standard of life

T. S. Ashton, *The Industrial Revolution 1760–1830* (1948), pp. 157–161. Reprinted by permission of Oxford University Press, London.

of the British worker had been forced down to Asiatic levels. Mr. Colin Clark can hardly have looked at the statistics which more than a generation of research has produced. The careful studies of Mrs. Gilboy indicate that, over the eighteenth century, the material well-being of the labourer in the woollen area of the South-West had, indeed, fallen, but that the lot of his fellow in the textile region of the North had steadily improved, and that the labourer of London more than held his own. It is true that the rise of prices after 1793 made many humble people poorer. But before the end of the war (as Professor Silberling has shown) industrial wages in England caught up with retail prices, and in the 'twenties the gain was pronounced. In 1831 the cost of living was 11 per cent higher than in 1790, but over this span of time urban wages had increased, it appears, by no less than 43 per cent.

It would have been strange, indeed, if the industrial revolution had simply made the rich richer and the poor poorer. For the commodities to which it gave rise were not, in general, luxuries, but necessaries and capital goods. The tardiness with which the last of these yielded their fruit to the consumer has already been explained. But by the 'twenties the effects of the war were passing away and the cottons and woollens, and food and drink, which now became available, were consumed not by the few, but by the masses. Some of the products of the factories and ironworks were sent abroad, but the return cargoes did not consist, in the main, of wines and silks, but of sugar, grain, coffee, and tea for the people at large. Much has been made of the suggestion that the prices of the things Britain exported fell more rapidly than those of the things she brought back: there was no revolution to reduce costs in overseas agriculture; and British lending abroad may also have helped to give the terms of trade an unfavourable turn. But, though such influences may explain why, in the 'thirties and 'forties, real wages were lower than might have been expected, they had little effect, it would seem, between 1815 and 1830. The diet of the worker almost certainly improved: there was a substitution of "flower of wheat" for rye and oatmeal; and meat, which had been a rarity, became, with potatoes, the staple dish on the artisan's table. Not all the coal raised from the pits went to feed the furnaces and steam-engines: a warm hearth and a hot meal were of no small consequence to the man who came home wet from the fields.

In 1802 George Chalmers remarked that the laborious classes were "too wealthy to covet the pittance of the soldier, or too independent to court the dangers of the sailor." There were, true enough, many vagrants and paupers, but, even before the new Poor Law came in, the hordes of the "indigent and distressed" had probably shrunk. Hours of labour were long, and holidays few; there is a mass of evidence that employment in factories was harmful to the health and morals of the young. A leading politician has recently spoken of the "mechanized horrors of the industrial revolution," and there can be little doubt that the deeper mines and more complicated machines brought new risks of mutilation and death. But against all this must be set the lessening of strain on those who worked in the heavy trades, and the decline in the number of crippled and deformed people that followed the introduction of power in places like Sheffield. There must be set, also, the reduction of sweating of women and young children, the rise in family earnings, the greater regularity of pay, and the gain in welfare that came as industrial work was taken out of the home.

Whether the houses themselves were becoming better or worse is difficult to determine: much depends on the periods compared. Many of the dwellings provided for the workers by the country factory masters have survived—at Cromford, Mellor, and Styal. They have design and proportion, and, even by modern standards, are not wanting in amenity and comfort. But these were put up when building materials were plentiful, wages relatively low, and money relatively cheap. After 1793 the import of timber from the Baltic was restricted, and the price of labour of bricklayers and carpenters went up. At least two-thirds of the rent of a dwelling consists of interest charges: rates of interest were rising, and for more than a generation they remained high. This meant that if dwellings were to be let at rents which the workers could afford to pay they had to be smaller and less durable than those of the 'eighties. The rows of ill-built, back-to-back houses, into which the rapidly growing population of the towns was pressed, were largely the product of wartime conditions.

After 1815 matters were made worse by the influx of Irish, who, gregarious by instinct, crowded into the seaports and the towns of the North. Careful estimates made by members of the Manchester Statistical Society in the middle 'thirties led to the conclusion that about one-sixth of the families in Manchester were Irish, and that the percentage of the people living in cellars was 11.75. In Liverpool, where again there were many Irish, no less than 15 per cent of the inhabitants were in cellars. But in the newer towns, which were the special creation of the industrial revolution, conditions were far less grim. In Bury, where there were few Irish (and few hand-loom weavers), only 3.75 per cent, and in Ashton-under-Lyne only 1.25 per cent, of the people were housed in this way. In these places, the investigators reported, the houses of the workers were not only less crowded, but also better furnished and cleaner than those of the cities.

An historian has written of "the disasters of the industrial revolution." If by this he means that the years 1760–1830 were darkened by wars and made cheerless by dearth, no objection can be made to the phrase. But if he means that the technical and economic changes were themselves the source of calamity the opinion is surely perverse. The central problem of the age was how to feed and clothe and employ generations of children outnumbering by far those of any earlier time. Ireland was faced by the same problem. Failing to solve it, she lost in the 'forties about a fifth of her people by emigration or starvation and disease. If England had remained a nation of cultivators and craftsmen, she could hardly have escaped the same fate, and, at best, the weight of a growing population must have pressed down the spring of her spirit. She was delivered, not by her rulers, but by those who, seeking no doubt their own narrow ends, had the wit and resource to devise new instruments of production and new methods of administering industry. There are to-day on the plains of India and China men and women, plague-ridden and hungry, living lives little better, to outward appearance, than those of the cattle that toil with them by day and share their places of sleep by night. Such Asiatic standards, and such unmechanized horrors, are the lot of those who increase their numbers without passing through an industrial revolution.

THE MARXISTS
REVOLUTIONARIES OR REFORMERS?

CONTENTS

QUESTIONS FOR STUDY

1. *How do Marx and Engels define social classes in the* Communist Manifesto? *Why does this definition make class conflict inevitable?*

2. *What is the goal of revolution in the* Communist Manifesto?

3. *How has Engels' position changed from the time of the* Communist Manifesto *to that of the letter to Van Patten?*

4. *Why did Engels feel, in 1894, that revolution could be avoided?*

5. *What is the basis for the disagreement between Carr and Ulam?*

6. *What function does revolution play in Lenin's system?*

The Industrial Revolution caused an upheaval in England of almost the same scale as that created in Europe by the French Revolution. Its effects could not be ignored, especially as they appeared to be almost entirely evil as far as the common man was concerned. Not all those who raised their voices against industrialization were wild-eyed radicals. The leader of the reform movement in England was the Earl of Shaftesbury, who simply felt it was un-Christian to force women and children to work fourteen hours a day in mines and factories. Among the other reformers were men like Robert Owen, who argued that exploitation was simply bad for production and went on to prove his point by paying his workers unheard-of wages, providing them with clean, neat housing, and still making a profit.

In the nineteenth century the air was filled with similar partial "solutions" to the problems created by the Industrial Revolution. It was Karl Marx and Friedrich Engels who saw furthest into the total situation created by industrialization. To them, the Industrial Revolution was no mere accident but a necessary step in the economic development of Great Britain and, ultimately, of the world. It was the culmination of the rise of the bourgeoisie, which had begun in the waning years of the Middle Ages. Its evils were clear, but only Marx and Engels (they maintained) knew how to interpret them properly. Exploitation caused pain and misery, but in the long run this pain and misery were both necessary and good. It was pain and misery that would force self-consciousness upon the working class. As industrialization spread over the world, it would create an ever-larger proletariat whose increasing self-consciousness would provide the bonds necessary to unite it against capitalism. The bourgeoisie, far from triumphing over the working class through the imposition of the factory system, was really digging its own grave. When the proletariat became large enough and conscious of its unity, it would rise up and overthrow the bourgeois state, use the instruments of capitalism for its own liberation, and finally usher in a new era of human history in which, for the first time, no man would be exploited by another.

All this was spelled out in masterful prose in the *Manifesto of the Communist Party*, which burst upon the world in the revolutionary year of 1848. The coincidence of the publication of the *Communist Manifesto* and the outbreak of revolutions in France, Germany, Austria, Poland, and Italy was enough to put fear of Marx into the heart of the most confident capitalist. Even some "Socialists" found Marx's gleeful prediction of world cataclysm rather hard to take and sought somehow to soften the Marxist message. Almost immediately, therefore, the politically aware in the industrialized nations divided into two opposing camps vis-à-vis Marxism. On the one side were those who took Marx seriously when he insisted upon the necessity of revolution; on the other were those who argued that the goal of Marxism was control of the state and that revolution was merely one means, perhaps not the best, for attaining this end. This split created odd bedfellows. Both the robber baron and Lenin, for example, could agree that Marxism necessarily meant violent revolution, and both acted accordingly. The robber baron insisted upon repressive legislation to nip Marxist socialism in the bud; Lenin insisted upon creating a small, elite cadre of revolutionary leaders who would know what to do when the opportunity presented itself.

The opponents of violent revolution included those who deplored violence in any form as well as those who felt that revolution from below was doomed in an age of increasing military sophistication. Marx himself was equivocal, and Engels appears to have abandoned his early revolutionary position late in life. So the revisionists could and did cite Marx and Engels as support for their view.

As the arguments that follow illustrate, the purpose of revolution is not an academic quibble. The whole Socialist strategy will ultimately be determined by one's answer to the question: Is violent revolution necessary for the triumph of socialism? During the course of the debate, which involved both competing theories of history and competing evaluations of contemporary political situations, the meanings of key words appeared to change. Did violent revolution really mean open warfare, or could seizure of power by means of the vote also qualify as a revolution? And what, precisely, was revolution necessary for—merely the attainment of power? Or was the revolution itself the crucible in which the unity of the proletariat was to be achieved? And if this were the case, would not periodic "revolutions" be necessary even after power was seized by the people in order to preserve the unity without which the Socialist ideal could never be achieved? This last question brings us beyond Marx and even Lenin to Mao Tse-tung.

1
THE ROAD TO
REVOLUTION

In 1848 Karl Marx (1818-1883) and Friedrich Engels (1820–1895) brought out the *Manifesto of the Communist Party*. It could not have appeared at a more opportune time; the manuscript was delivered to the printer in London a few weeks before the revolution of February 1848 in France. A French translation was published shortly before the insurrection of the workers in Paris in June 1848. Thought and deed thus seemed to go together, and the *Communist Manifesto* became the rallying point for those who saw in revolution the only course for the oppressed workers of the world.

FROM Manifesto of the Communist Party
BY KARL MARX AND FRIEDRICH ENGELS

A spectre is haunting Europe—the spectre of Communism. All the Powers of old Europe have entered into a holy alliance to exorcise this spectre; Pope and Czar, Metternich and Guizot, French Radicals and German police-spies.

Where is the party in opposition that has not been decried as communistic by its opponents in power? Where the Opposition that has not hurled back the branding reproach of Communism, against the more advanced opposition parties, as well as against its re-actionary adversaries?

Two things result from this fact.

1. Communism is already acknowledged by all European Powers to be itself a Power.

2. It is high time that Communists should openly, in the face of the whole

Karl Marx and Friedrich Engels, *Manifesto of the Communist Party* (1911), pp. 11–30, 32–36, 42–47.

world, publish their views, their aims, their tendencies, and meet this nursery tale of the Spectre of Communism with a Manifesto of the party itself.

To this end, Communists of various nationalities have assembled in London, and sketched the following manifesto, to be published in the English, French, German, Italian, Flemish and Danish languages.

I. BOURGEOIS AND PROLETARIANS

The history of all hitherto existing society is the history of class struggles.

Freeman and slave, patrician and plebeian, lord and serf, guild-master and journeyman, in a word, oppressor and oppressed, stood in constant opposition to one another, carried on an uninterrupted, now hidden, now open fight, a fight that each time ended either in a revolutionary re-constitution of society at large, or in the common ruin of the contending classes.

In the earlier epochs of history, we find almost everywhere a complicated arrangement of society into various orders, a manifold gradation of social rank. In ancient Rome we have patricians, knights, plebeians, slaves; in the middle ages, feudal lords, vassals, guild-masters, journeymen, apprentices, serfs; in almost all of these classes, again, subordinate gradations.

The modern bourgeois society that has sprouted from the ruins of feudal society, has not done away with class antagonisms. It has but established new classes, new conditions of oppression, new forms of struggle in place of the old ones.

Our epoch, the epoch of the bourgeoisie, possesses, however, this distinctive feature: it has simplified the class antagonisms. Society as a whole is more and more splitting up into two great hostile camps, into two great classes directly facing each other: Bourgeoisie and Proletariat.

From the serfs of the Middle Ages sprang the chartered burghers of the earliest towns. From these burgesses the first elements of the bourgeoisie were developed.

The discovery of America, the rounding of the Cape, opened up fresh ground for the rising bourgeoisie. The East-Indian and Chinese markets, the colonisation of America, trade with the colonies, the increase in the means of exchange and in commodities generally, gave to commerce, to navigation, to industry, an impulse never before known, and thereby, to the revolutionary element in the tottering feudal society, a rapid development.

The feudal system of industry, under which industrial production was monopolised by close guilds, now no longer sufficed for the growing wants of the new markets. The manufacturing system took its place. The guild-masters were pushed on one side by the manufacturing middle-class; division of labour between the different corporate guilds vanished in the face of division of labour in each single workshop.

Meantime the markets kept ever growing, the demand, ever rising. Even

manufacture no longer sufficed. Thereupon, steam and machinery revolutionised industrial production. The place of manufacture was taken by the giant,
Modern Industry, the place of the industrial middle-class, by industrial millionaires, the leaders of whole industrial armies, the modern bourgeois.

Modern industry has established the world-market, for which the discovery
of America paved the way. This market has given an immense development
to commerce, to navigation, to communication by land. This development
has, in its turn, reacted on the extension of industry; and in proportion as
industry, commerce, navigation, railways extended, in the same proportion
the bourgeoisie developed, increased its capital, and pushed into the background every class handed down from the Middle Ages.

We see, therefore, how the modern bourgeoisie is itself the product of a
long course of development, of a series of revolutions in the modes of production and of exchange.

Each step in the development of the bourgeoisie was accompanied by a
corresponding political advance of that class. An oppressed class under the
sway of the feudal nobility, an armed and self-governing association in the
medieval commune, here independent urban republic (as in Italy and Germany), there taxable "third estate" of the monarchy (as in France), afterwards, in the period of manufacture proper, serving either the semi-feudal or
the absolute monarchy as a counterpoise against the nobility, and, in fact,
corner stone of the great monarchies in general, the bourgeoisie has at last,
since the establishment of Modern Industry and of the world-market, conquered for itself, in the modern representative State, exclusive political sway.
The executive of the modern State is but a committee for managing the
common affairs of the whole bourgeoisie.

The bourgeoisie, historically, has played a most revolutionary part.

The bourgeoisie, wherever it has got the upper hand, has put an end to all
feudal, patriarchal, idyllic relations. It has pitilessly torn asunder the motley
feudal ties that bound man to his "natural superiors," and has left remaining
no other nexus between man and man than naked self-interest, than callous
"cash payment." It has drowned the most heavenly ecstasies of religious fer-
vour, of chivalrous enthusiasm, of philistine sentimentalism, in the icy water
of egotistical calculation. It has resolved personal worth into exchange value,
and in place of the numberless indefeasible chartered freedoms, has set up
that single, unconscionable freedom—Free Trade. In one word, for exploitation, veiled by religious and political illusions, it has substituted naked,
shameless, direct, brutal exploitation.

The bourgeoisie has stripped of its halo every occupation hitherto honoured and looked up to with reverent awe. It has converted the physician, the
lawyer, the priest, the poet, the man of science, into its paid wage-labourers.

The bourgeoisie has torn away from the family its sentimental veil, and has
reduced the family relation to a mere money relation.

The bourgeoisie has disclosed how it came to pass that the brutal display of
vigour in the Middle Ages, which Re-actionists so much admire, found its

fitting complement in the most slothful indolence. It has been the first to shew what man's activity can bring about. It has accomplished wonders far surpassing Egyptian pyramids, Roman aqueducts, and Gothic cathedrals; it has conducted expeditions that put in the shade all former Exoduses of nations and crusades.

The bourgeoisie cannot exist without constantly revolutionising the instruments of production, and thereby the relations of production, and with them the whole relations of society. Conservation of the old modes of production in unaltered form, was, on the contrary, the first condition of existence for all earlier industrial classes. Constant revolutionising of production, uninterrupted disturbance of all social conditions, everlasting uncertainty and agitation distinguish the bourgeois epoch from all earlier ones. All fixed, fast-frozen relations, with their train of ancient and venerable prejudices and opinions, are swept away, all new-formed ones become antiquated before they can ossify. All that is solid melts into air, all that is holy is profaned, and man is at last compelled to face with sober senses, his real conditions of life, and his relations with his kind.

The need of a constantly expanding market for its products chases the bourgeoisie over the whole surface of the globe. It must nestle everywhere, settle everywhere, establish connexions everywhere.

The bourgeoisie has through its exploitation of the world-market given a cosmopolitan character to production and consumption in every country. To the great chagrin of Re-actionists, it has drawn from under the feet of industry the national ground on which it stood. All old-established national industries have been destroyed or are daily being destroyed. They are dislodged by new industries, whose introduction becomes a life and death question for all civilised nations, by industries that no longer work up indigenous raw material, but raw material drawn from the remotest zones; industries whose products are consumed, not only at home, but in every quarter of the globe. In place of the old wants, satisfied by the productions of the country, we find new wants, requiring for their satisfaction the products of distant lands and climes. In place of the old local and national seclusion and self-sufficiency, we have intercourse in every direction, universal interdependence of nations. And as in material, so also in intellectual production. The intellectual creations of individual nations become common property. National one-sidedness and narrow-mindedness become more and more impossible, and from the numerous national and local literatures there arises a world-literature.

The bourgeoisie, by the rapid improvement of all instruments of production, by the immensely facilitated means of communication, draws all, even the most barbarian, nations into civilisation. The cheap prices of its commodities are the heavy artillery with which it batters down all Chinese walls, with which it forces the barbarian's intensely obstinate hatred of foreigners to capitulate. It compels all nations, on pain of extinction, to adopt the bourgeois mode of production; it compels them to introduce what it calls civilisation into their midst, i.e., to become bourgeois themselves. In a word, it creates a world after its own image.

The bourgeoisie has subjected the country to the rule of the towns. It has created enormous cities, has greatly increased the urban population as compared with the rural, and has thus rescued a considerable part of the population from the idiocy of rural life. Just as it has made the country dependent on the towns, so it has made barbarian and semi-barbarian countries dependent on the civilised ones, nations of peasants on nations of bourgeois, the East on the West.

The bourgeoisie keeps more and more doing away with the scattered state of the population, of the means of production, and of property. It has agglomerated population, centralised means of production, and has concentrated property in a few hands. The necessary consequence of this was political centralisation. Independent, or but loosely connected provinces, with separate interests, laws, governments and systems of taxation, became lumped together in one nation, with one government, one code of laws, one national class-interest, one frontier and one customs-tariff.

The bourgeoisie, during its rule of scarce one hundred years, has created more massive and more colossal productive forces than have all preceding generations together. Subjection of Nature's forces to man, machinery, application of chemistry to industry and agriculture, steam-navigation, railways, electric telegraphs, clearing of whole continents for cultivation, canalization of rivers, whole populations conjured out of the ground—what earlier century had even a presentiment that such productive forces slumbered in the lap of social labour?

We see then: the means of production and of exchange on whose foundation the bourgeoisie built itself up, were generated in feudal society. At a certain stage in the development of these means of production and of exchange, the conditions under which feudal society produced and exchanged, the feudal organisation of agriculture and manufacturing industry, in one word, the feudal relations of property became no longer compatible with the already developed productive forces; they became so many fetters. They had to burst asunder; they were burst asunder.

Into their places stepped free competition, accompanied by a social and political constitution adapted to it, and by the economical and political sway of the bourgeois class.

A similar movement is going on before our own eyes. Modern bourgeois society with its relations of production, of exchange and of property, a society that has conjured up such gigantic means of production and of exchange, is like the sorcerer, who is no longer able to control the powers of the nether world whom he has called up by his spells. For many a decade past the history of industry and commerce is but the history of the revolt of modern productive forces against modern conditions of production, against the property relations that are the conditions for the existence of the bourgeoisie and

of its rule. It is enough to mention the commercial crises that by their periodical return put on its trial, each time more threateningly, the existence of the
entire bourgeois society. In these crises a great part not only of the existing
products, but also of the previously created productive forces, are periodically
destroyed. In these crises there breaks out an epidemic that, in all earlier
epochs, would have seemed an absurdity—the epidemic of over-production.
Society suddenly finds itself put back into a state of momentary barbarism; it
appears as if a famine, a universal war of devastation had cut off the supply
of every means of subsistence; industry and commerce seem to be destroyed;
and why? Because there is too much civilisation, too much means of subsistence, too much industry, too much commerce. The productive forces at the
disposal of society no longer tend to further the development of the conditions of bourgeois property; on the contrary, they have become too powerful
for these conditions, by which they are fettered, and so soon as they overcome
these fetters, they bring disorder into the whole of bourgeois society, endanger
the existence of bourgeois property. The conditions of bourgeois society are
too narrow to comprise the wealth created by them. And how does the bourgeoisie get over these crises? On the one hand by enforced destruction of a
mass of productive forces; on the other, by the conquest of new markets, and
by the more thorough exploitation of the old ones. That is to say, by paving
the way for more extensive and more destructive crises, and by diminishing
the means whereby crises are prevented.

The weapons with which the bourgeoisie felled feudalism to the ground
are now turned against the bourgeoisie itself.

But not only has the bourgeoisie forged the weapons that bring death to
itself; it has also called into existence the men who are to wield those weapons—the modern working class—the proletarians.

In proportion as the bourgeoisie, i.e., capital, is developed, in the same proportion is the proletariat, the modern working class, developed, a class of
labourers, who live only so long as they find work, and who find work only
so long as their labour increases capital. These labourers, who must sell themselves piecemeal, are a commodity, like every other article of commerce, and
are consequently exposed to all the vicissitudes of competition, to all the fluctuations of the market.

Owing to the extensive use of machinery and to division of labour, the
work of the proletarians has lost all individual character, and, consequently,
all charm for the workman. He becomes an appendage of the machine, and it
is only the most simple, most monotonous, and most easily acquired knack
that is required of him. Hence, the cost of production of a workman is restricted, almost entirely, to the means of subsistence that he requires for his
maintenance, and for the propagation of his race. But the price of a commodity, and also of labour, is equal to its cost of production. In proportion, therefore, as the repulsiveness of the work increases, the wage decreases. Nay
more, in proportion as the use of machinery and division of labour increases,
in the same proportion the burden of toil also increases, whether by prolonga-

tion of the working hours, by increase of the work enacted in a given time, or by increased speed of the machinery, etc.

Modern industry has converted the little workshop of the patriarchal master into the great factory of the industrial capitalist. Masses of labourers, crowded into the factory, are organised like soldiers. As privates of the industrial army they are placed under the command of a perfect hierarchy of officers and sergeants. Not only are they the slaves of the bourgeois class, and of the bourgeois State, they are daily and hourly enslaved by the machine, by the over-looker, and, above all, by the individual bourgeois manufacturer himself. The more openly this despotism proclaims gain to be its end and aim, the more petty, the more hateful and the more embittering it is.

The less the skill and exertion or strength implied in manual labour, in other words, the more modern industry becomes developed, the more is the labour of men superseded by that of women. Differences of age and sex have no longer any distinctive social validity for the working class. All are instruments of labour, more or less expensive to use, according to their age and sex.

No sooner is the exploitation of the labourer by the manufacturer, so far, at an end, that he receives his wages in cash, than he is set upon by the other portions of the bourgeoisie, the landlord, the shopkeeper, the pawnbroker, etc.

The lower strata of the middle class—the small tradespeople, shopkeepers, and retired tradesmen generally, the handicraftsmen and peasants—all these sink gradually into the proletariat, partly because their diminutive capital does not suffice for the scale on which Modern Industry is carried on, and is swamped in the competition with the large capitalists, partly because their specialised skill is rendered worthless by new methods of production. Thus the proletariat is recruited from all classes of the population.

The proletariat goes through various stages of development. With its birth begins its struggle with the bourgeoisie. At first the contest is carried on by individual labourers, then by the workpeople of a factory, then by the operatives of one trade, in one locality, against the individual bourgeois who directly exploits them. They direct their attacks not against the bourgeois conditions of production, but against the instruments of production themselves; they destroy imported wares that compete with their labour, they smash to pieces machinery, they set factories ablaze, they seek to restore by force the vanished status of the workman of the Middle Ages.

At this stage the labourers still form an incoherent mass scattered over the whole country, and broken up by their mutual competition. If anywhere they unite to form more compact bodies, this is not yet the consequence of their own active union, but of the union of the bourgeoisie, which class, in order to attain its own political ends, is compelled to set the whole proletariat in motion, and is moreover yet, for a time, able to do so. At this stage, therefore, the proletarians do not fight their enemies, but the enemies of their enemies, the remnants of absolute monarchy, the landowners, the nonindustrial bourgeois, the petty bourgeoisie. Thus the whole historical movement is concentrated in the hands of the bourgeoisie, every victory so obtained is a victory for the bourgeoisie.

But with the development of industry the proletariat not only increases in number; it becomes concentrated in greater masses, its strength grows, and it feels that strength more. The various interests and conditions of life within the ranks of the proletariat are more and more equalised, in proportion as machinery obliterates all distinctions of labour, and nearly everywhere reduces wages to the same low level. The growing competition among the bourgeois, and the resulting commercial crises, make the wages of the workers ever more fluctuating. The unceasing improvement of machinery, ever more rapidly developing, makes their livelihood more and more precarious; the collisions between individual workmen and individual bourgeois take more and more the character of collisions between two classes. Thereupon the workers begin to form combinations (Trades' Unions) against the bourgeois; they club together in order to keep up the rate of wages; they found permanent associations in order to make provision beforehand for these occasional revolts. Here and there the contest breaks out into riots.

Now and then the workers are victorious, but only for a time. The real fruit of their battles lies, not in the immediate result, but in the ever expanding union of the workers. This union is helped on by the improved means of communication that are created by modern industry, and that place the workers of different localities in contact with one another. It was just this contact that was needed to centralise the numerous local struggles, all of the same character, into one national struggle between classes. But every class struggle is a political struggle. And that union, to attain which the burghers of the Middle Ages, with their miserable highways, required centuries, the modern proletarians, thanks to railways, achieve in a few years.

This organisation of the proletarians into a class, and consequently into a political party, is continually being upset again by the competition between the workers themselves. But it ever rises up again, stronger, firmer, mightier. It compels legislative recognition of particular interests of the workers, by taking advantage of the divisions among the bourgeoisie itself. Thus the ten-hours'-bill in England was carried.

Altogether collisions between the classes of the old society further, in many ways, the course of development of the proletariat. The bourgeoisie finds itself involved in a constant battle. At first with the aristocracy; later on, with those portions of the bourgeoisie itself, whose interests have become antagonistic to the progress of industry; at all times, with the bourgeoisie of foreign countries. In all these battles it sees itself compelled to appeal to the proletariat, to ask for its help, and thus, to drag it into the political arena. The bourgeoisie itself, therefore, supplies the proletariat with its own elements of political and general education, in other words, it furnishes the proletariat with weapons for fighting the bourgeoisie.

Further, as we have already seen, entire sections of the ruling classes are, by the advance of industry, precipitated into the proletariat, or are at least threatened in their conditions of existence. These also supply the proletariat with fresh elements of enlightenment and progress.

Finally, in times when the class struggle nears the decisive hour, the process of dissolution going on within the ruling class, in fact within the whole range of old society, assumes such a violent, glaring character, that a small section of the ruling class cuts itself adrift, and joins the revolutionary class, the class that holds the future in its hands. Just as, therefore, at an earlier period, a section of the nobility went over to the bourgeoisie, so now a portion of the bourgeoisie goes over to the proletariat, and in particular, a portion of the bourgeois ideologists, who have raised themselves to the level of comprehending theoretically the historical movements as a whole.

Of all the classes that stand face to face with the bourgeoisie to-day, the proletariat alone is a really revolutionary class. The other classes decay and finally disappear in the face of modern industry; the proletariat is its special and essential product.

* * *

Though not in substance, yet in form, the struggle of the proletariat with the bourgeoisie is at first a national struggle. The proletariat of each country must, of course, first of all settle matters with its own bourgeoisie.

In depicting the most general phases of the development of the proletariat, we traced the more or less veiled civil war, raging within existing society, up to the point where that war breaks out into open revolution, and where the violent overthrow of the bourgeoisie lays the foundation for the sway of the proletariat.

Hitherto, every form of society has been based, as we have already seen, on the antagonism of oppressing and oppressed classes. But in order to oppress a class, certain conditions must be assured to it under which it can, at least, continue its slavish existence. The serf, in the period of serfdom, raised himself to membership in the commune, just as the petty bourgeois, under the yoke of feudal absolutism, managed to develop into a bourgeois. The modern labourer, on the contrary, instead of rising with the progress of industry, sinks deeper and deeper below the conditions of existence of his own class. He becomes a pauper, and pauperism develops more rapidly than population and wealth. And here it becomes evident, that the bourgeoisie is unfit any longer to be the ruling class in society, and to impose its conditions of existence upon society as an over-riding law. It is unfit to rule, because it is incompetent to assure an existence to its slave within his slavery, because it cannot help letting him sink into such a state that it has to feed him, instead of being fed by him. Society can no longer live under this bourgeoisie, in other words, its existence is no longer compatible with society.

The essential condition for the existence, and for the sway of the bourgeois class, is the formation and augmentation of capital; the condition for capital is wage-labour. Wage-labour rests exclusively on competition between the labourers. The advance of industry, whose involuntary promoter is the bourgeoisie, replaces the isolation of the labourers, due to competition, by their involuntary combination, due to association. The development of Modern Industry, therefore, cuts from under its feet the very foundation on which the bourgeoisie produces and appropriates products. What the bourgeoisie therefore produces, above all, are its own grave-diggers. Its fall and the victory of the proletariat are equally inevitable.

II. PROLETARIANS AND COMMUNISTS

In what relation do the Communists stand to the proletarians as a whole?

The Communists do not form a separate party opposed to other working-class parties.

They have no interests separate and apart from those of the proletariat as a whole.

They do not set up any sectarian principles of their own, by which to shape and mould the proletarian movement.

The Communists are distinguished from the other working-class parties by this only: 1. In the national struggles of the proletarians of the different countries, they point out and bring to the front the common interests of the entire proletariat, independently of all nationality. 2. In the various stages of development which the struggle of the working class against the bourgeoisie has to pass through, they always and everywhere represent the interests of the movement as a whole.

The Communists, therefore, are on the one hand, practically, the most advanced and resolute section of the working-class parties of every country, that section which pushes forward all others; on the other hand, theoretically, they have over the great mass of the proletariat the advantage of clearly understanding the line of march, the conditions, and the ultimate general results of the proletarian movement.

The immediate aim of the Communists is the same as that of all the other proletarian parties: formation of the proletariat into a class, overthrow of the bourgeois supremacy, conquest of political power by the proletariat.

The theoretical conclusions of the Communists are in no way based on ideas or principles that have been invented, or discovered, by this or that would-be universal reformer.

They merely express, in general terms, actual relations springing from an existing class struggle, from a historical movement going on under our very eyes. The abolition of existing property-relations is not at all a distinctive feature of Communism.

All property relations in the past have continually been subject to historical change consequent upon the change in historical conditions.

The French Revolution, for example, abolished feudal property in favour of bourgeois property.

The distinguishing feature of Communism is not the abolition of property generally, but the abolition of bourgeois property. But modern bourgeois private property is the final and most complete expression of the system of producing and appropriating products, that is based on class antagonism, on the exploitation of the many by the few.

In this sense, the theory of the Communists may be summed up in the single sentence: Abolition of private property.

We Communists have been reproached with the desire of abolishing the right of personally acquiring property as the fruit of a man's own labour, which property is alleged to be the ground work of all personal freedom, activity and independence.

Hard-won, self-acquired, self-earned property! Do you mean the property of the petty artisan and of the small peasant, a form of property that preceded the bourgeois form? There is no need to abolish that; the development of industry has to a great extent already destroyed it, and is still destroying it daily.

Or do you mean modern bourgeois private property?

But does wage-labour create any property for the labourer? Not a bit. It creates capital, i.e., that kind of property which exploits wage-labour, and which cannot increase except upon condition of getting a new supply of wage-labour for fresh exploitation. Property, in its present form, is based on the antagonism of capital and wage-labour. Let us examine both sides of this antagonism.

To be a capitalist, is to have not only a purely personal, but a social status in production. Capital is a collective product, and only by the united action of many members, nay, in the last resort, only by the united action of all members of society, can it be set in motion.

Capital is therefore not a personal, it is a social power.

When, therefore, capital is converted into common property, into the property of all members of society, personal property is not thereby transformed into social property. It is only the social character of the property that is changed. It loses its class-character.

Let us now take wage-labour.

The average price of wage-labour is the minimum wage, i.e., that quantum of the means of subsistence, which is absolutely requisite to keep the labourer in bare existence as a labourer. What, therefore, the wage-labourer appropriates by means of his labour, merely suffices to prolong and reproduce a bare existence. We by no means intend to abolish this personal appropriation of the products of labour, an appropriation that is made for the maintenance and reproduction of human life, and that leaves no surplus wherewith to command the labour of others. All that we want to do away with is the miserable character of this appropriation, under which the labourer lives merely to increase capital, and is allowed to live only in so far as the interest of the ruling class requires it.

In bourgeois society, living labour is but a means to increase accumulated labour. In Communist society, accumulated labour is but a means to widen, to enrich, to promote the existence of the labourer.

In bourgeois society, therefore, the past dominates the present; in Communist society, the present dominates the past. In bourgeois society capital is independent and has individuality, while the living person is dependent and has no individuality.

And the abolition of this state of things is called by the bourgeois, abolition of individuality and freedom! And rightly so. The abolition of bourgeois individuality, bourgeois independence, and bourgeois freedom is undoubtedly aimed at.

By freedom is meant, under the present bourgeois conditions of production, free trade, free selling and buying.

* * *

The charges against Communism made from a religious, a philosophical, and generally, from an ideological standpoint, are not deserving of serious examination.

Does it require deep intuition to comprehend that man's ideas, views, and conceptions, in one word, man's consciousness, changes with every change in the conditions of his material existence, in his social relations and in his social life?

What else does the history of ideas prove, than that intellectual production changes in character in proportion as material production is changed? The ruling ideas of each age have ever been the ideas of its ruling class.

When people speak of ideas that revolutionize society, they do but express the fact, that within the old society, the elements of a new one have been created, and that the dissolution of the old ideas keeps even pace with the dissolution of the old conditions of existence.

When the ancient world was in its last throes, the ancient religions were overcome by Christianity. When Christian ideas succumbed in the 18th century to rationalist ideas, feudal society fought its death-battle with the then revolutionary bourgeoisie. The ideas of religious liberty and freedom of conscience, merely gave expression to the sway of free competition within the domain of knowledge.

"Undoubtedly," it will be said, "religious, moral, philosophical and juridical ideas have been modified in the course of historical development. But religion, morality, philosophy, political science, and law, constantly survived this change.

"There are, besides, eternal truths, such as Freedom, Justice, etc., that are common to all states of society. But Communism abolishes eternal truths, it abolishes all religion, and all morality, instead of constituting them on a new basis; it therefore acts in contradiction to all past historical experience."

What does this accusation reduce itself to? The history of all past society has consisted in the development of class antagonisms, antagonisms that assumed different forms at different epochs.

But whatever form they may have taken, one fact is common to all past ages, viz., the exploitation of one part of society by the other. No wonder, then, that the social consciousness of past ages, despite all the multiplicity and variety it displays, moves within certain common forms, or general ideas, which cannot completely vanish except with the total disappearance of class antagonisms.

The Communist revolution is the most radical rupture with traditional property-relations; no wonder that its development involves the most radical rupture with traditional ideas.

But let us have done with the bourgeois objections to Communism.

We have seen above, that the first step in the revolution by the working class is to raise the proletariat to the position of ruling class, to win the battle of democracy.

The proletariat will use its political supremacy to wrest, by degrees, all capital from the bourgeoisie, to centralise all instruments of production in the hands of the State, i.e., of the proletariat organised by the ruling class; and to increase the total of productive forces as rapidly as possible.

Of course, in the beginning, this cannot be effected except by means of despotic inroads on the rights of property, and on the conditions of bourgeois production; by means of measures, therefore, which appear economically insufficient and untenable, but which, in the course of the movement, outstrip themselves, necessitate further inroads upon the old social order, and are unavoidable as a means of entirely revolutionising the mode of production.

These measures will of course be different in different countries.

Nevertheless in the most advanced countries the following will be pretty generally applicable:

1. Abolition of property in land and application of all rents of land to public purposes.
2. A heavy progressive or graduated income tax.
3. Abolition of all right of inheritance.
4. Confiscation of the property of all emigrants and rebels.
5. Centralisation of credit in the hands of the State, by means of a national bank with State capital and an exclusive monopoly.
6. Centralisation of the means of communication and transport in the hands of the State.
7. Extension of factories and instruments of production owned by the State; the bringing into cultivation of waste lands, and the improvement of the soil generally in accordance with a common plan.
8. Equal liability of all to labour. Establishment of industrial armies, especially for agriculture.
9. Combination of agriculture with manufacturing industries; gradual abolition of the distinction between town and country, by a more equable distribution of the population over the country.
10. Free education for all children in public schools. Abolition of children's

factory labour in its present form. Combination of education with industrial production, etc., etc.

When, in the course of development, class distinctions have disappeared, and all production has been concentrated in the hands of a vast association of the whole nation, the public power will lose its political character. Political power, properly so called, is merely the organised power of one class for oppressing another. If the proletariat during its contest with the bourgeoisie is compelled, by the force of circumstances, to organise itself as a class, if, by means of a revolution, it makes itself the ruling class, and, as such, sweeps away by force the old conditions of production, then it will, along with these conditions, have swept away the conditions for the existence of class antagonisms, and of classes generally, and will thereby have abolished its own supremacy as a class.

In place of the old bourgeois society, with its classes and class antagonisms, we shall have an association in which the free development of each is the condition for the free development of all.

The Marxist condemnation of bourgeois society had unexpected results. Marx and Engels had used all their rhetoric to prove that capitalist society was evil. Moreover, they had proven that the state as such was the instrument of oppression. It should not have surprised them to find that their conclusions were eagerly grasped by a group—the anarchists—who saw the whole purpose of the coming struggle between proletariat and bourgeoisie as the destruction of the state. It was this view that Engels countered in the selection that follows. What must be gained is the control of the state, not its destruction. This principle, in turn, left the door open to those who argued that control could come by means other than revolution.

Friedrich Engels' Letter to Philip van Patten

London, April 18, 1883

Dear Comrade:

My reply to your inquiry of April 2 regarding Karl Marx's attitude toward the anarchists in general and toward Johann Most in particular will be brief and to the point.

Frederick Engels, *Letters to Americans, 1848–1895: A Selection*, pp. 137–138. Reprinted by permission of International Publishers Co., Inc. Copyright 1953 International Publishers Co., Inc.

Since 1845 Marx and I have held the view that one of the ultimate results of the future proletarian revolution will be the gradual dissolution of the political organization known by the name of *state*. The main object of this organization has always been to secure, by armed force, the economic oppression of the laboring majority by the minority which alone possesses wealth. With the disappearance of an exclusive wealth-possessing minority there also disappears the need for an armed force of suppression, or state power. At the same time, however, it was always our opinion that in order to attain this and the other far more important aims of the future social revolution, the working class must first take possession of the organized political power of the state and by its aid crush the resistance of the capitalist class and organize society anew. This is to be found as early as the *Communist Manifesto* of 1847, Chapter II, conclusion.

The anarchists stand the thing on its head. They declare that the proletarian revolution must *begin* by abolishing the political organization of the state. But the only organization that the proletariat finds ready to hand after its victory is precisely the state. This state may require very considerable alterations before it can fulfill its new functions. But to destroy it at such a moment would mean to destroy the only organism by means of which the victorious proletariat can assert its newly conquered power, hold down its capitalist adversaries, and carry out that economic revolution of society without which the whole victory must end in a new defeat and in a mass slaughter of the workers similar to that after the Paris Commune.

Does it require my express assurance that Marx opposed this anarchist nonsense from the first day it was put forward in its present form by Bakunin? The whole internal history of the International Workingmen's Association proves it. Ever since 1867 the anarchists tried, by the most infamous methods, to seize the leadership of the International; the main hindrance in their way was Marx. The five-year struggle ended, at the Hague Congress in September 1872, with the expulsion of the anarchists from the International; and the man who did most to effect this expulsion was Marx. Our old friend, Friedrich Anton Sorge, in Hoboken, who was present as a delegate, can give you further details if you wish.

By 1895, when Engels wrote this introduction, the position of the left had changed considerably. Many of the revolutionary demands of the *Communist Manifesto* had been written into law, as the result not of violent revolution but of peaceful politicking. Was it possible that the "inevitability" of revolution, to which all Marx's and Engels' writings in the 1840s logically led, was a mistake? Engels took a long look at the question in the selection that follows.

FROM Introduction to Marx's The Class Struggles in France BY FRIEDRICH ENGELS

In judging the events and series of events of day-to-day history, it will never be possible for anyone to go right back to the final economic causes. Even today, when the specialised technical press provides such rich materials, in England itself it still remains impossible to follow day by day the movement of industry and trade in the world market and the changes which take place in the methods of production, in such a way as to be able to draw the general conclusion, at any point of time, from these very complicated and ever changing factors: of these factors, the most important, into the bargain, generally operate a long time in secret before they suddenly and violently make themselves felt on the surface. A clear survey of the economic history of a given period is never contemporaneous; it can only be gained subsequently, after collecting and sifting of the material has taken place. Statistics are a necessary help here, and they always lag behind. For this reason, it is only too often necessary, in the current history of the time, to treat the most decisive factor as constant, to treat the economic situation existing at the beginning of the period concerned as given and unalterable for the whole period, or else to take notice only of such changes in this situation as themselves arise out of events clearly before us, and as, therefore, can likewise be clearly seen. Hence, the materialist method has here often to limit itself to tracing political conflicts back to the struggles between the interests of the social classes and fractions of classes encountered as the result of economic development, and to show the particular political parties as the more or less adequate political expression of these same classes and fractions of classes.

It is self-evident that this unavoidable neglect of contemporaneous changes in the economic situation, of the very basis of all the proceedings subject to examination, must be a source of error. But all the conditions of a comprehensive presentation of the history of the day unavoidably imply sources of error—which, however, keeps nobody from writing contemporary history.

When Marx undertook this work, the sources of error mentioned were, to a still greater degree, impossible to avoid. It was quite impossible during the period of the Revolution of 1848–49 to follow the economic transformations which were being consummated at the same time, or even to keep a general view of them. It was just the same during the first months of exile in Lon-

---

Karl Marx, *The Class Struggles in France* (1848–50) (1895), pp. 9–10, 13–14, 15, 19–28.

don, in the autumn and winter of 1849–50. But that was just the time when Marx began this work. And in spite of these unfavourable circumstances, his exact knowledge both of the economic situation in France and of the political history of that country since the February Revolution, made it possible for him to give a picture of events which laid bare their inner connections in a way never attained since, and which later brilliantly withstood the double test instituted by Marx himself.

* * *

When the Paris upheaval found its echo in the victorious insurrections in Vienna, Milan and Berlin; when the whole of Europe right up to the Russian frontier was swept into the movement; when in Paris the first great battle for power between the proletariat and the bourgeoisie was joined; when the very victory of their class so shook the bourgeoisie of all countries that they fled back into the arms of the monarchist-feudal reaction which had just been overthrown—for us under the circumstances of the time, there could be no doubt that the great decisive struggle had broken out, that it would have to be fought out in a single, long and changeful period of revolution, but that it could only end with the final victory of the proletariat.

* * *

But we, too, have been shown to have been wrong by history, which has revealed our point of view of that time to have been an illusion. It has done even more: it has not merely destroyed our error of that time; it has also completely transformed the conditions under which the proletariat has to fight. The mode of struggle of 1848 is today obsolete from every point of view, and this is a point which deserves closer examination on the present occasion.

* * *

History has proved us, and all who thought like us, wrong. It has made it clear that the state of economic development on the Continent at that time was not, by a long way, ripe for the removal of capitalist production; it has proved this by the economic revolution which, since 1848, has seized the whole of the Continent, has really caused big industry for the first time to take root in France, Austria, Hungary, Poland and, recently, in Russia, while it has made Germany positively an industrial country of the first rank—all on a capitalist basis, which in the year 1848, therefore, still had great capacity for expansion. But it is just this industrial revolution which has everywhere for the first time produced clarity in the class relationships, which has removed a number of transition forms handed down from the manufacturing period and in Eastern Europe even from guild handicraft, and has created a genuine bourgeoisie and a genuine large-scale industrial proletariat and pushed them into the foreground of social development. But owing to this, the struggle of these two great classes, which, apart from England, existed in 1848 only in

Paris and, at the most, a few big industrial centres, has been spread over the whole of Europe and has reached an intensity such as was unthinkable in 1848. At that time the many obscure evangels of the sects, with their panaceas; today the one generally recognised, transparently clear theory of Marx, sharply formulating the final aims of the struggle. At that time the masses, sundered and differing according to locality and nationality, linked only by the feeling of common suffering, undeveloped, tossed to and fro in their perplexity from enthusiasm to despair; today a great international army of Socialists, marching irresistibly on and growing daily in number, organisation, discipline, insight and assurance of victory. If even this mighty army of the proletariat has still not reached its goal, if, a long way from winning victory with one mighty stroke, it has slowly to press forward from position to position in a hard, tenacious struggle, this only proves, once and for all, how impossible it was in 1848 to win social reconstruction by a simple surprise attack.

* * *

The war of 1870–71 and the defeat of the Commune had transferred the centre of gravity of the European workers' movement for the time being from France to Germany, as Marx foretold. In France it naturally took years to recover from the bloodletting of May 1871. In Germany, on the other hand, where industry was, in addition, furthered (in positively hot-house fashion) by the blessing of the French milliards and developed more and more quickly, Social-Democracy experienced a much more rapid and enduring growth. Thanks to the understanding with which the German workers made use of the universal suffrage introduced in 1866, the astonishing growth of the Party is made plain to all the world by incontestable figures: 1871, 102,000; 1874, 352,000; 1877, 493,000 Social-Democratic votes. Then came recognition of this advance by high authority in the shape of the Anti-Socialist Law: the Party was temporarily disrupted; the number of votes sank to 312,000 in 1881. But that was quickly overcome, and then, though oppressed by the Exceptional Law, without press, without external organisation and without the right of combination or meeting, the rapid expansion really began: 1884, 550,-000; 1887, 763,000; 1890, 1,427,000 votes. Then the hand of the state was paralysed. The Anti-Socialist Law disappeared; socialist votes rose to 1,787,000— over a quarter of all the votes cast. The government and the ruling classes had exhausted all their expedients—uselessly, to no purpose, and without success. The tangible proofs of their impotence, which the authorities, from night watchman to the imperial chancellor, had had to accept—and that from the despised workers—these proofs were counted in millions. The state was at the end of its Latin [sic—L. P. W.], the workers only at the beginning of theirs.

But the German workers did a second great service to their cause in addition to the first, which they rendered by their mere existence as the strongest, best disciplined, and most rapidly growing Socialist Party. They supplied their comrades of all countries with a new weapon, and one of the sharpest, when they showed them how to use universal suffrage.

There had long been universal suffrage in France, but it had fallen into disrepute through the misuse to which the Bonapartist government had put it. After the Commune there was no workers' party to make use of it. Also in Spain it had existed since the republic, but in Spain boycott of the elections was ever the rule of all serious opposition parties. The Swiss experiences of universal suffrage, also, were anything but encouraging for a workers' party. The revolutionary workers of the Latin countries had been wont to regard the suffrage as a snare, as an instrument of government trickery. It was otherwise in Germany. *The Communist Manifesto* had already proclaimed the winning of universal suffrage, of democracy, as one of the first and most important tasks of the militant proletariat, and Lassalle had again taken up this point. When Bismarck found himself compelled to introduce the franchise as the only means of interesting the mass of the people in his plans, our workers immediately took it in earnest and sent August Bebel to the first constituent Reichstag. And from that day on, they have used the franchise in a way which has paid them a thousandfold and has served as a model to the workers of all countries. The franchise has been, in the words of the French Marxist programme, . . . transformed from a means of deception, which it was heretofore, into an instrument of emancipation. And if universal suffrage had offered no other advantage than that it allowed us to count our numbers every three years; that by the regularly established, unexpectedly rapid rise in the number of votes it increased in equal measure the workers' certainty of victory and the dismay of their opponents, and so became our best means of propaganda; that it accurately informed us concerning our own strength and that of all hostile parties, and thereby provided us with a measure of proportion for our action second to none, safeguarding us from untimely timidity as much as from untimely foolhardiness—if this had been the only advantage we gained from the suffrage, then it would still have been more than enough. But it has done much more than this. In election agitation it provided us with a means, second to none, of getting in touch with the mass of the people, where they still stand aloof from us; of forcing all parties to defend their views and actions against our attacks before all the people; and, further, it opened to our representatives in the Reichstag a platform from which they could speak to their opponents in Parliament and to the masses without, with quite other authority and freedom than in the press or at meetings. Of what avail to the government and the bourgeoisie was their Anti-Socialist Law when election agitation and socialist speeches in the Reichstag continually broke through it?

With this successful utilisation of universal suffrage, an entirely new mode of proletarian struggle came into force, and this quickly developed further. It was found that the state institutions, in which the rule of the bourgeoisie is organised, offer still further opportunities for the working class to fight these very state institutions. They took part in elections to individual diets, to municipal councils and to industrial courts; they contested every post against the bourgeoisie in the occupation of which a sufficient part of the proletariat had its say. And so it happened that the bourgeoisie and the government came to be much more afraid of the legal than of the illegal action of the workers' party, of the results of elections than of those of rebellion.

For here, too, the conditions of the struggle had essentially changed. Rebellion in the old style, the street fight with barricades, which up to 1848 gave everywhere the final decision, was to a considerable extent obsolete.

Let us have no illusions about it; a real victory of an insurrection over the military in street fighting, a victory as between two armies, is one of the rarest exceptions. But the insurgents, also, counted on it just as rarely. For them it was solely a question of making the troops yield to moral influences, which, in a fight between the armies of two warring countries do not come into play at all, or do so to a much less degree. If they succeed in this, then the troops fail to act, or the commanding officers lose their heads, and the insurrection wins. If they do not succeed in this, then, even where the military are in the minority, the superiority of better equipment and training, of discipline makes itself felt. The most that the insurrection can achieve in actual tactical practice is the correct construction and defence of a single barricade. Mutual support; the disposition and defence of a single barricade. Mutual support; the disposition and employment of reserves; in short, the cooperation and harmonious working of the individual detachments, indispensable even for the defence of one quarter of the town, not to speak of the whole of a large town, are at best defective, and mostly not attainable at all; concentration of the military forces at a decisive point is, of course, impossible. Hence the passive defence is the prevailing form of fight: the attack will rise here and there, but only by way of exception, to occasional advances and flank assaults; as a rule, however, it will be limited to occupation of the positions abandoned by the retreating troops. In addition, the military have, on their side, the disposal of artillery and fully equipped corps of skilled engineers, resources of war which, in nearly every case, the insurgents entirely lack. No wonder, then, that even the barricade struggles conducted with the greatest heroism— Paris, June 1848; Vienna, October 1848; Dresden, May 1849—ended with the defeat of the insurrection, so soon as the leaders of the attack, unhampered by political considerations, acted from the purely military standpoint, and their soldiers remained reliable.

The numerous successes of the insurgents up to 1848 were due to a great variety of causes. In Paris in July 1830 and February 1848, as in most of the Spanish street fights, there stood between the insurgents and the military a civic militia, which either directly took the side of the insurrection, or else by its lukewarm, indecisive attitude caused the troops likewise to vacillate, and supplied the insurrection with arms into the bargain. Where this citizens' guard opposed the insurrection from the outset, as in June 1848 in Paris, the insurrection was vanquished. In Berlin in 1848, the people were victorious partly through a considerable accession of new fighting forces during the night and the morning of the 19th, partly as a result of the exhaustion and bad victualling of the troops, and, finally, partly as a result of the paralysed command. But in all cases the fight was won because the troops failed to obey, because the officers lost their power of decision or because their hands were tied.

Even in the classic time of street fighting, therefore, the barricade produced more of a moral than a material effect. It was a means of shaking the steadfastness of the military. If it held out until this was attained, then victory was won; if not, there was defeat. This is the main point, which must be kept in view, likewise when the chances of contingent future street fights are examined.

* * *

But since then there have been very many more changes, and all in favour of the military. If the big towns have become considerably bigger, the armies have become bigger still. Paris and Berlin have, since 1848, grown less than fourfold, but their garrisons have grown more than that. By means of the railways, the garrisons can, in twenty-four hours, be more than doubled, and in forty-eight hours they can be increased to huge armies. The arming of this enormously increased number of troops has become incomparably more effective. In 1848 the smooth-bore percussion muzzle-loader, today the small-calibre magazine breech-loading rifle, which shoots four times as far, ten times as accurately and ten times as fast as the former. At that time the relatively ineffective round-shot and grape-shot of the artillery; today the percussion shells, of which one is sufficient to demolish the best barricade. At that time the pick-axe of the sapper for breaking through walls; today the dynamite cartridge.

On the other hand, all the conditions on the insurgents' side have grown worse. An insurrection with which all sections of the people sympathise, will hardly recur; in the class struggle all the middle sections will never group themselves round the proletariat so exclusively that the reactionary parties gathered round the bourgeoisie well-nigh disappear. The "people," therefore, will always appear divided, and with this a powerful lever, so extraordinarily effective in 1848, is lacking. Even if more soldiers who have seen service were to come over to the insurrectionists, the arming of them becomes so much the more difficult. The hunting and luxury guns of the gunshops—even if not previously made unusable by removal of part of the lock by the police—are far from being a match for the magazine rifle of the soldier, even in close fighting. Up to 1848 it was possible to make the necessary ammunition oneself out of powder and lead; today the cartridges differ for each rifle, and are everywhere alike only in one point, that they are a special product of big industry, and therefore not to be prepared *ex tempore,* with the result that most rifles are useless as long as one does not possess the ammunition specially suited to them. And, finally, since 1848 the newly built quarters of the big towns have been laid out in long, straight, broad streets, as though made to give full effect to the new cannons and rifles. The revolutionary would have to be mad, who himself chose the working class districts in the North and East of Berlin for a barricade fight.

* * *

Does the reader now understand why the ruling classes decidedly want to bring us to where the guns shoot and the sabres slash? Why they accuse us today of cowardice, because we do not betake ourselves without more ado into the street, where we are certain of defeat in advance? Why they so earnestly implore us to play for once the part of cannon fodder?

* * *

Of course, our foreign comrades do not renounce their right to revolution. The right to revolution is, after all, the only real "historical right" the only right on which all modern states without exception rest. . . .

But whatever may happen in other countries, German Social-Democracy has a special situation and therewith, at least in the first instance, a special task. The two million voters, whom it sends to the ballot box, together with the young men and women who stand behind them as non-voters, form the most numerous, most compact mass, the decisive *"shock force"* of the international proletarian army. This mass already supplies over a fourth of the recorded votes; and as the by-elections to the Reichstag, the diet elections in individual states, the municipal council and industrial court elections demonstrate, it increases uninterruptedly. Its growth proceeds as spontaneously, as steadily, as irresistibly, and at the same time as tranquilly as a natural process. All government interventions have proved powerless against it. We can count even today on two and a half million voters. If it continues in this fashion, by the end of the century we shall conquer the greater part of the middle section of society, petty bourgeois and small peasants, and grow into the decisive power in the land, before which all other powers will have to bow, whether they like it or not. To keep this growth going without interruption until of itself it gets beyond the control of the ruling governmental system *not to fritter away this daily increasing shock force in advance guard fighting, but to keep it intact until the day of the decision,* that is our main task. And there is only one means by which the steady rise of the socialist fighting forces in Germany could be momentarily halted, and even thrown back for some time: a clash on a big scale with the military, a bloodbath like that of 1871 in Paris. In the long run that would also be overcome. To shoot out of the world a party which numbers millions—all the magazine rifles of Europe and America are not enough for this. . . .

The irony of world history turns everything upside down. We, the "revolutionaries," the "rebels"—we are thriving far better on legal methods than on illegal methods and revolt. The parties of order, as they call themselves, are perishing under the legal conditions created by themselves. They cry despairingly with Odilon Barrot: . . . legality is the death of us; whereas we, under this legality, get firm muscles and rosy cheeks and look like eternal life. And if we are not so crazy as to let ourselves be driven into street fighting in order to please them, then nothing else is finally left for them but themselves to break through this legality so fatal to them.

2
THE
SCHOLARS'
VIEWS

Marxism is both a program of political action and a theoretical analysis of society. The two are inextricably intertwined. This has created the problem of determining what is merely politically expedient and what follows necessarily from the theoretical premises of the Marxist argument. One of the central problems is that of the place of revolution in the coming of the Marxist society. Scholars have argued for a generation over this point: Must revolutionary action necessarily be taken, or can the Marxist society evolve from that of the bourgeoisie?

E. H. Carr is one of the foremost historians of Soviet Russia; from this vantage point he assesses the message of the *Communist Manifesto*.

FROM Studies in Revolution BY E. H. CARR

THE COMMUNIST MANIFESTO

The winter of 1847–48 (it is difficult to fix a more precise date for the celebration of the centenary) saw the birth of one of the capital documents of the nineteenth century—the *Communist Manifesto*. In the summer of 1847 a group consisting mainly of German craftsmen in London held the first congress of a new "Communist League." They had been in touch with Marx, then living in Brussels, for some time; and Engels attended the congress, which adjourned to a future congress the drafting of a programme for the

E. H. Carr, *Studies in Revolution* (1962), pp. 15–37. Reprinted by permission of Macmillan & Company, Ltd., London, and The Macmillan Company of Canada, Ltd., Toronto.

League. Inspired by this prospect, Engels tried his hand and produced a catechism in twenty-five questions, which Marx and he took with them to the second League congress in London at the end of November. The congress thereupon charged Marx and Engels to draft their programme for them: it was to take the form of a manifesto. Marx worked away in Brussels through December and January. The "Manifesto of the Communist Party" was published in London in German in February 1848, a few days before the revolution broke out in Paris.

The *Communist Manifesto* is divided into four parts. The first reviews the rise of the bourgeoisie on the ruins of the feudal system of property relations, government and morality which it destroyed; shows how "the powerful and colossal productive forces" which the bourgeoisie itself created have now grown to a point where they are no longer compatible with bourgeois property relations and bourgeois supremacy; and finally demonstrates that the proletariat is the new revolutionary class which can alone master the forces of modern industry and end the exploitation of man by man. The second part proclaims the policy of the Communist Party, as "the most progressive and resolute section of the working class of all countries," to promote the proletarian revolution which will destroy bourgeois power and "raise the proletariat to the position of the ruling class." The third part surveys and condemns other recent and existing schools of socialism; and the fourth is a brief tactical postscript on the relations of Communists to other left-wing parties.

A historic document like the *Communist Manifesto* invites examination from the point of view both of its antecedents and of its consequences. On the former count the *Manifesto* owes as much to predecessors and contemporaries as most great pronouncements; and the worst that can be said is that Marx's sweeping denunciations of predecessors and contemporaries sometimes mask the nature of the debt. Babeuf, who also called his proclamation a "manifesto," had announced the final struggle between rich and poor, between "a tiny minority" and "the huge majority." Blanqui had anticipated the class interpretation of history and the idea of the dictatorship of the proletariat (the phrase was not used by Marx himself till 1850). Lorenz von Stein had written that the history of freedom, society and political order was essentially dependent on the distribution of economic goods among the classes of the population. Proudhon also knew that "the laws of political economy are the laws of history" and measured the progress of society "by the development of industry and the perfection of its instruments"; and Pecqueur had predicted that, with the spread of commerce, "the barriers between nation and nation will be broken down" until the day when "every man becomes a citizen of the world." Such ideas were current coin in advanced circles when Marx wrote. But neither such borrowings, nor Marx's overriding debt to Hegel's immense synthesis, detract from the power of the conception presented to the world in the *Communist Manifesto*.

To-day it is more appropriate to study the famous manifesto in the light of its hundred-year influence on posterity. Though written when Marx was in his thirtieth year and Engels two years younger, it already contains the quintessence of Marxism. Beginning with a broad historical generalization ("the history of all hitherto existing society is the history of class struggles") and ending with an inflammatory appeal to the workers of all countries to unite for "the forcible overthrow of all existing social conditions," it presents Marxist methodology in its fully developed form—an interpretation of history which is at the same time a call to action. Some passages in Marx's writings, especially at the revolutionary crises of 1848 and 1871, appear to commend revolutionary action as a good thing in itself. Some passages, both earlier and later, appear to dwell on the iron laws of historical development in such a way as to leave little place for the initiative of the human will. But these momentary shifts of emphasis cannot be taken to impair the dual orthodoxy established by the *Communist Manifesto,* where interpretation and action, predestination and free will, revolutionary theory and revolutionary practice march triumphantly hand in hand. It propounds a philosophy of history, a dogma of revolution, belief in which will take the spontaneous form of appropriate action in the believer.

The *Communist Manifesto* is thus no broadsheet for the hoardings or the hustings. Marx—and many others who are not Marxists—would deny the possibility of any rigid separation of emotion and intellect; but using the terms in a popular sense, it is to the intellect rather than to the emotions that the *Manifesto* makes its primary appeal. The overwhelming impression which it leaves on the reader's mind is not so much that the revolution is desirable (that, like the injustice of capitalism in *Das Kapital,* is taken for granted as something not requiring argument) but that the revolution is inevitable. For successive generations of Marxists the *Manifesto* was not a plea for revolution—that they did not need—but a prediction about the way in which the revolution would inevitably happen combined with a prescription for the action required of revolutionaries to make it happen. The controversies of a hundred years ranged round the questions as to what Marx actually said or meant and how what he said should be applied to conditions diverging widely from those of his own time and place. Only the bold offered openly to "revise" Marx; the sagacious interpreted him. The *Communist Manifesto* has thus remained a living document. The centenary of the *Communist Manifesto* cannot be celebrated otherwise than in the light, and in the shadow, of the Russian revolution which was its culminating embodiment in history.

The *Communist Manifesto* sets out a coherent scheme of revolution. "The history of all hitherto existing society is the history of class struggles." In modern times Marx detects two such struggles—the struggle between feudalism and the bourgeoisie, ending in the victorious bourgeois revolution, and the struggle between the bourgeoisie and the proletariat, destined to end in the victorious proletarian revolution. In the first struggle a nascent proletariat is mobilized by the bourgeoisie in support of bourgeois aims, but is incapable of pursuing independent aims of its own: "every victory so obtained is a victory for the bourgeoisie." In the second struggle Marx recognizes the presence of the lower middle class—"the small manufacturer, the shopkeeper, the artisan, the peasant"—which plays a fluctuating role between bourgeoisie and proletariat, and a "slum proletariat" which is liable to "sell itself to reactionary forces." But these complications do not seriously affect the ordered simplicity of the main pattern of revolution.

The pattern had been framed in the light of Marx's reading in modern English and French history and in the works of French and British economists, and of Engels's study of factory conditions in England. The English bourgeois revolution, winning its victory in the seventeenth century, had fully consolidated itself by 1832. The French bourgeois revolution, more suddenly and dramatically triumphant after 1789, had succumbed to reaction only to reemerge once more in 1830. In both countries the first revolutionary struggle of the modern age—the struggle between feudalism and bourgeoisie—was virtually over; the stage was set for the second struggle—between bourgeoisie and proletariat.

The events of 1848, coming hard on the heels of the *Manifesto,* did much to confirm its diagnosis and nothing to refute it. In England the collapse of Chartism was a set-back which none the less marked a stage in the consolidation of a class-conscious workers' movement. In France the proletariat marched shoulder to shoulder with the bourgeoisie in February 1848, as the *Manifesto* had said it would, so long as the aim was to consolidate and extend the bourgeois revolution. But once the proletariat raised its own banner of social revolution the line was crossed. Bourgeoisie and proletariat, allies until the bourgeois revolution had been completed and made secure, were now divided on opposite sides of the barricades by the call for proletarian revolution. The first revolutionary struggle was thus over: the second was impending. In Paris, in the June days of 1848, Cavaignac saved the bourgeoisie and staved off the proletarian revolution by massacring, executing and transporting the class-conscious workers. The pattern of the *Communist Manifesto* had been precisely followed. As Professor Namier, who is no Marxist, puts it: "The working classes touched off, and the middle classes cashed in on it."

The June revolution [as Marx wrote at the time] for the first time split the whole of society into two hostile camps—east and west Paris. The unity of the February revolution no longer exists. The February fighters are now warring against each other—something that has never happened before; the former indifference has vanished and every man capable of bearing arms is fighting on one side or other of the barricades.

The events of February and June 1848 had provided a classic illustration of the great gulf fixed between bourgeois and proletarian revolutions.

Farther east the pattern of England and France did not fully apply, as the concluding section of the *Manifesto* admitted—almost by way of an after-thought.

In Germany the bourgeois revolution had not yet begun. The German bourgeoisie had not yet won the fundamental political rights which the English bourgeoisie had achieved in 1689 and the French a hundred years later. The task of the German proletariat was still therefore to support the bourgeoisie in the first revolutionary struggle against feudalism; in Germany, in the words of the *Manifesto*, "the Communist Party fights with the bourgeoisie whenever it acts in a revolutionary manner against the absolute monarchy, the feudal landlords and the petty bourgeoisie." But it could not be argued that Germany would simply follow the same path as England and France at a greater or less distance of time. The German revolution would occur "under the most advanced conditions of European civilization" which would give it a special character. Where the proletariat was already so advanced, thought Marx, the bourgeois revolution "can only be the immediate prelude to the proletarian revolution."

When Marx, in the brief concluding section of the *Manifesto,* devoted to Communist Party tactics, thus announced the prospect in Germany of an immediate transition from bourgeois to proletarian revolution without the intervening period of bourgeois rule, he showed a keen historical perception, even at the expense of undermining the validity of his own theoretical analysis. The events of 1848 in the German-speaking lands confirmed Marx's intuition of the impossibility in Germany of a period of established bourgeois supremacy comparable with that which has set so strong a mark on English and French history. This impossibility was due not so much to the strength of the German proletariat, which Marx perhaps exaggerated, as to the weakness of the German bourgeoisie. Whatever the prospects of an eventual proletarian revolution such as England and France had long ago achieved was still conspicuously absent. Indeed, the bourgeoisie, far from bidding for power for itself, was plainly ready to ally itself with the surviving elements of feudalism for defence against the proletarian menace. It need hardly be added that the same symptoms, in a still more pronounced form, repeated themselves in Russia more than half a century afterwards.

The problem, therefore, which Germany presented in 1848 to the authors of the *Communist Manifesto* was the same which Russia would one day present to the theorists of her revolution. According to the revolutionary pattern of the *Communist Manifesto,* the function of the bourgeoisie was to destroy feudal society root and branch preparatory to its own destruction in the final phase of the revolutionary struggle by the proletariat. But what was to happen if the bourgeoisie through weakness or cowardice—or perhaps through some untimely premonition of its own eventual fate—was unable or unwilling to perform its essential function? Marx never provided a categorical answer to this question. But his answer was implicit in the doctrine of "permanent revolution," which he propounded in an address to the Communist League in 1850:

While the democratic petty bourgeoisie wants to end the revolution as rapidly as possible . . . our interests and our task consist in making the revolution permanent until all the more or less possessing classes are removed from authority, until the proletariat wins State power.

The responsibility was thus placed on the proletariat to complete the task, which the bourgeoisie had failed to perform, of liquidating feudalism.

What form the liquidation was to take when the proletariat found itself directly confronted by a feudal society without any effective and independent bourgeoisie was not altogether clear. But if one insisted—as Marx apparently did, and Engels continued to do down to the end of his life—that "our party can come to power only under some such form as a democratic republic," then the conclusion followed that the immediate aim of the proletariat must be limited to the establishment of a political democracy in which it was interested only as a necessary stepping-stone to the proletarian social revolution. This was, however, a theoretical construction unlikely to be realized in practice—as the experience of both the German and the Russian revolutions was one day to show. Marx never really fitted his analysis of revolution to countries where the bourgeoisie was incapable of making its own revolution; and acrimonious controversy about the relation between bourgeois and proletarian revolutions continued to divide the Russian revolutionaries for several decades.

The economic corollary of this conclusion was still more startling. If the establishment of a democratic republic was a prerequisite of the proletarian revolution, so also was the full development of capitalism; for capitalism was the essential expression of bourgeois society and inseparable from it. Marx certainly held this view as late as 1859 when he wrote in the preface to the *Critique of Political Economy:* "No social form perishes until all the productive forces for which it provides scope have been developed." It appeared to follow, paradoxically enough, that in backward countries the interest of the nascent proletariat was to promote the most rapid development of capitalism and capitalist exploitation at its own expense.

Such was the view seriously propounded by Russian Marxists, Bolshevik and Menshevik alike, down to 1905—perhaps even down to 1917. Meanwhile, however, in the spring of 1905, Lenin's practical mind worked out a new scheme under which the proletariat was to seize power in conjunction with the peasantry, creating a "democratic dictatorship" of workers and peasants; and this became the official doctrine of the October revolution. The Mensheviks stuck to their guns, and their survivors and successors to-day attribute the shortcomings of the Russian revolution to its failure to pass through the bourgeois-democratic, bourgeois-capitalist phase on its way to the achievement of socialism. The issue is not to be settled by reference to Marx, who can hardly be acquitted of inconsistency on this point. Either he made a mistake in suggesting, in the last section of the *Communist Manifesto,* that Germany might pass immediately from the bourgeois to the proletarian revolution; or he failed to fit this new conception into the revolutionary framework of the earlier part of the *Manifesto*.

Marx was to encounter similar difficulties in applying the generalizations of the *Communist Manifesto* about nationalism, which were also based on British and French experience, to central and eastern Europe. The charge often brought against Marx of ignoring or depreciating national sentiment rests indeed on a misunderstanding. The famous remark that "the workers have no country," read in its context, is neither a boast nor a programme; it is a complaint which had long been a commonplace among socialist writers. Babeuf had declared that the multitude "sees in society only an enemy, and loses even the possibility of having a country"; and Weitling had connected the notion of country with the notion of property:

He alone has a country who is a property owner or at any rate has the liberty and the means of becoming one. He who has not that, has no country.

In order to remedy this state of affairs (to quote once more from the *Manifesto*) "the proletariat must first conquer political power, must rise to be the dominant class of the nation, must constitute itself the nation, so that the proletariat is so far national itself, though not in the bourgeois sense."

The passage of the *Manifesto* in which these sentences occur is not free from ambiguities. But the thought behind it is clear. In Marx's view, which corresponded to the facts of English and French history, nationalism grew up as an attribute of bourgeois society at a time when the bourgeoisie was a revolutionary and progressive force. Both in England and in France the bourgeoisie, invoking the national spirit to destroy a feudalism which was at once particularist and cosmopolitan, had through a period of centuries built up a centralized State on a national basis. But the advance of capitalism was already making nations obsolete.

National differences and antagonisms are to-day vanishing ever more and more with the development of the bourgeoisie, free trade in the world market, the uniformity of industrial production and the conditions of life corresponding thereto.

With the victory of the proletariat they will vanish still faster. . . . With the disappearance of classes within the nation the state of enmity between nations will come to an end.

Hence the first step was for the proletariat of every country to "settle accounts with its own bourgeoisie." The way would then be open for a true international communist order. Like Mazzini and other nineteenth-century thinkers, Marx thought of nationalism as a natural stepping-stone to internationalism.

Unfortunately the national pattern of the *Manifesto,* far from being universal, proved difficult to extend beyond the narrow limits of the place (western Europe) or the time (the age of Cobden) in which it was designed. Beyond western Europe the same conditions which prevented the rise of a powerful bourgeoisie also prevented the development of an orderly bourgeois national-ism. In central Europe (the Hapsburg Empire, Prussia) as well as in Russia the centralized State had been brought into being under pressure of military necessity by feudal overlords indifferent to national feeling; and when in the nineteenth century, under the impetus of the French revolution, nationalism became for the first time a force to be reckoned with in central and eastern Europe, it appeared not—as in England and France—as an attribute and complement of the State but as a sentiment independent of any existing State organization.

Moreover, the relation of nation to State worked itself out in different ways and sometimes involved even the same national group in inconsistent atti-tudes. This was particularly true of the Hapsburg Empire. The growing na-tional consciousness of the German-Austrian bourgeoisie did not diminish its support of imperial unity; the bourgeoisie of the other constituent national groups sought to destroy that unity or at least to dissolve it into a federation. The Hungarians asserted the rights of the Magyar nation against the Ger-man-Austrians, but denied the national rights of Croats and Slovaks.

In these circumstances it is not surprising that Marx and Engels never succeeded in working out, even for their own day and generation, a consistent theory of nationalism which would hold good throughout Europe. They sup-ported the Polish claim to national independence; no revolutionary, no lib-eral, of the nineteenth century could have done otherwise. But Engels, at any rate, seemed mainly concerned that this claim should be satisfied at the ex-pense of Russia rather than of Prussia, proposing on one occasion to offer the Poles Riga and Mitau in exchange for Danzig and Elbing; and in the candid outburst of a private letter to Marx he referred to the Poles as *"une nation foutue,* a serviceable instrument only until Russia herself is swept into the agrarian revolution." In the same spirit he rejected outright the national aspi-rations of the Slavs of the Hapsburg Empire, whose triumph would be, in his eyes, a subjugation "of the civilized west by the barbaric east."

In these judgments, from which Marx is not known to have dissented, Engels was indubitably swayed by national prejudice and in particular by hostility to Russia as the most reactionary Power of the day. But he was also moved by the recognition that these nationalisms of central and eastern Eu-rope, whose economic basis was agrarian, had little or nothing to do with the bourgeois nationalism of which Marx and he had taken cognizance in the *Communist Manifesto.* It was not only a question of "the civilized west" and "the barbaric east": it was a question of the subjugation "of town by the country, of trade, manufacture and intelligence by the primitive agriculture of Slavonic serfs." On the presuppositions of the *Manifesto,* this seemed nec-essarily a retrograde step. The failure of Marx and Engels to take account of agrarian nationalism was one aspect of the other great lacuna of the *Mani-festo*—the question of the peasant.

If, however, the theory of nationalism propounded in the *Communist Manifesto* could not be transplanted from western to central and eastern Eu-

rope, it equally failed to stand the test of time. The *Manifesto* contains indeed
one reference to "the exploitation of one nation by another" and declares, by
what seems a tautology in one sense and a *non sequitur* in another, that it
will end when the exploitation of one individual by another ends. But Marx
has little to say (nothing at all in the *Manifesto* itself) about the colonial
question, touching on it in detail only in the case of Ireland; and here it is
perhaps significant that, while in 1848 he was prepared to sacrifice the Irish in
the same way as the Austrian Slavs, he had become convinced by 1869 that
"the direct absolute interest of the English working class demands a rupture
of the present connexion with Ireland." Marx did not, however, live to see the
full development of the process by which the great nations, already victims of
the contradictions of capitalism, vied with one another in bringing the whole
world under their yoke in a desperate attempt to save themselves and the
capitalist system—the process which Lenin was afterwards to analyse in his
famous work on *Imperialism as the Highest Stage of Capitalism;* nor could
he foresee that rise to national consciousness of innumerable "unhistorical"
nations of which the Austrian Slavs had been the harbingers. The Soviet
theory of nationality, in which the colonial question and the question of
small nations divide the honours between them, can derive only a pale and
faltering light from the simple and far-away formulation of the *Communist
Manifesto*. But critics of the national theories, whether of Marx or of the
Bolsheviks, may do well to reflect that bourgeois thinkers and statesmen have
also not been able to formulate, and still less to apply, a consistent doctrine of
national rights.

Marx's attitude to the tiller of the soil is more seriously open to criticism.
Here too there is a foretaste of subsequent controversy—both the Mensheviks
and Trotsky were accused, rightly from Lenin's point of view, of "underestimating" the peasant; and here too Marx ran into trouble because his initial
theories had been primarily framed to fit western conditions. The *Communist Manifesto* praised the bourgeoisie for having, through its development of
factories and towns, "delivered a great part of the population from the idiocy
of country life"; and it classed peasant or peasant proprietor with handicraftsmen, small traders and shopkeepers as members of the "petty bourgeoisie"—an unstable and reactionary class, since it struggled against the greater
bourgeoisie, not for revolutionary ends, but only in order to maintain its own
bourgeois status. In England, in France (which in revolutionary circles was
generally thought of as Paris writ large) and in Germany, the *Communist
Manifesto* upheld the strict pattern of successive revolutions of which the
bourgeoisie and the proletariat would be the respective driving forces, and
reserved no independent place for the peasant.

Events were soon to show up the lacuna left by this scheme of things even
in western Europe. The French peasants were unmoved when the revolutionary workers of Paris were shot down in June 1848 by the agents of the
bourgeoisie, and voted solidly for the bourgeois dictatorship of Louis Napo-

leon. In fact they behaved exactly as the *Communist Manifesto* expected them to behave (which did not save them from incurring some of Marx's fiercest invective in *The Eighteenth Brumaire of Louis Napoleon*); but in so doing they showed how far things would have to travel before the French proletariat would be able to make another French revolution.

In Prussia and throughout Germany the revolution of 1848 was in the hands of intellectuals who thought as little of the peasants as Marx himself; and the peasants failed to move. In Austria the peasants did move. They rose in Galicia against the landlords and would have risen elsewhere with the right leadership. They formed a large and vocal group in the new democratic Reichstag. But the claims of the peasant encountered the hostility of the bourgeoisie and the indifference of the urban workers. Peasantry and proletariat were crushed separately in the absence of a leader and a programme to unite them; and in central Europe the surest moral of 1848 was that no revolution could succeed which did not win the peasant and give a high priority to his concerns.

In eastern Europe this was still more abundantly clear. As regards Poland, even the *Communist Manifesto* declared that "the Communists support the party that sees in agrarian revolution the means to national freedom, the party which caused the Cracow insurrection of 1846." But this passage, which occurs in the tactical postscript, is the only incursion of the *Manifesto* into eastern Europe and the only reference to agrarian revolution; and even here agrarian revolution is regarded as the ally of a bourgeois revolution leading to "national freedom," not of a proletarian revolution.

Spending the rest of his years in England, where there was no peasantry and no agrarian question, Marx never felt any strong impulse to fill this lacuna in the *Communist Manifesto*. In 1856, drawing a moral from the failure of 1848 in Germany, he spoke casually of the importance of backing up the future proletarian German revolution "with some second edition of the Peasants' War." But even here only a subsidiary role was assigned to the peasantry. It was towards the end of his life that Marx was called on to pass judgment on a controversy just opening in far-away Russia. The leading Russian revolutionaries, the Narodniks, regarded the Russian peasant commune with its system of common tenure of land as the seed-bed of the future Russian Socialist order. On the other hand, the first Russian Marxists were already beginning to argue that the way to socialism could only lie, in Russia as elsewhere, through a development of capitalism and the proletariat.

Four times did the Marx-Engels partnership attack this ticklish issue. In 1874, before the Russian Marxists had raised their head, Engels had recognized the possibility in favourable conditions of the direct transformation of the communal system into a higher form, "avoiding the intermediate stage of individualized bourgeois property." In 1877, in reply to an attack in a Russian journal, Marx confined himself to a doubtful admission that Russia had "the finest chance which history ever presented to a nation of avoiding the ups-and-downs of the capitalist order." In 1881 Marx gave a more positive response to a direct personal inquiry from Vera Zasulich; and in the following year the last and most authoritative pronouncement appeared in the preface to a Russian translation of the *Communist Manifesto,* signed jointly by both its authors:

If the Russian revolution is the signal for a workers' revolution in the west so that these complement each other, then the contemporary Russian system of communal ownership can serve as the starting-point for a Communist development.

Russian Social-Democrats of a later generation, both Bolshevik and Menshevik, looked askance at this quasi-Narodnik deviation, and returned to the purer theoretical pattern of the *Manifesto* with its clear-cut dialectic of bourgeois and proletarian revolutions; and Lenin himself, not less than the Mensheviks, sternly maintained the paradox that the further development of capitalism in Russia was a necessary prelude to social revolution. Nevertheless, Lenin, like Marx in his later years, recognized that no revolution, and no revolutionary, in eastern Europe could afford to ignore the peasant and his demands. After 1905—and before and after 1917—the Bolsheviks were obliged to devote an immense amount of energy and controversy to the task of fitting the Russian peasant into the western formulae of the *Communist Manifesto*.

Franz Mehring, Marx's best and most sympathetic biographer, remarks of the *Communist Manifesto* that "in many respects historical development has proceeded otherwise, and above all has proceeded more slowly, than its authors expected." This is true of the expectations of the two young men who composed the *Manifesto*. But how far were these expectations modified? As regards pace, Marx in later life certainly no longer believed in the imminence of the proletarian revolution with all the eager confidence of 1848. But even the *Manifesto* in one of its more cautious passages had predicted temporary successes followed by set-backs and a slow process of "growing unity" among the workers before the goal was achieved. Marx came, with advancing years, to accept the necessity of a long course of education for the proletariat in revolutionary principles; and there is the famous *obiter dictum* in a speech of the 1870s, which admits that in certain advanced countries the victory of the proletariat may be achieved without revolutionary violence.

As regards the scheme of historical development, it would be difficult to prove that Marx, speaking theoretically and *ex cathedra,* ever abandoned the strict analysis of revolution which he had worked out in the *Communist Manifesto*. But he was not a pure theorist. He was willy-nilly the leader of a political party; and it was when he found himself compelled to make pronouncements in this capacity that he sometimes appeared to derogate from his principles. Thus in the last section of the *Manifesto* itself he had already foreseen that in Germany the bourgeois revolution would be the "immediate prelude" of the proletarian revolution, thus skipping over the period of bourgeois supremacy; in the next few years he was drawn into some uncomfortable compromises and inconsistencies on the national question; and towards the end of his life he was constrained to admit that a predominantly peasant country like Russia had the chance of achieving the social revolution without passing through the bourgeois-capitalist phase at all, thus not merely modifying but side-tracking altogether the revolutionary analysis of the *Manifesto*.

It is curious and significant of the vitality of Marx's thought to watch how accurately this evolution was repeated in the Russian Social-Democratic Party. Its first leaders—Plekhanov and Axelrod, Lenin and Martov—accepted without question the scheme of the *Communist Manifesto*. After 1903 the Mensheviks, remaining consistent with themselves and with the Marxist scheme, ended in bankruptcy because they could find no way of applying it to Russian conditions. The more flexible Lenin took the scheme and brilliantly adapted it to those conditions; and the adaptations which he made followed —in broad outline, though not in every detail—those which Marx himself had admitted in his later years. The process can be justified. Marxism was never offered to the world as a static body of doctrine; Marx himself once confessed that he was no Marxist; and the constant evolution of doctrine in response to changing conditions is itself a canon of Marxism.

It is on such grounds that the Russian revolution can claim to be a legitimate child of the *Communist Manifesto*. The *Manifesto* challenged bourgeois society and offered a revaluation of bourgeois values. The Bolshevik revolution, with all its deviations, all its adaptations to specifically Russian conditions and all the impurities which always disfigure practice as opposed to theory, has driven home the challenge and sought to apply the revaluation. That bourgeois society has been put progressively on the defensive in the past hundred years, that its fate still hangs in the balance, few to-day will deny; and until that fate is settled, until some new synthesis has been achieved, the *Communist Manifesto* will not have said its last word.

Eduard Bernstein (1850–1932) was a German journalist and an important member of the German Social Democratic party. Like Engels, he was an ardent Marxist, but unlike Engels, he was not an apologist for Marx. Bernstein's views of the essential truths of Marxism were based upon an intimate study of the important texts, as well as on a close acquaintance with German political reality in the 1890s. The work from which the following selection is drawn was first published in 1899.

FROM Evolutionary Socialism BY EDUARD BERNSTEIN

THE MARXIST DOCTRINE OF CLASS WAR AND OF THE EVOLUTION OF CAPITAL

The doctrine of the class wars rests on the foundation of the materialist conception of history. "It was found," writes Engels in *Anti-Dühring,* "that all history hitherto was the history of class wars, that the classes fighting each other are, each time, the outcome of the conditions of production and commerce—in one word, of the economic conditions of their epoch." . . . In modern society it is the class war between the capitalist owners of the means of production and the producers without capital, the wage workers, which imprints its mark on history in this respect. For the former class Marx took from France the term "bourgeoisie," and for the latter the term "proletariat." This class struggle between bourgeoisie and proletariat is accordingly the antagonism, transferred to men, which is in the conditions of production today, that is, in the private character of the method of appropriation and the social character of the method of production. The means of production are the property of individual capitalists who appropriate to themselves the results of the production, but the production itself has become a social process; that means, a production of commodities for use made by many workers on a basis of systematic division and organisation of labour. And this antagonism conceals in itself, or has, a second conflict, as a supplement: the systematic division and organisation of work within the establishments for production (workshop, factory, combination of factories, etc.) is opposed by the unsystematic disposal of the produce on the market.

The starting point of the class struggle between capitalists and workers is the antagonism of interests which follows from the nature of the utilisation of the labour of the latter by the former for profit.

* * *

The capitalist sells the products (manufactured with the help of the worker—that is, by the whole of the workers employed by him) in the goods

Eduard Bernstein, *Evolutionary Socialism: A Criticism and Affirmation* (1909), pp. 18–20, 24–25, 146–150, 153–157, 159–165, translated by Edith C. Harvey. Reprinted by permission of the Independent Labour Party, London.

market at a price which, as a rule and as a condition of the continuance of his undertaking, yields a surplus above the amount which the manufacture costs. What is, then, this surplus?

According to Marx it is the surplus value of the labour accomplished by the worker. The goods are exchanged on the market at a value which is fixed by the labour embodied in them, measured according to time. What the capitalist has put in in past—we would even say dead—labour in the form of raw material, auxiliary material, wear and tear of machinery, rent, and other costs of production, appears again unchanged in the value of the product. It is otherwise with the living work expended on it. This costs the capitalist wages; it brings him an amount beyond these, the equivalent of the value of labour. The labour value is the value of the quantity of labour worked into the product; the worker's wages is the selling price of the labour power used up in production. Prices, or the value of labour power, are determined by the cost of maintenance of the worker as it corresponds with his historically developed habits of life. The difference between the equivalent . . . of the labour-value and the labour-wage is the surplus value which it is the natural endeavour of the capitalist to raise as high as possible and in any case not to allow to sink.

* * *

So far, in the most concise compression possible, I have endeavoured to set forth the most important propositions of that part of the Marxist theory which we have to consider as essential to his socialism. Just as little as—or, rather, still less than—the materialist theory of history has this part of the theory sprung from the beginning in a perfected form from the head of its authors. Even more than in the former case can a development of the theory be shown which, whilst firmly maintaining the chief points of view, consists of limiting the propositions at first represented as absolute. In the preface to *Capital* (1867), in the preface to the new edition of the *Communist Manifesto* (1872), in the preface and a note to the new edition of the *Poverty of Philosophy* (1884), and in the preface to the *Class Struggles in the French Revolution* (1895), some of the changes are shown which in the course of time have been brought to pass with regard to various corresponding matters in the views of Marx and Engels. But not all the changes to be cited here and elsewhere with reference to single portions or hypotheses of the theory have found full consideration in its final elaboration. Marx and Engels confined themselves sometimes merely to hinting at, sometimes only to stating in regard to single points, the changes recognised by them in facts, and in the better analyses of these facts, which influenced the form and application of their theory. And even in the last respect contradictions are not wanting in their writings. They have left to their successors the duty of bringing unity again into their theory and of co-ordinating theory and practice.

But this duty can only be accomplished if one gives an account unreservedly of the gaps and contradictions in the theory. In other words, the further development and elaboration of the Marxist doctrine must begin with criticism of it.

* * *

The whole practical activity of social democracy is directed towards creating circumstances and conditions which shall render possible and secure a transition (free from convulsive outbursts) of the modern social order into a higher one. From the consciousness of being the pioneers of a higher civilisation, its adherents are ever creating fresh inspiration and zeal. In this rests also, finally, the moral justification of the socialist expropriation towards which they aspire. But the "dictatorship of the classes" belongs to a lower civilisation, and apart from the question of the expediency and practicability of the thing, it is only to be looked upon as a reversion, as political atavism. If the thought is aroused that the transition from a capitalist to a socialist society must necessarily be accomplished by means of the development of forms of an age which did not know at all, or only in quite an imperfect form, the present methods of the initiating and carrying of laws, and which was without the organs fit for the purpose, reaction will set in.

I say expressly transition from a capitalist to a socialist society, and not from a "civic society," as is so frequently the expression used to-day. This application of the word "civic" is also much more an atavism, or in any case an ambiguous way of speaking, which must be considered an inconvenience in the phraseology of German social democracy, and which forms an excellent bridge for mistakes with friend and foe. The fault lies partly in the German language, which has no special word for the idea of the citizen with equal civic rights separate from the idea of privileged citizens.

What is the struggle against, or the abolition of, a civic society? What does it mean specially in Germany, in whose greatest and leading state, Prussia, we are still constantly concerned with first getting rid of a great part of feudalism which stands in the path of civic development? No man thinks of destroying civic society as a civilised ordered system of society. On the contrary, social democracy does not wish to break up this society and make all its members proletarians together; it labours rather incessantly at raising the worker from the social position of a proletarian to that of a citizen, and thus to make citizenship universal. It does not want to set up a proletarian society instead of a civic society, but a socialist order of society instead of a capitalist one. It would be well if one, instead of availing himself of the former ambiguous expression, kept to the latter quite clear declaration. Then one would be quite free of a good portion of other contradictions which opponents, not quite without reason, assert do exist between the phraseology and the practice of social democracy. . . .

Finally, it is to be recommended that some moderation should be kept in the declaration of war against "liberalism." It is true that the great liberal movement of modern times arose for the advantage of the capitalist bourgeoisie first of all, and the parties which assumed the names of liberals were, or became in due course, simple guardians of capitalism. Naturally, only opposition can reign between these parties and social democracy. But with respect to liberalism as a great historical movement, socialism is its legitimate heir, not only in chronological sequence, but also in its spiritual qualities, as is shown moreover in every question of principle in which social democracy has had to take up an attitude.

Wherever an economic advance of the socialist programme had to be carried out in a manner, or under circumstances, that appeared seriously to imperil the development of freedom, social democracy has never shunned taking up a position against it. The security of civil freedom has always seemed to it to stand higher than the fulfilment of some economic progress.

The aim of all socialist measures, even of those which appear outwardly as coercive measures, is the development and the securing of a free personality. Their more exact examination always shows that the coercion included will raise the sum total of liberty in society, and will give more freedom over a more extended area than it takes away. The legal day of a maximum number of hours' work, for example, is actually a fixing of a minimum of freedom, a prohibition to sell freedom longer than for a certain number of hours daily, and, in principle, therefore, stands on the same ground as the prohibition agreed to by all liberals against selling oneself into personal slavery.

* * *

Liberalism had historically the task of breaking the chains which the fettered economy and the corresponding organisations of law of the middle ages had imposed on the further development of society. That it at first strictly maintained the form of bourgeois liberalism did not stop it from actually expressing a very much wider-reaching general principle of society whose completion will be socialism.

Socialism will create no new bondage of any kind whatever. The individual is to be free, not in the metaphysical sense, as the anarchists dreamed—*i.e.,* free from all duties towards the community—but free from every economic compulsion in his action and choice of a calling. Such freedom is only possible for all means of organisation. In this sense one might call socialism "organising liberalism," for when one examines more closely the organizations that socialism wants and how it wants them, he will find that what distinguishes them above all from the feudalistic organisations, outwardly like them, is just their liberalism, their democratic constitution, their accessibility. Therefore the trade union, striving after an arrangement similar to a guild, is, in the eyes of the socialist, the product of self-defence against the tendency of capitalism to overstock the labour market; but, at the same time, just on account of its tendency towards a guild, and to the degree in which that obtains, is it an unsocialistic corporate body.

* * *

To create the organisations described—or, so far as they are already begun, to develop them further—is the indispensable preliminary to what we call socialism of production. Without them the so-called social appropriation of the means of production would only result presumably in reckless devastation of productive forces, insane experimentalising and aimless violence, and the political sovereignty of the working class would, in fact, only be carried out in the form of a dictatorial, revolutionary, central power, supported by the terrorist dictatorship of revolutionary clubs. As such it hovered before the Blanquists, and as such it is still represented in the *Communist Manifesto* and in the publications for which its authors were responsible at that time. But "in presence of the practical experiences of the February revolution and much more of those of the Paris Commune when the proletariat retained political power for two months," the revolutionary programme given in the *Manifesto* has "here and there become out of date." "The Commune notably offers a proof that the working class cannot simply take possession of the state machinery and set it in motion for their own ends."

So wrote Marx and Engels in 1872 in the preface to the new edition of the *Manifesto*. And they refer to the work, *The Civil War in France,* where this is developed more fully. But if we open the work in question and read the part referred to (it is the third), we find a programme developed which, according to its political contents, shows in all material features the greatest similarity to the federalism of Proudhon.

"The unity of the nation was not to be broken, but on the contrary it was to be organised by the destruction of that power of the state which pretended to be the personification of that unity but wanted to be independent of, and superior to, the nation on whose body it was after all only a parasitic growth. Whilst they were occupied in cutting off the merely oppressive organs of the old governing power its rightful functions as a power which claimed to stand above the community were to be taken away and given over to the responsible servants of the community. Instead of deciding once in three or six years what member of the ruling class should trample on and crush the people in Parliament, universal suffrage should serve the people constituted in communities, as individual suffrage serves every other employer to select for his business workers, inspectors, and clerks.

"The antagonism between the commune and the power of the state has been looked on as an exaggerated form of the old fight against over-centralisation. . . . The constitution of the commune, on the contrary, would have restored to the community all the powers which until now the parasitic growth, the state, which lives on the community and hinders its free action, has absorbed."

Thus Marx wrote in the *Civil War in France*.

* * *

There is not the least doubt (and it has since then been proved many times practically) that the general development of modern society is along the line of a constant increase of the duties of municipalities and the extension of municipal freedom, that the municipality will be an ever more important lever of social emancipation. It appears to me doubtful if it was necessary for the first work of democracy to be such a dissolution of the modern state system and complete transformation of its organisation as Marx . . . pictured (the formation of the national assembly out of delegates from provincial or district assemblies, which in their turn were composed of delegates from municipalities) so that the form the national assemblies had hitherto taken had to be abolished. Evolution has given life to too many institutions and bodies corporate, whose sphere has outgrown the control of municipalities and even of provinces and districts for it to be able to do without the control of the central governments unless or before their organisation is transformed. . . .

But we are less concerned here with a criticism of separate items in the quoted programme than with bringing into prominence the energy with which it emphasises autonomy as the preliminary condition of social emancipation, and with showing how the democratic organisation from the bottom upwards is depicted as the way to the realisation of socialism, and how the antagonists Proudhon and Marx meet again in—liberalism.

The future itself will reveal how far the municipalities and other self-governing bodies will discharge their duties under a complete democracy, and how far they will make use of these duties. But so much is clear: the more suddenly they come in possession of their freedom, the more experiments they will make in number and in violence and therefore be liable to greater mistakes, and the more experience the working class democracy has had in the school of self-government, the more cautiously and practically will it proceed.

Simple as democracy appears to be at the first glance, its problems in such a complicated society as ours are in no way easy to solve. Read only in the volumes of *Industrial Democracy* by Mr. and Mrs. Webb how many experiments the English trade unions had to make and are still making in order to find out the most serviceable forms of government and administration, and of what importance this question of constitution is to trade unions. The English trade unions have been able to develop in this respect for over seventy years in perfect freedom. They began with the most elementary form of self-government and have been forced to convince themselves that this form is only suited to the most elementary organisms, for quite small, local unions. As they grew they gradually learned to renounce as injurious to their successful development certain cherished ideas of doctrinaire democracy (the imperative mandate, the unpaid official, the powerless central representation), and to form instead of it a democracy capable of governing with representative assemblies, paid officials, and central government with full powers.

* * *

Meantime we are not yet so far on, and it is not my intention to unfold pictures of the future. I am not concerned with what will happen in the more distant future, but with what can and ought to happen in the present, for the present and the nearest future. And so the conclusion of this exposition is the very banal statement that the conquest of the democracy, the formation of political and social organs of the democracy, is the indispensable preliminary condition to the realisation of socialism.

Feudalism, with its unbending organisations and corporations, had to be destroyed nearly everywhere by violence. The liberal organisations of modern society are distinguished from those exactly because they are flexible, and capable of change and development. They do not need to be destroyed, but only to be further developed. For that we need organisation and energetic action, but not necessarily a revolutionary dictatorship. . . .

The present is a revolutionary age, and the place of revolutions on the Marxist plan raises questions of global concern. Dr. Ulam, professor of government at Harvard University, views the Marxist analysis of the ills of contemporary society through modern (and somewhat jaundiced) eyes.

FROM The Unfinished Revolution BY ADAM B. ULAM

The eternal battle array of history always ranges the oppressor against the oppressed, most commonly the owner of the means of production against the man who works with them. Only in the very beginning of human society was there no class struggle, just as there will be none in its culmination. Between the most primitive tribal community and the socialist-communist era, "the history of all hitherto existing society is the history of class struggles." Capitalism witnesses this struggle in the most simplified form: the proletariat against the capitalists. The victory of the proletariat will bring with it the abolition of the class struggle. The discovery of private property disrupted the social innocence of mankind. The full utilization of mankind's productive powers under socialism will restore it. With the disappearance of private property and of the class struggle, most of the social evils will disappear and with them the rationale for oppressive institutions, including the state.

This is the most clear-cut and internally consistent of all Marxist arguments. From its ringing formulation in the *Communist Manifesto* to the end of their lives, Marx and Engels never doubted that they had found the operat-

From *The Unfinished Revolution*, pp. 32–44, by Adam B. Ulam. © Copyright 1960 by Adam B. Ulam. Reprinted by permission of Random House, Inc.

ing pattern of history, that the reality of social and political life is expressed, not in the struggle of ideas, dynasties, or nations, but in the class struggle grounded in economic motivation. To their followers, the principle was a satisfactory explanation and a reliable guide to action, with none of the puzzling qualities of Marxist economics or overall philosophy. Class struggle became, in effect, the major portion of the revolutionary appeal of Marxism. Workers do not strike or storm the barricades in order to abolish surplus value. They strike and revolt against oppressive conditions, against the capitalists. From the point of view of political action, the slogan of class struggle is the simplest guide. It is also the simplest, most convincing revolutionary explanation of politics and history.

A deceptive simplicity! It has misled both the critics and the followers of Marxism. It has led Marxist movements too often to identify Marxist politics with a simple posture of opposition to the exploiting classes. The dominant faction of the German Social Democrats before World War I defined their Marxism as hostility to the imperial institutions and middle-class parties of their country. It led the Bolsheviks, in the first flush of their victory in 1917, to believe that by destroying the capitalists they were destroying capitalism. It has led people versed in Marxism to express surprise that many secondary features of capitalism "suddenly" made their appearance in Soviet Russia in the 1930's. Marxism became identified with insurrectionary action or with hostility, open and uncompromising, to capitalism and to everything and everyone connected with it.

It is necessary to repeat (as it will be again) what is perhaps the most pregnant sentence in Marx's view of social revolution, describing the role of the capitalist: "He thus forces the development of the productive powers of society, and creates *those material conditions, which alone can form the real basis of a higher form of society,* a society in which the full and free development of every individual forms the ruling principle." Nothing in the *main body* of Marx and Engels' writing suggests that any political development, even a seizure of power by the proletariat, can abrogate the laws governing the material development of mankind. From the earliest days of their association, the days filled with the most immediate revolutionary hope, Marx and Engels believed in the primacy of material factors over political action. It is always possible to find an incident or a statement by one or the other that would range them in the camp of believers in revolution pure and simple and hang the stage of economic development. (Thus the brief "Blanquist" period of Marx's early revolutionary activity, and, late in his life, his opinion that Russia might skip the full capitalist phase and pass into socialism from precapitalism.) But it is impossible to claim that such incidents or utterances represent the main tendency of Marxism or, as M. Rubel claims in his excellent biography, that Marx ultimately abandoned economic determinism in favor of unconditional faith in the ideal of human liberation.[1]

---

[1] Maximilien Rubel, *Karl Marx: Essai de biographie intellectuelle,* Paris, 1957.

What bridges the gap between economic determinism on the one hand and class struggle and the call to the proletariat to seize power on the other is Marx's revolutionary optimism. In the 1840's and early '50's, he believed that capitalism was on its last legs, that the economic as well as the political conditions for its downfall were at hand. It is true, as M. Rubel reminds us, that Marx was a socialist long before he discovered his economic system. It is true that the fascination of political economy engrossed and captured him, pushing his thought in directions he had perhaps not envisaged as a young man. But his socialism and his "discovery" of the class struggle did not precede his distaste for the existing moralistic brands of socialism and the determination to place *his* socialism on a firm, materialistic, scientific basis.

Again, what is difficult for us to understand from the perspective of a hundred years becomes easier if we immerse ourselves in the feeling of the period. How could a man believe both that capitalism was a necessary phase of the development of mankind and that Western European capitalism circa 1850 had played its role and was ready to leave the stage? The simple answer is that Marx and Engels shared not only the expectations of many radicals and socialists of the day, but also the apprehensions of many capitalists and liberal economists. Social and economic unrest had risen in ascending proportion from the introduction of what are *to us* the rudimentary institutions of capitalism to the middle of the nineteenth century. Was it entirely unreasonable to expect a fairly early economic collapse as well as a political revolution? Or to see a democratic revolution as a far-reaching step toward socialism? Many revolutionaries live expecting their revolution to take place any day. In Marx the faith of a revolutionary was complemented by the analysis of a social scientist. It is easy for us to say that Marx was wrong: capitalism did not collapse in Europe in 1850 or in 1860. But he was also right, though on wrong premises: what he assumed were relatively late stages of capitalism in France and England were in effect the early stages of industrialization and modernization in those countries, and in those stages capitalism is most vulnerable to class struggle.

Without revolutionary optimism, the doctrine of the class struggle, when joined with economic determinism, is a somber and tragic lesson. Except at the turning points in history, there is nothing the oppressed can do against the oppressor. The slave cannot prevail against his master, the serf against the landowner; and one type of oppression disappears only to be reborn in a different form of exploitation of man by man. Class struggle is compounded in the character of law and civilization imposed by each dominant class. Systems of religion and ethics serve to reinforce and to conceal at the same time the interest of the dominant class. Ever since he had seen, as a young man, the diet of his province discuss draconic laws against the removal of timber from state and private forests by the poor, all of Marx's instincts rebelled at the myth of the impartial state, impartial law. The system of private property under capitalism embodies best the double deception by which each exploiting class masks its exploiting role. It protects the capitalist against any tampering with his property, and it seeks to create the illusion of equality and impartiality for all. The plea for democratic franchise that the bourgeoisie makes is likewise a weapon of its class struggle. It seeks to strip the landlords of the remnants of their power and to delude the proletariat into believing that the essential issues are political in nature. The principle of class struggle illuminates world history by stripping it of its theatrical aspects of national struggles or contests about principles, and by demonstrating its material nature. Marx's is the "inside story" of world history, with economic interest its moving principle.

The "exposure" of history and politics was not unique to Marx. The dominant role of "interest" in politics and recent history was a cardinal tenet of the liberalism of his time. The sense of politics consisted in the struggle of classes seeking the advancement of their material interests. Thus the political struggle in the England of the thirties and forties between the Whigs and the Tories was interpreted as centering around the contest between the agricultural and the manufacturing interests. Liberal economists saw in their doctrine a guide to public policies that would secure a "harmony of interests," but they were far from assuming that the correctness of their theories would of itself secure their adoption, or that a collusion of vested interests could not—as well as ignorance—hamper public welfare. The liberal version was already a "suspicious" theory of history, with the material interests of classes lurking behind the struggle for politics and principles.

Marx elevates this suspicion into certainty. Thus, for example, the Glorious Revolution of 1688 is not primarily a victory of parliamentarianism over royal despotism, but a harbinger of bourgeois domination, with the Stock Exchange and other rudimentary institutions of capitalism soon to be established. In a sense, the Marxist class-struggle interpretation of history is more "historical" than the liberal one. In the liberal outlook, history had been a period of darkness and superstition until the sixteenth and seventeenth centuries, and only then had scientific principle begun to assert itself in thinking about human affairs. To Marx, on the other hand, the class struggle provided the rationale of social systems and philosophies from earliest times; the pattern of history is always meaningful if we follow the class-struggle principle and its economic underpinning. The Middle Ages are thus not merely a period of darkness and obscurantism: their social and religious ideas are perfectly understandable in terms of the then dominant mode of production and system of property. Marxist historical analysis and methods of investigation have had an influence on many historians, some of whom would repudiate indignantly the charge of having anything to do with Marxism.

* * *

Marx cannot be reproached with having overlooked the differentiation and proliferation of social classes in his society. Indeed, ostensible political activity consists in various classes and subclasses playing for, or being played for, power in the state. But the essence of the class struggle and its eventual determination is much simpler. Only two classes really count—the capitalists and the proletariat. Other classes and subclasses play increasingly minor roles in the drama of capitalism. Sooner or later they retire into the wings, leaving the stage to the two great antagonists. Insofar as it is the logic of history, i.e., the development of productive forces, and not the temporary whims or affiliations of groups of population that ordain social stratifications, only two classes will remain, and they are "really" the only classes in the true sense of the word. Capitalism is already destroying the landowning nobility, and it will destroy the peasants.

*　*　*

The two classes that are to square off in the last phase of the class struggle are quite dissimilar in many characteristics. The capitalist class is forever growing smaller in numbers; the proletariat, the exploited, ever larger. The rationale of the capitalist process, while it makes the capitalists aware of certain interests they have in common, still obliges them to engage in suicidal competition. The capitalist-industrial process makes the workers more and more unified in the realization of their common interest and in their class solidarity. The peasants, for instance, because of their dispersion, because of the peculiarity of their way of living, can never achieve real solidarity and a real community of interest and feeling; and thus, apart from their marginal economic significance, they can never constitute a true class. The workers, on the contrary, are disciplined by the circumstances of their work, brought together in great aggregations where they can feel the community of their privations and realize the logic of capitalism as leading to socialism. The *spontaneous growth* of class consciousness accompanies the growth of the captialist-industrial system. . . .

Here we may observe certain interesting connotations of the concept. It is *rationalistic* in the extreme. The working class will not be distracted from the obligation and the realization of the inevitability of the class struggle by nationalistic or religious slogans and considerations. Only a degenerate, rootless portion of it, the *Lumpenproletariat,* may capitulate to the schemes of reactionaries and adventurers. The vast majority of the workers will understand their historical position and historical mission. The vision of the working class is Hegelian in its underpinnings. The proletariat is the universal class, carrying in its future the destiny of mankind, thus parallel in its function to Rousseau's General Will and Hegel's State. The loss of individuality caused and made inevitable by factory labor, the worker's *alienation,* carries in it the seeds of the fullest assertion of individuality under socialism, which comes as a Hegelian "negation of a negation." In more prosaic terms, the factory system is inevitably oppressive and inevitably felt by the worker as such. This oppression *inherent* in the system produces the class feeling. Capitalism = factory system = class consciousness is the line of argument, and a closer examination of each term of the triad will illuminate the nature and conditions of the appeal of Marxism.

The doctrines of the classes and the class struggle have, within the context of the Marxist system, some further rather unexpected connotations. Take the class struggle between the bourgeoisie and the proletariat. The latter, through strikes and political action, resists the inevitable tendency of the capitalists to increase the exploitation of the workers. Yet nothing is clearer according to the logic of the doctrine than that the class struggle cannot paralyze capitalism until the system is fully developed and ready to pass on, or until the proletariat is fully capable of wresting power from the bourgeoisie. What might be called guerrilla class warfare, endemic industrial strife, which would paralyze the system, is clearly against the logic of Marxist thought, even if paradoxically within its spirit: the worker has to get used to the hated factory system, has to undergo exploitation, before the material conditions of the society will allow the transition to socialism. From the perspective of a hundred years, we may appreciate how the Russian and Chinese Communists have taken to heart the logic of the last proposition.

There is no *mystique* of the working class in early Marxism, no extolling of humble material circumstances as being conducive to virtue. Workers are not asserted or called upon to be heroic. They are asserted and called upon to be rational, to develop class consciousness. To Marx, nothing would have been more distasteful than the emotional undertones of later syndicalism. The ideal (in Weber's sense of the term) Marxist worker is a curiously unemotional creature. He has no country, no real family life; and his main objective in life is not an amelioration of his conditions, but the overthrow of the whole capitalist system. His sense of suffering injustice, of being exploited, does not deceive him into immediate action against the immediate agents of oppression—the factory and the employer—but into a *planned* struggle against capitalism and the capitalist state. In his political writings and speeches, Marx makes eloquent and emotion-tinged appeals, but the fact is that the main tenet of his theory about the worker and the class struggle is coldly rational in its logic. Human passion and generosity cannot in the last analysis prevail against the facts of history. The drama of the class struggle and the heroic exploits of the working-class revolutionaries are secondary to the working out of material forces. One cannot divorce economic evolution from the human drama that underlies it, but one must not ignore the laws of economics in revolutionary action. It is only a superficial reader of Marxism who would read into it the assumption that the proletariat may by political or insurrectionary action void the laws of history and avoid, say, by seizing power before capitalism is fully established, the hardships and privation of the factory system.

The idea of the class struggle serves to disprove the facile optimism of the liberals for whom, in all the clashes of interests, an "invisible hand" assured in a rationally organized society the harmony of individual and class self-interest with the general welfare. Marx's "invisible hand" is the very visible forces of production, which by their evolution confront each succeeding civilization with a different type of class warfare until, finally developed, they bring about classless society.

The centering of the social problem around the individual is, according to Marx, another pious hypocrisy of liberalism. Individual liberty and due process of law are, within a capitalist society, simply contradictions in terms. They are at most scraps of concessions thrown by the bourgeois state to deceive the proletariat, and in the circumstances of the workers' life under capitalism, they are of no value to them. This contemptuous attitude toward civil liberties, of such great historical significance to Marxism, is attuned to the circumstances of the worst period of the Industrial Revolution: with the proletarian working twelve and fourteen hours a day, and his wife and underage children also in unregulated industrial labor, the Bill of Rights did not, in fact, appear of overwhelming importance to the working class. The class struggle becomes the doctrine of total distrust of the capitalist state, with its laws, bureaucracy, and ideology. The violence of this distrust and opposition, the difficulty Marx and Engels experienced in acknowledging even the slightest social-welfare aspect of the bourgeois state, have often led to the optical illusion that Marxism was opposed to the state as such. It has enabled the revolutionary Marxists to denounce *the state,* with all the accents and conviction of anarchists, forgetting, for the moment, that the centralized state, like the capitalism of which it is a necessary ingredient, is an inevitable part of the historical process.

* * *

Here, then, is a theory attuned even more closely than other parts of Marxism to the facts and feelings of an early period of industrialization. The class struggle is the salt of Marxism, its most operative revolutionary part. As a historical and psychological concept, it expresses a gross oversimplification, but it is the oversimplification of a genius. The formula of the class struggle seizes the essence of the mood of a great historical moment—a revolution in basic economy—and generalizes it into a historical law. It extracts the grievances of groups of politically conscious workers in Western Europe, then a very small part of the whole proletariat, and sees in it the portent and meaning of the awakening of the whole working class everywhere. The first reaction of the worker to industrialization, his feelings of grievance and impotence before the machine, his employer, and the state which stands behind the employer, are assumed by Marx to be typical of the general reactions of the worker to industrialization. What does change in the process of the development of industry is that the worker's feeling of impotence gives way to class consciousness, which in turn leads him to class struggle and socialism. Marx's worker is the historical worker, but he is the historical worker of a specific period of industrial and political development.

Even in interpreting the psychology of the worker of the transitional period, Marx exhibited a rationalistic bias. The worker's opposition to the capitalist order is a total opposition to its laws, its factories, and its government. But this revolutionary consciousness of the worker is to take him next to Marxist socialism, where he will accept the factory system and the state, the *only* difference being the abolition of capitalism. Why shouldn't the revolutionary protest of the worker flow into other channels: into rejection of industrialism as well as capitalism, into rejection of the socialist as well as the capitalist state? It is here that Marx is most definitely the child of his age, the child of rationalistic optimism: the workers will undoubtedly translate their anarchistic protests and grievances into a sophisticated philosophy of history. They will undoubtedly realize that the forces of industrialism and modern life, which strip them of property, status, and economic security, are in themselves benevolent in their ultimate effects and that it is only capitalism and the capitalists which make them into instruments of oppression. The chains felt by the proletariat are the chains of the industrial system. The chains Marx urges them to throw off are those of capitalism. Will the workers understand the difference? And if they do, will they still feel that in destroying capitalism they have a "world to win"?

3
THE PARTICIPANTS' VIEWS

The real teachings of Marxism on revolution were of more than academic importance. The Marxist in many countries was betting his life on the truth of the system; a misinterpretation could lead not only to the failure of the Socialist movement but also to imprisonment or death. It was a high price to pay for misreading the Marxist texts, and the leaders of the Socialist movement in the various countries of Europe were concerned to establish an official reading.

The selections that follow illustrate two approaches: the "hard" one of Nikolai Lenin (1870–1924), to whom revolution was fundamental, and the "soft" one of Karl Kautsky (1854–1938), to whom revolution was no longer necessary.

FROM State and Revolution BY NIKOLAI LENIN

We must . . . note that Engels quite definitely regards universal suffrage as a means of bourgeois domination. Universal suffrage, he says, obviously summing up the long experience of German Social-Democracy, is "an index of the maturity of the working class; it cannot, and never will, be anything else but that in the modern state."

The petty-bourgeois democrats, such as our Socialist-Revolutionaries and Mensheviks, and also their twin brothers, the social-chauvinists and opportunists of Western Europe, all expect "more" from universal suffrage. They themselves share, and instil into the minds of the people, the wrong idea that

V. I. Lenin, *State and Revolution*, pp. 14–20. Reprinted by permission of International Publishers Co., Inc. Copyright 1932 by International Publishers Co., Inc.

universal suffrage "in the *modern* state" is really capable of expressing the will of the majority of the toilers and of assuring its realisation.

We can here only note this wrong idea, only point out that this perfectly clear, exact and concrete statement by Engels is distorted at every step in the propaganda and agitation of the "official" (*i.e.,* opportunist) Socialist parties. A detailed analysis of all the falseness of this idea, which Engels brushes aside, is given in our further account of the views of Marx and Engels on the "modern" state.

A general summary of his views is given by Engels in the most popular of his works in the following words:

The state, therefore, has not existed from all eternity. There have been societies which managed without it, which had no conception of the state and state power. At a certain stage of economic development, which was necessarily bound up with the cleavage of society into classes, the state became a necessity owing to this cleavage. We are now rapidly approaching a stage in the development of production at which the existence of these classes has not only ceased to be a necessity, but is becoming a positive hindrance to production. They will disappear as inevitably as they arose at an earlier stage. Along with them, the state will inevitably disappear. The society that organises production anew on the basis of a free and equal association of the producers will put the whole state machine where it will then belong: in the museum of antiquities, side by side with the spinning wheel and the bronze axe.

It is not often that we find this passage quoted in the propaganda and agitation literature of contemporary Social-Democracy. But even when we do come across it, it is generally quoted in the same manner as one bows before an icon, *i.e.,* it is done merely to show official respect for Engels, without any attempt to gauge the breadth and depth of revolutionary action presupposed by this relegating of "the whole state machine . . . to the museum of antiquities." In most cases we do not even find an understanding of what Engels calls the state machine.

* * *

Without fear of committing an error, it may be said that of this argument by Engels so singularly rich in ideas, only one point has become an integral part of Socialist thought among modern Socialist parties, namely, that, unlike the Anarchist doctrine of the "abolition" of the state, according to Marx the state "withers away." To emasculate Marxism in such a manner is to reduce it to opportunism for such an "interpretation" only leaves the hazy conception of a slow, even, gradual change, free from leaps and storms, free from revolution. The current popular conception, if one may say so, of the "withering away" of the state undoubtedly means a slurring over, if not a negation, of revolution.

Yet, such an "interpretation" is the crudest distortion of Marxism, which is advantageous only to the bourgeoisie; in point of theory, it is based on a disregard for the most important circumstances and considerations pointed out in the very passage summarising Engels' ideas, which we have just quoted in full.

In the first place, Engels at the very outset of his argument says that, in assuming state power, the proletariat by that very act "puts an end to the state as the state." One is "not accustomed" to reflect on what this really means Generally, it is either ignored altogether, or it is considered as a piece of "Hegelian weakness" on Engels' part. As a matter of fact, however, these words express succinctly the experience of one of the greatest proletarian revolutions—the Paris Commune of 1871, of which we shall speak in greater detail in its proper place. As a matter of fact, Engels speaks here of the destruction of the bourgeois state by the proletarian revolution, while the words about its withering away refer to the remains of *proletarian* statehood *after* the Socialist revolution. The bourgeois state does not "wither away," according to Engels, but is "put an end to" by the proletariat in the course of the revolution. What withers away after the revolution is the proletarian state or semi-state.

Secondly, the state is a "special repressive force." This splendid and extremely profound definition of Engels' is given by him here with complete lucidity. It follows from this that the "special repressive force" of the bourgeoisie for the suppression of the proletariat, of the millions of workers by a handful of the rich, must be replaced by a "special repressive force" of the proletariat for the suppression of the bourgeoisie (the dictatorship of the proletariat). It is just this that constitutes the "act" of "the seizure of the means of production in the name of society." And it is obvious that such a substitution of one (proletarian) "special repressive force" for another (bourgeois) "special repressive force" can in no way take place in the form of a "withering away."

Thirdly, as to the "withering away" or, more expressively and colourfully, as to the state "becoming dormant," Engels refers quite clearly and definitely to the period *after* "the seizure of the means of production [by the state] in the name of society," that is, *after* the Socialist revolution. We all know that the political form of the "state" at that time is complete democracy. But it never enters the head of any of the opportunists who shamelessly distort Marx that when Engels speaks here of the state "withering away," or "becoming dormant," he speaks of *democracy*. At first sight this seems very strange. But it is "unintelligible" only to one who has not reflected on the fact that democracy is *also* a state and that, consequently, democracy will *also* disappear when the state disappears. The bourgeois state can only be "put an end to" by a revolution. The state in general, *i.e.,* most complete democracy, can only "wither away."

Fourthly, having formulated his famous proposition that "the state withers away," Engels at once explains concretely that this proposition is directed equally against the opportunists and the Anarchists. In doing this, however,

Engels puts in the first place that conclusion from his proposition about the "withering away" of the state which is directed against the opportunists.

One can wager that out of every 10,000 persons who have read or heard about the "withering away" of the state, 9,990 do not know at all, or do not remember, that Engels did not direct his conclusions from this proposition against the Anarchists *alone*. And out of the remaining ten, probably nine do not know the meaning of a "people's free state" nor the reason why an attack on this watchword contains an attack on the opportunists. This is how history is written! This is how a great revolutionary doctrine is imperceptibly adulterated and adapted to current philistinism! The conclusion drawn against the Anarchists has been repeated thousands of times, vulgarised, harangued about in the crudest fashion possible until it has acquired the strength of a prejudice, whereas the conclusion drawn against the opportunists has been hushed up and "forgotten"!

The "people's free state" was a demand in the programme of the German Social-Democrats and their current slogan in the 'seventies. There is no political substance in this slogan other than a pompous middle-class circumlocution of the idea of democracy. In so far as it referred in a lawful manner to a democratic republic, Engels was prepared to "justify" its use "at times" from a propaganda point of view. But this slogan was opportunist, for it not only expressed an exaggerated view of the attractiveness of bourgeois democracy, but also a lack of understanding of the Socialist criticism of every state in general. We are in favour of a democratic republic as the best form of the state for the proletariat under capitalism, but we have no right to forget that wage slavery is the lot of the people even in the most democratic bourgeois republic. Furthermore, every state is a "special repressive force" for the suppression of the oppressed class. Consequently, *no* state is either "free" or a "people's state." Marx and Engels explained this repeatedly to their party comrades in the 'seventies.

Fifthly, in the same work of Engels, from which every one remembers his argument on the "withering away" of the state, there is also a disquisition on the significance of a violent revolution. The historical analysis of its rôle becomes, with Engels, a veritable panegyric on violent revolution. This, of course, "no one remembers"; to talk or even to think of the importance of this idea is not considered good form by contemporary Socialist parties, and in the daily propaganda and agitation among the masses it plays no part whatever. Yet it is indissolubly bound up with the "withering away" of the state in one harmonious whole.

Here is Engels' argument:

. . . That force, however, plays another rôle (other than that of a diabolical power) in history, a revolutionary rôle; that, in the words of Marx, it is the midwife of every old society which is pregnant with the new; that it is the instrument with whose aid social movement forces its way through and shatters the dead, fossilised political forms—of this there is not a word in Herr Dühring. It is only with sighs and groans that he admits the possibility that force will perhaps be necessary for the overthrow of the economic system of exploitation—unfortunately! because all use of force, forsooth, demoralises the person who uses it. And this in spite of the immense moral and spiritual impetus which has resulted from every victorious revolution! And this in Germany, where a violent collision—which indeed may be forced on the people—would at least have the advantage of wiping out the servility which has permeated the national consciousness as a result of the humiliation of the Thirty Years' War. And this parson's mode of thought—lifeless, insipid and impotent—claims to impose itself on the most revolutionary party which history has known?

How can this panegyric on violent revolution, which Engels insistently brought to the attention of the German Social-Democrats between 1878 and 1894, *i.e.*, right to the time of his death, be combined with the theory of the "withering away" of the state to form one doctrine?

Usually the two views are combined by means of eclecticism, by an unprincipled, sophistic, arbitrary selection (to oblige the powers that be) of either one or the other argument, and in ninety-nine cases out of a hundred (if not more often), it is the idea of the "withering away" that is specially emphasised. Eclecticism is substituted for dialectics—this is the most usual, the most widespread phenomenon to be met with in the official Social-Democratic literature of our day in relation to Marxism. Such a substitution is, of course, nothing new; it may be observed even in the history of classic Greek philosophy. When Marxism is adulterated to become opportunism, the substitution of eclecticism for dialectics is the best method of deceiving the masses; it gives an illusory satisfaction; it seems to take into account all sides of the process, all the tendencies of development, all the contradictory factors and so forth, whereas in reality it offers no consistent and revolutionary view of the process of social development at all.

We have already said above and shall show more fully later that the teaching of Marx and Engels regarding the inevitability of a violent revolution refers to the bourgeois state. It *cannot* be replaced by the proletarian state (the dictatorship of the proletariat) through "withering away," but, as a general rule, only through a violent revolution. The panegyric sung in its honour by Engels and fully corresponding to the repeated declarations of Marx (remember the concluding passages of the *Poverty of Philosophy* and the *Communist Manifesto,* with its proud and open declaration of the inevitability of a violent revolution; remember Marx's *Critique of the Gotha Programme* of 1875 in which, almost thirty years later, he mercilessly castigates the opportunist character of that programme)—this praise is by no means a mere "impulse," a mere declamation, or a polemical sally. The necessity of systematically fostering among the masses *this* and just this point of view about violent revolution lies at the root of the *whole* of Marx's and Engels' teaching. The neglect of such propaganda and agitation by both the present predominant social-chauvinist and the Kautskyist currents brings their betrayal of Marx's and Engels' teaching into prominent relief.

The replacement of the bourgeois by the proletarian state is impossible without a violent revolution. The abolition of the proletarian state, *i.e.,* of all states, is only possible through "withering away."

Marx and Engels gave a full and concrete exposition of these views in studying each revolutionary situation separately, in analysing the lessons of the experience of each individual revolution. We now pass to this, undoubtedly the most important part of their work.

Karl Kautsky (1854–1938) was one of the leading theoreticians of the German Social Democratic party. The selection that follows—Kautsky's attempt to come to grips with the problem of the necessity of revolution in a state with democratic institutions—is from a book review written by him in 1893.

from A Social Democratic Catechism by karl kautsky

We are revolutionaries, and not merely in the sense that the steam engine is revolutionary. The social overturn at which we aim can only be achieved through a political revolution, through the conquest of political power by the fighting proletariat. And the specific form of government in which alone socialism can be realized is the republic, that is—as the phrase is commonly understood—in the democratic republic.

* * *

Social Democracy is a revolutionary—but not a revolution-making—party. We know that our aims can only be achieved through a revolution, but we also know that it is as little in our power to make that revolution as it is in the power of our enemies to prevent it. It does not occur to us, therefore, to want to either plot or instigate a revolution. And since the revolution cannot arbitrarily be made by us, we cannot even attempt to describe when, under what circumstances, and in which form it will break out. We do know that the class struggle between bourgeoisie and proletariat will not end before the latter has come into full possession of political power, which it will use to establish the socialist society. We do know that this class struggle must be-

Karl Kautsky, "Ein Sozialdemokratischer Katechismus," *Neue Zeit* (December 1893), pp. 368–369, 402–405, 409–410, translated by Walter R. Weitzmann.

come more intensive and extensive, that the proletariat will grow in numbers and in moral and economic power and that, therefore, its victory and capitalism's defeat are inevitable. But we can venture only the vaguest guesses about how the last decisive battles in this social war will be fought.

* * *

Since we know nothing about the decisive battles of the social war we can, of course, say little about their character—whether they will be bloody, whether physical violence will play a dominant rôle, or whether they will be fought exclusively by means of economic, legislative, and moral pressures.

But we can say that it is very probable that in the revolutionary struggles of the proletariat the latter [non-violent] means will have greater predominance over the use of physical, i.e., military, force, than was the case in the revolutionary struggles of the bourgeoisie.

One reason why the coming revolutionary struggles will be fought less and less with military means is, as has often been said, that the equipment of government troops is today vastly superior to the weapons available to the "civilians." As a rule, this disparity makes all the latters' resistance hopeless from the start. On the other hand, today's revolutionary strata have available to them better weapons of economic, political and moral resistance than had those of the previous century. The only exception to this is Russia.

Freedom of association, of press, and universal suffrage (under some circumstances, universal military service, as well), are, however, not merely weapons that give the proletariat of modern nations an advantage not possessed by the classes that fought the revolutionary battles of the bourgeoisie. These institutions also spread over the power relations of individual classes and parties, and the spirit which animates them is a light which was missing during the absolutist era.

Then, the ruling classes as well as the revolutionary classes groped about in the dark. Because the expression of opposition was made impossible, neither the governments nor the revolutionaries had any way to measure their strengths. Each of the two groups was therefore in danger of overestimating its strength before it had tested it in battle with its opponent, and equally, of underestimating it when it suffered a single defeat—quickly throwing in the towel. This is probably the main reason why we find, in the era of the revolutionary bourgeoisie, so many *coups* so easily put down, and so many governments so easily toppled—a succession, therefore, of revolution and counterrevolution.

It is entirely different today, at least in countries with somewhat democratic institutions. These institutions have been called the safety valve of society. If one means by this that the proletariat in a democracy ceases to be revolutionary, that it remains satisfied with merely expressing its resentment and its suffering publicly, and that it renounces political and social revolution, then this designation is wrong. Democracy cannot do away with the class contradictions of capitalist society, and it cannot prevent their necessary final result, the overthrow of this social system. But it can do one thing: though it cannot prevent the revolution, it can prevent some foredoomed revolutionary attempts and forestall some revolutionary uprisings. Democracy produces clarity about the relative strength of different parties and classes; though it cannot resolve their opposition nor transform their final aims, it does tend to prevent the rising classes from attempting to solve problems which they are not yet strong enough to tackle, and it tends, in turn, to keep the ruling classes from denying concessions which they are no longer strong enough to do. The direction of development is not thereby changed, but its pace becomes steadier and calmer. In states with democratic institutions the advance of the proletariat will be accompanied by less striking successes than was the rise of the bourgeoisie during its revolutionary epoch. But neither will it be marked by as severe defeats. Since the awakening of the modern social democratic workers' movement in the sixties the European proletariat has suffered only one great defeat—in the Paris Commune of 1871. At that time France was still suffering from the imprint of the Empire which had deprived the people of truly democratic institutions; the French proletariat had reached only a low level of self-consciousness, and the uprising had been forced upon them.

The democratic parliamentary method of struggle may appear more tedious than the method used in the revolutionary epoch of the bourgeoisie. It is true that it is less dramatic and showy, but it also produces fewer casualties. This may be a matter of indifference to that aestheticised group of literati which dabbles in socialism solely to find interesting sport and copy, but it is not unimportant to those who have to wage the struggle.

The more effective the democratic institutions and the greater the political and economic awareness and self-control of the populace, the better are the chances that so-called peaceful means of class struggle, those that limit themselves to non-violent means such as parliamentarianism, strikes, demonstrations, use of the press and other means of pressure, will be used.

Given any two opponents and everything else being equal, the one who feels superior to the other will most likely maintain his *sang-froid*. Someone who does not believe in himself and his cause is only too likely to lose his equanimity and control.

Now the class which in every modern country has the greatest faith in itself and its cause is the proletariat. To attain it it needs no false illusions. It needs only to examine the history of the last generation to see itself everywhere in uninterrupted advance. It needs only to study contemporary developments to gain the assurance that its victory is unavoidable. Hence, we should not expect the highly developed proletariat of a given country to easily lose its equanimity and self-control, or to inaugurate a policy of adventurism. The more educated and aware the working class and the more democratic the state, the less likely a policy of adventurism becomes.

But one cannot place equal confidence in the ruling class. Seeing and feeling themselves grow weaker every day, they become ever more anxious, and therefore unpredictable. Increasingly they sink into a mood where one must be prepared to see them seized by attacks of madness during which they fall upon their enemy in blind rage, intent upon finishing him off, mindless of the wounds they will thereby inflict upon all of society including themselves, and of the devastation they will wreak.

The political position of the proletariat is such that it will attempt as long as possible to advance by the aforementioned "legal" means. The danger that this aim will be frustrated lies in the jittery mood of the ruling classes.

The political leaders of the ruling classes hope for such madness to lay hold not just of the ruling classes but the indifferent masses as well, before Social Democracy is strong enough to resist. This is their only hope to delay the victory of socialism for at least another few years. But this is a desperate gamble. For if the bourgeoisie should fail in their mad attempt to suppress the proletariat, they will have exhausted their strength and will collapse even sooner while the proletariat triumphs even more quickly. But the predominant mood among many politicians of the ruling classes has already reached the point where they believe that nothing else can be done but to gamble everything on one card. They want to provoke civil war because they fear the revolution.

Social Democracy, on the other hand, has no reason to adopt such a policy of despair. It has every reason to avoid—and failing this to postpone—such madness in its rulers as long as possible. Ultimately, it must be delayed until the proletariat is strong enough to subdue and tame the maniacs, so that the havoc and its victims will be reduced and their attack be the last.

Social Democrats must, therefore, avoid and even combat anything that might be a purposeless provocation of the ruling classes; anything that might give their leaders an excuse to drive the bourgeoisie and its followers into a socialist-hating frenzy. Thus, when we declare that revolutions cannot be "made," when we condemn as nonsensical and dangerous the instigation of a revolution and act accordingly, we do this not to please the German state attorneys, but in the interest of the fighting proletariat. And in this position German Social Democrats stand united with their sister parties. Because of this stand it has so far been impossible for the leaders of the ruling classes to proceed against the fighting proletariat as they would have wished.

Though the political power of Social Democracy is still relatively small, socialists in modern nations are powerful enough to prevent bourgeois politicians from arbitrary actions. Minor regulations and ordinances cannot help them; they only embitter their subjects without discouraging them or reducing their fighting ability. Any attempt, however, to enact legislation that would seriously affect the proletariat's fighting capacity conjures up the danger of civil war which, whatever its outcome, would bring frightful devastation. This is fairly common knowledge. And though the bourgeois politicians may wish for a trial of strength with socialists before the latter are prepared, the bourgeois businessmen will have nothing to do with experiments which would ruin every one of them; at least in a rational state unaffected by the aforementioned madness. In a state of frenzy, the bourgeois can be gotten to support any measure, and the greater his fear, the wilder his cry for blood.

The interests of the proletariat demand even more authoritatively today than ever before that anything that might provoke the ruling classes into a policy of violence be avoided. Social Democrats act accordingly.

[*Kautsky then speaks of a tendency calling itself proletarian that advocates such a policy of provocation. This he calls "anarchism" and he spends the next five pages showing that Socialists must reject this anarchist direction, which has been responsible for all the setbacks of socialism since the Paris Commune—L. P. W.*]

The main lever of our success is our revolutionary enthusiasm. We shall need it even more in the future for the most difficult days lie not behind, but ahead of us. Thus anything that might immobilize this lever would be most detrimental to our cause.

Our present position, by making us appear more "moderate" than we really are, carries with it a certain danger. The stronger we are, the more the practical tasks take precedence: the more we must extend our agitation beyond the circle of the industrial wage workers, and the more we must guard against useless provocations or hollow threats. This makes it extremely difficult to maintain the proper balance; to give full attention to the needs of the present without losing sight of the future; to engage in a dialogue with the peasantry and lower middle class and yet not surrender the proletarian standpoint; to avoid all provocation and yet to convince everyone that we are a party of struggle in irreconcilable opposition to the existing social system.

THE ORIGINS
OF MODERN
IMPERIALISM

IDEOLOGICAL OR
ECONOMIC?

CONTENTS

QUESTIONS FOR STUDY

1. *What are the arguments in favor of imperialism offered by Chamberlain?*
2. *Do they lend support to Lenin's analysis?*
3. *What is the nature of Langer's criticism of the Marxist analysis?*
4. *What is the relation of Kipling's poem to the attitude of Strong?*
5. *In what ways does Schumpeter disagree with Lenin?*
6. *Is there a legitimate argument in favor of imperialism?*

For millennia tribes, peoples, and nations have engaged in aggressive expansion at the expense of their neighbors. In the period from about 1870 to World War I the nations of Europe, the United States, and Japan were all particularly active in extending their influence and control over many areas of the world. These nations had many things in common: they were all industrial powers for whom commerce was very important; they extended their power over countries that were generally less industrial or not industrial at all; their control was sometimes not territorial but merely commercial. This "new imperialism," a consequence of the industrial era, quickly brought about the partition of the underdeveloped regions of the world among the great industrial powers and soon produced theories of imperialism. What were its causes? its purposes? its results?

Probably the most influential attempt to account for modern imperialism was that put forward by Lenin (pp. 401–409). Based on the work of the English historian J. A. Hobson but altered in a more Marxian direction, Lenin's theory considers imperialism as uniquely and necessarily associated with capitalism. In brief, he defines imperialism as "the monopoly stage of capitalism." That stage is characterized, according to Lenin, by the concentration of production and capital to form monopolies, the emergence of "finance capital" and a "financial oligarchy," the growth of capital as an export, the formation of international capitalist monopolies, and the division of the world among the great capitalist powers. In its fullest form the Marxist-Leninist theory argues that imperialism is inevitable in a capitalist world. Overpopulation leads to the search for new markets for both products and capital. The ensuing competition must lead to imperialism and finally to war.

There is certainly some evidence in support of Lenin's thesis. Much of the imperialism of the nineteenth and twentieth centuries was, or claimed to be, economic in its purpose. Such advocates of empire as Joseph Chamberlain in England (pp. 410–420) and Jules Ferry in France argued openly for the economic advantages of an imperial policy. Naturally, they also stressed political and spiritual purposes as well, but they spoke unashamedly of their economic aims. There were, however, other advocates of imperialism who supported it for different reasons. Men like Rudyard Kipling (pp. 421–422) and the American clergyman Josiah Strong (pp. 423–429), influenced by Christianity, Social Darwinism, and theories of racial superiority, urged that the "advanced" powers of the West had a moral responsibility to uplift "less civilized" peoples. Their defense of imperialism may have been less rational, but it was no less vigorous than that of men like Chamberlain.

The nonrational basis for imperialism is seized upon and expounded by Joseph Schumpeter (pp. 430–436). He examines imperialism as a historical phenomenon of great antiquity and concludes that it was not necessarily associated with capitalism, not economic, and not even rational in its causes. He explains it as a form of "social atavism," a regression to "psychological dispositions and social structure acquired in the dim past." Schumpeter argues that modern capitalism produces attitudes and structures that are increasingly rational; thus he is led to a conclusion diametrically opposed to that of Lenin —"that capitalism is by nature anti-imperialist."

William Langer (pp. 437–451) challenges the Marxist analysis of Lenin not as a theorist but as a historian. He examines the history of European imperialism since the nineteenth century and argues that the facts refute the theory. Export of goods and capital was far greater to areas in no way controlled by the exporting power than it was to areas under colonial domination. Colonies, for the most part, proved bad economic investments. Economic and other rational considerations, according to Langer, do not support a satisfactory cause for Europe's imperial expansion. Nationalism, that great irrational and indefinable force in the modern world, seems to play a large part in the story of imperialism, and the strength of nationalist feeling in formerly colonial areas does not lead Langer to optimistic expectations for peace in the future.

1
IMPERIALISM
AND
CAPITALISM

The first full-scale economic explanation of imperialism was offered by John A. Hobson in 1902. It strongly influenced Lenin, who adapted it to suit Marxist principles and presented it in a form that has been very influential ever since.

FROM Imperialism, the Highest Stage of Capitalism
BY V. I. LENIN

We must now try to sum up and put together what has been said above on the subject of imperialism. Imperialism emerged as the development and direct continuation of the fundamental attributes of capitalism in general. But capitalism only became capitalist imperialism at a definite and very high stage of its development, when certain of its fundamental attributes began to be transformed into their opposites, when the features of a period of transition from capitalism to a higher social and economic system began to take shape and reveal themselves all along the line. Economically, the main thing in this process is the substitution of capitalist monopolies for capitalist free competition. Free competition is the fundamental attribute of capitalism, and of commodity production generally. Monopoly is exactly the opposite of free competition; but we have seen the latter being transformed into monopoly before our very eyes, creating large-scale industry and eliminating small industry, replacing large-scale industry by still larger-scale industry, finally leading to such a concentration of production and capital that monopoly has been and is the result: cartels, syndicates and trusts, and merging with them, the

V. I. Lenin, *Imperialism, the Highest Stage of Capitalism* (1939), pp. 88–98. Reprinted by permission of International Publishers Co., Inc.

capital of a dozen or so banks manipulating thousands of millions. At the same time monopoly, which has grown out of free competition, does not abolish the latter, but exists over it and alongside of it, and thereby gives rise to a number of very acute, intense antagonisms, friction and conflicts. Monopoly is the transition from capitalism to a higher system.

If it were necessary to give the briefest possible definition of imperialism we should have to say that imperialism is the monopoly stage of capitalism. Such a definition would include what is most important, for, on the one hand, finance capital is the bank capital of a few big monopolist banks, merged with the capital of the monopolist combines of manufacturers; and, on the other hand, the division of the world is the transition from a colonial policy which has extended without hindrance to territories unoccupied by any capitalist power, to a colonial policy of monopolistic possession of the territory of the world which has been completely divided up.

But very brief definitions, although convenient, for they sum up the main points, are nevertheless inadequate, because very important features of the phenomenon that has to be defined have to be especially deduced. And so, without forgetting the conditional and relative value of all definitions, which can never include all the concatenations of a phenomenon in its complete development, we must give a definition of imperialism that will embrace the following five essential features:

1. The concentration of production and capital developed to such a high stage that it created monopolies which play a decisive role in economic life.
2. The merging of bank capital with industrial capital, and the creation, on the basis of this "finance capital," of a "financial oligarchy."
3. The export of capital, which has become extremely important, as distinguished from the export of commodities.
4. The formation of international capitalist monopolies which share the world among themselves.
5. The territorial division of the whole world among the greatest capitalist powers is completed.

Imperialism is capitalism in that stage of development in which the dominance of monopolies and finance capital has established itself; in which the export of capital has acquired pronounced importance; in which the division of the world among the international trusts has begun; in which the division of all territories of the globe among the great capitalist powers has been completed.

We shall see later that imperialism can and must be defined differently if consideration is to be given, not only to the basic, purely economic factors—to which the above definition is limited—but also to the historical place of this stage of capitalism in relation to capitalism in general, or to the relations between imperialism and the two main trends in the working class movement. The point to be noted just now is that imperialism, as interpreted above, undoubtedly represents a special stage in the development of capitalism. In order to enable the reader to obtain as well grounded an idea of imperialism as possible, we deliberately quoted largely from *bourgeois* economists who are obliged to admit the particularly incontrovertible facts regarding modern capitalist economy. With the same object in view, we have produced detailed statistics which reveal the extent to which bank capital, etc., has developed, showing how the transformation of quantity into quality, of developed capitalism into imperialism, has expressed itself. Needless to say, all boundaries in nature and in society are conditional and changeable, and, consequently, it would be absurd to discuss the exact year or the decade in which imperialism "definitely" became established.

In this matter of defining imperialism, however, we have to enter into controversy, primarily, with K. Kautsky, the principal Marxian theoretician of the epoch of the so-called Second International—that is, of the twenty-five years between 1889 and 1914.

Kautsky, in 1915 and even in November 1914, very emphatically attacked the fundamental ideas expressed in our definition of imperialism. Kautsky said that imperialism must not be regarded as a "phase" or stage of economy, but as a policy; a definite policy "preferred" by finance capital; that imperialism cannot be "identified" with "contemporary capitalism"; that if imperialism is to be understood to mean "all the phenomena of contemporary capitalism"—cartels, protection, the domination of the financiers and colonial policy—then the question as to whether imperialism is necessary to capitalism becomes reduced to the "flattest tautology"; because, in that case, "imperialism is naturally a vital necessity for capitalism," and so on. The best way to present Kautsky's ideas is to quote his own definition of imperialism, which is diametrically opposed to the substance of the ideas which we have set forth (for the objections coming from the camp of the German Marxists, who have been advocating such ideas for many years already, have been long known to Kautsky as the objections of a definite trend in Marxism).

Kautsky's definition is as follows:

Imperialism is a product of highly developed industrial capitalism. It consists in the striving of every industrial capitalist nation to bring under its control and to annex increasingly big *agrarian* [Kautsky's italics] regions irrespective of what nations inhabit those regions.

This definition is utterly worthless because it one-sidedly, *i.e.,* arbitrarily, brings out the national question alone (although this is extremely important in itself as well as in its relation to imperialism), it arbitrarily and *inaccurately* relates this question *only* to industrial capital in the countries which annex other nations, and in an equally arbitrary and inaccurate manner brings out the annexation of agrarian regions.

Imperialism is a striving for annexations—this is what the *political* part of Kautsky's definition amounts to. It is correct, but very incomplete, for politically, imperialism is, in general, a striving towards violence and reaction. For the moment, however, we are interested in the *economic* aspect of the ques-

tion, which Kautsky *himself* introduced into *his* definition. The inaccuracy of
Kautsky's definition is strikingly obvious. The characteristic feature of imperialism is *not* industrial capital, *but* finance capital. It is not an accident that
in France it was precisely the extraordinarily rapid development of *finance*
capital, and the weakening of industrial capital, that, from 1880 onwards,
gave rise to the extreme extension of annexationist (colonial) policy. The
characteristic feature of imperialism is precisely that it strives to annex *not
only* agricultural regions, but even highly industrialised regions (German appetite for Belgium; French appetite for Lorraine), because 1) the fact that the
world is already divided up obliges those contemplating a *new* division to
reach out for *any kind* of territory, and 2) because an essential feature of
imperialism is the rivalry between a number of great powers in the striving
for hegemony, *i.e.,* for the conquest of territory, not so much directly for
themselves as to weaken the adversary and undermine *his* hegemony. (Belgium is chiefly necessary to Germany as a base for operations against England; England needs Bagdad as a base for operations against Germany, etc.)

Kautsky refers especially—and repeatedly—to English writers who, he alleges, have given a purely political meaning to the word "imperialism" in the
sense that Kautsky understands it. We take up the work by the Englishman
Hobson, *Imperialism,* which appeared in 1902, and therein we read:

The new imperialism differs from the older, first, in substituting for the ambition of a single growing empire the theory and the practice of competing empires,
each motivated by similar lusts of political aggrandisement and commercial gain;
secondly, in the dominance of financial or investing over mercantile interests.

We see, therefore, that Kautsky is absolutely wrong in referring to English writers generally (unless he meant the vulgar English imperialist writers,
or the avowed apologists for imperialism). We see that Kautsky, while claiming that he continues to defend Marxism, as a matter of fact takes a step
backward compared with the *social-liberal* Hobson, who *more correctly* takes
into account two "historically concrete" (Kautsky's definition is a mockery of
historical concreteness) features of modern imperialism: 1) the competition
between *several* imperialisms, and 2) the predominance of the financier over
the merchant. If it were chiefly a question of the annexation of agrarian countries by industrial countries, the role of the merchant would be predominant.

Kautsky's definition is not only wrong and un-Marxian. It serves as a basis
for a whole system of views which run counter to Marxian theory and Marxian practice all along the line. We shall refer to this again later. The argument about words which Kautsky raises as to whether the modern stage of
capitalism should be called "imperialism" or "the stage of finance capital" is
of no importance. Call it what you will, it matters little. The fact of the
matter is that Kautsky detaches the politics of imperialism from its economics, speaks of annexations as being a policy "preferred" by finance capital, and opposes to it another bourgeois policy which, he alleges, is possible

on this very basis of finance capital. According to his argument, monopolies in economics are compatible with non-monopolistic, non-violent, non-annexationist methods in politics. According to his argument, the territorial division of the world, which was completed precisely during the period of finance capital, and which constitutes the basis of the present peculiar forms of rivalry between the biggest capitalist states, is compatible with a non-imperialist policy. The result is a slurring-over and a blunting of the most profound contradictions of the latest stage of capitalism, instead of an exposure of their depth; the result is bourgeois reformism instead of Marxism.

Kautsky enters into controversy with the German apologist of imperialism and annexations, Cunow, who clumsily and cynically argues that: imperialism is modern capitalism, the development of capitalism is inevitable and progressive; therefore imperialism is progressive; therefore, we should cringe before and eulogise it. This is something like the caricature of Russian Marxism which the Narodniki drew in 1894-95. They used to argue as follows: if the Marxists believe that capitalism is inevitable in Russia, that it is progressive, then they ought to open a public-house and begin to implant capitalism! Kautsky's reply to Cunow is as follows: imperialism is not modern capitalism. It is only one of the forms of the policy of modern capitalism. This policy we can and should fight; we can and should fight against imperialism, annexations, etc.

The reply seems quite plausible, but in effect it is a more subtle and more disguised (and therefore more dangerous) propaganda of conciliation with imperialism; for unless it strikes at the economic basis of the trusts and banks, the "struggle" against the policy of the trusts and banks reduces itself to bourgeois reformism and pacifism, to an innocent and benevolent expression of pious hopes. Kautsky's theory means refraining from mentioning existing contradictions, forgetting the most important of them, instead of revealing them in their full depth; it is a theory that has nothing in common with Marxism. Naturally, such a "theory" can only serve the purpose of advocating unity with the Cunows.

Kautsky writes: "from the purely economic point of view it is not impossible that capitalism will yet go through a new phase, that of the extension of the policy of the cartels to foreign policy, the phase of ultra-imperialism," *i.e.,* of a super-imperialism, a union of world imperialisms and not struggles among imperialisms; a phase when wars shall cease under capitalism, a phase of "the joint exploitation of the world by internationally combined finance capital."

We shall have to deal with this "theory of ultra-imperialism" later on in order to show in detail how definitely and utterly it departs from Marxism. In keeping with the plan of the present work, we shall examine the exact economic data on this question. Is "ultra-imperialism" possible "from the purely economic point of view" or is it ultra-nonsense?

If, by purely economic point of view a "pure" abstraction is meant, then all that can be said reduces itself to the following proposition: evolution is proceeding towards monopoly; therefore the trend is towards a single world monopoly, to a universal trust. This is indisputable, but it is also as completely meaningless as is the statement that "evolution is proceeding" towards the manufacture of foodstuffs in laboratories. In this sense the "theory" of ultra-imperialism is no less absurd than a "theory of ultra-agriculture" would be.

If, on the other hand, we are discussing the "purely economic" conditions of the epoch of finance capital as an historically concrete epoch which opened at the beginning of the twentieth century, then the best reply that one can make to the lifeless abstractions of "ultra-imperialism" (which serve an exclusively reactionary aim: that of diverting attention from the depth of *existing* antagonisms) is to contrast them with the concrete economic realities of present-day world economy. Kautsky's utterly meaningless talk about ultra-imperialism encourages, among other things, that profoundly mistaken idea which only brings grist to the mill of the apologists of imperialism, *viz.,* that the rule of finance capital *lessens* the unevenness and contradictions inherent in world economy, whereas in reality it *increases* them.

R. Calwer, in his little book, *An Introduction to World Economics,* attempted to compile the main, purely economic, data required to understand in a concrete way the internal relations of world economy at the end of the nineteenth and beginning of the twentieth centuries. He divides the world into five "main economic areas," as follows: 1) Central Europe (the whole of Europe with the exception of Russia and Great Britain); 2) Great Britain; 3) Russia; 4) Eastern Asia; 5) America; he includes the colonies in the "areas" of the state to which they belong and "leaves out" a few countries not distributed according to areas, such as Persia, Afghanistan and Arabia in Asia; Morocco and Abyssinia in Africa, etc.

Here is a brief summary of the economic data he quotes on these regions:

Principal Economic Areas	1 Central European	2 British	3 Russian	4 East Asian	5 American
AREA Million Sq. Km.	27.6 (23.6) *	28.9 (28.6) †	22	12	30
POPULATION Millions	388 (146)	398 (355)	131	389	148
TRANSPORT [*Railways*] Thous. Km.	204	140	63	8	379
[*Mercantile Fleet*] Million Tons	8	11	1	1	6

* R. Calwer, *Einfuhrung in die Weltwirtschaft,* Berlin, 1906.
† The figures in parentheses show the area and population of the colonies.

Principal Economic Areas	1 Central European	2 British	3 Russian	4 East Asian	5 American
TRADE					
Imports & Exports Billion Marks	41	25	3	2	14
INDUSTRY					
Output of Coal Million Tons	251	249	16	8	245
Output of Pig Iron Million Tons	15	9	3	0.02	14
No. of Cotton Spindles Millions	26	51	7	2	19

We notice three areas of highly developed capitalism with a high development of means of transport, of trade and of industry, the Central European, the British and the American areas. Among these are three states which dominate the world: Germany, Great Britain, the United States. Imperialist rivalry and the struggle between these countries have become very keen because Germany has only a restricted area and few colonies (the creation of "Central Europe" is still a matter for the future; it is being born in the midst of desperate struggles). For the moment the distinctive feature of Europe is political disintegration. In the British and American areas, on the other hand, political concentration is very highly developed, but there is a tremendous disparity between the immense colonies of the one and the insignificant colonies of the other. In the colonies, capitalism is only beginning to develop. The struggle for South America is becoming more and more acute.

There are two areas where capitalism is not strongly developed: Russia and Eastern Asia. In the former, the density of population is very low, in the latter it is very high; in the former political concentration is very high, in the latter it does not exist. The partition of China is only beginning, and the struggle between Japan, U.S.A., etc., in connection therewith is continually gaining in intensity.

Compare this reality, the vast diversity of economic and political conditions, the extreme disparity in the rate of development of the various countries, etc., and the violent struggles of the imperialist states, with Kautsky's silly little fable about "peaceful" ultra-imperialism. Is this not the reactionary attempt of a frightened philistine to hide from stern reality? Are not the international cartels which Kautsky imagines are the embryos of "ultra-imperialism" (with as much reason as one would have for describing the manufacture of tabloids in a laboratory as ultra-agriculture in embryo) an example of the division and the *redivision* of the world, the transition from peaceful division to non-peaceful division and *vice versa?* Is not American and other finance capital, which divided the whole world peacefully, with Germany's participation, for example, in the international rail syndicate, or in the international mercantile shipping trust, now engaged in *redividing* the world on the basis of a new relation of forces, which has been changed by methods *by no means* peaceful?

Finance capital and the trusts are increasing instead of diminishing the differences in the rate of development of the various parts of world economy. When the relation of forces is changed, how else, *under capitalism,* can the solution of contradictions be found, except by resorting to *violence?* Railway statistics provide remarkably exact data on the different rates of development of capitalism and finance capital in world economy. In the last decades of imperialist development, the total length of railways has changed as follows:

RAILWAYS (Thousand Kilometres)

	1890	1913	Increase
EUROPE	224	346	122
U.S.A.	268	411	143
COLONIES (TOTAL)	82 ⎫	210 ⎫	128 ⎫
INDEPENDENT AND SEMI-DEPENDENT STATES OF ASIA AND AMERICA	43 ⎬ 125	137 ⎬ 347	94 ⎬ 222
TOTAL	617	1,104	

Thus, the development of railways has been more rapid in the colonies and in the independent (and semi-dependent) states of Asia and America. Here, as we know, the finance capital of the four or five biggest capitalist states reigns undisputed. Two hundred thousand kilometres of new railways in the colonies and in the other countries of Asia and America represent more than 40,000,000,000 marks in capital, newly invested on particularly advantageous terms, with special guarantees of a good return and with profitable orders for steel works, etc., etc.

Capitalism is growing with the greatest rapidity in the colonies and in overseas countries. Among the latter, *new* imperialist powers are emerging (*e.g.,* Japan). The struggle of world imperialism is becoming more acute. The tribute levied by finance capital on the most profitable colonial and overseas enterprises is increasing. In sharing out this "booty," an exceptionally large part goes to countries which, as far as the development of productive forces is concerned, do not always stand at the top of the list. In the case of the biggest countries, considered with their colonies, the total length of railways was as follows (in thousands of kilometres):

	1890	1913	Increase
U.S.A.	268	413	145
BRITISH EMPIRE	107	208	101
RUSSIA	32	78	46
GERMANY	43	68	25
FRANCE	41	63	22
TOTAL	491	830	339

Thus, about 80 per cent of the total existing railways are concentrated in the hands of the five Great Powers. But the concentration of the *ownership* of these railways, of finance capital, is much greater still: French and English millionaires, for example, own an enormous amount of stocks and bonds in American, Russian and other railways.

Thanks to her colonies, Great Britain has increased the length of "her" railways by 100,000 kilometres, four times as much as Germany. And yet, it is well known that the development of productive forces in Germany, and especially the development of the coal and iron industries, has been much more rapid during this period than in England—not to mention France and Russia. In 1892, Germany produced 4,900,000 tons of pig iron and Great Britain produced 6,800,000 tons; in 1912, Germany produced 17,600,000 tons and Great Britain 9,000,000 tons. Germany, therefore, had an overwhelming superiority over England in this respect. We ask, is there *under capitalism* any means of removing the disparity between the development of productive forces and the accumulation of capital on the one side, and the division of colonies and "spheres of influence" for finance capital on the other side— other than by resorting to war?

2
THE
ECONOMIC
ELEMENT

The most obvious motive for imperialism, economic gain, has not been neglected by theorists. Such contemporary proponents of empire as the English businessman and Liberal politician Joseph Chamberlain were not ashamed to admit to such a purpose. In the following selection he offers other practical advantages of empire as well. The speech was delivered to a sympathetic audience at Glasgow on October 6, 1903.

FROM Imperial Union and Tariff Reform
BY JOSEPH CHAMBERLAIN

My first duty is to thank this great and representative audience for having offered to me an opportunity of explaining for the first time in some detail the views which I hold upon the subject of our fiscal policy (cheers). I would desire no better platform than this ("hear, hear," and cheers). I am in a great city, the second of the Empire; the city which by the enterprise and intelligence which it has always shown is entitled to claim something of a representative character in respect of British industry (cheers). I am in that city in which Free Trade took its birth ("hear, hear"), in that city in which Adam Smith taught so long, and where he was one of my most distinguished predecessors in the great office of Lord Rector of your University (cheers) which it will always be to me a great honour to have filled. Adam Smith was a great man. It was not given to him, it never has been given to mortals to foresee all the changes that may occur in something like a century and a half, but with a

---

Joseph Chamberlain, *Imperial Union and Tariff Reform* (1903), pp. 19–34.

broad and far-seeing intelligence which is not common among men, Adam Smith did at any rate anticipate many of our modern conditions, and when I read his books I see how even then he was aware of the importance of home markets as compared with foreign ("hear, hear"); how he advocated retaliation under certain conditions; how he supported the Navigation Laws; how he was the author of a sentence which we ought never to forget, that "Defence is greater than opulence" (cheers). When I remember, also, how he, entirely before his time, pressed for reciprocal trade between our Colonies and the Mother Country, I say he had a broader mind, a more Imperial conception of the duties of the citizens of a great Empire, than some of those who have taught also as professors (laughter and cheers), and who claim to be his successors (renewed laughter and cheering). Ladies and gentlemen, I am not afraid to come here (cheers, and a voice "Bravo!") to the home of Adam Smith, and to combat free imports (cheers), and still less am I afraid to preach to you preference with our Colonies ("hear, hear," and cheers)—to you in this great city whose whole prosperity has been founded upon its colonial relations (cheers). But I must not think only of the city, I must think of the country. It is known to every man that Scotland has contributed out of all proportion to its population to build up the great Empire of which we are all so proud—an Empire which took genius and capacity and courage to create ("hear, hear")—and which requires now genius and capacity and courage to maintain (loud cheers).

I do not regard this as a party meeting. I am no longer a party leader (laughter). I am an outsider (renewed laughter), and it is not my intention— I do not think it would be right—to raise any exclusively party issues. But after what has occurred in the last few days, after the meeting at Sheffield (cheers), a word or two may be forgiven to me, who, although no longer a leader, am still a loyal servant of the party to which I belong (cheers).

I say to you, ladies and gentlemen, that that party whose continued existence, whose union, whose strength I still believe to be essential to the welfare of the country and to the welfare of the Empire (cheers), has found a leader whom every member may be proud to follow (loud cheers). Mr. Balfour (cheers) in his position has responsibilities which he cannot share with us, but no one will contest his right—a right to which his high office, his ability, and his character alike entitle him—to declare the official policy of the party which he leads ("hear, hear"), to fix its limits, to settle the time at which application shall be given to the principles which he has put forward (loud cheers). For myself, I agree with the principles that he has stated. I approve of the policy to which he proposes to give effect, and I admire the courage and the resource with which he faces difficulties which even in our varied political history have hardly ever been surpassed ("hear, hear"). It ought not to be necessary to say any more. But it seems as though in this country there have always been men who do not know what loyalty and friendship mean ("hear, hear"), and to them I say that nothing that they can do will have the slightest influence or will affect in the slightest degree the friendship and confidence which exist and have existed for so many years between the Prime Minister and myself (loud cheers). Let them do their worst. Their insinuations pass us by like the idle wind, and I would say to my friends, to those who support me in the great struggle on which I have entered, I would say to them also, I beg of you to give no encouragement to these mean and libellous insinuations. Understand that in no conceivable circumstances will I allow myself to be put in any sort of competition, direct or indirect, with my friend and leader, whom I mean to follow (cheers). What is my position? I have invited a discussion upon a question which comes peculiarly within my province, owing to the office which I have so recently held. I have invited discussion upon it. I have not pretended that a matter of this importance is to be settled offhand. I have been well aware that the country has to be educated, as I myself have had to be educated before I saw, or could see, all the bearings of this great matter; and therefore I take up the position of a pioneer. I go in front of the army, and if the army is attacked, I go back to it (loud and prolonged cheers).

Meanwhile, putting aside all these personal and party questions, I ask my countrymen, without regard to any political opinions which they may have hitherto held, to consider the greatest of all great questions that can be put before the country, to consider it impartially if possible, and to come to a decision—and it is possible—I am always an optimist (laughter)—it is possible that the nation may be prepared to go a little further than the official programme ("hear, hear," and cheers). I have known them to do it before (laughter), and no harm has come to the party; no harm that I know has come to those who as scouts, or pioneers, or investigators, or discoverers have gone a little before it. Well, one of my objects in coming here is to find an answer to this question. Is the country prepared to go a little further? (Cries of "Yes," and cheers.)

I suppose that there are differences in Scotland, differences in Glasgow, as there are certainly in the southern country, but those differences, I hope, are mainly differences as to methods ("hear, hear"). For I cannot conceive that, so far as regards the majority of the country at any rate, there can be any differences as to our objects. What are our objects? They are two. In the first place, we all desire the maintenance and increase of the national strength and the prosperity of the United Kingdom (cheers). That may be a selfish desire; but in my mind it carries with it something more than mere selfishness. You cannot expect foreigners to take the same views as we of our position and duty. To my mind Britain has played a great part in the past in the history of the world, and for that reason I wish Britain to continue (cheers). Then, in the second place, our object is, or should be, the realisation of the greatest ideal which has ever inspired statesmen in any country or in any age—the creation of an Empire such as the world has never seen (loud cheers). We have to cement the union of the States beyond the seas; we have to consolidate the British race; we have to meet the clash of competition, commercial now—sometimes in the past it has been otherwise—it may be again in the future. Whatever it be, whatever danger threatens, we have to meet it no longer as an isolated country; we have to meet it fortified and strengthened, and buttressed by all those of our kinsmen, all those powerful and continually rising States which speak our common tongue and glory in our common flag (cheers).

Those are two great objects, and, as I have said, we all should have them in view. How are we to attain them? In the first place, let me say one word as to the method in which this discussion is to be carried on. Surely it should be treated in a manner worthy of its magnitude, worthy of the dignity of the theme ("hear, hear"). For my part I disclaim any imputation of evil motive and unworthy motive on the part of those who may happen to disagree with me; and I claim equal consideration from them ("hear, hear"). I claim that this matter should be treated on its merits—without personal feeling, personal bitterness, and, if possible, without entering upon questions of purely party controversy (cheers), and I do that for the reason I have given; but also because, if you are to make a change in a system which has existed for nearly sixty years, which affects more or less every man, woman, and child in the kingdom, you can only make that change successfully if you have behind you not merely a party support—if you do not attempt to force it by a small majority on a large and unwilling minority, but if it becomes, as I believe it will become (cheers), a national policy in consonance with the feelings, the aspirations, and the interests of the overwhelming proportion of the country (cheers).

I was speaking just now of the characteristics of Glasgow as a great city; I am not certain whether I mentioned that I believe it is one of the most prosperous of cities, that it has had a great and continuous prosperity; and if that be so, here, more than anywhere else, I have to answer the question, Why cannot you let well alone? ("Hear, hear.") Well, I have been in Venice—the beautiful city of the Adriatic—which had at one time a commercial supremacy quite as great in proportion as anything we have ever enjoyed. Its glories have departed; but what I was going to say was that when I was there last I saw the great tower of the Campanile rising above the city which it had overshadowed for centuries, and looking as though it was as permanent as the city itself. And yet the other day, in a few minutes, the whole structure fell to the ground. Nothing was left of it but a mass of ruin and rubbish. I do not say to you, gentlemen, that I anticipate any catastrophe so great or so sudden for British trade; but I do say to you that I see signs of decay; that I see cracks and crevices in the walls of the great structure; that I know that the foundations upon which it has been raised are not broad enough or deep enough to sustain it (cheers). Now, do I do wrong, if I know this—if I even think I know it—do I do wrong to warn you? Is it not a most strange and inconsistent thing that while certain people are indicting the Government in language which, to say the least of it, is extravagant, for not having been prepared for the great war from which we have recently emerged with success (cheers)—is it not strange that these same people should be denouncing me in language equally extravagant because I want to prepare you now, while there is time, for a struggle greater in its consequences than that to which I have referred ("hear, hear")—a struggle from which, if we emerge defeated, this country will lose its place, will no longer count among the great nations of the world—a struggle which we are asked to meet with antiquated weapons and with old-fashioned tactics? (Cheers.)

I tell you that it is not well to-day with British industry ("hear, hear"). We have been going through a period of great expansion. The whole world has been prosperous. I see signs of a change, but let that pass. When the change comes I think even the Free Fooders will be converted (laughter). But meanwhile, what are the facts? The year 1900 was the record year of British trade. The exports were the largest we had ever known. The year 1902—last year— was nearly as good, and yet, if you will compare your trade in 1872, thirty years ago, with the trade of 1902—the export trade—you will find that there has been a moderate increase of twenty-two millions. That, I think, is something like 7½ per cent. Meanwhile, the population has increased 30 per cent. Can you go on supporting your population at that rate of increase, when even in the best of years you can only show so much smaller an increase in your foreign trade? The actual increase was twenty-two millions under our Free Trade. In the same time the increase in the United States of America was 110 millions, and the increase in Germany was fifty-six millions. In the United Kingdom our export trade has been practically stagnant for thirty years. It went down in the interval. It has now gone up in the most prosperous times. In the most prosperous times it is hardly better than it was thirty years ago.

Meanwhile the protected countries which you have been told, and which I myself at one time believed, were going rapidly to wreck and ruin, have progressed in a much greater proportion than ours. That is not all; not merely the amount of your trade remained stagnant, but the character of your trade has changed. When Mr. Cobden preached his doctrine, he believed, as he had at that time considerable reason to suppose, that while foreign countries would supply us with our food-stuffs and raw materials, we should remain the mart of the world, and should send them in exchange our manufactures. But that is exactly what we have not done. On the contrary, in the period to which I have referred, we are sending less and less of our manufactures to them, and they are sending more and more of their manufactures to us (cheers).

I know how difficult it is for a great meeting like this to follow figures. I shall give you as few as I can, but I must give you some to lay the basis of my argument. I have had a table constructed, and upon that table I would be willing to base the whole of my contention. I will take some figures from it. You have to analyse your trade. It is not merely a question of amount; you have to consider of what it is composed. Now what has been the case with regard to our manufactures? Our existence as a nation depends upon our manufacturing capacity and production. We are not essentially or mainly an agricultural country. That can never be the main source of our prosperity.

We are a great manufacturing country. In 1872, we sent to the protected countries of Europe and to the United States of America, £116,000,000 of exported manufactures. In 1882, ten years later, it fell to £88,000,000. In 1892, ten years later, it fell to £75,000,000. In 1902, last year, although the general exports had increased, the exports of manufactures to these countries had decreased again to £73,500,000, and the total result of this is that, after thirty years, you are sending £42,500,000 of manufactures less to the great protected countries than you did thirty years ago (cheers). Then there are the neutral countries, that is, the countries which, although they may have tariffs, have no manufactures, and therefore the tariffs are not protective—such countries as Egypt and China, and South America, and similar places. Our exports of manufactures have not fallen in these markets to any considerable extent. They have practically remained the same, but on the whole they have fallen £3,500,000. Adding that to the loss in the protected countries, and you have lost altogether in your exports of manufactures £46,000,000.

How is it that that has not impressed the people before now? Because the change has been concealed by our statistics. I do not say they have not shown it, because you could have picked it out, but they are not put in a form which is understanded of the people. You have failed to observe that the maintenance of your trade is dependent entirely on British possessions. While to these foreign countries your export of manufactures has declined by £46,000,-000, to your British possessions it has increased £40,000,000 (cheers), and at the present time your trade with the Colonies and British possessions is larger in amount, very much larger in amount, and very much more valuable in the categories I have named, than our trade with the whole of Europe and the United States of America. It is much larger than our trade to those neutral countries of which I have spoken, and it remains at the present day the most rapidly increasing, the most important, the most valuable of the whole of our trade (cheers). One more comparison. During this period of thirty years in which our exports of manufactures have fallen £46,000,000 to foreign countries, what has happened as regards their exports of manufactures to us? They have risen from £63,000,000 in 1872 to £149,000,000 in 1902. They have increased £86,000,000. That may be all right. I am not for the moment saying whether that is right or wrong, but when people say that we ought to hold exactly the same opinion about things that our ancestors did, my reply is that I daresay we should do so if circumstances had remained the same (cheers).

But now, if I have been able to make these figures clear, there is one thing which follows—that is, that our Imperial trade is absolutely essential to our prosperity at the present time ("hear, hear"). If that trade declines, or if it does not increase in proportion to our population and to the loss of trade with foreign countries, then we sink at once into a fifth-rate nation (cheers). Our fate will be the fate of the empires and kingdoms of the past. We shall have reached our highest point, and indeed I am not certain that there are some of my opponents who do not regard that with absolute complacency (laughter). I do not (loud cheers). As I have said, I have the misfortune to be an opti-

mist. I do not believe in the setting of the British star (cheers), but then, I do
not believe in the folly of the British people (laughter). I trust them. I trust
the working classes of this country (cheers), and I have confidence that they
who are our masters, electorally speaking, will have the intelligence to see
that they must wake up. They must modify their policy to suit new conditions. They must meet those conditions with altogether a new policy
(cheers).

I have said that if our Imperial trade declines we decline. My second point
is this. It will decline inevitably unless while there is still time we take the
necessary steps to preserve it ("hear, hear"). Have you ever considered why it
is that Canada takes so much more of the products of British manufacturers
than the United States of America does per head? When you answer that, I
have another conundrum (laughter). Why does Australia take about three
times as much per head as Canada? And to wind up, why does South Africa
—the white population of South Africa—take more per head than Australasia? When you have got to the bottom of that—and it is not difficult—you
will see the whole argument. These countries are all protective countries. I see
that the Labour leaders, or some of them, in this country are saying that the
interest of the working class is to maintain our present system of free imports.
The moment those men go to the Colonies they change. I will undertake to
say that no one of them has ever been there for six months without singing a
different tune (laughter). The vast majority of the working men in all the
Colonies are Protectionists, and I am not inclined to accept the easy explanation that they are all fools (laughter). I do not understand why an intelligent
man—a man who is intelligent in this country—becomes an idiot when he
goes to Australasia (laughter). But I will tell you what he does do. He gets
rid of a good number of old-world prejudices and superstitions (laughter). I
say they are Protectionist, all these countries. Now, what is the history of
Protection? In the first place a tariff is imposed. There are no industries, or
practically none, but only a tariff; then gradually industries grow up behind
the tariff wall. In the first place they are primary industries, the industries for
which the country has natural aptitude or for which it has some special advantage—mineral or other resources. Then when those are established the
secondary industries spring up, first the necessaries, then the luxuries, until at
last all the ground is covered. These countries of which I have been speaking
to you are in different stages of the protective process. In America the process
has been completed. She produces everything; she excludes everything
(laughter). There is no trade to be done with her beyond a paltry 6s. per
head. Canada has been protective for a long time. The protective policy has
produced its natural result. The principal industries are there, and you can
never get rid of them. They will be there for ever, but up to the present time
the secondary industries have not been created, and there is an immense deal
of trade that is still open to you, that you may still retain, that you may
increase. In Australasia the industrial position is still less advanced. The agricultural products of the country have been first of all developed. Accordingly,

Australasia takes more from you per head than Canada. In South Africa there are, practically speaking, no industries at all. Now, I ask you to suppose that we intervene in any stage of the process. We can do it now. We might have done it with greater effect ten years ago ("hear, hear"). Whether we can do it with any effect or at all twenty years hence I am very doubtful. We can intervene now. We can say to our great Colonies: "We understand your views and conditions. We do not attempt to dictate to you. We do not think ourselves superior to you. We have taken the trouble to learn your objections, to appreciate and sympathise with your policy. We know that you are right in saying you will not always be content to be what the Americans call a one-horse country, with a single industry and no diversity of employment. We can see that you are right not to neglect what Providence has given you in the shape of mineral or other resources. We understand and we appreciate the wisdom of your statesmen when they say they will not allow their country to be solely dependent on foreign supplies for the necessities of life. We understand all that, and therefore we will not propose to you anything that is unreasonable or contrary to this policy, which we know is deep in your hearts; but we will say to you, 'After all, there are many things which you do not now make, many things for which we have a great capacity of production—leave them to us as you have left them hitherto. Do not increase your tariff walls against us. Pull them down where they are unnecessary to the success of this policy to which you are committed. Do that because we are kinsmen—without injury to any important interest—because it is good for the Empire as a whole, and because we have taken the first step and have set you the example ("hear, hear"). We offer you a preference; we rely on your patriotism, your affection, that we shall not be losers thereby'" (cheers).

Now, suppose that we had made an offer of that kind—I won't say to the Colonies, but to Germany, to the United States of America—ten or twenty years ago. Do you suppose that we should not have been able to retain a great deal of what we have now lost and cannot recover? (Cheers.)

I will give you an illustration. America is the strictest of protective nations. It has a tariff which to me is an abomination. It is so immoderate, so unreasonable, so unnecessary, that, though America has profited enormously under it, yet I think it has been carried to excessive lengths, and I believe now that a great number of intelligent Americans would gladly negotiate with us for its reduction. But until very recent times even this immoderate tariff left to us a great trade. It left to us the tin-plate trade, and the American tin-plate trade amounted to millions per annum, and gave employment to thousands of British workpeople. If we had gone to America ten or twenty years ago and had said, "If you will leave the tin-plate trade as it is, put no duty on tin-plate— you have never had to complain either of our quality or our price—we in return will give you some advantage on some articles which you produce," we might have kept the tin-plate trade ("hear, hear"). It would not have been worth America's while to put a duty on an article for which it had no particular or special aptitude or capacity. If we had gone to Germany in the same sense there are hundreds of articles which are now made in Germany which are sent to this country, which are taking the place of goods employing British labour, which they might have left to us in return for our concessions to them.

We did not take that course. We were not prepared for it as a people. We allowed matters to drift. Are we going to let them drift now? ("No.") Are we going to lose the colonial trade? (Cries of "No.") This is the parting of the ways. You have to remember that if you do not take this opportunity it will not recur (cheers). If you do not take it I predict, and I predict with certainty, that Canada will fall to the level of the United States, that Australia will fall to the level of Canada, that South Africa will fall to the level of Australia, and that will only be the beginning of the general decline which will deprive you of your most important customers, of your most rapidly increasing trade (cheers). I think that I have some reason to speak with authority on this subject. The Colonies are prepared to meet us (cheers). In return for a very moderate preference they will give us a substantial advantage. They will give us in the first place, I believe they will reserve to us, much at any rate of the trade which we already enjoy. They will not—and I would not urge them for a moment to do so—they will not injure those of their industries which have already been created. They will maintain them, they will not allow them to be destroyed or injured even by our competition, but outside that there is still a great margin, a margin which has given us this enormous increase of trade to which I have referred. That margin I believe we can permanently retain ("hear, hear")—and I ask you to think, if that is of so much importance to us now, when we have only eleven millions of white fellow-citizens in these distant Colonies, what will it be when in the course of a period which is a mere moment of time in the history of States, what will it be when that population is forty millions or more? ("Hear, hear.") Is it not worth while to consider whether the actual trade which you may retain, whether the enormous potential trade which you and your descendants may enjoy, be not worth a sacrifice, if sacrifice be required? ("Hear, hear.") But they will do a great deal more for you. This is certain. Not only will they enable you to retain the trade which you have, but they are ready to give you preference on all the trade which is now done with them by foreign competitors (cheers). I never see any appreciation by the free importers of the magnitude of this trade. It will increase. It has increased greatly in thirty years, and if it goes on with equally rapid strides we shall be ousted by foreign competition, if not by protective tariffs, from our Colonies. It amounts at the present time to £47,000,000. But it is said that a great part of that £47,000,000 is in goods which we cannot supply. That is true, and with regard to that portion of the trade we have no interest in any preferential tariff, but it has been calculated, and I believe it to be accurate, that £26,000,000 a year of that trade might come to this country which now goes to Germany and France and other foreign countries, if reasonable preference were given to British manufactures (cheers). What does that mean? The Board of

Trade assumes that of manufactured goods one-half the value is expended in labour—I think it is a great deal more, but take the Board of Trade figures—£13,000,000 a year of new employment. What does that mean to the United Kingdom? It means the employment of 166,000 men at 30s. a week (cheers). It means the subsistence, if you include their families, of 830,000 persons; and now, if you will only add to that our present export to the British possessions of £96,000,000, you will find that that gives, on the same calculation, £48,000,000 for wages, or employment at 30s. a week to 615,000 workpeople, and it finds subsistence for 3,075,000 persons ("hear, hear"). In other words, your Colonial trade as it stands at present with the prospective advantage of a preference against the foreigner means employment and fair wages for three-quarters of a million of workmen, and subsistence for nearly four millions of our population (cheers).

Ladies and gentlemen, I feel deeply sensible that the argument I have addressed to you is one of those which will be described by the Leader of the Opposition as a squalid argument (laughter). A squalid argument! I have appealed to your interests, I have come here as a man of business (loud cheers), I have appealed to the employers and the employed alike in this great city. I have endeavoured to point out to them that their trade, their wages, all depend on the maintenance of this Colonial trade, of which some of my opponents speak with such contempt, and, above all, with such egregious ignorance (loud laughter and cheers). But now I abandon that line of argument for the moment, and appeal to something higher, which I believe is in your hearts as it is in mine. I appeal to you as fellow-citizens of the greatest Empire that the world has ever known; I appeal to you to recognise that the privileges of Empire bring with them great responsibilities (cheers). I want to ask you to think what this Empire means, what it is to you and your descendants. I will not speak, or, at least, I will not dwell, on its area, greater than that which has been under one dominion in the history of the world. I will not speak of its population, of the hundreds of millions of men for whom we have made ourselves responsible. But I will speak of its variety, and of the fact that here we have an Empire which with decent organisation and consolidation might be absolutely self-sustaining (loud cheers). Nothing of the kind has ever been known before. There is no article of your food, there is no raw material of your trade, there is no necessity of your lives, no luxury of your existence which cannot be produced somewhere or other in the British Empire, if the British Empire holds together, and if we who have inherited it are worthy of our opportunities.

There is another product of the British Empire, that is, men (cheers). You have not forgotten the advantage, the encouragement, which can be given by the existence of loyal men (cheers), inhabitants, indeed, of distant States, but still loyal to the common flag (cheers). It is not so long since these men, when the old country was in straits, rushed to her assistance (cheers). No persuasion was necessary; it was a voluntary movement. That was not a squalid assistance (loud cheers). They had no special interest. They were interested indeed, as sons of the Empire. If they had been separate States they would have had no interest at all. They came to our assistance and proved themselves indeed men of the old stock (cheers); they proved themselves worthy of the best traditions of the British army (cheers), and gave us an assistance, a material assistance, which was invaluable. They gave us moral support which was even more grateful (loud cheers). That is the result of Empire (cheers). I should be wrong if, in referring to our white fellow-subjects, I did not also say, that in addition to them, if any straits befell us, there are millions and hundreds of millions of men born in tropical climes, and of races very different from ours, who, although they were prevented by political considerations from taking part in our recent struggle, would be in any death-throe of the Empire (loud cheers) equally eager to show their loyalty and their devotion (cheers). Now, is such a dominion, are such traditions, is such a glorious inheritance, is such a splendid sentiment—are they worth preserving? (Cheers.) They have cost us much. They have cost much in blood and treasure; and in past times, as in recent, many of our best and noblest have given their lives, or risked their lives, for this great ideal. But it has also done much for us. It has ennobled our national life, it has discouraged that petty parochialism which is the defect of all small communities. I say to you that all that is best in our present life, best in this Britain of ours, all of which we have the right to be most proud, is due to the fact that we are not only sons of Britain, but we are sons of Empire. I do not think, I am not likely to do you the injustice to believe, that you would make this sacrifice fruitless, that you would make all this endeavour vain. But if you want to complete it, remember that each generation in turn has to do its part, and you are called to take your share in this great work. Others have founded the Empire; it is yours to build firmly and permanently the great edifice of which others have laid the foundation (cheers). And I believe we have got to change somewhat our rather insular habits. When I have been in the Colonies I have told them that they are too provincial, but I think we are too provincial also. We think too much of ourselves ("hear, hear"), and we forget—and it is necessary we should remember—that we are only part of a larger whole ("hear, hear"). And when I speak of our Colonies, it is an expression; they are not ours—they are not ours in a possessory sense. They are sister States, able to treat with us from an equal position, able to hold to us, willing to hold to us, but also able to break with us. I have had eight years' experience (cheers). I have been in communication with many of the men, statesmen, orators, writers, distinguished in our Colonies. I have had intimate conversation with them. I have tried to understand them and I think I do understand them (cheers), and I say that none of them desire separation. There are none of them who are not loyal to this idea of Empire which they say they wish us to accept more fully in the future, but I have found none who do not believe that our present colonial relations cannot be permanent. We must either draw closer together or we shall drift apart.

3
THE MISSION
OF EMPIRE

At least some imperialists were moved by motives that were not economic. Honor, decency, responsibility, and uplift were all offered as reasons for empire.

The White Man's Burden BY RUDYARD KIPLING

1899

(The United States and the Philippine Islands)

Take up the White Man's burden—
  Send forth the best ye breed—
Go bind your sons to exile
  To serve your captives' need;
To wait in heavy harness
  On fluttered folk and wild—
Your new-caught, sullen peoples,
  Half devil and half child.

Take up the White Man's burden—
  In patience to abide,
To veil the threat of terror
  And check the show of pride;
By open speech and simple,
  An hundred times made plain,
To seek another's profit,
  And work another's gain.

"The White Man's Burden" (1899), from *Rudyard Kipling's Verse: Definitive Edition.* Reprinted by permission of Mrs. George Bambridge and Doubleday & Company, Inc. Reprinted from *The Five Nations* by permission of Mrs. George Bambridge, Methuen & Co. Ltd., London, and Macmillan Co. of Canada Ltd., Toronto.

Take up the White Man's burden—
    The savage wars of peace—
Fill full the mouth of Famine
    And bid the sickness cease;
And when your goal is nearest
    The end for others sought,
Watch Sloth and heathen Folly
    Bring all your hope to nought.

Take up the White Man's burden—
    No tawdry rule of kings,
But toil of serf and sweeper—
    The tale of common things.
The ports ye shall not enter,
    The roads ye shall not tread,
Go make them with your living,
    And mark them with your dead!

Take up the White Man's burden—
    And reap his old reward:
The blame of those ye better,
    The hate of those ye guard—
The cry of hosts ye humour
    (Ah, slowly!) toward the light:—
"Why brought ye us from bondage,
    "Our loved Egyptian night?"

Take up the White Man's burden—
    Ye dare not stoop to less—
Nor call too loud on Freedom
    To cloak your weariness;
By all ye cry or whisper,
    By all ye leave or do,
The silent, sullen peoples
    Shall weigh your Gods and you.

Take up the White Man's burden—
    Have done with childish days—
The lightly proffered laurel,
    The easy, ungrudged praise.
Comes now, to search your manhood
    Through all the thankless years,
Cold-edged with dear-bought wisdom,
    The judgment of your peers!

4
RACE AND
CHRISTIANITY

The advocates of imperialism included men convinced that the domination of backward areas by the more developed nations was a duty imposed upon the advanced countries by their racial superiority. According to the American clergyman Josiah Strong, the Anglo-Saxon race, and especially the American branch of it, was morally bound to bring the message of Christianity and individual liberty to less favored peoples.

FROM Our Country BY JOSIAH STRONG

Every race which has deeply impressed itself on the human family has been the representative of some great idea—one or more—which has given direction to the nation's life and form to its civilization. Among the Egyptians this seminal idea was life, among the Persians it was light, among the Hebrews it was purity, among the Greeks it was beauty, among the Romans it was law. The Anglo-Saxon is the representative of two great ideas, which are closely related. One of them is that of civil liberty. Nearly all of the civil liberty in the world is enjoyed by Anglo-Saxons: the English, the British colonists, and the people of the United States. To some, like the Swiss, it is permitted by the sufferance of their neighbors; others, like the French, have experimented with it; but, in modern times, the peoples whose love of liberty has won it, and whose genius for self-government has preserved it, have been Anglo-Saxons. The noblest races have always been lovers of liberty. That love ran strong in early German blood, and has profoundly influenced the institutions of all the branches of the great German family; but it was left for the Anglo-

Josiah Strong, *Our Country* (1885), pp. 159–162, 165, 172–180.

Saxon branch fully to recognize the right of the individual to himself, and
formally to declare it the foundation stone of government.

The other great idea of which the Anglo-Saxon is the exponent is that of a
pure *spiritual* Christianity. It was no accident that the great reformation of
the sixteenth century originated among a Teutonic, rather than a Latin
people. It was the fire of liberty burning in the Saxon heart that flamed up
against the absolutism of the Pope. Speaking roughly, the peoples of Europe
which are Celtic are Catholic, and those which are Teutonic are Protestant;
and where the Teutonic race was purest, there Protestantism spread with the
greatest rapidity. But, with rare and beautiful exceptions, Protestantism on
the continent has degenerated into mere formalism. By confirmation at a
certain age, the state churches are filled with members who generally know
nothing of a personal spiritual experience. In obedience to a military order, a
regiment of German soldiers files into church and partakes of the sacrament,
just as it would shoulder arms or obey any other word of command. It is said
that, in Berlin and Leipsic, only a little over one per cent. of the Protestant
population are found in church. Protestantism on the continent seems to be
about as poor in spiritual life and power as Catholicism. That means that
most of the spiritual Christianity in the world is found among the Anglo-
Saxons and their converts; for this is the great missionary race. If we take all
of the German missionary societies together, we find that, in the number of
workers and amount of contributions, they do not equal the smallest of the
three great English missionary societies. The year that Congregationalists in
the United States gave one dollar and thirty-seven cents per caput to foreign
missions, the members of the great German State Church gave only three-
quarters of a cent per caput to the same cause. Evidently it is chiefly to the
English and American peoples that we must look for the evangelization of
the world.

It is not necessary to argue to those for whom I write that the two great
needs of mankind, that all men may be lifted up into the light of the highest
Christian civilization, are, first, a pure, spiritual Christianity, and, second,
civil liberty. Without controversy, these are the forces which, in the past, have
contributed most to the elevation of the human race, and they must continue
to be, in the future, the most efficient ministers to its progress. It follows,
then, that the Anglo-Saxon, as the great representative of these two ideas, the
depository of these two greatest blessings, sustains peculiar relations to the
world's future, is divinely commissioned to be, in a peculiar sense, his brother's keeper. Add to this the fact of his rapidly increasing strength in modern
times, and we have well nigh a demonstration of his destiny. In 1700 this
race numbered less than 6,000,000 souls. In 1800, Anglo-Saxons (I use the term
somewhat broadly to include all English-speaking peoples) had increased to
about 20,500,000, and in 1880 they numbered nearly 100,000,000, having multiplied almost five-fold in eighty years. At the end of the reign of Charles II,
the English colonists in America numbered 200,000. During these two
hundred years, our population has increased two hundred and fifty-fold.

And the expansion of this race has been no less remarkable than its multiplication. In one century the United States has increased its territory tenfold, while the enormous acquisition of foreign territory by Great Britain—and chiefly within the last hundred years—is wholly unparalleled in history. This mighty Anglo-Saxon race, though comprising only one-fifteenth part of mankind, now rules more than one-third of the earth's surface, and more than one-fourth of its people. And if this race, while growing from 6,000,000 to 100,000,000, thus gained possession of a third portion of the earth, is it to be supposed that when it numbers 1,000,000,000, it will lose the disposition, or lack the power to extend its sway? . . . It is not unlikely that, before the close of the next century, this race will outnumber all the other civilized races of the world. Does it not look as if God were not only preparing in our Anglo-Saxon civilization the die with which to stamp the peoples of the earth, but as if he were also massing behind that die the mighty power with which to press it? My confidence that this race is eventually to give its civilization to mankind is not based on mere numbers—China forbid! I look forward to what the world has never yet seen united in the same race; viz., the greatest numbers, *and* the highest civilization.

* * *

It may be easily shown, and is of no small significance, that the two great ideas of which the Anglo-Saxon is the exponent are having a fuller development in the United States than in Great Britain. There the union of Church and State tends strongly to paralyze some of the members of the body of Christ. Here there is no such influence to destroy spiritual life and power. Here, also, has been evolved the form of government consistent with the largest possible civil liberty. Furthermore, it is significant that the marked characteristics of this race are being here emphasized most. Among the most striking features of the Anglo-Saxon is his money-making power—a power of increasing importance in the widening commerce of the world's future . . . although England is by far the richest nation of Europe, we have already outstripped her in the race after wealth, and we have only begun the development of our vast resources.

Again, another marked characteristic of the Anglo-Saxon is what may be called an instinct or genius for colonizing. His unequaled energy, his indomitable perseverance, and his personal independence, made him a pioneer. He excels all others in pushing his way into new countries. It was those in whom this tendency was strongest that came to America, and this inherited tendency has been further developed by the westward sweep of successive generations across the continent. So noticeable has this characteristic become that English visitors remark it. Charles Dickens once said that the typical American would hesitate to enter heaven unless assured that he could go further west.

Again, nothing more manifestly distinguishes the Anglo-Saxon than his intense and persistent energy; and he is developing in the United States an energy which, in eager activity and effectiveness, is peculiarly American. This is due partly to the fact that Americans are much better fed than Europeans, and partly to the undeveloped resources of a new country, but more largely to our climate, which acts as a constant stimulus. Ten years after the landing of the Pilgrims, the Rev. Francis Higginson, a good observer, wrote: "A sup of New England air is better than a whole flagon of English ale." Thus early had the stimulating effect of our climate been noted. Moreover, our social institutions are stimulating. In Europe the various ranks of society are, like the strata of the earth, fixed and fossilized. There can be no great change without a terrible upheaval, a social earthquake. Here society is like the waters of the sea, mobile; as General Garfield said, and so signally illustrated in his own experience, that which is at the bottom to-day may one day flash on the crest of the highest wave. Every one is free to become whatever he can make of himself; free to transform himself from a rail-splitter or a tanner or a canal-boy, into the nation's President. Our aristocracy, unlike that of Europe, is open to all comers. Wealth, position, influence, are prizes offered for energy; and every farmer's boy, every apprentice and clerk, every friendless and penniless immigrant, is free to enter the lists. Thus many causes co-operate to produce here the most forceful and tremendous energy in the world.

What is the significance of such facts? These tendencies infold the future; they are the mighty alphabet with which God writes his prophecies. May we not, by a careful laying together of the letters, spell out something of his meaning? It seems to me that God, with infinite wisdom and skill, is training the Anglo-Saxon race for an hour sure to come in the world's future. Heretofore there has always been in the history of the world a comparatively unoccupied land westward, into which the crowded countries of the East have poured their surplus populations. But the widening waves of migration, which millenniums ago rolled east and west from the valley of the Euphrates, meet to-day on our Pacific coast. There are no more new worlds. The unoccupied arable lands of the earth are limited, and will soon be taken. The time is coming when the pressure of population on the means of subsistence will be felt here as it is now felt in Europe and Asia. Then will the world enter upon a new stage of its history—*the final competition of races, for which the Anglo-Saxon is being schooled*. Long before the thousand millions are here, the mighty *centrifugal* tendency, inherent in this stock and strengthened in the United States, will assert itself. Then this race of unequaled energy, with all the majesty of numbers and the might of wealth behind it—the representative, let us hope, of the largest liberty, the purest Christianity, the highest civilization—having developed peculiarly aggressive traits calculated to impress its institutions upon mankind, will spread itself over the earth. If I read not amiss, this powerful race will move down upon Mexico, down upon Central and South America, out upon the islands of the sea, over upon Africa and beyond. And can any one doubt that the result of this competition of races will be the "survival of the fittest"? "Any people," says Dr. Bushnell, "that is physiologically advanced in culture, though it be only in a degree beyond another which is mingled with it on strictly equal terms, is sure to live down and finally live out its inferior. Nothing can save the inferior race but a ready and pliant assimilation. Whether the feebler and more abject races are going to be regenerated and raised up, is already very much of a question. What if it should be God's plan to people the world with better and finer material? Certain it is, whatever expectations we may indulge, that there is a tremendous overbearing surge of power in the Christian nations, which, if the others are not speedily raised to some vastly higher capacity, will inevitably submerge and bury them forever. These great populations of Christendom—what are they doing, but throwing out their colonies on every side, and populating themselves, if I may so speak, into the possession of all countries and climes?" To this result no war of extermination is needful; the contest is not one of arms, but of vitality and of civilization. "At the present day," says Mr. Darwin, "civilized nations are everywhere supplanting barbarous nations, excepting where the climate opposes a deadly barrier; and they succeed mainly, though not exclusively, through their arts, which are the products of the intellect." Thus the Finns were supplanted by the Aryan races in Europe and Asia, the Tartars by the Russians, and thus the aborigines of North America, Australia and New Zealand are now disappearing before the all-conquering Anglo-Saxons. It would seem as if these inferior tribes were only precursors of a superior race, voices in the wilderness crying: "Prepare ye the way of the Lord!" The savage is a hunter; by the incoming of civilization the game is driven away and disappears before the hunter becomes a herder or an agriculturist. The savage is ignorant of many diseases of civilization which, when he is exposed to them, attack him before he learns how to treat them. Civilization also has its vices, of which the uninitiated savage is innocent. He proves an apt learner of vice, but dull enough in the school of morals. Every civilization has its destructive and preservative elements. The Ango-Saxon race would speedily decay but for the salt of Christianity. Bring savages into contact with our civilization, and its destructive forces become operative at once, while years are necessary to render effective the saving influences of Christian instruction. Moreover, the pioneer wave of our civilization carries with it more scum than salt. Where there is one missionary, there are hundreds of miners or traders or adventurers ready to debauch the native. Whether the extinction of inferior races before the advancing Anglo-Saxon seems to the reader sad or otherwise, it certainly appears probable. I know of nothing except climatic conditions to prevent this race from populating Africa as it has peopled North America. And those portions of Africa which are unfavorable to Anglo-Saxon life are less extensive than was once supposed. The Dutch Boers, after two centuries of life there, are as hardy as any race on earth. The Anglo-Saxon has established himself in climates totally diverse—Canada, South Africa, and India—and, through several generations, has preserved his essential race characteristics. He is not, of course, superior to climatic influences; but, even in warm climates, he is likely to retain his aggressive vigor long enough to supplant races already enfeebled. Thus, in what Dr. Bushnell calls "the out-populating power of the Christian stock," may be found God's final and complete solution of the dark problem of heathenism among many inferior peoples.

Some of the stronger races, doubtless, may be able to preserve their integrity; but, in order to compete with the Anglo-Saxon, they will probably be forced to adopt his methods and instruments, his civilization and his religion. Significant movements are now in progress among them. While the Christian religion was never more vital, or its hold upon the Anglo-Saxon mind stronger, there is taking place among the nations a wide-spread intellectual revolt against traditional beliefs. "In every corner of the world," says Mr. Froude, "there is the same phenomenon of the decay of established religions. . . . Among Mohammedans, Jews, Buddhists, Brahmins, traditionary creeds are losing their hold. An intellectual revolution is sweeping over the world, breaking down established opinions, dissolving foundations on which historical faiths have been built up." The contact of Christian with heathen nations is awaking the latter to new life. Old superstitions are loosening their grasp. The dead crust of fossil faiths is being shattered by the movements of life underneath. In Catholic countries, Catholicism is losing its influence over educated minds, and in some cases the masses have already lost all faith in it. Thus, while on this continent God is training the Anglo-Saxon race for its mission, a complemental work has been in progress in the great world beyond. God has two hands. Not only is he preparing in our civilization the die with which to stamp the nations, but, by what Southey called the "timing of Providence," he is preparing mankind to receive our impress.

Is there room for reasonable doubt that this race, unless devitalized by alcohol and tobacco, is destined to dispossess many weaker races, assimilate others, and mold the remainder, until, in a very true and important sense, it has Anglo-Saxonized mankind? Already "the English language, saturated with Christian ideas, gathering up into itself the best thought of all the ages, is the great agent of Christian civilization throughout the world; at this moment affecting the destinies and molding the character of half the human race." Jacob Grimm, the German philologist, said of this language: "It seems chosen, like its people, to rule in future times in a still greater degree in all the corners of the earth." He predicted, indeed, that the language of Shakespeare would eventually become the language of mankind. Is not Tennyson's noble prophecy to find its fulfillment in Anglo-Saxondom's extending its dominion and influence—

> Till the war-drum throbs no longer, and the battle-flags are furl'd
> In the Parliament of man, the Federation of the world.

In my own mind, there is no doubt that the Anglo-Saxon is to exercise the commanding influence in the world's future; but the exact nature of that influence is, as yet, undetermined. How far his civilization will be materialistic and atheistic, and how long it will take thoroughly to Christianize and sweeten it, how rapidly he will hasten the coming of the kingdom wherein dwelleth righteousness, or how many ages he may retard it, is still uncertain; but *it is now being swiftly determined*. Let us weld together in a chain the various links of our logic which we have endeavored to forge. Is it manifest that the Anglo-Saxon holds in his hands the destinies of mankind for ages to come? Is it evident that the United States is to be the home of this race, the principal seat of his power, the great center of his influence? Is it true . . . that the great West is to dominate the nation's future? Has it been shown . . . that this generation is to determine the character, and hence the destiny, of the West? Then may God open the eyes of this generation! When Napoleon drew up his troops before the Mamelukes, under the shadow of the Pyramids, pointing to the latter, he said to his soldiers: "Remember that from yonder heights forty centuries look down on you." Men of this generation, from the pyramid top of opportunity on which God has set us, *we look down on forty centuries!* We stretch our hand into the future with power to mold the destinies of unborn millions.

> We are living, we are dwelling,
> In a grand and awful time,
> In an age on ages telling—
> To be living is sublime!

Notwithstanding the great perils which threaten it, I cannot think our civilization will perish; but I believe it is fully in the hands of the Christians of the United States, during the next fifteen or twenty years, to hasten or retard the coming of Christ's kingdom in the world by hundreds, and perhaps thousands, of years. We of this generation and nation occupy the Gibraltar of the ages which commands the world's future.

5
IMPERIALISM
AS A SOCIAL
ATAVISM

As evidence for noneconomic and even nonrational motives for empire accumulated, the limits of the economic interpretation became obvious. Joseph Schumpeter offered a broader interpretation based on his understanding of world history since antiquity.

FROM Imperialism and Social Classes BY JOSEPH SCHUMPETER

Our analysis of the historical evidence has shown, first, the unquestionable fact that "objectless" tendencies toward forcible expansion, without definite, utilitarian limits—that is, non-rational and irrational, purely instinctual inclinations toward war and conquest—play a very large role in the history of mankind. It may sound paradoxical, but numberless wars—perhaps the majority of all wars—have been waged without adequate "reason"—not so much from the moral viewpoint as from that of reasoned and reasonable interest. The most herculean efforts of the nations, in other words, have faded into the empty air. Our analysis, in the second place, provides an explanation for this drive to action, this will to war—a theory by no means exhausted by mere references to an "urge" or an "instinct." The explanation lies, instead, in the vital needs of situations that molded peoples and classes into warriors—if they wanted to avoid extinction—and in the fact that psychological dispositions and social structures acquired in the dim past in such situations, once firmly established, tend to maintain themselves and to continue in effect long after they have lost their meaning and their life-preserving function. Our analysis,

Reprinted by permission of the President and Fellows of Harvard College from Joseph Schumpeter, *Imperialism and Social Classes* (1955), pp. 64–73, translated by Heinz Norden.

in the third place, has shown the existence of subsidiary factors that facilitate the survival of such dispositions and structures—factors that may be divided into two groups. The orientation toward war is mainly fostered by the domestic interests of ruling classes, but also by the influence of all those who stand to gain individually from a war policy, whether economically or socially. Both groups of factors are generally overgrown by elements of an altogether different character, not only in terms of political phraseology, but also of psychological motivation. Imperialisms differ greatly in detail, but they all have at least these traits in common, turning them into a single phenomenon in the field of sociology, as we noted in the introduction.

Imperialism thus is atavistic in character. It falls into that large group of surviving features from earlier ages that play such an important part in every concrete social situation. In other words, it is an element that stems from the living conditions, not of the present, but of the past—or, put in terms of the economic interpretation of history, from past rather than present relations of production. It is an atavism in the social structure, in individual, psychological habits of emotional reaction. Since the vital needs that created it have passed away for good, it too must gradually disappear, even though every warlike involvement, no matter how non-imperialist in character, tends to revive it. It tends to disappear as a structural element because the structure that brought it to the fore goes into a decline, giving way, in the course of social development, to other structures that have no room for it and eliminate the power factors that supported it. It tends to disappear as an element of habitual emotional reaction, because of the progressive rationalization of life and mind, a process in which old functional needs are absorbed by new tasks, in which heretofore military energies are functionally modified. If our theory is correct, cases of imperialism should decline in intensity the later they occur in the history of a people and of a culture. Our most recent examples of unmistakable, clear-cut imperialism are the absolute monarchies of the eighteenth century. They are unmistakably "more civilized" than their predecessors.

It is from absolute autocracy that the present age has taken over what imperialist tendencies it displays. And the imperialism of absolute autocracy flourished before the Industrial Revolution that created the modern world, or rather, before the consequences of that revolution began to be felt in all their aspects. These two statements are primarily meant in a historical sense, and as such they are no more than self-evident. We shall nevertheless try, within the framework of our theory, to define the significance of capitalism for our phenomenon and to examine the relationship between present-day imperialist tendencies and the autocratic imperialism of the eighteenth century.

The floodtide that burst the dams in the Industrial Revolution had its sources, of course, back in the Middle Ages. But capitalism began to shape society and impress its stamp on every page of social history only with the second half of the eighteenth century. Before that time there had been only islands of capitalist economy imbedded in an ocean of village and urban economy. True, certain political influences emanated from these islands, but they were able to assert themselves only indirectly. Not until the process we term the Industrial Revolution did the working masses, led by the entrepreneur, overcome the bonds of older life-forms—the environment of peasantry, guild, and aristocracy. The causal connection was this: A transformation in the basic economic factors (which need not detain us here) created the objective opportunity for the production of commodities, for large-scale industry, working for a market of customers whose individual identities were unknown, operating solely with a view to maximum financial profit. It was this opportunity that created an economically oriented leadership—personalities whose field of achievement was the organization of such commodity production in the form of capitalist enterprise. Successful enterprises in large numbers represented something new in the economic and social sense. They fought for and won freedom of action. They compelled state policy to adapt itself to their needs. More and more they attracted the most vigorous leaders from other spheres, as well as the manpower of those spheres, causing them and the social strata they represented to languish. Capitalist entrepreneurs fought the former ruling circles for a share in state control, for leadership in the state. The very fact of their success, their position, their resources, their power, raised them in the political and social scale. Their mode of life, their cast of mind became increasingly important elements on the social scene. Their actions, desires, needs, and beliefs emerged more and more sharply within the total picture of the social community. In a historical sense, this applied primarily to the industrial and financial leaders of the movement— the bourgeoisie. But soon it applied also to the working masses which this movement created and placed in an altogether new class situation. This situation was governed by new forms of the working day, of family life, of interests—and these, in turn, corresponded to new orientations toward the social structure as a whole. More and more, in the course of the nineteenth century, the typical modern worker came to determine the overall aspect of society; for competitive capitalism, by its inherent logic, kept on raising the demand for labor and thus the economic level and social power of the workers, until this class too was able to assert itself in a political sense. The working class and its mode of life provided the type from which the intellectual developed. Capitalism did not create the intellectuals—the "new middle class." But in earlier times only the legal scholar, the cleric, and the physician had formed a special intellectual class, and even they had enjoyed but little scope for playing an independent role. Such opportunities were provided only by capitalist society, which created the industrial and financial bureaucrat, the journalist, and so on, and which opened up new vistas to the jurist and physician. The "professional" of capitalist society arose as a class type. Finally, as a class type, the rentier, the beneficiary of industrial loan capital, is also a creature of capitalism. All these types are shaped by the capitalist mode of production, and they tend for this reason to bring other types—even the peasant—into conformity with themselves.

These new types were now cast adrift from the fixed order of earlier times, from the environment that had shackled and protected people for centuries, from the old associations of village, manor house, clan fellowship, often even from families in the broader sense. They were severed from the things that had been constant year after year, from cradle to grave—tools, homes, the countryside, especially the soil. They were on their own, enmeshed in the pitiless logic of gainful employment, mere drops in the vast ocean of industrial life, exposed to the inexorable pressures of competition. They were freed from the control of ancient patterns of thought, of the grip of institutions and organs that taught and represented these outlooks in village, manor, and guild. They were removed from the old world, engaged in building a new one for themselves—a specialized, mechanized world. Thus they were all inevitably democratized, individualized, and rationalized. They were democratized, because the picture of time-honored power and privilege gave way to one of continual change, set in motion by industrial life. They were individualized, because subjective opportunities to shape their lives took the place of immutable objective factors. They were rationalized, because the instability of economic position made their survival hinge on continual, deliberately rationalistic decisions—a dependence that emerged with great sharpness. Trained to economic rationalism, these people left no sphere of life unrationalized, questioning everything about themselves, the social structure, the state, the ruling class. The marks of this process are engraved on every aspect of modern culture. It is this process that explains the basic features of that culture.

These are things that are well known today, recognized in their full significance—indeed, often exaggerated. Their application to our subject is plain. Everything that is purely instinctual, everything insofar as it is purely instinctual, is driven into the background by this development. It creates a social and psychological atmosphere in keeping with modern economic forms, where traditional habits, merely because they were traditional, could no more survive than obsolete economic forms. Just as the latter can survive only if they are continually "adapted," so instinctual tendencies can survive only when the conditions that gave rise to them continue to apply, or when the "instinct" in question derives a new purpose from new conditions. The "instinct" that is *only* "instinct," that has lost its purpose, languishes relatively quickly in the capitalist world, just as does an inefficient economic practice. We see this process of rationalization at work even in the case of the strongest impulses. We observe it, for example, in the facts of procreation. We must therefore anticipate finding it in the case of the imperialist impulse as well; we must expect to see this impulse, which rests on the primitive contingencies of physical combat, gradually disappear, washed away by new exigencies of daily life. There is another factor too. The competitive system absorbs the full energies of most of the people at all economic levels. Constant application, attention, and concentration of energy are the conditions of survival within it, primarily in the specifically economic professions, but also in other activities organized on their model. There is much less excess energy to be vented in war and conquest than in any precapitalist society. What excess energy there is flows largely into industry itself, accounts for its shining figures—the type of the captain of industry—and for the rest is applied to art, science, and the social struggle. In a purely capitalist world, what was once energy for war becomes simply energy for labor of every kind. Wars of conquest and adventurism in foreign policy in general are bound to be regarded as troublesome distractions, destructive of life's meaning, a diversion from the accustomed and therefore "true" task.

A purely capitalist world therefore can offer no fertile soil to imperialist impulses. That does not mean that it cannot still maintain an interest in imperialist expansion. We shall discuss this immediately. The point is that its people are likely to be essentially of an unwarlike disposition. Hence we must expect that anti-imperialist tendencies will show themselves wherever capitalism penetrates the economy and, through the economy, the mind of modern nations—most strongly, of course, where capitalism itself is strongest, where it has advanced furthest, encountered the least resistance, and preeminently where its types and hence democracy—in the "bourgeois" sense—come closest to political dominion. We must further expect that the types formed by capitalism will actually be the carriers of these tendencies. Is such the case? The facts that follow are cited to show that this expectation, which flows from our theory, is in fact justified.

Throughout the world of capitalism, and specifically among the elements formed by capitalism in modern social life, there has arisen a fundamental opposition to war, expansion, cabinet diplomacy, armaments, and socially-entrenched professional armies. This opposition had its origin in the country that first turned capitalist—England—and arose coincidentally with that country's capitalist development. "Philosophical radicalism" was the first politically influential intellectual movement to represent this trend successfully, linking it up, as was to be expected, with economic freedom in general and free trade in particular. Molesworth became a cabinet member, even though he had publicly declared—on the occasion of the Canadian revolution—that he prayed for the defeat of his country's arms. In step with the advance of capitalism, the movement also gained adherents elsewhere—though at first only adherents without influence. It found support in Paris—indeed, in a circle oriented toward capitalist enterprise (for example, Frédéric Passy). True, pacifism as a matter of principle had existed before, though only among a few small religious sects. But modern pacifism, in its political foundations if not its derivation, is unquestionably a phenomenon of the capitalist world.

Wherever capitalism penetrated, peace parties of such strength arose that virtually every war meant a political struggle on the domestic scene. The exceptions are rare—Germany in the Franco-Prussian war of 1870–1871, both belligerents in the Russo-Turkish war of 1877–1878. That is why every war is carefully justified as a defensive war by the governments involved, and by all the political parties, in their official utterances—indicating a realization that a war of a different nature would scarcely be tenable in a political sense. (Here too the Russo-Turkish war is an exception, but a significant one.) In former times this would not have been necessary. Reference to an interest or pretense at moral justification was customary as early as the eighteenth century, but only in the nineteenth century did the assertion of attack, or the threat of attack, become the only avowed occasion for war. In the distant past, imperialism had needed no disguise whatever, and in the absolute autocracies only a very transparent one; but today imperialism is carefully hidden from public view—even though there may still be an unofficial appeal to warlike instincts. No people and no ruling class today can openly afford to regard war as a normal state of affairs or a normal element in the life of nations. No one doubts that today it must be characterized as an abnormality and a disaster. True, war is still glorified. But glorification in the style of King Tuglâi-palisharra is rare and unleashes such a storm of indignation that every practical politician carefully dissociates himself from such things. Everywhere there is official acknowledgment that peace is an end in itself—though not necessarily an end overshadowing all purposes that can be realized by means of war. Every expansionist urge must be carefully related to a concrete goal. All this is primarily a matter of political phraseology, to be sure. But the necessity for this phraseology is a symptom of the popular attitude. And that attitude makes a policy of imperialism more and more difficult—indeed, the very word imperialism is applied only to the enemy, in a reproachful sense, being carefully avoided with reference to the speaker's own policies.

The type of industrial worker created by capitalism is always vigorously anti-imperialist. In the individual case, skillful agitation may persuade the working masses to approve or remain neutral—a concrete goal or interest in self-defense always playing the main part—but no initiative for a forcible policy of expansion ever emanates from this quarter. On this point official socialism unquestionably formulates not merely the interests but also the conscious will of the workers. Even less than peasant imperialism is there any such thing as socialist or other working-class imperialism.

Despite manifest resistance on the part of powerful elements, the capitalist age has seen the development of methods for preventing war, for the peaceful settlement of disputes among states. The very fact of resistance means that the trend can be explained only from the mentality of capitalism as a mode of life. It definitely limits the opportunities imperialism needs if it is to be a powerful force. True, the methods in question often fail, but even more often they are successful. I am thinking not merely of the Hague Court of Arbitration but of the practice of submitting controversial issues to conferences of the major powers or at least those powers directly concerned—a course of action that has become less and less avoidable. True, here too the individual case may become a farce. But the serious setbacks of today must not blind us to the real importance or sociological significance of these things.

Among all capitalist economies, that of the United States is least burdened with precapitalist elements, survivals, reminiscences, and power factors. Certainly we cannot expect to find imperialist tendencies altogether lacking even in the United States, for the immigrants came from Europe with their convictions fully formed, and the environment certainly favored the revival of instincts of pugnacity. But we can conjecture that among all countries the United States is likely to exhibit the weakest imperialist trend. This turns out to be the truth. The case is particularly instructive, because the United States has seen a particularly strong emergence of capitalist interests in an imperialist direction—those very interests to which the phenomenon of imperialism has so often been reduced, a subject we shall yet touch on. Nevertheless the United States was the first advocate of disarmament and arbitration. It was the first to conclude treaties concerning arms limitations (1817) and arbitral courts (first attempt in 1797)—doing so most zealously, by the way, when economic interest in expansion was at its greatest. Since 1908 such treaties have been concluded with twenty-two states. In the course of the nineteenth century, the United States had numerous occasions for war, including instances that were well calculated to test its patience. It made almost no use of such occasions. Leading industrial and financial circles in the United States had and still have an evident interest in incorporating Mexico into the Union. There was more than enough opportunity for such annexation—but Mexico remained unconquered. Racial catch phrases and working-class interests pointed to Japan as a possible danger. Hence possession of the Philippines was not a matter of indifference—yet surrender of this possession is being discussed. Canada was an almost defenseless prize—but Canada remained independent. Even in the United States, of course, politicians need slogans—especially slogans calculated to divert attention from domestic issues. Theodore Roosevelt and certain magnates of the press actually resorted to imperialism—and the result, in that world of high capitalism, was utter defeat, a defeat that would have been even more abject, if other slogans, notably those appealing to anti-trust sentiment, had not met with better success.

These facts are scarcely in dispute. And since they fit into the picture of the mode of life which we have recognized to be the necessary product of capitalism, since we can grasp them adequately from the necessities of that mode of life and industry, it follows that capitalism is by nature anti-imperialist.

$$6$$

A CRITIQUE
OF THE MARXIST
ANALYSIS

By 1935 the course of the "new imperialism" had largely been run, and a proper historical evaluation was possible. The theories could be tested by facts, and the two did not necessarily agree.

A Critique of Imperialism BY W. L. LANGER

It is now roughly fifty years since the beginning of that great outburst of expansive activity on the part of the Great Powers of Europe which we have come to call "imperialism." And it is about a generation since J. A. Hobson published his "Imperialism: a Study," a book which has served as the starting point for most later discussions and which has proved a perennial inspiration for writers of the most diverse schools. A reappraisal of it is therefore decidedly in order. The wonder is that it has not been undertaken sooner.

Since before the outbreak of the World War the theoretical writing on imperialism has been very largely monopolized by the so-called Neo-Marxians, that is, by those who, following in the footsteps of the master, have carried on his historical analysis from the critique of capitalism to the study of this further phase, imperialism, the significance of which Marx himself did not appreciate and the very existence of which he barely adumbrated. The Neo-Marxians, beginning with Rudolf Hilferding and Rosa Luxemburg, have by this time elaborated a complete theory, which has recently been expounded in several ponderous German works. The theory hinges upon the idea of the accumulation of capital, its adherents holding that imperialism is

William L. Langer, "A Critique of Imperialism," reprinted by permission from *Foreign Affairs*, XIV (1935–1936), 102–119. Copyright by The Council on Foreign Relations, Inc., New York. Some footnotes omitted by permission.

nothing more nor less than the last stage in the development of capitalism—
the stage in which the surplus capital resulting from the system of production
is obliged by ever diminishing returns at home to seek new fields for investment abroad. When this surplus capital has transformed the whole world
and remade even the most backward areas in the image of capitalism, the
whole economic-social system will inevitably die of congestion.

That the classical writers of the socialistic school derived this basic idea
from Hobson's book there can be no doubt.[1] Lenin himself admitted, in his
"Imperialism, the Latest Stage of Capitalism," that Hobson gave "a very
good and accurate description of the fundamental economic and political
traits of imperialism," and that Hobson and Hilferding had said the essentials on the subject. This, then, has been the most fruitful contribution of
Hobson's essay. When we examine his ideas on this subject we refer indirectly to the larger part of the writing on imperialism since his day.

As a matter of pure economic theory it is most difficult to break down the
logic of the accumulation theory. It is a fact that since the middle of the last
century certain countries—first England, then France, Germany and the
United States—have exported large amounts of capital, and that the financial
returns from these investments in many instances came to overshadow completely the income derived by the lending countries from foreign trade. It is
also indisputable that industry embarked upon the road to concentration and
monopoly, that increased efficiency in production led to larger profits and to
the amassing of ever greater surpluses of capital. We must recognize further
that, as a general rule, the return from investments abroad was distinctly
above the return on reinvestment in home industry. In other words, the postulates of the socialist theory undoubtedly existed. There is no mentionable
reason why the development of the capitalist system should not have had the
results attributed to it.

But, as it happens, the actual course of history refutes the thesis. The course
of British investment abroad shows that there was a very considerable export
of capital before 1875, that is, during the climax of anti-imperialism in England. Between 1875 and 1895, while the tide of imperialism was coming to the
full, there was a marked falling off of foreign investment. Capital export was
then resumed on a large scale in the years before the war, though England
was, in this period, already somewhat disillusioned by the outcome of the
South African adventure and rather inclined to be skeptical about imperialism. Similar observations hold true of the United States. If the promulgation
of the Monroe Doctrine was an act of imperialism, where was the export of
capital which ought to have been its condition? Let us concede that the war
with Spain was an imperialist episode. At that time the United States was
still a debtor nation, importing rather than exporting capital. In Russia, too,

---

[1] I strongly suspect that Hobson, in turn, took over the idea from the very bourgeois American
financial expert, Charles A. Conant, whose remarkable article, "The Economic Basis of
Imperialism," in the *North American Review*, September 1898, p. 326–340, is now forgotten,
but deserves recognition.

the heyday of imperialism coincided with a period of heavy borrowing rather than of lending.

There is this further objection to be raised against the view of Hobson and his Neo-Marxian followers, that the export of capital seems to have little direct connection with territorial expansion. France, before the war, had plenty of capital to export, and some of her earliest and most vigorous imperialists, like Jules Ferry, declared that she required colonies in order to have adequate fields for the placement of this capital. But when France had secured colonies, she did not send her capital to them. By far the larger part of her exported funds went to Russia, Rumania, Spain and Portugal, Egypt and the Ottoman Empire. In 1902 only two or two and a half billion francs out of a total foreign investment of some 30 or 35 billion francs was placed in the colonies. In 1913 Britain had more money invested in the United States than in any colony or other foreign country. Less than half of her total export of capital had been to other parts of the Empire. The United States put more capital into the development of Canada than did England; and when, after the war, the United States became a great creditor nation, 43 percent of her investment was in Latin America, 27 percent in Canada and Newfoundland, and 22 percent in European countries. What she sent to her colonies was insignificant. Or let us take Germany, which in 1914 had about 25 billion marks placed abroad. Of this total only three percent was invested in Asia and Africa, and of that three percent only a small part in her colonies. Prewar Russia was a great imperialist power, but Russia had to borrow from France the money invested in her Far Eastern projects. In our own day two of the most outspokenly imperialist powers, Japan and Italy, are both nations poor in capital. Whatever the urge that drives them to expansion, it cannot be the need for the export of capital.

At the height of the imperialist tide, let us say from 1885 to 1914, there was much less talk among the advocates of expansion about the need for foreign investment fields than about the need for new markets and for the safeguarding of markets from the tariff restrictions of competitors. It is certain that in the opinion of contemporaries that was the mainspring of the whole movement. But this economic explanation, like the other, has not been borne out by the actual developments. Very few colonies have done even half of their trading with the mother country and many have done less. Taken in the large it can be proved statistically that the colonial trade has always played a relatively unimportant part in the total foreign commerce of the great industrial nations. These nations have always been each other's best customers and no amount of rivalry and competition has prevented their trade from following, not the flag, but the price-list. The position of Canada within the British Empire did not prevent her from levying tariffs against British goods, nor from developing exceedingly close economic relations with the United States. In the pre-war period German commerce with the British possessions was expanding at a relatively higher rate than was Britain's.

If one must have an economic interpretation of imperialism, one will prob-

ably find its historical evolution to have been something like this: In the days
of England's industrial preëminence she was, the very nature of the case,
interested in free trade. In the palmiest days of Cobdenism she exported manufactured goods to the four corners of the earth, but she exported also machinery and other producers' goods, thereby preparing the way for the
industrialization of the continental nations and latterly of other regions of the
world. In order to protect their infant industries from British competition,
these new industrial Powers threw over the teachings of the Manchester
school and began to set up tariffs. The result was that the national markets
were set aside, to a large extent, for home industry. British trade was driven
to seek new markets, where the process was repeated. But the introduction of
protective tariffs had this further effect, that it made possible the organization
of cartels and trusts, that is, the concentration of industry, the increase of
production and the lowering of costs. Surplus goods and low prices caused
the other industrial Powers likewise to look abroad for additional markets,
and, while this development was taking place, technological improvements
were making transportation and communication safer and more expeditious.
The exploration of Africa at that time was probably a pure coincidence, but it
contributed to the movement toward trade and expansion and the growth of
a world market. Fear that the newly opened areas of the world might be
taken over by others and then enclosed in tariff walls led directly to the
scramble for territory in Asia and Africa.

The socialist writers would have us believe that concentration in industry
made for monopoly and that the banks, undergoing the same process of evolution, were, through their connection with industry, enabled to take over
control of the whole capitalist system. They were the repositories of the surplus capital accumulated by a monopolistic system and they were therefore
the prime movers in the drive for imperial expansion, their problem being to
find fields for the investment of capital. This is an argument which does
violence to the facts as they appear historically. The socialist writers almost to
a man argue chiefly from the example of Germany, where cartellization came
early and where the concentration of banking and the control of industry by
the banks went further than in most countries. But even in Germany the
movement towards overseas expansion came before the growth of monopoly
and the amalgamation of the banks. In England, the imperialist country *par
excellence,* there was no obvious connection between the two phenomena.
The trust movement came late and never went as far as in Germany. The
same was true of the consolidation of the banking system. One of the perennial complaints in England was the lack of proper coördination between the
banks and industry. To a certain extent the English exported capital because
the machinery for foreign investment was better than the organization for
home investment. In the United States, to be sure, there was already a pronounced concentration of industry when the great outburst of imperialism
came in the last years of the past century, but in general the trust movement
ran parallel to the movement for territorial expansion. In any event, it would

be hard to disprove the contention that the growth of world trade and the world market brought on the tendency toward better organization and concentration in industry, rather than the reverse. It is obvious not only that one large unit can manufacture more cheaply than many small ones, but that it can act more efficiently in competition with others in the world market.

But this much is clear—that territorial control of extra-European territory solved neither the trade problem nor the question of surplus capital. The white colonies, which were the best customers, followed their own economic interests and not even tariff restrictions could prevent them from doing so. In the backward, colored, tropical colonies, which could be more easily controlled and exploited, it proved difficult to develop a market, because of the low purchasing power of the natives. The question of raw materials, of which so much has always been made, also remained open. The great industrial countries got but a fraction of their raw materials from the colonies, and the colonies themselves continued to show a tendency to sell products in the best market. As for the export of capital, that continued to flow in an ever broader stream, not because the opportunities for investment at home were exhausted, but because the return from foreign investment was apt to be better and because, in many cases, foreign investment was the easier course. Capital flowed from the great industrial countries of Europe, but it did not flow to their colonies. The United States and Canada, Latin America (especially the Argentine) and even old countries like Austria-Hungary and Russia, got the bulk of it. The export of capital necessarily took the form of the extension of credit, which in turn implied the transfer of goods. Not infrequently the granting of loans was made conditional on trade concessions by the borrowing country. So we come back to the question of trade and tariffs. In a sense the export of capital was nothing but a device to stimulate trade and to circumvent tariff barriers, which brings us back to the coincidence of the movement for protection and the movement toward imperialism.

This may seem like an oversimplified explanation and it probably is. Some may argue that imperialism is more than a movement toward territorial expansion and that financial imperialism in particular lays the iron hand of control on many countries supposedly independent. But if you try to divorce imperialism from territorial control you will get nowhere. Practically all writers on the subject have been driven to the conclusion that the problem cannot be handled at all unless you restrict it in this way. When Hobson wrote on imperialism, he had reference to the great spectacle of a few Powers taking over tremendous areas in Africa and Asia. Imperialism is, in a sense, synonymous with the appropriation by the western nations of the largest part of the rest of the world. If you take it to be anything else, you will soon be lost in nebulous concepts and bloodless abstractions. If imperialism is to mean any vague interference of traders and bankers in the affairs of other countries, you may as well extend it to cover any form of influence. You will have to admit cultural imperialism, religious imperialism, and what not. Personally I prefer to stick by a measurable, manageable concept.

But even though Hobson's idea, that imperialism "is the endeavor of the great controllers of industry to broaden the channel for the flow of their surplus wealth by seeking foreign markets and foreign investments to take off the goods and capital they cannot sell or use at home," proved to be the most stimulating and fertile of his arguments, he had the very correct idea that imperialism was also a "medley of aims and feelings." He had many other contributory explanations of the phenomenon. For example, he was keenly aware of the relationship between democracy and imperialism. The enfranchisement of the working classes and the introduction of free education had brought the rank and file of the population into the political arena. One result of this epoch-making change was the rise of the so-called yellow press, which catered to the common man's love of excitement and sensationalism. Northcliffe was one of the first to sense the value of imperialism as a "talking point." Colonial adventure and far-away conflict satisfied the craving for excitement of the industrial and white-collar classes which had to find some outlet for their "spectatorial lust." The upper crust of the working class, as Lenin admitted, was easily converted to the teaching of imperialism and took pride in the extension of empire.

No doubt this aspect of the problem is important. The mechanization of humanity in an industrial society is a phenomenon with which we have become all too familiar, and every thoughtful person now recognizes the tremendous dangers inherent in the powers which the demagogue can exercise through the press, the motion picture and the radio. In Hobson's day propaganda was still carried on primarily through the press, but later developments were already foreshadowed in the activities of a Northcliffe or a Hearst. Hobson himself was able to show how, during the war in South Africa, the English press took its information from the South African press, which had been brought very largely under the control of Rhodes and his associates. Even at that time Hobson and others were pointing out how imperialistic capital was influencing not only the press, but the pulpit and the universities. Indeed, Hobson went so far as to claim that the great inert mass of the population, who saw the tangled maze of world improvements through dim and bewildered eyes, were the inevitable dupes of able, organized interests who could lure or scare or drive them into any convenient course.

Recognizing as we do that control of the public mind involves the most urgent political problems of the day, it is nevertheless important to point out that there is nothing inexorable about the connection of propaganda and imperialism. Even if you admit that a generation ago moneyed interests believed that imperialism was to their advantage, that these interests exercised a far-reaching control over public opinion, and that they used this control to dupe the common man into support of imperial ventures, it is obvious that at some other time these same interests might have different ideas with regard to their own welfare, just as it is evident that public opinion may be controlled by some other agency—the modern dictator, for example.

But the same thing is not true of another influence upon which Hobson laid great stress, namely the biological conception of politics and international relations. During the last years of the nineteenth century the ideas of "social Darwinism," as it was called, carried everything before them. Darwin's catchwords—the struggle for existence and the survival of the fittest—which he himself always refused to apply to the social organism, were snapped up by others who were less scrupulous, and soon became an integral part of popular and even official thought on foreign affairs. It not only served to justify the ruthless treatment of the "backward" races and the carving up *in spe* of the Portuguese, Spanish, Ottoman and Chinese Empires and of other "dying nations," as Lord Salisbury called them, but it put the necessary imprimatur on the ideas of conflict between the great imperialistic Powers themselves, and supplied a divine sanction for expansion. It was currently believed, in the days of exuberant imperialism, that the world would soon be the preserve of the great states—the British, the American and the Russian—and it was deduced from this belief that survival in the struggle for existence was in itself adequate evidence of superiority and supernatural appointment. The British therefore looked upon their empire as a work of the divine will, while the Americans and Russians were filled with the idea of a manifest destiny. It will be at once apparent that glorification of war and joy in the conflict was intimately connected with the evolutionary mentality. Hobson, the most determined of anti-imperialists, was finally driven to define the whole movement as "a depraved choice of national life, imposed by self-seeking interests which appeal to the lusts of quantitative acquisitiveness and of forceful domination surviving in a nation from early centuries of animal struggle for existence."

The last phrases of this quotation will serve to lead us to the consideration of what has proved to be another fruitful thought of Hobson. He speaks, in one place, of imperialism as a sociological atavism, a remnant of the roving instinct, just as hunting and sport are left-overs of the physical struggle for existence. This idea of the roving instinct has made but little appeal to later writers, but the basic interpretation of imperialism as an atavism underlies the ingenious and highly intelligent essay of Joseph Schumpeter, "Zur Soziologie der Imperialismus," the only work from the bourgeois side which has had anything like the influence exerted by the writers of the socialist school. Schumpeter, who is an eminent economist, worked out a most convincing argument to prove that imperialism has nothing to do with capitalism, and that it is certainly not a development of capitalism. Capitalism, he holds, is by nature opposed to expansion, war, armaments and professional militarism, and imperialism is nothing but an atavism, one of those elements of the social structure which cannot be explained from existing conditions, but only from the conditions of the past. It is, in other words, a hang-over from a preceding economic order. Imperialism antedates capitalism, going back at least to the time of the Assyrians and Egyptians. It is, according to Schumpeter, the disposition of a state to forceful expansion without any special object and without a definable limit. Conquests are desired not so much because of their advantages, which are often questionable, but merely for the sake of conquest, success and activity.

Schumpeter's theory is in some ways extravagant, but it has served as the starting point for some very interesting speculation, especially among German scholars of the liberal persuasion. It is now fairly clear, I think, that the Neo-Marxian critics have paid far too little attention to the imponderable, psychological ingredients of imperialism. The movement may, without much exaggeration, be interpreted not only as an atavism, as a remnant of the days of absolute monarchy and mercantilism, when it was to the interest of the prince to increase his territory and the number of his subjects, but also as an aberration, to be classed with the extravagances of nationalism. Just as nationalism can drive individuals to the point of sacrificing their very lives for the purposes of the state, so imperialism has driven them to the utmost exertions and the extreme sacrifice, even though the stake might be only some little known and at bottom valueless part of Africa or Asia. In the days when communication and economic interdependence have made the world one in so many ways, men still interpret international relations in terms of the old cabinet policies, they are still swayed by out-moded, feudalistic ideas of honor and prestige.

In a sense, then, you can say that there is, in every people, a certain indefinable national energy, which may find expression in a variety of ways.

As a general rule great domestic crises and outbursts of expansion follow each other in the history of the world. In many of the continental countries of Europe, and for that matter in our own country, great internal problems were fought out in the period before 1870. The energies which, in Germany and Italy, went into the victory of the national cause, soon began to project themselves beyond the frontiers. While the continental nations were settling great issues between them, England sat "like a bloated Quaker, rubbing his hands at the roaring trade" he was carrying on. In those days the British cared very little for their empire. Many of them would have felt relieved if the colonies had broken away without a fuss. But, says Egerton, the best-known historian of British colonial policy, when the Germans and the French began to show an interest in colonial expansion, then the British began to think that there must be some value as yet undiscovered in the colonies. They not only started a movement to bind the colonies and the mother country more closely together, but they stretched out their hands for more. In the end they, who had the largest empire to begin with, got easily the lion's share of the yet unappropriated parts of the world. Some thought they were engaged in the fulfilment of a divine mission to abolish slavery, to spread the gospel, to clothe and educate the heathen. Others thought they were protecting the new markets from dangerous competitors, securing their supply of raw materials, or finding new fields for investment. But underlying the whole imperial outlook there was certainly more than a little misapprehension of economics, much self-delusion and self-righteousness, much misapplication of evolutionary teaching and above all much of the hoary tradition of honor, prestige, power

and even plain combativeness. Imperialism always carries with it the connotation of the *Imperator* and of the tradition of rule. It is bound up with
conscious or subconscious ideas of force, of brutality, of ruthlessness. It was
these traits and tendencies that were so vividly expressed in the poetry and
stories of Kipling, and it was his almost uncanny ability to sense the emotions
of his time and people that made him the greatest apostle of imperialism.

We shall not go far wrong, then, if we stress the psychological and political
factors in imperialism as well as its economic and intellectual elements. It
was, of course, connected closely with the great changes in the social structure
of the western world, but it was also a projection of nationalism beyond the
boundaries of Europe, a projection on a world scale of the time-honored
struggle for power and for a balance of power as it had existed on the Continent for centuries. The most casual perusal of the literature of imperialism
will reveal the continued potency of these atavistic motives. In a recent number of this very journal a leading Italian diplomat [*Dino Grandi—D. K.*],
explaining the policy of the Duce, recurred again and again to the failure
of the other countries to appreciate the fact that Italy is a young and active
country "animated by new spiritual values." By the much-decried Corfu episode of 1923, Mussolini, to give a concrete example, "called Europe's attention
to the respect due to the new Italy and to the reawakened energies of the
Italian people." In the present Ethiopian crisis there is not very much suggestion of economic or civilizing motives on the part of the Italians; rather
the Duce holds before his followers the prospect of revenge for the defeat at
Adua (reminiscent of Britain's thirst to avenge Gordon) and promises them
a glorious future. Not long ago he spoke to a group of veterans among the
ruins of ancient Rome and told them that every stone surrounding them
should remind them that Rome once dominated the world by the wisdom of
her rule and the might of her arms and that "nothing forbids us to believe
that what was our destiny yesterday may again become our destiny tomorrow." In much the same spirit an eminent Japanese statesman expressed himself recently in FOREIGN AFFAIRS: "As soon as the Meiji Restoration lifted the
ban on foreign intercourse, the long-pent-up energy of our race was released,
and with fresh outlook and enthusiasm the nation has made swift progress.
When you know this historical background and understand this overflowing
vitality of our race, you will see the impossibility of compelling us to stay still
within the confines of our little island home. We are destined to grow and
expand overseas." It is the same emphasis given by the Italian diplomat to the
need for an outlet for surplus energies.

It is, of course, true that both Italy and Japan have a serious population
problem and that Japan, at any rate, has an economic argument to back her
imperialistic enterprises in Manchuria and China. But it has been shown long
ago that the acquisition of new territory has no direct bearing on the population problem and that emigrants go where their interest calls them, not where
their governments would like to have them go. As for Japan's economic
needs, it may at least be questioned whether she would not be better off if she

avoided political and military commitments in China. Her cheap goods have made very extensive inroads in all the markets of the world, and her eventual conquest of the whole Chinese market is perhaps inevitable. Far from having gained much from her recent policy, she has had to face boycotts and other forms of hostility. In this case, certainly, one might debate whether the game is worth the candle.

Baron Wakatsuki, whose statement is quoted above, was careful to avoid mention of a factor in Japanese imperialism which, as every well-informed person knows, is probably the real explanation of Japanese policy. After the Meiji Restoration it was more the exuberance and bellicosity of the military caste in Japan than the enthusiasm of the country at large which determined the policy of the government. If one reads modern Japanese history aright one will find that from 1870 onward the military classes were constantly pressing upon the government for action in Korea. Only with the greatest difficulty did the civil authorities stave off this pressure. In 1894 the Tokyo government more or less rushed into the war with China in order to avoid a dangerous domestic crisis. In other words, the ideas of honor and patriotism were appealed to in order to divert attention from the parliamentary conflict which was then raging. After the Japanese victory it was the military men who, against the better judgment of men like Count Ito and Baron Mutsu, insisted on the cession of the Liaotung Peninsula, which netted Japan nothing but the intervention of Russia, Germany, and France. We need not pursue this subject in all its minute details. The point I want to make is that in the case of Japan, as in the case of many other countries, it is easier to show that the military and official classes are a driving force behind the movement for expansion than to show that a clique of nefarious bankers or industrialists is the determining factor. Business interests may have an interest in the acquisition of territory, or they may not. But military and official classes almost always have. War is, for the soldiers, a profession, and it is no mere chance that war and imperialism are so commonly lumped together. For officials, expansion means new territories to govern and new jobs to be filled.

Hobson, with his pronouncedly economic approach to the problem, held that "the struggle for markets, the greater eagerness of producers to sell than of consumers to buy, is the crowning proof of a false economy of distribution," of which imperialism is the fruit. The remedy, he thought, lay in "social reform." "There is no necessity to open up new foreign markets," he maintained; "the home markets are capable of indefinite expansion." These contentions sound familiar enough in this day of world depression. Whether the home markets are capable of indefinite expansion is a question on which the economic internationalists and the advocates of autarchy hold different opinions. The interesting thing for us to consider, however, is the fact that movements towards autarchy should have developed at all and that so much stress should now be laid upon the problems of redistribution of wealth, of building up purchasing power, and, in general, of domestic social reform. The current of activity has shifted distinctly from expansion to revolution, peaceful or violent. Perhaps it may be argued from this that the socialist thesis regarding imperialism is now being proved; that capitalism has already transformed the backward areas to such an extent that the markets are ruined, and that the capitalist system is rapidly choking. This view might be acceptable if it were not for the fact that the colonies and backward areas are still very far from developed and if it were not for the further fact that before the depression the colonial trade with the older countries was steadily increasing. In the last five years, to be sure, international commerce has sunk to an unbelievably low point, but the difficulty has been chiefly with the trade between the great industrial Powers themselves. It is quite conceivable that the crisis is primarily due to the special situation arising from the World War and that the root of the trouble lies in the impossibility of fitting tremendous international payments into the existing framework of trade relations. The fantastic tariff barriers which have been set up on all sides have simply aggravated a situation which has been developing since the teachings of Cobdenism first began to fall into disrepute.

But whatever the true explanation of our present difficulties, very few voices are raised in favor of a solution by the methods of imperialism. Indeed, the movement toward autarchy is in a way a negation of imperialism. Economically we have been disillusioned about imperialism. We have learned that colonies do not pay. Britain's expenditure for the defense of the empire alone is enormous, yet she has never yet devised a method by which anything like a commensurate return could be secured. The French military outlay on the colonies in 1913 was more than five hundred million francs, at a time when the entire trade of France with her colonies came to hardly three times that figure. Similar statistics could be quoted for Germany, and it is a well-known fact that the colonies of both Spain and Portugal were much more of a liability than an asset.

In the same way it has turned out that foreign investments of capital are not all that they were expected to be. The higher returns from colonial investments have often been counterbalanced by the greater insecurity that went with them. European countries had more than one opportunity to learn the lesson even before the war. We need only recall the Argentine fiasco of 1890 and the wildcat Kaffir Boom in South African securities in 1895 as classical examples of what might happen. But of course all these instances are completely dwarfed by the experiences of the postwar—or perhaps better, the pre-depression—decade. Foreign investments have caused acute international tensions and have resulted in phenomena like American dollar diplomacy in Latin America. The expenditure has been immense and what has been salvaged has been unimpressive enough. The nations of the world are still on the lookout for markets, as they have been for centuries, but the peoples of the world have become more or less convinced that the markets, if they can be got at all, can be got only by the offering of better and cheaper goods and not by occupation, political control or forceful exploitation. As for foreign investments, no one has any stomach for them and most of those fortunate enough to have money to invest would be glad to learn of a safe investment at home. The assurance of needed sources for raw materials is as much if not more of a problem today than it was a generation ago, but there is little sense in taking over the expensive administration of tropical or other territory to guarantee a source of raw materials, because somehow or other it usually turns out that the other fellow has the materials that you want, and it has long since become obvious that the idea of controlling sources of all the materials you may need is a snare and a delusion.

In 1919, at the Paris Peace Conference, the struggle among the victors for the colonial spoils of the vanquished reached the proportions of the epic and the heroic. It seems like a long time ago, because so much has happened since and because we have come to see that in large measure it was a case of much ado about nothing. To meet the demands for some sort of ethics in imperialism, the German colonies and large parts of the Ottoman Empire were set up as mandates under the League, the principle being wholly in consonance with the demand already put forward by Hobson that there be an "international council" which should "accredit a civilized nation with the duty of educating a lower race." But no one will deny that the mandate-seeking nations had other than purely altruistic motives. Though they should have known better, they still proceeded on the principle that some good was to be gotten out of colonies. But the sequel has shown that, just as the more backward regions imported producers' as well as consumers' goods from Europe and thereby laid the foundation for an independent economy by no means favorable to European industrialism, so they imported from Europe the ideas of self-determination and nationalism. Since the disaster suffered by the Italians at Adua in 1896 Europe has had ample evidence of what may happen when these ideas are taken up by native populations and defended with European implements of war. The story of the last generation has been not only the story of the westernization of the world, but also the story of the revolt of Asia and Africa against the western nations. True to Hobson's prediction, the attacks of imperialism on the liberties and existence of weaker races have stimulated in them a corresponding excess of national self-consciousness. We have had much of this in India and China and we have lived to witness the rise of Mustapha Kemal and Ibn Saud, to whom, for all we know, may be added the name of Hailé Selassié. France has had her battles in Morocco and the United States has at last come to appreciate the depth of resentment and ill-feeling against her in Latin America.

That these are not matters to be trifled with has by this time penetrated not only the minds of the governing classes and of the industrial and financial magnates, but also the mind of the man in the street. Who is there in England, for example, who puts much store by the mandates? Since the war England has allowed Ireland to cut loose and she is trying, as best she can, to put India on her own. Egypt has been given her independence and the mandate over Iraq has been abandoned. It would probably not be overshooting the mark to say that the British would be glad to get out of the Palestine hornet's nest if they could, and it is whispered that they would not be averse to turning back to Germany some of the African colonies. But it is not at all clear that Hitler really wants the colonies back. There obviously are other things that he wants more and the return of the colonies is more a question of vindication and prestige than anything else. In like fashion the United States has reversed the rambunctious policy of interference and disguised control in Mexico, the Caribbean and Latin America. We are about to withdraw from the Philippines with greater haste than the Filipinos desire or than many Americans think wise or decent. Neither Britain nor America has shown much real appetite for interfering against Japan in the Far East. Public opinion would not tolerate it, and even among those who have interests at stake there seems to be a growing opinion that if the Japanese wish to make the expenditure in blood and money necessary to restore order and security in China, they ought to be given a universal blessing.

France, to be sure, has shown no inclination to give up any of her vast colonial possessions, while Italy and Japan are both on the war-path. But the case of France is a very special one. Being less industrialized than England, Germany or the United States, she never felt to the same extent as those countries the urge for markets and sources of raw material. The imperialist movement was in France always something of an artificial and fictitious thing, fanned by a small group of enthusiasts. It takes a great and splendid colonial exposition to arouse much popular interest in the Greater France. It might be supposed, therefore, that France would be among the first nations to beat the retreat. But there is a purely military consideration that holds her back. Like England, she can draw troops from her colonies in time of crisis. In the British case this is always something of a gambling proposition. England has no choice but to defend the empire so long as it exists, but whether the dominions and colonies will support England is a question which they decide in each case as they choose. They elected to support the mother country in the Boer War and in the World War, but they did not choose to support her in the Near East when Mustapha Kemal drove the Greeks from Anatolia and appeared at the Straits in 1922.

With France the situation is different. In 1896 an eminent French statesman told Tsar Nicholas II, in reply to an inquiry, that France needed her colonies if only because they could supply her with man-power. The exploitation of that man-power reached large dimensions during the World War and it is now an important and generally recognized factor in France's military establishment. So far, so good, but the French must realize, and no doubt they do realize, that this may not go on forever. Who can say how long the "Senegalese" will be willing to pour out their blood in defense of French interests? Who can say when they will make use of the training and equipment that has been given them and turn upon their own masters? The spectacle of black troops holding down the population in the Rhineland was one which roused misgivings in the minds of many who think of western civilization in terms other than those of might and political exigency.

As for Japan and Italy, perhaps the less said the better. Japan is motivated by ideas which were current in Europe a generation ago and which are now being discarded. She has serious economic problems which have come with industrialism, and she is trying to solve them by means of territorial expansion and political control. But the peculiar thing is that, with all her progress, little headway has been made in the direction of breaking the power of the former feudal, military caste. Ideas of conquest, power and prestige are still dominant and they explain, more perhaps than economic considerations, the rampant imperialism of the present day.

The Italians, on the other hand, have involved themselves deeply in the Ethiopian affair for reasons which are hardly at all economic. If they were to conquer Abyssinia, what good would it really do them? The country is populated by some six to eight million warlike natives and it would cost a fortune in blood and treasure, poured out over a long term of years, to hold them in subjection. Can anyone seriously maintain that such an area would prove a suitable one for the settlement of very considerable numbers of Italian colonists, or that emigrants from Italy would choose Ethiopia so long as the door in Latin America is even the least bit open? It may be that there are oil reserves or gold in the country, but talk on this point is to a large extent speculation. The story of Ethiopia's wealth will, in all probability, be exploded as was the myth of Yunnan's treasure in the nineties. Taken in the large, it has been proved on many an occasion that "pegging out claims for the future" is in the long run a poor proposition. But Dino Grandi has said in so many words, in the article quoted above, that Italy's claims to empire were ignored and neglected at Paris in 1919 and that Italy must now teach the world to respect her. If that is indeed the object, Mussolini has failed to note the trend of world opinion since the war. The greatness of a nation is no longer necessarily measured by the extent of the national color on the maps of the world, and on many sides empire has come to be regarded indeed as the "white man's burden." In other words, Il Duce is behind the times. I think much of the disapproval of the Italian policy in the world at large is due to the fact that other nations have grown out of the mentality that has produced the Ethiopian crisis.

Imperialism as it existed in the last two generations will never again be possible, for the world has been definitely divided up and there are but very few unclaimed areas still to be appropriated. There may be exchanges of territory between the imperial Powers, and there will undoubtedly be aggression by one against another, but, in the large, territory has, in this age of rabid nationalism, become so sacred that its permanent transference has become more and more difficult and in many places almost impossible. The tightness of the territorial settlement in Europe long since became such that changes were possible only as the result of a great cataclysm, and the same petrifaction of the territorial *status quo* now tends to hold good of the general world settlement. If we are to give up empire, it will probably be to the natives to whom the territory originally belonged. If the tide of native resistance continues to rise, as it is likely to do, that course will become inevitable. We shall have more and more nations and more and more margin for conflict between them unless the mentality of nationalism undergoes a modification and there is some divorce of the ideas of nationalism and territory. In the interval the hope of the world would seem to be in the gradual evolution of voluntary federative combinations between groups of nations, regional pacts. The British Commonwealth, the Soviet Federation and the Pan-American bloc may point the way to a transition to some form of super-national organization for which the present League of Nations will have served as a model and a guide. But all this may be merely wishful thinking.

THE OUTBREAK OF THE FIRST WORLD WAR

WHO WAS RESPONSIBLE?

CONTENTS

QUESTIONS FOR STUDY

1. *Which documents provide evidence for the Austrian responsibility? for the German? for the Russian? for the English? for the French?*
2. *What is the importance of the Sarajevo affair?*
3. *What is the importance of the Hoyos mission?*
4. *Is the "blank check" appropriately named?*
5. *What action made war inevitable?*
6. *What role did the Kaiser play in bringing on the war? Lord Grey? Sazonov?*
7. *Which nation is most to blame? least to blame?*

The discussion of the ultimate causes of World War I is enduring and possibly fruitless. The European system of alliances, nationalism, economic competition, and imperialism all played an important role. The fact remains that in the century between the Congress of Vienna and Sarajevo, Europe had overcome one crisis after another without recourse to a major war. Yet the assassination of the Archduke Francis Ferdinand, heir to the Austro-Hungarian Empire, in a Bosnian town on June 28, 1914, produced a crisis that led to a general and catastrophic war. It is interesting to focus attention on the crisis of July 1914, for if we cannot apportion precise shares of the blame for the war, we can at least trace the steps that turned a Balkan incident into a major disaster. The following section examines the July crisis in some detail and attempts to place it in its proper perspective. Its analysis is crucial for understanding the larger problem of responsibility for the war.

The problem of assigning responsibility for World War I took on unusual importance when the victorious Allies fixed exclusive blame on Germany in the famous Article 231 of the Treaty of Versailles (p. 458). German leaders naturally rejected this assertion and argued against it vigorously not only because they thought it unjust but, even more important, because it served as the moral basis for the imposition of reparations payments and other sanctions on the defeated Germans. The resulting debate led to the publication of secret documents by each nation in an attempt to prove its own innocence and the guilt of others. As a consequence, the question of responsibility for World War I is probably the best documented problem among those studied by historians.

The assassination of Archduke Francis Ferdinand at Sarajevo, which set off the crisis, was certainly a shocking event, but it need not have led to war. The assassins were Bosnian and therefore citizens of the Austro-Hungarian Empire. To be sure, they were south Slavic nationalists, and the center of south Slavic agitation against Austria was Serbia, but at no time during the crisis could the Austrians produce evidence that the Serbian government was involved in the plot. Nevertheless, there were forces in Vienna who were eager to seize on the assassination as a pretext for attacking Serbia and eliminating it as a threat to the very existence of the Austro-Hungarian Empire. The Austrians, however, could not proceed alone, for there was the threat that if Austria attacked Serbia, Russia, the self-proclaimed protector of the Slavs and a power with a strong interest in the Balkans, would intervene. Before Austria could act, it needed a promise of support from Germany.

On July 5 the Austrian Foreign Minister met with the Kaiser and the German Chancellor and received what has been called a "blank check." Some scholars now argue that the check was not blank but that the Austrians were urged to move ahead with their plans to attack Serbia and to do so quickly. The Germans were led to take this position by a combination of considerations. For some time they had felt themselves "encircled" by the Triple Entente powers—France, Russia, and Great Britain. Their only reliable ally was Austria-Hungary, and they feared that it might collapse unless the agitation of the Slavs in the empire ceased. They could not, they believed, allow Austrian influence in the Balkans to wane and Russian influence to increase without endangering Germany's security. They hoped to confine any war that came out of the Sarajevo crisis to the Balkans, keeping the great powers out. Failing that, they hoped to keep Great Britain neutral. In any event, they did not entertain the thought of restraining or abandoning Austria.

Much of the evidence on which this analysis is based was known quite early; some was not, and some of what was known was treated with suspicion. In the 1920s a wave of attacks was launched against Article 231 and the theory of German war guilt, chiefly by American scholars. The most influential of these "revisionist" histories was that of Sidney B. Fay (pp. 501–508), who argued that the blame must be shared by all the powers but emphasized Russia's decision to order general mobilization on July 29 as the step "which finally rendered the European War inevitable." A. J. P. Taylor (pp. 509–516), benefiting from the work of scholars like Luigi Albertini and from the publication of new documents, came to a conclusion closer to that of the Treaty of Versailles. In his view, although the Germans did not plan a war for August 1914, "they welcomed it when the occasion offered." Laurence Lafore (pp. 517–521) took a view at longer range. While accepting Germany's predominant role in the July crisis, he regarded the continuing problem of Austria-Hungary as the true cause of the war.

1
THE
QUESTION OF
RESPONSIBILITY

Article 231 of the Treaty of Versailles firmly placed all the blame for the war on Germany, thus opening the debate.

Article 231 of the Treaty of Versailles

The Allied and Associated Governments affirm and Germany accepts the responsibility of Germany and her allies for causing all the loss and damage to which the Allied and Associated Governments and their nationals have been subjected as a consequence of the war imposed upon them by the aggression of Germany and her allies.

U.S. Department of State, *The Treaty of Versailles and After: Annotations of the Text of the Treaty* (1947), p. 413.

2
A DEFENSE
OF THE CENTRAL
POWERS

The following selection is an early and direct refutation of the war-guilt clause. Count Montgelas was an official spokesman for the German republic at the Versailles discussions of responsibility for the war. He helped to draft the German answer to the charge of war guilt.

FROM The Case for the Central Powers
BY MAX MONTGELAS

I.

Germany pursued no aim either in Europe or elsewhere which could only be achieved by means of war.

Austria-Hungary's only aim was to maintain the *status quo*. Her first intention of rectifying her frontiers at Serbia's expense was immediately abandoned at Germany's instance and even Sazonov was convinced of her territorial *désintéressement* by her definite statements . . .

France aimed at recovering Alsace Lorraine, and many leading French politicians also hoped to annex the Saar basin, whilst Russia aspired to possession of Constantinople and the Straits, both Powers knowing well that these aims could not be achieved without a European war.

Count Max Montgelas, *The Case for the Central Powers: An Impeachment of the Versailles Verdict*, Part III, Section 15 (1925), pp. 200–203, translated by Constantine Versey. Reprinted by permission of George Allen & Unwin Ltd., London.

2.

Germany's preparations for war were on a considerably smaller scale than those made by France, having regard to the political constellation, her geographical position, the extent of her unprotected frontiers, and the number of her population. From 1913 onwards, even her actual numerical peace strength was less, in respect of white troops, quite apart from the steadily increasing strength of the French coloured troops.

As compared with Russia's armaments, those of Austria-Hungary were absolutely inadequate.

The Franco-Russian allies were far superior to the Central Powers as regards the amount of war material, as well as of man power at their disposal.

3.

It was a political mistake to construct a German battle fleet, instead of completing the naval defences, but even in London the proportion of ten to sixteen Dreadnoughts finally proposed by Germany was not regarded as a menace.

4.

Even after Bismarck's time the German Empire repeatedly omitted to take advantage of favourable opportunities for a war of prevention.

5.

The Russian suggestion of the first Hague Conference was not based on pure love of peace. All the Great Powers, without exception, were most sceptical as regards the question of reducing armaments; the Russian proposal of 1899 was unanimously rejected, and public opinion in France strongly opposed Campbell-Bannerman's 1907 suggestion.

Neither at the first nor the second Hague Conference was any proposal to adjust serious international conflicts, affecting the honour and vital interests of a nation, brought forward or supported by any Great Power.

6.

The world war was not decided upon at Potsdam on the 5th of July, 1914; Germany merely assented to Austria's going to war with Serbia.

The possibility that the Austro-Serbian war, like others—the Boer, Moroccan, Tripolitan, and Balkan wars—might lead to further complications, was well weighed, but the risk was thought very small, in view of the special provocation.

7.

After the publication of the Serbian reply, Germany no longer thought war advisable, even against Serbia, and only favoured strictly limited military operations, which were considered justifiable, even in London.

8.

It is true that Germany did not support the proposal to extend the time limit, and rejected the idea of a conference. She not only, however, accepted every other proposal of mediation which came from London, but proposed on her own initiative the two most suitable methods of negotiation, namely, direct conversations between Vienna and St. Petersburg, and the idea of not going beyond Belgrade, which was adopted by Grey.

Sazonov's first formula was considered unacceptable, even in London, and the second was far worse than the first.

9.

An understanding had almost been reached by the methods Germany had been the first to propose, namely, direct discussions between Vienna and St. Petersburg, and limiting the military operations against Serbia, when the Russian mobilization suddenly tore the threads asunder.

10.

The leading men knew just as well in Paris and St. Petersburg as in Berlin, that this mobilization must inevitably lead to war.

Viviani telegraphed to London on the 1st of August that the one who first orders general mobilization is the aggressor, and he saddled Germany with this responsibility, knowing that the accusation was false.

11.

France did not advise moderation in St. Petersburg during the crisis. Finding that the first attempt to do so had annoyed Sazonov, the French Government refrained from taking any further steps in this direction.

12.

France not only did not advise Russia against ordering general mobilization, but gave surreptitious advice as to how she could carry on her military preparations secretly without provoking Germany to take timely countermeasures.

13.

Russia was the first Power to order general mobilization.
    France was the first Power to inform another Power officially of her decision to take part in a European war.

14.

England was never as firm in advising moderation in St. Petersburg as Germany in giving this advice to Vienna.
    Unlike other British diplomats, Sir Edward Grey only realized the meaning of the Russian mobilization when it was too late, and St. Petersburg was no longer willing to put a stop to it.

15.

Germany's premature declaration of war on Russia was a political error, which can be accounted for by the immense danger of the position on two fronts; her declaration of war on France was a pure formality.
    The decisive event was not this or that declaration of war, but the action which made the declaration of war inevitable, and this action was Russia's general mobilization.

16.

England declared war on Germany because she did not consider it compatible with her interests that France should be defeated a second time. Belgian interests, and the treaty of 1839, which Lord Salisbury had been prepared to sacrifice in 1887, were the reasons adduced to make it popular.

Over and above this, the naval agreement of 1912 with France compelled England to abandon her neutrality before Belgium's neutrality was violated.

17.

Greater diplomatic skill was shown by the Entente than by the Triple Alliance Powers.

By her false statements regarding Germany's preparations for war, particularly regarding the alleged priority of the German mobilization, by magnifying insignificant incidents on the frontier into invasions of French territory, and by withdrawing her covering troops to a distance of ten kilometres from the frontier, France created the prior condition in London, which Benckendorff had indicated, as far back as at the end of 1912, as necessary for England's intervention. An impression was produced in London that "the opponents of the Entente were the aggressors."

3
THE JULY
CRISIS

The following Austrian account describes the setting of the murder at Sarajevo and the Serbian response.

FROM Austrian Red Book

Ritter von Storck, Secretary of Legation, to Count Berchtold [1]

Belgrade, June 29, 1914.

Under the terrible shock of yesterday's catastrophe it is difficult for me to give any satisfactory judgment on the bloody drama of Serajevo with the necessary composure and judicial calm. I must ask you, therefore, to allow me for the moment to limit myself to putting on record certain facts.

Yesterday, the 15/28, the anniversary of the battle of the Amselfeld, was celebrated with greater ceremony than usual, and there were celebrations in honour of the Servian patriot, Miloš Obilić, who in 1389 with two companions treacherously stabbed the victorious Murad.

Among all Servians, Obilić is regarded as the national hero. In place of the Turks, however, we are now looked on as the hereditary enemy, thanks to the propaganda which has been nourished under the aegis of the Royal Government and the agitation which has for many years been carried on in the press.

A repetition of the drama on the field of Kossovo seems, therefore, to have hovered before the minds of the three young criminals of Serajevo, Princip,

---

Austrian Red Book, in *Collected Diplomatic Documents Relating to the Outbreak of the European War,* No. 1 (1915), p. 448. Reprinted by permission of Harrison & Sons Ltd., London.
[1] Count Leopold von Berchtold, Austro-Hungarian Minister for Foreign Affairs, 1912–1915.

Čabrinović and the third person still unknown, who also threw a bomb. They also shot down an innocent woman, and may therefore think that they have surpassed their model.

For many years hatred against the Monarchy has been sown in Servia. The crop has sprung up and the harvest is murder.

The news arrived at about 5 o'clock; the Servian Government at about 10 o'clock caused the Obilić festivities to be officially stopped. They continued, however, unofficially for a considerable time after it was dark. The accounts of eye-witnesses say that people fell into one another's arms in delight, and remarks were heard, such as: "It serves them right, we have been expecting this for a long time," or "This is revenge for the annexation."

This document is a note from the German ambassador at Vienna, Tschirschky, to the German Chancellor, Bethmann-Hollweg. The marginal remarks are by Kaiser Wilhelm II.

Tschirschky's Report of Austrian Opinion

The Ambassador at Vienna[1] to the Imperial Chancellor[2]

Vienna, June 30, 1914.

I hope not.

Count Berchtold told me today that *everything* pointed to the fact that the threads of the conspiracy to which the Archduke fell a sacrifice, *ran together at Belgrade*. The affair was so well thought out that very young men were intentionally selected for the perpetration of the crime, against whom *only a mild punishment could be decreed*. The Minister spoke very bitterly about the Serbian plots.

Now or never. Who authorized him to act that way? That is very stupid! It is none of his business, as it is solely the affair of Austria, what she plans to do in this case.

I frequently hear expressed here, even among serious people, the wish that *at last a final and fundamental reckoning should be had with the Serbs*. The Serbs should first be presented with a number of demands, and in case they should not accept these, energetic measures should be taken. *I take opportunity of every such occasion to advise quietly*

Max Montgelas and Walther Schücking, eds., *Outbreak of the World War: German Documents Collected by Karl Kautsky*, No. 7 (1924), p. 61, translated by Carnegie Endowment for International Peace. Reprinted by permission of Carnegie Endowment for International Peace.
[1] Heinrich Leonhard von Tschirschky und Bögendorff, German Ambassador to Austria-Hungary, 1907–1916.
[2] Dr. Theobald von Bethmann-Hollweg, Chancellor of the German Empire, 1909–1917.

Later, if plans go wrong, it will be said that Germany did not want it! Let Tschirschky be good enough to drop this nonsense! The Serbs must be disposed of, AND *that right* SOON! *Goes without saying; nothing but truisms.*

but very impressively and seriously against too hasty steps. First of all, they must make sure what they want to do, for so far I have heard only indefinite expressions of opinion. Then the chances of every kind of action should be carefully weighed, and it should be kept in mind that Austria-Hungary does not stand alone in the world, that it is her duty to think not only of her allies, but to take into consideration the entire European situation, and especially to bear in mind the attitude of Italy and Roumania on all questions that concern Serbia.

Von Tschirschky

On July 5 Count Ladislaus Hoyos, Secretary for Balkan Affairs at the Austro-Hungarian Ministry of Foreign Affairs, arrived in Berlin to confer with the Germans. Hoyos' version of what he learned is presented here by Luigi Albertini, an Italian historian. Since there has been some doubt about the reliability of the Hoyos account, Albertini cites an interview with Alfred Zimmermann, German Undersecretary of Foreign Affairs, who took part in the talks.

FROM The Origins of the War of 1914 BY LUIGI ALBERTINI

When questioned by the present writer Hoyos stated that at his interview with Zimmermann on the afternoon of the 5th he delivered himself of the mission entrusted to him by Berchtold, handing over a copy of Francis Joseph's letter and of the Austrian memorandum. He explained to Zimmermann that the Sarajevo outrage touched vital Austrian interests in both home and foreign affairs, that Vienna found itself compelled to arrive at a definite settlement of accounts with Serbia, but that before taking a decisive step the Austrian Government needed to be certain that its intentions met with the full approval of Berlin. Hoyos assured the present writer that he had been surprised to find Zimmermann in wholehearted agreement that Austria-Hungary could no longer tolerate Serbian provocation. The decision of the Kaiser and Bethmann-Hollweg was still awaited but there was little doubt that they would give Austria the assurance of unconditional support from

Luigi Albertini, *The Origins of the War of 1914,* II (1953), 144–145, translated and edited by Isabella M. Massey. Reprinted by permission of The Clarendon Press, Oxford.

Germany. Zimmermann inquired what steps Vienna proposed to take and Hoyos replied that so far no decision had been taken but that the idea was to impose severe conditions on Serbia and, if these were not accepted, go to war. Zimmermann replied that if Austria meant to act she must do so immediately without diplomatic delays which would waste precious time and give the alarm to *Entente* diplomacy.

We at Vienna—he said—have the defect of arguing too much and changing our minds. Once a decision was taken, there should be no time lost in going into action so as to take Serbia and the chancelleries of Europe by surprise. Austrian reprisals were amply justified by the Sarajevo crime.

Zimmermann felt sure that, if this course were pursued, the conflict would remain localized, but that, should France and Russia intervene, Germany alone with her increased military strength would be able to meet them. Hoyos told him that as soon as he was in possession of the German reply he would return to Vienna, and a Council of Joint Ministers would be summoned. Zimmermann replied that after the Council meeting it would be desirable that no further time should be lost.

Hoyos thus continues his narrative:

And as Tschirschky at Vienna had advised me to be very firm and detailed in my account of Austrian plans at Berlin, I carried out Berchtold's instructions by stating that, once we had beaten Serbia, we intended to partition her territory among Austria-Hungary, Bulgaria, and Albania. Zimmermann replied with a smile of satisfaction that this was a question concerning only ourselves and that he would raise no objections. Next day Bethmann officially informed Szögyény and myself in the presence of Zimmermann that it was entirely for us to decide on the measures we were to take: in whatever circumstances and whatever our decision we should find Germany unconditionally at our side in allied loyalty. Twice over he said to me, however, that in his personal opinion, with things as they were, only "immediate action against Serbia" could solve our difficulties with her. "The international situation was entirely in our favour." When I started out from Vienna, despite all that had been said by Naumann and Ganz, I did not expect to find in Berlin such instantaneous and complete understanding of our difficulties. Our design of a decisive settlement of accounts with Serbia met with no objection. On the contrary we were told that this was also the opinion of Germany and we were advised to take "immediate action." This incitement, expressed to me first by Zimmermann and then by Bethmann, made a great impression on me and I did not fail to draw attention to it in the telegram which I sent to Vienna over Szögyény's signature after the conversation.

Zimmermann, in answer to an inquiry from the present writer, wrote on 17 June 1938:

The Wilhelmstrasse, in coming to the conclusion that the war would remain confined to Austria-Hungary and Serbia and that its spread to Europe would be avoided, went on the assumption that the Dual Monarchy would lose no time in proceeding against Serbia. To avoid the impression of exercising constraint, we unfortunately refrained from explicitly influencing our ally in the sense of this assumption. Austria-Hungary failed to act without delay and under the powerful impression of the Sarajevo murder. She allowed precious weeks to slip by in useless investigations; finally she sent an ultimatum to Serbia without making the necessary military preparations to invade Serbia immediately and occupy Belgrade in the event of a rejection, which was surely to be expected. This mistake gave the *Entente* Powers the welcome chance to exchange views and arrive at an understanding.

Bethmann-Hollweg's Relay of Kaiser Wilhelm's Position

The Imperial Chancellor to the Ambassador at Vienna

Telegram 113.
Confidential. For Your Excellency's personal information and guidance.

Berlin, July 6, 1914.

The Austro-Hungarian Ambassador yesterday delivered to the Emperor a confidential personal letter from the Emperor Franz Joseph, which depicts the present situation from the Austro-Hungarian point of view, and describes the measures which Vienna has in view. A copy is now being forwarded to Your Excellency.

I replied to Count Szögyény[1] today on behalf of His Majesty that His Majesty sends his thanks to the Emperor Franz Joseph for his letter and would soon answer it personally. In the meantime His Majesty desires to say that he is not blind to the danger which threatens Austria-Hungary and thus the Triple Alliance as a result of the Russian and Serbian Panslavic agitation. Even though His Majesty is known to feel no unqualified confidence in Bulgaria and her ruler, and naturally inclines more toward our old ally Roumania and her Hohenzollern prince, yet he quite understands that the Emperor Franz Joseph, in view of the attitude of Roumania and of the danger of a new Balkan alliance aimed directly at the Danube Monarchy, is anxious to bring about an understanding between Bulgaria and the Triple Alliance. His

Max Montgelas and Walther Schücking, eds., *Outbreak of the World War: German Documents Collected by Karl Kautsky,* No. 15 (1924), pp. 78–79, translated by the Carnegie Endowment for International Peace. Reprinted by permission of Carnegie Endowment for International Peace.
[1] Austro-Hungarian Ambassador to Germany.

Majesty will, therefore, direct his minister at Sofia to lend the Austro-Hungarian representative such support as he may desire in any action taken to this end. His Majesty will, furthermore, make an effort at Bucharest, according to the wishes of the Emperor Franz Joseph, to influence King Carol to the fulfillment of the duties of his alliance, to the renunciation of Serbia, and to the suppression of the Roumanian agitations directed against Austria-Hungary.

Finally, as far as concerns Serbia, His Majesty, of course, can not interfere in the dispute now going on between Austria-Hungary and that country, as it is a matter not within his competence. The Emperor Franz Joseph may, however, rest assured that His Majesty will faithfully stand by Austria-Hungary, as is required by the obligations of his alliance and of his ancient friendship.

Bethmann-Hollweg.

Already on July 1 Victor Naumann, a German publicist close to the German Foreign Secretary, had met with Hoyos and urged an attack on Serbia. In the following selection Albertini shows that similar views were communicated by the German ambassador.

FROM The Origins of the War of 1914 BY LUIGI ALBERTINI

But Berlin gave Austria-Hungary not only what Lutz describes as the "curse" of a free hand. It also gave her incitement and encouragement to take action against Serbia. We have already noted Naumann's call of 1 July on Hoyos. On 4 July Forgach drafted a note stating that he had seen Ganz, the Vienna correspondent of the *Frankfurter Zeitung*, who had that day been received by Tschirschky. Ganz had said that the German Ambassador had several times repeated to him with the obvious intention that the Ballplatz should be told of it

that Germany would support the Monarchy through thick and thin in whatever it might decide regarding Serbia. The Ambassador had added that the sooner Austria-Hungary went into action the better. Yesterday would have been better than to-day, and to-day would be better than to-morrow.

Luigi Albertini, *The Origins of the War of 1914*, II (1953), 150–151, translated and edited by Isabella M. Massey. Reprinted by permission of The Clarendon Press, Oxford.

To his English colleague Bunsen, as the latter on 5 July reported to the Foreign Office, Tschirschky said that relations between Austria and Serbia

must be bad, and that nothing could mend them. He added that he had tried in vain to convince Berlin of this fundamental truth. Some people in Germany still persisted in believing in the efficacy of a conciliatory policy on the part of Austria towards Serbia. He himself knew better.

But after Sarajevo, even in Germany those in authority were converted to Tschirschky's thesis and he, in consequence, could speak a very different language to Berchtold than he had used on 2 July. This is shown by what Berchtold wrote to Tisza on 8 July:

Tschirschky has just left after having told me that he has received a telegram from Berlin containing instructions from his Imperial master to emphasize here that Berlin expects the Monarchy to take action against Serbia and that Germany would not understand our letting the opportunity slip without striking a blow. . . . From other utterances of the Ambassador I could see that Germany would interpret any compromise on our part with Serbia as a confession of weakness, which would not remain without repercussions on our position in the Triple Alliance and the future policy of Germany.

On July 18 Dr. H. von Schoen, the Bavarian *chargé d'affaires* at Berlin, wrote an account of the discussions between the Germans and the Austrians based on conversations with well-informed German officials.

Von Schoen's Account of the Austro-German Discussions

The Chargé d'Affaires at Berlin to the President of the Ministerial Council

Report 386.

Berlin, July 18, 1914.

I have the honor most respectfully to report as follows to Your Excellency concerning the prospective settlement between the Austro-Hungarian Government and Serbia, on the basis of conversations I have had with Under-

Max Montgelas and Walther Schücking, eds., *Outbreak of the World War: German Documents Collected by Karl Kautsky*, Supplement IV, No. 2 (1924), pp. 616–618, translated by Carnegie Endowment for International Peace. Reprinted by permission of Carnegie Endowment for International Peace.

Secretary of State Zimmermann, and further with the Foreign Office reporter for the Balkans and the Triple Alliance, and with the counselor of the Austro-Hungarian Embassy.

The step which the Vienna Cabinet has decided to undertake at Belgrade, and which will consist in the presentation of a note, will take place on the twenty-fifth instant. The reason for the postponement of the action to that date is that they wish to await the departure of Messrs. Poincaré and Viviani from Petersburg, in order not to facilitate an agreement between the Dual Alliance Powers on any possible counter-action. Until then, by the granting of leave of absence simultaneously to the Minister of War and the Chief of the General Staff, the Vienna authorities will have the appearance of being peacefully inclined; and they have not failed of success in their attempts to influence the press and the exchange. It is recognized here that the Vienna Cabinet has been proceeding quite cleverly in this matter, and it is only regretted that Count Tisza, who at first is said to have been against any severe action, has somewhat raised the veil of secrecy by his statement in the Hungarian House of Deputies.

As Mr. Zimmermann told me, the note, so far as has yet been determined, will contain the following demands:

1. The issuing of a proclamation by the King of Serbia which shall state that the Serbian Government has nothing to do with the Greater-Serbia movement, and fully disapproves of it.
2. The initiation of an inquiry to discover those implicated in the murder of Serajevo, and the participation of Austrian officials in this inquiry.
3. Proceedings against all who have participated in the Greater-Serbia movement.

A respite of forty-eight hours is to be granted for the acceptance of these demands.

It is perfectly plain that Serbia can not accept any such demands, which are incompatible with her dignity as a sovereign state. Thus the result would be war.

Here they are absolutely willing that Austria should take advantage of this favorable opportunity, even at the risk of further complications. But whether they will actually rise to the occasion in Vienna, still seems doubtful to Mr. von Jagow, as it does to Mr. Zimmermann. The Under-Secretary of State made the statement that Austria-Hungary, thanks to her indecision and her desultoriness, had really become the Sick Man of Europe, as Turkey had once been, upon the partition of which, the Russians, Italians, Roumanians, Serbians and Montenegrins were now waiting. A powerful and successful move against Serbia would make it possible for the Austrians and Hungarians to feel themselves once more to be a national power, would again revive the country's collapsed economic life, and would set foreign aspirations back for years. To judge from the indignation at the bloody deed that was now dominant over the entire Monarchy, it looked as if they could even be sure of the

Slav troops. In a few years, with the continuance of the operation of the Slavic propaganda, this would no longer be the case, as even General Conrad von Hötzendorf himself had admitted.

So they are of the opinion here that Austria is face to face with an hour of fate, and for this reason they declared here without hesitation, in reply to an inquiry from Vienna, that we would agree to any method of procedure which they might determine on there, even at the risk of a war with Russia. The blank power of full authority that was given to Count Berchtold's Chief of the Cabinet, Count Hoyos, who came here to deliver a personal letter from the Emperor together with a detailed memorial, went so far that the Austro-Hungarian Government was empowered to deal with Bulgaria concerning her entrance into the Triple Alliance.

In Vienna they do not seem to have expected such an unconditional support of the Danube Monarchy by Germany, and Mr. Zimmermann has the impression that it is almost embarrassing to the always timid and undecided authorities at Vienna not to be admonished by Germany to caution and self-restraint. To what extent they waver in their decisions at Vienna is shown by the circumstance that Count Berchtold, three days after he had had inquiries made here concerning the alliance with Bulgaria, telegraphed that he still had scruples about closing with Bulgaria.

So it would have been liked even better here, if they had not waited so long with their action against Serbia, and the Serbian Government had not been given time to make an offer of satisfaction on its own account, perhaps acting under Russo-French pressure.

What attitude the other Powers will take toward an armed conflict between Austria and Serbia will chiefly depend, according to the opinion here, on whether Austria will content herself with a chastisement of Serbia, or will demand territorial compensation for herself. In the first case, it might be possible to localize the war; in the other case, on the other hand, more serious complications would probably be inevitable.

The administration will, immediately upon the presentation of the Austrian note at Belgrade, initiate diplomatic action with the Powers, in the interest of the localization of the war. It will claim that the Austrian action has been just as much of a surprise to it as to the other Powers, pointing out the fact that the Emperor is on his northern journey and that the Prussian Minister of War, as well as the Chief of the Grand General Staff are away on leave of absence. (As I take the liberty to insert here, not even the Italian Government has been taken into confidence.) It will lay stress upon the fact that it is a matter of interest for all the monarchical Governments that "the Belgrade nest of anarchists" be once and for all rooted out; and it will make use of its influence to get all the Powers to take the view that the settlement between Austria and Serbia is a matter concerning those two nations alone. The mobilization of the German Army is to be refrained from, and they are also going to work through the military authorities to prevent Austria from mobilizing her entire Army, and especially not those troops stationed in Galicia, in order to avoid bringing about automatically a counter-mobilization on the part of Russia, which would force, first ourselves, and then France, to take similar measures and thereby conjure up a European war.

The attitude of Russia will, above all else, determine the question whether the attempt to localize the war will succeed.

If Russia is not determined on war against Austria and Germany, in any case, she can, in that event—and that is the most favorable factor in the present situation—very well remain inactive, and justify herself toward the Serbs by announcing that she approves of the kind of fighting that goes to work with the throwing of bombs and with revolver shots just as little as any of the other civilized nations; this, especially, so long as Austria does not render doubtful Serbia's national independence. Mr. Zimmermann assumes that both England and France, to neither of whom a war would be acceptable at the present moment, will try to exert a pacifying influence on Russia; besides that, he is counting on the fact that "bluffing" constitutes one of the most favored requisites of Russian policy, and that while the Russian likes to threaten with the sword, he still does not like so very much to draw it in behalf of others at the critical moment.

England will not prevent Austria from calling Serbia to account; it is only the destruction of the nation that she would scarcely permit, being far more likely—true to her traditions—presumably to take a stand, even in this case, for the principles of nationality. A war between the Dual Alliance and the Triple Alliance would be unwelcome to England at the present time, if only in consideration of the situation in Ireland. Should it, however, come to that, according to all opinion here, we should find our English cousins on the side of our enemies, inasmuch as England fears that France, in the event of a new defeat, would sink to the level of a Power of the second class, and that the "balance of power," the maintenance of which England considers to be necessary for her own interests, would be upset thereby.

This report from Pourtalès, German Ambassador to Russia, to Bethmann-Hollweg, describes the attitude of Sazonoff, Russian Minister for Foreign Affairs, to the growing crisis. The marginal remarks are by Kaiser Wilhelm.

Pourtalès' Report of the Russian Response

The Ambassador at Petersburg to the Imperial Chancellor

St. Petersburg, July 21, 1914.

Mr. Sazonoff, who spent several days last week at his country estate in the Government of Grodno, has been quite anxious since his return from there on account of the relations between Austria-Hungary and Serbia. He told me that he had received very alarming reports from London, Paris and Rome, and that Austria-Hungary's attitude was inspiring an increasing worry everywhere. Mr. Schebeko, too, who was in general a calm observer, reported that the feeling in Vienna against Serbia was constantly growing more bitter.

The Minister took the opportunity of giving his wrath at the Austro-Hungarian policy free rein, as usual. That the Emperor Franz Joseph and even Count Berchtold were friends of peace, Mr. Sazonoff was, it is true, willing to admit, but he said that there were very powerful and dangerous influences at work, which were constantly gaining ground in both halves of the Empire, and which did not hesitate at the idea of plunging Austria into a war, even at the risk of starting a general world conflagration. One anxiously asked oneself the question whether the aged Monarch and his week Foreign Minister would always be able to successfully oppose these influences.

The picture fits Petersburg much better!

Previously the belligerent elements, among which clerical intrigues also played an especially important rôle, had set their hopes on the dead Archduke, Franz Ferdinand. The death of the Archduke had in no way discouraged them; on the other hand, they were the very ones who were inspiring[1] the dangerous policy which Austria-Hungary

---

Max Montgelas and Walther Schücking, eds., *Outbreak of the World War: German Documents Collected by Karl Kautsky*, No. 120 (1924), pp. 159–162, translated by Carnegie Endowment for International Peace. Reprinted by permission of Carnegie Endowment for International Peace.
[1] Exclamation-point by the Emperor in the margin.

was pursuing at the present moment. The actual leaders in this policy were two men, particularly, whose increasing influence appeared to the highest degree dubious—namely, Count Forgach, who is "an intriguer of the basest sort," and Count Tisza, who "is half a fool."

Fool yourself, Mr. Sazonoff!

I replied to Mr. Sazonoff that his unmeasured reproaches against Austro-Hungarian policy appeared to me to be strongly influenced by his too great sympathy for the Serbs, and to be utterly unjustified. No sensible man could refuse to recognize the complete restraint observed by the Vienna Cabinet since the assassination at Serajevo. It seemed to me that to decide just how far Austria-Hungary was justified in holding the Serbian Government responsible for the Greater-Serbia agitations, as early as this, before the result of the inquiry concerning the assassination was known, was absolutely premature. But according to everything that was already known, one could scarcely doubt *that the Greater-Serbia agitation was stirred up under the very eyes of the Serbian Government, and that even the shameless assassination itself had been planned in Serbia*. No great nation, however, could possibly tolerate permanently the existence along its borders of a propaganda which directly threatened its own security. Should, therefore, as appearances now seemed to indicate, traces be discovered at the inquiry into the origin of the crime which pointed back to Serbia, and should it be proved that the Serbian Government had regrettably connived at the intrigues directed against Austria, then the Austro-Hungarian Government would unquestionably be justified in using strong language at Belgrade. I could not conceive that in such a case the representations of the Vienna Cabinet to the Serbian Government could meet with the objection of any Power whatsoever.

Yes.

Right.

Yes.

Good.

The Minister met these arguments with the assertion that the support of the Greater-Serbia propaganda in Austria-Hungary by Serbia or by the Serbian Government in any way, *had in nowise been proved*. A whole country *could not be held responsible* for *the acts of individuals*. Furthermore, the murderer of the Archduke was not even a Serbian subject. There *certainly* was a Greater-Serbia propaganda *in Austria,* but it was the result of the *bad* methods of government by which Austria had distinguished herself for ages back. Just as there was a Greater-Serbia propaganda, one heard talk also of the Italian Irredenta and of the Free-from-Rome movement. The Vienna Cabi-

Genuinely Russian.

net had not the slightest reason for complaining of the *attitude of the Serbian Government,* which, on the contrary, *was behaving itself with entire propriety.*

Damnation!

I interjected here that it did not suffice for members of the Serbian Government themselves to refrain from participation in the anti-Austrian propaganda. Austria-Hungary had far more reason to require that the Serbian authorities should proceed actively against the anti-Austrian propaganda, for it was impossible that the Government should refuse responsibility for everything that was going on in the country.

Right.

And Russia for her spies that are being apprehended everywhere!

According to that principle, returned Mr. Sazonoff, Russia ought to hold the Swedish Government responsible for the *anti-Russian agitation* that has been *going on in Sweden* for about a year and a half.

I pointed out that in Sweden the matter merely concerned a political agitation, and not, as in Serbia, a propaganda of action.

Mr. Sazonoff remarked in reply that those people in Austria who were advocating proceeding against Serbia would apparently not content themselves with making representations at Belgrade, but that their object was the annihilation of Serbia. I answered that I had never heard of any object but one, namely, the "clarification" of Austria-Hungary's relations with Serbia.

And the best thing, too.

No! with Russia, yes! as the perpetrator and advocate of regicide!!!

The Minister continued excitedly, saying that in any case, Austria-Hungary, if she was absolutely determined to disturb the peace, ought not to forget that in that event she would *have to reckon with Europe.* Russia could not look indifferently on at a move at Belgrade which aimed at the humiliation (of) Serbia. I remarked that I was able [to] *see no humiliation* in serious representations by which Serbia was reminded of her international obligations. Mr. Sazonoff answered that it would all depend on how the move was carried out; that in no case *should there be any talk of an ultimatum.*

Right.

It's already there!

The Minister repeatedly called attention in the course of the conversation to the fact that, according to information he had received, the situation was being very seriously regarded in Paris and London also, and he was visibly attempting to give me the impression that even in England Austria's attitude was strongly disapproved.

He is wrong!

At the conclusion of our conversation I asked Mr. Sazonoff what there was, in his opinion, to the alleged plan for the union of Serbia and Montenegro, lately so much discussed in the papers. The Minister remarked that such a union was desired only by Montenegro, which would of course benefit most by it. Such a union was not being considered at all in Serbia, as the late Mr. Hartwig had specifically emphasized in one of his last reports. At the most, all that was wanted was a closer economic relation with Montenegro, but a personal union was not in any way desired.

Qui vivra verra!

Mr. Sazonoff has also expressed to my Italian colleague his anxiety about the Austro-Serbian tension, and remarked at the time that Russia would *not be able to permit* Austria-Hungary to *make any threats against Serbia* or to *take any military measures*. "*La politique de la Russie*," said Mr. Sazonoff, "*est pacifique, mais pas passive*."

F. Pourtalès.

On the afternoon of July 23 the Austrians presented a list of demands to Serbia and the Serbs were given forty-eight hours to reply. The Austrian ambassador at Belgrade was instructed to leave the country and break off diplomatic relations unless the demands were met without reservations.

The Austrian Ultimatum

The results brought out by the inquiry no longer permit the Imperial and Royal Government to maintain the attitude of patient tolerance which it has observed for years toward those agitations which center at Belgrade and are spread thence into the territories of the Monarchy. Instead, these results impose upon the Imperial and Royal Government the obligation to put an end to those intrigues, which constitute a standing menace to the peace of the Monarchy.

In order to attain this end, the Imperial and Royal Government finds itself compelled to demand that the Serbian Government give official assurance that it will condemn the propaganda directed against Austria-Hungary, that is to say, the whole body of the efforts whose ultimate object it is to separate

Max Montgelas and Walther Schücking, eds., *Outbreak of the World War: German Documents Collected by Karl Kautsky*, Supplement I (1924), pp. 604–605, translated by Carnegie Endowment for International Peace. Reprinted by permission of Carnegie Endowment for International Peace.

from the Monarchy territories that belong to it; and that it will obligate itself to suppress with all the means at its command this criminal and terroristic propaganda.

In order to give these assurances a character of solemnity, the Royal Serbian Government will publish on the first page of its official organ of July 26/13, the following declaration:

The Royal Serbian Government condemns the propaganda directed against Austria-Hungary, that is to say, the whole body of the efforts whose ultimate object it is to separate from the Austro-Hungarian Monarchy territories that belong to it, and it most sincerely regrets the dreadful consequences of these criminal transactions.

The Royal Serbian Government regrets that Serbian officers and officials should have taken part in the above-mentioned propaganda and thus have endangered the friendly and neighborly relations, to the cultivation of which the Royal Government had most solemnly pledged itself by its declaration of March 31, 1909.

The Royal Government, which disapproves and repels every idea and every attempt to interfere in the destinies of the population of whatever portion of Austria-Hungary, regards it as its duty most expressly to call the attention of the officers, officials, and the whole population of the Kingdom to the fact that for the future it will proceed with the utmost rigor against any persons who shall become guilty of any such activities, activities to prevent and to suppress which, the Government will bend every effort.

This declaration shall be brought to the attention of the Royal army simultaneously by an order of the day from His Majesty the King, and by publication in the official organ of the army.

The Royal Serbian Government will furthermore pledge itself:

1. to suppress every publication which shall incite to hatred and contempt of the Monarchy, and the general tendency of which shall be directed against the territorial integrity of the latter;
2. to proceed at once to the dissolution of the *Narodna Odbrana*, to confiscate all of its means of propaganda, and in the same manner to proceed against the other unions and associations in Serbia which occupy themselves with propaganda against Austria-Hungary; the Royal Government will take such measures as are necessary to make sure that the dissolved associations may not continue their activities under other names or in other forms;
3. to eliminate without delay from public instruction in Serbia, everything, whether connected with the teaching corps or with the methods of teaching, that serves or may serve to nourish the propaganda against Austria-Hungary;
4. to remove from the military and administrative service in general all officers and officials who have been guilty of carrying on the propaganda against Austria-Hungary, whose names the Imperial and Royal Government reserves the right to make known to the Royal Government when communicating the material evidence now in its possession;

5. to agree to the cooperation in Serbia of the organs of the Imperial and Royal Government in the suppression of the subversive movement directed against the integrity of the Monarchy;

6. to institute a judicial inquiry against every participant in the conspiracy of the twenty-eighth of June who may be found in Serbian territory; the organs of the Imperial and Royal Government delegated for this purpose will take part in the proceedings held for this purpose;

7. to undertake with all haste the arrest of Major Voislav Tankositch and of one Milan Ciganovitch, a Serbian official, who have been compromised by the results of the inquiry;

8. by efficient measures to prevent the participation of Serbian authorities in the smuggling of weapons and explosives across the frontier; to dismiss from the service and to punish severely those members of the Frontier Service at Schabats and Losnitza who assisted the authors of the crime of Serajevo to cross the frontier;

9. to make explanations to the Imperial and Royal Government concerning the unjustifiable utterances of high Serbian functionaries in Serbia and abroad, who, without regard for their official position, have not hesitated to express themselves in a manner hostile toward Austria-Hungary since the assassination of the twenty-eighth of June;

10. to inform the Imperial and Royal Government without delay of the execution of the measures comprised in the foregoing points.

The Imperial and Royal Government awaits the reply of the Royal Government by Saturday, the twenty-fifth instant, at 6 P.M., at the latest.

A mémoire concerning the results of the inquiry at Serajevo, as far as they concern the functionaries referred to in Points 7 and 8, is appended to this note.

This is a report from the German ambassador at St. Petersburg to the Foreign Office in Berlin. Marginal remarks are by Kaiser Wilhelm.

Pourtalès' Report on Russia's Reaction to Austria's Ultimatum

The Ambassador at Petersburg to the Foreign Office

Telegram 149.

St. Petersburg, July 25, 1914.

Good.

Have just had long interview with Sazonoff at which subject of dispatch 592 figured exhaustively. Minister, who was *very much excited* and gave vent to boundless reproaches against Austria-Hungary, stated in the most determined manner that it would be impossible for Russia to admit that the Austro-Serb quarrel could be settled between the two parties concerned. The obligations which Serbia had assumed after the Bosnian crisis and to which the Austrian note refers, were assumed toward Europe, consequently the affair was a European affair, and it was for *Europe* to investigate as to whether Serbia had lived up to these obligations. He therefore proposes that the documents in relation to the inquiry be laid before the Cabinets of the six Powers. Austria could not be both accuser and judge in her own case. Sazonoff announced that he could in no way consider as proven the facts alleged by Austria in her note, that the inquiry, on the other hand, inspired him with the greatest (suspicion). He continued by saying that, in case the facts asserted should be proved to be true, Serbia could give Austria satisfaction in the purely legal questions, but not, on the other hand, in the matter of the demands of a political nature. I called attention to the fact that it was impossible to separate the legal from the political side of the matter, as the assassination was inseparably connected with the Greater-Serbia propaganda.

Rot!

That's a question of the point of view!

Cannot be separated.

Max Montgelas and Walther Schücking, eds., *Outbreak of the World War: German Documents Collected by Karl Kautsky,* No. 160 (1924), pp. 186–187, translated by Carnegie Endowment for International Peace. Reprinted by permission of Carnegie Endowment for International Peace.

Right.
Panslavistic.
Most certainly not!

    I promised to lay his ideas before my Government, but did not believe that we would suggest to our ally to submit the results of an inquiry conducted by her *once more to a European tribunal.* Austria would object to this suggestion just as any Great Power would have to refuse to submit

Bravo!
Well said!

itself to a court of arbitration in a case in which its vital interests were at stake.

Not since her fraternizing with the French socialist republic!

    My references to the monarchical principle made little impression on the Minister. Russia *knew* what she *owed to the monarchical principle,* with which, however, this case had nothing to do. I requested Sazonoff very seriously, avoiding everything that might have the appearance of a threat, not to let himself be led astray by his hatred of

Regicide.
Very good.

Austria and *"not to defend a bad cause." Russia could not possibly constitute herself the advocate of regicides.*

Well, go to it!

    In the course of the conversation Sazonoff exclaimed: "If Austria-Hungary devours Serbia, we will go to war with her." From this it may perhaps be concluded that Rus-

That it wants to do, it seems.

sia will only take up arms in the event of Austria's attempting to acquire territory at the expense of Serbia. The expressed desire to Europeanize the question also seems to point to the fact that immediate intervention on the part

Not correct.

of Russia is not to be anticipated.

Pourtalès.

Here is a telegram from Sir Edward Grey, British Secretary of State for Foreign Affairs, to the British ambassador at Vienna.

Grey's Conveyal of the British Response to Austria's Ultimatum

Grey to Bunsen

Tel. (No. 148)

Foreign Office, July 24, 1914

Austro-Hungarian Ambassador has communicated to me the note addressed to Servia with the explanation of the Austro-Hungarian Government upon it.

I said that the murder of the Archduke and some of the circumstances stated in the Austro-Hungarian note with regard to Servia naturally aroused sympathy with Austria, but I thought it a great pity that a time-limit, and such a short time-limit, had been introduced at this stage, and the note seemed to me the most formidable document I had ever seen addressed by one State to another that was independent. Demand No. 5 might mean that the Austro-Hungarian Government were to be entitled to appoint officials who should have authority in Servian territory and this would hardly be consistent with the maintenance of independent sovereignty of Servia.

I was not, however, making these comments in order to discuss the merits of the dispute between Austria-Hungary and Servia; that was not our concern. It was solely from the point of view of the peace of Europe that I should concern myself with the matter, and I felt great apprehension.

I must wait to hear the views of other Powers and no doubt we should consult with them to see what could be done to mitigate difficulties.

The Austro-Hungarian Ambassador observed that there had been so much procrastination on the part of Servia that a time-limit was essential. Some weeks had passed since the murder of the Archduke and Servia had made no sign of sympathy or help; if she had held out a hand after the murder the present situation might have been prevented.

I observed that a time-limit could have been introduced at any later stage if Servia had procrastinated about a reply; as it was, the Austro-Hungarian Government not only demanded a reply within forty-eight hours, but dictated the terms of the reply.

Grey's Proposal for a Conference

Sir Edward Grey to Sir F. Bertie

Tel. (No. 232)

Foreign Office, July 26, 1914

Ask Minister for Foreign Affairs if he would be disposed to instruct Ambassador here to join with representatives of Italy, Germany, France, and myself in a conference to be held here at once in order to endeavour to find an issue to prevent complications. With this view representatives at Vienna, St. Petersburg, and Belgrade should be authorised in informing Governments to which they are accredited of above suggestion to request that pending results of conference all active military operations shall be suspended.

(Repeated to Vienna, St. Petersburg, and Nish.)
(Sent also to Berlin, and Rome.)

Prince Lichnowsky, the German ambassador at London, was in close touch with the ruling circles of England and better informed on British opinion than were his colleagues in Berlin. The following report is one of several in which he argues against war on the grounds that England would be likely to fight against Germany.

Lichnowsky's Appraisal of the British Position

The Ambassador at London to the Foreign Office

Telegram 161.

London, July 26, 1914

Have just talked with Sir A. Nicolson and Sir W. Tyrrell. According to reports at hand here, a general calling to the colors of the Russian reservists is not projected, but only a partial mobilization far from our frontiers. Both gentlemen see in Sir E. Grey's proposal to hold a conference *à quatre* here, the only possibility of avoiding a general war, and hope that in this way it would be possible to get full satisfaction for Austria, as Serbia would be more apt to give in to the pressure of the Powers and to submit to their united will than to the threats of Austria. But the absolute prerequisite to the bringing about of the conference and the maintenance of peace would be the cessation of all military activities. Once the Serbian border was crossed, everything would be at an end, as no Russian Government would be able to tolerate this, and would be forced to move to the attack on Austria unless she wanted to see her status among the Balkan nations lost forever. Sir W. Tyrrell, who saw Sir E. Grey last evening and is fully cognizant of his views, pointed out to me repeatedly and with emphasis the immense importance of Serbia's territory remaining unviolated until the question of the conference had been settled, as otherwise every effort would have been in vain and the world war would be inevitable. The localization of the conflict as hoped for in Berlin was wholly impossible, and must be dropped from the calculations of practical politics. If we two should succeed—that is, His Majesty the Emperor or his Government and representatives in conjunction with Sir E. Grey—in preserving the peace of Europe, German-English relations would be placed on a firm foundation for time everlasting. If we did not succeed, everything would be doubtful.

Max Montgelas and Walther Schücking, eds., *Outbreak of the World War: German Documents Collected by Karl Kautsky*, No. 236 (1924), pp. 230–231, translated by Carnegie Endowment for International Peace. Reprinted by permission of Carnegie Endowment for International Peace.

I would like to offer an urgent warning against believing any further in the possibility of localization, and to express the humble wish that our policy be guided solely and alone by the need of sparing the German nation a struggle in which it has nothing to gain and everything to lose.

Sir E. Grey returns this evening.

Lichnowsky.

Serbia's Answer to the Ultimatum

The Royal Servian Government have received the communication of the Imperial and Royal Government of the 10th instant, and are convinced that their reply will remove any misunderstanding which may threaten to impair the good neighbourly relations between the Austro-Hungarian Monarchy and the Kingdom of Servia.

Conscious of the fact that the protests which were made both from the tribune of the national Skuptchina and in the declarations and actions of the responsible representatives of the State—protests which were cut short by the declarations made by the Servian Government on the 18th March, 1909—have not been renewed on any occasion as regards the great neighbouring Monarchy, and that no attempt has been made since that time, either by the successive Royal Governments or by their organs, to change the political and legal state of affairs created in Bosnia and Herzegovina, the Royal Government draw attention to the fact that in this connection the Imperial and Royal Government have made no representation except one concerning a school book, and that on that occasion the Imperial and Royal Government received an entirely satisfactory explanation. Servia has several times given proofs of her pacific and moderate policy during the Balkan crisis, and it is thanks to Servia and to the sacrifice that she has made in the exclusive interest of European peace that that peace has been preserved. The Royal Government cannot be held responsible for manifestations of a private character, such as articles in the press and the peaceable work of societies—manifestations which take place in nearly all countries in the ordinary course of events, and which, as a general rule, escape official control. The Royal Government are all the less responsible, in view of the fact that at the time of the solution of a series of questions which arose between Servia and Austria-Hungary they gave proof of a great readiness to oblige, and thus succeeded in settling the majority of these questions to the advantage of the two neighbouring countries.

For these reasons the Royal Government have been pained and surprised at the statements, according to which members of the Kingdom of Servia are

British Diplomatic Correspondence, in *Collected Diplomatic Documents Relating to the Outbreak of the European War*, No. 39 (1915), pp. 31–37.

supposed to have participated in the preparations for the crime committed at Serajevo; the Royal Government expected to be invited to collaborate in an investigation of all that concerns this crime, and they were ready, in order to prove the entire correctness of their attitude, to take measures against any persons concerning whom representations were made to them. Falling in, therefore, with the desire of the Imperial and Royal Government, they are prepared to hand over for trial any Servian subject, without regard to his situation or rank, of whose complicity in the crime of Serajevo proofs are forthcoming, and more especially they undertake to cause to be published on the first page of the "Journal officiel," on the date of the 13th (26th) July, the following declaration:—

"The Royal Government of Servia condemn all propaganda which may be directed against Austria-Hungary, that is to say, all such tendencies as aim at ultimately detaching from the Austro-Hungarian Monarchy territories which form part thereof, and they sincerely deplore the baneful consequences of these criminal movements. The Royal Government regret that, according to the communication from the Imperial and Royal Government, certain Servian officers and officials should have taken part in the above-mentioned propaganda and thus compromised the good neighbourly relations to which the Royal Servian Government was solemnly engaged by the declaration of the 31st March, 1909, which declaration disapproves and repudiates all idea or attempt at interference with the destiny of the inhabitants of any part whatsoever of Austria-Hungary, and they consider it their duty formally to warn the officers, officials, and entire population of the kingdom that henceforth they will take the most rigorous steps against all such persons as are guilty of such acts, to prevent and to repress which they will use their utmost endeavour."

This declaration will be brought to the knowledge of the Royal Army in an order of the day, in the name of His Majesty the King, by his Royal Highness the Crown Prince Alexander, and will be published in the next official army bulletin.

The Royal Government further undertake:—

1. To introduce at the first regular convocation of the Skuptchina a provision into the press law providing for the most severe punishment of incitement to hatred or contempt of the Austro-Hungarian Monarchy, and for taking action against any publication the general tendency of which is directed against the territorial integrity of Austria-Hungary. The Government engage at the approaching revision of the Constitution to cause an amendment to be introduced into article 22 of the Constitution of such a nature that such publication may be confiscated, a proceeding at present impossible under the categorical terms of article 22 of the Constitution.

2. The Government possess no proof, nor does the note of the Imperial and Royal Government furnish them with any, that the "Narodna Odbrana" and other similar societies have committed up to the present any criminal

act of this nature through the proceedings of any of their members. Nevertheless, the Royal Government will accept the demand of the Imperial and Royal Government, and will dissolve the "Narodna Odbrana" Society and every other society which may be directing its efforts against Austria-Hungary.

3. The Royal Servian Government undertake to remove without delay from their public educational establishments in Servia all that serves or could serve to foment propaganda against Austria-Hungary, whenever the Imperial and Royal Government furnish them with facts and proofs of this propaganda.

4. The Royal Government also agree to remove from military service all such persons as the judicial enquiry may have proved to be guilty of acts directed against the integrity of the territory of the Austro-Hungarian Monarchy, and they expect the Imperial and Royal Government to communicate to them at a later date the names and the acts of these officers and officials for the purposes of the proceedings which are to be taken against them.

5. The Royal Government must confess that they do not clearly grasp the meaning or the scope of the demand made by the Imperial and Royal Government that Servia shall undertake to accept the collaboration of the organs of the Imperial and Royal Government upon their territory, but they declare that they will admit such collaboration as agrees with the principle of international law, with criminal procedure, and with good neighbourly relations.

6. It goes without saying that the Royal Government consider it their duty to open an enquiry against all such persons as are, or eventually may be, implicated in the plot of the 15th June, and who happen to be within the territory of the kingdom. As regards the participation in this enquiry of Austro-Hungarian agents or authorities appointed for this purpose by the Imperial and Royal Government, the Royal Government cannot accept such an arrangement, as it would be a violation of the Constitution and of the law of criminal procedure; nevertheless, in concrete cases communications as to the results of the investigation in question might be given to the Austro-Hungarian agents.

7. The Royal Government proceeded, on the very evening of the delivery of the note, to arrest Commandant Voislav Tankossitch. As regards Milan Ziganovitch, who is a subject of the Austro-Hungarian Monarchy and who up to the 15th June was employed (on probation) by the directorate of railways, it has not yet been possible to arrest him.

The Austro-Hungarian Government are requested to be so good as to supply as soon as possible, in the customary form, the presumptive evidence of guilt, as well as the eventual proofs of guilt which have been collected up to the present, at the enquiry at Serajevo for the purposes of the later enquiry.

8. The Servian Government will reinforce and extend the measures which

have been taken for preventing the illicit traffic of arms and explosives across the frontier. It goes without saying that they will immediately order an enquiry and will severely punish the frontier officials on the Schabatz-Loznitza line who have failed in their duty and allowed authors of the crime of Serajevo to pass.

9. The Royal Government will gladly give explanations of the remarks made by their officials whether in Servia or abroad, in interviews after the crime which according to the statement of the Imperial and Royal Government were hostile towards the Monarchy, as soon as the Imperial and Royal Government have communicated to them the passages in question in these remarks, and as soon as they have shown that the remarks were actually made by the said officials, although the Royal Government will itself take steps to collect evidence and proofs.

10. The Royal Government will inform the Imperial and Royal Government of the execution of the measures comprised under the above heads, in so far as this has not already been done by the present note, as soon as each measure has been ordered and carried out.

If the Imperial and Royal Government are not satisfied with this reply, the Servian Government, considering that it is not to the common interest to precipitate the solution of this question, are ready, as always, to accept a pacific understanding, either by referring this question to the decision of the International Tribunal of The Hague, or to the Great Powers which took part in the drawing up of the declaration made by the Servian Government on the 18th (31st) March, 1909.

Belgrade, July 12 (25), 1914

Bethmann-Hollweg's Reaction to the British Proposal

The Imperial Chancellor to the Ambassador at Vienna

Telegram 169.

Berlin, July 27, 1914.

Prince Lichnowsky has just telegraphed:

Sir E. Grey had me call on him just now and requested me to inform Your Excellency as follows:

The Serbian Chargé d'Affaires had just transmitted to him the text of the Serbian reply to the Austrian note. It appeared from the reply that Serbia had

Max Montgelas and Walther Schücking, eds., *Outbreak of the World War: German Documents Collected by Karl Kautsky*, No. 277 (1924), pp. 255–256, translated by Carnegie Endowment for International Peace. Reprinted by permission of Carnegie Endowment for International Peace.

agreed to the Austrian demands to an extent such as he would never have believed possible; except in one point, the participation of Austrian officials in the judicial investigation, Serbia had actually agreed to everything that had been demanded of her. It was plain that this compliance of Serbia's *was to be attributed solely to the pressure exerted from Petersburg.*

Should Austria fail to be satisfied with this reply, in other words, should this reply not be accepted at Vienna as a foundation for peaceful negotiations, or should Austria even proceed to the occupation of Belgrade, which lay quite defenseless before her, it would then be absolutely evident that Austria was only seeking an excuse for crushing Serbia. And thus, that Russia and Russian influence in the Balkans were to be struck at through Serbia. It was plain that Russia could not regard such action with equanimity, and would have to accept it as a direct challenge. The result would be the most frightful war that Europe had ever seen, and no one could tell to what such a war might lead.

We had repeatedly, and even yesterday, stated the Minister, turned to him with the request that he *make a plea for moderation at Petersburg. He had always gladly complied with this request* and during the last crisis had subjected himself to reproaches from Russia to the effect that he was placing himself too much on our side and too little on theirs. Now he was turning to us with the request that we should make use of our influence at Vienna either to get them to accept the reply from Belgrade as satisfactory or as the basis for conferences. He was convinced that it lay in our hands to bring the matter to a settlement by means of the proper representations, and he would regard it as a good augury for the future *if we two should once again succeed in assuring the peace of Europe by means of our mutual influence on our allies.*

I found the Minister irritated for the first time. He spoke with great seriousness and seemed absolutely to expect that we should successfully make use of our influence to settle the matter. He is also going to make a statement in the House of Commons today in which he is to express his point of view. In any event, I am convinced that in case it should come to war after all, we should no longer be able to count on British sympathy or British support, as every evidence of ill-will would be seen in Austria's procedure.

Since we have already refused one English proposal for a conference, it is impossible for us to waive *a limine* this English suggestion also. By refusing every proposition for mediation, we should be held responsible for the conflagration by the whole world, and be set forth as the original instigators of the war. That would also make our position impossible in our own country, where we must appear as having been forced into the war. Our situation is all the more difficult, inasmuch as Serbia has apparently yielded to a very great degree. Therefore we cannot refuse the mediator's rôle, and must submit the English proposal to the consideration of the Vienna Cabinet, especially as London and Paris continue to make their influence felt in Petersburg. I request Count Berchtold's opinion on the English suggestion, as likewise his views on Mr. Sazonoff's desire to negotiate directly with Vienna.

Bethmann-Hollweg.

Goschen was the British ambassador at Berlin. In the following telegram he reports the German answer to the proposal for a conference to Grey.

Goschen's Transmission of the German Refusal

Sir E. Goschen to Sir Edward Grey

Tel. (No. 96)

Berlin, July 27, 1914

Your telegram No. 232 of 26th of July to Paris.

Secretary of State for Foreign Affairs says that conference you suggest would practically amount to a court of arbitration and could not, in his opinion, be called together except at the request of Austria and Russia. He could not therefore, desirous though he was to cooperate for the maintenance of peace, fall in with your suggestion. I said I was sure that your idea had nothing to do with arbitration, but meant that representatives of the four nations not directly interested should discuss and suggest means for avoiding a dangerous situation. He maintained, however, that such a conference as you proposed was not practicable. He added that news he had just received from St. Petersburg showed that there was an intention on the part of M. Sazonof to exchange views with Count Berchtold. He thought that this method of procedure might lead to a satisfactory result, and that it would be best, before doing anything else, to await outcome of the exchange of views between the Austrian and Russian Governments.

In the course of a short conversation Secretary of State for Foreign Affairs said that as yet Austria was only partially mobilising, but that if Russia mobilised against Germany latter would have to follow suit. I asked him what he meant by "mobilising against Germany." He said that if Russia only mobilised in south Germany would not mobilise, but if she mobilised in north Germany would have to do so too, and Russian system of mobilisation was so complicated that it might be difficult exactly to locate her mobilisation. Germany would therefore have to be very careful not to be taken by surprise.

In the crucial days following the rejection of the ultimatum, France seems not to have tried to restrain Russia. The following telegram was omitted from the *Russian Orange Book*.

French Full Support of Russia

The Russian Ambassador at Paris, M. Isvolsky,
to the Russian Foreign Secretary, M. Sazonov

Telegram. Secret. No. 195

Paris, July 14/27, 1914

Immediately upon my return to Paris, I saw the Minister of Justice [Bienvenu-Martin] in the presence of Abel Ferry and Berthelot. They confirmed the details of the steps taken by the German Ambassador, of which you have been informed by Sevastopoulo's telegrams Nos. 187 and 188. This morning, Baron Schoen confirmed in writing the declaration made by him yesterday, to wit:

1. "Austria has declared to Russia that she is not seeking territorial acquisitions and will respect the integrity of Serbia. Her only aim is to assure her own security;
2. "The prevention of war consequently rests upon Russia;
3. "Germany and France entirely united in the ardent desire to maintain peace, ought to press Russia to be moderate."

In this connection Baron Schoen particularly emphasized the expression "united" [*solidaire*] applied to Germany and France. According to the conviction of the Minister of Justice, these steps on the part of Germany are taken with the evident object of disuniting Russia and France, of inducing the French Government to make representations at St. Petersburg, and of thus compromising our ally in our eyes, and, in case of war, of throwing the responsibility not on Germany, who is ostensibly making every effort to preserve peace, but on Russia and France. Today, two hours before the steps taken by the Austrian Ambassador reported in my telegram 191, the German Ambassador paid a visit to Abel Ferry and made him, in the name of his Government, a new proposition "of intervention of France and Germany between Russia and Austria." Abel Ferry replied to him that he would bring

"French Full Support of Russia," from *Readings in European International Relations*, pp. 361–362, edited by W. Henry Cooke and Edith P. Stickney. Copyright 1931 by Harper & Brothers; renewed 1959 by W. Henry Cooke. Reprinted by permission of Harper & Row, Publishers.

this proposal to the attention of the Minister of Justice and merely observed that it would be opportune to leave the initiative of intervention to the four Powers, to which Baron Schoen acquiesced. The Minister of Justice has told me that he does not understand the sense of the new proposal of Baron Schoen, but that he viewed it with defiance and proposed to tell him tomorrow that a reply would be given him on the return to Paris of the Minister of Foreign Affairs on Wednesday. Altogether, I am struck by the way the Minister of Justice and his colleagues correctly understand the situation and how firm and calm is their decision to give us the most complete support and to avoid the least appearance of divergence of view between us.

Isvolsky

The Kaiser's Reaction to Serbia's Reply

The Emperor to the Secretary of State for Foreign Affairs

Your Excellency:

New Palace, July 28, 1914, 10 A.M.

After reading over the Serbian reply, which I received this morning, I am convinced that on the whole the wishes of the Danube Monarchy have been acceded to. The few reservations that Serbia makes in regard to individual points could, according to my opinion, be settled by negotiation. But it contains the announcement *orbi et urbi* of a capitulation of the most humiliating kind, and as a result, *every cause for war* falls to the ground.

Nevertheless, the piece of paper, like its contents, can be considered as of little value so long as it is not translated into *deeds*. The Serbs are Orientals, therefore liars, tricksters, and masters of evasion. In order that these beautiful promises may be turned to truth and facts, a *douce violence* must be exercised. This should be so arranged that Austria would receive a HOSTAGE (Belgrade), as a guaranty for the enforcement and carrying out of the promises, and should occupy it until the *petita* had ACTUALLY been complied with. This is also necessary in order to give the army, now UNNECESSARILY mobilized for the third time, the external *satisfaction d'honneur* of an ostensible success in the eyes of the world, and to make it possible for it to feel that it had at least stood on foreign soil. Unless this were done, the abandonment of the campaign might be the cause of a wave of bad feeling against the Monarchy, which would be dangerous in the highest degree. In case Your Excellency

Max Montgelas and Walther Schücking, eds., *Outbreak of the World War: German Documents Collected by Karl Kautsky,* No. 293 (1924), pp. 273–274, translated by Carnegie Endowment for International Peace. Reprinted by permission of Carnegie Endowment for International Peace.

shares my views, I propose that we say to Austria: Serbia has been forced to retreat in a very humiliating manner, and we offer our congratulations. Naturally, as a result, EVERY CAUSE FOR WAR HAS VANISHED. But a GUARANTY that the promises WILL BE CARRIED OUT is unquestionably necessary. That could be secured by means of the TEMPORARY military occupation of a portion of Serbia, similar to the way we kept troops stationed in France in 1871 until the billions were paid. ON THIS BASIS, I am ready to MEDIATE FOR PEACE with Austria. Any proposals or protests to the contrary by other nations I should refuse regardless, especially as all of them have made more or less open appeals to me to assist in maintaining peace. This I will do in my own way, and as sparingly of Austria's NATIONALISTIC FEELING, and of the HONOR OF HER ARMS as possible. For the latter has already been appealed to on the part of the highest War Lord, and is about to respond to the appeal. Consequently it is absolutely necessary that it receive a visible *satisfaction d'honneur;* this is the *prerequisite* of my mediation. Therefore Your Excellency will submit a proposal to me along the lines sketched out; which shall be communicated to Vienna. I have had Plessen write along the lines indicated above to the Chief of the General Staff, who is entirely in accord with my views.

Wilhelm I. R.

Austria's Reception of Serbia's Reply

The Austro-Hungarian Ambassador to the Foreign Office

Memorandum

Berlin, July 27, 1914.

The Royal Serbian Government has refused to agree to the demands which we were forced to make for the lasting assurance of those of our vital interests threatened by that Government, and has thus given evidence that it is not willing to desist from its destructive efforts directed toward the constant disturbance of some of our border territories and their eventual separation from the control of the Monarchy. We are therefore compelled, to our regret and much against our will, to force Serbia by the sharpest means to a fundamental alteration of her hitherto hostile attitude. That in so doing, aggressive intentions are far from our thoughts, and that it is merely in self-defense that we have finally determined, after years of patience, to oppose the Greater-Serbia intrigues with the sword, is well known to the Imperial German Government.

Max Montgelas and Walther Schücking, eds., *Outbreak of the World War: German Documents Collected by Karl Kautsky,* No. 268 (1924), p. 249, translated by Carnegie Endowment for International Peace. Reprinted by permission of Carnegie Endowment for International Peace.

It is a cause of honest satisfaction to us that we find both in the Imperial German Government and in the entire German people a complete comprehension of the fact that our patience was of necessity exhausted after the assassination at Serajevo, which, according to the results of the inquiry, was planned at Belgrade and carried out by emissaries from that city; and that we are now forced to the task of securing ourselves by every means against the continuation of the present intolerable conditions on our southeastern border.

We confidently hope that our prospective difference with Serbia will be the cause of no further complications; but in the event that such should nevertheless occur, we are gratefully certain that Germany, with a fidelity long proven, will bear in mind the obligations of her alliance and lend us her support in any fight forced upon us by another opponent.

The following telegrams from Bethmann-Hollweg to Tschirschky have often been taken as evidence for a change of heart at Berlin and the beginning of a policy of restraining Austria.

Bethmann-Hollweg's Telegrams to Tschirschky

The Imperial Chancellor to the Ambassador at Vienna

Telegram 174.
Urgent.

Berlin, July 28, 1914.

The Austro-Hungarian Government has distinctly informed Russia that it is not considering any territorial acquisitions in Serbia. This agrees with Your Excellency's report to the effect that neither the Austrian nor the Hungarian statesmen consider the increase of the Slavic element in the Monarchy to be desirable. On the other hand, the Austro-Hungarian Government has left us in the dark concerning its intentions, despite repeated interrogations. The reply of the Serbian Government to the Austrian ultimatum, which has now been received, makes it clear that Serbia has agreed to the Austrian demands to so great an extent that, in case of a completely uncompromising attitude on the part of the Austro-Hungarian Government, it will become necessary to

Max Montgelas and Walther Schücking, eds., *Outbreak of the World War: German Documents Collected by Karl Kautsky*, No. 323 (1924), pp. 288–289, and No. 395 (1924), pp. 344–345, translated by Carnegie Endowment for International Peace. Reprinted by permission of Carnegie Endowment for International Peace.

reckon upon the gradual defection from its cause of public opinion throughout all Europe.

According to the statements of the Austrian General Staff, an active military movement against Serbia will not be possible before the 12th of August. As a result, the Imperial Government is placed in the extraordinarily difficult position of being exposed in the meantime to the mediation and conference proposals of the other Cabinets, and if it continues to maintain its previous aloofness in the face of such proposals, it will incur the odium of having been responsible for a world war, even, finally, among the German people themselves. A successful war on three fronts cannot be commenced and carried on on any such basis. It is imperative that the responsibility for the eventual extension of the war among those nations not originally immediately concerned should, under all circumstances, fall on Russia. At Mr. Sazonoff's last conversation with Count Pourtalès the Minister already conceded that Serbia would have to receive her "deserved lesson." At any rate the Minister was no longer so unconditionally opposed to the Austrian point of view as he had been earlier. From this fact it is not difficult to draw the conclusion that the Russian Government might even realize that, once the mobilization of the Austro-Hungarian Army had begun, the very honor of its arms demanded an invasion of Serbia. But it will be all the better able to compromise with this idea if the Vienna Cabinet repeats at Petersburg its distinct declaration that she is far from wishing to make any territorial acquisitions in Serbia, and that her military preparations are solely for the purpose of a temporary occupation of Belgrade and certain other localities on Serbian territory in order to force the Serbian Government to the complete fulfilment of her demands, and for the creation of guaranties of future good behavior—to which Austria-Hungary has an unquestionable claim after the experiences she has had with Serbia. An occupation like the German occupation of French territory after the Peace of Frankfurt, for the purpose of securing compliance with the demands for war indemnity, is suggested. As soon as the Austrian demands should be complied with, evacuation would follow. Should the Russian Government fail to recognize the justice of this point of view, it would have against it the public opinion of all Europe, which is now in the process of turning away from Austria. As a further result, the general diplomatic, and probably the military, situation would undergo material alteration in favor of Austria-Hungary and her allies.

Your Excellency will kindly discuss the matter along these lines thoroughly and impressively with Count Berchtold, and instigate an appropriate move at St. Petersburg. You will have to avoid very carefully giving rise to the impression that we wish to hold Austria back. The case is solely one of finding a way to realize Austria's desired aim, that of cutting the vital cord of the Greater-Serbia propaganda, without at the same time bringing on a world war, and, if the latter cannot be avoided in the end, of improving the conditions under which we shall have to wage it, in so far as is possible.

Wire report.

Bethmann-Hollweg.

The Imperial Chancellor to the Ambassador at Vienna

Telegram 192.
Urgent.

Berlin, July 30, 1914.

The Imperial Ambassador at London telegraphs:

Sir E. Grey just sent for me again. The Minister was entirely calm, but very grave, and received me with the words that the situation was continuing to grow more acute. Sazonoff had stated that after the declaration of war he will no longer be in a position to negotiate with Austria direct, and *had requested them here to take up the mediation efforts again.* The Russian Government regards the cessation of hostilities for the present as a necessary preliminary to mediation.

Sir E. Grey repeated his suggestion already reported, that we take part in a mediation *à quatre,* such as we had already accepted in principle. It would seem to him to be a suitable basis for mediation, if Austria, after occupying Belgrade, for example, or other places, should announce her conditions. Should Your Excellency, however, undertake mediation, a prospect I was able early this morning to put before him, this would of course suit him equally well. But *mediation* seemed now to him to be urgently necessary, if *a European catastrophe were not to result.*

Sir E. Grey then said to me that he had a friendly and private communication to make to me, namely, that he did not want our warm personal relations and the intimacy of our talks on all political matters to lead me astray, and he would *like to spare himself later the reproach (of) bad faith.* The British Government desired now as before to cultivate our previous friendship, and it could *stand aside as long as the conflict remained confined to Austria and Russia. But if we and France* should *be involved,* the situation would immediately be altered, and the British Government would, *under the circumstances, find itself forced to make up its mind quickly.* In that event *it would not be practicable to stand aside and wait for any length of time.* "If war breaks out, it will be *the greatest catastrophe that the world has ever seen."* It was far from his desire to express any kind of a threat; he only wanted to protect me from disappointments and *himself* from the *reproach of bad faith,* and had therefore chosen the form of a private explanation.

As a result we stand, in case Austria refuses all mediation, before a conflagration in which England will be against us; Italy and Roumania to all appearances will not go with us, and we two shall be opposed to four Great Powers. On Germany, thanks to England's opposition, the principal burden of the fight would fall. Austria's political prestige, the honor of her arms, as well as her just claims against Serbia, could all be amply satisfied by the occupation of Belgrade or of other places. She would be strengthening her status in the Balkans as well as in relation to Russia by the humiliation of Serbia. Under these circumstances we must urgently and impressively suggest to the consideration of the Vienna Cabinet the acceptance of mediation on the above-mentioned honorable conditions. The responsibility for the consequences that would otherwise follow would be an uncommonly heavy one both for Austria and for us.

Bethmann-Hollweg.

At 9:15 on July 27, more than two hours before Bethmann-Hollweg sent his telegram to Tschirschky, Count Laszlo Szögyény, the Austrian ambassador at Berlin, sent the following report to Vienna. The reliability of Szögyény's account has been challenged, but Luigi Albertini defends it and thinks that "no stronger shaft of light could fall on the guilt and duplicity of the German Government."

FROM The Origins of the War of 1914 BY LUIGI ALBERTINI

The Secretary of State told me very definitely in a strictly confidential form that in the immediate future mediation proposals from England will possibly (*eventuell*) be brought to Your Excellency's knowledge by the German Government. The German Government, he says, tenders the most binding assurances that it in no way associates itself with the proposals, is even decidedly against their being considered, and only passes them on in order to conform to the English request. In so doing the Government proceeds from the standpoint that it is of the greatest importance that England at the present moment should not make common cause with Russia and France. Consequently everything must be avoided that might disconnect the telegraph line between Germany and England which till now has been in good working order. Were Germany to say flatly to Sir E. Grey that she is not willing to pass on his wishes to Austria-Hungary, by whom England believes these wishes will sooner find consideration if Germany is the intermediary, then the situation would arise which, as has just been said, must at all costs be avoided. The German Government would, moreover, in respect of any other request of England to Vienna, assure the latter most emphatically that it in no way supports any such demands for intervention in regard to Austria-Hungary

Luigi Albertini, *The Origins of the War of 1914,* II (1953), 445–446, translated and edited by Isabella M. Massey. Reprinted by permission of The Clarendon Press, Oxford.

and only passes them on to comply with the wish of England. For instance only yesterday the English Government approached him, the Secretary of State, through the German Ambassador to London and directly through its own representative here, asking him to support the wish of England in regard to a toning down by us of the note to Serbia. He, Jagow, gave answer that he would certainly fulfil Sir E. Grey's wish and pass on England's desire to Your Excellency, but that he could not support it himself, since the Serbian conflict was a question of prestige for the Austro-Hungarian Monarchy in which Germany was also involved. He, the Secretary of State, had therefore passed on Sir E. Grey's note to Herr von Tschirschky, but without giving him instructions to submit it to Your Excellency; thereupon he had been able to inform the English Cabinet, that he did not directly decline the English wish, and had even forwarded it to Vienna. In conclusion the Secretary of State reiterated his standpoint to me and, in order to prevent any misunderstanding, asked me to assure Your Excellency that, also in the case just adduced, he, in acting as intermediary, was not in the slightest degree in favour of consideration being given to the English wish.

On July 28 Austria declared war on Serbia. Further attempts at negotiation were made, but once mobilization began military considerations became paramount. Germany had always insisted that Russian mobilization would mean war, for the Schlieffen Plan demanded a quick victory before France—and particularly Russia—could fully prepare for war. After Russia's total mobilization, the war was unavoidable. The marginal notes are once again those of the Kaiser.

Pourtalès' Report of Russian Mobilization

The Ambassador at Petersburg to the Foreign Office

Telegram 189.
Urgent.

Petersburg, July 30, 1914.

Just had one and a half hours' conference with Sazonoff, who sent for me at midnight. Minister's purpose was to

Max Montgelas and Walther Schücking, eds., *Outbreak of the World War: German Documents Collected by Karl Kautsky,* No. 401 (1924), pp. 348–350, translated by Carnegie Endowment for International Peace. Reprinted by permission of Carnegie Endowment for International Peace.

*Is Russian mobiliza-
tion a friendly
means?!*

persuade me to advocate participation by my Government in a conference of four, in order to find a way to *move Austria by friendly means to drop those demands which infringe on the sovereignty of Serbia.* I confined myself to promising to report the conversation, and took the stand that any exchange of opinions appeared to me to be a very difficult if not an impossible matter now that Russia had *decided to take the fateful step of mobilization.* Russia was demanding of us to do that to Austria which Austria was being reproached for doing to Serbia; to wit, *infringing upon her rights of sovereignty.* Since Austria had promised to *consider Russian interests* by her declaration of territorial disinterestedness, which, on the part of a nation at war *meant a great deal,* the Austro-Hungarian Monarchy ought to be let alone while settling her affairs with Serbia. It would be time enough to return to the question of sparing Serbia's sovereign rights when *peace* was concluded. I added very earnestly that the whole Austro-Serbian matter took a *back seat* for the moment in the face of the *danger of a European conflagration.* I took great pains to impress the magnitude of this danger upon the Minister. Sazonoff was not to be diverted from the idea that Russia could not leave Serbia in the lurch. No Government could follow such a policy here *without seriously endangering the Monarchy.*

Right.

Very good.

Good.

*Yes.
Nonsense! that
sort of policy
conceals within
itself the greatest
dangers for the
Czar!*

During the course of the conversation *Sazonoff wanted* to *argue* the inconsistency between the telegram of His Majesty the Emperor to the Czar and Your Excellency's telegraphic instructions number 134. I decidedly denied any, and pointed out that *even if we had already mobilized,* an appeal by my Most Gracious Master to the common interests of monarchs *would not be inconsistent* with such a measure. I said that the communication I had made him this afternoon according to the instructions of Your Excellency, had been no threat, but a friendly warning in the shape of a reference to the *automatic effect that the mobilization here would have to have on us in consequence of the German-Austrian alliance.* Sazonoff stated that the order for mobilization *could no longer possibly be retracted,* and that the *Austrian mobilization was to blame for it.*

*Nothing done
as yet.
Right.*

*That was a
partial mobiliza-
tion of six corps
for a limited
purpose!*

From Sazonoff's statements I received the impression that His Majesty's telegram did not fail of an effect on the Czar, but that the Minister is busily striving to make sure that the Czar stands firm.

Pourtalès.

If mobilization can no longer be retracted—WHICH IS NOT TRUE—*why, then, did the Czar appeal for my mediation three days afterward without mention of the issuance of the mobilization order? That shows plainly that the mobilization appeared to him to have been precipitate, and that after it he made this move* pro forma *in our direction for the sake of quieting his uneasy conscience, although he knew that it would no longer be of any use, as he did not feel himself to be strong enough to* STOP *the mobilization. Frivolity and weakness are to plunge the world into the most frightful war, which eventually aims at the destruction of Germany. For I have no doubt left about it: England, Russia and France have* AGREED *among themselves— after laying the foundation of the* casus foederis *for us through Austria—to take the Austro-Serbian conflict for an* EXCUSE *for waging a* WAR OF EXTERMINATION *against us. Hence Grey's cynical observation to Lichnowsky "as long as the war is* CONFINED *to Russia and Austria, England would sit quiet, only when we and France* MIXED INTO IT *would he be compelled to make an active move against us(");* i.e., *either we are shamefully to betray our allies,* SACRIFICE *them to Russia—thereby breaking up the Triple Alliance, or we are to be attacked in common by the Triple Entente for our* FIDELITY TO OUR ALLIES *and punished, whereby they will satisfy their jealousy by joining in totally* RUINING *us. That is the real naked situation in* nuce, *which, slowly and cleverly set going, certainly by Edward VII, has been carried on, and systematically built up by disowned conferences between England and Paris and Petersburg; finally brought to a conclusion by George V and set to work. And thereby the stupidity and ineptitude of our ally is turned into a snare for us. So the famous "*CIRCUMSCRIPTION*" of Germany has finally become a complete fact, despite every effort of our politicians and diplomats to prevent it. The net has been suddenly thrown over our head, and England sneeringly reaps the most brilliant success of her persistently prosecuted purely* ANTI-GERMAN WORLD-POLICY, *against which we have proved ourselves helpless, while she twists the noose of our political and economic destruction out of our fidelity to Austria, as we squirm* ISOLATED *in the net. A great achievement, which arouses the admiration even of him who is to be destroyed as its result! Edward VII is stronger after his death than am I who am still alive! And there have been people who believed that England could be won over or pacified, by this or that puny measure!!! Unremittingly, relentlessly she has pursued her object, with notes, holiday proposals, scares, Haldane, etc., until this point was reached. And we walked into the net and even went into the one-ship-program in construction with the ardent hope of thus pacifying England!!! All my warnings, all my pleas were voiced for nothing. Now comes England's so-called gratitude for it! From the dilemma raised by our fidelity to the venerable old Emperor of Austria we are brought into a situation which offers England the desired pretext for annihilating us under the hypocritical cloak of justice, namely, of helping France on account of the reputed "balance of power" in Europe,* i.e., *playing the card of all the European* *nations in England's favor against us! This whole business must now be ruthlessly uncovered and the mask of Christian peaceableness publicly and brusquely torn from its face in public, and the pharisaical hypocrisy exposed on the pillory!! And our consuls in Turkey and India, agents, etc., must fire the whole Mohammedan world to fierce rebellion against this hated, lying, conscienceless nation of shop-keepers; for if we are to be bled to death, England shall at least lose India.*

W.

4
THE
REVISIONIST
POSITION

The 1920s witnessed a reassessment of the question of war guilt. In England and America particularly, scholars began to revise the general opinion that Germany and Austria were exclusively responsible. Sidney B. Fay was one of the leaders of the revisionist movement.

FROM Origins of the World War BY SIDNEY B. FAY

None of the Powers wanted a European War. Their governing rulers and ministers, with very few exceptions, all foresaw that it must be a frightful *NO* struggle, in which the political results were not absolutely certain, but in which the loss of life, suffering, and economic consequences were bound to be terrible. This is true, in a greater or less degree, of Pashitch, Berchtold, Bethmann, Sazonov, Poincaré, San Giuliano and Sir Edward Grey. Yet none of them, not even Sir Edward Grey, could have foreseen that the political results were to be so stupendous, and the other consequences so terrible, as was actually the case.

For many of the Powers, to be sure, a European War might seem to hold out the possibility of achieving various desired advantages: for Serbia, the achievement of national unity for all Serbs; for Austria, the revival of her waning prestige as a Great Power, and the checking of nationalistic tendencies which threatened her very existence: for Russia, the accomplishment of her historic mission of controlling Constantinople and the Straits; for Germany, new economic advantages and the restoration of the European balance

Reprinted with permission of The Macmillan Company from *Origins of the World War*, II (1930), 547–558, by Sidney B. Fay. Copyright 1928 and 1930 by The Macmillan Company.

which had changed with the weakening of the Triple Alliance and the tightening of the Triple Entente; for France, the recovery of Alsace-Lorraine and the ending of the German menace; and for England, the destruction of the German naval danger and of Prussian militarism. All these advantages, and many others, were feverishly striven and intrigued for, on all sides, the moment the War actually broke out, but this is no good proof that any of the statesmen mentioned deliberately aimed to bring about a war to secure these advantages. One cannot judge the motives which actuated men before the War, by what they did in an absolutely new situation which arose as soon as they were overtaken by a conflagration they had sought to avert. And in fact, in the case of the two Powers between whom the immediate conflict arose, the postponement or avoidance of a European War would have facilitated the accomplishment of the ultimate advantages aimed at: Pashitch knew that there was a better chance for Serbian national unity after he had consolidated Serbian gains in the Balkan Wars, and after Russia had completed her military and naval armaments as planned for 1917; and Berchtold knew that he had a better chance of crushing the Greater Serbia danger and strengthening Austria, if he could avoid Russian intervention and a general European War.

It is also true, likewise, that the moment war was declared, it was hailed with varying demonstrations of enthusiasm on the part of the people in every country—with considerable in Serbia, Austria, Russia and Germany, with less in France, and with almost none in England. But this does not mean that the peoples wanted war or exerted a decisive influence to bring it about. It is a curious psychological phenomenon that as soon as a country engages in war, there develops or is created among the masses a frenzy of patriotic excitement which is no index of their pre-war desires. And in the countries where the demonstrations of enthusiasm were greatest, the political influence of the people on the Government was least.

Nevertheless, a European War broke out. Why? Because in each country political and military leaders did certain things, which led to mobilizations and declarations of war, or failed to do certain things which might have prevented them. In this sense, all the European countries, in a greater or less degree, were responsible. One must abandon the dictum of the Versailles Treaty that Germany and her allies were solely responsible. It was a dictum exacted by victors from vanquished, under the influence of the blindness, ignorance, hatred, and the propagandist misconceptions to which war had given rise. It was based on evidence which was incomplete and not always sound. It is generally recognized by the best historical scholars in all countries to be no longer tenable or defensible. They are agreed that the responsibility for the War is a divided responsibility. But they still disagree very much as to the relative part of this responsibility that falls on each country and on each individual political or military leader.

Some writers like to fix positively in some precise mathematical fashion the exact responsibility for the War. This was done in one way by the framers of Article 231 of the Treaty of Versailles. It has been done in other ways by those who would fix the responsibility in some relative fashion, as, for instance, Austria first, then Russia, France and Germany and England. But the present writer deprecates such efforts to assess by a precise formula a very complicated question, which is after all more a matter of delicate shading than of definite white and black. Oversimplification, as Napoleon once said in framing his Code, is the enemy of precision. Moreover, even supposing that a general consensus of opinion might be reached as to the relative responsibility of any individual country or man for immediate causes connected with the July crisis of 1914, it is by no means necessarily true that the same relative responsibility would hold for the underlying causes, which for years had been tending toward the creation of a dangerous situation.

One may, however, sum up very briefly the most salient facts in regard to each country.

Serbia felt a natural and justifiable impulse to do what so many other countries had done in the nineteenth century—to bring under one national Government all the discontented Serb people. She had liberated those under Turkish rule; the next step was to liberate those under Hapsburg rule. She looked to Russia for assistance, and had been encouraged to expect that she would receive it. After the assassination, Mr. Pashitch took no steps to discover and bring to justice Serbians in Belgrade who had been implicated in the plot. One of them, Ciganovitch, was even assisted to disappear. Mr. Pashitch waited to see what evidence the Austrian authorities could find. When Austria demanded cooperation of Austrian officials in discovering, though not in trying, implicated Serbians, the Serbian Government made a very conciliatory but negative reply. They expected that the reply would not be regarded as satisfactory, and, even before it was given, ordered the mobilization of the Serbian army. Serbia did not want war, but believed it would be forced upon her. That Mr. Pashitch was aware of the plot three weeks before it was executed, failed to take effective steps to prevent the assassins from crossing over from Serbia to Bosnia, and then failed to give Austria any warning or information which might have averted the fatal crime, were facts unknown to Austria in July, 1914; they cannot therefore be regarded as in any way justifying Austria's conduct; but they are part of Serbia's responsibility, and a very serious part.

Austria was more responsible for the immediate origin of the war than any other Power. Yet from her own point of view she was acting in self-defence—not against an immediate military attack, but against the corroding Greater Serbia and Jugoslav agitation which her leaders believed threatened her very existence. No State can be expected to sit with folded arms and await dismemberment at the hands of its neighbors. Russia was believed to be intriguing with Serbia and Rumania against the Dual Monarchy. The assassination of the heir to the throne, as a result of a plot prepared in Belgrade, demanded severe retribution; otherwise Austria would be regarded as incapable of action, "Worm-eaten" as the Serbian Press expressed it, would sink in prestige, and hasten her own downfall. To avert this Berchtold determined to

crush Serbia with war. He deliberately framed the ultimatum with the expectation and hope that it would be rejected. He hurriedly declared war against
Serbia in order to forestall all efforts at mediation. He refused even to answer
his own ally's urgent requests to come to an understanding with Russia, on
the basis of a military occupation of Belgrade as a pledge that Serbia would
carry out the promises in her reply to the ultimatum. Berchtold gambled on a
"local" war with Serbia only, believing that he could rattle the German
sword; but rather than abandon his war with Serbia, he was ready to drag
the rest of Europe into war.

It is very questionable whether Berchtold's obstinate determination to diminish Serbia and destroy her as a Balkan factor was, after all, the right
method, even if he had succeeded in keeping the war "localized" and in temporarily strengthening the Dual Monarchy. Supposing that Russia in 1914,
because of military unpreparedness or lack of support, had been ready to
tolerate the execution of Berchtold's designs, it is quite certain that she would
have aimed within the next two or three years at wiping out this second
humiliation, which was so much more damaging to her prestige than that of
1908–09. In two or three years, when her great program of military reform
was finally completed, Russia would certainly have found a pretext to reverse
the balance in the Balkans in her own favor again. A further consequence of
Berchtold's policy, even if successful, would have been the still closer consolidation of the Triple Entente, with the possible addition of Italy. And, finally,
a partially dismembered Serbia would have become a still greater source of
unrest and danger to the peace of Europe than heretofore. Serbian nationalism, like Polish nationalism, would have been intensified by partition. Austrian power and prestige would not have been so greatly increased as to be
able to meet these new dangers. Berchtold's plan was a mere temporary improvement, but could not be a final solution of the Austro-Serbian antagonism. Franz Ferdinand and many others recognized this, and so long as he
lived, no step in this fatal direction had been taken. It was the tragic fate of
Austria that the only man who might have had the power and ability to
develop Austria along sound lines became the innocent victim of the crime
which was the occasion of the World War and so of her ultimate disruption.

Germany did not plot a European War, did not want one, and made genuine, though too belated efforts, to avert one. She was the victim of her alliance
with Austria and of her own folly. Austria was her only dependable ally,
Italy and Rumania having become nothing but allies in name. She could not
throw her over, as otherwise she would stand isolated between Russia, where
Panslavism and armaments were growing stronger every year, and France,
where Alsace-Lorraine, Delcassé's fall, and Agadir were not forgotten. Therefore, Bethmann felt bound to accede to Berchtold's request for support and
gave him a free hand to deal with Serbia; he also hoped and expected to
"localize" the Austro-Serbian conflict. Germany then gave grounds to the
Entente for suspecting the sincerity of her peaceful intentions by her denial of
any foreknowledge of the ultimatum, by her support and justification of it

when it was published, and by her refusal to Sir Edward Grey's conference proposal. However, Germany by no means had Austria so completely under her thumb as the Entente Powers and many writers have assumed. It is true that Berchtold would hardly have embarked on his gambler's policy unless he had been assured that Germany would fulfil the obligations of the alliance, and to this extent Germany must share the great responsibility of Austria. But when Bethmann realized that Russia was likely to intervene, that England might not remain neutral, and that there was danger of a world war of which Germany and Austria would appear to be the instigators, he tried to call a halt on Austria, but it was too late. He pressed mediation proposals on Vienna, but Berchtold was insensible to the pressure, and the Entente Powers did not believe in the sincerity of his pressure, especially as they produced no results.

Germany's geographical position between France and Russia, and her inferiority in number of troops, had made necessary the plan of crushing the French army quickly at first and then turning against Russia. This was only possible, in the opinion of her strategists, by marching through Belgium, as it was generally anticipated by military men that she would do in case of a European War. On July 29, after Austria had declared war on Serbia, and after the Tsar had assented to general mobilization in Russia (though this was not known in Berlin and was later postponed for a day owing to the Kaiser's telegram to the Tsar), Bethmann took the precaution of sending to the German Minister in Brussels a sealed envelope. The Minister was not to open it except on further instructions. It contained the later demand for the passage of the German army through Belgium. This does not mean, however, that Germany had decided for war. In fact, Bethmann was one of the last of the statesmen to abandon hope of peace and to consent to the mobilization of his country's army. General mobilization of the continental armies took place in the following order: Serbia, Russia, Austria, France and Germany. General mobilization by a Great Power was commonly interpreted by military men in every country, though perhaps not by Sir Edward Grey, the Tsar, and some civilian officials, as meaning that the country was on the point of making war—that the military machine had begun to move and would not be stopped. Hence, when Germany learned of the Russian general mobilization, she sent ultimatums to St. Petersburg and Paris, warning that German mobilization would follow unless Russia suspended hers within twelve hours, and asking what would be the attitude of France. The answers being unsatisfactory, Germany then mobilized and declared war. It was the hasty Russian general mobilization, assented to on July 29 and ordered on July 30, while Germany was still trying to bring Austria to accept mediation proposals, which finally rendered the European War inevitable.

Russia was partly responsible for the Austro-Serbian conflict because of the frequent encouragement which she had given at Belgrade—that Serbian national unity would be ultimately achieved with Russian assistance at Austrian expense. This had led the Belgrade Cabinet to hope for Russian support in case of a war with Austria, and the hope did not prove vain in July, 1914. Before this, to be sure, in the Bosnian Crisis and during the Balkan Wars, Russia had put restraint upon Serbia, because Russia, exhausted by the effects of the Russo-Japanese War, was not yet ready for a European struggle with the Teutonic Powers. But in 1914 her armaments, though not yet completed, had made such progress that the militarists were confident of success, if they had French and British support. In the spring of 1914, the Minister of War, Sukhomlinov, had published an article in a Russian newspaper, though without signing his name, to the effect, "Russia is ready, France must be ready also." Austria was convinced that Russia would ultimately aid Serbia, unless the Serbian danger were dealt with energetically after the Archduke's murder; she knew that Russia was growing stronger every year; but she doubted whether the Tsar's armaments had yet reached the point at which Russia would dare to intervene; she would therefore run less risk of Russian intervention and a European War if she used the Archduke's assassination as an excuse for weakening Serbia, than if she should postpone action until the future.

Russia's responsibility lay also in the secret preparatory military measures which she was making at the same time that she was carrying on diplomatic negotiations. These alarmed Germany and Austria. But it was primarily Russia's general mobilization, made when Germany was trying to bring Austria to a settlement, which precipitated the final catastrophe, causing Germany to mobilize and declare war.

The part of France is less clear than that of the other Great Powers, because she has not yet made a full publication of her documents. To be sure, M. Poincaré, in the fourth volume of his memories, has made a skilful and elaborate plea, to prove *"La France innocente."* But he is not convincing. It is quite clear that on his visit to Russia he assured the Tsar's Government that France would support her as an ally in preventing Austria from humiliating or crushing Serbia. Paléologue renewed these assurances in a way to encourage Russia to take a strong hand. He did not attempt to restrain Russia from military measures which he knew would call forth German counter-measures and cause war. Nor did he keep his Government promptly and fully informed of the military steps which were being taken at St. Petersburg. President Poincaré, upon his return to France, made efforts for peace, but his great preoccupation was to minimize French and Russian preparatory measures and emphasize those of Germany, in order to secure the certainty of British support in a struggle which he now regarded as inevitable.

Sir Edward Grey made many sincere proposals for preserving peace; they all failed owing partly, but not exclusively, to Germany's attitude. Sir Edward could probably have prevented war if he had done either of two things. If, early in the crisis, he had acceded to the urging of France and Russia and given a strong warning to Germany that, in a European War, England would take the side of the Franco-Russian Alliance, this would probably have led Bethmann to exert an earlier and more effective pressure on Austria; and it would perhaps thereby have prevented the Austrian declaration of war on Serbia, and brought to a successful issue the "direct conversations" between Vienna and St. Petersburg. Or, if Sir Edward Grey had listened to German urging, and warned France and Russia early in the crisis, that if they became involved in war, England would remain neutral, probably Russia would have hesitated with her mobilizations, and France would probably have exerted a restraining influence at St. Petersburg. But Sir Edward Grey could not say that England would take the side of France and Russia, because he had a Cabinet nearly evenly divided, and he was not sure, early in the crisis, that public opinion in England would back him up in war against Germany. He could resign, and he says in his memoirs that he would have resigned, but that would have been no comfort or aid to France, who had come confidently to count upon British support. He was determined to say and do nothing which might encourage her with a hope which he could not fulfil. Therefore, in spite of the pleadings of the French, he refused to give them definite assurances until the probable German determination to go through Belgium made it clear that the Cabinet, and Parliament, and British public opinion would follow his lead in war on Germany. On the other hand, he was unwilling to heed the German pleadings that he exercise restraint at Paris and St. Petersburg, because he did not wish to endanger the Anglo-Russian Entente and the solidarity of the Triple Entente, because he felt a moral obligation to France, growing out of the Anglo-French military and naval conversations of the past years, and because he suspected that Germany was backing Austria up in an unjustifiable course and that Prussian militarists had taken the direction of affairs at Berlin out of the hands of Herr von Bethmann-Hollweg and the civilian authorities.

Italy exerted relatively little influence on the crisis in either direction.

Belgium had done nothing in any way to justify the demand which Germany made upon her. With commendable prudence, at the very first news of the ominous Austrian ultimatum, she had foreseen the danger to which she might be exposed. She had accordingly instructed her representatives abroad as to the statements which they were to make in case Belgium should decide very suddenly to mobilize to protect her neutrality. On July 29, she placed her army upon "a strengthened war footing," but did not order complete mobilization until two days later, when Austria, Russia, and Germany had already done so, and war appeared inevitable. Even after being confronted with the terrible German ultimatum, at 7 P.M. on August 2, she did not at once invite the assistance of English and French troops to aid her in the defense of her soil and her neutrality against a certain German assault; it was not until German troops had actually violated her territory, on August 4, that she appealed for the assistance of the Powers which had guaranteed her neutrality. Belgium was the innocent victim of German strategic necessity. Though the German violation of Belgium was of enormous influence in forming public opinion as to the responsibility for the War after hostilities began, it was not a cause of the War, except in so far as it made it easier for Sir Edward Grey to bring England into it.

In the forty years following the Franco-Prussian War, as we have seen, there developed a system of alliances which divided Europe into two hostile groups. This hostility was accentuated by the increase of armaments, economic rivalry, nationalist ambitions and antagonisms, and newspaper incitement. But it is very doubtful whether all these dangerous tendencies would have actually led to war, had it not been for the assassination of Franz Ferdinand. That was the factor which consolidated the elements of hostility and started the rapid and complicated succession of events which culminated in a World War, and for that factor Serbian nationalism was primarily responsible.

But the verdict of the Versailles Treaty that Germany and her allies were responsible for the War, in view of the evidence now available, is historically unsound. It should therefore be revised. However, because of the popular feeling widespread in some of the Entente countries, it is doubtful whether a formal and legal revision is as yet practicable. There must first come a further revision by historical scholars, and through them of public opinion.

5
THE CASE AGAINST THE CENTRAL POWERS

FROM The Struggle for the Mastery of Europe
BY A. J. P. TAYLOR

It has been strongly argued that the Germans deliberately timed war for August 1914. There is little evidence for this, and a decisive argument against it. Bethmann and William II were incapable of consistent policy; Moltke, the chief-of-staff, could not conduct a campaign, let alone make a war. The Germans were involved in war by Austria-Hungary, but they went with her willingly. It was easy to co-operate with her; it would have needed a statesman to refuse. On 28 June Francis Ferdinand was assassinated at Sarejevo, the capital of Bosnia, by a Bosnian Serb. Berchtold was weary of being jeered at by Conrad as irresolute and feeble. Moreover, when Turkey-in-Asia took the place of the Balkans as the centre of international rivalry, Austria-Hungary was pushed aside too; and the Germans had rejected with impatience Berchtold's claim to be allotted a "sphere" in Asia Minor. The murder at Sarejevo revived the Balkan question and enabled Austria-Hungary to reappear misleadingly as a Great Power. This time she could only hold the centre of the stage if she actually provoked a war. The German talk of writing off Austria-Hungary and of somehow restoring good relations with Russia at her expense had not escaped Austrian attention: and the Habsburg monarchy brought on its mortal crisis to prove that it was still alive.

Berchtold determined to force war on Serbia, though he had no proofs of Serbian complicity and never found any. Tisza, the Hungarian prime minis-

A. J. P. Taylor, *The Struggle for the Mastery of Europe 1848–1918* (1954), pp. 520–531. Reprinted by permission of The Clarendon Press, Oxford.

ter, opposed him. Berchtold wanted to restore the prestige of the monarchy; Tisza cared only for great Hungary. Like Kossuth before him, he looked to Germany, not to Vienna, as Hungary's ally and would not have much regretted the collapse of the Dual Monarchy, so long as great Hungary survived. Berchtold turned Tisza's opposition by appealing to Germany for support; Tisza could not hold out if Berlin, not Vienna, urged war. Berchtold took out his memorandum of 24 June, which had urged alliance with Bulgaria; added a postscript blaming Serbia for the assassination; and accompanied this with a letter from Francis Joseph to William II, which managed to blame Russian Panslavism as well. The conclusion: "Serbia must be eliminated as a political factor in the Balkans . . . friendly settlement is no longer to be thought of." These two documents were presented to William II on 5 July.

At Berlin there was no serious consultation. William II invited the Austro-Hungarian ambassador to lunch at Potsdam. At first he said that he must wait for Bethmann's opinion; then changed his mind after lunch and committed himself. Szögyény, the Austrian ambassador, reported: "Action against Serbia should not be delayed. . . . Even if it should come to a war between Austria and Russia, we could be convinced that Germany would stand by our side with her accustomed faithfulness as an ally." Bethmann arrived in the afternoon, went for a walk in the park with William II, and approved of what he had said. The next day he gave Szögyény official confirmation: "Austria must judge what is to be done to clear up her relations with Serbia; but whatever Austria's decision, she could count with certainty upon it, that Germany will stand behind her as an ally." Berchtold's plan of partitioning Serbia with Bulgaria was explained to Bethmann. He approved of it and added: "If war must break out, better now than in one or two years' time when the Entente will be stronger."

William II and Bethmann did more than give Austria-Hungary a free hand; they encouraged her to start a war against Serbia and to risk the greater consequences. They had grown used to Berchtold's irresolution during the Balkan wars and were determined not to be blamed for it. The most probable outcome of all the stir, they expected, would be an Austro-Hungarian alliance with Bulgaria. Further, both of them thought that Russia was not ready for war and that she would allow the humiliation of Serbia after some ineffective protest; then their position would be all the stronger to strike a bargain with Russia later. On the other hand, if it came to war, they were confident of winning it now and less confident of winning it later. They did not decide on war; but they did decide on 5 July to use their superior power either to win a war or to achieve a striking success. Bethmann had always said that Germany and Great Britain should cooperate to keep the peace. If he had wanted a peaceful solution of the present crisis, he would have approached the British at once. Instead he did nothing. He did not wish to alarm them. His aim, so far as he had one, was to keep them neutral in a continental war, not to enlist their support for a general peace.

The German reply gave Berchtold what he wanted: it enabled him to convert Tisza. He could now argue that Germany was urging them to war. On 14 July Tisza gave way: great Hungary had to keep German favour. He laid down one condition: Austria-Hungary should not acquire any Serbian territory. Though Berchtold accepted this condition, he meant to cheat Tisza, once Serbia had been crushed: her southern territories would be partitioned between Albania and Bulgaria, and the rest would become a dependency of the monarchy, even if it were not directly annexed. The one chance of success for Austria-Hungary would have been rapid action. Instead Berchtold dawdled, in the usual Viennese fashion. The ultimatum to Serbia was sent on 23 July, when all Europe had forgotten its first indignation at the archduke's murder. The Serbs replied on 25 July, accepting Berchtold's conditions much more nearly than had been expected. It made no difference. The Austrians were determined on war; and the Germans encouraged them to action. On 28 July Austria-Hungary declared war on Serbia. Military reasons were not the motive: the Austro-Hungarian army could not be ready even against Serbia until 12 August. But, as Berchtold said: "the diplomatic situation will not last as long as that." He needed a declaration of war in order to reject all attempts at mediation or a peaceful solution: they had now been "outstripped by events."

The Austro-Hungarian declaration of war on Serbia was the decisive act; everything else followed from it. Diplomacy had been silent between the assassination of Francis Ferdinand on 28 June and the Austro-Hungarian note of 23 July; there was nothing it could do until the Austro-Hungarian demands were known. Then the statesmen tried to avert the crisis. The Russians advised Serbia not to resist, but to trust to the Great Powers; Grey offered to mediate between Serbia and Austria-Hungary. But the Russians had repeatedly declared that they would not allow Serbia to be crushed; they could do no other if they were to maintain the buffer of independent Balkan states. Poincaré and Viviani were in St. Petersburg just before the Austro-Hungarian note to Serbia was sent off. They emphasized again French loyalty to the alliance; but there is no evidence that they encouraged Russia to provoke a war, if a peaceful settlement could be found. When Austria-Hungary declared war on Serbia, the Russians attempted to mobilize against her alone, although they had no plans except for total mobilization. They were, in fact, still acting in terms of diplomacy; they were raising their bid, not preparing for war. The Germans now entered the field. They had assured the Austrians that they would keep Russia out of things, and they set out to do so. On 29 July they warned Sazonov that "further continuation of Russian mobilization would force us to mobilize also."

This time the Russians were determined not to retreat; they raised their bid still higher. On 30 July they resolved on general mobilization. This, too, was a diplomatic move; the Russian armies could not be ready for many weeks. But, in Jagow's words, "the German asset was speed." Their only military plan was to defeat France in six weeks and then to turn against Russia before she was fully prepared. Therefore they had to precipitate events and to force a rupture on both Russia and France. William II might still carry on a private telegraphic correspondence with Nicholas II, which was prolonged even after the declaration of war; Bethmann might still seek an impossible diplomatic success. They were both swept aside by the generals; and they had no answer to the military argument that immediate war was necessary for Germany's security. Yet even the generals did not want war; they wanted victory. When Bethmann urged caution at Vienna and Moltke at the same time urged speedier action, Berchtold exclaimed: "What a joke! Who rules at Berlin?" The answer was: nobody. German statesmen and generals alike succumbed to the demands of technique.

On 31 July the Germans took the preliminary step towards general mobilization on their side. From this moment, diplomacy ceased so far as the continental Powers were concerned. The only German concern was to get the war going as soon as possible. On 31 July they demanded from Russia the arrest of all war measures; when this was refused, a declaration of war followed on 1 August. The French were asked for a promise of neutrality in a Russo-German war; if they had agreed, they would also have been told to surrender their principal fortresses on the frontier, Toul and Verdun, as pledge of their neutrality. Viviani merely replied: "France will act in accordance with her interests." The Germans had no plausible excuse for war against France. They therefore trumped up some false stories of French violation of German territory; and with these decked out a declaration of war on 3 August.

Negotiations between Germany and Great Britain were more prolonged. Their object, on the German side, was to secure British neutrality, not to avert a continental war. All along, Bethmann had urged Berchtold to appear conciliatory in order to impress the British, not in order to find a compromise. On 29 July he offered not to annex any French territory if Great Britain remained neutral; the offer did not extend to the French colonies. As well, Germany would respect the integrity of Belgium after the war, provided that "she did not take sides against Germany." Grey stuck to his line of policy to the end. He made repeated attempts to settle the original Austro-Serb dispute by negotiation; later he tried to assemble a conference of the Great Powers. He warned the Germans not to count on British neutrality; equally he warned the French and Russians not to count on her support.

It is sometimes said that Grey could have averted the war if he had defined his policy one way or the other. This is not so. The German general staff had long planned to invade France through Belgium and would not have been deterred by any British threat. Indeed they had always assumed that Great Britain would enter the war; they did not take her military weight seriously, and naval questions did not interest them. Bethmann had wanted a British declaration of neutrality in order to discourage France and Russia; once it was clear that they would go to war in any case, British policy ceased to interest him. Emotionally he deplored the breach with Great Britain; but he did nothing to avert it and, in any case, was impotent to influence the German generals. On the other side, France and Russia decided on war without counting firmly on British support; the French believed that they could defeat Germany, and the Russians could not risk their own diplomatic defeat. A British declaration of neutrality would not have influenced their policy. Besides, Grey was resolved that they should decide their policy without encouragement from him; war must spring from their independent resolve.

Those who urged a clear British line did so from contradictory motives. Nicolson feared that Russia and France would win a complete victory and that the British empire would then be at their mercy. Eyre Crowe, more representative of official opinion, feared that France would be defeated and that Great Britain would then be at the mercy of Germany. In any case it was impossible for Grey to make any clear declaration; public opinion would not have allowed it. If there is a criticism of Grey, it must be that he had not educated the British public enough in the previous years. No doubt he had shrunk from increasing the tension in Europe; but, as well, the unity of the liberal party and the survival of the liberal government had ranked higher in his mind than a decisive foreign policy. It was common form to regret discussion of foreign issues. Eyre Crowe, for instance, "deplored all public speeches on foreign affairs"; and Grey agreed with him. As a result, in July 1914, the cabinet overruled any commitment. On 27 July Lloyd George said: "there could be no question of our taking part in any war in the first instance. He knew of no Minister who would be in favour of it."

Moreover, Grey supposed that British intervention would not carry much weight. He thought solely of naval action; it seemed impossible to him to send even an expeditionary force to France, and he certainly never imagined military intervention on a continental scale. On 2 August the cabinet authorized him to warn the Germans that their fleet would not be allowed to attack France in the Channel. Even this condition was not decisive; the Germans would have gladly agreed to it, in exchange for British neutrality. But on 3 August they sent an ultimatum to Belgium, demanding free passage to invade France; the British answered on 4 August demanding that Belgian neutrality be respected. Here again Grey has been criticised for not acting earlier; he should, it is said, have made British neutrality conditional on respect for Belgium. It would have made no difference. The German ultimatum to Belgium was drafted on 26 July, that is, even before the Austro-Hungarian declaration of war on Serbia; invasion of Belgium was an essential, indeed the essential, part of their plans. Only a French surrender could have held them from it. If Grey had acted earlier he would have achieved nothing, except perhaps the break-up of the liberal government; if he had delayed longer he would not have saved Belgium and he would have lost the inestimable value of moral superiority.

On 4 August the long Bismarckian peace ended. It had lasted more than a generation. Men had come to regard peace as normal; when it ended, they looked for some profound cause. Yet the immediate cause was a good deal simpler than on other occasions. Where, for instance, lay the precise responsibility for the Crimean war, and when did that war become inevitable? In 1914 there could be no doubt. Austria-Hungary had failed to solve her national problems. She blamed Serbia for the South Slav discontent; it would be far truer to say that this discontent involved Serbia, against her will, in Habsburg affairs. In July 1914 the Habsburg statesmen took the easy course of violence against Serbia, as their predecessors had taken it (though with more justification) against Sardinia in 1859. Berchtold launched war in 1914, as consciously as Buol launched it in 1859 or Gramont in 1870. There was this difference. Buol counted on support from Prussia and Great Britain; Gramont on support from Austria-Hungary. They were wrong. Berchtold counted rightly on support from Germany; he would not have persisted in a resolute line if it had not been for the repeated encouragements which came from Berlin. The Germans did not fix on war for August 1914, but they welcomed it when the occasion offered. They could win it now; they were more doubtful later. Hence they surrendered easily to the dictates of a military time-table. Austria-Hungary was growing weaker; Germany believed herself at the height of her strength. They decided on war from opposite motives; and the two decisions together caused a general European war.

The Powers of the Triple Entente all entered the war to defend themselves. The Russians fought to preserve the free passage of the Straits, on which their economic life depended; France for the sake of the Triple Entente, which she believed, rightly, alone guaranteed her survival as a Great Power. The British fought for the independence of sovereign states and, more remotely, to prevent a German domination of the Continent. It is sometimes said that the war was caused by the system of alliances or, more vaguely, by the Balance of Power. This is a generalization without reality. None of the Powers acted according to the letter of their commitments, though no doubt they might have done so if they had not anticipated them. Germany was pledged to go to war if Russia attacked Austria-Hungary. Instead, she declared war before Russia took any action; and Austria-Hungary only broke with Russia, grudgingly enough, a week afterwards. France was pledged to attack Germany, if the latter attacked Russia. Instead she was faced with a German demand for unconditional neutrality and would have had to accept war even had there been no Franco-Russian alliance, unless she was prepared to abdicate as a Great Power. Great Britain had a moral obligation to stand by France and a rather stronger one to defend her Channel coast. But she went to war for the sake of Belgium and would have done so, even if there had been no Anglo-French entente and no exchange of letters between Grey and Cambon in November 1912. Only then, the British intervention would have been even less effective than it was.

As to the Balance of Power, it would be truer to say that the war was caused by its breakdown rather than by its existence. There had been a real European Balance in the first decade of the Franco-Russian alliance; and peace had followed from it. The Balance broke down when Russia was weakened by the war with Japan; and Germany got in the habit of trying to get her way by threats. This ended with the Agadir crisis. Russia began to recover her strength, France her nerve. Both insisted on being treated as equals, as they had been in Bismarck's time. The Germans resented this and resolved to end it by war, if they could end it no other way. They feared that the Balance was being re-created. Their fears were exaggerated. Certainly, Russia would have been a more formidable Power by 1917, if her military plans had been carried through and if she had escaped internal disturbance—two formidable hypotheses. But it is unlikely that the three-year service would have been maintained in France; and, in any case, the Russians might well have used their strength against Great Britain in Asia rather than to attack Germany, if they had been left alone. In fact, peace must have brought Germany the mastery of Europe within a few years. This was prevented by the habit of her diplomacy and, still more, by the mental outlook of her people. They had trained themselves psychologically for aggression.

The German military plans played a vital part. The other Great Powers thought in terms of defending themselves. No Frenchman thought seriously of recovering Alsace and Lorraine; and the struggle of Slav and Teuton in the Balkans was very great nonsense so far as most Russians were concerned. The German generals wanted a decisive victory for its own sake. Though they complained of "encirclement," it was German policy that had created this encirclement. Absurdly enough, the Germans created their own problem when they annexed Alsace and Lorraine in 1871. They wanted an impregnable frontier; and they got one, as was shown in August 1914, when a small German force held its own there against the bulk of the French army. After 1871 the Germans could easily have fought Russia and stood on the defensive in the west; this was indeed the strategical plan of the elder Moltke. It was not a strategy which guaranteed final, decisive, victory; and Schlieffen therefore rejected it. In 1892 he insisted that France must be defeated first; ten years later he drew the further inevitable conclusion that the German armies must go through Belgium. If the strategy of the elder Moltke had been adhered to with all its political consequences, it would have been very difficult to persuade French and British opinion to go to the assistance of Russia; instead, it appeared in 1914 that Russia was coming to the assistance of France and even of Great Britain. Schlieffen first created the Franco-Russian alliance; and then ensured that Great Britain would enter the war as well. The Germans complained that the war could not be "localized" in 1914; Schlieffen's strategy prevented it. He would be content with nothing less than total victory; therefore he exposed Germany to total defeat.

There is a deeper explanation still. No one in 1914 took the dangers of war seriously except on a purely military plane. Though all, except a few fighting men, abhorred its bloodshed, none expected a social catastrophe. In the days of Metternich, and even afterwards, statesmen had feared that war would produce "revolution"—and revolutionaries had sometimes advocated it for that very reason. Now they were inclined to think that war would stave off their social and political problems. In France it produced the "sacred union";

in Germany William II was able to say: "I do not see parties any more; I see only Germans." All thought that war could be fitted into the existing framework of civilization, as the wars of 1866 and 1870 had been. Indeed, these wars had been followed by stabler currencies, freer trade, and more constitutional governments. War was expected to interrupt the even tenor of civilian life only while it lasted. Grey expressed this outlook in extreme form, when he said in the house of commons on 3 August: "if we are engaged in war, we shall suffer but little more than we shall suffer if we stand aside"; and by suffering he meant only the interruption of British trade with the continent of Europe. No country made serious economic preparations for war. In England the cry was raised of "business as usual" to mitigate the unemployment which war was expected to cause. The Germans so little understood the implications of total war that they abstained from invading Holland in August 1914, so as to be able to trade freely with the rest of the world.

The Balkan wars had taught a deceptive lesson. Everyone supposed that decisive battles would be fought at once, and a dictated peace would follow. The Germans expected to take Paris; the French expected to break through in Lorraine. The Russian "steam-roller" would reach Berlin; more important, from the Russian point of view, their armies would cross the Carpathians and take Budapest. Even the Austrians expected to "crush" Serbia. The British expected to destroy the German fleet in an immediate naval engagement and then to establish a close blockade of the German coast; apart from that, they had no military plans, except to applaud the victories of their allies and perhaps to profit from them.

None of these things happened. The French armies failed to make headway in Lorraine and suffered enormous casualties. The Germans marched through Belgium and saw from afar the Eiffel Tower. On 6 September they were halted on the Marne and driven back in defeat. But though the French won the battle of the Marne, they could not exploit their victory; the Germans were neither destroyed nor even expelled from French soil. By November there was a line of trenches running from Switzerland to the sea. The Russians invaded east Prussia; they were catastrophically defeated at Tannenberg on 27 August, and their armies in Galicia failed to reach the Carpathians. The Austrians occupied Belgrade, from which the Serbs had withdrawn; they were driven out again in November, and Serbian forces entered southern Hungary. The German fleet remained in harbour; and the British fleet was similarly imprisoned in order to balance it. Everywhere siege warfare superseded decisive battles. The machine-gun and the spade changed the course of European history. Policy had been silenced by the first great clash; but in the autumn of 1914 diplomacy was renewed. All the Powers sought to consolidate their alliances; to enlist new allies; and, more feebly, to shake the opposing coalition.

6

THE
FAILURE OF
IMAGINATION

FROM The Long Fuse BY LAURENCE LAFORE

The course of events that led to this general war are perfectly clear, though the motives and in some cases the timing are not. Austria-Hungary, at the urging of its ally, Germany, undertook strong measures against Serbia in order to protect its existence and its position as a Great Power. The exact purpose of these measures was not clearly agreed upon in Vienna, but they were of a sort to convince the Russians that Austria intended to extinguish Serbian sovereignty and to establish Austro-German predominance in the Balkans. To prevent this, and perhaps to frighten Austria into a more reasonable frame of mind, the Russians adopted military measures. The Germans felt absolutely obliged to stand by their ally, and they believed, from the moment of the assassination, that the safest course of action for Austria-Hungary to adopt would be a quick, decisive one, a *fait accompli*. They were prepared to incur the risk of fighting Russia, although they believed that it could be avoided. They urged—fruitlessly, most of the time—speed and decision in Vienna, and they continued to urge it after the Russian reaction to the ultimatum had showed that the risks were very serious. The Austrians responded by speeding up the declaration of war against Serbia; the Russians reacted, according to schedule, by mobilizing. Military considerations made it expedient that their mobilization be general, and this constituted a direct threat to Germany that could be met only by German mobilization. The French felt absolutely obliged to stand by *their* ally; it would almost certainly have been impossible for them to abstain from participation if they had wanted to, since the Germans almost certainly would have attacked them anyway as part of their plan for war against Russia. But the French did not consider abstention; instead, they gave the Russians unchanging, and sometimes provocative, assurances of their loyalty. German mobilization meant French mobilization, and German war against Russia meant a war between France and Germany. And since war between France and Germany involved the German violation of Belgium, it meant, too, war between Germany and Great Britain.

In this summary of events, stripped of the fruitless proposals for negotiation, may be discerned several elementary facts.

First, the vital interests of Germany and of France required loyalty to their respective allies; betrayal, or even a suggestion of weakness, would have incurred charges of treachery and led to a vulnerable and invidious isolation in a dangerous world. *The strength of their allies was part—an essential part— of their own strength and safety;* the preservation of that strength was deemed to demand not only loyal support but assistance in executing the policy of the ally. Prestige was part of strength; the Germans feared, rightly, a diminution of Austro-Hungarian authority; the French feared a diminution of Russian authority. Neither believed that the two were wholly incompatible, but they had very different views as to the minimum requirements of their allies' needs.

Second, the safety of each Power depended upon the execution, within very narrow time limits, of a very complicated and unalterable military plan. Not only could the plans not be changed; they must be put into effect as rapidly as possible to prevent grave military disadvantage, once the threat of war became serious.

Third, the Russians were absolutely convinced that Austria had sinister plans in the Balkans seriously menacing to their own interests, and they were convinced that the sovereignty of Serbia, however much of a nuisance they thought that nation might be, was indispensable to their own security and dignity.

Fourth, the Austrians were convinced that the sovereignty of Serbia was a serious and permanent threat to their own existence.

Fifth, the irretrievable steps were military measures, and these were taken in most cases at the urgent behest of the chiefs of staff and their advisers. The generals appear in a very unfavorable light in most narratives of events. There is no doubt that some of them—most conspicuously, Conrad—inclined to rabid bellicosity. But none of them acted except when ordered by civilian ministers. And the advice of most of them, of Janushkevich, of Moltke, of Joffre, was given as a matter of duty when facts drove them, correctly, to the conclusion that they could not safeguard their countries without preparing for war. This had nothing to do with their views as to whether war was or was not wise. They, like the ministers they advised, were merely performing their necessary function. As Winston Churchill was to say some twenty years later, "The responsibility of ministers for the public safety is absolute and needs no mandate."

But this is not to suggest that the course of events was preordained or that nothing could have been done to prevent its developing as it did. There are hundreds of suppositious changes that might have prevented the war from taking place when it did and on the terms it did. To discuss them is profitless, but to suggest a few possibilities, chosen at random, may be instructive.

For one thing, the French Ambassador at Saint Petersburg, Maurice Paléologue, repeatedly pressed on Sazonov the need for a "firm policy." His position was very influential—both because he represented Russia's ally and because, since his chiefs were inaccessible, it was necessary for him to act on his own responsibility. He was, for a time, *making* French policy toward Russia, and the policy he made was incitement to war. A different ambassador might well have altered the course of events. Paléologue went far beyond the terms of the alliance, beyond the need to show diplomatic solidarity, beyond the limits of previous French policy. His actions and influences offer a precise counterpart to those of Tschirschky in Vienna.

To take another example, it has frequently been said by both sides that a clearer stand by Sir Edward Grey would have saved the peace. If the Germans had been told, early and with conviction, that Britain would take part in the war, they would very probably have averted instead of encouraging the Austrian ultimatum and declaration of war. There is strong evidence for this; some Germans have even taken the weird moral stand that Grey was responsible for starting the war because if he had made his position clear the Germans would never have permitted it to start. The ethics of this attitude are not convincing, but the facts are. A less fastidious, conciliatory, and correct statesman might have acted more effectively. A modest measure of duplicity, such as many diplomats regard as a proper tool of their trade, would have permitted him to make much stronger representations much sooner than he did. No absolute commitment was necessary; he could have told both Lichnowsky and his own Ambassador at Berlin that Great Britain *did* regard the Austro-Serbian problem as of European and British concern (that would have been a matter of judgment, not of propriety) and that if war broke out Great Britain would almost certainly take part in it on the allied side. This would have been tricky, in both senses of the word, but experienced diplomats of the utmost rectitude like Nicolson and Eyre Crowe were urging something like it. Sir Edward suffered from an excess of scruples and perhaps an insufficiency of grasp; his case is a demonstration for the argument that there is at times nothing so dangerous as pacific punctilio.

If either Sazonov or Berchtold had behaved differently, on any of several occasions, the course of events would certainly have been different. A less volatile and more judicious statesman than Sazonov, and one surer of his own ground, might not have reacted with so much emotion and so little regard for political realities as he did on hearing of the Austrian ultimatum.

A smaller concern for Russia's prestige and his own might have prevented his urging the Serbs to reject the ultimatum, and it might have delayed the Period Preparatory to War and given time for fruitful negotiation. A less indecisive statesman than Berchtold, and one with a clearer vision of the future, might have formulated concrete demands for Serbia that would secure Austria's ends without leaving so much scope for uncertainty, even apparently in his own mind, about what really was intended as an objective. The problem of Austria-Hungary was in some ways comparable to that of Great Britain: there were too many disagreements and cross-currents and deterrents to clear-cut action. But a different sort of statesman in either country might have overcome them and produced a definite and rapid solution to the difficulties.

Most important, there were in Germany many occasions when different events would have followed if even slightly different decisions had been made. At all times the Germans treated the prospective war as if it were a rather inviting prospect. From July 5 on, the Germans behaved unwisely in regard to Austria; they first pressed for decisive action and, when it was not forthcoming, continued to press for it without regard to changing circumstances. They seem to have been wildly optimistic about the chances of French and British pressure being exerted at Saint Petersburg. They were certainly wildly irresponsible in acting on the belief that they could win a European war if one broke out. Such unwisdom was an understandable but not a necessary component of German policy. If the German leaders had not been widely dispersed around the middle of July, if the Emperor had returned a few days earlier from his cruise, if Bethmann-Hollweg and Jagow had not been caught up in the established policy that a *fait accompli* was possible, Austria-Hungary might not have rejected out of hand the Serbian reply, might not have broken diplomatic relations with Serbia, might not have declared war, might not have provoked the Russian mobilization.

All these involve reproaches to the statesmen for deficiencies in their stature. But the basic reproach must be the failure of imagination; the statesmen were thinking of the defense of visible interests that seemed vital; they failed to discern that invisible and much larger interests were involved in their decisions. There were, in Russia, those who foresaw a threat to the regime in the war, but the defense of the regime seemed to Sazonov and the Emperor Nicholas to demand not peace but prestige. No one, let it be said again, realized that the war they were consciously risking would be the first World War.

Two things happened to turn war into cataclysm. First, the breakdown of the German strategy in France and the establishment of stable lines in early September, 1914: instead of a decision there was an indecision, made perennial by the peculiar equilibrium of military technology. Second, the accumulated tensions and conflicts of the European State System, long repressed or stabilized, all broke out the moment that war was a fact; the war could not be ended until they were resolved. Most of these tensions had nothing to do with the events that caused the war to break out; they were buried at the bottom of the rivalries and the institutions that made it possible. There was Alsace-Lorraine: once a Franco-German war had started, France could not make peace until Alsace-Lorraine was restored, except after a military disaster; without a military disaster, Germany would never concede the loss of the provinces. There was the Anglo-German naval rivalry: once war had started, Great Britain would not make peace until the threat of a strong German Navy had been permanently dispersed. There was Constantinople: once war broke out, the Russian government could not make peace until it was assured that the centuries-old ambition for Constantinople would be satisfied. There was Germany's encirclement: once war broke out, Germany could not, short of military disaster, make peace until the encirclement had been broken, which meant the decisive crushing of both France and Russia.

These needs and ambitions had underlaid the tensions of Europe and had shaped the alliance system and the policies of the Powers. But they none of them had led to actions that produced war. They were either negotiable or repressible. The one problem that was neither negotiable nor repressible was that raised by threats to the integrity of Austria-Hungary. The composition of the Habsburg Monarchy made it fatally vulnerable to the activities of the Serbs; at the same time, it made it difficult to eliminate those activities by rapid and resolute action; and it made it difficult for the government of Austria-Hungary—or its ally, Germany—to retreat, to equivocate, to delay, once the decision to take action had been made, ill defined and unsatisfactory as the decision was. It was this problem that caused the war which became the first World War.

THE ORIGINS OF NAZI GERMANY

GERMAN HISTORY OR CHARISMATIC LEADERSHIP?

CONTENTS

QUESTIONS FOR STUDY

1. *What elements of German history and tradition contributed to the Nazi victory?*
2. *What external forces were responsible?*
3. *How did the Nazi program and propaganda exploit these elements and forces?*
4. *What was the importance of anti-Semitism to the Nazi victory?*
5. *How and why did the Communists and businessmen aid the Nazis?*
6. *Was the destruction of the Weimar Republic inevitable?*

On January 30, 1933, Adolf Hitler took office as Chancellor of Germany. In March of the same year a compliant Reichstag passed an Enabling Act, which suspended the constitution, established Hitler's dictatorship, and put an end to Germany's attempt at democratic republican government. It also introduced a reign of terror, a policy of racism and military adventurism the likes of which the world had never seen. The problem in this section is to decide why this disaster befell Germany. Some scholars maintain that the evil aspects and consequences of Nazism are inherent in the German character, which was created by the unique course of German history. Others find the causes of the Nazi rise to power in the peculiar problems faced by the Weimar Republic and suggest that any nation faced by such conditions and problems might well follow Germany's pattern. Still others hold that Nazism was largely the product of the evil genius of Adolf Hitler himself. The selections that follow illustrate some of the difficulties that Germany faced after World War I and the nature of the solutions offered by Hitler and the Nazis. They also indicate which elements of the German people helped Hitler to power.

Alan Bullock (pp. 528–537) presents a clear statement of one view of the problem in his magisterial biography of the dictator. Bullock is fully aware of the conditions in Europe and Germany that made the victory of the Nazis possible, but he argues that the peculiar talents of "the greatest demagogue in history"—rhetorical skill, insight into mass psychology, and shrewd, unprincipled opportunism—were necessary to forge the political movement that conquered Germany.

That movement, of course, was made up of many strands of Germany's past as well as the discontent of the 1920s. The Treaty of Versailles stripped Germany of some of its territory and all its overseas colonies, limited its military forces to the point that it could hardly defend itself, imposed a heavy war indemnity that hampered economic recovery, and added insult to injury by placing exclusive responsibility for World War I on the German side. The Weimar Republic was the result of that peace, and the democratic parties that governed for most of its history had been compelled to sign the treaty and accept its provisions. Hitler's rhetoric placed all the blame for Germany's troubles on the treaty and on the politicians and constitution that accepted and tried to live by it. He helped to create and manipulate German resentment against the treaty and the republic (pp. 538–540). The terrible inflation of 1921–1923, which devastated the middle class and weakened confidence in the Weimar regime, played right into Hitler's hands. He was able to depict it as part of the international Jewish-Communist conspiracy, which was a central theme of his ideology. In their desperation many Germans who might ordinarily have known better were converted (pp. 540–543).

The democratic parties that tried to govern Germany during the Weimar period were hampered by several facts of political life. One was that Germany, only legally unified since 1871, was not yet unified in fact. The local states retained an important degree of local autonomy under the Weimar constitution. Bavaria, for instance, was Catholic and conservative and always suspicious of centralized government lest it be dominated by Prussia, which was Protestant and liberal or even socialistic. As a result, the Bavarian government made little effort to suppress the illegal activities of the Nazis, and some of its officials secretly supported Hitler. In addition, the Weimar constitution was so structured as to give rise to a multiparty system, and no single party was strong enough to rule alone. The ever-shifting coalitions found it hard to achieve the stability needed to meet Germany's problems. But the remarkable thing is that the governments of Social Democrats, Catholic Centralists, and Liberals did achieve a great deal. Reparations were reduced, loans from America were negotiated, and the economy was restored to stability and a degree of prosperity. Under its ablest chief, Gustav Stresemann, Weimar Germany was on the verge of becoming internationally respectable and domestically stable. The democratic parties in Germany who looked back to the liberal revolution of 1848 were enthusiastic in their support of the infant democracy, which promised to bring peace, progress, and prosperity (pp. 559–560), but they were too few. Even many of the supporters of the Weimar constitution were *Vernunft Republikaner*—republicans from calculation—who supported the regime out of necessity but without passion.

The enemies of the republic, however, were unswervingly dedicated to its destruction. The German Communist party, for instance, even as late as 1932, rejected any thought of cooperation with the Social Democrats to save the republic from the Nazis. Instead, it regarded the major supporters of the Weimar regime as "Social Fascists" who had to be smashed on the way to the true Socialist revolution (pp. 551–552). The Nazis, of course, never deviated from their purpose of destroying the democratic republic. They seized upon the real problems of the time and combined them with a brilliant demagogic appeal to the fears and prejudices that had been present among the German people for some time. Nationalism, militarism, racial consciousness, and anti-Semitism, all of which existed outside of Germany, were put together by Hitler with resentment against the Treaty of Versailles and the economic disaster of the 1920s in a program intended to have broad appeal (pp. 561–564). When the Weimar Republic seemed unable to deal effectively with the problems created by the severe depression that began in 1929, the Nazis came to power, aided by the support of influential businessmen (pp. 553–558), by the divisions among their opponents, and, perhaps, by certain tendencies arising from German history.

1
HITLER, THE GREATEST DEMAGOGUE IN HISTORY

Alan Bullock presents a sophisticated version of a widely held opinion that Nazism was the product of the demagogic genius of Adolf Hitler.

FROM Hitler BY ALAN BULLOCK

Hitler lived through the exciting days of April and May 1919 in Munich itself. What part he played, if any, is uncertain. According to his own account in *Mein Kampf,* he was to have been put under arrest at the end of April, but drove off with his rifle the three men who came to arrest him. Once the Communists had been overthrown, he gave information before the Commission of Inquiry set up by the 2nd Infantry Regiment, which tried and shot those reported to have been active on the other side. He then got a job in the Press and News Bureau of the Political Department of the Army's VII (Munich) District Command, a centre for the activities of such men as Röhm. After attending a course of "political instruction" for the troops, Hitler was himself appointed a *Bildungsoffizier* (Instruction Officer) with the task of inoculating the men against contagion by socialist, pacifist, or democratic ideas. This was an important step for Hitler, since it constituted the first recognition of the fact that he had any political ability at all. Then, in September, he was instructed by the head of the Political Department to investigate a small group meeting in Munich, the German Workers' Party, which might possibly be of interest to the Army.

Hitler: A Study in Tyranny, Completely Revised Edition, pp. 63–71, 805–808, by Alan Bullock. Copyright © 1962 by Alan Bullock. Reprinted by permission of Harper & Row, Publishers, and Odhams Books Ltd., London.

The German Workers' Party had its origins in a Committee of Independent Workmen set up by a Munich locksmith, Anton Drexler, on 7 March 1918. Drexler's idea was to create a party which would be both working class and nationalist. He saw what Hitler had also seen, that a middle-class movement like the Fatherland Front (to which Drexler belonged) was hopelessly out of touch with the mood of the masses, and that these were coming increasingly under the influence of anti-national and anti-militarist propaganda. Drexler made little headway with his committee, which recruited forty members, and in October 1918 he and Karl Harrer, a journalist, founded the Political Workers' Circle which, in turn, was merged with the earlier organization in January 1919 to form the German Workers' Party. Harrer became the Party's first chairman. Its total membership was little more than Drexler's original forty, activity was limited to discussions in Munich beer-halls, and the committee of six had no clear idea of anything more ambitious. It can scarcely have been a very impressive scene when, on the evening of 12 September 1919, Hitler attended his first meeting in a room at the Sterneckerbräu, a Munich beer-cellar in which a handful of twenty or twenty-five people had gathered. One of the speakers was Gottfried Feder, an economic crank well known in Munich, who had already impressed Hitler at one of the political courses arranged for the Army. The other was a Bavarian separatist, whose proposals for the secession of Bavaria from the German Reich and a union with Austria brought Hitler to his feet in a fury. He spoke with such vehemence that when the meeting was over Drexler went up to him and gave him a copy of his autobiographical pamphlet, *Mein politisches Erwachen*.[1] A few days later Hitler received a postcard inviting him to attend a committee meeting of the German Workers' Party.

After some hesitation Hitler went. The committee met in an obscure beer-house, the Alte Rosenbad, in the Herrnstrasse. "I went through the badly lighted guest-room, where not a single guest was to be seen, and searched for the door which led to the side room; and there I was face to face with the Committee. Under the dim light shed by a grimy gas-lamp I could see four people sitting round a table, one of them the author of the pamphlet."[2]

The rest of the proceedings followed in the same key: the Party's funds were reported to total 7.50 marks, minutes were read and confirmed, three letters were received, three replies read and approved.

Yet, as Hitler frankly acknowledges, this very obscurity was an attraction. It was only in a party which, like himself, was beginning at the bottom that he had any prospect of playing a leading part and imposing his ideas. In the established parties there was no room for him, he would be a nobody. After two days' reflection he made up his mind and joined the Committee of the German Workers' Party as its seventh member.

---

[1] *My Political Awakening.*
[2] *Mein Kampf*, p. 189.

The energy and ambition which had been hitherto unharnessed now found an outlet. Slowly and painfully he pushed the Party forward, and prodded his cautious and unimaginative colleagues on the committee into bolder methods of recruitment. A few invitations were multigraphed and distributed, a small advertisement inserted in the local paper, a larger hall secured for more frequent meetings. When Hitler himself spoke for the first time in the Hofbräuhaus in October, a hundred and eleven people were present. The result was to confirm the chairman, Karl Harrer, in his belief that Hitler had no talent for public speaking. But Hitler persisted and the numbers rose. In October there were a hundred and thirty when Hitler spoke on Brest-Litovsk and Versailles, a little later there were two hundred.

At the beginning of 1920 Hitler was put in charge of the Party's propaganda and promptly set to work to organize its first mass meeting. By the use of clever advertising he got nearly two thousand people into the *Festsaal* of the Hofbräuhaus on 24 February. The principal speaker was a Dr Dingfelder, but it was Hitler who captured the audience's attention and used the occasion to announce the Party's new name, the National Socialist German Workers' Party, and its twenty-five point programme. Angered by the way in which Hitler was now forcing the pace, Harrer resigned from the office of chairman. On 1 April 1920, Hitler at last left the Army and devoted all his time to building up the Party, control of which he now more and more arrogated to himself.

Hitler's and Drexler's group in Munich was not the only National Socialist party. In Bavaria itself there were rival groups, led by Streicher in Nuremberg and Dr Otto Dickel in Augsburg, both nominally branches of the German Socialist Party founded by Alfred Brunner in 1919. Across the frontier in Austria and in the Sudetenland the pre-war German Social Workers' Party had been reorganized and got in touch with the new Party in Munich. A number of attempts had been made in Austria before 1914 to combine a working-class movement with a Pan-German nationalist programme. The most successful was this Deutsch Arbeiterpartei which, led by an Austrian lawyer, Walther Riehl, and a railway employee named Rudolf Jung, won three seats in the Reichsrat at the Austrian elections of 1911. The Party's programme was formulated at the Moravian town of Iglau in 1913, and reflected the bitterness of the German struggle with the Czechs as well as the attraction of Pan-German and anti-Semitic ideas.

In May 1918, this Austrian party took the title of D.N.S.A.P.—the German National Socialist Workers' Party—and began to use the Hakenkreuz, the swastika, as its symbol. When the Austro-Hungarian monarchy was broken up, and a separate Czech State formed, the National Socialists set up an inter-State bureau with one branch in Vienna, of which Riehl was chairman, and another in the Sudetenland. It was this inter-State bureau which now invited the cooperation of the Bavarian National Socialists, and a Munich delegation attended the next joint meeting at Salzburg in August 1920. Shortly afterwards the Munich Party, too, adopted the name of the National Socialist German Workers' Party.

Up to August 1923, when Hitler attended the last of the inter-State meetings at Salzburg, there were fairly frequent contacts between these different National Socialist groups, but little came of them. Hitler was too jealous of his independence to submit to interference from outside, and the last meeting of the conference, at Salzburg in 1923, led to Riehl's resignation.

Much more important to Hitler was the support he received from Captain Röhm, on the staff of the Army District Command in Munich. Röhm, a tough, scar-faced soldier of fortune with real organizing ability, exercised considerable influence in the shadowy world of the Freikorps, Defence Leagues, and political conspiracies. He had actually joined the German Workers' Party before Hitler, for, like Hitler, he saw that it would be impossible to re-create a strong, nationalist Germany until the alienation of the mass of the people from their old loyalty to the Fatherland and the Army could be overcome. Any party which could recapture the working classes for a nationalist and militarist allegiance interested him. He admired the spirit and toughness of the Communists, who were prepared to fight for what they believed in: what he wanted was working-class organizations with the same qualities on his own side.

Röhm had little patience with the view that the Army should keep out of politics. The Army, he believed, had to go into politics if it wanted to create the sort of State which would restore its old privileged position, and break with the policy of fulfilling the terms of the Peace Treaty. This was a view accepted by only a part of the Officer Corps; others, especially among the senior officers, viewed Röhm's activities with mistrust. But there was sufficient sympathy with his aims to allow a determined man to use the opportunities of his position to the full.

When Hitler began to build up the German Workers' Party, Röhm pushed in ex-Freikorps men and ex-servicemen to swell the Party's membership. From these elements the first "strong-arm" squads were formed, the nucleus of the S.A. In December 1920, Röhm had persuaded his commanding officer, Major-General Ritter von Epp—himself a former Freikorps leader and a member of the Party—to help raise the sixty thousand marks needed to buy the Party a weekly paper, the *Völkischer Beobachter*. Dietrich Eckart provided half, but part of the rest came from Army secret funds. Above all, Röhm was the indispensable link in securing for Hitler the protection, or at least the tolerance, of the Army and of the Bavarian Government, which depended on the local Army Command as the ultimate arbiter of public order. Without the unique position of the Army in German, and especially in Bavarian, politics—its ability to extend powerful support to the political groups and activities it favoured—Hitler would never have been able to exercise with impunity his methods of incitement, violence and intimidation. At every step from 1914 to 1945 Hitler's varying relationship to the Army was of the greatest importance to him: never more so than in these early years in Munich when, without the Army's patronage, Hitler would have found the greatest difficulty in climbing the first steps of his political career. Before his death the Army was to learn the full measure of his ingratitude.

Yet however important this help from outside, the foundation of Hitler's success was his own energy and ability as a political leader. Without this, the help would never have been forthcoming, or would have produced insignificant results. Hitler's genius as a politician lay in his unequalled grasp of what could be done by propaganda, and his flair for seeing how to do it. He had to learn in a hard school, on his feet night after night, arguing his case in every kind of hall, from the smoke-filled back room of a beer-cellar to the huge auditorium of the Zirkus Krone; often, in the early days, in the face of opposition, indifference or amused contempt; learning to hold his audience's attention, to win them over; most important of all, learning to read the minds of his audiences, finding the sensitive spots on which to hammer. "He could play like a virtuoso on the well-tempered piano of lower-middle-class hearts," says Dr Schacht. Behind that virtuosity lay years of experience as an agitator and mob orator. Hitler came to know Germany and the German people at first hand as few of Germany's other leaders ever had. By the time he came to power in 1933 there were few towns of any size in the Reich where he had not spoken. Here was one great advantage Hitler had over nearly all the politicians with whom he had to deal, his immense practical experience of politics, not in the Chancellery or the Reichstag, but in the street, the level at which elections are won, the level at which any politician must be effective if he is to carry a mass vote with him.

Hitler was the greatest demagogue in history. Those who add "only a demagogue" fail to appreciate the nature of political power in an age of mass politics. As he himself said: "To be a leader, means to be able to move masses."

The lessons which Hitler drew from the activities of the Austrian Social Democrats and Lueger's Christian Socialists were now tried out in Munich. Success was far from being automatic. Hitler made mistakes and had much to learn before he could persuade people to take him seriously, even on the small stage of Bavarian politics. By 1923 he was still only a provincial politician, who had not yet made any impact on national politics, and the end of 1923 saw the collapse of his movement in a fiasco. But Hitler learned from his mistakes, and by the time he came to write *Mein Kampf* in the middle of the 1920s he was able to set down quite clearly what he was trying to do, and what were the conditions of success. The pages in *Mein Kampf* in which he discusses the technique of mass propaganda and political leadership stand out in brilliant contrast with the turgid attempts to explain his entirely unoriginal political ideas.

The first and most important principle for political action laid down by

Hitler is: Go to the masses. "The movement must avoid everything which may lessen or weaken its power of influencing the masses . . . because of the simple fact that no great idea, no matter how sublime or exalted, can be realized in practice without the effective power which resides in the popular masses."

Since the masses have only a poor acquaintance with abstract ideas, their reactions lie more in the domain of the feelings, where the roots of their positive as well as their negative attitudes are implanted. . . . The emotional grounds of their attitude furnish the reason for their extraordinary stability. It is always more difficult to fight against faith than against knowledge. And the driving force which has brought about the most tremendous revolutions on this earth has never been a body of scientific teaching which has gained power over the masses, but always a devotion which has inspired them, and often a kind of hysteria which has urged them into action. Whoever wishes to win over the masses must know the key that will open the door to their hearts. It is not objectivity, which is a feckless attitude, but a determined will, backed up by power where necessary.

Hitler is quite open in explaining how this is to be achieved. "The receptive powers of the masses are very restricted, and their understanding is feeble. On the other hand, they quickly forget. Such being the case, all effective propaganda must be confined to a few bare necessities and then must be expressed in a few stereotyped formulas." Hitler had nothing but scorn for the intellectuals who are always looking for something new. "Only constant repetition will finally succeed in imprinting an idea on the memory of a crowd." For the same reason it is better to stick to a programme even when certain points in it become out of date: "As soon as one point is removed from the sphere of dogmatic certainty, the discussion will not simply result in a new and better formulation, but may easily lead to endless debates and general confusion."

When you lie, tell big lies. This is what the Jews do, working on the principle, "which is quite true in itself, that in the big lie there is always a certain force of credibility; because the broad masses of a nation are always more easily corrupted in the deeper strata of their emotional nature than consciously or voluntarily, and thus in the primitive simplicity of their minds they more readily fall victims to the big lie than the small lie, since they themselves often tell small lies in little matters, but would be ashamed to resort to large-scale falsehoods. It would never come into their heads to fabricate colossal untruths and they would not believe that others could have the impudence to distort the truth so infamously. . . . The grossly impudent lie always leaves traces behind it, even after it has been nailed down."

Above all, never hesitate, never qualify what you say, never concede an inch to the other side, paint all your contrasts in black and white. This is the "very first condition which has to be fulfilled in every kind of propaganda: a systematically one-sided attitude towards every problem that has to be dealt with. . . . When they see an uncompromising onslaught against an adversary, the people have at all times taken this as proof that right is on the side of the active aggressor; but if the aggressor should go only halfway and fail to push home his success . . . the people will look upon this as a sign that he is uncertain of the justice of his own cause."

Vehemence, passion, fanaticism, these are "the great magnetic forces which alone attract the great masses; for these masses always respond to the compelling force which emanates from absolute faith in the ideas put forward, combined with an indomitable zest to fight for and defend them. . . . The doom of a nation can be averted only by a storm of glowing passion; but only those who are passionate themselves can arouse passion in others."

Hitler showed a marked preference for the spoken over the written word. "The force which ever set in motion the great historical avalanches of religious and political movements is the magic power of the spoken word. The broad masses of a population are more amenable to the appeal of rhetoric than to any other force." The employment of verbal violence, the repetition of such words as "smash," "force," "ruthless," "hatred," was deliberate. Hitler's gestures and the emotional character of his speaking, lashing himself up to a pitch of near-hysteria in which he would scream and spit out his resentment, had the same effect on an audience. Many descriptions have been given of the way in which he succeeded in communicating passion to his listeners, so that men groaned or hissed and women sobbed involuntarily, if only to relieve the tension, caught up in the spell of powerful emotions of hatred and exaltation, from which all restraint had been removed.

It was to be years yet before Hitler was able to achieve this effect on the scale of the Berlin Sportpalast audiences of the 1930s, but he had already begun to develop extraordinary gifts as a speaker. It was in Munich that he learned to address mass audiences of several thousands. In *Mein Kampf* he remarks that the orator's relationship with his audience is the secret of his art. "He will always follow the lead of the great mass in such a way that from the living emotion of his hearers the apt word which he needs will be suggested to him and in its turn this will go straight to the hearts of his hearers." A little later he speaks of the difficulty of overcoming emotional resistance: this cannot be done by argument, but only by an appeal to the "hidden forces" in an audience, an appeal that the orator alone can make.

Many attempts have been made to explain away the importance of Hitler, from Chaplin's brilliant caricature in *The Great Dictator* to the much less convincing picture of Hitler the pawn, a front man for German capitalism. Others have argued that Hitler was nothing in himself, only a symbol of the restless ambition of the German nation to dominate Europe; a creature flung to the top by the tides of revolutionary change, or the embodiment of the collective unconscious of a people obsessed with violence and death.

These arguments seem to me to be based upon a confusion of two different questions. Obviously, Nazism was a complex phenomenon to which many factors—social, economic, historical, psychological—contributed. But whatever the explanation of this episode in European history—and it can be no simple one—that does not answer the question with which this book has been concerned, what was the part played by Hitler. It may be true that a mass movement, strongly nationalist, anti-Semitic, and radical, would have sprung up in Germany without Hitler. But so far as what actually happened is concerned—not what might have happened—the evidence seems to me to leave no doubt that no other man played a role in the Nazi revolution or in the history of the Third Reich remotely comparable with that of Adolf Hitler.

The conception of the Nazi Party, the propaganda with which it must appeal to the German people, and the tactics by which it would come to power—these were unquestionably Hitler's. After 1934 there were no rivals left and by 1938 he had removed the last checks on his freedom of action. Thereafter, he exercised an arbitrary rule in Germany to a degree rarely, if ever, equalled in a modern industrialized state.

At the same time, from the re-militarization of the Rhineland to the invasion of Russia, he won a series of successes in diplomacy and war which established an hegemony over the continent of Europe comparable with that of Napoleon at the height of his fame. While these could not have been won without a people and an Army willing to serve him, it was Hitler who provided the indispensable leadership, the flair for grasping opportunities, the boldness in using them. In retrospect his mistakes appear obvious, and it is easy to be complacent about the inevitability of his defeat; but it took the combined efforts of the three most powerful nations in the world to break his hold on Europe.

Luck and the disunity of his opponents will account for much of Hitler's success—as it will of Napoleon's—but not for all. He began with few advantages, a man without a name and without support other than that which he acquired for himself, not even a citizen of the country he aspired to rule. To achieve what he did Hitler needed—and possessed—talents out of the ordinary which in sum amounted to political genius, however evil its fruits.

His abilities have been sufficiently described in the preceding pages: his mastery of the irrational factors in politics, his insight into the weaknesses of his opponents, his gift for simplification, his sense of timing, his willingness to take risks. An opportunist entirely without principle, he showed both consistency and an astonishing power of will in pursuing his aims. Cynical and calculating in the exploitation of his histrionic gifts, he retained an unshaken belief in his historic role and in himself as a creature of destiny.

The fact that his career ended in failure, and that his defeat was preeminently due to his own mistakes, does not by itself detract from Hitler's claim to greatness. The flaw lies deeper. For these remarkable powers were combined with an ugly and strident egotism, a moral and intellectual cretinism. The passions which ruled Hitler's mind were ignoble: hatred, resentment, the lust to dominate, and, where he could not dominate, to destroy. His career did not exalt but debased the human condition, and his twelve years' dictatorship was barren of all ideas save one—the further extension of his own power and that of the nation with which he had identified himself. Even power he conceived of in the crudest terms: an endless vista of military roads, S.S. garrisons, and concentration camps to sustain the rule of the Aryan "master race" over the degraded subject peoples of his new empire in the east.

The great revolutions of the past, whatever their ultimate fate, have been identified with the release of certain powerful ideas: individual conscience, liberty, equality, national freedom, social justice. National Socialism produced nothing. Hitler constantly exalted force over the power of ideas and delighted to prove that men were governed by cupidity, fear, and their baser passions. The sole theme of the Nazi revolution was domination, dressed up as the doctrine of race, and, failing that, a vindictive destructiveness, Rauschning's *Revolution des Nihilismus*.

It is this emptiness, this lack of anything to justify the suffering he caused rather than his own monstrous and ungovernable will which makes Hitler both so repellent and so barren a figure. Hitler will have his place in history, but it will be alongside Attila the Hun, the barbarian king who was surnamed, not "the Great," but "the Scourge of God," and who boasted "in a saying," Gibbon writes, "worthy of his ferocious pride, that the grass never grew on the spot where his horse had stood." [3]

The view has often been expressed that Hitler could only have come to power in Germany, and it is true—without falling into the same error of racialism as the Nazis—that there were certain features of German historical development, quite apart from the effects of the Defeat and the Depression, which favoured the rise of such a movement.

This is not to accuse the Germans of Original Sin, or to ignore the other sides of German life which were only grossly caricatured by the Nazis. But Nazism was not some terrible accident which fell upon the German people out of a blue sky. It was rooted in their history, and while it is true that a majority of the German people never voted for Hitler, it is also true that thirteen millions did. Both facts need to be remembered.

From this point of view Hitler's career may be described as a *reductio ad absurdum* of the most powerful political tradition in Germany since the Unification. This is what nationalism, militarism, authoritarianism, the worship of success and force, the exaltation of the State, and *Realpolitik* lead to, if they are projected to their logical conclusion.

There are Germans who reject such a view. They argue that what was wrong with Hitler was that he lacked the necessary skill, that he was a bungler. If only he had listened to the generals—or Schacht—or the career diplomats—if only he had not attacked Russia, and so on. There is some point, they feel, at which he went wrong. They refuse to see that it was the ends themselves, not simply the means, which were wrong: the pursuit of unlimited power, the scorn for justice or any restraint on power; the exaltation of will over reason and conscience; the assertion of an arrogant supremacy, the

---

[3] Gibbon: *Decline and Fall of the Roman Empire*, c. 34.

contempt for others' rights. As at least one German historian, Professor Meinecke, has recognized, the catastrophe to which Hitler led Germany points to the need to re-examine the aims as well as the methods of German policy as far back as Bismarck.

The Germans, however, were not the only people who preferred in the 1930s not to know what was happening and refused to call evil things by their true names. The British and French at Munich; the Italians, Germany's partners in the Pact of Steel; the Poles, who stabbed the Czechs in the back over Teschen; the Russians, who signed the Nazi-Soviet Pact to partition Poland, all thought they could buy Hitler off, or use him to their own selfish advantage. They did not succeed, any more than the German Right or the German Army. In the bitterness of war and occupation they were forced to learn the truth of the words of John Donne which Ernest Hemingway set at the beginning of his novel of the Spanish Civil War:

No man is an Iland, intire of it selfe; every man is a peece of the Continent, a part of the maine; If a clod bee washed away by the Sea, Europe is the lesse, as well as if a Promontorie were, as well as if a Mannor of thy friends or of thine own were; Any man's death diminishes me, because I am involved in Mankinde; And therefore never send to know for whom the bell tolls; It tolls for thee.

Hitler, indeed, was a European, no less than a German phenomenon. The conditions and the state of mind which he exploited, the *malaise* of which he was the symptom, were not confined to one country, although they were more strongly marked in Germany than anywhere else. Hitler's idiom was German, but the thoughts and emotions to which he gave expression have a more universal currency.

Hitler recognized this relationship with Europe perfectly clearly. He was in revolt against "the System" not just in Germany but in Europe, against the liberal bourgeois order, symbolized for him in the Vienna which had once rejected him. To destroy this was his mission, the mission in which he never ceased to believe; and in this, the most deeply felt of his purposes, he did not fail. Europe may rise again, but the old Europe of the years between 1789, the year of the French Revolution, and 1939, the year of Hitler's War, has gone for ever—and the last figure in its history is that of Adolf Hitler, the architect of its ruin. *"Si monumentum requiris, circumspice"*—"If you seek his monument, look around."

2
THE
WEAKNESSES
OF WEIMAR

Article 231 of the Treaty of Versailles, which assigned all responsibility for the recent war to Germany and her allies, was a thorn in the side of those Germans who defended the Weimar democracy. The clause was widely rejected by the Germans, and enemies of the republic used it to fix the blame for all Germany's troubles on the republican officials who had signed the treaty. The following remarks of Adolf Hitler are examples of the rhetoric that was employed.

FROM Hitler's Speeches on War Guilt

In a speech delivered at Munich on 13 April 1923 Hitler said:

"In the winter of the year 1919–20 we National Socialists publicly for the first time put to the German people the question, whose is the guilt for the War? . . . And we received pat from all sides the stereotyped answer of despicable self-humiliation: 'We confess it: the guilt for the War is ours!' . . . Yes, the whole Revolution was made artificially on the basis of this truly monstrous lie. For if it had not been possible to bring this lie into the field as a propaganda formula against the old Reich, what sense could one give at all to the November treason? They needed this slander of the existing system in order to justify before the people their own deed of shame. The masses, under the

The Speeches of Adolf Hitler, I (1942), 54–57, translated and edited by Norman Baynes, published by Oxford University Press under the auspices of the Royal Institute of International Affairs, London.

influence of a criminal incitement, were prepared without any hesitation to believe whatever the men of the new Government told them."

In his speech delivered in Munich on 17 April 1923 Hitler discussed "The Peace Treaty of Versailles as the perpetual curse of the November-Republic."

Who, *he asked,* were the real rulers of Germany in 1914 to whom war guilt might be attributed: not the Kaiser, not the Pan-Germans, but Messrs. Ballin, Bleichröder, Mendelssohn, &c., a whole brood of Hebrews who formed the unofficial Government. And in 1914 the real ruler of the Reich was Herr Bethmann-Hollweg, "a descendant of a Jewish family of Frankfurt—the genuine article, and in his every act the Yiddish philosopher all over. Those were the leaders of the State, not the Pan-Germans."

* * *

After discussing the mistakes of German politicians during the course of the War Hitler continued:

"With the armistice begins the humiliation of Germany. If the Republic on the day of its foundation had appealed to the country: 'Germans, stand together! Up and resist the foe! The Fatherland, the Republic expects of you that you fight to your last breath,' then millions who are now the enemies of the Republic would be fanatical Republicans. To-day they are the foes of the Republic not because it is a Republic but because this Republic was founded at the moment when Germany was humiliated, because it so discredited the new flag that men's eyes must turn regretfully towards the old flag."

"It was no Treaty of Peace which was signed, but a betrayal of Peace."

"The Treaty was signed which demanded from Germany that she should perform what was for ever impossible of performance. But that was not the worst: after all that was only a question of material values. This was not the end: Commissions of Control were formed! For the first time in the history of the modern world there were planted on a State agents of foreign Powers to act as hangmen, and German soldiers were set to serve the foreigner. And if one of these Commissions was 'insulted,' a company of the German army (*Reichswehr*) had to defile before the French flag. We no longer feel the humiliation of such an act; but the outside world says, 'What a people of curs!'"

"So long as this Treaty stands there can be no resurrection of the German people: no social reform of any kind is possible! The Treaty was made in order to bring 20 million Germans to their deaths and to ruin the German nation. But those who made the Treaty cannot set it aside. At its foundation our Movement formulated three demands:

1. Setting aside of the Peace Treaty.
2. Unification of all Germans.
3. Land and soil (*Grund und Boden*) to feed our nation.

Our Movement could formulate these demands, since it was not our Movement which caused the War, it has not made the Republic, it did not sign the Peace Treaty."

"There is thus one thing which is the first task of this Movement: it desires to make the German once more National, that his Fatherland shall stand for him above everything else. It desires to teach our people to understand afresh the truth of the old saying: He who will not be a hammer must be an anvil. An anvil are we today, and that anvil will be beaten until out of the anvil we fashion once more a hammer, a German sword!"

A major role in the weakening of the republic and in the destruction of the German people's confidence in it was played by the severe inflation that struck between 1921 and 1923. It wreaked havoc on the economy and wiped out the savings of the middle class. The following account is from the autobiography of a woman who lived through that difficult time in Germany.

FROM Restless Days BY LILO LINKE

The time for my first excursions into life was badly chosen. Rapidly Germany was precipitated into the inflation, thousands, millions, milliards of marks whirled about, making heads swim in confusion. War, revolution, and the wild years after had deprived everyone of old standards and the possibility of planning a normal life. Again and again fate hurled the helpless individual into the boiling kettle of a wicked witch. Now the inflation came and destroyed the last vestige of steadiness. Hurriedly one had to make use of the moment and could not consider the following day.

The whole population had suddenly turned into maniacs. Everyone was buying, selling, speculating, bargaining, and dollar, dollar, dollar was the magic word which dominated every conversation, every newspaper, every poster in Germany. Nobody understood what was happening. There seemed to be no sense, no rules in the mad game, but one had to take part in it if one did not want to be trampled underfoot at once. Only a few people were able to carry through to the end and gain by the inflation. The majority lost everything and broke down, impoverished and bewildered.

The middle class was hurt more than any other, the savings of a lifetime and their small fortunes melted into a few coppers. They had to sell their most precious belongings for ten milliard inflated marks to buy a bit of food or an absolutely necessary coat, and their pride and dignity were bleeding out of many wounds. Bitterness remained for ever in their hearts. Full of hatred, they accused the international financiers, the Jews and Socialists—their old enemies—of having exploited their distress. They never forgot and never forgave and were the first to lend a willing ear to Hitler's fervent preaching.

In the shops, notices announced that we should receive our salaries in weekly parts, after a while we queued up at the cashier's desk every evening, and before long we were paid twice daily and ran out during the lunch hour to buy a few things, because as soon as the new rate of exchange became known in the early afternoon our money had again lost half its value.

In the beginning I did not concern myself much with these happenings. They merely added to the excitement of my new life, which was all that mattered to me. Living in the east of Berlin and in hard times, I was long accustomed to seeing people around me in hunger, distress, and poverty. My mother was always lamenting that it was impossible for her to make both ends meet, my father—whenever he was at home—always asking what the deuce she had done with all the money he had given her yesterday. A few tears, a few outbreaks more did not make a difference great enough to impress me deeply.

Yet, in the long run, the evil influence of the inflation, financially as well as morally, penetrated even to me. Berlin had become the centre of international profiteers and noisy new rich. For a few dollars they could buy the whole town, drinks and women, horses and houses, virtue and vice, and they made free use of these possibilities. The evening when I had gone with the Count to the restaurant and the Pacific Bar I had watched them with surprised eyes, although certainly my lack of experience exaggerated the impression, as it had done many years before on the Rummel, and although the bar and the people there would in any circumstances have seemed luxurious and astonishing to me. During the next months I had many opportunities of witnessing their lavish life because I went often to expensive places, a modest grey sparrow, watching in a crowd of radiant peacocks.

The following remarks were made by Hitler in 1923 at the height of the inflation.

FROM Hitler's Speeches

It was the height of the inflation period and of the manufacture of paper money:
"Germany is a people of children; a grown-up people would say: 'We don't care a fig for your paper-money. Give us something of value—gold! What have you after all to give us? Nothing? Thus have you defrauded us, you rogues and swindlers!' An awakened people with its last thirty marks—all that is left of the millions of its glory—would buy a rope and with it string up 10,000 of its defrauders!" Even the farmer will no longer sell his produce. "When you offer him your million scraps of paper with which he can cover the walls of his closet on his dung-heap, can you wonder that he says, 'Keep your millions and I will keep my corn and my butter.'" "The individual and the nation are delivered over to the international capital of the banks; despair seizes the whole people. We are on the eve of a second revolution. Some are setting their hopes on the star of the Soviet: that is the symbol of those who began the Revolution, to whom the Revolution has brought untold wealth, who have exploited it until to-day. It is the star of David, the sign of the Synagogue. The symbol of the race high over the world, a lordship which stretches from Vladivostok to the West—the lordship of Jewry. The golden star which for the Jew means the glittering gold."

"And when the people in its horror sees that one can starve though one may have milliards of marks, then it will perforce make up its mind and say: 'We will bow down no longer before an institution which is founded on the delusory majority principle, we want a dictatorship.' Already the Jew has a premonition of things to come: . . . he is saying to himself: If there must be a dictatorship, then it shall be a dictatorship of Cohen or Levi."

The payment of reparations by Germany to the victorious powers was disruptive in several ways. It was based on the war-guilt clause and therefore was a tangible reminder of Germany's defeat and the shameful peace; it

The Speeches of Adolf Hitler, I (1942), 72–73, translated and edited by Norman Baynes, published by Oxford University Press under the auspices of the Royal Institute of International Affairs, London.

slowed economic recovery; it was a device that enabled France to occupy the Saar and the Rhineland and thus a weapon that could be used by Nationalists against the republic. In 1929 a group of international experts met at Paris to resolve the reparations problem and produced the relatively lenient Young Plan. This plan was adopted by the powers and Germany at a conference at The Hague. The plan evoked great hostility on the right, and a committee, headed by the Nationalist Hugenberg; Hitler; Seldte, the leader of the Stahlhelm; and Class, the leader of the Pan-German League, was organized to fight it. They proposed a plebiscite to give the people a chance to repudiate the reparations settlement. In September 1929 they published the following draft of a law. The bill was defeated, but its language shows the intensity of the animosity felt toward reparations in some quarters.

Law Against the Enslavement of the German People

1. The government of the Reich must immediately give notice to the foreign powers that the forced acknowledgment of war guilt in the Versailles Treaty contradicts historical truth, rests on false assumptions, and is not binding in international law.
2. The government of the Reich must work toward the formal abrogation of the war-guilt clause of Article 231 as well as Articles 429 and 430 of the Versailles Treaty. It must further work toward immediate and unconditional evacuation of the occupied territories and the removal of all control over German territory independent of the acceptance or rejection of the resolutions of the Hague Conference.
3. New burdens and obligations toward foreign powers which rest on the war-guilt clause must not be undertaken. Under this category fall the burdens and obligations that may be taken by Germany on the basis of the experts at Paris and according to the agreements coming from them.
4. Reichschancellors and Reichsministers as well as plenipotentiaries of the German Reich who sign treaties with foreign powers contrary to the prescription of clause number three are subject to the penalties of clause ninety-two, section three of the civil code [*dealing with treason—D. K.*].
5. This law goes into effect at the time of its proclamation.

Deutsche Allgemeine Zeitung, No. 422 (September 12, 1929), translated by Donald Kagan.

Part of the reason for the failure of the Weimar Republic may be found in its constitution. The following selections from it are translated, edited, and introduced by Louis Snyder.

FROM The Constitution of the German Republic

After the German imperial government had been overthrown and the Communist Spartacist revolt put down by force, Germans over nineteen years of age went to the polls on January 19, 1919, to elect a National Constituent Assembly. More than thirty million men and women elected 423 representatives, with the Majority Socialists leading with 165 seats, the Centrists second with 91 seats, and the Democrats third with 75 seats. The Assembly was controlled by these three top groups (the "Weimar Coalition") out of a dozen or more parties.

The National Constituent Assembly convened at Weimar on February 6, 1919. Weimar was chosen for sentimental reasons: It was believed that the spirit of Goethe had triumphed finally over that of Frederick the Great's Potsdam. The Assembly's sessions were turned by the German nationalists into riotous brawls. After electing Friedrich Ebert as President of the Republic (February 11th), the Assembly began to discuss the Constitution drafted by Dr. Hugo Preuss, a professor of constitutional law and Minister of the Interior. The article causing most heated discussion, that relating to the national colors, was settled by a compromise. The document, passed on July 31st at its third reading, went into effect on August 11, 1919, as the fundamental law of the German Republic.

The Weimar Constitution was a letter-perfect document, seemingly embodying the best features of the British Bill of Rights, the French Declaration of the Rights of Man, and the first Ten Amendments of the American Constitution. However, this magnificent Constitution planned for every contingency except that of preserving itself. Article 48, the "suicide clause," empowered the President to assume dictatorial powers in an emergency. This escape clause proved to be of inestimable value to Hitler later on.

The Weimar Constitution, "the formulation of a stalemate," was a compromise that accepted the outward forms of democracy but breathed no life into the form that had been created. It was attacked bitterly from both the Right and the Left.

The Weimar Republic was burdened by difficulties from its inception. The

Social Democratic party had a program, but, in action, it was pitifully impotent. Its leaders, though undeniably men of good intentions, were unable adequately to meet the responsibilities placed upon them: the liquidation of the war, the Treaty of Versailles, reparations, the Ruhr invasion, the collapse of the mark, and the catastrophic decline of the middle class. These men were ruined in public opinion because they had been forced to accept the mission of advocating the conditions that had been imposed upon their fellow citizens. The victorious Allies, who had demanded a German democratic state, now gave but grudging assistance to the fledgling republic. In the Allied countries the suspicion persisted that the Germans had not willingly broken with their imperialist and a militaristic past and that the Weimar Republic was devised merely as a necessary expedient in troublous times.

Preamble:

The German people, united in all their racial elements, and inspired by the will to renew and strengthen their Reich in liberty and justice, to preserve peace at home and abroad and to foster social progress, have established the following Constitution:

CHAPTER I: STRUCTURE AND FUNCTIONS OF THE REICH

Section I: Reich and States

ARTICLE 1. The German Reich is a Republic. Political authority emanates from the people.

ARTICLE 2. The territory of the Reich consists of the territories of the German member states. . . .

ARTICLE 3. The Reich colors are black, red, and gold. The merchant flag is black, white, and red, with the Reich colors in the upper inside corner.

ARTICLE 4. The generally accepted rules of international law are to be considered as binding integral parts of the German Reich.

ARTICLE 5. Political authority is exercised in national affairs by the national government in accordance with the Constitution of the Reich, and in state affairs by the state governments in accordance with state constitutions. . . .

ARTICLE 12. Insofar as the Reich does not exercise its jurisdiction, such jurisdiction remains with the states . . . with the exception of cases in which the Reich possesses exclusive jurisdiction. . . .

ARTICLE 17. Every state must have a republican constitution. The representatives of the people must be elected by universal, equal, direct, and secret suffrage of all German citizens, both men and women, in accordance with the principles of proportional representation.

Section II: The Reichstag

ARTICLE 20. The Reichstag is composed of the delegates of the German people.

ARTICLE 21. The delegates are representatives of the whole people. They are subject only to their own conscience and are not bound by any instructions.

ARTICLE 22. The delegates are elected by universal, equal, direct, and secret suffrage by men and women over twenty years of age, according to the principle of proportional representation. Election day must be a Sunday or a public holiday.

ARTICLE 23. The Reichstag is elected for four years. New elections must take place at the latest on the sixtieth day after this term has run its course. . . .

ARTICLE 32. For decisions of the Reichstag a simple majority vote is necessary, unless the Constitution prescribes another proportion of votes. . . .

ARTICLE 33. The Reichstag and its committees may require the presence of the Reich Chancellor and every Reich Minister. . . .

Section III: The Reich President and the Reich Cabinet

ARTICLE 41. The Reich President is elected by the whole German people. Every German who has completed his thirty-fifth year is eligible for election. . . .

ARTICLE 42. On assuming office, the Reich President shall take the following oath before the Reichstag:

I swear to devote my energies to the well-being of the German people, to further their interests, to guard them from injury, to maintain the Constitution and the laws of the Reich, to fulfill my duties conscientiously, and to administer justice for all.

It is permissible to add a religious affirmation.

ARTICLE 43. The term of office of the Reich President is seven years. Re-election is permissible.

Before the expiration of his term, the Reich President, upon motion of the Reichstag, may be recalled by a popular vote. The decision of the Reichstag shall be by a two-thirds majority. Through such decision the Reich President is denied any further exercise of his office. The rejection of the recall motion by the popular referendum counts as a new election and results in the dissolution of the Reichstag.

ARTICLE 48. If any state does not fulfill the duties imposed upon it by the Constitution or the laws of the Reich, the Reich President may enforce such duties with the aid of the armed forces.

In the event that the public order and security are seriously disturbed or endangered, the Reich President may take the measures necessary for their restoration, intervening, if necessary, with the aid of the armed forces. For this purpose he may temporarily abrogate, wholly or in part, the fundamental principles laid down in Articles 114, 115, 117, 118, 123, 124, and 153.

The Reich President must, without delay, inform the Reichstag of all measures taken under Paragraph 1 or Paragraph 2 of this Article. These measures may be rescinded on demand of the Reichstag. . . .

ARTICLE 50. All orders and decrees of the Reich President, including those relating to the armed forces, must, in order to be valid, be countersigned by the Reich Chancellor or by the appropriate Reich Minister. Responsibility is assumed through the countersignature. . . .

ARTICLE 52. The Reich Cabinet consists of the Reich Chancellor and the Reich Ministers.

ARTICLE 53. The Reich Chancellor and, on his recommendation, the Reich Ministers, are appointed and dismissed by the Reich President.

ARTICLE 54. The Reich Chancellor and the Reich Ministers require for the exercise of their office the confidence of the Reichstag. Any one of them must resign if the Reichstag by formal resolution withdraws its confidence.

ARTICLE 55. The Reich Chancellor presides over the government of the Reich and conducts its affairs according to the rules of procedure laid down by the government of the Reich and approved by the Reich President.

ARTICLE 56. The Reich Chancellor determines the political program of the Reich and assumes responsibility to the Reichstag. Within this general policy each Reich Minister conducts independently the office entrusted to him and is held individually responsible to the Reichstag.

Section IV: The Reichsrat

ARTICLE 60. A Reichsrat is formed to give the German states representation in the law-making and administration of the Reich.

ARTICLE 61. Each state has at least one vote in the Reichsrat. In the case of the larger states one vote shall be assigned for every million inhabitants. . . . No single state shall have more than two fifths of the total number of votes. . . .

ARTICLE 63. The states shall be represented in the Reichsrat by members of their governments. . . .

Section V: Reich Legislation

ARTICLE 68. Bills are introduced by the Reich cabinet, with the concurrence of the Reichsrat, or by members of the Reichstag. Reich laws shall be enacted by the Reichstag. . . .

ARTICLE 73. A law of the Reichstag must be submitted to popular referendum before its proclamation, if the Reich President, within one month of its passage, so decides. . . .

ARTICLE 74. The Reichsrat may protest against laws passed by the Reichstag. In case of such protest, the law is returned to the Reichstag, which may override the objection by a two-thirds majority. The Reich President must either promulgate the law within three months or call for a referendum. . . .

ARTICLE 76. The Constitution may be amended by law, but acts . . . amending the Constitution can only take effect if two thirds of the legal number of members are present and at least two thirds of those present consent. . . .

Section VI: The Reich Administration

[Articles 78–101 cover the jurisdiction of the Reich Administration in such matters as foreign affairs, national defense, colonial policies, customs, national budgets, postal and telegraph services, railroads, and waterways.]

Section VII: Administration of Justice

[Articles 102–108 provide for a hierarchy of Reich and state courts, with judges appointed by the Reich President for life.]

CHAPTER II: FUNDAMENTAL RIGHTS AND DUTIES OF THE GERMANS

Section I: The Individual

ARTICLE 109. All Germans are equal before the law. Men and women have the same fundamental civil rights and duties. Public legal privileges or disadvantages of birth or of rank are abolished. Titles of nobility . . . may be bestowed no longer. . . . Orders and decorations shall not be conferred by the state. No German shall accept titles or orders from a foreign government.

ARTICLE 110. Citizenship of the Reich and the states is acquired in accordance with the provisions of a Reich law. . . .

ARTICLE 111. All Germans shall enjoy liberty of travel and residence throughout the whole Reich. . . .

ARTICLE 112. Every German is permitted to emigrate to a foreign country. . . .

ARTICLE 114. Personal liberty is inviolable. Curtailment or deprivation of personal liberty by a public authority is permissible only by authority of law.

Persons who have been deprived of their liberty must be informed at the latest on the following day by whose authority and for what reasons they have been held. They shall receive the opportunity without delay of submitting objections to their deprivation of liberty.

ARTICLE 115. The house of every German is his sanctuary and is inviolable. Exceptions are permitted only by authority of law. . . .

ARTICLE 117. The secrecy of letters and all postal, telegraph, and telephone communications is inviolable. Exceptions are inadmissible except by national law.

ARTICLE 118. Every German has the right, within the limits of the general laws, to express his opinion freely by word, in writing, in print, in picture form, or in any other way. . . . Censorship is forbidden. . . .

Section II: The General Welfare

ARTICLE 123. All Germans have the right to assemble peacefully and unarmed without giving notice and without special permission. . . .

ARTICLE 124. All Germans have the right to form associations and societies for purposes not contrary to the criminal law. . . .

ARTICLE 126. Every German has the right to petition. . . .

Section III: Religion and Religious Societies

ARTICLE 135. All inhabitants of the Reich enjoy full religious freedom and freedom of conscience. The free exercise of religion is guaranteed by the Constitution and is under public protection. . . .

ARTICLE 137. There is no state church. . . .

Section IV: Education and the Schools

ARTICLE 142. Art, science, and the teaching thereof are free. . . .

ARTICLE 143. The education of the young is to be provided for by means of public institutions. . . .

ARTICLE 144. The entire school system is under the supervision of the state. . . .

ARTICLE 145. Attendance at school is compulsory. . . .

Section V: Economic Life

ARTICLE 151. The regulation of economic life must be compatible with the principles of justice, with the aim of attaining humane conditions of existence for all. Within these limits the economic liberty of the individual is assured. . . .

ARTICLE 152. Freedom of contract prevails . . . in accordance with the laws. . . .

ARTICLE 153. The right of private property is guaranteed by the Constitution. . . . Expropriation of property may take place . . . by due process of law. . . .

ARTICLE 159. Freedom of association for the preservation and promotion of labor and economic conditions is guaranteed to everyone and to all vocations. All agreements and measures attempting to restrict or restrain this freedom are unlawful. . . .

ARTICLE 161. The Reich shall organize a comprehensive system of [social] insurance. . . .

ARTICLE 165. Workers and employees are called upon to cooperate, on an equal footing, with employers in the regulation of wages and of the conditions of labor, as well as in the general development of the productive forces. . . .

CONCLUDING PROVISIONS

ARTICLE 181. . . . The German people have passed and adopted this Constitution through their National Assembly. It comes into force with the date of its proclamation.

Schwarzburg, August 11, 1919.

The Reich President
EBERT
The Reich Cabinet
BAUER

ERZBERGER	HERMANN MÜLLER	DR. DAVID
	NOSKE SCHMIDT	
SCHLICKE	GIESBERTS	DR. BAYER
	DR. BELL	

One of the advantages held by the Nazis was that their opponents were badly divided. The left was particularly weakened by the split between the Social Democrats and the Communists. In the following statement Ernst Thälmann, head of the Communist party, expresses the party's position with respect to the Nazis and the Socialists.

The Revolutionary Alternative and the KPD
BY ERNST THÄLMANN

What is the current relationship between the policy of Hitler's party and Social Democracy? The eleventh plenum [*of the German Communist Party—D. K.*] has already spoken of an involvement of both these factors in the service of finance capital. Already in 1924 Comrade Stalin most clearly

Ernst Thälmann, "Der Revolutionäre Ausweg und die KPD," in Hermann Weber, *Der Deutsche Kommunismus Dokumente* (1963), pp. 185–186. Translated by Donald Kagan by permission of Verlag Kiepenheuer & Witsch, Cologne.

characterized the role of both these wings when he spoke of them as twins who supplement each other.

At present this development is revealed unmistakably in Germany. . . . In the question of terror organizations, too, the SPD [*German Socialist party—D. K.*] increasingly copies Hitlerism. In this respect one need only think of the creation of the Reichsbanner or, more recently, of the so-called "hammer units" of the Iron Front, which were to be used as instruments to help the capitalist dictatorship in the defense of the capitalistic system against the revolutionary proletariat.

But above all it is the Prussian government of the SPD and the ADGB [*Free Trade Unions—D. K.*] that, through their actions, fully and completely confirm the role of the Social Democracy as the most active factor in making Germany Fascistic, as the eleventh plenum has stated.

Thus, while the Social Democrats increasingly approach Hitlerite Fascism, Fascism, in turn, emphasizes its legality and lately even steps onto the platform of Brüning's foreign policy. . . .

All these points reveal the far-reaching mutual rapprochement of the SPD and the National Socialists toward the line of Fascism.

WHY MUST WE DIRECT THE CHIEF BLOW AGAINST THE SOCIAL DEMOCRATS?

Our strategy, which directs the chief blow against the Social Democrats without thereby weakening the struggle against Hitlerite Fascism; our strategy, which provides the first assumption of an effective fight against Hitlerite Fascism precisely through the chief blow against the Social Democrats—this strategy is not comprehensible if one has not clearly understood the role of the proletarian classes as the only class that is revolutionary to the end. . . .

The practical application of this strategy in Germany calls for the chief blow against the Social Democracy. With its "left" branches it is the most dangerous support of the enemy of the revolution. It is the major social support of the bourgeoisie; it is the most active factor in creating Fascism, as the eleventh plenum has correctly declared. At the same time it understands in the most dangerous way, as the "more moderate wing of Fascism," how to capture the masses, by its fraudulent maneuvers, for the dictatorship of the bourgeoisie and for its Fascistic methods. To strike the Social Democrats is the same as to conquer the majority of the proletariat and to create the preconditions for the proletarian revolution. . . .

WHAT DOES A POLICY OF A UNITED FRONT MEAN?

To carry out a policy of the revolutionary united front means to pursue a merciless struggle against Social Fascists of every shade, especially against the most dangerous "left" variety of Social Fascism, against the SAPD [*Socialist*

Workers party—D. K.], against the Brandler Group and similar cliques and tendencies.

To pursue a policy of the revolutionary united front means to mobilize the masses for the struggle really from below, in the factories and in the unemployment offices.

A policy of a revolutionary united front cannot come to pass through parliamentary negotiations. It cannot happen through accommodation with other parties or groups, but it must grow from the movement of the masses and be supported by that movement and present a really living fighting front.

There is no negotiation of the KDP with the SDP, SAPD, or Brandler Group; there must be none!

One important source of support for Hitler came from the German business community, which helped him both politically and financially. The following documents illustrate the nature of this support.

Poechlinger's Letter to Krupp

Director of the Leading Department,
Certified Engineer JOSEF POECHLINGER
Press Representative of the
    Reichsminister, Dr. TODT.

Berlin, W.8   12.3.41.
Pariser Place, 3,
Telephone No. 11 6481.
[note in pencil: For attention of Mr. Goerferns]
[Stamp: Reply given as per enclosure, 14.3.41.]

Dr. Krupp von Bohlen und Halbach,
Essen.
at the Huegel.

Dear Dr. Krupp,

By request of the Reichs Minister, Dr. Todt, I am preparing to publish a presentation book for the German armament worker, in which he will be honoured on the account of his hard work for the German armament industry.

The structure of the book is as follows:—

1. Dr. Todt Introduction.
2. Josef Weinheber. Ode to the German Armaments Worker.
3. Josef Poechlinger. "The Meaning of Work."
4. M. Schulze-Fielitz (Reichs Ministry for Arms and Munitions). "The Organization of the German Armament Industry."
5. Reichs Department Leader Fuehrer (Chief Department of Technology, NSDAP). "The Employment of the Parties for the German Armament Industry."
6. ———— "Works Leader and Armament Worker."
7. Maier-Dorn, Reichs School Trustee of the National Socialist Union of German Technology. "Front Line Soldier and Armament Worker."
8. Gauleiter Krebs. "Your Contribution to the Great Reich."

May I ask whether you would be prepared to compile the chapter "Works Leader and Armament Worker"? A work of approximately twenty typewritten pages would be sufficient, in which you would briefly and pleasantly describe, in your capacity of the best-known and most authoritative representative of the German armament industry, the relationship between the works leader and armament worker, as well as your observations, adventures and experiences in connection with the workers.

The article would have to reach me in about four weeks.

I shall be grateful for a brief notification whether you are prepared to take on this work.

Heil Hitler:
Yours very sincerely,
(Sgd.) *Poechlinger.*

FROM Draft of Works Leader and Armaments Works
BY GUSTAV KRUPP

Everyone can gather the significance of the outcome of the war, for the Krupp works as well as for my wife and myself, without my writing about it at great length. It is general knowledge that hardly any works were so badly hit by the Treaty of Versailles as Krupp. At this point, once more, I should like to reiterate a few shattering figures. After the signing of the peace, values amounting to 104 million goldmarks were destroyed at our works. Nine thousand three hundred machines, with a total weight of 60,000 tons were demolished or destroyed amounting to nearly half of our entire machinery of November 1918. Eight hundred and one thousand, four hundred and twenty

Office of United States Chief Counsel for Prosecution of Axis Criminality, *Nazi Conspiracy and Aggression*, VI (1946), 1031–1034.

pieces of gauges, moulds, jigs and tools, with a total weight of 9588 tons were destroyed. Three hundred and seventy-nine plants, such as presses, hardening ovens, oil and water tanks, cooling plants and cranes were smashed.

In those days the situation seemed hopeless at times. It appeared even more desperate if one remained as firmly convinced as I was that "Versailles" could not represent the end.

Everything in me revolted against believing, and many many Germans felt likewise, that the German people should remain enslaved forever.

I knew German history only too well, and I believed, particularly with my experiences in other parts of the world, that I knew the German people. For that reason, I never believed that, in spite of all existing evidence to the contrary, a change would come one day; I did not know, nor did I ask myself that question, but I believed in it; but owing to this—and today I can talk about these things, and this is the first time that I do so publicly and at length—owing to this, I emphasize, I, as the responsible leader of the Krupp Works, had to come to conclusions of great significance. If ever there should be a resurrection for Germany, if ever she were to shake off the chains of Versailles, then Krupp would have to be prepared.

The machines were demolished; the tools were destroyed; but one thing had remained—the men, the men at the drawing boards and in the workshops, who in happy co-operation had brought the manufacture of guns to its last perfection. Their skill would have to be saved, these immense resources of knowledge and experience. The decisions of that period were, probably, amongst the most difficult ones of my life. Even though camouflaged I had to maintain Krupps as an armament factory for the distant future, in spite of all obstacles. Only in a very small and most trustworthy circle could I speak about the actual reasons which caused me to pursue this intention of reorganizing the works for the production of certain definite articles. I had to be prepared, therefore, to be generally misunderstood, probably have ridicule heaped upon myself—as it promptly occurred, of course—but never in my life have I felt the inner urge for my actions as strongly as in those fateful weeks and months of the years 1919–20. Just then I felt myself fully part of the magic circle of the solid community of the workers. I understood the sentiments of my workers, who until now had so proudly worked for Germany's defense and who now were suddenly to undergo what, from their point of view, meant some sort of degradation. I owed it to them, too, to keep my chin up, and think of a better future. Without losing time or skilled men the necessary preparations were made and measures taken. Thus, to the surprise of many people, Krupps concentrated on the manufacture of articles which seemed to be particularly remote from the activities of the weapon-smithy. Even the Allied spying commission was fooled. Padlocks, milk cans, cash registers, rail mending machines, refuse carts and similar rubbish appeared really innocent, and locomotives and motor cars appeared perfectly "peaceful."

In this manner, during years of unobtrusive work, we created the scientific and material conditions which were necessary in order to be ready to work for the Armed Forces of the Reich at the right hour, and without loss of time and experience. Many a fellow worker will have had his own private thoughts and often have been without a clue, just why he was employed in this and that manner.

The whole reorganization, furthermore, was not only a personnel problem and of a purely technical character, but was also of immense economic significance. Our new production had to meet competition, far superior because of its considerable start.

It was my aim at all times, even when measures for the reduction of personnel were simply unavoidable, to maintain the nucleus of the workers at Krupp, whom we would need one day,—and nothing could deter me from that contention—for the purpose of rearmament.

After the assumption of power by Adolf Hitler I had the satisfaction of being able to report to the Fuehrer that Krupp needed only a short period to get ready for the re-arming of the German people and that there were no gaps in our experience. The blood of our comrades had not been shed in vain on that Passion Saturday of 1923. Thus, many a time I was able to walk through the old and new work-shops with him and to experience the gratitude expressed in the cheers of the workers of Krupps.

We worked with incredible zeal during those years after 1933, and finally when war broke out, speed and output increased still further. We are, all of us, proud that we have thus been able to contribute to the tremendous successes of our Forces.

It may appear that this record of mine is of too personal a character. But when I spoke of myself and the business concern in my trust, when I spoke of my experiences and impressions during a long life, I only did so to make the subject "Works Leader and Armament Worker" more colourful and descriptive, in preference to treating it under general headings.

I am standing here not wanting to make myself an example, for many another man who has been put into his key position in the German armament industry through fate, and, I think, his suitability. Like the workers of Krupps, these workers, too, are doing their duty faithfully in many other works. I have always considered it an honour, as well as an obligation, to be the leader of an armaments plant, and I know that the workers of Krupps share these sentiments.

This, thanks to the educational work of the National Socialist Leaders of the State, this is the same everywhere in Germany. What I have said especially about the armament worker applies, and this I know, to simply every German worker; with the help of these men and women, working with all their hearts, cool heads and skilled hands for the great whole, we shall succeed whatever our fate may be.

FROM Interrogation of Dr. Hjalmar Schacht at "Dustbin"

INTERROGATOR: C. J. HYNNING

Q. When did you next see Goering?

A. He invited me to a party in his house for the first of January 1931, where I met Hitler.

Q. Did you meet anybody else?

A. At that party Fritz Thyssen was also present, and that evening Hitler made a long speech, for almost two hours, although the company was a small one.

Q. Was that a monologue?

A. An entire monologue and everything that he said was reasonable and moderate that night.

Q. What did he say?

A. Oh, ideas he expressed before, but it was full of will and spirit.

Q. What did he say?

A. He elaborated his program as it was outlined more extensively in his book.

Q. And in the party platform?

A. Yes, also the party platform. But the platform is very short and brief, it is not so full of general phrases.

Q. Were there any prominent officers present?

A. No.

Q. Any industrialists like Fritz Thyssen?

A. No.

Q. What was your impression at the end of that evening?

A. I thought Hitler was a man with whom one could cooperate.

Q. Did you think he was a man of the future and that you had to deal with him as a man of the future?

A. Well, I could not know that at the time.

Q. Did you think it desirable to join the Nazi Party at that time?

A. I can't tell you as to that time, but if his ideas, which he developed that night, were backed by a big party, as it seemed to be, I think that one could join that group for public purposes.

Q. Let us then direct our attention to February and March 1933. I have been told by Goering and by Funk and Baron von Schnizler and also by Thyssen, that there was a meeting held in the house of Goering of certain prominent German industrialists at which you were also present in 1933. This was after Hitler became chancellor but before the elections of that

Office of United States Chief Counsel for Prosecution of Axis Criminality, *Nazi Conspiracy and Aggression*, VI (1946), 464–465.

spring. Hitler came into the meeting and made a short speech and left. Then, according to the testimony of Funk, you passed the hat. You asked the industrialists to support the Nazi Party financially to the tune of approximately 7, 8, 9 or 10 million marks. Do you recall that?

A. I recall that meeting very well. And I have answered the same question to Major Tilley. It must be in one of my former memorandums or in the hearings done by Major Tilley. As far as I remember, the meeting was not in Goering's house, but in some hotel room I think, or some other more public room. After Hitler had made his speech the old Krupp von Bohlen answered Hitler and expressed the unanimous feeling of the industrialists to support Hitler. After that I spoke for the financial part only, not on political principles or intentions. And the amount which I collected was 3 million marks. The apportionment amongst the industrialists was made not by me but by they themselves and the payments afterwards were made to the bank of Delbruck Schickler. The books will certainly show the amounts which were paid in and which went to the party. I had nothing to do with that account. I just played the role of cashier or financial treasurer at the meeting itself.

3
THE DEMOCRATIC SPIRIT IN GERMANY

It is important to remember that many Germans were loyal to the republic and its constitution and determined to make German democracy a success and a reality. The following excerpt from Lilo Linke's account of her youth illustrates the enthusiasm some Germans felt for the new German state.

FROM Restless Days BY LILO LINKE

The University was one of the centres of liberal thought and welcomed us heartily. So did half a dozen high officials from the Republic of Baden, the town, the Reichsbanner, the Democratic Party. In their united opinion we were the hope of Germany, born into a nation which our fathers had freed and refounded seven years ago on the principles of liberty and democracy. In this new Germany there was room for all, the hand of brotherhood was stretched out and encouragement was given to those who were full of goodwill. Our task, the task of the young, was to grow up as true and worthy citizens of this free Republic.

When the last speaker had concluded his address, the signal for the fireworks was given, and a few minutes later the ruins seemed to be burning again in red flames and smoke, golden stars shot up into the air, silver waterfalls sparkled, orange-coloured wheels rolled over the sky, rising and descending to make room for the next. But before the final cascade had died away, torch-bearers ran over the courtyard to kindle the two thousand torches

Reprinted by permission of the publisher from *Restless Days*, pp. 278–280, by Lilo Linke. Copyright 1935 by Alfred A. Knopf, Inc. Renewed 1965 by Lilo Linke.

which meanwhile had been distributed among all of us, rousing a waving ocean of light.

A procession was formed, headed by the military band with triangles and drums and clarinets and followed by the members of the movement, two abreast, holding their torches in their upraised hands. We marched through the town, our ghostly magnified shadows moving restlessly over the fronts of the houses.

Never before had I followed the flag of the Republic, which was now waving thirty yards in front of me, spreading its colours overhead, the black melting in one with the night, the red glowing in the light of the torches, and the gold overshining them like a dancing sun. It was not just a torchlight march for me, it was a political confession. I had decided to take part in the struggle for German democracy, I wanted to fight for it although I knew that this meant a challenge to my parents and my whole family, who all lived with their eyes turned towards the past and thought it disloyal and shameful to help the Socialists.

From the band a song floated back through the long columns, a defiant determined song:

> We do not call it liberty
> When mercy grants us right,
> When our cunning enemy
> Is checked today by fright.
> Not king alone and army,
> But strong-box we must fight.
> Powder is black,
> Blood is red,
> Golden flickers the flame.

We marched out of the town to the cemetery, where the first President of the Republic, Fritz Ebert, had been buried. Silently we assembled round the grave. Wilhelm Wismar, national leader of the Young Democrats and youngest member of the Reichstag, stepped forward and spoke slowly the oath:

"We vow to stand for the Republic with all our abilities and strength.

"We vow to work for the fulfilment of the promises given to the German people in the Weimar Constitution.

"We vow to shield and defend democracy against all its enemies and attackers whoever they might be."

And out of the night in a rolling echo two thousand citizens of tomorrow answered, repeating solemnly word for word:

"We vow to stand for the Republic with all our abilities and strength.

"We vow to work for the fulfilment of the promises given to the German people in the Weimar Constitution.

"We vow to shield and defend democracy against all its enemies and attackers whoever they might be."

4
THE NAZI
PROGRAM

FROM National Socialistic Yearbook 1941

THE PROGRAM OF THE NSDAP

The program is the political foundation of the NSDAP and accordingly the primary political law of the State. It has been made brief and clear intentionally.

All legal precepts must be applied in the spirit of the party program.

Since the taking over of control, the Fuehrer has succeeded in the realization of essential portions of the Party program from the fundamentals to the detail.

The Party Program of the NSDAP was proclaimed on the 24 February 1920 by Adolf Hitler at the first large Party gathering in Munich and since that day has remained unaltered. Within the national socialist philosophy is summarized in 25 points:

1. We demand the unification of all Germans in the Greater Germany on the basis of the right of self-determination of peoples.
2. We demand equality of rights for the German people in respect to the other nations; abrogation of the peace treaties of Versailles and St. Germain.
3. We demand land and territory (colonies) for the sustenance of our people, and colonization for our surplus population.
4. Only a member of the race can be a citizen. A member of the race can only be one who is of German blood, without consideration of creed. Consequently no Jew can be a member of the race.
5. Whoever has no citizenship is to be able to live in Germany only as a guest, and must be under the authority of legislation for foreigners.

Office of United States Chief Counsel for Prosecution of Axis Criminality, *Nazi Conspiracy and Aggression*, IV (1946), 208–211.

6. The right to determine matters concerning administration and law belongs only to the citizen. Therefore we demand that every public office, of any sort whatsoever, whether in the Reich, the county or municipality, be filled only by citizens. We combat the corrupting parliamentary economy, office-holding only according to party inclinations without consideration of character or abilities.

7. We demand that the state be charged first with providing the opportunity for a livelihood and way of life for the citizens. If it is impossible to sustain the total population of the State, then the members of foreign nations (non-citizens) are to be expelled from the Reich.

8. Any further immigration of non-citizens is to be prevented. We demand that all non-Germans, who have immigrated to Germany since the 2 August 1914, be forced immediately to leave the Reich.

9. All citizens must have equal rights and obligations.

10. The first obligation of every citizen must be to work both spiritually and physically. The activity of individuals is not to counteract the interests of the universality, but must have its result within the framework of the whole for the benefit of all.

Consequently we demand:

11. Abolition of unearned (work and labour) incomes. Breaking of rent-slavery.

12. In consideration of the monstrous sacrifice in property and blood that each war demands of the people personal enrichment through a war must be designated as a crime against the people. Therefore we demand the total confiscation of all war profits.

13. We demand the nationalization of all (previous) associated industries (trusts).

14. We demand a division of profits of all heavy industries.

15. We demand an expansion on a large scale of old age welfare.

16. We demand the creation of a healthy middle class and its conservation, immediate communalization of the great warehouses and their being leased at low cost to small firms, the utmost consideration of all small firms in contracts with the State, county or municipality.

17. We demand a land reform suitable to our needs, provision of a law for the free expropriation of land for the purposes of public utility, abolition of taxes on land and prevention of all speculation in land.

18. We demand struggle without consideration against those whose activity is injurious to the general interest. Common national criminals, usurers, Schieber and so forth are to be punished with death, without consideration of confession or race.

19. We demand substitution of a German common law in place of the Roman Law serving a materialistic world-order.

20. The state is to be responsible for a fundamental reconstruction of our whole national education program, to enable every capable and industrious

German to obtain higher education and subsequently introduction into leading positions. The plans of instruction of all educational institutions are to conform with the experiences of practical life. The comprehension of the concept of the State must be striven for by the school [Staatsbuergerkunde] as early as the beginning of understanding. We demand the education at the expense of the State of outstanding intellectually gifted children of poor parents without consideration of position or profession.

21. The State is to care for the elevating of national health by protecting the mother and child, by outlawing child-labor, by the encouragement of physical fitness, by means of the legal establishment of a gymnastic and sport obligation, by the utmost support of all organizations concerned with the physical instruction of the young.

22. We demand abolition of the mercenary troops and formation of a national army.

23. We demand legal opposition to known lies and their promulgation through the press. In order to enable the provision of a German press, we demand, that: a. All writers and employees of the newspapers appearing in the German language be members of the race: b. Non-German newspapers be required to have the express permission of the State to be published. They may not be printed in the German language: c. Non-Germans are forbidden by law any financial interest in German publications, or any influence on them, and as punishment for violations the closing of such a publication as well as the immediate expulsion from the Reich of the non-German concerned. Publications which are counter to the general good are to be forbidden. We demand legal prosecution of artistic and literary forms which exert a destructive influence on our national life, and the closure of organizations opposing the above made demands.

24. We demand freedom of religion for all religious denominations within the State so long as they do not endanger its existence or oppose the moral senses of the Germanic race. The Party as such advocates the standpoint of a positive Christianity without binding itself confessionally to any one denomination. It combats the Jewish-materialistic spirit with and around us, and is convinced that a lasting recovery of our nation can only succeed from within on the framework: common utility precedes individual utility.

25. For the execution of all of this we demand the formation of a strong central power in the Reich. Unlimited authority of the central parliament over the whole Reich and its organizations in general. The forming of state and profession chambers for the execution of the laws made by the Reich within the various states of the confederation. The leaders of the Party promise, if necessary by sacrificing their own lives, to support by the execution of the points set forth above without consideration.

Adolf Hitler proclaimed the following explanation for this program on the 13 April 1928:

EXPLANATION

Regarding the false interpretations of Point 17 of the Program of the NSDAP on the part of our opponents, the following definition is necessary:

"Since the NSDAP stands on the platform of private ownership it happens that the passage" gratuitous expropriation concerns only the creation of legal opportunities to expropriate if necessary, land which has been illegally acquired or is not administered from the view-point of the national welfare. This is directed primarily against the Jewish land-speculation companies.

5
THE INFLUENCE OF GERMANY'S PAST

Some scholars have suggested that one of the great appeals of Nazism was its ardent militarism and war spirit, which corresponded with similar sentiments embedded in the history and character of Germany. In the following selection Louis Snyder introduces evidence of the cultivation of such notions in both Weimar and Hitler Germany.

FROM Documents of German History

All nations have at one time or another been victims of the diseases of jingoism and chauvinism. The glorification of war has been the prime aim of super-patriots everywhere. But in Germany the phenomenon has been so persistent that it merits the special attention of the historian. Such historians as Heinrich von Treitschke ("Those who preach the nonsense of eternal peace do not understand Aryan national life"), such militarists as Friedrich von Bernhardi ("War is a biological necessity"), and such leaders as Adolf Hitler ("In eternal peace, mankind perishes") expressed a point of view that was not unique but widespread. In both world wars, Allied propagandists published bulky collections of German quotations glorifying war, which were strongly effective in solidifying world public opinion against Germany.

The war spirit infected institutions both of higher and lower education. In the first extract quoted here, a superintendent of schools during the era of the

Louis L. Snyder, ed., *Documents of German History*, pp. 408–410. Copyright 1958 by Rutgers, the State University. Reprinted by permission of Rutgers University Press.

Weimar Republic gave his suggestion for a student's composition on the advantages of war. The following two poems show how first-grade children during the Hitler regime were encouraged to imbibe the war spirit.

DRAFT FOR A STUDENT COMPOSITION ON THE ADVANTAGES OF WAR, 1927

I. For the Nation:

1. War is the antidote for the weeds of peace, during which intellectualism takes precedence over idealism and puts everything to sleep.
2. Patriotism is stimulated, and a sacred enthusiasm for the Fatherland is awakened.
3. The triumphant nation obtains a position of power, as well as the prestige and influence it deserves; the honor of the defeated nation is not affected at all if it has defended itself with courage.
4. Peoples learn to know each other better and to respect one another. There is an exchange of ideas, opinions, points of view.
5. Trade finds new routes, often favorable ones.
6. The arts, especially poetry and painting, are given excellent subjects.

II. For the Citizens:

1. War gives them the opportunity to develop their talents. Without war the world would have fewer great men.
2. War enables many virtues to assert themselves.
3. Many active persons get the opportunity to make great fortunes.
4. It is sweet to die for the Fatherland. The dead of the enemy live in the memory of the victor.

POEMS FROM FIRST-YEAR READERS, 1940

A

> Trum, trum, trum!
> There they march,
> Always in step,
> One, two, one, two,
> Teo is also there.
> Dieter plays the drums.
> Trum, trum, trum!

B

> He who wants to be a soldier,
> That one must have a weapon,
> Which he must load with powder,
> And with a good hard bullet.
> Little fellow, if you want to be a recruit,
> Take good care of this little song!

Both racism and anti-Semitism had roots in German history and were not confined to the Nazis. Hitler, however, made brilliant use of these sentiments to win support for his own party.

FROM Hitler's Speeches

The German people was once clear thinking and simple: why has it lost these characteristics? Any inner renewal is possible only if one realizes that this is a question of race: America forbids the yellow peoples to settle there, but this is a lesser peril than that which stretches out its hand over the entire world—the Jewish peril. "Many hold that the Jews are not a race, but is there a second people anywhere in the wide world which is so determined to maintain its race?"

"As a matter of fact the Jew can never become a German however often he may affirm that he can. If he wished to become a German, he must surrender the Jew in him. And that is not possible: he cannot, however much he try, become a German at heart, and that for several reasons: first because of his blood, second because of his character, thirdly because of his will, and fourthly because of his actions. His actions remain Jewish: he works for the 'greater idea' of the Jewish people. Because that is so, because it cannot be otherwise, therefore the bare existence of the Jew as part of another State rests upon a monstrous lie. It is a lie when he pretends to the peoples to be a German, a Frenchman, &c."

"What then are the specifically Jewish aims?"

"To spread their invisible State as a supreme tyranny over all other States in the whole world. The Jew is therefore a disintegrator of peoples. To realize

The Speeches of Adolf Hitler, I (1942), 59–61, translated and edited by Norman Baynes, published by Oxford University Press under the auspices of the Royal Institute of International Affairs, London.

his rule over the peoples he must work in two directions: in economics he dominates peoples when he subjugates them politically and morally: in politics he dominates them through the propagation of the principles of democracy and the doctrines of Marxism—the creed which makes a Proletarian a Terrorist in the domestic sphere and a Pacifist in foreign policy. Ethically the Jew destroys the peoples both in religion and in morals. He who wishes to see that can see it, and him who refuses to see it no one can help."

"The Jew, whether consciously or unconsciously, whether he wishes it or not, undermines the platform on which alone a nation can stand."

"We are now met by the question: Do we wish to restore Germany to freedom and power? If 'yes': then the first thing to do is to rescue it from him who is ruining our country. Admittedly it is a hard fight that must be fought here. We National Socialists on this point occupy an extreme position: but we know only one people: it is for that people we fight and that is our own people. . . . We want to stir up a storm. Men must not sleep: they ought to know that a thunder-storm is coming up. We want to prevent our Germany from suffering, as Another did, the death upon the Cross."

"We may be inhumane, but if we rescue Germany we have achieved the greatest deed in the world! We may work injustice, but if we rescue Germany then we have removed the greatest injustice in the world. We may be immoral, but if our people is rescued we have once more opened up the way for morality!"

In a speech on "Race and Economics: the German Workman in the National Socialist State," delivered on 24 April 1923, Hitler said:

"I reject the word 'Proletariat.' The Jew who coined the word meant by 'Proletariat,' not the oppressed, but those who work with their hands. And those who work with their intellects are stigmatized bluntly as 'Bourgeois.' It is not the character of a man's life which forms the basis of this classification, it is simply the occupation—whether a man works with his brain or with his body. And in this turbulent mass of the hand-workers the Jew recognized a new power which might perhaps be his instrument for the gaining of that which is his ultimate goal: World-supremacy, the destruction of the national States."

"And while the Jew 'organizes' these masses, he organizes business (*Wirtschaft*), too, at the same time. Business was depersonalized, i.e., Judaized. Business lost the Aryan character of work: it became an object of speculation. Master and man (*Unternehmer und Arbeiter*) were torn asunder . . . and he who created this class-division was the same person who led the masses in their opposition to this class-division, led them not against his Jewish brethren, but against the last remnants of independent national economic life (*Wirtschaft*)."

"And these remnants, the *bourgeoisie* which also was already Judaized, resisted the great masses who were knocking at the door and demanding better conditions of life. And so the Jewish leaders succeeded in hammering into the minds of the masses the Marxist propaganda: 'Your deadly foe is the *bourgeois,* if he were not there, you would be free.' If it had not been for the boundless blindness and stupidity of our *bourgeoisie* the Jew would never have become the leader of the German working-classes. And the ally of this stupidity was the pride of the 'better stratum' of society which thought it would degrade itself if it condescended to stoop to the level of the 'Plebs.' The millions of our German fellow-countrymen would never have been alienated from their people if the leading strata of society had shown any care for their welfare."

It has been suggested that the Germans have always been peculiarly susceptible to autocratic government. Whatever truth there may be in this assertion, there is no question that Hitler openly announced and advertised the dictatorial and autocratic nature of his proposed regime and contrasted it to the weak and inefficient democratic republic of Weimar.

FROM Organization Book of the NSDAP

THE ORGANIZATION OF THE NSDAP AND ITS AFFILIATED ASSOCIATIONS

The Party was created by the Fuehrer out of the realization that if our people were to live and advance towards an era of prosperity they had to be led according to an ideology suitable for our race. They must have as supporters men above average, that means, men who surpass others in self-control, discipline, efficiency, and greater judgment. The party will therefore always constitute a minority, the order of the National Socialist ideology which comprises the leading elements of our people.

Therefore the party comprises only fighters, at all times prepared to assume and to give everything for the furtherance of the National Socialist ideology. Men and women whose primary and most sacred duty is to serve the people.

The NSDAP as the leading element of the German people control the entire public life, from an organizational point of view, as well as from that of affiliates, the organizations of the State administration, and so forth.

Office of United States Chief Counsel for Prosecution of Axis Criminality, *Nazi Conspiracy and Aggression,* IV (1946), 411–414.

In the long run it will be impossible to let leaders retain responsible offices if they have not been recognized by the Party.

Furthermore, the party shall create the prerequisites for a systematic selection of potential "Fuehrers."

The reconstruction of the National Socialist organizational structure itself is demonstrated by the observation of the following principles:

The Fuehrer Principle.

The subordination and coordination within the structure of the entire organization.

The regional unity.

The expression of the practical community thought.

I. Fuehrer Principle [Fuehrer Prinzip]

The Fuehrer Principle requires a pyramidal organization structure in its details as well as in its entirety.

The Fuehrer is at the top.

He nominates the necessary leaders for the various spheres of work of the Reich's direction, the Party apparatus and the State administration.

Thus a clear picture of the tasks of the party is given.

The Party is the order of "Fuehrers." It is furthermore responsible for the spiritual-ideological National Socialist direction of the German people. The right to organize people for their own sake emanates from these reasons.

This also justifies the subordination to the party of the organizations concerned with the welfare of the people, besides the inclusion of people in the affiliates of the party, the SA, SS, NSKK, the Hitler Youth, the NS Womanhood, the NS German Student Association and the NS German "Dozentenbund" [University teachers association].

This is where the National Socialist Fuehrer structure becomes more strongly apparent.

Every single affiliate is cared for by an office of the NSDAP.

The leadership of the individual affiliates is appointed by the Party.

The Reich Organization Leader [Reichsorganisationsleiter] of the NSDAP is simultaneously leader of the DAF. The NSBO is the organization bearer of the DAF.

The Leader of the Head-Office for Public Welfare also handles within the "Personalunion" the National Socialist Welfare and the Winter Relief.

The same applies to:

The Reich Justice Office [Reichsrechtsamt] for the NS "Rechtswahrerbund,"
The head office for public health for the NS. German Medical Association,
The head office for educators for the NS Teachers Association,
The head office for civil servants for the Reich Association of Civil Servants,
The head office for war victims for the NS War Victim Relief,
The head office for technology for the NS. Association of German Technology.

The Racial Political Office handles the Reich Association of families with many children, the NS Womanhood [Frauenschaft] and the "Deutsches Frauenwerk."

The Reich Office for agrarian politics of the NSDAP remains furthermore in closest touch with the "Reichnaehrstand" [Reich Nutrition Office] which is anchored in the State. Direct handling and personal contact of the leaders is also provided in this manner.

All attached affiliates, as well as the offices of the Party, have their foundation, in the same manner as in the Reich direction, in the sovereign territories, in the "Gaue" and furthermore in the districts (Kreise) and if required in the local groups of the NSDAP. This applies also to cells and blocks in the case of the NS Womanhood, the DAF, and the NSV. The members of the attached affiliates will be included in local administrations, respectively district sectors or district comradeships which correspond geographically to local groups of the Party.

II. Fuehrer Principle. Subordination and Coordination within the Total Organizational Structure

The Fuehrer structure would be split, though, if all subdivisions, including attached affiliates, were completely independent in their structure from the smallest unit up to the "Reichsfuehrung" and were they to come only at the top directly under the Fuehrer.

Like a four-story building, if we consider the four Sovereign territories [Reich, Gau, etc.] whose pillars and walls go up to the roof without having supporting joists (wooden stays) or connections on the various floors. Furthermore, it would not be reconcilable with the Fuehrer principle, which assumes complete responsibility, to assume that the Leader of a sub-division, as well as an affiliated organization, would be in the position to guarantee beyond a professional and factual responsibility the political and ideological attitude of *all* the sub-leaders down to the smallest unit on the basis of his Reich leadership. The total independence of individual organizations would necessitate furthermore, the creation of an organizational, personal and educational apparatus for each one of them. This, in turn, would create eventually, in spite of the best will of the responsible "Reichsleiters" [Reich Leaders], central offices and office leaders in the Reich Leadership [Reichsfuehrung] of the party, differences in the various organizations. Those differences would later on of necessity take the shape of completely different systems in regional, vertical, and personal respects, etc. within the National Socialist regime.

The Subdivisions NS German Student Association, NS Womanhood Association, NSD [Dozentenbund] and the affiliates and their leaders come therefore under the authority of the competent sovereign leaders of the NSDAP. At the same time their structure is professionally effectuated from the bottom up and they are subordinated to their immediately superior organization in the sovereign divisions of the Party, from a disciplinary point of view, that is to say insofar as organization, ideology, politics, supervision and personal questions are concerned.

Thus a solid anchorage for all the organizations within the party structure is provided and a firm connection with the sovereign leaders of the NSDAP is created in accordance with the Fuehrer Principle.

6

THE BURDEN
OF GERMANY'S
PAST

A. J. P. Taylor argues that the destruction of the republic and the coming
of Nazism were inherent in the history of Germany.

FROM The Course of German History BY A. J. P. TAYLOR

In 1930 parliamentary rule ceased in Germany. There followed, first, temporary dictatorship, then permanent dictatorship. Technically the Reichstag remained sovereign (as it does to the present day); actually Germany was ruled
by emergency decrees, which the democratic parties tolerated as the "lesser
evil"—the greater evil being to provoke a civil conflict in defence of democracy. Unemployment, the result of the economic crisis, sapped the spirit of the
skilled workers, who were the only reliable republicans. Their skill had been
the one secure possession to survive the inflation; unemployment made it as
worthless as the paper savings of the middle classes. Therefore, though still
loyal to the republic, they became half-hearted, indifferent to events, feeling
that they stood for a cause which was already lost, ready to respond, though
with shame, to a "national" appeal. The depression, too, completed the demoralization of the respectable middle class. The brief period of prosperity
had stimulated a tendency, or its beginning, to postpone "revenge" to a distant future—just as French pacifism after 1871 began as a very temporary
affair. Of course Versailles had to be destroyed, but not while profits were
mounting, not while salaries were good, not while more and more bureaucratic posts were being created; the German bourgeoisie felt that their gener-

ation had done enough for Germany. But in 1930, with the ending of prosperity, the distant future of "revenge" arrived: the crisis seemed almost a punishment for the wickedness of neglecting the restoration of German honour and power. As for the great capitalists, they welcomed the depression, for it enabled them to carry still further the process of rationalization, which had been its cause. As one of them exclaimed: "This is the crisis we need!" They could shake off both the remnants of Allied control and the weak ineffective brake of the republic, could make their monopolies still bigger, could compel even the Allies to welcome German rearmament as the only alternative to social revolution.

The republic had been an empty shell; still its open supersession in 1930 created a revolutionary atmosphere, in which projects of universal upheaval could flourish. Now, if ever, was the time of the Communists, who saw their prophecies of capitalist collapse come true. But the Communists made nothing of their opportunity: they still regarded the Social Democrats as their chief enemy, still strove to increase confusion and disorder in the belief that a revolutionary situation would carry them automatically into power. The German Communists, with their pseudo-revolutionary jargon, were silly enough to evolve this theory themselves; but they were prompted on their way by the orders of the Comintern, which was still obsessed with the fear of a capitalist intervention against the Soviet Union and so desired above everything else to break the democratic link between Germany and western Europe. The Soviet leaders, with their old-fashioned Marxist outlook, thought that the German army leaders were still drawn exclusively from the Prussian Junkers and therefore counted confidently on a renewal of the old Russo-Prussian friendship. In 1930 German democracy was probably too far gone to have been saved by any change of policy; still the Communist line prevented the united front of Communist and Social Democratic workers which was the last hope of the republic. The Communists were not very effective; so far as they had an effect at all it was to add to the political demoralization, to act as the pioneers for violence and dishonesty, to prepare the way for a party which had in very truth freed itself from the shackles of "bourgeois morality," even from the morality devised by the German bourgeois thinker, Karl Marx.

To talk of a "party," however, is to echo the misunderstandings of those lamentable years. The National Socialists were not a party in any political sense, but a movement: they were action without thought, the union of all those who had lost their bearings and asked only a change of circumstances no matter what. At the heart of the National Socialists were the Free Corps, the wild mercenaries of the post-war years, whose "patriotism" had taken the form of shooting German workers. The Munich rising in November 1923 had been the last splutter of their Free Corps days. Since then they had been taught discipline by a ruthless gangster leader, Hitler, a man bent on destruction, "the unknown soldier of the last war," but unfortunately not buried, expressing in every turn of his personality the bitter disillusionment of the trenches; and a greater master of hysteric oratory than either Frederick William IV or William II. The National Socialists had no programme, still less a defined class interest; they stood simply for destruction and action, not contradictory but complementary. They united in their ranks the disillusioned of every class: the army officer who had failed to find a place in civil life; the ruined capitalist; the unemployed worker; but, most of all, the "white collar" worker of the lower middle class, on whom the greatest burden of the postwar years had fallen. The unemployed clerk; the university student who had failed in his examinations; the incompetent lawyer and the blundering doctor: all these could exchange their shabby threadbare suits for the smart uniforms of the National Socialist army and could find in Hitler's promise of action new hope for themselves. In England they would have been shipped off to the colonies as remittance men: their presence in Germany was the high price which the victors of 1918 paid for the worthless tracts of German colonial territory.

The failure of the Munich rising in 1923 had taught Hitler a bitter lesson: he must not run head on against the army and the possessing classes. From that moment until September 1933 he used the method of intrigue, of terror and persuasion, not the method of open assault. Just as the Communists had tried to outbid the "national" parties in whipping up nationalist passion, so now Hitler outbid the Communists, but with the added attraction, for the upper classes, that this nationalist passion would be turned against the German working classes as well. He was at once everyone's enemy and everyone's friend: his programme of contradictory principles could succeed only in a community which had already lost all unity and self-confidence. To the workers he offered employment; to the lower-middle classes a new self-respect and importance; to the capitalists vaster profits and freedom from trade union restraints; to the army leaders a great army; to all Germans German supremacy; to all the world peace. In reality it mattered little what he offered: to a Germany still bewildered by defeat he offered action, success, undefined achievement, all the sensations of a revolution without the pains. In September 1930, when the economic crisis had hardly begun, but when the French had evacuated the Rhineland, the National Socialists were already hot on the heels of the Social Democrats as the largest party in the Reichstag; the "national" card was irresistible.

This moral was drawn too by Brüning, who, in his hatred of National Socialist paganism, adopted in succession almost every item of the National Socialist creed. Called in to save German capitalism and to promote German rearmament, Brüning went further on the path already marked out by Stresemann. Stresemann had tried to make the republic popular by winning concessions in foreign affairs. Brüning demanded concessions in foreign affairs in order to win support for his system of presidential dictatorship. If Germany was allowed to rearm, the Germans might not notice the reductions in their wages. More than that, if Germans were brought together in a campaign of hatred against Poland, the disparities between rich and poor would be over-

looked. Where Stresemann had tried to conciliate the Allies, Brüning black-
mailed them: if they did not make concessions to him, they would have to
deal with Hitler and the National Socialists. Brüning knew that the economic
crisis was due to deflation, the decline of prices and wages; still, far from
attempting to arrest or even alleviate this deflation, he drove it on—forced
wages and, less effectively, prices, still lower—perhaps to get the crisis over all
the sooner, perhaps to threaten the Allies with the prospect of German ruin.
For the Brüning Cabinet was primarily a cabinet of "front-line fighters," officers of the Four Years' War, who were dominated by the resolve to reverse
the verdict of 1918. Stresemann too had desired to liquidate Versailles, but he
had cared also for democracy; Brüning was for the undoing of Versailles pure
and simple, hoping, no doubt, to win popularity with the German people,
satisfying still more his own deepest feelings. For him, as much as for the
great capitalists, the crisis was welcome, the crisis he needed. His most ambitious effort was the customs union with Austria in March 1931, ostensibly a
measure against the depression, though it is difficult to see the use of a customs union between two countries both suffering from unemployment and
impoverishment. In reality the purpose of the customs union was not economic, but demagogic, an evocation of the programme of Greater Germany,
and, so far as it had any sense, a move of economic war against Czechoslovakia, exposed outpost of the system of Versailles. France and her central
European allies protested and, almost for the last time, got their way: the
separation of Austria from Germany was the only remaining guarantee
against an overwhelming German power, and this last fragment of victory
was shored up for a few more years.

The Brüning policy of combating evil by taking homoeopathic doses of the
same medicine, far from checking the National Socialists, aided their advance. If the Allies trembled before Brüning's blackmail, they would collapse
altogether before the blackmail of Hitler. Brüning made everyone in Germany talk once more of rearmament, of union with Austria, of the injustice
of the eastern frontier; and every sentence of their talk made them turn, not
to Brüning, but to the movement of radical revision. Above all, Brüning had
overlooked the lesson of the Four Years' War which Ludendorff had learnt
too late—that a programme of German power must rest on a demagogic
basis. Austria, Poland, Bohemia, could not be conquered, and Versailles de-
fied, by a Chancellor supported only by a section of the Centre party; for that,
a united German will was needed. Captain Brüning was halfway between
General Ludendorff and Corporal Hitler, with the weaknesses of both, the
advantages of neither. Brüning, the defender of the Roman Catholic Church,
shared the error of Stresemann, the defender of the republic: both thought to
draw the sting of nationalism by going with it, to silence demagogy by trying
to capture its tone. Neither grasped that his every step strengthened his
enemy; neither understood that the only security for German democracy, or
for German Christian civilization, lay in a full and sincere acceptance of the
Treaty of Versailles. Only if Germany made reparation; only if Germany

remained disarmed; only if the German frontiers were final; only, above all, if the Germans accepted the Slav peoples as their equals, was there any chance of a stable, peaceful, civilized Germany. No man did more than Brüning to make this Germany impossible.

The decay, disappearance indeed, of peaceful Germany was openly revealed in 1932 when the time came to elect a new President. The candidate of upheaval and violence was Hitler; the candidate of the peaceful constitutional Left was Hindenburg, hero of the Four Years' War and candidate in 1925 of the "national" parties. The "left" had moved immeasurably to the "right" in the last seven years: what was then a defeat would now rank as a dazzling victory—for it could not be supposed that a senile soldier of over eighty and never mentally flexible had changed his outlook since 1925, or for that matter since 1918. The German people had accepted militarism: the only dispute was between the orderly militarism of a field-marshal and the unrestrained militarism of a hysterical corporal. Hindenburg carried the day, evidence that the Germans still craved to reconcile decency and power, militarism and the rule of law. Yet Hindenburg's victory, strangely enough, was the prelude to National Socialist success. Brüning drew from the presidential election the moral that his government must win greater popularity by some demagogic stroke; and, as a stroke in foreign policy was delayed, he sought for achievement in home affairs. His solution was his undoing. He planned to satisfy Social Democratic workers and Roman Catholic peasants by an attack on the great estates of eastern Germany, breaking them up for the benefit of exservicemen; and as a first step he began to investigate the affairs of the *Osthilfe,* the scheme of agrarian relief inaugurated in 1927 by which tens of millions of pounds had been lavished on the Junker landowners. This was a programme of social revolution, and it could be carried out only with the backing of enthusiastic and united democratic parties. But Brüning's solution of Germany's ills was the restoration of the monarchy, and he would not condescend to democracy by a single gesture; he relied solely on Hindenburg, and this reliance was his undoing. For Hindenburg, once himself the patron of land settlement for ex-servicemen, had been long won over by the Junker landowners, who in 1927 had launched a plan for presenting Hindenburg with an estate at Neudeck, once a Hindenburg property, but long alienated. It was characteristic of the Junkers that even for their own cause they would not pay: all the estate owners of eastern Germany only subscribed 60,000 marks, the rest of the required million was provided by the capitalists of the Ruhr—principally by Duisberg, manufacturer of paints and cosmetics. But thereafter Hindenburg counted himself a Junker landowner; and he turned against Brüning the moment that he was persuaded that Brüning's plans threatened the great estates. On May 29th, 1932, Brüning was summarily dismissed.

With the dismissal of Brüning there began eight months of intrigue and confusion, in which the old order in Germany, which had now come into its own, struggled to escape from the conclusion that, to achieve its ends, it must

strike a bargain with the gangsters of National Socialism. Fragments of past
policies were resurrected haphazard, as a dying man recalls chance echoes of
his life. First device was the Roman Catholic cavalry officer, Papen, and his
"cabinet of barons," a collection of antiquarian conservatism unparalleled
since the days of Frederick William IV, the sort of government which might
have existed for a day if a few romantic officers had refused to acknowledge
the abdication of William II in 1918. Papen's great achievement in the eyes of
the Prussian landowners was to end constitutional government in Prussia:
the Socialist ministers were turned out without a murmur. It was both curious and appropriate that Prussian constitutionalism, which had originated in
the Junkers' selfish interest in the *Ostbahn,* should owe its death to the
Junkers' selfish interest in the *Osthilfe.* Papen, in his daring, blundering
way, continued, too, Brüning's undoing of Versailles, and accomplished the
two decisive steps: reparations were scrapped in September 1932; German
equality of armaments recognized in December. But it was impossible for a
government of frivolous aristocrats, which would have been hard put to it to
survive in 1858, to keep Germany going in 1932. Even the Centre, with its
readiness to support any government, dared not offend its members by supporting Papen and expelled him from the party. The Germans, divided in all
else, were united against the "cabinet of barons."

The army was forced to the last expedient of all: it took over the government itself. In December, Papen in his turn was ordered out of office and
succeeded by General Schleicher, forced into office by his own intrigues.
Schleicher, too, intended to do without the National Socialists, though he had
often flirted with them in the past. He was the first professional soldier to
rule Germany without an intermediary since Caprivi. Like Caprivi he was a
"social general," intelligent enough to see the advantages of an alliance between the army and the Left, not intelligent enough to see its impossibility.
To win over the Social Democrats, he revived the proposal for agrarian reform in eastern Germany and proposed to publish the report of the Reichstag
committee on the *Osthilfe* at the end of January; in return he asked the trade
union leaders to stand by him in his quarrel with the National Socialists. The
prospect of the publication of the *Osthilfe* report made the Junkers around
Hindenburg abandon all caution. The agent of reconciliation between the
conservatives of the old order and the demagogic National Socialists was
none other than Papen, who now hoped somehow to manoeuvre himself into
the key position of power. Papen not only swung the Junkers behind Hitler.
Early in January 1933 he negotiated an alliance between Hitler and the great
industrialists of the Ruhr: Hitler was to be made Chancellor; the debts of the
National Socialists were to be paid; and in return Hitler promised not to do
anything of which Papen or the Ruhr capitalists disapproved. Papen's sublime self-confidence had already landed him in many disasters; but even he
never made a more fantastic mistake than to suppose that Hitler's treachery
and dishonesty, immutable as the laws of God, would be specially suspended
for Franz von Papen. Against this combination Schleicher was helpless. He

could not even count on the support of the Reichswehr; for though the army leaders had often acted independently of the Junkers and sometimes gone against them in great issues of foreign policy, they were not prepared to become the agents of agrarian revolution. They returned to the union of generals and landowners from which Bismarck had started. The *Osthilfe* report was to be published on January 29th. On January 28th Schleicher was dismissed and publication held up; and on January 30th Hindenburg, a field-marshal and a Prussian landowner, made Hitler Chancellor.

It was a symbolic act. The privileged classes of old Germany—the landowners, the generals, the great industrialists—made their peace with demagogy: unable themselves to give "authority" a popular colour, they hoped to turn to their own purposes the man of the people. In January 1933 the "man from the gutter" grasped the "crown from the gutter" which Frederick William IV had refused in April 1849. The great weakness of the Bismarckian order, the weakness which caused its final liquidation in January 1933, was that the interests of the "national" classes could never correspond to the deepest wishes of the German people. It was the Centre and the Social Democrats, not the Conservatives and still less the National Liberals, who had gained mass support. There was no need for a new party or a new leader to carry out the wishes of the landowners and the industrialists; but there was need for a new party and a new leader who would capture the mass enthusiasm, formerly possessed by the Centre and the Social Democrats, for the "national" programme. This was Hitler's achievement, which made him indispensable to the "national" classes, and so ultimately their master. He stole the thunder of the two parties which even Bismarck had never been able to master. The sham Socialism of his programme captured the disillusioned followers of the Social Democrats; the real paganism of his programme rotted the religious basis of the Centre.

There was nothing mysterious in Hitler's victory; the mystery is rather that it had been so long delayed. The delay was caused by the tragic incompatibility of German wishes. The rootless and irresponsible, the young and the violent embraced the opportunity of licensed gangsterdom on a heroic scale; but most Germans wanted the recovery of German power, yet disliked the brutality and lawlessness of the National Socialists, by which alone they could attain their wish. Thus Brüning was the nominee of the Reichswehr and the enemy of the republic, the harbinger both of dictatorship and of German rearmament. Yet he hated the paganism and barbarity of the National Socialists and would have done anything against them—except breaking with the generals. Schleicher, in control of the Reichswehr, was obsessed with German military recovery; yet he contemplated an alliance with the trade unions against the National Socialists and, subsequently, paid for his opposition with his life. The generals, the judges, the civil servants, the professional classes, wanted what only Hitler could offer—German mastery of Europe. But they did not want to pay the price. Hence the delay in the National Socialist rise to power; hence their failure to win a clear majority of votes even at the general election in March 1933. The great majority of German people wanted German domination abroad and the rule of law at home, irreconcilables which they had sought to reconcile ever since 1871, or rather ever since the struggles against Poles, Czechs, and Danes in 1848.

In January 1933 the German upper classes imagined that they had taken Hitler prisoner. They were mistaken. They soon found that they were in the position of a factory owner who employs a gang of roughs to break up a strike: he deplores the violence, is sorry for his workpeople who are being beaten up, and intensely dislikes the bad manners of the gangster leader whom he has called in. All the same, he pays the price and discovers, soon enough, that if he does not pay the price (later, even if he does) he will be shot in the back. The gangster chief sits in the managing director's office, smokes his cigars, finally takes over the concern himself. Such was the experience of the owning classes in Germany after 1933. The first act of the new dictators won the game. When the terror of their private armies looked like failing, the National Socialists set fire to the Reichstag, proclaimed the discovery of a Communist plot, and so suspended the rule of law in Germany. The Reichstag fire, burning away the pretentious home of German sham-constitutionalism, was the unexpected push by which the old order in Germany, hesitating on the brink, was induced to take the plunge into gangster rule. The new Reichstag, still, despite the outlawing of the Communists, with no clear National Socialist majority, met under open terror. Hitler asked for an Enabling Bill, to make him legal dictator. He was supported by the "national" parties, and the Centre, faithful to its lack of principles to the last, also voted for Hitler's dictatorship, in the hope of protecting the position of the Roman Catholic Church; impotent to oppose, they deceived themselves with the prospect of a promise from Hitler, which was in fact never given. Only the Social Democrats were loyal to the republic which they had failed to defend and by a final gesture, impotent but noble, voted unitedly against the bill. But even the Social Democrats went on to show the fatal weakness which had destroyed German liberties. When in May 1933 the Reichstag was recalled to approve Hitler's foreign policy, the Social Democrats did not repeat their brave act: some abstained, most voted with the National Socialists. This was an absurdity. If Germany intended to undo the system of Versailles, she must organize for war, and she could organize for war only on a totalitarian basis. Only by renouncing foreign ambitions could Germany become a democracy; and as even the Social Democrats refused to make this renunciation the victory of the National Socialists was inevitable.

This is the explanation of the paradox of the "Third Reich." It was a system founded on terror, unworkable without the secret police and the concentration camp; but it was also a system which represented the deepest wishes of the German people. In fact it was the only system of German government ever created by German initiative. The old empire had been imposed by the arms of Austria and France; the German Confederation by the armies of Austria and Prussia. The Hohenzollern empire was made by the victories of

Prussia, the Weimar republic by the victories of the Allies. But the "Third Reich" rested solely on German force and German impulse; it owed nothing to alien forces. It was a tyranny imposed upon the German people by themselves. Every class disliked the barbarism or the tension of National Socialism; yet it was essential to the attainment of their ends. This is most obvious in the case of the old "governing classes." The Junker landowners wished to prevent the expropriation of the great estates and the exposure of the scandals of the *Osthilfe;* the army officers wanted a mass army, heavily equipped; the industrialists needed an economic monopoly of all Europe if their great concerns were to survive. Yet many Junkers had an old-fashioned Lutheran respectability; many army officers knew that world conquest was beyond Germany's strength; many industrialists, such as Thyssen, who had financed the National Socialists, were pious and simple in their private lives. But all were prisoners of the inescapable fact that if the expansion of German power were for a moment arrested, their position would be destroyed.

But the National Socialist dictatorship had a deeper foundation. Many, perhaps most, Germans were reluctant to make the sacrifices demanded by rearmament and total war; but they desired the prize which only total war would give. They desired to undo the verdict of 1918; not merely to end reparations or to cancel the "war guilt" clause, but to repudiate the equality with the peoples of eastern Europe which had then been forced upon them. During the preceding eighty years the Germans had sacrificed to the Reich all their liberties; they demanded as reward the enslavement of others. No German recognized the Czechs or Poles as equals. Therefore every German desired the achievement which only total war could give. By no other means could the Reich be held together. It had been made by conquest and for conquest; if it ever gave up a career of conquest, it would dissolve. Patriotic duty compelled even the best of Germans to support a policy which was leading Germany to disaster.

7
AGAINST
A FATALISTIC VIEW
OF GERMAN
HISTORY

Eugene Anderson takes a view different from that of Taylor.

FROM Freedom and Authority in German History
BY EUGENE N. ANDERSON

By a kind of inverted racialism, the German people are often branded as irretrievably authoritarian in government and politics and in the manifestations of social life. The father of the family and the labor leader, the social worker and the school teacher, all are accused of conforming to a pattern of authoritarianism set by the long domination of monarchism and militarism and of their servant, bureaucracy. The goose step is regarded as the normal manner of walking, thinking, and acting; and the sharp and rude precision of its jerky progress is found to be reflected in the gruff, staccato accents of the German language. The conclusion from this view follows illogically but inevitably: the Germans cannot be trusted to live peaceably with the rest of the world; they will succumb to the violent promises and deeds of another *Führer;* one must either reduce them to a harmless number or prevent the rise of another Hitler by assuming over them authoritarian power.

Since both prospects are repulsive to the Western world, it is essential that the premises on which such conclusions rest be re-examined. Are the German people congenitally authoritarian? Do elements of freedom find any support

Eugene N. Anderson, "Freedom and Authority in German History," in Gabriel A. Almond, ed., *The Struggle for German Democracy* (1949), pp. 3–5, 22–32. Reprinted by permission of University of North Carolina Press.

among them? The definitive answer cannot be found by turning to the study of the past alone; but as history supplies one of the few available sources of evidence, an analysis of German past experience with respect to freedom and authority should indicate the degree of permanence of National Socialist behavior and the dimensions of the German problem.

Taken as a whole, German historical tradition is rich enough to supply evidence in support of any thesis about the German people. It seems irrelevant and unnecessary for the purpose in hand, however, to explore any period prior to that which has exercised an immediate influence upon the present day. There are times in the history of every country when habits are formed, institutions are established, social classes and groups are fixed in relation to one another, legal systems and norms are created, and ideals are accepted which inaugurate a new period in the life of the country. These changes fundamentally condition the character of that period and incorporate into its living forms all that is relevant from earlier times. This period of history, with its particular institutions and ways, then endures until the course of time changes the foundations and evolves a new age.

In the case of Germany the present evidence indicates that the years between the unification of the country in the third quarter of the nineteenth century and the overthrow of Nazism may be called a historical period with a particular life of its own. It is the period of the rise and fall of the second German Reich, and its essential characteristics were developed during the unification of the country. That Nazism would actually be the climax of the period no one could foresee. Even though certain German nationalistic writers envisaged such a future occurrence, it would be attributing to Germany an omnipotence which neither it nor any other country ever possessed to assume that Nazism grew inevitably out of Bismarckian Germany. Since hindsight is not difficult, the historian can find many origins and a superficially convincing logical course for the degeneration of modern Germany into National Socialism. However, the interplay, particularly of international power politics, has been so sharp during the past three quarters of a century, not merely at Germany's instigation but at that of all the great Powers, and the course of economic life has been subject to such unexpected and violent depressions, that no one country can be credited with the full responsibility for its own history. One can at most state that, without being able to control the course of events in all its richness, Germany received through Bismarck's actions the social and political organization and ways out of which under favorable circumstances Nazism could develop. For Bismarck's work of national unification fixed the political, social, and institutional framework within which or against which German events have since then moved.

The three wars of German unification, in common with all other European wars after the French Revolution, affected both international and internal affairs. A unified Germany pushed her way authoritatively into the family of nations and assumed a position of power. At the same time a hierarchical relationship of social groups in Germany, in contrast to the free relationship in a democracy, became fixed for decades to come, and governmental institutions of authoritarianism were firmly established. In 1914–18 it required the combined power of the rest of the world to undermine these dominant social groups and institutions, and even then the social groups escaped destruction. Able to revive and exploit the general despair of the economic crisis of 1930–31, these groups assisted National Socialism to power and without entirely identifying themselves with Nazism contributed elements essential for enabling it to wreck Germany and Europe and to menace the world.

The effect of World War I upon the relative strength of freedom and authoritarianism in Germany cannot be summed up in a formula. The concentration of power incident upon the necessities of fighting set precedents in new institutions and habits for authoritarian rule which were essential as a basis for the rise of National Socialism. The war blended military and civilian methods and ideals to a degree not before experienced in German history and supplied the future Nazis with the pattern of a society organized exclusively for war. At the same time the growing aversion to the war aroused the proletariat and increasingly large elements of the middle classes and bourgeoisie to new recognition of the value of freedom from authoritarian control.

The postwar (1918–33) course of German history does not lend itself to adequate explanation in terms of class conflicts and material interests. The psychological effects of war, defeat, and revolution cut across class and occupational lines and left tensions which within a short time transformed the acceptance of freedom and democracy into a furious endeavor on the part of the old conservative forces and the lower middle class to destroy them. Groups picked up extreme ideals, of which German history had a copious variety, as a means of solving their problems; and the period is full of ists and isms, crisscrossing, merging, fighting, each with its own troubled history.

The Social Democrats, who supplied the force of the revolution, stopped with a transformation of government. Their leaders wished to establish a constitutional regime based on parliamentary control and the rule of law, and operating by way of political parties. They used these means to develop model instruments for handling labor-management relations and to transform the authoritarian state into a state concerned with the welfare of all its members. They established the conditions of intellectual and spiritual freedom, to which the response was immediate. The theatre, literature, and the arts flourished during the short life of the Weimar Republic as nowhere else in Europe. Educational reforms were vigorously discussed and experimental schools of a progressive type emerged. In spite of the recent war, the cultural ties with the rest of the world were closer than in any age since the time of Goethe. In internal organization and policy the Weimar Republic was endeavoring to align with Western democracies, and in its international relations it was striving to overcome German nationalism in favor of world cooperation and understanding. Democratic Catholics in the Centrist party and many of the middle classes and bourgeoisie supported this policy, and the world witnessed the extraordinary sight of political cooperation between

Marxian Socialists and Catholic Centrists in the government of a democratic republic.

The Social Democrats and their new allies opposed a thorough social revolution with a fundamental change in the ownership of property and in the distribution of social power. Social Democrats in the revolutionary government used the old military leaders and forces to prevent the feeble attempts at the kind of revolution which, in theory, the workers had advocated for decades. The standards and ideals of the authoritarian groups had affected Socialist leaders like Ebert and Noske to the extent that they agreed on the necessity of preserving order. The war had not diminished the Social Democrats' faith in the essential reasonableness of man, and they apparently expected the former ruling elements suddenly to become converted to the same belief and to practice it. A democratic government thus established itself in a society which had little experience with democracy, which had suffered through four years of war and an accentuated form of authoritarian rule, and which was neither morally nor politically prepared for defeat. This society teemed with bitterness, inner conflicts, and fear. A majority was willing to accept democracy if it brought peace, full employment, and a high standard of living; that is, if it immediately established better living conditions than had obtained under the empire. The people, trained to look to others for leadership and to throw responsibility on them, expected a miracle to occur by the grace of the victorious and occupying Powers, with no more effort on their part than the formulation of a constitution and the erection of a new government. They did not know that they had to earn democracy; that they must practice democracy in every-day life, where it meant more than a formal structure of government and the secret ballot.

The Weimar Republic failed to teach all Germans that political parties, as well as all other organized groups, can live together in peace only by learning the ways of compromise, of respecting the views of others, of accepting defeat without recourse to violence. The Social Democrats and the Catholic Centrist party, and even certain middle class and bourgeois parties, had learned this elementary lesson; but the extreme groups on left and right, the Communists, the Nationalists, and all those elements rapidly turning to Nazism and similar organizations, never were willing to admit that their opponents might have some justice and truth on their side.

The course of developments during the Weimar Republic sadly disappointed almost everyone. When the miracle failed to appear, a large number of voters, especially from the lower middle classes, wandered from party to party, seeking a panacea, landing finally in National Socialism. The forces of conservatism and reaction revived and fought with their accustomed bitterness and ruthlessness to restore their control. Political freedom permitted them to do so. Economic interests re-established their affiliation with political groups. The Junkers and the big landowners remained as powerful economically as before and determined to regain through ardent nationalism their social and political dominance. In comparison with their prewar position they suffered under the handicap of having a Social Democratic laborer in place of the Kaiser and his court; but they soon found a thoroughly satisfactory substitute in Field Marshal von Hindenburg, president after 1925 of the German Republic. Loss of control by an authoritarian government and the lack of a disproportionate influence in the representative assemblies could not yet be overcome; but the bureaucracy, with the exception of a few departments, remained loyal to conservative ideals and never operated in a democratic way. Whenever a former army officer or other reactionary nationalist assassinated a democratic member of the Cabinet or political leader, or instigated a rebellion, the judges could be relied upon to free him entirely or impose a gentle sentence; after all, it would be said, he had killed from the finest patriotic motives. Most of the upper bourgeoisie, except for the Catholics, sided with the conservatives and financed the many patriotic groups bent on undermining or overthrowing the Weimar regime. The bourgeoisie disliked the so-called workers' republic, imposed, as most Germans believed, by the victorious Powers and alien to true Germanism. The numerous professional army officers, unemployed because of the Treaty of Versailles, provided invaluable men of action for these authoritarian groups and served efficiently as private and illegal adjuncts to the small professional army left to Germany. The educational system continued to be organized mainly on a class basis, and teachers and professors remained on the whole as staunchly conservative and nationalistic as before the war.

The democratic forces had to contend not merely with these authoritarian powers. They confronted the problem common to every state, whether victor or vanquished, in the postwar period; namely, how to balance the necessity for large-scale governmental planning and action in order to cope with the numerous and unprecedented difficulties in economic and cultural life with the necessity for leaving an equally wide area for freedom of action on the part of individuals and private groups in order to allow the people the opportunity for training themselves in the ways of freedom and democracy. The Germans had to learn not to look to the state for guidance on all matters; they had to learn to rely on individual and private activities in civic affairs; they had to transform the bureaucracy into a servant, tolerant, at the least, of cordial relations with a respected and confident public; they had to overcome and awesome deference toward officialdom and to bring themselves to the point of taking the initiative or participating vigorously in affairs which they had formerly left to the government and bureaucracy. The problem acquired enhanced significance in Germany where statesmanship of rare quality would have been needed to prevent the powerful authoritarian elements from exploiting present needs for the revival and accentuation of traditional authoritarian forms of control as the sole means of salvation. The war, defeat, and revolution left vast difficulties on a national scale which an authoritarian government seemed most competent to handle. Every inducement, reasonable as well as emotional, seemed to lead the Germans, unaccustomed to self-government, to throw all their pressing burdens upon the state. Taxes were high while wages and salaries were low; the Weimar Republic was blamed. Social Security was expensive; the state was blamed. Foreign markets did not materialize; the state had failed to do its duty. Labor conflicts arose; if the state interfered it did not settle them properly or fairly, if it did not interfere, it should have. Credit was tight; the state should help out. Bankruptcy threatened; the state must save the firm. The schools must be left alone, the schools must be reformed; the state was blamed for doing one or the other. Newspapers published too much scandal; the state should forbid it. And so on and on. The times were full of uncertainty—as to economic conditions, markets, sources of raw materials, credit; as to social standards and social power; as to political control; as to governmental structure. It seems true that the majority of Germans disliked with more or less intensity the Weimar government and constitution and all that they stood for; but the opponents of Weimar could not go back to the old regime, and they did not know what kind of a new order they wanted. The realistic and immediate problems caused them to fight for control of the powerful machinery of government in order to use it for special interests. Those who thought that they had most to gain from reconquering the government, namely, the authoritarian groups, most loudly asserted their nationalism. The supporters of a democratic Germany had increasing difficulty in maintaining themselves.

The emotional currents of the Weimar period were rich and varied, with moral standards in flux. The war had brutalized many groups and individuals ready for any sadistic action. It had accustomed even the rest of society to acquiesce in legal arbitrariness and murder in times of stress, and, although most were appalled at the thought of another war and wished the lawlessness to stop, the odor of blood remained in the air. Almost all Germans believed that they had lost the war unjustly. Even more of them refused to accept the thesis of German guilt and regarded the Treaty of Versailles as a wicked imposition. When the inflation wiped out the savings of a lifetime, made some unjustly rich and others unjustly poor overnight, the economic order of life seemed shattered. The economic depression of 1930–31 completed the work of disillusionment. Germans came to believe that this was a world of hazard, of no fixed principles, a world in which the individual confronted overwhelming, arbitrary powers. Forces beyond one's control appeared too strong. The moral order seemed to have degenerated into moral chaos. The rule of law had given way to arbitrariness. Reason could not be trusted as a guide, for it had succumbed to the forces of blind and cruel chance. Intelligence offered no salvation. Compromise failed when others would not compromise; or if agreement was reached, some alien force or unpredictable economic crisis might nullify the result. Democracy meant, therefore, so it seemed, the continued shackling of Germany for the advantage of mean, selfish foreign Powers. Millions of Germans came to believe that the country could be saved only by repudiating the Weimar system and turning to a new messiah, a man of miracles, a leader, arbitrary and cruel, determined and ruthless, like the rest of the world. The problems of the Germans as individuals and as a people seemed insoluble without such a leader. Nationalism arose like a flame to help the Germans escape from freedom, to guide them into the hysteria of Nazism.

The Germans accepted National Socialism as a last act of desperation. A nation which appreciated its own excellent qualities and high abilities thought its existence menaced by chaos. It could not understand the reason for this plight and refused to acquiesce. Millions of Germans from all classes and occupations felt the crisis to be so acute that the Nazis were quickly transformed from a small group of crackpots into a mass party led by a messiah determined upon action to restore the vigor and the rightful glory of the German people. The ingredients of National Socialism were derived in sufficient strength from the German past to be acceptable as German. The *Führerprinzip* enjoyed the traditional prestige of centuries of absolute or strong monarchism, of Bismarckian authoritarianism, and of the traditions and habits of military and even bureaucratic command. It had been practiced, in an appropriate form, by Krupp, Stumm, and many other big industrialists. The new popular element in it was exalted as a sign of democratic equality and became immediately a powerful asset accepted even by the upper classes. The Germans also knew that in every crisis among every people the executive head becomes increasingly important as the instrument for quick and effective action. The relegation of parliament to an insignificant position seemed necessary and was fully approved by the millions of conservatives who had never liked representative government and by the middle classes and even many of the workers who cared less about it than about steady employment. Responsible representative government had had a short history, from 1919 to 1933, and had scarcely been crowned with success. The Germans were accustomed to a wide range of governmental authority, and in the crisis the individual wished the state to take even more responsibility away from him. The absence of tradition of private initiative and responsibility in civic affairs among most of the people and the dislike of politics and political parties as degrading influences led them to reject the potentialities of the Weimar Republic in favor of the wild promises of Nazism. They lacked democratic safeguards in the habits and standards of their private lives against the enticement of a seemingly easy way out of an unexpected and overwhelming crisis like that of the world economic depression. Certainly for some years until the destructive qualities of Nazism became apparent, few manifested any interest in defending moral principles against the nihilism of the National Socialist.

The qualities which German tradition regarded as the highest virtues became means of totalitarian domination. The Germans made a fetish of order, cleanliness, performance of duty, efficiency in craft or profession, concentration on the business in hand without interference in affairs about which they knew little, being obedient to officers and officials and to the law irrespective of the validity or morality of the order, ardent love of the nation and supreme loyalty to it. All peoples of our civilization have these traits in varying degrees, but in Western democracies they are balanced by a strong sense of civic responsibility and of individual worth as a citizen. In no other country than Germany did such a combination of qualities obtain on such a broad scale, qualities which in favorable circumstances could be exploited to the ruin of a people.

One important line of German political and social philosophy for at least a century and a half had been basically concerned with the problem of the relation of the individual and the state. Scholars and popular writers at all levels of intelligence had discussed the subject. It permeated the cheap pamphlet literature which Hitler read as an embittered, unemployed ex-soldier. At times of prosperity the rights of the individual might be emphasized; but at every period of crisis—the Napoleonic era, 1848, the 1860's, the Bismarckian era, World War I, the economic depression of 1930–31, the Nazi seizure of power—the belief in the subordination of the individual to the welfare of the nation-state became widespread. This exaggeration seems logical and understandable for a crisis situation where the individual finds no way to solve his problems alone and throws himself upon the mercy of the state. The view forms the core of nationalistic thought in every country, France, England, Italy, Russia, Germany, or any other. It is the peculiar fate of German history, however, that the idea, derived easily from a class society struggling to maintain hierarchy, suited nicely the needs of the upper classes, especially the monarchy and the aristocrats, in their effort to keep control over the rest of the population. Since they dominated, or believed that with a little more action they could restore their domination over the lower classes, they kept alive the ideal of the superior interests of the state over those of the individual.

When National Socialism arose, it adopted for its own purposes this rich tradition. For the first time in history a nation sought to organize and run itself according to the ideals of nationalism. The process of nationalism which characterized European history after the French Revolution thereby reached its culmination. As stated above, the National Socialists could have found most of their ideals in the nationalistic writings of any country; there is nothing peculiarly German in them. No other people, however, has attempted to realize these ideals, for in no other country has the combination of conditions, inherited and present, been comparable to that which gave National Socialism its opportunity. Only one further step is possible in the unfolding of nationalism and of authoritarianism. That step may be described as national bolshevism. Although one strong faction wished to go so far, the National Socialists were unable to force the German people into the final act of destruction of their social and institutional heritage.

It would be wrong to conclude that Nazism grew inevitably from the German past. This theory would imply a fatalism which is entirely out of place in any serious study of history. A careful analysis of the events of 1932–33 shows that at that time a substantial majority of the German people favored an extraordinary increase in governmental authority necessary to solve their problems but opposed National Socialism, that this majority was increasing, and that the recession of the economic crisis would have entailed further losses of Nazi popular support. A relatively small group of Junkers, industrialists, and militarists actually achieved Hitler's appointment as Chancellor and utilized the senility of President von Hindenburg to accomplish its purpose. The group expected to control the Nazis and to exploit the Nazi power for its own purposes; but the National Socialists proved too clever and too ruthless for it, giving the next twelve years their own imprint. It would also be wrong to equate the conservative authoritarianism of the Hohenzollerns, Bismarck, the Junkers, the big industrialists, and the army officers with National Socialist authoritarianism. The conservatives believed in and practiced authoritarianism as a means of preserving their social, economic, and political status, a status quite different from that of Nazism. Their way of life included respect for at least some of the Christian virtues and for the qualities of their own type of cultured personality. It implied a certain reasonableness and a disinclination on the whole to run desperate risks. Perhaps one may counter by asserting that totalitarianism in all its fulness and with its extreme ruthlessness lay dormant in these groups and awaited the utilization of a Hitler. The growing evidence does not bear out this accusation. Rather it points to a milder view that these conservatives sympathized strongly with a popular totalitarian movement, the full import of which they did not understand, that their nationalism and their craving for power induced them to take a chance with Hitler, and that the authoritarian forms of their own thinking and acting and of those of the German people made possible the easy acceptance of National Socialism. The obedience of the German conservatives and all other elements to the Nazis through twelve years of hell does not prove the identity of all the German people with National Socialism. It merely reveals how politically irresponsible two generations of conservative authoritarianism had left a great nation and how susceptible the people were to nationalistic and military success, how unable they were to distinguish between a form of authoritarianism in the old Christian tradition which might have helped to solve their problems without violating the ideals and standards of Western culture and the violent, sadistic ultra-nationalism of Nazi nihilism.

Few Germans seemed to regret the disappearance of freedom after 1933. The overwhelming majority of the population either joyfully accepted dictatorship or acquiesced in it. While history helps to explain this fact, it also offers the assurance that the Germans have not always approved authoritarianism, that they have not always been nationalistic, indeed, that a large percentage opposed vigorously the Hohenzollern authoritarianism and militarism and preferred the ideals of freedom. History shows that on several occasions the adherents to freedom were powerful enough almost to gain a decisive victory. Historical conditions differed markedly in Germany's development over the past century from those of Britain and France and produced the peculiar mixture of elements from the *ancien régime,* modern industrial capitalism, and mass social movements which reached its fullest authoritarian form in National Socialism. History offers the assurance that under new and favorable conditions the Germans have the elements of a liberal and even democratic tradition of sufficient strength to encourage and assist them in turning toward democracy. There is no historical reason to doubt that they are able and would be willing to learn the ways of living in social and political freedom; but it is equally clear that their experience since national unification does not offer them much positive guidance. Conservative authoritarianism provides no assurance against a resurgence of totalitarianism. The fate of the Weimar Republic demonstrates that democracy depends upon more than a free constitution and free political instruments; it must permeate likewise individual conduct and social relations. It is this conception of democracy that the Germans must for the first time and on a national scale learn how to practice.

THE
COLD WAR

WHO IS TO
BLAME?

CONTENTS

QUESTIONS FOR STUDY

1. *In what ways does Fleming disagree on the facts of the cold war?*
2. *What was the part played by the Baruch Plan in the cold war?*
3. *Why did Russia reject it?*
4. *What was the beginning of the breach between Russia and the United States?*

5. *What is the importance of the coup in Czechoslovakia?*

6. *Compare the views of Fleming and Lukacs on the importance of the Truman Doctrine, the Marshall Plan, and NATO.*

During World War II the United States, Great Britain, and the Soviet Union were allied in a fight for survival against the Axis powers. From the beginning there were differences in strategy, aims, and ideology, accompanied by mutual distrust. Nevertheless, the alliance held together; at Teheran and Yalta conferences were held and joint plans made for the conduct of the war and for the shape of the peace to come. A United Nations organization was envisaged in which all nations would participate to maintain peace and harmony. But within a few years hopes for friendship and cooperation had been dashed and the world was divided into two hostile armed camps; the cold war had begun.

At first, people in the West had little doubt that Communist Russia, led by Stalin, was to blame. His insistence on Russian domination of Eastern Europe through satellite governments, his refusal to cooperate with the Baruch Plan for controlling atomic energy, the Communist coup that brought Czechoslovakia behind the iron curtain, all seemed evidence of an intransigent Russian attitude that made continued friendship impossible and conflict inevitable. From this point of view, all the measures taken by the United States to oppose communism were merely responses to aggressive challenges. The Truman Doctrine was thus aimed at preventing the fall of Greece and Turkey to international communism, the Marshall Plan and NATO an effort to prevent Western Europe from falling under communism and therefore Russian domination, and the whole policy of containment merely a necessary reply to aggressive Soviet communism.

The last decade, however, has seen the rise of a "revisionist" school of historians of the cold war. It is made up chiefly of young American historians who have examined American policy and found it to be largely at fault for the growth of estrangement between East and West. They discern a change in America's attitude with the death of Roosevelt and the advent of Truman. They cite the sudden cessation of lend-lease shipments to the Soviet Union (pp. 614–615) and the use of the atomic bomb (pp. 615–618) as evidence of American responsibility for the beginning of distrust and hostility. From their point of view the Truman Doctrine, the Marshall Plan, and NATO were not defensive responses but hostile actions aimed at gaining or preserving American spheres of political and economic influence. Although many historians of the "new left" have taken up this theme in recent years, their efforts have not added substantially to the pioneering work done for the cause of revisionism by D. F. Fleming (pp. 597–610).

The most influential rebuttal of the new revisionism has been Arthur Schlesinger, Jr.'s article "Origins of the Cold War" (pp. 641–666). Schlesinger emphasizes the one-sided nature of the revisionist analysis, which almost disregards Russian actions while focusing critically on Western motives and behavior. The debate has far from run its course and continues to produce both light and heat. One thing that has become clear is that the evidence is not balanced. We know a great deal about Western actions and motives, for the sources are largely available, but evidence for the behavior of the Soviet Union is for the most part not available. In such circumstances it is all the more helpful to have the views of a sophisticated European observer like John Lukacs (pp. 667–677), who looks upon the quarrel between the United States and the Soviet Union with subtlety and detachment.

1
AMERICA'S RESPONSIBILITY

In the following selection D. F. Fleming presents the view that the United States was largely responsible for the coming of the cold war and establishes the nature of the controversy.

FROM The Cold War and Its Origins BY D. F. FLEMING

THE CHRONOLOGY OF THE COLD WAR

There can be no real understanding of the Cold War unless chronology is kept in mind. What came first? What was action and what reaction? Not everything that came after a given act was due to that act, but a later event could not be the cause of an earlier one.

Below are the principal events of the Cold War in the order in which they occurred.

1. September 1938—Control of East Europe achieved by Hitler at Munich.
2. December 5, 1941 to February 4, 1942—State Department decisions not to make any wartime agreements about Russia's western boundaries.
3. April 1942 to June 1944—The second front postponed. Peripheral war conducted in Africa and Italy.
4. October 9, 1944—Churchill and Stalin agreed on spheres of influence in the Balkans: Greece to Britain; Bulgaria and Rumania to Russia; Yugoslavia 50–50.
5. December 3, 1944 to January 15, 1945—The British crushed the Greek leftists in heavy fighting.

From *The Cold War and Its Origins, 1917–1960*, II (1961), 1038–1051, by D. F. Fleming. Reprinted by permission of Doubleday & Company, Inc., and George Allen & Unwin Ltd., London.

6. December 24, 1944 to May 14, 1945—Bulgarian purge trials executed 2000 rightists and imprisoned 3000.

7. March 29, 1944 to February 1945—Soviet armies occupied East Europe.

8. February 1945—The Yalta Conference conceded friendly governments in East Europe to Russia, but with free elections and a reorganization of the Polish Government.

9. March 6, 1945—Russia imposed a communist-led coalition in Rumania.

10. March 1945—Friction with Russia over German surrender negotiations in Italy.

11. April 12, 1945—Franklin D. Roosevelt's death, four months after Cordell Hull's resignation.

12. April 23, 1945—Truman's White House lecture to Molotov on the Polish Government.

13. July 17–25, 1945—The Potsdam Conference failed to alter Russian arrangements in East Europe.

14. August 6, 1945—The first American A-bomb upset the expected world strategic balance.

15. August 18, 1945—Beginning of the Byrnes-Bevin diplomatic drive to force free elections in East Europe.

16. September 1945—First Council of Foreign Ministers deadlocked over East Europe.

17. March 5, 1946—Churchill's Fulton speech demanded an Anglo-American preponderance of power against Russia, with reference to East Europe.

18. April 1946—Russian troops forced from Iran through the United Nations.

19. August 1946—Soviet demands upon Turkey for the return of two provinces and for a base in the Straits.

20. July to December 1946—Peace treaties for Italy, Hungary, Rumania, Bulgaria and Finland hammered out.

21. November 1946—The Republicans won control of the Congress, aided by charges of widespread communist infiltration in the United States.

22. Late December 1946—General relaxation and expectation of peace.

23. March 12, 1947—The Truman Doctrine, calling for the containment of the Soviet Union and communism.

24. March 23, 1947—Truman's order providing for the loyalty investigation of *all* government employees.

25. March to August 1947—The freely elected Smallholder's Party Government of Hungary disintegrated by communist pressure.

26. June 5, 1947—The Marshall Plan announced. Rejected by Russia August 2, 1947.

27. November 1947—The Cominform organized, uniting all the principal communist parties of Europe, including those of France and Italy.

28. January 22, 1948—A plan for a Western Union in Europe announced by Bevin.

29. February 25, 1948—A communist coup seized control of Czechoslovakia.

30. March 25, 1948—Western Union treaty signed. Devil theory address by President Truman.
31. June 28, 1948—Yugoslavia expelled by the Cominform. Received help from the West.
32. June 1948 to May 1949—The Berlin blockade.
33. March to August 1949—The signing and ratification of the North Atlantic Treaty creating NATO.
34. September 23, 1949—The first Soviet A-bomb hung the threat of total destruction over West Europe.
35. February 1, 1950—Drive for the H-bomb announced by Truman.
36. February 9, March 9 and 16, 1950—Acheson explained the policy of no negotiation with the Russian river of aggression until strength had been accumulated.
37. October 1948 to January 1950—The Chinese Nationalist armies captured or destroyed by the Communists.
38. February to May 1950—The first explosion of McCarthyism.
39. June 25, 1950—The outbreak of the Korean War.
40. September 12, 1950—The United States demanded the rearmament of Germany and began a vast rearmament.
41. October 1950—Having liberated South Korea, we decided to conquer the North Korean Republic.
42. February 1952—Acheson's Lisbon NATO arms goals overstrained our allies.
43. May to November 1952—Our allies escaped from control during the long American election campaign.
44. November 1952—The first American H-bomb exploded, on the ground.
45. March 6, 1953—The death of Stalin created uncertainty and a desire for relaxation in Russia.
46. May 11, 1953—Churchill repealed his Fulton address and called for an end of the Cold War on the basis of guaranteeing Russia's security in East Europe.
47. July 26, 1953—Korean cease-fire signed.
48. August 9, 1953—The first air-borne H-bomb achieved by Russia, and growing Russian air power brought the threat of incineration to all large American cities.
49. November 6, 1953—Ex-President Truman officially charged with knowingly harboring a communist spy.
50. May 1952 to January 1954—A growing realization that the world power struggle had become a stalemate.
51. April 22 to June 15, 1954—The crest of McCarthyism.
52. July 18–24, 1955—The First Summit Conference recognized the atomic arms stalemate and the inevitability of competitive coexistence.
53. February 15–20, 1956—Khrushchev's denunciation of Stalin accelerated a wave of reforms behind the iron curtain, relaxing police state controls and giving greater incentives to individuals.

54. March 7, 1956—President Eisenhower urged that we counter the threat to us "more by positive measures that people throughout the world will trust, than just by trying to answer specific thrusts."

55. October–November 1956—Revolution in Poland and Hungary against Soviet control and communism.

56. November 1956—Attacks upon Egypt by Israel, France and Britain.

57. August 26, 1957—The first intercontinental ballistic rocket claimed by the Soviet Union.

58. October 4, 1957—The first of the increasingly heavy Sputniks demonstrated Russia's ability to lay down large pay-loads accurately across great distances.

59. April 1958—The pro-American Liberal Party ousted in Canada by the strongly nationalistic Conservatives.

60. May 1958—Vice President Nixon mobbed in Peru and Venezuela.

61. July 1958—Revolution in Iraq and the sending of American troops to Lebanon.

62. August–October 1958—The second Quemoy crisis, ending in China's defeat.

63. November 1958 to July 1959—The second Berlin crisis.

64. April 16, 1959—The resignation of Secretary of State John Foster Dulles.

65. September 1959—Khrushchev's visit to the United States, inaugurating President Eisenhower's effort to move toward making peace and ending the Cold War.

66. September–October 1959—A Soviet *Lunik* rocket hit the moon and another went around it relaying to earth pictures of its hidden side, emphasizing Russia's continued leadership in rocketry and the conquest of space.

67. November 16, 1959—Secretary of State Herter's appeal for keeping the great competition of our time with communism "within the bounds set by the conditions of co-survival."

68. December 1959—Eisenhower's eleven nation crusade for a new international climate and peace, climaxed by his statement to the Parliament of India on December 10 that the mistrusts, fixations and tensions that exist in the world "are the creations of Governments, cherished and nourished by Governments. Nations would never feel them if they were given freedom from propaganda and pressure."

69. October 1955 to May 1960—The Second Summit Conference frustrated by the steady erosion in the West of the expectation of serious negotiations about West Berlin and by the U-2 spy plane incident at Sverdlovsk.

70. June 16, 1960—President Eisenhower turned back from a visit to Japan by the inability of the Japanese Government to protect him from great hostile demonstrations.

It is of cardinal importance to remember that East Europe was given away not at Yalta but at Munich. Before that the curbing of Hitler might have cost the West the same territories which Hitler yielded to Russia. After Munich the marching armies would grind back and forth across the face of Europe until the Red armies came to rest in Berlin and Vienna.

Decisions During the War

This was not foreseen in the State Department as late as December 5, 1941, and February 1942 when the Atherton-Dunn memoranda reasoned that Stalin might not be able to recover all of his lost territories and ruled against recognizing his seizure of the Baltic states and half of Poland. Our fear of another uproar in this country over "secret treaties," such as had been raised after World War I, and of the outcry of Polish and other citizens, combined with aversion to any extension of the area of communism to prevent the British from making a more realistic agreement with Russia in April 1942.

Then the British managed to lead Western war operations through peripheral warfare in North Africa, Sicily, and Italy until May 1944. This was justifiable strategy for us, but it left the main brunt of the land war on the Russians to the end and created in their minds lasting suspicions of being deliberately sacrificed. More important, it gave the Russian armies time to come into Central Europe, at the cost of many hundreds of thousands of casualties, losses which we would have suffered had we struck sooner and directly at Germany.

All during the war years Churchill sought manfully to retrieve in East Europe what Chamberlain had given away. His eyes were always on the nonexistent "soft underbelly" of Europe, then in the late stages of the war on an invasion through Trieste, and finally for lunges into Germany to seize areas beyond the agreed zones of occupation for bargaining purposes. But always the actual balance of forces defeated him. The Russians were required to maul the bulk of the German forces to the last day of the war. Allied forces thrown through Trieste might well have enabled the Russians to skirt the Baltic Sea and appear on the English Channel. Furthermore, attempts to change the zones of occupation against the Russians would have been rejected by allied public opinion. Long afterward General Bedell Smith, one of General Eisenhower's most trusted generals, recorded his conviction that it "would have been quite impossible in the light of world public opinion in our own country," and his advice to Churchill at the time was "that I didn't think his own public opinion would permit it."

Soviet control of East Europe was the price we paid for the years of appeasement of Hitler, and it was not a high price. In Toynbee's judgment "the Nazis would have conquered the world," if we and the Soviets had not combined our efforts. They would eventually have crossed the narrow gap of the South Atlantic to Brazil and the rest of South America, where strong fifth columns could have been organized in more than one country. By our war alliance with the Soviets we prevented the unification of the world by the Nazis. That was a victory beyond price, but, says Toynbee, we "could not have put down Hitler without consequently producing the situation with which all of us now find ourselves confronted."

All this was fully evident during the war and it is still true. C. B. Marshall has reminded us that we do not have to guess what the Axis powers would have done had they won. They set it down plainly in their Tripartite Alliance on September 27, 1940—"a pattern for the conquest of the rest of the world and the beleaguerment of the United States." Why then did we have ten years of cold war over Russia's control of East Europe and over her desire to have a military base on the Turkish Straits?

East Europe Divided by Churchill and Stalin

Early in October 1944 Churchill sought to come to terms with the inevitable. Over the strong opposition of our State Department, but with Roosevelt's permission, he went to Moscow to make a temporary agreement for three months concerning the Balkans.

On October 9 he proposed to Stalin that Russia have 90 per cent predominance in Rumania, others 10 per cent, and 75 per cent predominance in Bulgaria, others 25 per cent. In Greece Britain would have 90 per cent predominance, and others 10 per cent. The "predominance" was to be divided 50–50 in Hungary and Yugoslavia. Nothing was said about this division of influence being temporary.

Stalin accepted this proposal without a word. He permitted a really free election in Hungary, which the old ruling classes duly won, and he did his best to force Tito to honor the bargain about Yugoslavia. Also he held his hand completely while Churchill promptly crushed the left forces in Greece, thereby sealing his agreement with Churchill and committing Roosevelt to it, before Yalta.

The communist revolution in Bulgaria was already in full cry when the Yalta conference met. The overthrow in the preceding December of the mighty ELAS movement in Greece by the British army and the Greek officer caste had suggested to the Russians that something very similar could occur in Bulgaria, where the Bulgarian army officers used the coup d'état "as a normal political instrument." "People's Court" trials began on December 24, 1944, and cut down the Bulgarian army officers as with a scythe until the end of February 1945.

On March 6 the Soviet Government imposed a communist-led government upon Rumania, deposing the Rumanian conservatives. It was "very hard to think of any constructive alternative," since free elections in Rumania under their control would have been "an invitation to Fascism here more than elsewhere."

The situation was worst in Rumania, where government was notoriously "so corrupt that it is a synonym for corrupt government," but there was no country in East Europe, with the exception of Greece, where the kind of free elections we wanted would not have been controlled by the old ruling classes. They had manipulated the elections for generations. No free election had ever been held. The Hungarian landlords had been ruthless rulers for a thousand years, and elsewhere the cliques which ruled for their own benefit had virtually all of the knowledge of political manipulations. The Hungarian and Rumanian ruling groups had also sent two million conscripted troops deep into Russia, behind Hitler's armies.

Free Elections

In these circumstances the question arises, why did Stalin agree at Yalta to conduct "free elections" in Eastern Europe? Why we demanded them was clear. That is the American way of doing things, subject to the operations of political machines, and we wanted very much to prevent East Europe from being communized. No one at Yalta dreamed of denying that the region must cease to be a hostile *cordon sanitaire* against the Soviet Union and become "friendly" politically to the Soviet Union. No one could deny that, with the Red armies at that moment across Poland, within thirty miles of Berlin, and beyond Budapest sweeping up the Danube, while the Western allies were still in France, set back by the Ardennes offensive.

But could governments friendly to Russia be obtained in this region by "free elections" in which the ruling groups participated freely? It was inconceivable that these groups could be friendly to Russia, or that communist Russia could think of depending on them. That was as incredible as that we should freely arrange for a communist government in France or Italy. The Soviets also happened to believe that their system of government was as valid as ours, and that they could really depend only upon it to stop East Europe from being used as an invasion corridor into the Soviet Union.

If the Americans at Yalta committed a fault, it was not in "giving away" East Europe. That had been done at Munich long before. It was in trying to achieve the impossible under the formula of "free elections." Yet free elections were in their blood and they could do no other than to believe that this was a solution which all must accept. On his side, it is not likely that Stalin thought the formula would prevent him from purging the long dominant elements in East Europe, whose hostility to Red Russia needed no further demonstration. These elections might be managed and "people's democracies" set up which would be acceptable to the Americans. He knew that the decisive settlement for the area had been made in his gentleman's agreement with Churchill, on October 9, 1944, and that its execution was already far advanced on both sides.

He was loyally holding to his side of the bargain with Churchill and he could hardly have believed that the Yalta formulas would disrupt allied relations as soon as the war was over and lead to long years of bitter cold war.

Truman's Reversal of the Roosevelt-Hull Policy

It is possible that if Roosevelt had lived the same deadly quarrel would have developed, though it is far more likely that he already understood the deeper forces involved and the impossibility of frustrating them. What made a clash certain was the accession of Truman just at the close of the war. He intended to carry out Roosevelt's engagements, loyally and fully, and to exact from Stalin the same complete fulfilment, including free elections in East Europe. This theme runs through the first volume of his memoirs.

However his methods were poles apart from those of Roosevelt and Hull. All through 1944, his last year in office, Hull had conducted off-the-record conferences with groups of editors, clergymen, and members of Congress, to explain to them how far the Russians had come with us, how they had been "locked up and isolated for a quarter of a century," used to receiving violent epithets. It would "take time for them to get into step," but they would do it. He urged that "we must be patient and forbearing. We cannot settle questions with Russia by threats. We must use friendly methods."

No one was more opposed than Hull to Soviet control of East Europe, "interfering with her neighbors," but as he left office his policy rested on two bases: to show the Russians by example how a great power should act and to continue in constant friendly discussion with them. "Consult them on every point. Engage in no 'cussin matches' with them."

Nothing could have been further from President Truman's approach. He quickly read all the dispatches about friction with Russia over German surrenders, listened to everybody who wanted to get tough with the Russians, and when Molotov came by on April 23, 1945, to pay his respects to the new President, he received such a dressing down that he complained at the end of it that no one had ever talked like that to him before.

This was exactly eleven days after Roosevelt's death. It took Truman just that long to reverse the entire Roosevelt-Hull approach to Russia and to inaugurate an era of toughness and ever greater toughness in our dealings with her. Then on August 6, 1945, the Hiroshima explosion gave him the means to back insistence on free elections in East Europe and when the London Conference of September 1945 deadlocked over this issue he made up his mind at once to contain Russia. It was at this moment that Lippmann, noting that we had terminated lend-lease "abruptly and brutally" and had drifted into an arms race with the Soviet Union, warned: "Let no one deceive himself. We are drifting toward a catastrophe."

To the already deep fears of Russia for her own security, thrice justified since 1914, was added a new and dreadful fear of a fourth Western attack, backed by the atomic bomb. From the psychological point of view the policy of toughness was "the worst treatment" that could have been devised. "If a patient is suffering from genuine fear, you do not cure his fears and establish a rational relationship with him by making him more afraid. You endeavor to show him patiently and by your actions toward him that he has nothing to fear."

Exactly the opposite course was followed, with increasing momentum. In the following spring of 1946 Churchill issued at Fulton, Missouri, and in President Truman's applauding presence, his call for an overwhelming preponderance of power against Russia, hinting broadly at later forcible interventions in East Europe. Nevertheless, peace was made in Europe during the remainder of 1946. In three sessions of the Council of Foreign Ministers and a conference of 21 nations in Paris, peace treaties were hammered out in substantially the terms established by the various armistices. Really free elections had been held in Hungary and there were many signs of relaxation of tension as the year closed.

Results of the Truman Doctrine

However, in February the British turned the burden of supporting Greece over to us and Truman seized the occasion to proclaim the doctrine of containment, on March 12, 1947, which George F. Kennan spelled out fully in the July issue of *Foreign Affairs* as "long term, patient but firm and vigilant containment of Russian expansive tendencies." Otherwise the Kremlin would take its time about filling every "nook and cranny available to it in the basin of world power."

On its face this was the rashest policy ever enunciated by any American leader. For the first time in history the encirclement of a great power was openly proclaimed. This power, too, was in firm possession of the great heartland of Eurasia. It had already demonstrated that it could industrialize itself quickly and enough to defeat Hitler's armies. What it would do, after the Cold War was declared by Churchill and Truman, was easily predictable by any average man. The Soviet Union would put up a bold front to cover its frightening post-war weakness and work mightily to gain strength to hold what it had and then break the encirclement.

This was a difficult undertaking, for not only was the Soviet Union frightfully devastated, but Eastern Europe was in nearly as bad shape. However, what the Soviet peoples had done twice already they could do again under the lash of containment. After the two gruelling forced marches, before 1941 and after the German invasion, they undertook still a third and within eleven years from 1946 they had achieved first their A-bomb in 1949, then the H-bomb in 1953 and the first ICBM in 1957. In all other vital respects also they had gained that position of strength which was our announced goal after March 1950.

In the course of containment, "negotiation from strength" and liberation, we revivified fully the machinery of totalitarian rule in Russia. As William A. Williams has pointed out: "Appearing as a classic and literal verification of Marx's most apocalyptic prophecy, the policy of containment strengthened the hand of every die-hard Marxist and every extreme Russian nationalist among the Soviet leadership."

Containment also gave Stalin total power over the Soviet peoples. Williams continues: "Armed with the language and actions of containment, which underwrote and extended his existing power, Stalin could and did drive the Soviet people to the brink of collapse and, no doubt, to the thought of open resistance. But the dynamic of revolt was always blocked, even among those who did have access to the levels of authority, by the fact of containment and the open threat of liberation. Thus protected by his avowed enemies, Stalin was able to force his nation through extreme deprivations and extensive purges to the verge of physical and psychological exhaustion. But he also steered it through the perils of reconstruction to the security of nuclear parity with the United States."

Stalin's first reply to containment was the destruction of the Smallholder's Party in Hungary, between March and August 1947, into which he had allowed the dispossessed landlords to go, and to take over the Hungarian government in its first free elections. The ending of this government was not difficult, since a topnotch American newsman found in Hungary that the "political sterility" of these elements was so great and their inclinations toward corruption so "incorrigible" that an astonishing number of anti-communists accepted the communist claim to represent the people. The kind of democracy for which we had fought throughout East Europe might have been destroyed in Hungary anyway, but the Truman Doctrine made it a matter of life and death for the Hungarian Reds to end it.

FROM THE MARSHALL PLAN TO TOTAL DIPLOMACY

The Marshall Plan

Meanwhile the yawning economic void in West Europe had led to the American Marshall Plan, an offer of economic help to all the nations of Europe, a "policy not directed against any country or doctrine, but against hunger, poverty, desperation and chaos."

If this magnificent conception had come earlier, while the Russians were asking in vain for a six billion dollar loan, before UNRRA was abolished and before the Truman Doctrine had drawn the lines of conflict tightly, there would have been no Cold War. In the context of the declared Cold War, Russia not only rejected the Marshall Plan for herself but forbade her East European satellites to participate, foreseeing that the American largesse would dissolve shaky loyalties to her satellite governments in more than one East European quarter.

Molotov's angry departure from the Marshall Plan conference in Paris, on August 2, 1947, convinced much of Western opinion that Russia was hostile to the West and that she had deliberately split the world in two. Three months later Russia created the Cominform, an organization of all the Communist parties in East Europe, plus those of France and Italy, to back the Molotov Plan for East European reconstruction, to oppose the Marshall Plan and to fight the Cold War generally. This response to the Truman Doctrine and the Marshall Plan convinced many people throughout the West that the Russians had reverted to the world revolution and were plotting to take over the earth.

Then the Communist seizure of Czechoslovakia hardened this fear into frightened certainty. This high peak of the Cold War, in late February 1948, had been preceded by the announcement on January 22 of a plan for a Western Union in Europe, which the London *Times* later thought might have "provoked the Soviet Union to hurry forward its own plans" for the consolidation of the Communist bloc.

Czechoslovakia

But Czechoslovakia had been lost to the West at Munich, and in the successive events of the German occupation, which had destroyed most of the conservative classes and made it impossible for the Czechs to wish to oppose Russia. Both the Truman Doctrine and the Marshall Plan had also made it certain that Russia would bring Czechoslovakia behind the Iron Curtain before long. When this happened, the West lost nothing from the power standpoint. On broader grounds it was a time for sorrow and remorse that big power politics had twice deprived the Czechs of the democracy and freedom they did not deserve to lose either time.

However, all this was forgotten in the wave of shock, alarm and anger which swept over the West. Within a month the five power Western Union treaty was signed and on the same day, March 25, 1948, President Truman made an address in which he developed the devil theory fully. One nation, and one alone, had refused to cooperate in making peace, had broken the agreements it did make, had obstructed the United Nations and destroyed both the independence and the democratic character of a whole series of nations in Central and East Europe. To stop this nation Truman demanded prompt passage of ERP, more funds for Greece, Turkey and Chiang Kaishek, and universal military training.

Thereafter the United States proceeded rapidly along an essentially negative course, in which we rushed to counter each communist move, tied up our resources in blocking efforts, selected our friends on one test alone, and rapidly adopted at home the methods and weapons of "the enemy."

Berlin Blockade

There is more cause for satisfaction in our handling of the Berlin blockade from June 1948 to May 1949. The Russians had a strong case for terminating the four power occupation of Berlin, because the West had announced plans on June 7 for the creation of a West German government. Since the four power occupation of Berlin was based on the assumption that Berlin would be the capital of a united Germany, the quadripartite occupation did become an anomaly when the assumption was destroyed. Thereafter West Berlin became from the Russian standpoint only a listening post and spy center for the West in the center of East Germany, and an ideological thorn in her side.

The announcement of a new currency for West Germany, imperatively needed, also created urgent problems for East Germany, since it would circulate in Berlin.

These were real grievances, but from the Western standpoint they did not justify an attempt to starve out 2,000,000 West Berliners. The crisis was grave and it was met by the West imaginatively, boldly and resolutely. The advocates of sending an army of tanks to Berlin were silenced and the air-lift did the job, dramatically lifting allied prestige to new heights. In this engagement of the Cold War the action of the West was a model of combined courage and restraint, and President Truman deserves his large share of the credit for it.

"Total Diplomacy"

The Cold War as proclaimed by Churchill and Truman would have been impractical from the start had it not been for the American A-bomb monopoly, in which both leaders took the deepest satisfaction. When it was abruptly ended in September 1949, long before the expected time, a severe crisis of confidence shook Washington, a crisis which was ended by the decision to produce H-bombs and rearm further for the successful prosecution of the Cold War. It would be a long pull and take very steady nerves, Secretary of State Acheson explained on three occasions early in 1950, but the Russian river of aggression would be contained.

Restored confidence was expressed in Acheson's Berkeley speech of March 16, 1950, in which he laid down seven pre-conditions for negotiation with Russia amounting to Soviet surrender of its positions before negotiation.

Korea

Then on June 25, 1950, the Russian river of aggression actually moved into Western held territory for the first time when the North Koreans invaded South Korea. Hardly anyone in the West questioned this verdict. Yet there were two other equally strong probabilities: that the North Koreans plunged southward on their own initiative, and that Syngman Rhee provoked them to do so by taking the initiative along the border in the day or two after the UN observers returned to Seoul. That he would be wholly capable of precipitating a war for the unification of Korea has been amply demonstrated several times since. Both sides in Korea were highly keyed for civil war, each intent on unification its way.

Ingram's conclusion is sound when he says: "Nor are we in possession of any positive proof that in Korea or elsewhere she (Russia) has conspired to instigate minor war against the Western allies through one of her satellites." He adds that "suspicions are not proof" and doubts that any evidence can be found later to sustain the charge that the Korean trouble arose as the result of a plot by China, or the Soviet Union, or both, to embarrass the West.

No doubts on this score entered the minds of our leaders in June 1950. It was assumed at once that the Kremlin had ordered the invasion and that this was the first of a series of satellite wars which would stampede both Asia and eventually West Europe into the Soviet camp, unless this attempt were promptly scotched. The United Nations was instantly mobilized, to minimize the shock of our intervention in an Asiatic civil war.

If our cold war purpose had not been predominant, the defeat of the North Korean aggression would have been a great victory for collective security and the United Nations. As the crisis did develop the UN Security Council approved our military action before it had heard the North Koreans, and it never did hear them—a serious breach of normal, fair procedure.

Then when the 38th Parallel was recovered, within three months and relatively painlessly, the monumental error was committed of trying to abolish the North Korean state. This mistake ranks close behind our failure to lead the League of Nations and our enunciation of the Truman Doctrine among the foreign policy errors committed by the United States. It was a political mistake of the first magnitude because it challenged both China and Russia in the North Korean triangle, a strategic area of the utmost importance to them. Moreover, it challenged them as communist powers to permit the Americans to destroy a communist state in their own front yards and set up a model capitalist democracy. It was a military gamble because it launched our armies precipitately into untenable territory. It was a moral blunder because it invalidated the central idea of the United Nations that it is a police force and not a partisan belligerent. When the United Nations invaded North Korea "they were no longer acting as police, but as co-belligerents on the side of the South Koreans."

Consequently, when China intervened on behalf of the North Koreans "the United Nations by becoming belligerents instead of a police force were no longer morally entitled to indict China." But she was indicted as an aggressor, under total pressure from Washington, and is still excluded from the United Nations on that ground.

Thus what should have been a brief, successful UN police operation was converted into a full-scale war which dragged on for three more years, always on the edge of a world war, until neutralism had been made a world movement, until the whole idea of the United Nations being a policeman had been made highly doubtful, and until President Truman and his party had been driven from office, more because of "Truman's war," never declared by Congress, than for any other reason. The war had become to the American people a never ending horror in a far country, for veiled cold war reasons.

Truman's Leadership

The tragedy of the second war in Korea brought out sharply both the defects and the good qualities of President Truman's leadership. His ability to make up his mind and act is a great quality in a ruler. Without it he is lost. But it is not the only quality necessary. There are occasions, perhaps more of them, when restraint is what is needed. There are even times when a President must have "the courage to be timid" or to seem so. Restraint is a far greater virtue than rashness. Truman could plunge in easily and too far, but he did not expand the second Korean war into World War III, as so many urged him to do, and he finally recalled General MacArthur who had flagrantly exceeded his instructions and was leading the cry for a greater war. Thus Truman did not compound his great Korean error into an irretrievable one, even when there was a widespread, angry belief that the Kremlin planned to bleed us white in a series of satellite wars around Russia's vast perimeter—accepting the challenge and logic of the Truman Doctrine.

On the great issue of the Chinese Revolution Truman also avoided disaster. His Doctrine was breached in gigantic fashion by the Communist Revolution in China, and his political enemies pushed him relentlessly to enforce it there, but he had the good sense to send his greatest lieutenant, General Marshall, to China for a long effort to mediate the Chinese civil war, and afterwards he accepted Marshall's report that we could not settle that gigantic conflict. It must have been difficult to put his Doctrine into abeyance, in the place where it was violated on the greatest scale, but he did it and avoided inaugurating a third world war by that route.

By 1950, an experienced editor and biographer could write of Truman: "In 1945 the moral hegemony of the world was within his grasp, but it has slipped from his fingers."

At the close of his presidency the moral leadership of the world had passed in large part to Nehru, the neutral opponent of the Cold War, but much of it went begging for lack of a truly powerful voice. Truman, who might have voiced it, had become only the belligerent leader of an anti-Soviet, anti-communist crusade.

2
THE DEVELOPMENT OF THE COLD WAR

Not long after the Yalta conference it became clear that the Allies disagreed on the interpretation of its terms. The Russians had promised self-determination and free elections in Eastern Europe. It soon became apparent that by Western standards these promises were not being kept. In the following letter written shortly before his death Roosevelt complains to Stalin.

President Roosevelt's Letter to Marshal Stalin

Received on April 1, 1945

Personal and Top Secret for Marshal Stalin
from President Roosevelt

I cannot conceal from you the concern with which I view the developments of events of mutual interest since our fruitful meeting at Yalta. The decisions we reached there were good ones and have for the most part been welcomed with enthusiasm by the peoples of the world who saw in our ability to find a common basis of understanding the best pledge for a secure and peaceful world after this war. Precisely because of the hopes and expectations that these decisions raised, their fulfillment is being followed with the closest at-

Ministry of Foreign Affairs of the U.S.S.R., *Correspondence Between the Chairman of the Council of Ministers of the U.S.S.R. and the Presidents of the U.S.A. and the Prime Ministers of Great Britain During the Great Patriotic War of 1941–1945*, II (1957), 201–204.

tention. We have no right to let them be disappointed. So far there has been a discouraging lack of progress made in the carrying out, which the world expects, of the political decisions which we reached at the conference particularly those relating to the Polish question. I am frankly puzzled as to why this should be and must tell you that I do not fully understand in many respects the apparent indifferent attitude of your Government. Having understood each other so well at Yalta I am convinced that the three of us can and will clear away any obstacles which have developed since then. I intend, therefore, in this message to lay before you with complete frankness the problem as I see it.

Although I have in mind primarily the difficulties which the Polish negotiations have encountered, I must make a brief mention of our agreement embodied in the Declaration on Liberated Europe. I frankly cannot understand why the recent developments in Roumania should be regarded as not falling within the terms of that Agreement. I hope you will find time personally to examine the correspondence between our Governments on this subject.

However, the part of our agreements at Yalta which has aroused the greatest popular interest and is the most urgent relates to the Polish question. You are aware of course that the Commission which we set up has made no progress. I feel this is due to the interpretation which your Government is placing upon the Crimea decisions. In order that there shall be no misunderstanding I set forth below my interpretations of the points of the Agreement which are pertinent to the difficulties encountered by the Commission in Moscow.

In the discussions that have taken place so far your Government appears to take the position that the new Polish Provisional Government of National Unity which we agreed should be formed should be little more than a continuation of the present Warsaw Government. I cannot reconcile this either with our agreement or our discussions. While it is true that the Lublin Government is to be reorganized and its members play a prominent role, it is to be done in such a fashion as to bring into being a new government. This point is clearly brought out in several places in the text of the Agreement. I must make it quite plain to you that any such solution which would result in a thinly disguised continuance of the present Warsaw régime would be unacceptable and would cause the people of the United States to regard the Yalta Agreement as having failed.

It is equally apparent that for the same reason the Warsaw Government cannot under the Agreement claim the right to select or reject what Poles are to be brought to Moscow by the Commission for consultation. Can we not agree that it is up to the Commission to select the Polish leaders to come to Moscow to consult in the first instance and invitations be sent out accordingly. If this could be done I see no great objection to having the Lublin group come first in order that they may be fully acquainted with the agreed interpretation of the Yalta decisions on this point. It is of course understood that if the Lublin group come first no arrangements would be made independently with them before the arrival of the other Polish leaders called for consultation. In order to facilitate the agreement the Commission might first of all select a small but representative group of Polish leaders who could suggest other names for the consideration of the Commission. We have not and would not bar or veto any candidate for consultation which Mr. Molotov might propose, being confident that he would not suggest any Poles who would be inimical to the intent of the Crimea decision. I feel that it is not too much to ask that my Ambassador be accorded the same confidence and that any candidate for consultation presented by any one of the Commission be accepted by the others in good faith. It is obvious to me that if the right of the Commission to select these Poles is limited or shared with the Warsaw Government the very foundation on which our agreement rests would be destroyed.

While the foregoing are the immediate obstacles which in my opinion have prevented our Commission from making any progress in this vital matter, there are two other suggestions which were not in the agreement but nevertheless have a very important bearing on the result we all seek. Neither of these suggestions has been as yet accepted by your Government. I refer to:

(1) That there should be the maximum of political tranquility in Poland and that dissident groups should cease any measures and countermeasures against each other. That we should respectively use our influence to that end seems to me eminently reasonable.

(2) It would also seem entirely natural in view of the responsibilities placed upon them by the Agreement that representatives of the American and British members of the Commission should be permitted to visit Poland. As you will recall Mr. Molotov himself suggested this at an early meeting of the Commission and only subsequently withdrew it.

I wish I could convey to you how important it is for the successful development of our program of international collaboration that this Polish question be settled fairly and speedily. If this is not done all of the difficulties and dangers to Allied unity which we had so much in mind in reaching our decisions at the Crimea will face us in an even more acute form. You are, I am sure, aware that the genuine popular support in the United States is required to carry out any government policy, foreign or domestic. The American people make up their own mind and no government action can change it. I mention this fact because the last sentence of your message about Mr. Molotov's attendance at San Francisco made me wonder whether you give full weight to this factor.

One of the Russian grievances was America's cessation of lend-lease shipments after the end of the European war. In the following selection Secretary of State Byrnes reports Stalin's complaint and the American response.

FROM Speaking Frankly BY JAMES F. BYRNES

He [*Stalin—D. K.*] was particularly irritated by the manner in which lend-
lease shipments had been suspended at the end of the European war. The fact
that ships with supplies bound for Russia even had been unloaded indicated
to him that the cancellation order was an effort to put pressure on the Soviet
Union. This, he declared, was a fundamental mistake and the United States
should understand much could be gained from the Russians only if they were
approached on a friendly basis.

In the case of the German Navy and merchant fleet, he had sent a message
to the President and the Prime Minister suggesting that one-third be turned
over to the Soviets. Not only had he received no reply, he said, but he had
acquired instead an impression that the request was to be rejected.

These complaints were surprising to us at home. They revealed an extreme
sensitivity and an amazing degree of almost instinctive suspicion.

Mr. Hopkins forcefully and tactfully presented the position of the United
States. As for the German ships, it was our intention that they should be
divided equally among the three and we thought that the mater could be
settled at the forthcoming meeting of the Big Three. He explained that the
cancellation of lend-lease was necessary under the law because lend-lease was
authorized only for the purpose of prosecuting the war. With the German
war ended and with the Soviet Union not yet a participant in the Japanese
war, further shipment could not be justified. The order to unload the ships
was the mistake of an official who had nothing to do with policy, and the
order had been withdrawn quickly. He reminded the Marshal of how liber-
ally the United States had construed the law in sending foodstuffs and other
nonmilitary items to their aid.

Stalin readily acknowledged the accuracy of Hopkins' statement. If proper
warning had been given there would have been no feeling about the matter,
he said, pointing out that advance notice was important to them because their
economy is based on plans. The way in which the shipments had been halted
made it impossible for him to express, as he had intended, the great appreciation of the Soviets for the lend-lease aid given to them.

James F. Byrnes, *Speaking Frankly* (1947), pp. 62–63. Reprinted by permission of James F.
Byrnes Foundation.

Hopkins told the Marshal that what disturbed him most was the revelation that Stalin believed the United States would use lend-lease as a pressure weapon. The United States, he asserted, is a strong nation and does not need to indulge in such methods. With this, Stalin said he was fully satisfied with our explanation.

It is sometimes alleged that America's use of the atomic bomb to end the war in Asia was politically motivated and is evidence of American suspicion and hostility toward Russia even during the war. In the following selection Norman Cousins and Thomas Finletter argue for such an interpretation.

FROM A Beginning for Sanity
BY NORMAN COUSINS AND THOMAS K. FINLETTER

Summing up, the scientists expressed their conviction that a unilateral approach to the dropping of the bomb, even apart from moral considerations, however overwhelming, would almost inevitably result in unilateral action by other nations. And unilateralism in an atomic age was not merely a problem but a fatal disease. We would be undermining a possible common ground upon which common controls might later be built. As a corollary, we would be destroying whatever stand we might later decide to take on outlawing the use of atomic weapons in warfare. It would be naive to expect other nations to take such a plea seriously in view of our own lack of reticence in dropping the bomb when the war was on the very verge of being won without it.

Why, then, did we drop it? Or, assuming that the use of the bomb was justified, why did we not demonstrate its power in a test under the auspices of the UN, on the basis of which an ultimatum would be issued to Japan—transferring the burden of responsibility to the Japanese themselves?

In speculating upon possible answers to these questions, some facts available since the bombing may be helpful. We now know, for example, that Russia was scheduled to come into the war against Japan by August 8, 1945. Russia had agreed at Yalta to join the fight against Japan ninety days after V-E day. Going after the knockout punch, we bombed Hiroshima on August 5, Nagasaki on August 7. Russia came into the war on August 8, as specified. Japan asked for surrender terms the same day.

Norman Cousins and Thomas K. Finletter, "A Beginning for Sanity," *The Saturday Review of Literature*, XXIV (July 15, 1946), 7–8. Reprinted by permission of *Saturday Review*.

Can it be that we were more anxious to prevent Russia from establishing a claim for full participation in the occupation against Japan than we were to think through the implications of unleashing atomic warfare? Whatever the answer, one thing seems likely: There was not enough time between July 16, when we knew at New Mexico that the bomb would work, and August 8, the Russian deadline date, for us to have set up the very complicated machinery of a test atomic bombing involving time-consuming problems of area preparations; invitations and arrangements for observers (the probability being that the transportation to the South Pacific would in itself exceed the time limit); issuance of an ultimatum and the conditions of fulfillment, even if a reply limit was set at only forty-eight hours or less—just to mention a few.

No; any test would have been impossible if the purpose was to knock Japan out before Russia came in—or at least before Russia could make anything other than a token of participation prior to a Japanese collapse.

It may be argued that this decision was justified, that it was a legitimate exercise of power politics in a rough-and-tumble world, that we thereby avoided a struggle for authority in Japan similar to what we have experienced in Germany and Italy, that unless we came out of the war with a decisive balance of power over Russia, we would be in no position to checkmate Russian expansion.

There is a dangerous plausibility here—a plausibility as inseparable from the war system of sovereign nations as armaments are from armaments races. It is the plausibility of power politics, of action leading to reaction, reaction leading to counter-reaction, and counter-reaction leading to war; of competitive systems of security rather than of workable world organization. It is a plausibility that rests on the flat assumption that war with Russia is inevitable, and that we should fight it at a time and under terms advantageous to us.

Such "plausibilities" are rejected by those who feel that the big job is to avert the next war, rather than to win it—even assuming that the next war will be worth winning, a somewhat dubious proposition. And they see no way to avert the next war other than through a world organization having the power to back up its decisions by law and relying upon preponderant force as needed. Such an organization would attempt to dispose of the fear-begetting-fear, provocation-begetting-provocation cycle; and to substitute in its place a central authority from which no member could withdraw or secede under any circumstances. It would automatically deprive potential aggressors of their traditional excuse for aggression—namely, their own encirclement and insecurity—and be strong enough to deal with them should a real threat arise.

The following selection shows the confusion and contradictions in the American government over Russian participation in the Asiatic war.

FROM The Forrestal Diaries

Talked with Byrnes [now at Potsdam as American Secretary of State, having succeeded Mr. Stettinius on the conclusion of the San Francisco Conference]. . . . Byrnes said he was most anxious to get the Japanese affair over with before the Russians got in, with particular reference to Dairen and Port Arthur. Once in there, he felt, it would not be easy to get them out. . . .

Evidently on the question of Russian entry into the Pacific war the wheel was now coming full circle. Forrestal was to get a further sidelight on this two years later at a reminiscent luncheon gathering at which General Dwight D. Eisenhower was present. "When President Truman came to Potsdam in the summer of 1945," Forrestal noted, "he told Eisenhower he had as one of his primary objectives that of getting Russia into the Japanese war. Eisenhower begged him at that time not to assume that he had to give anything away to do this, that the Russians were desperately anxious to get into the Eastern war and that in Eisenhower's opinion there was no question but that Japan was already thoroughly beaten. When the President told him at the end of the Conference that he had achieved his objectives and was going home, Eisenhower again remarked that he earnestly hoped the President had not had to make any concessions to get them in."

Still later Forrestal recorded his own conclusion. In a note of June 23, 1947, he observed that the Russians would have to come into the Marshall Plan; "they could no more afford to be out of it than they could have afforded not to join in the war against Japan (fifty divisions could not have kept them *out* of this war)." While Forrestal was mistaken about Soviet participation in the Marshall Plan, it does not follow that his estimate as to the Pacific war was wrong.

Next day, a Sunday, Forrestal wandered through the ruins of Berlin and was as deeply impressed by that staggering scene of destruction as are all who have seen it. He also found that others did not share what would seem to have been the President's rather optimistic mood about the Russians.

Walter Millis, ed., with the collaboration of E. S. Duffield, *The Forrestal Diaries* (1951), pp. 78–79. Reprinted by permission of Princeton University.

On March 5, 1946, Winston Churchill, in a speech at Westminster College in Fulton, Missouri, gave public recognition to the division that had arisen between the former Allies.

FROM Winston Churchill's Speech at Fulton

EUROPE DIVIDED

A shadow has fallen upon the scenes so lately lighted by the Allied victory. Nobody knows what Soviet Russia and its Communist international organization intends to do in the immediate future, or what are the limits, if any, to their expansive and proselytizing tendencies. I have a strong admiration and regard for the valiant Russian people and for my war-time comrade, Marshal Stalin. There is sympathy and good will in Britain—and I doubt not here also —toward the peoples of all the Russias and a resolve to persevere through many differences and rebuffs in establishing lasting friendships. We understand the Russians need to be secure on her western frontiers from all renewal of German aggression. We welcome her to her rightful place among the leading nations of the world. Above all we welcome constant, frequent and growing contacts between the Russian people and our own people on both sides of the Atlantic. It is my duty, however, to place before you certain facts about the present position in Europe—I am sure I do not wish to, but it is my duty, I feel, to present them to you.

From Stettin in the Baltic to Trieste in the Adriatic, an iron curtain has descended across the Continent. Behind that line lie all the capitals of the ancient states of central and eastern Europe. Warsaw, Berlin, Prague, Vienna, Budapest, Belgrade, Bucharest and Sofia, all these famous cities and the populations around them lie in the Soviet sphere and all are subject in one form or another, not only to Soviet influence but to a very high and increasing measure of control from Moscow. Athens alone, with its immortal glories, is free to decide its future at an election under British, American and French observation. The Russian-dominated Polish government has been encouraged to make enormous and wrongful inroads upon Germany, and mass expulsions of millions of Germans on a scale grievous and undreamed of are now taking place. The Communist parties, which were very small in all these eastern states of Europe, have been raised to pre-eminence and power far beyond their numbers and are seeking everywhere to obtain totalitarian control. Po-

Vital Speeches of the Day, XII (March 15, 1946), 331–332. Reprinted by permission of City News Publishing Co.

lice governments are prevailing in nearly every case, and so far, except in Czechoslovakia, there is no true democracy. Turkey and Persia are both profoundly alarmed and disturbed at the claims which are made upon them and at the pressure being exerted by the Moscow government. An attempt is being made by the Russians in Berlin to build up a quasi-Communist party in their zone of occupied Germany by showing special favors to groups of Left-Wing German leaders. At the end of the fighting last June, the American and British armies withdrew westward, in accordance with an earlier agreement, to a depth at some points 150 miles on a front of nearly 400 miles to allow the Russians to occupy this vast expanse of territory which the western democracies had conquered. If now the Soviet government tries, by separate action, to build up a pro-Communist Germany in their areas this will cause new serious difficulties in the British and American zones, and will give the defeated Germans the power of putting themselves up to auction between the Soviets and western democracies. Whatever conclusions may be drawn from these facts—and facts they are—this is certainly not the liberated Europe we fought to build up. Nor is it one which contains the essentials of permanent peace.

The safety of the world, ladies and gentlemen, requires a new unity in Europe from which no nation should be permanently outcast.

It is impossible not to comprehend—twice we have seen them drawn by irresistible forces in time to secure the victory but only after frightful slaughter and devastation have occurred. Twice the United States has had to send millions of its young men to fight a war, but now war can find any nation between dusk and dawn. Surely we should work within the structure of the United Nations and in accordance with our charter. That is an open course of policy.

COMMUNIST FIFTH COLUMNS

In front of the iron curtain which lies across Europe are other causes for anxiety. In Italy the Communist party is seriously hampered by having to support the Communist trained Marshal Tito's claims to former Italian territory at the head of the Adriatic. Nevertheless the future of Italy hangs in the balance. Again one cannot imagine a regenerated Europe without a strong France. All my public life I have worked for a strong France and I never lost faith in her destiny, even in the darkest hours. I will not lose faith now. However, in a great number of countries, far from the Russian frontiers and throughout the world, Communist fifth columns are established and work in complete unity and absolute obedience to the directions they receive from the Communist center. Except in the British Commonwealth and in this United States, where Communism is in its infancy, the Communist parties or fifth columns constitute a growing challenge and peril to Christian civilization. These are somber facts for any one to have to recite on the morrow of a victory gained by so much splendid comradeship in arms and in the cause of freedom and democracy, and we should be most unwise not to face them squarely while time remains.

The outlook is also anxious in the Far East and especially in Manchuria. The agreement which was made at Yalta, to which I was a party, was extremely favorable to Soviet Russia, but it was made at a time when no one could say that the German war might not extend all through the summer and autumn of 1945 and when the Japanese war was expected to last for a further eighteen months from the end of the German war. In this country you are all so well informed about the Far East, and such devoted friends of China, that I do not need to expatiate on the situation there.

I have felt bound to portray the shadow which, alike in the West and in the East, falls upon the world. I was a minister at the time of the Versailles treaty and a close friend of Mr. Lloyd George. I did not myself agree with many things that were done, but I have a very vague impression in my mind of that situation, and I find it painful to contrast it with that which prevails now. In those days there were high hopes and unbounded confidence that the wars were over, and that the League of Nations would become all-powerful. I do not see or feel the same confidence or even the same hopes in the haggard world at this time.

WAR NOT INEVITABLE

On the other hand I repulse the idea that a new war is inevitable; still more that it is imminent. It is because I am so sure that our fortunes are in our own hands and that we hold the power to save the future, that I feel the duty to speak out now that I have an occasion to do so. I do not believe that Soviet Russia desires war. What they desire is the fruits of war and the indefinite expansion of their power and doctrines. But what we have to consider here today while time remains, is the permanent prevention of war and the establishment of conditions of freedom and democracy as rapidly as possible in all countries. Our difficulties and dangers will not be removed by closing our eyes to them. They will not be removed by mere waiting to see what happens; nor will they be relieved by a policy of appeasement. What is needed is a settlement and the longer this is delayed the more difficult it will be and the greater our dangers will become. From what I have seen of our Russian friends and allies during the war, I am convinced that there is nothing they admire so much as strength, and there is nothing for which they have less respect than for military weakness. For that reason the old doctrine of a balance of power is unsound. We cannot afford, if we can help it, to work on narrow margins, offering temptations to a trial of strength. If the western democracies stand together in strict adherence to the principles of the United Nations Charter, their influence for furthering these principles will be immense and no one is likely to molest them. If, however, they become divided or falter in their duty, and if these all-important years are allowed to slip away, then indeed catastrophe may overwhelm us all.

Last time I saw it all coming, and cried aloud to my fellow countrymen and to the world, but no one paid any attention. Up till the year 1933 or even 1935, Germany might have been saved from the awful fate which has overtaken her and we might all have been spared the miseries Hitler let loose upon mankind. There never was a war in all history easier to prevent by timely action than the one which has just desolated such great areas of the globe. It could have been prevented without the firing of a single shot, and Germany might be powerful, prosperous and honored today, but no one would listen and one by one we were all sucked into the awful whirlpool. We surely must not let that happen again. This can only be achieved by reaching now, in 1946, a good understanding on all points with Russia under the general authority of the United Nations Organization and by the maintenance of that good understanding through many peaceful years, by the world instrument, supported by the whole strength of the English-speaking world and all its connections.

Let no man underrate the abiding power of the British Empire and Commonwealth. Because you see the forty-six millions in our island harassed about their food supply, of which they grew only one half, even in war time, or because we have difficulty in restarting our industries and export trade after six years of passionate war effort, do not suppose that we shall not come through these dark years of privation as we have come through the glorious years of agony, or that half a century from now you will not see seventy or eighty millions of Britons spread about the world and united in defense of our traditions, our way of life and of the world causes we and you espouse. If the population of the English-speaking commonwealth be added to that of the United States, with all that such co-operation implies in the air, on the sea and in science and industry, there will be no quivering, precarious balance of power to offer its temptation to ambition or adventure. On the contrary, there will be an overwhelming assurance of security. If we adhere faithfully to the charter of the United Nations and walk forward in sedate and sober strength, seeking no one's land or treasure, or seeking to lay no arbitrary control on the thoughts of men, if all British moral and material forces and convictions are joined with your own in fraternal association, the highroads of the future will be clear, not only for us but for all, not only for our time but for a century to come.

In 1947 Britain informed the United States that it could no longer support the Greeks in their fight against a Communist insurrection supported from the outside. On March 12 of that year President Truman went before Congress and asked for legislation to undertake the support of both Greece and Turkey, which was also in danger. The Truman Doctrine marked a new step in American involvement in world affairs.

Message of the President to the Congress

Mr. President, Mr. Speaker, Members of the Congress of the United States:

The gravity of the situation which confronts the world today necessitates my appearance before a joint session of the Congress.

The foreign policy and the national security of this country are involved.

One aspect of the present situation, which I wish to present to you at this time for your consideration and decision, concerns Greece and Turkey.

The United States has received from the Greek Government an urgent appeal for financial and economic assistance. Preliminary reports from the American Economic Mission now in Greece and reports from the American Ambassador in Greece corroborate the statement of the Greek Government that assistance is imperative if Greece is to survive as a free nation.

I do not believe that the American people and the Congress wish to turn a deaf ear to the appeal of the Greek Government.

Greece is not a rich country. Lack of sufficient natural resources has always forced the Greek people to work hard to make both ends met. Since 1940 this industrious and peace-loving country has suffered invasion, four years of cruel enemy occupation, and bitter internal strife.

When forces of liberation entered Greece they found that the retreating Germans had destroyed virtually all the railways, roads, port facilities, communications, and merchant marine. More than a thousand villages had been burned. Eighty-five percent of the children were tubercular. Livestock, poultry, and draft animals had almost disappeared. Inflation had wiped out practically all savings.

As a result of these tragic conditions, a militant minority, exploiting human want and misery, was able to create political chaos which, until now, has made economic recovery impossible.

Greece is today without funds to finance the importation of those goods

---

Senate Committee on Foreign Relations, *A Decade of American Foreign Policy: Basic Documents 1941–1949* (1950), pp. 1235–1237.

which are essential to bare subsistence. Under these circumstances the people of Greece cannot make progress in solving their problems of reconstruction. Greece is in desperate need of financial and economic assistance to enable it to resume purchases of food, clothing, fuel, and seeds. These are indispensable for the subsistence of its people and are obtainable only from abroad. Greece must have help to import the goods necessary to restore internal order and security so essential for economic and political recovery.

The Greek Government has also asked for the assistance of experienced American administrators, economists, and technicians to insure that the financial and other aid given to Greece shall be used effectively in creating a stable and self-sustaining economy and in improving its public administration.

The very existence of the Greek state is today threatened by the terrorist activities of several thousand armed men, led by Communists, who defy the Government's authority at a number of points, particularly along the northern boundaries. A commission appointed by the United Nations Security Council is at present investigating disturbed conditions in northern Greece and alleged border violations along the frontier between Greece on the one hand and Albania, Bulgaria, and Yugoslavia on the other.

Meanwhile, the Greek Government is unable to cope with the situation. The Greek Army is small and poorly equipped. It needs supplies and equipment if it is to restore authority to the Government throughout Greek territory.

Greece must have assistance if it is to become a self-supporting and self-respecting democracy.

The United States must supply that assistance. We have already extended to Greece certain types of relief and economic aid, but these are inadequate.

There is no other country to which democratic Greece can turn.

No other nation is willing and able to provide the necessary support for a democratic Greek Government.

The British Government, which has been helping Greece, can give no further financial or economic aid after March 31. Great Britain finds itself under the necessity of reducing or liquidating its commitments in several parts of the world, including Greece.

We have considered how the United Nations might assist in this crisis. But the situation is an urgent one requiring immediate action, and the United Nations and its related organizations are not in a position to extend help of the kind that is required.

It is important to note that the Greek Government has asked for our aid in utilizing effectively the financial and other assistance we may give to Greece, and in improving its public administration. It is of the utmost importance that we supervise the use of any funds made available to Greece, in such a manner that each dollar spent will count toward making Greece self-supporting, and will help to build an economy in which a healthy democracy can flourish.

No government is perfect. One of the chief virtues of a democracy, however, is that its defects are always visible and under democratic processes can be pointed out and corrected. The Government of Greece is not perfect. Nevertheless it represents 85 percent of the members of the Greek Parliament who were chosen in an election last year. Foreign observers, including 692 Americans, considered this election to be a fair expression of the views of the Greek people.

The Greek Government has been operating in an atmosphere of chaos and extremism. It has made mistakes. The extension of aid by this country does not mean that the United States condones everything that the Greek Government has done or will do. We have condemned in the past, and we condemn now, extremist measures of the right or the left. We have in the past advised tolerance, and we advise tolerance now.

Greece's neighbor, Turkey, also deserves our attention.

The future of Turkey as an independent and economically sound state is clearly no less important to the freedom-loving peoples of the world than the future of Greece. The circumstances in which Turkey finds itself today are considerably different from those of Greece. Turkey has been spared the disasters that have beset Greece. And during the war the United States and Great Britain furnished Turkey with material aid.

Nevertheless, Turkey now needs our support.

Since the war Turkey has sought additional financial assistance from Great Britain and the United States for the purpose of effecting that modernization necessary for the maintenance of its national integrity.

That integrity is essential to the preservation of order in the Middle East.

The British Government has informed us that, owing to its own difficulties, it can no longer extend financial or economic aid to Turkey.

As in the case of Greece, if Turkey is to have the assistance it needs, the United States must supply it. We are the only country able to provide that help.

I am fully aware of the broad implications involved if the United States extends assistance to Greece and Turkey, and I shall discuss these implications with you at this time.

One of the primary objectives of the foreign policy of the United States is the creation of conditions in which we and other nations will be able to work out a way of life free from coercion. This was a fundamental issue in the war with Germany and Japan. Our victory was won over countries which sought to impose their will, and their way of life, upon other nations.

To insure the peaceful development of nations, free from coercion, the United States has taken a leading part in establishing the United Nations. The United Nations is designed to make possible lasting freedom and independence for all its members. We shall not realize our objectives, however, unless we are willing to help free peoples to maintain their free institutions and their national integrity against aggressive movements that seek to impose upon them totalitarian regimes. This is no more than a frank recognition that totalitarian regimes imposed upon free peoples, by direct or indirect aggression, undermine the foundations of international peace and hence the security of the United States.

The peoples of a number of countries of the world have recently had totalitarian regimes forced upon them against their will. The Government of the United States has made frequent protests against coercion and intimidation in violation of the Yalta agreement, in Poland, Rumania, and Bulgaria. I must also state that in a number of other countries there have been similar developments.

At the present moment in world history nearly every nation must choose between alternative ways of life. The choice is too often not a free one.

One way of life is based upon the will of the majority, and is distinguished by free institutions, representative government, free elections, guaranties, of individual liberty, freedom of speech and religion, and freedom from political oppression.

The second way of life is based upon the will of a minority forcibly imposed upon the majority. It relies upon terror and oppression, a controlled press and radio, fixed elections, and the suppression of personal freedoms.

I believe that it must be the policy of the United States to support free peoples who are resisting attempted subjugation by armed minorities or by outside pressures.

I believe that we must assist free peoples to work out their own destinies in their own way.

I believe that our help should be primarily through economic and financial aid which is essential to economic stability and orderly political processes.

The world is not static, and the *status quo* is not sacred. But we cannot allow changes in the *status quo* in violation of the Charter of the United Nations by such methods as coercion, or by such subterfuges as political infiltration. In helping free and independent nations to maintain their freedom, the United States will be giving effect to the principles of the Charter of the United Nations.

It is necessary only to glance at a map to realize that the survival and integrity of the Greek nation are of grave importance in a much wider situation. If Greece should fall under the control of an armed minority, the effect upon its neighbor, Turkey, would be immediate and serious. Confusion and disorder might well spread throughout the entire Middle East.

Moreover, the disappearance of Greece as an independent state would have a profound effect upon those countries in Europe whose peoples are struggling against great difficulties to maintain their freedoms and their independence while they repair the damages of war.

It would be an unspeakable tragedy if these countries, which have struggled so long against overwhelming odds, should lose that victory for which they sacrificed so much. Collapse of free institutions and loss of independence would be disastrous not only for them but for the world. Discouragement and possibly failure would quickly be the lot of neighboring peoples striving to maintain their freedom and independence.

Should we fail to aid Greece and Turkey in this fateful hour, the effect will be far-reaching to the West as well as to the East.

We must take immediate and resolute action.

I therefore ask the Congress to provide authority for assistance to Greece and Turkey in the amount of $400,000,000 for the period ending June 30, 1948. In requesting these funds, I have taken into consideration the maximum amount of relief assistance which would be furnished to Greece out of the $350,000,000 which I recently requested that the Congress authorize for the prevention of starvation and suffering in countries devastated by the war.

In addition to funds, I ask the Congress to authorize the detail of American civilian and military personnel to Greece and Turkey, at the request of those countries, to assist in the tasks of reconstruction, and for the purpose of supervising the use of such financial and material assistance as may be furnished. I recommend that authority also be provided for the instruction and training of selected Greek and Turkish personnel.

Finally, I ask that the Congress provide authority which will permit the speediest and most effective use, in terms of needed commodities, supplies, and equipment, of such funds as may be authorized.

If further funds, or further authority, should be needed for purposes indicated in this message, I shall not hesitate to bring the situation before the Congress. On this subject the Executive and Legislative branches of the Government must work together.

This is a serious course upon which we embark.

I would not recommend it except that the alternative is much more serious.

The United States contributed $341,000,000,000 toward winning World War II. This is an investment in world freedom and world peace.

The assistance that I am recommending for Greece and Turkey amounts to little more than one-tenth of one percent of this investment. It is only common sense that we should safeguard this investment and make sure that it was not in vain.

The seeds of totalitarian regimes are nurtured by misery and want. They spread and grow in the evil soil of poverty and strife. They reach their full growth when the hope of a people for a better life has died.

We must keep that hope alive.

The free peoples of the world look to us for support in maintaining their freedoms.

If we falter in our leadership, we may endanger the peace of the world— and we shall surely endanger the welfare of our own Nation.

Great responsibilities have been placed upon us by the swift movement of events.

I am confident that the Congress will face these responsibilities squarely.

The Russians did not fail to respond to the Truman Doctrine. The following editorial from *Izvestia* presents their view.

Editorial From Izvestia

On March 12, President Truman addressed a message to the U.S. Congress asking for 400 million dollars to be assigned for urgent aid to Greece and Turkey, and for authority to send to those countries American civil and military personnel, and to provide for the training by Americans by specially picked Greek and Turkish personnel.

Greece, said Truman, was in a desperate economic and political situation. Britain was no longer able to act as trustee for the Greeks. Turkey had requested speedy American aid. Turkey, unlike Greece, had not suffered from the Second World War, but she needed financial aid from Britain and from the U.S.A. in order to carry out that modernisation necessary for maintaining her national integrity. Since the British Government, on account of its own difficulties, was not capable of offering financial or other aid to the Turks, this aid must be furnished by the U.S.A.

Thus Congress was asked to do two "good deeds" at once—to save Greece from internal disorders and to pay for the cost of "modernising" Turkey.

The pathetic appeal of the Tsaldaris Government to the U.S.A. is clear evidence of the bankruptcy of the political regime in Greece. But the matter does not lie solely with the Greek Monarchists and their friends, now cracked up to American Congressmen as the direct descendents of the heroes of Thermopylae: it is well known that the real masters of Greece have been and are the British military authorities.

British troops have been on Greek territory since 1944. On Churchill's initiative, Britain took on herself the responsibility for "stabilising" political conditions in Greece. The British authorities did not confine themselves to perpetuating the rule of the reactionary, anti-democratic forces in Greece, making no scruple in supporting ex-collaborators with the Germans. The entire political and economic activities under a number of short-lived Greek Governments have been carried on under close British control and direction.

Today we can see the results of this policy—complete bankruptcy. British troops failed to bring peace and tranquillity to tormented Greece. The Greek people have been plunged into the abyss of new sufferings, of hunger and poverty. Civil war takes on ever fiercer forms.

Izvestia, March 13, 1947, in William A. Williams, *The Shaping of American Diplomacy* (1956), pp. 1003–1005.

Was not the presence of foreign troops on Greek territory instrumental in bringing about this state of affairs? Does not Britain, who proclaimed herself the guardian of Greece, bear responsibility for the bankruptcy of her charge?

The American President's message completely glosses over these questions. The U.S.A. does not wish to criticise Britain, since she herself intends to follow the British example. Truman's statement makes it clear that the U.S.A. does not intend to deviate from the course of British policy in Greece. So one cannot expect better results.

The U.S. Government has no intention of acting in the Greek question as one might have expected a member of UNO, concerned about the fate of another member, to act. It is obvious that in Washington they do not wish to take into account the obligations assumed by the U.S. Government regarding UNO. Truman did not even consider it necessary to wait for the findings of the Security Council Commission specially sent to Greece to investigate the situation on the spot.

Truman, indeed, failed to reckon either with the international organisation or with the sovereignty of Greece. What will be left of Greek sovereignty when the "American military and civilian personnel" gets to work in Greece by means of the 250 million dollars brought into that country? The sovereignty and independence of Greece will be the first victims of such singular "defence."

The American arguments for assisting Turkey base themselves on the existence of a threat to the integrity of Turkish territory—though no-one and nothing actually threatens Turkey's integrity. This "assistance" is evidently aimed at putting this country also under U.S. control.

Some American commentators admit this quite openly. Walter Lippmann, for example, frankly points out in the *Herald Tribune* that an American alliance with Turkey would give the U.S.A. a strategic position, incomparably more advantageous than any other, from which power could be wielded over the Middle East.

Commenting on Truman's message to Congress, the *New York Times* proclaims the advent of "the age of American responsibility." Yet what is this responsibility but a smokescreen for expansion? The cry of saving Greece and Turkey from the expansion of the so-called "totalitarian states" is not new. Hitler used to refer to the Bolsheviks when he wanted to open the road for his own conquests. Now they want to take Greece and Turkey under their control, they raise a din about "totalitarian states." This seems all the more attractive since, in elbowing in itself, the U.S.A. is pushing non-totalitarian Britain out of yet another country or two.

We are now witnessing a fresh intrusion of the U.S.A. into the affairs of other states. American claims to leadership in international affairs grow parallel with the growing appetite of the American quarters concerned. But the American leaders, in the new historical circumstances, fail to reckon with the fact that the old methods of the colonisers and diehard politicians have outlived their time and are doomed to failure. In this lies the chief weakness of Truman's message.

Aware that the threat of Communist revolution was greatest where poverty existed, Secretary of State Marshall proposed a plan whereby the United States would help the European nations return to prosperity. Although the iron curtain countries were included in the Marshall Plan, Russian hostility prevented their participation.

The European Recovery Program

REMARKS BY SECRETARY MARSHALL, JUNE 5, 1947

I need not tell you gentlemen that the world situation is very serious. That must be apparent to all intelligent people. I think one difficulty is that the problem is one of such enormous complexity that the very mass of facts presented to the public by press and radio make it exceedingly difficult for the man in the street to reach a clear appraisement of the situation. Furthermore, the people of this country are distant from the troubled areas of the earth and it is hard for them to comprehend the plight and consequent reactions of the long-suffering peoples, and the effect of those reactions on their governments in connection with our efforts to promote peace in the world.

In considering the requirements for the rehabilitation of Europe, the physical loss of life, the visible destruction of cities, factories, mines, and railroads was correctly estimated, but it has become obvious during recent months that this visible destruction was probably less serious than the dislocation of the entire fabric of European economy. For the past 10 years conditions have been highly abnormal. The feverish preparation for war and the more feverish maintenance of the war effort engulfed all aspects of national economies. Machinery has fallen into disrepair or is entirely obsolete. Under the arbitrary and destructive Nazi rule, virtually every possible enterprise was geared into the German war machine. Long-standing commercial ties, private institutions, banks, insurance companies, and shipping companies disappeared, through loss of capital, absorption through nationalization, or by simple destruction. In many countries, confidence in the local currency has been se-

Senate Committee on Foreign Relations, *A Decade of American Foreign Policy: Basic Documents, 1941–1949* (1950), pp. 1268–1270.

verely shaken. The breakdown of the business structure of Europe during the war was complete. Recovery has been seriously retarded by the fact that two years after the close of hostilities a peace settlement with Germany and Austria has not been agreed upon. But even given a more prompt solution of these difficult problems, the rehabilitation of the economic structure of Europe quite evidently will require a much longer time and greater effort than had been foreseen.

There is a phase of this matter which is both interesting and serious. The farmer has always produced the foodstuffs to exchange with the city dweller for the other necessities of life. This division of labor is the basis of modern civilization. At the present time it is threatened with breakdown. The town and city industries are not producing adequate goods to exchange with the food-producing farmer. Raw materials and fuel are in short supply. Machinery is lacking or worn out. The farmer or the peasant cannot find the goods for sale which he desires to purchase. So the sale of his farm produce for money which he cannot use seems to him an unprofitable transaction. He, therefore, has withdrawn many fields from crop cultivation and is using them for grazing. He feeds more grain to stock and finds for himself and his family an ample supply of food, however short he may be on clothing and the other ordinary gadgets of civilization. Meanwhile people in the cities are short of food and fuel. So the governments are forced to use their foreign money and credits to procure these necessities abroad. This process exhausts funds which are urgently needed for reconstruction. Thus a very serious situation is rapidly developing which bodes no good for the world. The modern system of the division of labor upon which the exchange of products is based is in danger of breaking down.

The truth of the matter is that Europe's requirements for the next three or four years of foreign food and other essential products—principally from America—are so much greater than her present ability to pay that she must have substantial additional help or face economic, social, and political deterioration of a very grave character.

The remedy lies in breaking the vicious circle and restoring the confidence of the European people in the economic future of their own countries and of Europe as a whole. The manufacturer and the farmer throughout wide areas must be able and willing to exchange their products for currencies the continuing value of which is not open to question.

Aside from the demoralizing effect on the world at large and the possibilities of disturbances arising as a result of the desperation of the people concerned, the consequences to the economy of the United States should be apparent to all. It is logical that the United States should do whatever it is able to do to assist in the return of normal economic health in the world, without which there can be no political stability and no assured peace. Our policy is directed not against any country or doctrine but against hunger, poverty, desperation, and chaos. Its purpose should be the revival of a working economy in the world so as to permit the emergence of political and social conditions in which free institutions can exist. Such assistance, I am convinced, must not be on a piecemeal basis as various crises develop. Any assistance that this Government may render in the future should provide a cure rather than a mere palliative. Any government that is willing to assist in the task of recovery will find full cooperation, I am sure, on the part of the United States Government. Any government which maneuvers to block the recovery of other countries cannot expect help from us. Furthermore, governments, political parties, or groups which seek to perpetuate human misery in order to profit therefrom politically or otherwise will encounter the opposition of the United States.

It is already evident that, before the United States Government can proceed much further in its efforts to alleviate the situation and help start the European world on its way to recovery, there must be some agreement among the countries of Europe as to the requirements of the situation and the part those countries themselves will take in order to give proper effect to whatever action might be undertaken by this Government. It would be neither fitting nor efficacious for this Government to undertake to draw up unilaterally a program designed to place Europe on its feet economically. This is the business of the Europeans. The initiative, I think, must come from Europe. The role of this country should consist of friendly aid in the drafting of a European program and of later support of such a program so far as it may be practical for us to do so. The program should be a joint one, agreed to by a number, if not all, European nations.

An essential part of any successful action on the part of the United States is an understanding on the part of the people of America of the character of the problem and the remedies to be applied. Political passion and prejudice should have no part. With foresight, and a willingness on the part of our people to face up to the vast responsibility which history has clearly placed upon our country, the difficulties I have outlined can and will be overcome.

In February 1948 democratic Czechoslovakia experienced a Communist *coup d'état* that effectively made it a Russian satellite. The following correspondence between President Beneš and the Communist party clearly indicates the course of events.

FROM President Beneš' Correspondence with the Presidium of the Communist Party

Letter from President Beneš to Presidium of the Communist Party

February 24, 1948

You sent me a letter on February 21 in which you express your attitude on a solution of the crisis and ask me to agree with it. Allow me to formulate my own attitude.

I feel fully the great responsibility of this fateful hour on our national and state life. From the beginning of this crisis I have been thinking about the situation as it was forming itself, putting these affairs of ours in connection with world affairs.

I am trying to see clearly not only the present situation but also the causes that led to it and the results that a decision can have. I am aware of the powerful forces through which the situation is being formed.

In a calm, matter of fact, impassionate and objective judgment of the situation I feel, through the common will of various groups of our citizens which turn their attention to me, that the will is expressed to maintain the peace and order and discipline voluntarily accepted to achieve a progressive and really socialist life.

How to achieve this goal? You know my sincerely democratic creed. I cannot but stay faithful to that creed even at this moment because democracy, according to my belief, is the only reliable and durable basis for a decent and dignified human life.

I insist on parliamentary democracy and parliamentary government as it limits democracy. I state I know very well it is necessary to social and economic content. I built my political work on these principles and cannot— without betraying myself—act otherwise.

The present crisis of democracy here too cannot be overcome but through democratic and parliamentary means. I thus do not overlook your demands. I

The Strategy and Tactics of World Communism, Supplement III, *The Coup d'État in Prague,* House of Representatives Committee on Foreign Affairs, National and International Movements, Subcommittee No. 5 Report (1948), pp. 25–27.

regard all our political parties associated in the National Front as bearers of political responsibility. We all accepted the principle of the National Front and this proved successful up to the recent time when the crisis began.

This crisis, however, in my opinion, does not deny the principle in itself. I am convinced that on this principle, even in the future, the necessary cooperation of all can be achieved. All disputes can be solved for the benefit of the national and common state of the Czechs and the Slovaks.

I therefore have been in negotiation with five political parties. I have listened to their views and some of them also have been put in writing. These are grave matters and I cannot ignore them.

Therefore, I again have to appeal to all to find a peaceful solution and new successful cooperation through parliamentary means and through the National Front.

That much for the formal side. As far as the personal side is concerned, it is clear to me, as I have said already, that the Prime Minister will be the chairman of the strongest party element, Gottwald.

Finally, on the factual side of this matter it is clear to me that socialism is a way of life desired by an overwhelming part of our nation. At the same time I believe that with socialism a certain measure of freedom and unity is possible and that these are vital principles to all in our national life.

Our nation has struggled for freedom almost throughout its history. History also has shown us where discord can lead.

I beg of you therefore to relive these facts and make them the starting point for our negotiations. Let us all together begin negotiations again for further durable cooperation and let us not allow prolongation of the split of the nation into two quarreling parts.

I believe that a reasonable agreement is possible because it is indispensable.

Reply by the Presidium of the Communist Party to Letter of President Beneš

February 25, 1948

The Presidium of the Central Committee of the Communist Party acknowledges your letter dated February 24 and states again that it cannot enter into negotiations with the present leadership of the National Socialist, People's and Slovak Democratic Parties because this would not conform to the interests of the unity of the people nor with the interests of further peaceful development of the republic.

Recent events indisputably proved that these three parties no longer represent the interests of the working people of the cities and countryside, that their leaders have betrayed the fundamental ideas of the people's democracy and National Front as they have been stated by the Kosice Government program and that they assumed the position of undermining the opposition.

This was shown again and again in the government, in the Constitutional National Assembly, in the press of these parties, and in actions that, with menacing levity, were organized by their central secretariats against the interests of the working people, against the security of the state, against the alliances of the republic, against state finance, against nationalized industry, against urgent agricultural reforms—in one word, against the whole constructive efforts of our people and against the very foundations, internal and external, of the security of the country.

These parties even got in touch with foreign circles hostile to our people's democratic order and our alliances, and in collaboration with these hostile foreign elements they attempted disruption of the present development of the republic.

This constantly increasing activity was crowned by an attempt to break up the government, an attempt that, as it was proved, should have been accompanied by actions aiming at a putsch.

Massive people's manifestations during the last few days clearly have shown our working people denounce, with complete unity and with indignation, the policy of these parties and ask the creation of a government in which all honest progressive patriots devoted to the republic and the people are represented.

Also among the members of the above-mentioned three parties an increasing amount of indignation can be seen. The members ask for a rebirth of their own parties and the National Front.

In conformity with this powerfully expressed will of the people, the Presidium of the Central Committee of the Communist Party approved the proposals of Premier Klement Gottwald according to which the government will be filled in with prominent representatives of all parties and also big nation-wide organizations.

We stress that a government filled in this way will present itself, with full agreement with the principles of parliamentary democracy, before the Constitutional National Assembly with its program and ask for its approval.

Being convinced that only such a highly constitutional and parliamentary process can guarantee the peaceful development of the republic and at the same time it corresponds to the ideas of a complete majority of the working people, the Presidium of the Central Committee hopes firmly after careful consideration that you will recognize the correctness of its conclusions and will agree with its proposals.

In 1949 the United States abandoned its traditional hostility toward entangling alliances and joined the North Atlantic Treaty Organization to counter Soviet pressure against Western Europe. It was the decisive recognition that the cold war was to be a lasting reality.

North Atlantic Treaty

The Parties to this Treaty reaffirm their faith in the purposes and principles of the Charter of the United Nations and their desire to live in peace with all peoples and all governments.

They are determined to safeguard the freedom, common heritage and civilization of their peoples, founded on the principles of democracy, individual liberty and the rule of law.

They seek to promote stability and well-being in the North Atlantic area.

They are resolved to unite their efforts for collective defense and for the preservation of peace and security.

They therefore agree to this North Atlantic Treaty:

ARTICLE 1

The Parties undertake, as set forth in the Charter of the United Nations, to settle any international disputes in which they may be involved by peaceful means in such a manner that international peace and security, and justice, are not endangered, and to refrain in their international relations from the threat or use of force in any manner inconsistent with the purposes of the United Nations.

ARTICLE 2

The Parties will contribute toward the further development of peaceful and friendly international relations by strengthening their free institutions, by bringing about a better understanding of the principles upon which these institutions are founded, and by promoting conditions of stability and well-being. They will seek to eliminate conflict in their international economic

Senate Committee on Foreign Relations, *A Decade of American Foreign Policy: Basic Documents, 1941–1949* (1950), pp. 1328–1331.

policies and will encourage economic collaboration between any or all of them.

ARTICLE 3

In order more effectively to achieve the objectives of this Treaty, the Parties, separately and jointly, by means of continuous and effective self-help and mutual aid, will maintain and develop their individual and collective capacity to resist armed attack.

ARTICLE 4

The Parties will consult together whenever, in the opinion of any of them, the territorial integrity, political independence or security of any of the Parties is threatened.

ARTICLE 5

The Parties agree that an armed attack against one or more of them in Europe or North America shall be considered an attack against them all; and consequently they agree that, if such an armed attack occurs, each of them, in exercise of the right of individual or collective self-defense recognized by Article 51 of the Charter of the United Nations, will assist the Party or Parties so attacked by taking forthwith, individually and in concert with the other Parties, such action as it deems necessary, including the use of armed force, to restore and maintain the security of the North Atlantic area.

Any such armed attack and all measures taken as a result thereof shall immediately be reported to the Security Council. Such measures shall be terminated when the Security Council has taken the measures necessary to restore and maintain international peace and security.

ARTICLE 6

For the purpose of Article 5 an armed attack on one or more of the Parties is deemed to include an armed attack on the territory of any of the Parties in Europe or North America, on the Algerian departments of France, on the occupation forces of any Party in Europe, on the islands under the jurisdiction of any Party in the North Atlantic area north of the Tropic of Cancer or on the vessels or aircraft in this area of any of the Parties.

ARTICLE 7

This Treaty does not affect, and shall not be interpreted as affecting, in any way the rights and obligations under the Charter of the Parties which are members of the United Nations, or the primary responsibility of the Security Council for the maintenance of international peace and security.

ARTICLE 8

Each Party declares that none of the international engagements now in force between it and any other of the Parties or any third state is in conflict with the provisions of this Treaty, and undertakes not to enter into any international engagement in conflict with this Treaty.

ARTICLE 9

The Parties hereby established a council, on which each of them shall be represented, to consider matters concerning the implementation of this Treaty. The council shall be so organized as to be able to meet promptly at any time. The council shall set up such subsidiary bodies as may be necessary; in particular it shall establish immediately a defense committee which shall recommend measures for the implementation of Articles 3 and 5.

ARTICLE 10

The Parties may, by unanimous agreement, invite any other European state in a position to further the principles of this Treaty and to contribute to the security of the North Atlantic area to accede to this Treaty. Any state so invited may become a party to the Treaty by depositing its instrument of accession with the Government of the United States of America. The Government of the United States of America will inform each of the Parties of the deposit of each such instrument of accession.

ARTICLE 11

This Treaty shall be ratified and its provisions carried out by the Parties in accordance with their respective constitutional processes. The instruments of ratification shall be deposited as soon as possible with the Government of the

United States of America, which will notify all the other signatories of each deposit. The Treaty shall enter into force between the states which have ratified it as soon as the ratifications of the majority of the signatories, including the ratifications of Belgium, Canada, France, Luxembourg, the Netherlands, the United Kingdom and the United States, have been deposited and shall come into effect with respect to other states on the date of the deposit of their ratifications.

ARTICLE 12

After the Treaty has been in force for ten years, or at any time thereafter, the Parties shall, if any of them so requests, consult together for the purpose of reviewing the Treaty, having regard for the factors then affecting peace and security in the North Atlantic area, including the development of universal as well as regional arrangements under the Charter of the United Nations for the maintenance of international peace and security.

ARTICLE 13

After the Treaty has been in force for twenty years, any Party may cease to be a party one year after its notice of denunciation has been given to the Government of the United States of America, which will inform the Governments of the other Parties of the deposit of each notice of denunciation.

ARTICLE 14

This Treaty, of which the English and French texts are equally authentic, shall be deposited in the archives of the Government of the United States of America. Duly certified copies thereof will be transmitted by that Government to the Governments of the other signatories.

In witness whereof, the undersigned plenipotentiaries have signed this Treaty.

Done at Washington, the fourth day of April, 1949.

For the Kingdom of Belgium:
P. H. Spaak
Silvercruys

For Canada:
Lester B. Pearson
H. H. Wrong

For the Kingdom of Denmark:
  Gustav Rasmussen
  Henrik Kauffmann

For France:
  Schuman
  H. Bonnet

For Iceland:
  Bjarni Benediktsson
  Thor Thors

For Italy:
  Sforza
  Alberto Tarchiani

For the Grand Duchy of Luxembourg:
  Jos Bech
  Hugues Le Gallais

For the Kingdom of the Netherlands:
  Stikker
  E. N. Van Kleffens

For the Kingdom of Norway:
  Halvard M. Lange
  Wilhelm Munthe Morgenstierne

For Portugal:
  José Caeiro da Matta
  Pedro Theotónio Pereira

For the United Kingdom of Great Britain and Northern Ireland:
  Ernest Bevin
  Oliver Franks

For the United States of America:
  Dean Acheson

I certify that the foregoing is a true copy of the North Atlantic Treaty signed at Washington on April 4, 1949 in the English and French languages, the signed original of which is deposited in the archives of the Government of the United States of America.

In testimony whereof, I, Dean Acheson, Secretary of State of the United States of America, have hereunto caused the seal of the Department of State to be affixed and my name subscribed by the Authentication Officer of the said Department, at the city of Washington, in the District of Columbia, this fourth day of April, 1949.

Dean Acheson
Secretary of State
By *M. P. Chauvin*
Authentication Officer
Department of State

3
RUSSIA'S
RESPONSIBILITY

Origins of the Cold War BY ARTHUR SCHLESINGER, JR.

I

The Cold War in its original form was a presumably mortal antagonism, arising in the wake of the Second World War, between two rigidly hostile blocs, one led by the Soviet Union, the other by the United States. For nearly two somber and dangerous decades this antagonism dominated the fears of mankind; it may even, on occasion, have come close to blowing up the planet. In recent years, however, the once implacable struggle has lost its familiar clarity of outline. With the passing of old issues and the emergence of new conflicts and contestants, there is a natural tendency, especially on the part of the generation which grew up during the Cold War, to take a fresh look at the causes of the great contention between Russia and America.

Some exercises in reappraisal have merely elaborated the orthodoxies promulgated in Washington or Moscow during the boom years of the Cold War. But others, especially in the United States (there are no signs, alas, of this in the Soviet Union), represent what American historians call "revisionism"—that is, a readiness to challenge official explanations. No one should be surprised by this phenomenon. Every war in American history has been followed in due course by skeptical reassessments of supposedly sacred assumptions. So the War of 1812, fought at the time for the freedom of the seas, was in later years ascribed to the expansionist ambitions of Congressional war hawks; so the Mexican War became a slaveholders' conspiracy. So the Civil War has been pronounced a "needless war," and Lincoln has even been accused of manoeuvring the rebel attack on Fort Sumter. So too the Spanish-American War and the First and Second World Wars have, each in its turn,

Arthur Schlesinger, Jr., "Origins of the Cold War," *Foreign Affairs*, XLIV (October 1967), 22–52, reprinted by permission of Arthur Schlesinger, Jr.

undergone revisionist critiques. It is not to be supposed that the Cold War would remain exempt.

In the case of the Cold War, special factors reinforce the predictable historiographical rhythm. The outburst of polycentrism in the communist empire has made people wonder whether communism was ever so monolithic as official theories of the Cold War supposed. A generation with no vivid memories of Stalinism may see the Russia of the forties in the image of the relatively mild, seedy and irresolute Russia of the sixties. And for this same generation the American course of widening the war in Viet Nam—which even non-revisionists can easily regard as folly—has unquestionably stirred doubts about the wisdom of American foreign policy in the sixties which younger historians may have begun to read back into the forties.

It is useful to remember that, on the whole, past exercises in revisionism have failed to stick. Few historians today believe that the war hawks caused the War of 1812 or the slaveholders the Mexican War, or that the Civil War was needless, or that the House of Morgan brought America into the First World War or that Franklin Roosevelt schemed to produce the attack on Pearl Harbor. But this does not mean that one should deplore the rise of Cold War revisionism.[1] For revisionism is an essential part of the process by which history, through the posing of new problems and the investigation of new possibilities, enlarges its perspectives and enriches its insights.

More than this, in the present context, revisionism expresses a deep, legitimate and tragic apprehension. As the Cold War has begun to lose its purity of definition, as the moral absolutes of the fifties become the moralistic clichés of the sixties, some have begun to ask whether the appalling risks which humanity ran during the Cold War were, after all, necessary and inevitable; whether more restrained and rational policies might not have guided the energies of man from the perils of conflict into the potentialities of collaboration. The fact that such questions are in their nature unanswerable does not mean that it is not right and useful to raise them. Nor does it mean that our sons and daughters are not entitled to an accounting from the generation of Russians and Americans who produced the Cold War.

II

The orthodox American view, as originally set forth by the American government and as reaffirmed until recently by most American scholars, has been that the Cold War was the brave and essential response of free men to communist aggression. Some have gone back well before the Second World War to lay open the sources of Russian expansionism. Geopoliticians traced the Cold War to imperial Russian strategic ambitions which in the nineteenth

---

[1] As this writer somewhat intemperately did in a letter to *The New York Review of Books,* October 20, 1966.

century led to the Crimean War, to Russian penetration of the Balkans and the Middle East and to Russian pressure on Britain's "lifeline" to India. Ideologists traced it to the Communist Manifesto of 1848 ("the violent overthrow of the bourgeoisie lays the foundation for the sway of the proletariat"). Thoughtful observers (a phrase meant to exclude those who speak in Dullese about the unlimited evil of godless, atheistic, militant communism) concluded that classical Russian imperialism and Pan-Slavism, compounded after 1917 by Leninist messianism, confronted the West at the end of the Second World War with an inexorable drive for domination.[2]

The revisionist thesis is very different.[3] In its extreme form, it is that, after the death of Franklin Roosevelt and the end of the Second World War, the United States deliberately abandoned the wartime policy of collaboration

---

[2] Every student of the Cold War must acknowledge his debt to W. H. McNeill's remarkable account, "America, Britain and Russia: Their Cooperation and Conflict, 1941–1946" (New York, 1953) and to the brilliant and indispensable series by Herbert Feis: "Churchill, Roosevelt, Stalin: The War They Waged and the Peace They Sought" (Princeton, 1957); "Between War and Peace: The Potsdam Conference" (Princeton, 1960); and "The Atomic Bomb and the End of World War II" (Princeton, 1966). Useful recent analyses include André Fontaine, "Histoire de la Guerre Froide (2 v., Paris, 1965, 1967); N. A. Graebner, "Cold War Diplomacy, 1945–1960" (Princeton, 1962); L. J. Halle, "The Cold War as History" (London, 1967); M. F. Herz, "Beginnings of the Cold War" (Bloomington, 1966) and W. L. Neumann, "After Victory: Churchill, Roosevelt, Stalin and the Making of the Peace" (New York, 1967).

[3] The fullest statement of this case is to be found in D. F. Fleming's voluminous "The Cold War and Its Origins" (New York, 1961). For a shorter version of this argument, see David Horowitz, "The Free World Colossus" (New York, 1965); the most subtle and ingenious statements come in W. A. Williams' "The Tragedy of American Diplomacy" (rev. ed., New York, 1962) and in Gar Alperowitz's "Atomic Diplomacy: Hiroshima and Potsdam" (New York, 1965) and in subsequent articles and reviews by Mr. Alperowitz in *The New York Review of Books*. The fact that in some aspects the revisionist thesis parallels the official Soviet argument must not, of course, prevent consideration of the case on its merits, nor raise questions about the motives of the writers, all of whom, so far as I know, are independent-minded scholars.

I might further add that all these books, in spite of their ostentatious display of scholarly apparatus, must be used with caution. Professor Fleming, for example, relies heavily on newspaper articles and even columnists. While Mr. Alperowitz bases his case on official documents or authoritative reminiscences, he sometimes twists his material in a most unscholarly way. For example, in describing Ambassador Harriman's talk with President Truman on April 20, 1945, Mr. Alperowitz writes, "He argued that a reconsideration of Roosevelt's policy was necessary" (p. 22, repeated on p. 24). The citation is to p. 70–72 in President Truman's "Years of Decision." What President Truman reported Harriman as saying was the exact opposite: "Before leaving, Harriman took me aside and said, 'Frankly, one of the reasons that made me rush back to Washington was the fear that you did not understand, as I had seen Roosevelt understand, that Stalin is breaking his agreements.'" Similarly, in an appendix (p. 271) Mr. Alperowitz writes that the Hopkins and Davies missions of May 1945 "were opposed by the 'firm' advisers." Actually the Hopkins mission was proposed by Harriman and Charles E. Bohlen, who Mr. Alperowitz elsewhere suggests were the firmest of the firm—and was proposed by them precisely to impress on Stalin the continuity of American policy from Roosevelt to Truman. While the idea that Truman reversed Roosevelt's policy is tempting dramatically, it is a myth. See, for example, the testimony of Anna Rosenberg Hoffman, who lunched with Roosevelt on March 24, 1945, the last day he spent in Washington. After luncheon, Roosevelt was handed a cable. "He read it and became quite angry. He banged his fists on the arms of his wheelchair and said, 'Averell is right; we can't do business with Stalin. He has broken every one of the promises he made at Yalta.' He was very upset and continued in the same vein on the subject."

and, exhilarated by the possession of the atomic bomb, undertook a course of aggression of its own designed to expel all Russian influence from Eastern Europe and to establish democratic-capitalist states on the very border of the Soviet Union. As the revisionists see it, this radically new American policy—or rather this resumption by Truman of the pre-Roosevelt policy of insensate anti-communism—left Moscow no alternative but to take measures in defense of its own borders. The result was the Cold War.

These two views, of course, could not be more starkly contrasting. It is therefore not unreasonable to look again at the half-dozen critical years between June 22, 1941, when Hitler attacked Russia, and July 2, 1947, when the Russians walked out of the Marshall Plan meeting in Paris. Several things should be borne in mind as this reëxamination is made. For one thing, we have thought a great deal more in recent years, in part because of writers like Roberta Wohlstetter and T. C. Schelling, about the problems of communication in diplomacy—the signals which one nation, by word or by deed, gives, inadvertently or intentionally, to another. Any honest reappraisal of the origins of the Cold War requires the imaginative leap—which should in any case be as instinctive for the historian as it is prudent for the statesman—into the adversary's viewpoint. We must strive to see how, given Soviet perspectives, the Russians might conceivably have misread our signals, as we must reconsider how intelligently we read theirs.

For another, the historian must not overindulge the man of power in the illusion cherished by those in office that high position carries with it the easy ability to shape history. Violating the statesman's creed, Lincoln once blurted out the truth in his letter of 1864 to A. G. Hodges: "I claim not to have controlled events, but confess plainly that events have controlled me." He was not asserting Tolstoyan fatalism but rather suggesting how greatly events limit the capacity of the statesman to bend history to his will. The physical course of the Second World War—the military operations undertaken, the position of the respective armies at the war's end, the momentum generated by victory and the vacuums created by defeat—all these determined the future as much as the character of individual leaders and the substance of national ideology and purpose.

Nor can the historian forget the conditions under which decisions are made, especially in a time like the Second World War. These were tired, overworked, aging men: in 1945, Churchill was 71 years old, Stalin had governed his country for 17 exacting years, Roosevelt his for 12 years nearly as exacting. During the war, moreover, the importunities of military operations had shoved postwar questions to the margins of their minds. All—even Stalin, behind his screen of ideology—had become addicts of improvisation, relying on authority and virtuosity to conceal the fact that they were constantly surprised by developments. Like Eliza, they leaped from one cake of ice to the next in the effort to reach the other side of the river. None showed great tactical consistency, or cared much about it; all employed a certain ambiguity to preserve their power to decide big issues; and it is hard to know how to interpret anything any one of them said on any specific occasion. This was partly because, like all princes, they designed their expressions to have particular effects on particular audiences; partly because the entirely genuine intellectual difficulty of the questions they faced made a degree of vacillation and mind-changing eminently reasonable. If historians cannot solve their problems in retrospect, who are they to blame Roosevelt, Stalin and Churchill for not having solved them at the time?

III

Peacemaking after the Second World War was not so much a tapestry as it was a hopelessly raveled and knotted mess of yarn. Yet, for purposes of clarity, it is essential to follow certain threads. One theme indispensable to an understanding of the Cold War is the contrast between two clashing views of world order: the "universalist" view, by which all nations shared a common interest in all the affairs of the world, and the "sphere-of-influence" view, by which each great power would be assured by the other great powers of an acknowledged predominance in its own area of special interest. The universalist view assumed that national security would be guaranteed by an international organization. The sphere-of-interest view assumed that national security would be guaranteed by the balance of power. While in practice these views have by no means been incompatible (indeed, our shaky peace has been based on a combination of the two), in the abstract they involved sharp contradictions.

The tradition of American thought in these matters was universalist—*i.e.* Wilsonian. Roosevelt had been a member of Wilson's subcabinet; in 1920, as candidate for Vice President, he had campaigned for the League of Nations. It is true that, within Roosevelt's infinitely complex mind, Wilsonianism warred with the perception of vital strategic interests he had imbibed from Mahan. Moreover, his temperamental inclination to settle things with fellow princes around the conference table led him to regard the Big Three—or Four—as trustees for the rest of the world. On occasion, as this narrative will show, he was beguiled into flirtation with the sphere-of-influence heresy. But in principle he believed in joint action and remained a Wilsonian. His hope for Yalta, as he told the Congress on his return, was that it would "spell the end of the system of unilateral action, the exclusive alliances, the spheres of influence, the balances of power, and all the other expedients that have been tried for centuries—and have always failed."

Whenever Roosevelt backslid, he had at his side that Wilsonian fundamentalist, Secretary of State Cordell Hull, to recall him to the pure faith. After his visit to Moscow in 1943, Hull characteristically said that, with the Declaration of Four Nations on General Security (in which America, Russia, Britain and China pledged "united action . . . for the organization and maintenance of peace and security"), "there will no longer be need for spheres of influence, for alliances, for balance of power, or any other of the special arrangements through which, in the unhappy past, the nations strove to safeguard their security or to promote their interests."

Remembering the corruption of the Wilsonian vision by the secret treaties of the First World War, Hull was determined to prevent any sphere-of-influence nonsense after the Second World War. He therefore fought all proposals to settle border questions while the war was still on and, excluded as he largely was from wartime diplomacy, poured his not inconsiderable moral energy and frustration into the promulgation of virtuous and spacious general principles.

In adopting the universalist view, Roosevelt and Hull were not indulging personal hobbies. Sumner Welles, Adolf Berle, Averell Harriman, Charles Bohlen—all, if with a variety of nuances, opposed the sphere-of-influence approach. And here the State Department was expressing what seems clearly to have been the predominant mood of the American people, so long mistrustful of European power politics. The Republicans shared the true faith. John Foster Dulles argued that the great threat to peace after the war would lie in the revival of sphere-of-influence thinking. The United States, he said, must not permit Britain and Russia to revert to these bad old ways; it must therefore insist on American participation in all policy decisions for all territories in the World. Dulles wrote pessimistically in January 1945, "The three great powers which at Moscow agreed upon the 'closest coöperation' about European questions have shifted to a practice of separate, regional responsibility."

It is true that critics, and even friends, of the United States sometimes noted a discrepancy between the American passion for universalism when it applied to territory far from American shores and the preëminence the United States accorded its own interests nearer home. Churchill, seeking Washington's blessing for a sphere-of-influence initiative in Eastern Europe, could not forbear reminding the Americans, "We follow the lead of the United States in South America"; nor did any universalist of record propose the abolition of the Monroe Doctrine. But a convenient myopia prevented such inconsistencies from qualifying the ardency of the universalist faith.

There seem only to have been three officials in the United States Government who dissented. One was the Secretary of War, Henry L. Stimson, a classical balance-of-power man, who in 1944 opposed the creation of a vacuum in Central Europe by the pastoralization of Germany and in 1945 urged "the settlement of all territorial acquisitions in the shape of defense posts which each of these four powers may deem to be necessary for their own safety" in advance of any effort to establish a peacetime United Nations. Stimson considered the claim of Russia to a preferred position in Eastern Europe as not unreasonable: as he told President Truman, "he thought the Russians perhaps were being more realistic than we were in regard to their own security." Such a position for Russia seemed to him comparable to the preferred American position in Latin America; he even spoke of "our respective orbits." Stimson was therefore skeptical of what he regarded as the prevailing tendency "to hang on to exaggerated views of the Monroe Doctrine and at the same time butt into every question that comes up in Central Europe." Acceptance of spheres of influence seemed to him the way to avoid "a head-on collision."

A second official opponent of universalism was George Kennan, an eloquent advocate from the American Embassy in Moscow of "a prompt and clear recognition of the division of Europe into spheres of influence and of a policy based on the fact of such division." Kennan argued that nothing we could do would possibly alter the course of events in Eastern Europe; that we were deceiving ourselves by supposing that these countries had any future but Russian domination; that we should therefore relinquish Eastern Europe to the Soviet Union and avoid anything which would make things easier for the Russians by giving them economic assistance or by sharing moral responsibility for their actions.

A third voice within the government against universalism was (at least after the war) Henry A. Wallace. As Secretary of Commerce, he stated the sphere-of-influence case with trenchancy in the famous Madison Square Garden speech of September 1946 which led to his dismissal by President Truman:

On our part, we should recognize that we have no more business in the *political* affairs of Eastern Europe than Russia has in the *political* affairs of Latin America, Western Europe, and the United States. . . . Whether we like it or not, the Russians will try to socialize their sphere of influence just as we try to democratize our sphere of influence. . . . The Russians have no more business stirring up native Communists to political activity in Western Europe, Latin America, and the United States than we have in interfering with the politics of Eastern Europe and Russia.

Stimson, Kennan and Wallace seem to have been alone in the government, however, in taking these views. They were very much minority voices. Meanwhile universalism, rooted in the American legal and moral tradition, overwhelmingly backed by contemporary opinion, received successive enshrinements in the Atlantic Charter of 1941, in the Declaration of the United Nations in 1942 and in the Moscow Declaration of 1943.

IV

The Kremlin, on the other hand, thought *only* of spheres of interest; above all, the Russians were determined to protect their frontiers, and especially their border to the west, crossed so often and so bloodily in the dark course of their history. These western frontiers lacked natural means of defense—no great oceans, rugged mountains, steaming swamps or impenetrable jungles. The history of Russia had been the history of invasion, the last of which was by now horribly killing up to twenty million of its people. The protocol of Russia therefore meant the enlargement of the area of Russian influence. Kennan himself wrote (in May 1944), "Behind Russia's stubborn expansion lies only the age-old sense of insecurity of a sedentary people reared on an exposed plain in the neighborhood of fierce nomadic peoples," and he called this "urge" a "permanent feature of Russian psychology."

In earlier times the "urge" had produced the tsarist search for buffer states and maritime outlets. In 1939 the Soviet-Nazi pact and its secret protocol had enabled Russia to begin to satisfy in the Baltic states, Karelian Finland and Poland, part of what it conceived as its security requirements in Eastern Europe. But the "urge" persisted, causing the friction between Russia and Germany in 1940 as each jostled for position in the area which separated them. Later it led to Molotov's new demands on Hitler in November 1940—a free hand in Finland, Soviet predominance in Rumania and Bulgaria, bases in the Dardanelles—the demands which convinced Hitler that he had no choice but to attack Russia. Now Stalin hoped to gain from the West what Hitler, a closer neighbor, had not dared yield him.

It is true that, so long as Russian survival appeared to require a second front to relieve the Nazi pressure, Moscow's demand for Eastern Europe was a little muffled. Thus the Soviet government adhered to the Atlantic Charter (though with a significant if obscure reservation about adapting its principles to "the circumstances, needs, and historic peculiarities of particular countries"). Thus it also adhered to the Moscow Declaration of 1943, and Molotov then, with his easy mendacity, even denied that Russia had any desire to divide Europe into spheres of influence. But this was guff, which the Russians were perfectly willing to ladle out if it would keep the Americans, and especially Secretary Hull (who made a strong personal impression at the Moscow conference), happy. "A declaration," as Stalin once observed to Eden, "I regard as algebra, but an agreement as practical arithmetic. I do not wish to decry algebra, but I prefer practical arithmetic."

The more consistent Russian purpose was revealed when Stalin offered the British a straight sphere-of-influence deal at the end of 1941. Britain, he suggested, should recognize the Russian absorption of the Baltic states, part of Finland, eastern Poland and Bessarabia; in return, Russia would support any special British need for bases or security arrangements in Western Europe. There was nothing specifically communist about these ambitions. If Stalin achieved them, he would be fulfilling an age-old dream of the tsars. The British reaction was mixed. "Soviet policy is amoral," as Anthony Eden noted at the time; "United States policy is exaggeratedly moral, at least where non-American interests are concerned." If Roosevelt was a universalist with occasional leanings toward spheres of influence and Stalin was a sphere-of-influence man with occasional gestures toward universalism, Churchill seemed evenly poised between the familiar realism of the balance of power, which he had so long recorded as an historian and manipulated as a statesman, and the hope that there must be some better way of doing things. His

1943 proposal of a world organization divided into regional councils represented an effort to blend universalist and sphere-of-interest conceptions. His initial rejection of Stalin's proposal in December 1941 as "directly contrary to the first, second and third articles of the Atlantic Charter" thus did not spring entirely from a desire to propitiate the United States. On the other hand, he had himself already reinterpreted the Atlantic Charter as applying only to Europe (and thus not to the British Empire), and he was, above all, an empiricist who never believed in sacrificing reality on the altar of doctrine.

So in April 1942 he wrote Roosevelt that "the increasing gravity of the war" had led him to feel that the Charter "ought not to be construed so as to deny Russia the frontiers she occupied when Germany attacked her." Hull, however, remained fiercely hostile to the inclusion of territorial provisions in the Anglo-Russian treaty; the American position, Eden noted, "chilled me with Wilsonian memories." Though Stalin complained that it looked "as if the Atlantic Charter was directed against the U.S.S.R.," it was the Russian season of military adversity in the spring of 1942, and he dropped his demands.

He did not, however, change his intentions. A year later Ambassador Standley could cable Washington from Moscow: "In 1918 Western Europe attempted to set up a *cordon sanitaire* to protect it from the influence of bolshevism. Might not now the Kremlin envisage the formation of a belt of pro-Soviet states to protect it from the influences of the West?" It well might; and that purpose became increasingly clear as the war approached its end. Indeed, it derived sustenance from Western policy in the first area of liberation.

The unconditional surrender of Italy in July 1943 created the first major test of the Western devotion to universalism. America and Britain, having won the Italian war, handled the capitulation, keeping Moscow informed at a distance. Stalin complained:

The United States and Great Britain made agreements but the Soviet Union received information about the results . . . just as a passive third observer. I have to tell you that it is impossible to tolerate the situation any longer. I propose that the [tripartite military-political commission] be established and that Sicily be assigned . . . as its place of residence.

Roosevelt, who had no intention of sharing the control of Italy with the Russians, suavely replied with the suggestion that Stalin send an officer "to General Eisenhower's headquarters in connection with the commission." Unimpressed, Stalin continued to press for a tripartite body; but his Western allies were adamant in keeping the Soviet Union off the Control Commission for Italy, and the Russians in the end had to be satisfied with a seat, along with minor Allied states, on a meaningless Inter-Allied Advisory Council. Their acquiescence in this was doubtless not unconnected with a desire to establish precedents for Eastern Europe.

Teheran in December 1943 marked the high point of three-power collaboration. Still, when Churchill asked about Russian territorial interests, Stalin replied a little ominously, "There is no need to speak at the present time about any Soviet desires, but when the time comes we will speak." In the next weeks, there were increasing indications of a Soviet determination to deal unilaterally with Eastern Europe—so much so that in early February 1944 Hull cabled Harriman in Moscow:

Matters are rapidly approaching the point where the Soviet Government will have to choose between the development and extension of the foundation of international cooperation as the guiding principle of the postwar world as against the continuance of a unilateral and arbitrary method of dealing with its special problems even though these problems are admittedly of more direct interest to the Soviet Union than to other great powers.

As against this approach, however, Churchill, more tolerant of sphere-of-influence deviations, soon proposed that, with the impending liberation of the Balkans, Russia should run things in Rumania and Britain in Greece. Hull strongly opposed this suggestion but made the mistake of leaving Washington for a few days; and Roosevelt, momentarily free from his Wilsonian conscience, yielded to Churchill's plea for a three-months' trial. Hull resumed the fight on his return, and Churchill postponed the matter.

The Red Army continued its advance into Eastern Europe. In August the Polish Home Army, urged on by Polish-language broadcasts from Moscow, rose up against the Nazis in Warsaw. For 63 terrible days, the Poles fought valiantly on, while the Red Army halted on the banks of the Vistula a few miles away, and in Moscow Stalin for more than half this time declined to coöperate with the Western effort to drop supplies to the Warsaw Resistance. It appeared a calculated Soviet decision to let the Nazis slaughter the anti-Soviet Polish underground; and, indeed, the result was to destroy any substantial alternative to a Soviet solution in Poland. The agony of Warsaw caused the most deep and genuine moral shock in Britain and America and provoked dark forebodings about Soviet postwar purposes.

Again history enjoins the imaginative leap in order to see things for a moment from Moscow's viewpoint. The Polish question, Churchill would say at Yalta, was for Britain a question of honor. "It is not only a question of honor for Russia," Stalin replied, "but one of life and death. . . . Throughout history Poland had been the corridor for attack on Russia." A top postwar priority for any Russian régime must be to close that corridor. The Home Army was led by anti-communists. It clearly hoped by its action to forestall the Soviet occupation of Warsaw and, in Russian eyes, to prepare the way for an anti-Russian Poland. In addition, the uprising from a strictly operational viewpoint was premature. The Russians, it is evident in retrospect, had real military problems at the Vistula. The Soviet attempt in September to send Polish units from the Red Army across the river to join forces with the Home Army was a disaster. Heavy German shelling thereafter prevented the ferrying of tanks necessary for an assault on the German position. The Red Army itself did not take Warsaw for another three months. None the less, Stalin's indifference to the human tragedy, his effort to blackmail the London Poles during the ordeal, his sanctimonious opposition during five precious weeks to aerial resupply, the invariable coldness of his explanations ("the Soviet command has come to the conclusion that it must dissociate itself from the Warsaw adventure") and the obvious political benefit to the Soviet Union from the destruction of the Home Army—all these had the effect of suddenly dropping the mask of wartime comradeship and displaying to the West the hard face of Soviet policy. In now pursuing what he grimly regarded as the minimal requirements for the postwar security of his country, Stalin was inadvertently showing the irreconcilability of both his means and his ends with the Anglo-American conception of the peace.

Meanwhile Eastern Europe presented the Alliance with still another crisis that same September. Bulgaria, which was not at war with Russia, decided to surrender to the Western Allies while it still could; and the English and Americans at Cairo began to discuss armistice terms with Bulgarian envoys. Moscow, challenged by what it plainly saw as a Western intrusion into its own zone of vital interest, promptly declared war on Bulgaria, took over the surrender negotiations and, invoking the Italian precedent, denied its Western Allies any role in the Bulgarian Control Commission. In a long and thoughtful cable, Ambassador Harriman meditated on the problems of communication with the Soviet Union. "Words," he reflected, "have a different connotation to the Soviets than they have to us. When they speak of insisting on 'friendly governments' in their neighboring countries, they have in mind something quite different from what we would mean." The Russians, he surmised, really believed that Washington accepted "their position that although they would keep us informed they had the right to settle their problems with their western neighbors unilaterally." But the Soviet position was still in flux: "the Soviet Government is not one mind." The problem, as Harriman had earlier told Harry Hopkins, was "to strengthen the hands of those around Stalin who want to play the game along our lines." The way to do this, he now told Hull, was to

be understanding of their sensitivity, meet them much more than half way, encourage them and support them wherever we can, and yet oppose them promptly with the greatest firmness where we see them going wrong. . . . The only way we can eventually come to an understanding with the Soviet Union on the question of non-interference in the internal affairs of other countries is for us to take a definite interest in the solution of the problems of each individual country as they arise.

As against Harriman's sophisticated universalist strategy, however, Churchill, increasingly fearful of the consequences of unrestrained competition in Eastern Europe, decided in early October to carry his sphere-of-influence proposal directly to Moscow. Roosevelt was at first content to have Churchill speak for him too and even prepared a cable to that effect. But Hopkins, a more rigorous universalist, took it upon himself to stop the cable and warn Roosevelt of its possible implications. Eventually Roosevelt sent a message to Harriman in Moscow emphasizing that he expected to "retain complete freedom of action after this conference is over." It was now that Churchill quickly proposed—and Stalin as quickly accepted—the celebrated division of southeastern Europe: ending (after further haggling between Eden and Molotov) with 90 percent Soviet predominance in Rumania, 80 percent in Bulgaria and Hungary, fifty-fifty in Jugoslavia, 90 percent British predominance in Greece.

Churchill in discussing this with Harriman used the phrase "spheres of influence." But he insisted that these were only "immediate wartime arrangements" and received a highly general blessing from Roosevelt. Yet, whatever Churchill intended, there is reason to believe that Stalin construed the percentages as an agreement, not a declaration; as practical arithmetic, not algebra. For Stalin, it should be understood, the sphere-of-influence idea did not mean that he would abandon all efforts to spread communism in some other nation's sphere; it did mean that, if he tried this and the other side cracked down, he could not feel he had serious cause for complaint. As Kennan wrote to Harriman at the end of 1944:

As far as border states are concerned the Soviet government has never ceased to think in terms of spheres of interest. They expect us to support them in whatever action they wish to take in those regions, regardless of whether that action seems to us or to the rest of the world to be right or wrong. . . . I have no doubt that this position is honestly maintained on their part, and that they would be equally prepared to reserve moral judgment on any actions which we might wish to carry out, i.e., in the Caribbean area.

In any case, the matter was already under test a good deal closer to Moscow than the Caribbean. The communist-dominated resistance movement in Greece was in open revolt against the effort of the Papandreou government to disarm and disband the guerrillas (the same Papandreou whom the Greek colonels have recently arrested on the claim that he is a tool of the communists). Churchill now called in British Army units to crush the insurrection. This action produced a storm of criticism in his own country and in the United States; the American Government even publicly dissociated itself from the intervention, thereby emphasizing its detachment from the sphere-of-influence deal. But Stalin, Churchill later claimed, "Adhered strictly and faithfully to our agreement of October, and during all the long weeks of fighting the Communists in the streets of Athens not one word of reproach came from *Pravda* or *Izvestia*," though there is no evidence that he tried to call off the Greek communists. Still, when the communist rebellion later broke out again in Greece, Stalin told Kardelj and Djilas of Jugoslavia in

1948, "The uprising in Greece must be stopped, and as quickly as possible."

No one, of course, can know what really was in the minds of the Russian leaders. The Kremlin archives are locked; of the primary actors, only Molotov survives, and he has not yet indicated any desire to collaborate with the Columbia Oral History Project. We do know that Stalin did not wholly surrender to sentimental illusion about his new friends. In June 1944, on the night before the landings in Normandy, he told Djilas that the English "find nothing sweeter than to trick their allies. . . . And Churchill? Churchill is the kind who, if you don't watch him, will slip a kopeck out of your pocket. Yes, a kopeck out of your pocket! . . . Roosevelt is not like that. He dips in his hand only for bigger coins." But whatever his views of his colleagues it is not unreasonable to suppose that Stalin would have been satisfied at the end of the war to secure what Kennan has called "a protective glacis along Russia's western border," and that, in exchange for a free hand in Eastern Europe, he was prepared to give the British and Americans equally free hands in their zones of vital interest, including in nations as close to Russia as Greece (for the British) and, very probably—or at least so the Jugoslavs believe—China (for the United States). In other words, his initial objectives were very probably not world conquest but Russian security.

V

It is now pertinent to inquire why the United States rejected the idea of stabilizing the world by division into spheres of influence and insisted on an East European strategy. One should warn against rushing to the conclusion that it was all a row between hard-nosed, balance-of-power realists and starry-eyed Wilsonians. Roosevelt, Hopkins, Welles, Harriman, Bohlen, Berle, Dulles and other universalists were tough and serious men. Why then did they rebuff the sphere-of-influence solution?

The first reason is that they regarded this solution as containing within itself the seeds of a third world war. The balance-of-power idea seemed inherently unstable. It had always broken down in the past. It held out to each power the permanent temptation to try to alter the balance in its own favor, and it built this temptation into the international order. It would turn the great powers of 1945 away from the objective of concerting common policies toward competition for postwar advantage. As Hopkins told Molotov at Teheran, "The President feels it essential to world peace that Russia, Great Britain and the United States work out this control question in a manner which will not start each of the three powers arming against the others." "The greatest likelihood of eventual conflict," said the Joint Chiefs of Staff in 1944 (the only conflict which the J.C.S., in its wisdom, could then glimpse "in the foreseeable future" was between Britain and Russia), ". . . would seem to grow out of either nation initiating attempts to build up its strength, by seeking to attach to herself parts of Europe to the disadvantage and possible danger of her potential adversary." The Americans were perfectly ready to acknowledge that Russia was entitled to convincing assurance of her national security—but not this way. "I could sympathize fully with Stalin's desire to protect his western borders from future attack," as Hull put it. "But I felt that this security could best be obtained through a strong postwar peace organization."

Hull's remark suggests the second objection: that the sphere-of-influence approach would, in the words of the State Department in 1945, "militate against the establishment and effective functioning of a broader system of general security in which all countries will have their part." The United Nations, in short, was seen as the alternative to the balance of power. Nor did the universalists see any necessary incompatibility between the Russian desire for "friendly governments" on its frontier and the American desire for self-determination in Eastern Europe. Before Yalta the State Department judged the general mood of Europe as "to the left and strongly in favor of far-reaching economic and social reforms, but not, however, in favor of a left-wing totalitarian regime to achieve these reforms." Governments in Eastern Europe could be sufficiently to the left "to allay Soviet suspicions" but sufficiently representative "of the center and *petit bourgeois* elements" not to seem a prelude to communist dictatorship. The American criteria were therefore that the government "should be dedicated to the preservation of civil liberties" and "should favor social and economic reforms." A string of New Deal states—of Finlands and Czechoslovakias—seemed a reasonable compromise solution.

Third, the universalists feared that the sphere-of-interest approach would be what Hull termed "a haven for the isolationists," who would advocate America's participation in Western Hemisphere affairs on condition that it did not participate in European or Asian affairs. Hull also feared that spheres of interest would lead to "closed trade areas or discriminatory systems" and thus defeat his cherished dream of a low-tariff, freely trading world.

Fourth, the sphere-of-interest solution meant the betrayal of the principles for which the Second World War was being fought—the Atlantic Charter, the Four Freedoms, the Declaration of the United Nations. Poland summed up the problem. Britain, having gone to war to defend the independence of Poland from the Germans, could not easily conclude the war by surrendering the independence of Poland to the Russians. Thus, as Hopkins told Stalin after Roosevelt's death in 1945, Poland had "become the symbol of our ability to work out problems with the Soviet Union." Nor could American liberals in general watch with equanimity while the police state spread into countries which, if they had mostly not been real democracies, had mostly not been tyrannies either. The execution in 1943 of Ehrlich and Alter, the Polish socialist trade union leaders, excited deep concern. "I have particularly in mind," Harriman cabled in 1944, "objection to the institution of secret police who may become involved in the persecution of persons of truly democratic convictions who may not be willing to conform to Soviet methods."

Fifth, the sphere-of-influence solution would create difficult domestic problems in American politics. Roosevelt was aware of the six million or more Polish votes in the 1944 election; even more acutely, he was aware of the broader and deeper attack which would follow if, after going to war to stop the Nazi conquest of Europe, he permitted the war to end with the communist conquest of Eastern Europe. As Archibald MacLeish, then Assistant Secretary of State for Public Affairs, warned in January 1945, "The wave of disillusionment which has distressed us in the last several weeks will be increased if the impression is permitted to get abroad that potentially totalitarian provisional governments are to be set up without adequate safeguards as to the holding of free elections and the realization of the principles of the Atlantic Charter." Roosevelt believed that no administration could survive which did not try everything short of war to save Eastern Europe, and he was the supreme American politician of the century.

Sixth, if the Russians were allowed to overrun Eastern Europe without argument, would that satisfy them? Even Kennan, in a dispatch of May 1944, admitted that the "urge" had dreadful potentialities: "If initially successful, will it know where to stop? Will it not be inexorably carried forward, by its very nature, in a struggle to reach the whole—to attain complete mastery of the shores of the Atlantic and the Pacific?" His own answer was that there were inherent limits to the Russian capacity to expand—"that Russia will not have an easy time in maintaining the power which it has seized over other people in Eastern and Central Europe unless it receives both moral and material assistance from the West." Subsequent developments have vindicated Kennan's argument. By the late forties, Jugoslavia and Albania, the two East European states farthest from the Soviet Union and the two in which communism was imposed from within rather than from without, had declared their independence of Moscow. But, given Russia's success in maintaining centralized control over the international communist movement for a quarter of a century, who in 1944 could have had much confidence in the idea of communist revolts against Moscow?

Most of those involved therefore rejected Kennan's answer and stayed with his question. If the West turned its back on Eastern Europe, the higher probability, in their view, was that the Russians would use their security zone, not just for defensive purposes, but as a springboard from which to mount an attack on Western Europe, now shattered by war, a vacuum of power awaiting its master. "If the policy is accepted that the Soviet Union has a right to penetrate her immediate neighbors for security," Harriman said in 1944, "penetration of the next immediate neighbors becomes at a certain time equally logical." If a row with Russia were inevitable, every consideration of prudence dictated that it should take place in Eastern rather than Western Europe.

Thus idealism and realism joined in opposition to the sphere-of-influence solution. The consequence was a determination to assert an American interest in the postwar destiny of all nations, including those of Eastern Europe.

In the message which Roosevelt and Hopkins drafted after Hopkins had stopped Roosevelt's initial cable authorizing Churchill to speak for the United States at the Moscow meeting of October 1944, Roosevelt now said, "There is in this global war literally no question, either military or political, in which the United States is not interested." After Roosevelt's death Hopkins repeated the point to Stalin: "The cardinal basis of President Roosevelt's policy which the American people had fully supported had been the concept that the interests of the U.S. were worldwide and not confined to North and South America and the Pacific Ocean."

VI

For better or worse, this was the American position. It is now necessary to attempt the imaginative leap and consider the impact of this position on the leaders of the Soviet Union who, also for better or for worse, had reached the bitter conclusion that the survival of their country depended on their unchallenged control of the corridors through which enemies had so often invaded their homeland. They could claim to have been keeping their own side of the sphere-of-influence bargain. Of course, they were working to capture the resistance movements of Western Europe; indeed, with the appointment of Oumansky as Ambassador to Mexico they were even beginning to enlarge underground operations in the Western Hemisphere. But, from their viewpoint, if the West permitted this, the more fools they; and, if the West stopped it, it was within their right to do so. In overt political matters the Russians were scrupulously playing the game. They had watched in silence while the British shot down communists in Greece. In Jugoslavia Stalin was urging Tito (as Djilas later revealed) to keep King Peter. They had not only acknowledged Western preëminence in Italy but had recognized the Badoglio régime; the Italian Communists had even voted (against the Socialists and the Liberals) for the renewal of the Lateran Pacts.

They would not regard anti-communist action in a Western zone as a *casus belli;* and they expected reciprocal license to assert their own authority in the East. But the principle of self-determination was carrying the United States into a deeper entanglement in Eastern Europe than the Soviet Union claimed as a right (whatever it was doing underground) in the affairs of Italy, Greece or China. When the Russians now exercised in Eastern Europe the same brutal control they were prepared to have Washington exercise in the American sphere of influence, the American protests, given the paranoia produced alike by Russian history and Leninist ideology, no doubt seemed not only an act of hypocrisy but a threat to security. To the Russians, a stroll into the neighborhood easily became a plot to burn down the house: when, for example, damaged American planes made emergency landings in Poland and Hungary, Moscow took this as attempts to organize the local resistance. It is not unusual to suspect one's adversary of doing what one is already doing oneself. At the same time, the cruelty with which the Russians executed their idea of spheres of influence—in a sense, perhaps, an unwitting cruelty, since Stalin treated the East Europeans no worse than he had treated the Russians in the thirties—discouraged the West from accepting the equation (for example, Italy = Rumania) which seemed so self-evident to the Kremlin.

So Moscow very probably, and not unnaturally, perceived the emphasis on self-determination as a systematic and deliberate pressure on Russia's western frontiers. Moreover, the restoration of capitalism to countries freed at frightful cost by the Red Army no doubt struck the Russians as the betrayal of the principles for which *they* were fighting. "That they, the victors," Isaac Deutscher has suggested, "should now preserve an order from which they had experienced nothing but hostility, and could expect nothing but hostility . . . would have been the most miserable anti-climax to their great 'war of liberation.' " By 1944 Poland was the critical issue; Harriman later said that "under instructions from President Roosevelt, I talked about Poland with Stalin more frequently than any other subject." While the West saw the point of Stalin's demand for a "friendly government" in Warsaw, the American insistence on the sovereign virtues of free elections (ironically in the spirit of the 1917 Bolshevik decree of peace, which affirmed "the right" of a nation "to decide the forms of its state existence by a free vote, taken after the complete evacuation of the incorporating or, generally, of the stronger nation") created an insoluble problem in those countries, like Poland (and Rumania), where free elections would almost certainly produce anti-Soviet governments.

The Russians thus may well have estimated the Western pressures as calculated to encourage their enemies in Eastern Europe and to defeat their own minimum objective of a protective glacis. Everything still hung, however, on the course of military operations. The wartime collaboration had been created by one thing, and one thing alone: the threat of Nazi victory. So long as this threat was real, so was the collaboration. In late December 1944, von Rundstedt launched his counter-offensive in the Ardennes. A few weeks later, when Roosevelt, Churchill and Stalin gathered in the Crimea, it was in the shadow of this last considerable explosion of German power. The meeting at Yalta was still dominated by the mood of war.

Yalta remains something of an historical perplexity—less, from the perspective of 1967, because of a mythical American deference to the sphere-of-influence thesis than because of the documentable Russian deference to the universalist thesis. Why should Stalin in 1945 have accepted the Declaration on Liberated Europe and an agreement on Poland pledging that "the three governments will jointly" act to assure "free elections of governments responsive to the will of the people"? There are several probable answers: that the war was not over and the Russians still wanted the Americans to intensify their military effort in the West; that one clause in the Declaration premised action on "the opinion of the three governments" and thus implied a Soviet veto, though the Polish agreement was more definite; most of all that the universalist algebra of the Declaration was plainly in Stalin's mind to be construed in terms of the practical arithmetic of his sphere-of-influence agreement with Churchill the previous October. Stalin's assurance to Churchill at Yalta that a proposed Russian amendment to the Declaration would not apply to Greece makes it clear that Roosevelt's pieties did not, in Stalin's mind, nullify Churchill's percentages. He could well have been strengthened in this supposition by the fact that *after* Yalta, Churchill himself repeatedly reasserted the terms of the October agreement as if he regarded it, despite Yalta, as controlling.

Harriman still had the feeling before Yalta that the Kremlin had "two approaches to their postwar policies" and that Stalin himself was "of two minds." One approach emphasized the internal reconstruction and development of Russia; the other its external expansion. But in the meantime the fact which dominated all political decisions—that is, the war against Germany— was moving into its final phase. In the weeks after Yalta, the military situation changed with great rapidity. As the Nazi threat declined, so too did the need for coöperation. The Soviet Union, feeling itself menaced by the American idea of self-determination and the borderlands diplomacy to which it was leading, skeptical whether the United Nations would protect its frontiers as reliably as its own domination in Eastern Europe, began to fulfill its security requirements unilaterally.

In March Stalin expressed his evaluation of the United Nations by rejecting Roosevelt's plea that Molotov come to the San Francisco conference, if only for the opening sessions. In the next weeks the Russians emphatically and crudely worked their will in Eastern Europe, above all in the test country of Poland. They were ignoring the Declaration on Liberated Europe, ignoring the Atlantic Charter, self-determination, human freedom and everything else the Americans considered essential for a stable peace. "We must clearly recognize," Harriman wired Washington a few days before Roosevelt's death, "that the Soviet program is the establishment of totalitarianism, ending personal liberty and democracy as we know and respect it."

At the same time, the Russians also began to mobilize communist resources in the United States itself to block American universalism. In April 1945 Jacques Duclos, who had been the Comintern official responsible for the Western communist parties, launched in *Cahiers du Communisme* an uncompromising attack on the policy of the American Communist Party. Duclos sharply condemned the revisionism of Earl Browder, the American Communist leader, as "expressed in the concept of a long-term class peace in the United States, of the possibility of the suppression of the class struggle in the postwar period and of establishment of harmony between labor and capital." Browder was specifically rebuked for favoring the "self-determination" of Europe "west of the Soviet Union" on a bourgeois-democratic basis. The excommunication of Browderism was plainly the Politburo's considered reaction to the impending defeat of Germany; it was a signal to the communist parties of the West that they should recover their identity; it was Moscow's alert to communists everywhere that they should prepare for new policies in the postwar world.

The Duclos piece obviously could not have been planned and written much later than the Yalta conference—that is, well before a number of events which revisionists now cite in order to demonstrate American responsibility for the Cold War: before Allen Dulles, for example, began to negotiate the surrender of the German armies in Italy (the episode which provoked Stalin to charge Roosevelt with seeking a separate peace and provoked Roosevelt to denounce the "vile misrepresentations" of Stalin's informants); well before Roosevelt died; many months before the testing of the atomic bomb; even more months before Truman ordered that the bomb be dropped on Japan. William Z. Foster, who soon replaced Browder as the leader of the American Communist Party and embodied the new Moscow line, later boasted of having said in January 1944, "A post-war Roosevelt administration would continue to be, as it is now, an imperialist government." With ancient suspicions revived by the American insistence on universalism, this was no doubt the conclusion which the Russians were reaching at the same time. The Soviet canonization of Roosevelt (like their present-day canonization of Kennedy) took place after the American President's death.

The atmosphere of mutual suspicion was beginning to rise. In January 1945 Molotov formally proposed that the United States grant Russia a $6 billion credit for postwar reconstruction. With characteristic tact he explained that he was doing this as a favor to save America from a postwar depression. The proposal seems to have been diffidently made and diffidently received. Roosevelt requested that the matter "not be pressed further" on the American side until he had a chance to talk with Stalin; but the Russians did not follow it up either at Yalta in February (save for a single glancing reference) or during the Stalin-Hopkins talks in May or at Potsdam. Finally the proposal was renewed in the very different political atmosphere of August. This time Washington inexplicably mislaid the request during the transfer of the records of the Foreign Economic Administration to the State Department. It did not turn up again until March 1946. Of course this was impossible for the Russians to believe; it is hard enough even for those acquainted with the capacity of the American government for incompetence to believe; and it only strengthened Soviet suspicions of American purposes.

The American credit was one conceivable form of Western contribution to Russian reconstruction. Another was lend-lease, and the possibility of reconstruction aid under the lend-lease protocol had already been discussed in 1944. But in May 1945 Russia, like Britain, suffered from Truman's abrupt termination of lend-lease shipments—"unfortunate and even brutal," Stalin told Hopkins, adding that, if it was "designed as pressure on the Russians in order to soften them up, then it was a fundamental mistake." A third form was German reparations. Here Stalin in demanding $10 billion in reparations for the Soviet Union made his strongest fight at Yalta. Roosevelt, while agreeing essentially with Churchill's opposition, tried to postpone the matter by accepting the Soviet figure as a "basis for discussion"—a formula which led to future misunderstanding. In short, the Russian hope for major Western assistance in postwar reconstruction foundered on three events which the Kremlin could well have interpreted respectively as deliberate sabotage (the loan request), blackmail (lend-lease cancellation) and pro-Germanism (reparations).

Actually the American attempt to settle the fourth lend-lease protocol was generous and the Russians for their own reasons declined to come to an agreement. It is not clear, though, that satisfying Moscow on any of these financial scores would have made much essential difference. It might have persuaded some doves in the Kremlin that the U.S. government was genuinely friendly; it might have persuaded some hawks that the American anxiety for Soviet friendship was such that Moscow could do as it wished without inviting challenge from the United States. It would, in short, merely have reinforced both sides of the Kremlin debate; it would hardly have reversed deeper tendencies toward the deterioration of political relationships. Economic deals were surely subordinate to the quality of mutual political confidence; and here, in the months after Yalta, the decay was steady.

The Cold War had now begun. It was the product not of a decision but of a dilemma. Each side felt compelled to adopt policies which the other could not but regard as a threat to the principles of the peace. Each then felt compelled to undertake defensive measures. Thus the Russians saw no choice but to consolidate their security in Eastern Europe. The Americans, regarding Eastern Europe as the first step toward Western Europe, responded by asserting their interest in the zone the Russians deemed vital to their security. The Russians concluded that the West was resuming its old course of capitalist encirclement; that it was purposefully laying the foundation for anti-Soviet régimes in the area defined by the blood of centuries as crucial to Russian survival. Each side believed with passion that future international stability depended on the success of its own conception of world order. Each side, in pursuing its own clearly indicated and deeply cherished principles, was only confirming the fear of the other that it was bent on aggression.

Very soon the process began to acquire a cumulative momentum. The impending collapse of Germany thus provoked new troubles: the Russians, for example, sincerely feared that the West was planning a separate surrender of the German armies in Italy in a way which would release troops for Hitler's eastern front, as they subsequently feared that the Nazis might succeed in surrendering Berlin to the West. This was the context in which the atomic bomb now appeared. Though the revisionist argument that Truman dropped the bomb less to defeat Japan than to intimidate Russia is not convincing, this thought unquestionably appealed to some in Washington as at least an advantageous side-effect of Hiroshima.

So the machinery of suspicion and counter-suspicion, action and counter-action, was set in motion. But, given relations among traditional national states, there was still no reason, even with all the postwar jostling, why this should not have remained a manageable situation. What made it unmanageable, what caused the rapid escalation of the Cold War and in another two years completed the division of Europe, was a set of considerations which this account has thus far excluded.

VII

Up to this point, the discussion has considered the schism within the wartime coalition as if it were entirely the result of disagreements among national states. Assuming this framework, there was unquestionably a failure of communication between America and Russia, a misperception of signals and, as time went on, a mounting tendency to ascribe ominous motives to the other side. It seems hard, for example, to deny that American postwar policy created genuine difficulties for the Russians and even assumed a threatening aspect for them. All this the revisionists have rightly and usefully emphasized.

But the great omission of the revisionists—and also the fundamental explanation of the speed with which the Cold War escalated—lies precisely in the fact that the Soviet Union was *not* a traditional national state.[4] This is where the "mirror image," invoked by some psychologists, falls down. For the Soviet Union was a phenomenon very different from America or Britain: it was a totalitarian state, endowed with an all-explanatory, all-consuming ideology, committed to the infallibility of government and party, still in a somewhat messianic mood, equating dissent with treason, and ruled by a dictator who, for all his quite extraordinary abilities, had his paranoid moments.

Marxism-Leninism gave the Russian leaders a view of the world according to which all societies were inexorably destined to proceed along appointed roads by appointed stages until they achieved the classless nirvana. Moreover, given the resistance of the capitalists to this development, the existence of any non-communist state was *by definition* a threat to the Soviet Union. "As long as capitalism and socialism exist," Lenin wrote, "we cannot live in peace: in the end, one or the other will triumph—a funeral dirge will be sung either over the Soviet Republic or over world capitalism."

Stalin and his associates, whatever Roosevelt or Truman did or failed to do, were bound to regard the United States as the enemy, not because of this deed or that, but because of the primordial fact that America was the leading capitalist power and thus, by Leninist syllogism, unappeasably hostile, driven

---

[4] This is the classical revisionist fallacy—the assumption of the rationality, or at least of the traditionalism, of states where ideology and social organization have created a different range of motives. So the Second World War revisionists omit the totalitarian dynamism of Nazism and the fanaticism of Hitler, as the Civil War revisionists omit the fact that the slavery system was producing a doctrinaire closed society in the American South. For a consideration of some of these issues, see "The Causes of the Civil War: A Note on Historical Sentimentalism" in my "The Politics of Hope" (Boston, 1963).

by the logic of its system to oppose, encircle and destroy Soviet Russia. Nothing the United States could have done in 1944–45 would have abolished this mistrust, required and sanctified as it was by Marxist gospel—nothing short of the conversion of the United States into a Stalinist despotism; and even this would not have sufficed, as the experience of Jugoslavia and China soon showed, unless it were accompanied by total subservience to Moscow. So long as the United States remained a capitalist democracy, no American policy, given Moscow's theology, could hope to win basic Soviet confidence, and every American action was poisoned from the source. So long as the Soviet Union remained a messianic state, ideology compelled a steady expansion of communist power.

It is easy, of course, to exaggerate the capacity of ideology to control events. The tension of acting according to revolutionary abstractions is too much for most nations to sustain over a long period: that is why Mao Tse-tung has launched his Cultural Revolution, hoping thereby to create a permanent revolutionary mood and save Chinese communism from the degeneration which, in his view, has overtaken Russian communism. Still, as any revolution grows older, normal human and social motives will increasingly reassert themselves. In due course, we can be sure, Leninism will be about as effective in governing the daily lives of Russians as Christianity is in governing the daily lives of Americans. Like the Ten Commandments and the Sermon on the Mount, the Leninist verities will increasingly become platitudes for ritual observance, not guides to secular decision. There can be no worse fallacy (even if respectable people practiced it diligently for a season in the United States) than that of drawing from a nation's ideology permanent conclusions about its behavior.

A temporary recession of ideology was already taking place during the Second World War when Stalin, to rally his people against the invader, had to replace the appeal of Marxism by that of nationalism. ("We are under no illusions that they are fighting for us," Stalin once said to Harriman. "They are fighting for Mother Russia.") But this was still taking place within the strictest limitations. The Soviet Union remained as much a police state as ever; the régime was as infallible as ever; foreigners and their ideas were as suspect as ever. "Never, except possibly during my later experience as ambassador in Moscow," Kennan has written, "did the insistence of the Soviet authorities on isolation of the diplomatic corps weigh more heavily on me . . . than in these first weeks following my return to Russia in the final months of the war. . . . [We were] treated as though we were the bearers of some species of the plague"—which, of course, from the Soviet viewpoint, they were: the plague of skepticism.

Paradoxically, of the forces capable of bringing about a modification of ideology, the most practical and effective was the Soviet dictatorship itself. If Stalin was an ideologist, he was also a pragmatist. If he saw everything through the lenses of Marxism-Leninism, he also, as the infallible expositor of the faith, could reinterpret Marxism-Leninism to justify anything he wanted to do at any given moment. No doubt Roosevelt's ignorance of Marxism-Leninism was inexcusable and led to grievous miscalculations. But Roosevelt's efforts to work on and through Stalin were not so hopelessly naïve as it used to be fashionable to think. With the extraordinary instinct of a great political leader, Roosevelt intuitively understood that Stalin was the *only* lever available to the West against the Leninist ideology and the Soviet system. If Stalin could be reached, then alone was there a chance of getting the Russians to act contrary to the prescriptions of their faith. The best evidence is that Roosevelt retained a certain capacity to influence Stalin to the end; the nominal Soviet acquiescence in American universalism as late as Yalta was perhaps an indication of that. It is in this way that the death of Roosevelt was crucial—not in the vulgar sense that his policy was then reversed by his successor, which did not happen, but in the sense that no other American could hope to have the restraining impact on Stalin which Roosevelt might for a while have had.

Stalin alone could have made any difference. Yet Stalin, in spite of the impression of sobriety and realism he made on Westerners who saw him during the Second World War, was plainly a man of deep and morbid obsessions and compulsions. When he was still a young man, Lenin had criticized his rude and arbitrary ways. A reasonably authoritative observer (N. S. Khrushchev) later commented, "These negative characteristics of his developed steadily and during the last years acquired an absolutely insufferable character." His paranoia, probably set off by the suicide of his wife in 1932, led to the terrible purges of the mid-thirties and the wanton murder of thousands of his Bolshevik comrades. "Everywhere and in everything," Khrushchev says of this period, "he saw 'enemies,' 'double-dealers' and 'spies.' " The crisis of war evidently steadied him in some way, though Khrushchev speaks of his "nervousness and hysteria . . . even after the war began." The madness, so rigidly controlled for a time, burst out with new and shocking intensity in the postwar years. "After the war," Khrushchev testifies,

the situation became even more complicated. Stalin became even more capricious, irritable and brutal; in particular, his suspicion grew. His persecution mania reached unbelievable dimensions. . . . He decided everything, without any consideration for anyone or anything.

Stalin's wilfulness showed itself . . . also in the international relations of the Soviet Union. . . . He had completely lost a sense of reality; he demonstrated his suspicion and haughtiness not only in relation to individuals in the USSR, but in relation to whole parties and nations.

A revisionist fallacy has been to treat Stalin as just another Realpolitik statesman, as Second World War revisionists see Hitler as just another Stresemann or Bismarck. But the record makes it clear that in the end nothing could satisfy Stalin's paranoia. His own associates failed. Why does anyone suppose that any conceivable American policy would have succeeded?

An analysis of the origins of the Cold War which leaves out these factors—the intransigence of Leninist ideology, the sinister dynamics of a totalitarian society and the madness of Stalin—is obviously incomplete. It was these factors which made it hard for the West to accept the thesis that Russia was moved only by a desire to protect its security and would be satisfied by the control of Eastern Europe; it was these factors which charged the debate between universalism and spheres of influence with apocalyptic potentiality.

Leninism and totalitarianism created a structure of thought and behavior which made postwar collaboration between Russia and America—in any normal sense of civilized intercourse between national states—inherently impossible. The Soviet dictatorship of 1945 simply could not have survived such a collaboration. Indeed, nearly a quarter-century later, the Soviet régime, though it has meanwhile moved a good distance, could still hardly survive it without risking the release inside Russia of energies profoundly opposed to communist despotism. As for Stalin, he may have represented the only force in 1945 capable of overcoming Stalinism, but the very traits which enabled him to win absolute power expressed terrifying instabilities of mind and temperament and hardly offered a solid foundation for a peaceful world.

VIII

The difference between America and Russia in 1945 was that some Americans fundamentally believed that, over a long run, a modus vivendi with Russia was possible; while the Russians, so far as one can tell, believed in no more than a short-run modus vivendi with the United States.

Harriman and Kennan, this narrative has made clear, took the lead in warning Washington about the difficulties of short-run dealings with the Soviet Union. But both argued that, if the United States developed a rational policy and stuck to it, there would be, after long and rough passages, the prospect of eventual clearing. "I am, as you know," Harriman cabled Washington in early April, "a most earnest advocate of the closest possible understanding with the Soviet Union so that what I am saying relates only to how best to attain such understanding." Kennan has similarly made it clear that the function of his containment policy was "to tide us over a difficult time and bring us to the point where we could discuss effectively with the Russians the dangers and drawbacks this status quo involved, and to arrange with them for its peaceful replacement by a better and sounder one." The subsequent careers of both men attest to the honesty of these statements.

There is no corresponding evidence on the Russian side that anyone seriously sought a modus vivendi in these terms. Stalin's choice was whether his long-term ideological and national interests would be better served by a short-run truce with the West or by an immediate resumption of pressure. In October 1945 Stalin indicated to Harriman at Sochi that he planned to adopt the second course—that the Soviet Union was going isolationist. No doubt the succession of problems with the United States contributed to this decision, but the basic causes most probably lay elsewhere: in the developing situations in Eastern Europe, in Western Europe and in the United States.

In Eastern Europe, Stalin was still for a moment experimenting with techniques of control. But he must by now have begun to conclude that he had underestimated the hostility of the people to Russian dominion. The Hungarian elections in November would finally convince him that the Yalta formula was a road to anti-Soviet governments. At the same time, he was feeling more strongly than ever a sense of his opportunities in Western Europe. The other half of the Continent lay unexpectedly before him, politically demoralized, economically prostrate, militarily defenseless. The hunting would be better and safer than he had anticipated. As for the United States, the alacrity of postwar demobilization must have recalled Roosevelt's offhand remark at Yalta that "two years would be the limit" for keeping American troops in Europe. And, despite Dr. Eugene Varga's doubts about the imminence of American economic breakdown, Marxist theology assured Stalin that the United States was heading into a bitter postwar depression and would be consumed with its own problems. If the condition of Eastern Europe made unilateral action seem essential in the interests of Russian security, the condition of Western Europe and the United States offered new temptations for communist expansion. The Cold War was now in full swing.

It still had its year of modulations and accommodations. Secretary Byrnes conducted his long and fruitless campaign to persuade the Russians that America only sought governments in Eastern Europe "both friendly to the Soviet Union and representative of all the democratic elements of the country." Crises were surmounted in Trieste and Iran. Secretary Marshall evidently did not give up hope of a modus vivendi until the Moscow conference of foreign secretaries of March 1947. Even then, the Soviet Union was invited to participate in the Marshall Plan.

The point of no return came on July 2, 1947, when Molotov, after bringing 89 technical specialists with him to Paris and evincing initial interest in the project for European reconstruction, received the hot flash from the Kremlin, denounced the whole idea and walked out of the conference. For the next fifteen years the Cold War raged unabated, passing out of historical ambiguity into the realm of good versus evil and breeding on both sides simplifications, stereotypes and self-serving absolutes, often couched in interchangeable phrases. Under the pressure even America, for a deplorable decade, forsook its pragmatic and pluralist traditions, posed as God's appointed messenger to ignorant and sinful man and followed the Soviet example in looking to a world remade in its own image.

In retrospect, if it is impossible to see the Cold War as a case of American aggression and Russian response, it is also hard to see it as a pure case of Russian aggression and American response. "In what is truly tragic," wrote Hegel, "there must be valid moral powers on both the sides which come into collision. . . . Both suffer loss and yet both are mutually justified." In this sense, the Cold War had its tragic elements. The question remains whether it was an instance of Greek tragedy—as Auden has called it, "the tragedy of necessity," where the feeling aroused in the spectator is "What a pity it had to be this way"—or of Christian tragedy, "the tragedy of possibility," where the feeling aroused is "What a pity it was this way when it might have been otherwise."

Once something has happened, the historian is tempted to assume that it had to happen; but this may often be a highly unphilosophical assumption. The Cold War could have been avoided only if the Soviet Union had not been possessed by convictions both of the infallibility of the communist word and of the inevitability of a communist world. These convictions transformed an impasse between national states into a religious war, a tragedy of possibility into one of necessity. One might wish that America had preserved the poise and proportion of the first years of the Cold War and had not in time succumbed to its own forms of self-righteousness. But the most rational of American policies could hardly have averted the Cold War. Only today, as Russia begins to recede from its messianic mission and to accept, in practice if not yet in principle, the permanence of the world of diversity, only now can the hope flicker that this long, dreary, costly contest may at last be taking on forms less dramatic, less obsessive and less dangerous to the future of mankind.

4
A EUROPEAN VIEW

FROM A History of the Cold War BY JOHN LUKACS

THE DIVISION OF EUROPE BECOMES RIGID (TO 1949)

I

Even before the end of the war Stalin alone of the Big Three remained in power. Because of the unexpected electoral victory of the British Labour Party, Churchill was replaced by Attlee during the closing days of the Potsdam Conference, where Truman had come to occupy Roosevelt's seat; soon thereafter General De Gaulle, disgusted with the new quagmire of French politics and parliaments, resigned and withdrew from public affairs. The conditions of defeated Germany and Italy were not yet auspicious for the emergence of important leaders; in China civil war was in development. Thus outside the Russian Empire the world suddenly seemed devoid of the impact of great personalities; but soon it became evident that Providence and political fortune had provided the English-speaking nations and, with them, the free world with two persons whose statesmanship proved adequate for halting the eventual spread of Russian Communist tyranny. Their integrity, bravery, and intelligence shine in retrospect through those murky years. They were Harry S Truman and Ernest Bevin, the provincial Midwestern politician who through a stroke of fate became President of the United States and the erstwhile dock worker who became Foreign Secretary of Britain in 1945. They soon made a strong and confident impression. There were many reasons to believe that, unlike Roosevelt, the inexperienced Truman would let the State Department and its Secretaries determine the ultimate conduct of American foreign policy; but Truman, who, unlike his successor, knew from

---

the first moment the historic traditions and necessity of strong presidential leadership, soon grasped the master wheel of the American ship of state with both hands. Meanwhile in Britain the somewhat colorless Prime Minister Attlee left to the Foreign Secretary the main task of insuring the continuity of British foreign policy in the best interests of the nation; and as early as in August 1945 Bevin's first speech in the House of Commons, direct and critical of Russian actions in Europe, dispelled the fears (or the hopes) of those who believed that the new Labour government would go to great lengths to accommodate the Russians.

Still, the United Kingdom, victorious in principle but impoverished in essence by the war, was no longer able to maintain her far-flung imperial and political commitments in all parts of the world. The British decision to grant full independence to India, Pakistan, Burma, and Palestine was made; from 1947 on, the British flag was hauled down in many places, while elsewhere the relationship of Britain with her colonial dependencies was newly reformed to the benefit of the latter in the name of the democratic principle. Yet none of these great transformations, including the dramatic birth of the Indian and Pakistani Republics on a vast subcontinent, and not even the birth of the State of Israel, had, as yet, an important bearing on the dreadful balance of the developing cold war. It was in Greece, the historic ally of Great Britain, that the turning point was reached.

2

By early 1947 President Truman and the American government finally concluded that the United States would not further acquiesce in the Communization—either by conquest, civil war, or subversion—of any portion of Europe or the Near East that lay outside the Russian imperial sphere in Eastern Europe. The so-called Truman Doctrine, the Marshall Plan, and the Containment Policy were the three principal instruments of this historic (though, in retrospect, hardly avoidable) decision.

In February 1947 the British government informed Washington that it could not alone sustain the armed struggle of the Greek state against the growing irregular tide of Communist guerrilla armies. Without hesitation Truman assumed the burden. His Message to Congress in March 1947 called for American military aid to a Greece and Turkey threatened by Russian pressure and eventual blackmail. After some debate congressional consent was given. Forthwith American military missions and abundant supplies were sent to these Eastern Mediterranean countries. In about a year the Greek Army defeated the Communist guerrillas everywhere. The prominence of American sea power in the Eastern Mediterranean, manifested by the Sixth Fleet, remained an important factor in world affairs ever since that time.

It was evident in 1945 that American statesmen were more responsive to economic than to political arguments when it came to the distressing problems of Europe. Predicated upon the belief that Communism would primarily prosper from economic chaos, fortified by strong inclinations of American common sense as well as by traditional American institutional generosity toward poverty and distress abroad, the so-called Marshall Plan was proposed in June 1947. The United States was willing to support, in the form of goods, gifts, and easy loans, the rebuilding of the war-torn economies of Britain and Europe. The aim of the Marshall Plan was the ultimate restoration of the balance in Europe by quickly getting the weakened nations of Western Europe to their feet again; but its purposes were broader politically and even more generous economically, since Marshall Plan Aid was offered to Eastern Europe, including Russia, too. But Stalin refused to take it; indeed, he forced his westernmost ally, the still semi-democratic republic of Czechoslovakia, to reverse its original acceptance.

His purpose of dividing Europe was now clearer than ever before. Peace Treaties were already signed with former German allies, Italy, Hungary, Rumania, Finland; but except for a few unimportant details these amounted about to a confirmation of the respective Armistice instruments signed before; moveover, Russian forces were not withdrawn from Hungary, Rumania, or Poland, where they were to guard communication lines to East Germany and Eastern Austria, pending a German and Austrian Peace Treaty. About the latter the Council of Foreign Ministers were getting nowhere during interminable debates. Through a variety of methods the Russians took ruthless advantage of the subject condition of their captive European neighbors; and in 1947 Stalin speeded up the gradual Sovietization of his prospective satellites. With crudest methods, on occasion not shunning even the open involvement of Russian police organs, the representatives of the remaining democratic forces in Hungary, Rumania, Poland, Bulgaria, and East Germany were sometimes deported, at times imprisoned, on occasion silenced, and frequently chased into Western exile. In Yugoslavia and Albania, where no Russian troops were stationed, the police control of the Communist regimes was most complete. In some of the other satellites, particularly Hungary, the unpopularity and the occasional ineptitude of local Communist satraps were still an obstacle despite the power of their Russian masters. In June 1947 the semi-democratic government of Hungary had to be transformed by force; thereafter unabashed police tactics were the main instruments for insuring Russia's mastery in Eastern Europe.

Though, except for increasingly angry protests and for individual actions of personal rescue, the Western Powers did little to intervene, Stalin's brutalities in Eastern Europe deeply affected the free world. There was, therefore, not much argument about the wisdom of the American Policy of Containment—in essence a political expression of the purpose that motivated the so-called Truman Doctrine and the Marshall Plan—formulated by the thoughtful American diplomatist George F. Kennan and first indicated in 1947 in an article under the cipher "X" in the American magazine *Foreign*

Affairs. Since Communism preaches a perpetual struggle against the non-Communist world, in certain historical situations this preaching may be rationalized into ruthless expansion unless it is met by the force of determined resistance. At least in Europe, it was now the supreme interest of the United States to prohibit the further overflow of Soviet influence beyond the already swollen limits of Stalin's new Russian Empire. This is the gist of the Policy of Containment. It sums up the events of the year 1947. It also suggests the principal direction of American world policy up to the present day.

3

By 1948 the leadership of Soviet Russia and of the United States over their respective halves of Europe (and also of Korea) was an accomplished fact. While Russian domination was welcomed by but a small minority of people in the eastern, American predominance was welcomed by most people in the western half of the continent, including Germany, where events were soon to test the measure of American determination. The American response to the Russian threat in Berlin was one of the finest American hours in the history of the cold war. A sense of relief and of Western Christian unity was diffused in the hearts of millions of Europeans. It was in 1948 that the term "cold war" became popular currency (I think the phrase was Walter Lippmann's). But it was also in 1948 that the term "West" acquired a new popular historical meaning: the cold wind of the Bolshevik threat from the steppes of Asia, instead of chilling the spirit into the mortal rigor of hopeless fear, suscitated significant new fires in the European spirit; and the unity of Western Christian civilization was first felt by thinking men in Europe and America together. In the American presidential election of 1948 (the first in a series of elections that were followed all over the free world with an interest that unconsciously reflected the knowledge that here the American people were choosing the leader of the West) foreign policy played no important part; and the unexpected victory of Harry Truman, no matter what its domestic electoral sources, assured the leadership of the free world of this vigorous personality for some years to come. In Western Europe the distressing aftermath of war and poverty still prevailed; but the spirit of people, especially of the young postwar generation, compared favorably with the radical and cynical mood of disillusionment that had followed the First World War. A genuine movement toward European Unity became current; together with constructive intellectual and religious tendencies, it was also manifest in politics through the broad emergence of Christian Democratic parties whose leadership was provided by the personal excellence of De Gasperi in Italy, Adenauer in Germany, Robert Schuman in France, Figl and Raab in Austria. Partly as a consequence of these developments and partly because of the blunders of Stalin's own brutalities, the Russians now suffered their first important setbacks in Europe.

Stalin's main blunders bear the names of Czechoslovakia, Yugoslavia, and Berlin: this order is chronological as well as one of ascending importance. In February 1948, nine years after the rapacious Hitler broke his word and incorporated the remains of a cowed Czech state, not knowing that his easy subjugation of Prague was an unnecessary act whose symbolic character galvanized resistance against him in the West, Stalin acted in a similar vein. The Czechoslovak Republic, whose pliant leaders had done everything not to arouse the ire or suspicion of their mastodon Russian neighbor, was not to be given the least opportunity to maintain certain traditional contacts with the West. Even without the pressuure of Russian armies, a Communist *coup d'état,* dramatized by the following suicide of the Foreign Minister, Jan Masaryk, effectively transformed Czechoslovakia into an all-out Soviet satellite. The Western Powers were not willing to intervene; but at least they took immediate steps to close their ranks and proceed with military preparations. A Western European military and political Instrument was signed in Brussels in March 1948. American military preparations in Germany increased while the still existing gradual differences in the Eastern European captive nations were being reduced to uniformity through drastic measures that indicated impatience and worrisomeness on Stalin's part. But on 28 June 1948 a Communist bulletin brought to the world the surprising news of a break between Stalin and Tito.

Few events indicate clearer the Russian national and imperialist, as distinct from Communist, motives and ambitions of Stalin than the dark (and at times almost comic) story of Russian-Yugoslav misunderstandings. In no Eastern European country was there a native Communist Party stronger than in Yugoslavia; Tito was indeed the most radical of the Communist leaders. But he was a junior partner, not a satellite; he had won his civil war, if not wholly without Russian help, at least not as a carpetbagger suppliant following behind the mighty hordes of the advancing Russian armies. Frequently Stalin preferred submissive Russian agents to steadfast Communist leaders; he grew dissatisfied with Tito's Communist South Slav nationalism from 1945 onward. As often before in history, the crudity of Russian intervention alienated those who had been her best friends in the Balkans. When his Russian agents proved unequal to the task of upsetting Tito, Stalin pronounced Communist anathema upon Yugoslavia; but his subsequent threats only united the still considerably divided Yugoslav nation behind their audacious leader, whose prestige, in contrast to Stalin's, now began to rise throughout the world.

In line with his policy to eliminate the last Western islands within his monochrome East European Empire, Stalin began to put pressure on Berlin in the spring of 1948. It will be remembered that Berlin, like Vienna, was divided into four occupational zones where for symbolic purposes all four Allies were keeping garrisons, an arrangement made in 1944 and which indeed had precedents going back to the occupation of Paris after Napoleon's fall. Unlike Vienna, where a central Austrian government resided, Berlin was not the seat of a German government. In its eastern suburbs the Russians were setting up the rudiments of an East German satellite "administration," while the West German government, after some debate, made its home in Bonn in 1949. These arrangements consequent to the practical division of Germany were not yet advanced when in May 1948 the Russians began to suspend supplies and communications between West Berlin and the Western Zones of Germany. The object of this Blockade was the starving of West Berlin into submission. It was broken from the very beginning by the resoluteness of the population in concert with Allied military determination to stand fast. Along the official highway connecting Berlin with the Western Zone, General Clark proposed to break through the Blockade with an American military column; but President Truman chose instead to depend on American ingenuity of material supply: the famous Berlin Air Lift was created. Throughout the dark autumn and winter days of 1948 a Berlin still largely in ruins drew hope and succor from the drone of American transport planes, piloted often by the same men who but a few years before cast bombs on that same city. Almost a hundred American, British, and French airmen gave their lives for the cause of freedom in Berlin. Their sacrifice was not in vain. The Russian bluff was called. In May 1949 the Russians lifted the "Blockade."

By that time, however, outside Berlin the division of Germany had begun to ossify. In Bonn in the West and in Berlin-Pankow in the East two rival German governments were installed. The Russians were beginning to give arms to their East German police and semi-military forces, while in the West the American military emphasis grew. In 1947–48 arrangements were made for American bombers to be installed on airfields in Britain. Increasing amounts of American military equipment were given to Western European nations. The permanent establishment of American forces in Europe was finally sealed by the instrument of the North Atlantic Treaty Organization, signed in March 1949. It was already foreseeable that unless important changes were to occur in the political relations of Moscow and Washington, at least a partial rearmament of West Germany by the United States and its allies would be but a matter of time.

Thus four years after the end of the Second World War within Russian Europe all resistance was crushed; but Russian and Communist expansion seemed to have come definitely to a halt. The Russification of Stalin's new Empire proceeded with its Communization; in 1949 a Russian Army Marshal was made Defense Minister of the Polish Republic, and the elimination of even proved and radical Communists who were not known Russian agents began in the rest of the satellite countries. Still, it was not Russian but American power that swayed the destinies of most of the world. The number and the extent of American—not of Russian—military, naval, and air bases were increasing. In Europe at least, Communism failed everywhere outside the iron curtain; strong American support insured the victory of the Christian Democrats in the important Italian elections of 1948. The European balance was becoming redressed—at the cost of the abandoned Eastern European nations, but at least altogether somewhat in favor of the West. In May 1949 Molotov, whose impregnable Soviet Russian conservatism was associated with a crucial decade of Russian history and expansion, left the Soviet Foreign Ministry; Stalin appointed Vishinsky in his place. This was at least a sign of his dissatisfaction with the way Russian foreign affairs were going.

Up to that time the United States had the atomic monopoly; but now in 1949 the Russians exploded their first atomic bomb—promptly monitored by American atomic agencies under whose aegis the plans for the construction of a Hydrogen Bomb had already begun.

4

At this point, with the first phase of the cold war closing, we must look at the ideas guiding the course of the now inimical Giant Powers of the world. Both the Russian and the American peoples were told by their leaders that the Second World War brought no real peace, that they might have to gird themselves anew for the dangers of war. This was possible without drastic interference with the domestic prosperity of America; it was not possible in Russia, where the regimen of privations continued well after the war. While the American people, relentlessly reminded of their new international responsibilities, tended more and more in an internationalist direction, Stalin's Russia became more national and isolationist than it had ever been since the Communist Revolution. By 1949 the similarities between Stalin's regime and that of Tsar Nicholas I, for example, were so obvious that pages and pages from books such as the Marquis de Custine's description of his travels in the Russia of the 1840s would apply to Stalin's Russia in the 1940s; but Americans sought the key to Soviet conduct in dogma rather than in history, in the internationalist, revolutionary, and agnostic doctrines of "Leninist" Communism, rather than in the nationalist, isolationist, and orthodox features that were emerging under Stalin, whose xenophobic, puritan, anti-Semitic terror suggested a Tsar rather than any international Communist revolutionary figure, and whose exhortations of Russian national pride had deep roots in Russian history but no source at all in Marx. The American reaction, concentrating on the dangers of international Communism rather than on the historical features of Russian aggressiveness, was of course only in part due to the myopic American intellectual tendency of taking dogmas and abstractions unduly seriously. It was also motivated by a strong domestic undercurrent, a political anti-Communist reaction against the more and more obvious falseness of wartime radical and Russophile propaganda. It was the reaction against the illusions of an intellectual and political generation now on trial: and such shocking developments as the evidence of amateur espionage practiced by people like Alger Hiss, an able young top organization man of the New Deal generation, now revealed to have been at least a Communist sympathizer, were to carry this popular anti-Communist reaction far.

Thus we find a curious and corresponding duality in American and Russian political tendencies by 1949. On one hand, the Soviet Union was, more than ever, the mighty leader of international Communism; but in reality the tendency of her tyrannical ruler was more national than international, more Russian than Communist, more isolationist than revolutionary; for example, there were (and, to some extent, there still are) two iron curtains, one separating the satellites from the rest of Europe, the other separating Russia from her Sovietized satellites, and the latter was even thicker than the first. On one hand, the United States was committing herself only to the defense of certain Western European and marginal strategic territories against the eventual armed aggression of Russia; but in reality the tendency of this American policy was becoming ideological rather than political, and world-wide rather than limited to America's admittedly vast national and Allied interests; for example, the United States, even though she had written off Eastern Europe, assumed the role of a coordinating center of Eastern European émigré political and propaganda activities, while her military intelligence organs were already involved in an underhand struggle with their Soviet counterparts throughout the whole world.

For on a vital point American intentions and purposes were not entirely clear. We have seen that while, during and even after the war, the Anglo-American purpose was, broadly speaking, the reconstruction of Europe, the Russian purpose was the division of Europe; now Europe was torn asunder, and Containment and NATO were to keep any more portions from going. But there was an important difference between NATO and Containment that has remained obscured and unresolved until the present day. The original purpose of Containment—at least in Kennan's concept—was to build up Western Europe and commit the United States in her defense so that after a while Russia's rulers would see how their aggressive behavior was leading them nowhere. Thereafter the growth of a peacefully prosperous Europe would modify the unnatural division of the continent into Russian and American military spheres, so that ultimately a mutual reduction of the more extreme Russian and American commitments and of some of their most advanced outposts could follow. These were not insubstantial speculations. They rested on political and geographical realities. In 1949 there was still an important marginal area in the middle of Europe that was not yet fully ranged within either the Russian or the American military system (indeed, until 1951 the only line where NATO's territories bordered on Russia was the short stretch of the Russian-Norwegian frontier in the extreme North). Finland was under the Russian shadow, and the Russians insisted on binding Pacts with Finland; but Stalin told the Finns that their country could remain outside the Soviet political sphere if Sweden, across the Baltic, was to stay outside NATO and the American military sphere. In 1948 neither West Germany nor, of course, Switzerland and Austria, were part of NATO; the latter, a battleground of competing intelligence agencies, was, like Germany, divided between Eastern and Western Zones but, unlike Germany, not quite hopelessly: there was a central Austrian government sitting in Vienna, recognized by both Washington and Moscow. Further to the south neither Yugoslavia nor Greece nor Turkey belonged to NATO (the latter two were then included in 1951), while it is significant that the multiple military alliances that the Russians were tying among their satellite neighbors were not extended to Albania, the only geographically isolated member of the Soviet group of states. Thus a motley but unbroken middle European zone separated the Russian and American spheres from the Arctic to the Aegean. This was the design of Kennan, who was the head of Policy Planning in the Department of State at the time; but this subtle and reasonable policy was soon superseded by the simple and military anti-Communist concept of NATO. Where the original purpose had been the ultimate dissolution of the division of Europe and Germany, NATO was to contribute to the hardening of that division into permanence. Absorbed by this newer purpose, the necessary imagination of American statesmanship began to falter; and we shall see how thereby the character of the American state and society began to develop in a centralized and military direction.

The question, therefore, arises whether American policy had understood Stalin's ambitions well enough. It was formulated at a time when Russia in Eastern Europe proceeded with shocking brutality. Around the edge of the new Russian Empire conditions were uncertain: the Red froth bubbled in northern Greece; France and Italy seemed withering in political and economic weakness. It was of the greatest importance to halt what was considered "the Red flood" before it could trickle and flow into Italy, France, Western Europe. But was this analysis sufficiently profound? There is no sufficient evidence that Stalin in 1947–48 had planned to advance into France and Italy or that he had even contemplated the imminent victory of the Communist Parties in those countries; indeed, the evidence points to the contrary. His actions were aimed at consolidating, in some cases with frantic haste, his imperial realms in Eastern Europe; and it is quite possible that the American preoccupation with Western Europe may have suited his purposes: for thus American attention was diverted from Eastern Europe.

Perhaps it would be well to put ourselves into Stalin's position in, say, 1947. He regarded Eastern Europe as his; he also felt somewhat justified in this possession. Russia had won the war against the German invaders. Her cities were devastated, her armies bled white; with age-old Russian suspicion, Stalin was prone to underestimate the Allied contribution to the victory over Germany. Russia had carried the main brunt of the war, while the United States, without wounds, emerged as the greatest and most powerful nation of the earth. It was the Americans, now in possession of the entire Western

European pastry shop, who a few years before let him have his Eastern European cake with such unconcern; why couldn't he eat it, after all? Now Stalin did not particularly contest American power: he did not challenge America's sphere; did it not seem to him, however, that the Americans were beginning to challenge *his* sphere? Always he was willing enough to go along with sphere-of-interest arrangements; he, again like Russian diplomacy in the past, was a *quid pro quo* politician of sorts. When Churchill, at Potsdam, complained about Rumania, Stalin would retort that he fulfilled their bargain by not intervening in Greece; when Churchill or Truman insisted upon Poland, Stalin answered that Poland involved Russian interests while he had not the slightest concern with how the British protected theirs in Belgium or Holland. But Churchill, that cunning old British Capitalist Enemy of Communism, at least understood him on that point; the Americans did not. Stalin did not really compete with them over Western Europe; but why were they now, after the war, two years after Yalta, getting worked up about Eastern Europe, protesting loudly about imprisoned Cardinals? He did not really challenge what to him amounted to the American domination of Western Europe; the financial assistance which Moscow had furnished the Italian Communist Party, for example, was far less than what the Americans poured into Italy before the 1948 elections. Why, then, the American meddling in Eastern Europe? Had they not won enough in the war? All of the Pacific and the Atlantic basins, plus Western and Southern Europe? With his narrow Oriental eyes looking westward from the Byzantine windows of the Kremlin, Stalin may have reasoned thus.

Thus an amused historian may say that the first few years—and perhaps even the first decade—of the Russian-American crisis over Europe might have been due to a fundamental, mutual misunderstanding: Washington presupposing that the immediate Russian aim was to upset and conquer Western Europe, Moscow presupposing that the American aim was to upset and reconquer Eastern Europe—and that both presuppositions were wrong.

Thus a cynical historian may say that Moscow and Washington did not make out so badly, after all. True, in 1945 and thereafter a more intelligent and imaginative American policy could have prevented the Russian advance into the very middle of Europe and thus spared much of the cost and the toil of the cold war; true, in 1945 and thereafter less crude and brutal Russian measures in Eastern Europe would not have provoked all of these countermeasures, including NATO, and Russian influence in Europe would not have been limited to the subject satellite capitals—but the cynic may say: so what? No cold war, no American dominion over one half, and no undisputed Russian dominion over the other half of Europe. No cold war, no rigid division of Europe—ah yes, a boon to Europe it may have been: but, if so, the Russians, for instance, would not be the masters of Hungary today, and the Americans would not be able to tie an armed Germany within their military system. Still, this imaginary cynic of a historian would not be entirely right— at least not yet. For, no matter how true is the maxim that one must want the

consequences of what one wants, this maxim is seldom put into practice in the affairs of men and of nations; and it is especially true in democratic ages that the discrepancy between intentions and ultimate results is great, very great indeed.